KORN/FERRY INTERNATIONAL

powered by LOMINGER

COMPETENCY

FYI

For Your Improvement™

A Guide for Development and Coaching

5th Edition

FOR LEARNERS, MANAGERS, MENTORS, AND FEEDBACK GIVERS

Michael M. Lombardo & Robert W. Eichinger

Tel. 952-345-3610
Fax. 952-345-3601
www.kornferry.com
www.lominger.com

ISBN 978-1-933578-17-0

Lominger reorder part number 11063

FYI For Your Improvement™ 5th Edition Printings:
version 09.1a 1st—01/09

Table of Contents

Competencies

**Note: Italicized words are not alphabetized.*

There are no competencies 68-80 or 91-100. Those numbers are reserved for future additions. Performance Dimensions (numbered 81-90) can be found in FYI for Performance Management.™

Career Stallers and Stoppers

There are no competencies numbered 120-160. Those numbers are reserved for future additions.

Global Focus Areas

Appendix A: Competency Connections

Appendix B: Developmental Difficulty Matrix

Appendix C: Creating a Development Plan

Table of Contents by Factor and Cluster

LEADERSHIP ARCHITECT® LIBRARY STRUCTURE:

Factor I: Strategic Skills

Factor II: Operating Skills

Factor VII: Trouble with People

Factor VIII: Trouble with Results

Introduction

Who is this book for?

We designed this book of development tips to support any motivated person with a need and to serve as a guide for managers, mentors, and feedback givers. It is a versatile resource intended for all levels of organizations, for problems at work or in one's personal life.

We know that anyone who has not yet recognized and accepted a need or limitation or weakness or developmental opportunity will not be helped by what's in this book. If you are still in denial, rationalizing, confused, or being defensive about having any needs, seek additional feedback and counsel before using this book.

We also find that people who do take personal responsibility for a need but lack motivation, drive, urgency, or energy to do anything about it won't be helped by what's in this book. If you don't think your need matters, talk to your mentor or someone higher up in the organization and ask them why this need is important for your development. See how the need plays out for you and any consequences that are unacceptable to you.

This book provides you with strategies to improve, substitute, or work around a need so that you can be as effective as possible. There are thousands of tips in this book that will help anyone who recognizes specific needs and is motivated to do something about them. If that's you, read on.

What is in this book? Where did it come from?

The content in this book covers three broad areas:

- Competencies
- Stallers and Stoppers
- Global Focus Areas

67 Competencies: These are the measurable characteristics of a person that are related to success at work. A competency may be a behavioral skill, a technical skill, an attribute (such as intelligence), or an attitude (such as optimism). The 67 Competencies are part of the Lominger Leadership Architect® and are grouped into 6 Factors and 21 Clusters. The competencies come from a content analysis of many sources: the major and continuing studies at the Center for Creative Leadership; long-term studies at AT&T and Sears; studies by Harry Levinson, Daniel Levinson, John Kotter, John Gabarro, Elliott Jaques, James Kouzes and Barry Posner, Warren Bennis, Noel Tichy, and Bernard Bass's *Handbook of Leadership*—a compendium of empirical studies.

19 Career Stallers and Stoppers: These are the negative characteristics or flame-out factors that can derail a person's career. The career stallers and stoppers come primarily from three sources: the continuing work of the Center for Creative Leadership, the work of Jon Bentz while he was at Sears, and from the executive development work and experiences of the authors.

7 Global Focus Areas: These are additional characteristics required for being successful in the global setting. After scanning the international literature, we found that for companies doing business globally, the competencies are basically the same. But there are some special skill sets that probably deserve emphasis. They are offered here to help those who need some focused assistance in the global setting. These 7 Global Focus Areas come from the research of Morgan McCall and George Hollenbeck, research done by the Center for Creative Leadership, and the work of John Fulkerson, who assisted in writing the seven chapters. Over time, as more research is available, this list will likely change.

Research with Lominger's VOICES®, a 360° feedback instrument using the competencies and stallers and stoppers, indicates they can be measured reliably and all are significantly related to current and long-term job performance. Additionally, many competencies and stallers have been related to profit, turnover reduction, bonus, stock options, potential for promotion, and actual promotion.

What's new for the 5th Edition?

While maintaining the integrity of the book, we're introducing new content to make it easier for you to identify the right needs to work on and create an effective development plan:

Questions and Action Statements in each chapter make it easy to create your own action plan. Hundreds of remedy titles have been rewritten as diagnostic questions and action statements so you can easily identify a need and transfer a remedy directly onto your development plan.

Develop-in-Place Assignments are job tasks that require application of certain competencies. Research shows that 70% of development happens on the job, and jobs differ in development power and in the competencies they address. You can't always change jobs for development reasons alone, but there is almost always a develop-in-place assignment that you can select in your current job to address your development need.

Other Causes show how stallers and stoppers can result from having too much or too little of certain competencies. Determine the direction of your development plan with these direct links back to the competencies that need to be improved or toned down.

Updated Quotes provide food for thought and inspiration.

Updated Suggested Readings were selected from expert reviews, best-seller lists, and reputable publishers based on their relevance, global perspective, and ROI. We selected readings that were current, available, organized well, and full of suggestions and examples. Plenty for you to choose from!

Competency Connections in Appendix A highlight how a development need or a career goal may be comprised of a few key competencies. For example, many learners are skilled in *Drive for* Results (53) but fail to make tough calls on people. This need can be addressed by developing skill in Conflict Management (12) and Confronting Direct Reports (13) to complement skill in *Drive for* Results. On the flip side, if you aspire to be someone who can convince people to take developmental assignments, you need to be skilled at Motivating Others (36) and complement that by also being skilled at Developing Direct Reports and Others (19) and Sizing Up People (56).

Developmental Difficulty Matrix in Appendix B shows on a 5-point scale how difficult it would be for a typical professional person to develop any of the 67 Competencies. It also shows the average skill rating of the general population for each competency. This information lets you know what you're up against so you can adjust your development plan, remedies, and time line accordingly.

Development Plan in Appendix C has a new format which allows you to organize your plan on an easy-to-use two-page layout. Three examples illustrate ways to maximize the plan's effectiveness when you are addressing unskilled, overused, or staller/stopper development needs.

An Index has been added to make this edition as user-friendly as possible and to help you cross-reference competencies, stallers/stoppers, and global focus areas as you determine your needs and create your development plan.

How do I use this book?

Strategies for Improvement

FIRST, DETERMINE THE NEED

The key to using this book is to identify the right development need. Try to determine what your real need is. Many times you may have to select a few that together equal your real need. Try to find the true underlying need, not just what's showing up on the surface. If you think you have a problem getting Results (53), ask yourself why. Maybe the real problem is lack of Composure (11) or Standing Alone (57) or Delegation (18). Perhaps you only have trouble with results when one of these is demanded. Also, look for a possible overused competency that's creating a weakness. If you get feedback that you lack Caring (7) and aren't Listening (33) to others for advice and counsel, perhaps it's because you're too Results (53) oriented.

Five of the most typical development needs fall into two major categories—the need to build skill or the need to reduce noise.

Developmental strategies to build skill in competencies and global focus areas are straightforward. In all cases, you can attack the need directly, or at least deal with it by working around the need. Consider these three cases that indicate a need to build skill:

1. You are average in a skill that is critically important and needs to be stronger.
2. You are weak (unskilled) in an important area and you'd like to get better (skilled) or move from negative to neutral.
3. You are untested (maybe unskilled) in an important area.

When your focus is to reduce noise in order to avoid derailment, it's a bit different. If you receive feedback that you are Insensitive to Others (112), this is a serious problem, and your goal should be to neutralize this potentially career-stopping issue. Working on a staller is not the same as building a competency. A staller is much more serious and likely results from many sources—what you underdo, such as Interpersonal Savvy (31) and what you overdo, such as Results (53) or Command Skills (9). For this reason, we have written separate remedies for the stallers and stoppers that cover tips you won't find if you simply go to Interpersonal Savvy (31), for example. Consider these two needs that require you to reduce noise:

1. You overuse a strength to the point that it is causing problems for you.
2. You have a staller/stopper that is causing serious problems for you that you need to neutralize.

THEN, TAKE ACTION

When you have identified a need, begin to fill in the development plan in Appendix C. List the competency and the "before" description that applies to you (from either the unskilled or overused definitions). Or, list the staller/stopper and the "before" description that applies to you from the problem definition. Review and record some causes as well as your learnings from the map for each chapter. Then you are ready to create an action plan. There are five possible strategies for taking action, depending on your need.

1. *Develop.* You don't have to be good at everything. Most successful leaders have four to six major strengths, but tend to lack glaring weaknesses. Developing in all 67 Competencies is unlikely, so select wisely. If directly working on improvement seems unlikely, use other indirect strategies such as substitutes, workarounds, or compensators detailed below. If you are committed to developing a competency, create a plan using these suggestions:
   - Choose from the Remedies. Look at the specific tips and pick the ones that apply. Each tip addresses a specific manifestation of being unskilled at the competency. It is unlikely that all of the topics or tips will apply to any one

person. Think back to the causes you checked and what you learned from the map. Most of the 93 chapters have cross-references to other competencies; consult the ones that are referenced for the specific topics you choose.

- Seek further feedback. Little happens without feedback. Get a developmental partner, get formal 360° feedback, and poll people you work with about what you should start doing, keep doing, keep doing with slight modifications, and stop doing.
- Use jobs or assignments for development. The number one developer of competence by far is stretching, challenging jobs—not feedback, not courses, not role models, but jobs where you develop and exercise significant and varied competencies. If you really want to grow, these are the best places to do it. You'll have to stretch in uncomfortable areas. A challenging job or assignment requires you to work on your downsides more vigorously because you either perform or fail. Real development happens when it's not practice but it's the real thing and the stakes are high. Use your new job or assignment to learn from experience—this ability has been shown to be linked to potential.
- Lay out a plan and a schedule. Your plan should include at least three items you will work on immediately. Write it in the "My Action Plan" section of your development plan.

2. *Substitute something else for the lack of skill.* You can use another skill to cover for, substitute for, or neutralize the negative effects of the lack of skill. This path requires using a strength to attack a weakness. For example, you could substitute a strength to attack a weakness in Presentation Skills (49) by upgrading the use of humor (already a high skill) in your presentations, facilitating (already a high skill) instead of presenting, or writing (already a high skill) out your points and distributing them ahead of the meeting so you can have a discussion instead of making a speech. Again, the outcome is to reduce the impact of being a marginal presenter by substituting things you are already good at to get the same thing done. This approach is relatively easy to do if you have the skills necessary to counter your need.
3. *Work around the need to neutralize the weakness.* Essential to this approach is self-knowledge. You have to know you have the need and acknowledge its importance. You can use any of these four workaround strategies to cover for your lack of skill. The goal of a workaround is to reduce the noise caused by the need. While there may or may not be any learning attached to the workaround, this accomplishes what must be done without directly addressing the personal need.

- People workarounds...
  Find an internal or external person to stand in for you when the weakness is in play. This could be a peer, a friend, someone from your staff, or a consultant. For example, if you are a marginal presenter, get someone who is a good presenter to present your material. Hire people for your team who are good in the areas you are not. Delegate the tasks that bring the weakness into play.
- Task workarounds...
  Trade tasks or share tasks with a peer. For example, you help a peer with his or her strategic planning, and he or she helps you with your presentations to senior management. Structure the weakness out. Redesign your job (with your boss) so that you are not responsible for the task(s) that brings your weakness into play. Change your job so that you no longer have to give lots of speeches to strangers. Assign that task to another unit.
- Change workarounds...
  If you decide that you don't want to work on your needs, do an honest assessment of your strengths and find an organization, a job, another unit, or another career that fits those strengths. If you are in sales promotion and are not a comfortable presenter or cold caller, then find a sales job where leads are provided or customers come to you, or consider marketing analysis where those two requirements are greatly decreased.
- Self workarounds...
  Acknowledge your weaknesses and be honest with yourself and others. Research shows that admitting weaknesses (within limits) actually increases people's evaluations of you. So if you start by saying, "As most of you know, speaking is not one of my strengths," people will not be as critical. Make a conscious decision to live with a weakness. If you decide not to address the need, concentrate harder on the things you do well.

4. *Compensate for an overused strength*. Using the strengths that got you where you are today is fine, of course, until something changes—a new strategy, a change in job responsibilities, a new leadership direction in the organization. Then new skills are called for, and the current skill portfolio needs an overhaul. You come to a fork in the road, and the path you choose makes a big difference. One path is taken by the open, learning agile, curious, continuous improvers. They detect that the assignment is going to require a break from the past, a new direction. They figure out what the new ways of thinking or new skills need to be and develop them or use workarounds or compensators. The other path is taken by the larger group. When things are not going the way they are used to, when they are stretched to their limit, they turn up the volume on the handful of

strengths that they already have. Their operating theory is that if a lot is good, more must be even better. If you have gotten feedback that you do too much of a good thing—here are some general strategies to address this problem:

- Isn't it obvious? Stop overdoing it. Do it less. But when your mentor says be less smart, be less results oriented, do less yourself, you have trouble with that advice. Why? Because those are the things that account for your success to date. Those are the things you have been rewarded for. It's pretty scary thinking about DOING LESS of what you are good at. It's really hard in real life to crank back on your strengths, but it can work.
- Add some other skills you have to lessen the noise and the damage you are causing by the overuse. Keep driving for results, but do so in a softer way by adding more listening skills and humor. The compensators listed after the overuse definitions decrease the negative effect of strengths that have gone into overdrive. Use as many compensators as it takes to get the noise down to a reasonable level.
- You also may not have the compensators you need. In that case, you can use a workaround strategy or develop the compensators that are needed. For that, use the developmental tips listed in the chapters of the compensators.

5. *Live with it*. You can just live with a weakness. At least you know what it is and are willing to admit that you have a lack of skills in this area. Recognize and deploy your strengths. In this case, find your highest competencies or performance dimensions and leverage them. If you excel at problem solving and strategy, get into more situations that allow you to use and hone your strengths. Get into roles, jobs, organizations, and career paths that use your specific current and existing strengths.

Finally, refer to Appendix C, Universal Ideas for Developing Any Competency, which lists 10 general ways to develop in any area and pick those that seem to fit. These universal ideas can be used as a basic core for any plan. You will also find three sample development plans focused on improving an unskilled competency, an overused competency, or a problem staller/stopper.

Development can also be all of the things we talked about above. After you know exactly what need you have, you could start with a substitute plan that has an immediate effect. Then midterm, you could use one or more workaround strategies to continue to cover for your lack of skill. While all of this is going on, you can use the development tips in this book to actually build the skill, as well as watch the people you use in your workaround plan to learn from what they do. Then, if even further development is needed, use tasks, special projects, part-time assignments, and even different jobs to finish your development.

Organization of *FYI For Your Improvement*™

Where do I find what I need?

Competency name and number as well as factor and cluster information to show where it fits in the Leadership Architect® Library.

Unskilled definitions provide a list of detailed behaviors that show what "unskilled" looks like for a competency. Read these to see if you may be unskilled at a competency. Which bullet points describe you the best? This is your "before" picture.

Substitutes – Under the unskilled definition, there are other skills that could substitute for the lack of skill in this area. One or more of those substitute skills (if you are high in them) can neutralize the negative effects of a lack of the skill. Use these in your development plan to address an unskilled competency. *(Competencies only)*

Skilled definitions provide a list of detailed behaviors that show what "skilled" looks like for a competency. Compare yourself to the skilled definition. What would you like to be able to do when you're done working on this need? This is your "after" picture.

Overused Skill definitions provide a list of detailed behaviors that show what "overused" looks like for a competency. Refer to these to determine whether you might be overusing one of your strengths.

Compensators – Under the overused skill definition, there are a number of compensator skills. If you are high on one or more of those skills, you can use them to neutralize the negative effects of overusing one of your strengths. Use these in your development plan to address an overused competency.
(Competencies and Global Focus Areas only)

Some Causes – We list numerous reasons why you might have this need. Use these to specify what your need looks like exactly. Check the causes that might apply to you. Many developmental efforts have floundered because the plan attacked the wrong problem. Write down your particular need—what it looks like, what causes it, whom it plays out with and in what situations. If your causes aren't listed, add them to the list.

Global Focus Area name and number as well as competency equivalents that are related.
(See example on page 529)

Quotes – Read the quotes for inspiration and to give yourself food for thought.

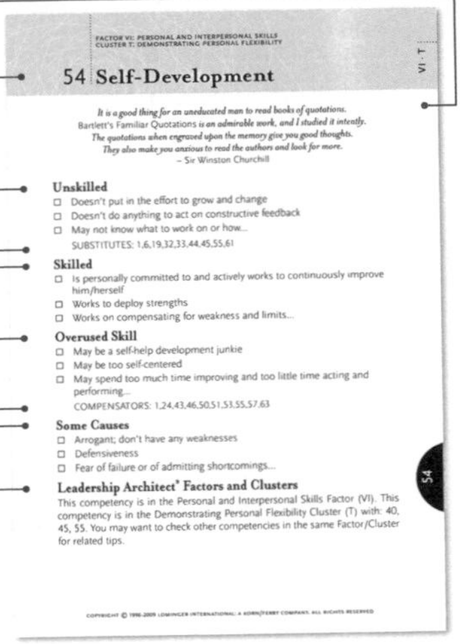

FACTOR VI: PERSONAL AND INTERPERSONAL SKILLS
CLUSTER T: DEMONSTRATING PERSONAL FLEXIBILITY

VI · T

54 Self-Development

It is a good thing for an uneducated man to read books of quotations.
Bartlett's Familiar Quotations *is an admirable work, and I studied it intently.*
The quotations when engraved upon the memory give you good thoughts.
They also make you anxious to read the authors and look for more.
– Sir Winston Churchill

Unskilled
- ☐ Doesn't put in the effort to grow and change
- ☐ Doesn't do anything to act on constructive feedback
- ☐ May not know what to work on or how...

SUBSTITUTES: 1,6,19,32,33,44,45,55,61

Skilled
- ☐ Is personally committed to and actively works to continuously improve him/herself
- ☐ Works to deploy strengths
- ☐ Works on compensating for weakness and limits...

Overused Skill
- ☐ May be a self-help development junkie
- ☐ May be too self-centered
- ☐ May spend too much time improving and too little time acting and performing...

COMPENSATORS: 1,24,43,46,50,51,53,55,57,63

Some Causes
- ☐ Arrogant; don't have any weaknesses
- ☐ Defensiveness
- ☐ Fear of failure or of admitting shortcomings...

Leadership Architect® Factors and Clusters
This competency is in the Personal and Interpersonal Skills Factor (VI). This competency is in the Demonstrating Personal Flexibility Cluster (T) with: 40, 45, 55. You may want to check other competencies in the same Factor/Cluster for related tips.

54

Factors and Clusters – All competencies and career stallers fall into one of 8 Factors and 26 Clusters. This means that a competency (or staller) in a particular cluster is somewhat similar to the others in that cluster. You may want to check for additional tips within the cluster (and perhaps the factor) for each competency.
(Competencies and Stallers and Stoppers only)

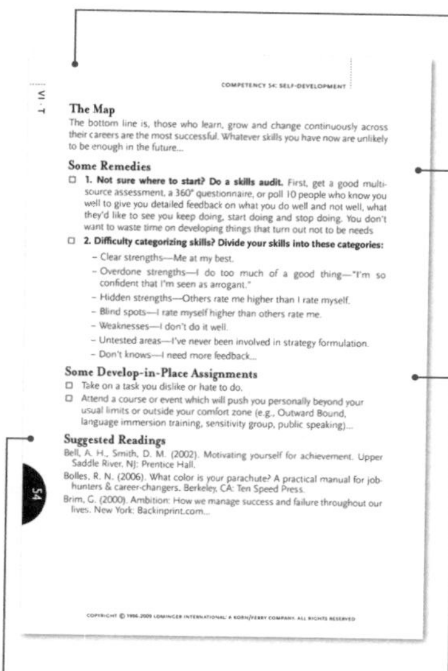

VI · T

COMPETENCY 54: SELF-DEVELOPMENT

The Map

The bottom line is, those who learn, grow and change continuously across their careers are the most successful. Whatever skills you have now are unlikely to be enough in the future...

Some Remedies

- ☐ 1. **Not sure where to start? Do a skills audit.** First, get a good multi-source assessment, a 360° questionnaire, or poll 10 people who know you well to give you detailed feedback on what you do well and not well, what they'd like to see you keep doing, start doing and stop doing. You don't want to waste time on developing things that turn out not to be needs
- ☐ 2. **Difficulty categorizing skills? Divide your skills into these categories:**
  - Clear strengths—Me at my best.
  - Overdone strengths—I do too much of a good thing—"I'm so confident that I'm seen as arrogant."
  - Hidden strengths—Others rate me higher than I rate myself.
  - Blind spots—I rate myself higher than others rate me.
  - Weaknesses—I don't do it well.
  - Untested areas—I've never been involved in strategy formulation.
  - Don't knows—I need more feedback...

Some Develop-in-Place Assignments

- ☐ Take on a task you dislike or hate to do.
- ☐ Attend a course or event which will push you personally beyond your usual limits or outside your comfort zone (e.g., Outward Bound, language immersion training, sensitivity group, public speaking)...

Suggested Readings

Bell, A. H., Smith, D. M. (2002). Motivating yourself for achievement. Upper Saddle River, NJ: Prentice Hall.

Bolles, R. N. (2006). What color is your parachute? A practical manual for job-hunters & career-changers. Berkeley, CA: Ten Speed Press.

Brim, G. (2000). Ambition: How we manage success and failure throughout our lives. New York: Backinprint.com...

54

COPYRIGHT © 1996-2009 LOMINGER INTERNATIONAL: A KORN/FERRY COMPANY. ALL RIGHTS RESERVED

The Map – The map gives you the lay of the land. It reviews the general case for the competency, how it operates, and why it's important. Especially important to remember are things about the competency you didn't understand before you read the map. Those added learnings will make a difference in your development plan.

Some Remedies were developed from research on competencies—what experiences teach them, what they look like, what their elements are. They are also tested ideas from working with executives on what's getting in their way and how to fix it. We kept these tips brief, doable, and action oriented. Ten or more tips are included to work directly on a need. Although a few may be longer-term, most are things you can start working on today. We wanted to give motivated people a way to get started right away and see results quickly. Based on our research and experience, these are the tips that are most likely to work. Choose one or two of these to include in your development plan.

Suggested Readings were selected from expert reviews, best-seller lists, and reputable publishers based on their relevance, global perspective, and ROI. We selected readings that were current, available, organized well, and full of suggestions and examples. Plenty for you to choose from!

Some Develop-in-Place Assignments are job tasks that require application of certain competencies. Research shows that 70% of development happens on the job, and jobs differ in development power and in the competencies they address. You can't always change jobs for development reasons alone, but there is almost always a develop-in-place assignment that you can select in your current job to address your development need.

Staller and Stopper name and number as well as factor and cluster information showing where it fits in the Leadership Architect® Library.

A Problem lists statements to describe detailed behaviors that illustrate what a staller/stopper looks like when it is "a problem." Read these to see if a staller/stopper might be an issue for you.

Not a Problem lists statements to describe detailed behaviors that illustrate what a staller/stopper looks like when it is "not a problem." Read these to see if a staller/stopper is not a concern for you.

Other Causes – A staller results from many sources—what you underdo (unskilled), such as Interpersonal Savvy (31) and what you overdo (overused), such as *Drive for* Results (53) or Command Skills (9). Review the list to see if any of the unskilled or overused competencies match your profile. Use this information to help you decide what to focus on in your development plan.

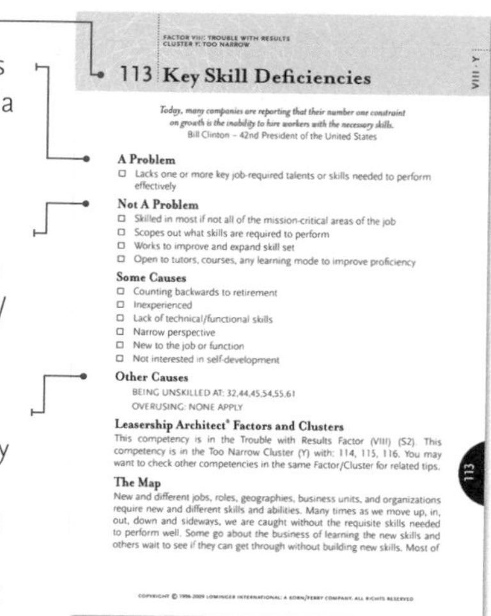

FACTOR VIII: TROUBLE WITH RESULTS
CLUSTER Y: TOO NARROW

113 Key Skill Deficiencies

VIII · Y

Today, many companies are reporting that their number one constraint on growth is the inability to hire workers with the necessary skills.
Bill Clinton – 42nd President of the United States

A Problem

- ☐ Lacks one or more key job-required talents or skills needed to perform effectively

Not A Problem

- ☐ Skilled in most if not all of the mission-critical areas of the job
- ☐ Scopes out what skills are required to perform
- ☐ Works to improve and expand skill set
- ☐ Open to tutors, courses, any learning mode to improve proficiency

Some Causes

- ☐ Counting backwards to retirement
- ☐ Inexperienced
- ☐ Lack of technical/functional skills
- ☐ Narrow perspective
- ☐ New to the job or function
- ☐ Not interested in self-development

Other Causes

BEING UNSKILLED AT: 32,44,45,54,55,61
OVERUSING: NONE APPLY

Leasership Architect® Factors and Clusters

This competency is in the Trouble with Results Factor (VIII) (S2). This competency is in the Too Narrow Cluster (Y) with: 114, 115, 116. You may want to check other competencies in the same Factor/Cluster for related tips.

The Map

New and different jobs, roles, geographies, business units, and organizations require new and different skills and abilities. Many times as we move up, in, out, down and sideways, we are caught without the requisite skills needed to perform well. Some go about the business of learning the new skills and others wait to see if they can get through without building new skills. Most of

113

COPYRIGHT © 1996-2009 LOMINGER INTERNATIONAL: A KORN/FERRY COMPANY. ALL RIGHTS RESERVED

About the Authors

Michael M. Lombardo

Mike Lombardo has over 30 years experience in executive and management research and in executive coaching. He is one of the founders of Lominger Limited, Inc., publishers of the Leadership Architect® Suite. With Bob Eichinger, Mike has authored 40 products for the suite, including *The Leadership Machine*, *FYI For Your Improvement*™, the *Career Architect®*, *Choices Architect®*, and VOICES®. During his 15 years at the Center for Creative Leadership, Mike was a coauthor of *The Lessons of Experience*, which detailed which learnings from experience can teach the competencies needed to be successful. He also coauthored the research on executive derailment revealing how personal flaws and overdone strengths caused otherwise effective executives to get into career trouble, Benchmarks®, a 360° feedback instrument, and the Looking Glass® simulation. Mike has won four national awards for research on managerial and executive development.

Robert W. Eichinger

Bob Eichinger is Vice Chairman of the Korn/Ferry Institute for Korn/Ferry International. Prior to Korn/Ferry's acquisition of Lominger International, he was cofounder and CEO of Lominger Limited, Inc. and cocreator of the Leadership Architect® Suite of management, executive, and organizational development tools. During his 40+ year career, he has worked inside companies such as PepsiCo and Pillsbury, and as a consultant in Fortune 500 companies in the United States, Europe, Japan, Canada, and Australia. Dr. Eichinger lectures extensively on the topic of executive and management development and has served on the Board of the Human Resource Planning Society. He has worked as a coach with more than 1,000 managers and executives. Some of his books include *The Leadership Machine*, written with Mike Lombardo, *100 Things You Need to Know: Best People Practices for Managers & HR*, written with Mike Lombardo and Dave Ulrich, and *FYI for Strategic Effectiveness*™, written with Kim Ruyle and Dave Ulrich.

1 Action Oriented

The world can only be grasped by action, not by contemplation.
The hand is the cutting edge of the mind.
Diane Arbus – American photographer

Unskilled

- ☐ Slow to act on an opportunity
- ☐ May be overly methodical, a perfectionist, or risk averse
- ☐ May procrastinate
- ☐ May not set very challenging goals
- ☐ May lack confidence to act
- ☐ May know what to do but hesitates to do it
- ☐ May not be motivated; may be bored with the work or burned out

Select one to three of the competencies listed below to use as a substitute for this competency if you decide not to work on it directly.

SUBSTITUTES: 9,12,16,18,32,34,36,43,50,52,53,57,62

Skilled

- ☐ Enjoys working hard
- ☐ Is action oriented and full of energy for the things he/she sees as challenging
- ☐ Not fearful of acting with a minimum of planning
- ☐ Seizes more opportunities than others

Overused Skill

- ☐ May be a workaholic
- ☐ May push solutions before adequate analysis
- ☐ May be non-strategic
- ☐ May overmanage to get things done too quickly
- ☐ May have personal and family problems due to disinterest and neglect
- ☐ May not attend to important but non-challenging duties and tasks
- ☐ May ignore personal life, burn out

Select one to three of the competencies listed below to work on to compensate for an overuse of this skill.

COMPENSATORS: 11,27,33,39,41,43,47,50,51,52,60,66

Some Causes

- ☐ Burned out
- ☐ Hang on to too much
- ☐ Not motivated; bored
- ☐ Not passionate enough about your work
- ☐ Not self-confident
- ☐ Perfectionist
- ☐ Procrastinate
- ☐ Slow to grab an opportunity
- ☐ Won't take a risk

Leadership Architect® Factors and Clusters

This competency is in the Energy and Drive Factor (IV). This competency is in the Focusing on the Bottom Line Cluster (J) with: 43, 53. You may want to check other competencies in the same Factor/Cluster for related tips.

The Map

One mission-critical competency for today and the future is action orientation. The need for speed and agility in the marketplace means that those individuals and organizations who hesitate will be overtaken by those who don't. Most successful senior managers count action orientation as one of their strengths. The hesitation mainly comes from perfectionism, procrastination or risk avoidance. All cause people to delay taking quick and timely action.

Some Remedies

☐ **1. Procrastinator? Get an early start.** Are you a lifelong procrastinator? Do you perform best in crises and impossible deadlines? Do you wait until the last possible moment? If you do, you will miss some deadlines and performance targets. You may be late taking action. Start earlier. Always do 10% of each task immediately after it is assigned so you can better gauge what it is going to take to finish the rest. Break the task down into smaller pieces. Commit to doing a piece a day. Don't even think of the larger goal. Just do something on it each day. One small step for a procrastinator, one giant step forward to being more action oriented. *More help? – See #16 Timely Decision Making and #47 Planning.*

☐ **2. Perfectionist? Curb your appetite for certainty.** Need to be 100% sure? Perfectionism is tough to let go of because it's a positive trait for most. Worried about what people will say when you mess up? When every "t" isn't crossed? Recognize your perfectionism for what it might be—collecting information to improve your confidence and avoid criticism, examining opportunities so long you miss them, or waiting for the perfect solution.

Try to decrease your need for all of the data and your need to be right all the time slightly every week, until you reach a more reasonable balance between thinking it through and taking action. Also, you may hold on to too much of the work, fail to delegate, and are becoming a bottleneck preventing action around you. One way to overcome this is to begin to believe in others and let them do some of the work for you. *More help? – See #18 Delegation and #19 Developing Direct Reports and Others.*

☐ **3. Struck by analysis paralysis? Balance thought with action.** Break out of your examine-it-to-death mode and just do it. Sometimes you hold back acting because you don't have all the information. Some like to be close to 100% sure before they act. Anyone with a brain and 100% of the data can make good decisions. The real test is who can act the soonest with a reasonable amount but not all of the data. Some studies suggest successful general managers are about 65% correct. If you learn to make smaller decisions more quickly, you can change course along the way to the correct decision. You may examine things to death because you are a chronic worrier who focuses on the downsides of action. Write down your worries, and for each one, write down the upside (a pro for each con). Once you consider both sides of the issue, you should be more willing to take action. Virtually any conceivable action has a downside, but it has an upside as well. Act, get feedback on the results, refine, and act again.

☐ **4. Not sure if you can do it? Build your confidence.** Maybe you're slow to act because you don't think you're up to the task. If you boldly act, others will shoot you down and find you out. Take a course or work with a tutor to bolster your confidence in one skill or area at a time. Focus on the strengths you do have; think of ways you can use these strengths when making nerve-wracking actions. If you are interpersonally skilled, for example, see yourself smoothly dealing with questions and objections to your actions. The only way you will ever know what you can do is to act and find out.

☐ **5. Don't like risk? Start small.** Sometimes taking action involves pushing the envelope, taking chances and trying bold new initiatives. Doing those things leads to more misfires and mistakes. Research says that successful executives have made more mistakes in their career than those who didn't make it. Treat any mistakes or failures as chances to learn. Nothing ventured, nothing gained. Up your risk comfort. Start small so you can recover more quickly. Go for small wins. Don't blast into a major task to prove your boldness. Break it down into smaller tasks. Take the easiest one for you first. Then build up to the tougher ones. Review each one to see what you did well and not well, and set goals so you'll do something differently and better each time. End up accomplishing the big goal and taking the bold action. Challenge yourself. See how creative you can be in taking action a number of different ways. *More help? – See #2 Dealing with Ambiguity, #14 Creativity, and #28 Innovation Management.*

☐ **6. Lost your passion? Focus on your interests.** Run out of gas? Heart's not in it anymore? Not 100% committed? Doing the same sort of work a long time and you're bored with it? Seen it all; done the same tasks, made the same decisions, worked with the same people? To make the best of this, make a list of what you like and don't like to do. Concentrate on doing at least a couple of liked activities each day. Work to delegate or task trade the things that are no longer motivating to you. Do your least preferred activities first; focus not on the activity, but your sense of accomplishment. Change your work activity to mirror your interests as much as you can. Volunteer for task forces and projects that would be motivating for you.

☐ **7. Moving, but in the wrong direction? Set better priorities.** You may not have the correct set of priorities. Some people take action but on the wrong things. Effective managers typically spend about half their time on two or three key priorities. What should you spend half your time on? Can you name five things that you have to do that are less critical? If you can't, you're not differentiating well. People without priorities see their jobs as 97 things that need to be done right now—that will actually slow you down. Pick a few mission-critical things and get them done. Don't get diverted by trivia. *More help? – See #50 Priority Setting.*

☐ **8. Not sure where to get started? Get organized.** Some don't know the best way to get things done. There is a well-established set of best practices for getting work done efficiently and effectively—TQM, ISO or Six Sigma. If you are not disciplined in how you design work for yourself and others, and are late taking action because of it, buy one book on each of these topics. Go to one workshop on efficient and effective work design. *More help? – See #52 Process Management and #63 Total Work Systems (e.g., TQM/ISO/Six Sigma).*

☐ **9. Afraid to get others involved? Polish your sales pitch.** Taking action requires that you get others on board. Work on your influence and selling skills. Lay out the business reason for the action. Think about how you can help everybody win with the action. Get others involved before you have to take action. Involved people are easier to influence. Learn better negotiation skills. Learn to bargain and trade. *More help? – See #31 Interpersonal Savvy, #37 Negotiating, and #39 Organizing.*

☐ **10. Not committed? Consider a shift.** Maybe you are giving as much to work as you care to give. Maybe you have made a life/work balance decision that leads you to a fair day's work for a fair day's pay mode of operating. No more. No less. That is an admirable decision. Certainly one you can and should make. Problem is, you may be in a job where that's not enough. Otherwise people would not have given you this rating. You might want to talk to your boss to get transferred to a more comfortable job for you; one that doesn't take as much effort and require as much action initiation on your part. You may even think about moving down to the job level where your balance between quality of life, and effort and hours required of you at work are more balanced.

Some Develop-in-Place Assignments

- ☐ Manage a group through a significant business crisis.
- ☐ Take on a task you dislike or hate to do.
- ☐ Take on a tough and undoable project, one where others who have tried it have failed.
- ☐ Resolve an issue in conflict between two people, units, geographies, functions, etc.
- ☐ Relaunch an existing product or service that's not doing well.

There are risks and costs to a program of action. But they are far less than the long-range risks and costs of comfortable inaction.
John F. Kennedy – 35th President of the United States

Suggested Readings

Allen, D. (2003). *Getting things done: The art of stress-free productivity*. New York: Penguin Group.

Allen, D. (2003). *Ready for anything: 52 Productivity principals for work and life*. New York: Penguin Group.

Bandrowski, J. F. (2000). *Corporate imagination plus: Five steps to translating innovative strategies into action*. New York: Free Press.

Block, P. (2001). *The answer to how is yes: Acting on what matters*. San Francisco: Berrett-Koehler Publishers.

Bossidy, L., & Charan, R. (with Burck, C.). (2002). *Execution: The discipline of getting things done*. New York: Crown Business.

Bryant, T. (2004). *Self-discipline in 10 days: How to go from thinking to doing*. Seattle, WA: HUB Publishing.

Burka, J. B. (2004). *Procrastination: Why you do it, what to do about it*. Cambridge, MA: Da Capo Press.

Collins, J. C. (2000). Turning goals into results: The power of catalytic mechanisms (HBR OnPoint Enhanced Edition). Boston: *Harvard Business Review*.

Collins, J. C. (2001). *Good to great: Why some companies make the leap...and others don't*. New York: HarperCollins.

Conger, J. A., Spreitzer, G. M., & Lawler, E. E., III (Eds.). (1999). *The leader's change handbook: An essential guide to setting direction and taking action*. San Francisco: Jossey-Bass.

Fiore, N. (2007). *The now habit: A strategic program for overcoming procrastination and enjoying guilt-free play*. New York: Tarcher/Putnam.

Gleeson, K. (2003). *The personal efficiency program: How to get organized to do more work in less time* (3rd ed.). Hoboken, NJ: John Wiley & Sons.

Huselid, M. A., Becker, B. E., & Beatty, R. W. (2005). *The workforce scorecard: Managing human capital to execute strategy*. Boston: Harvard Business School Press.

Kaplan, R. S., & Norton, D. P. (1996). *The balanced scorecard: Translating strategy into action*. Boston: Harvard Business School Press.

King, J. B. (2004). *Business plans to game plans: A practical system for turning strategies into action*. Hoboken, NJ: John Wiley & Sons.

Kotter, J. P., & Cohen, D. S. (2002). *The heart of change: Real-life stories of how people change their organizations*. Boston: Harvard Business School Press.

Niven, P. R. (2006). *Balanced scorecard step-by-step: Maximizing performance and maintaining results* (2nd ed.). Hoboken, NJ: John Wiley & Sons.

Pfeffer, J., & Sutton, R. I. (2000). *The knowing-doing gap: How smart companies turn knowledge into action*. Boston: Harvard Business School Press.

Torbert, W. R. (2004). *Action inquiry: The secret of timely and transforming leadership*. San Francisco: Berrett-Koehler Publishers.

2 *Dealing with* Ambiguity

Life is about not knowing, having to change, taking the moment and making the best of it, without knowing what's going to happen next. Delicious ambiguity.
Gilda Radner – Emmy Award-winning American comedienne and actress

Unskilled

- ☐ Not comfortable with change or uncertainty
- ☐ May not do well on fuzzy problems with no clear solution or outcome
- ☐ May prefer more data than others, and structure over uncertainty
- ☐ Prefers things tacked down and sure
- ☐ Less efficient and productive under ambiguity
- ☐ Too quick to close
- ☐ May have a strong need to finish everything
- ☐ May like to do things the same way time after time

Select one to three of the competencies listed below to use as a substitute for this competency if you decide not to work on it directly.

SUBSTITUTES: 1,5,12,14,16,28,30,32,36,39,40,46,47,50,51,52,53,58

Skilled

- ☐ Can effectively cope with change
- ☐ Can shift gears comfortably
- ☐ Can decide and act without having the total picture
- ☐ Isn't upset when things are up in the air
- ☐ Doesn't have to finish things before moving on
- ☐ Can comfortably handle risk and uncertainty

Overused Skill

- ☐ May move to conclusions without enough data
- ☐ May fill in gaps by adding things that aren't there
- ☐ May frustrate others by not getting specific enough
- ☐ May undervalue orderly problem solving
- ☐ May reject precedent and history
- ☐ May err toward the new and risky at the expense of proven solutions
- ☐ May over-complicate things

Select one to three of the competencies listed below to work on to compensate for an overuse of this skill.

COMPENSATORS: 5,17,24,30,35,39,40,47,50,51,52,59,61,63

Some Causes

- ☐ Avoid criticism
- ☐ Avoid risk
- ☐ Disorganized
- ☐ Get overwhelmed
- ☐ Like structure and control
- ☐ Perfectionist

Leadership Architect® Factors and Clusters

This competency is in the Strategic Skills Factor (I). This competency is in the Creating the New and Different Cluster (C) with: 14, 28, 46, 58. You may want to check other competencies in the same Factor/Cluster for related tips.

The Map

According to studies, 90% of the problems of middle managers and above are ambiguous—it's neither clear what the problem is nor what the solution is. The higher you go, the more ambiguous things get. Most people with a brain, given unlimited time and 100% of the information, could make accurate and good decisions. Most people, given access to how this specific problem has been solved hundreds of times before, could repeat the right decision. The real rewards go to those who can comfortably make more good decisions than bad with less than all of the information, in less time, with few or no precedents on how it was solved before.

Some Remedies

- ☐ **1. Overwhelmed? Take small, incremental steps.** The essence of dealing comfortably with uncertainty is the tolerance of errors and mistakes, and absorbing the possible heat and criticism that follow. Acting on an ill-defined problem with no precedents to follow means shooting in the dark with as informed a decision as you can make at the time. People who are good at this are incrementalists. They make a series of smaller decisions, get instant feedback, correct the course, get a little more data, move forward a little more, until the bigger problem is under control. They don't try to get it right the first time. Many problem-solving studies show that the second or third try is when we really understand the underlying dynamics of problems. They also know that the more uncertain the situation is, the more likely it is they will make mistakes in the beginning. So you need to work on two practices. Start small so you can recover more quickly. Do little somethings as soon as you can and get used to heat.
- ☐ **2. Perfectionist? Balance thinking with action.** Need or prefer or want to be 100% sure? Lots might prefer that. Perfectionism is tough to let go of

because most people see it as a positive trait for themselves. Recognize your perfectionism for what it might be—collecting more information than others to improve your confidence in making a fault-free decision and thereby avoiding risk and criticism. Try to decrease your need for data and your need to be right all the time slightly every week until you reach a more reasonable balance between thinking it through and taking action. Try making some small decisions on little or no data. Anyone with a brain and 100% of the data can make good decisions. The real test is who can act the soonest with a reasonable amount, but not all, of the data. Some studies suggest successful general managers are about 65% correct. Trust your intuition. Let your brain do the calculations.

☐ **3. Stuck with what you know? Broaden your horizon.** Do you feel best when you know everything that's going on around you and are in control? Most do. Few are motivated by uncertainty and chaos. But many are challenged by it. They enjoy solving problems no one has solved before. They enjoy cutting paths where no one has been before. You need to become more comfortable being a pioneer. Explore new ground. Learn new things. Practice in your life. Go to theme restaurants you know nothing about. Vacation at places without doing a lot of research. Go to ethnic festivals for groups you have little knowledge about.

☐ **4. Disorganized? Get organized.** Under uncertainty, you have to put the keel in the water yourself. You need to set tight priorities. Focus on the mission-critical few. Don't get diverted by trivia. Get better organized and disciplined. There is a well-established set of best practices for getting work done efficiently and effectively. If you are not disciplined in how you design work for yourself and others and are late taking action because of it, buy books on TQM, ISO and Six Sigma. Go to one workshop on efficient and effective work design. *More help? – See #50 Priority Setting, #52 Process Management, and #63 Total Work Systems (e.g., TQM/ISO/Six Sigma).*

☐ **5. Muddled problem definition? Ask the right questions to define the problem.** Under uncertainty, it really helps to get as firm a handle as possible on the problem. Figure out what causes it. Keep asking why. See how many causes you can come up with and how many organizing buckets you can put them in. This increases the chance of a better solution because you can see more connections. The evidence from decision-making research makes it clear that thorough problem definition with appropriate questions to answer leads to better decisions. Focusing on solutions or information first often slows things down since we have no conceptual buckets in which to organize our thinking. Learn to ask more questions. In one study of problem solving, 7% of comments were questions and about half were solutions.

- ☐ **6. Daunted by complexity? Visualize the problem.** Complex processes or problems with a lot of uncertainty are hard to understand. They tend to be a hopeless maze unless they are put in a visual format. One technique is a pictorial chart called a storyboard where a process or vision or strategy is illustrated by its components being depicted as pictures. A variation of this is to do the old pro and con, +'s and –'s of a problem and process, then flow chart those according to what's working and not working. Another is the fishbone diagram used in Total Quality Management. It is a method of breaking down the causes of a problem into categories. Buy a flow charting and/or project planning software program to help you visualize problems quickly.
- ☐ **7. Afraid to fail? Develop a philosophical stance toward failure/criticism.** After all, most innovations fail, most proposals fail, most change efforts fail, anything worth doing takes repeated effort. To increase learning from your mistakes, design feedback loops to be as immediate as possible. The faster and the more frequent the cycles, the more opportunities to learn—if we do one smaller thing a day for three days instead of one bigger thing in three, we triple our learning opportunities. There will be many mistakes and failures; after all, since you're not sure, it's very likely no one else knows what to do either. They just have a right to comment on your errors. The best tack when confronted with a mistake is to say "What can we learn from this?" *More help? – See #45 Personal Learning.*
- ☐ **8. Stressed out? Manage your stress.** Some get stressed with increased ambiguity and uncertainty. We lose our anchor. We are not at our best when we are anxious, frustrated, upset or when we lose our cool. What brings out your emotional response? Write down why you get anxious—when you don't know what to do; don't want to make a mistake; afraid of the unknown consequences; don't have the confidence to act. When you get emotional, drop the problem for a while. Go do something else. Come back to it when you are under better control. Let your brain work on it while you do something safer. *More help? – See #11 Composure and #107 Lack of Composure.*
- ☐ **9. Nothing to hold on to? Let go.** Change is letting go of one trapeze in the air to catch the next one. For a small amount of time, you have hold of nothing but thin air. The second gets you to a new platform and a new place. If you hang on to the first one, afraid you will fall, you will always return to the same old platform; safe but not new or different. Change is letting go. Stay informed about business/technological change and ask what it means for your work. Visualize a different and better outcome.

Talk about it. Invite ideas. Interview those who have successfully pulled off changes. Experiment. The more you do this, the more comfortable you'll feel. To better understand dealing with change, read *The Future of Leadership* by White, Hodgson and Crainer.

- ☐ **10. Want to check it off your list? Redefine progress.** Do you prefer to finish what you have started? Do you have a high need to complete tasks? Wrap them up in nice clean packages? Working well with ambiguity and under uncertainty means moving from incomplete task to incomplete task. Some may be abandoned, some may never be finished. They'll probably only ever get 80% done and you'll constantly have to edit your actions and decisions. Change your internal reward process toward feeling good about fixing mistakes and moving things forward incrementally, more than finishing any given project.

Some Develop-in-Place Assignments

- ☐ Make peace with an enemy or someone you've disappointed with a product or service or someone you've had some trouble with or don't get along with very well.
- ☐ Take on a task you dislike or hate to do.
- ☐ Take on a tough and undoable project, one where others who have tried it have failed.
- ☐ Go on a business trip to a foreign country you've not been to before.
- ☐ Integrate diverse systems, processes, or procedures across decentralized and/or dispersed units.

In the future, instead of striving to be right at a high cost, it will be more appropriate to be flexible and plural at a lower cost. If you cannot accurately predict the future, then you must flexibly be prepared to deal with various possible futures.

Edward de Bono – British physician, author, inventor, and consultant

Suggested Readings

Anderson, D., & Ackerman Anderson, L. S. (2001). *Beyond change management: Advanced strategies for today's transformational leaders.* San Francisco: Jossey-Bass.

Black, J. S., & Gregersen, H. B. (2002). *Leading strategic change: Breaking through the brain barrier.* Upper Saddle River, NJ: Financial Times/Prentice Hall.

Bolman, L. G., & Deal, T. E. (2008). *Reframing organizations: Artistry, choice, and leadership.* San Francisco: Jossey-Bass.

Calzada, L. (2007). *180 Ways to effectively deal with change: Get over it! Get with it! Get to it!* Flower Mound, TX: Walk the Talk Company.

Chapman, R. J. (2006). *Simple tools and techniques for enterprise risk management.* West Sussex, England: John Wiley & Sons, Ltd.

Chowdhury, S. (2000). *Management 21C: Someday we'll all manage this way.* Upper Saddle River, NJ: Financial Times/Prentice Hall.

Fullan, M. (2007). *Leading in a culture of change* (Rev. ed.). San Francisco: Jossey-Bass.

Gutzman, A. D. (2002). *Unforeseen circumstances.* New York: AMACOM.

Hillson, D., & Murray-Webster, R. (2007). *Understanding and managing risk attitude.* Burlington, VT: Gower Technical Press.

Koller, G. (2005). *Risk assessment and decision making in business and industry: A practical guide* (2nd ed.). Boca Raton, FL: Chapman & Hall/CRC.

Kotter, J. P., & Cohen, D. S. (2002). *The heart of change: Real-life stories of how people change their organizations.* Boston: Harvard Business School Press.

Kotter, J. P., & Rathgeber, H. (2006). *Our iceberg is melting: Changing and succeeding under any conditions.* New York: St. Martin's Press.

Kotter, J. P., & Schlesinger, L. A. (2008). Choosing strategies for change. *Harvard Business Review, 86,* 130-139.

Pascale, R. T., Millemann, M., & Gioja, L. (2001). *Surfing the edge of chaos: The laws of nature and the new laws of business.* New York: Three Rivers Press.

Shapiro, E., & Stevenson, H. H. (2005). *Make your own luck: 12 Practical steps to taking smarter risks in business.* New York: Portfolio.

Wilkinson, D. (2006). *The ambiguity advantage: What great leaders are great at.* Hampshire, England: Palgrave Macmillan.

3 Approachability

A true leader has to have a genuine open-door policy so that his people are not afraid to approach him for any reason.
Harold S. Geneen – American businessman

Unskilled

- ☐ Distant, not easy to be around
- ☐ Not comfortable with first contacts
- ☐ May be shy, cool or a person of few words
- ☐ Doesn't reveal much, hard to know what he/she is really like
- ☐ Doesn't build rapport, may be a "let's get on with it" type
- ☐ May be a poor listener or appear uninterested
- ☐ May not pick up on social cues that others would recognize
- ☐ May be tense
- ☐ Transactions don't go smoothly

Select one to three of the competencies listed below to use as a substitute for this competency if you decide not to work on it directly.

SUBSTITUTES: 4,7,10,11,15,21,23,27,31,33,36,41,42,60

Skilled

- ☐ Is easy to approach and talk to
- ☐ Spends the extra effort to put others at ease
- ☐ Can be warm, pleasant, and gracious
- ☐ Is sensitive to and patient with the interpersonal anxieties of others
- ☐ Builds rapport well
- ☐ Is a good listener
- ☐ Is an early knower, getting informal and incomplete information in time to do something about it

Overused Skill

- ☐ May waste too much time building rapport in meetings
- ☐ May be misinterpreted as easy-going or easy to influence
- ☐ May have too strong a desire to be liked
- ☐ May avoid necessary negative or unpleasant transactions
- ☐ May try to smooth over real issues and problems

Select one to three of the competencies listed below to work on to compensate for an overuse of this skill.

COMPENSATORS: 1,5,9,12,13,16,17,20,30,34,35,37,43,50,53,57,65

Some Causes

- ☐ Arrogant
- ☐ Insensitive
- ☐ Judgmental
- ☐ Not interpersonally skilled
- ☐ Not self-confident
- ☐ Shy
- ☐ Busy, busy, busy
- ☐ Too intense; can't relax

Leadership Architect® Factors and Clusters

This competency is in the Personal and Interpersonal Skills Factor (VI). This competency is in the Relating Skills Cluster (N) with: 31. You may want to check other competencies in the same Factor/Cluster for related tips.

The Map

Being approachable means putting others at ease so that they can be at their best. It means initiating rapport, listening, sharing, understanding and comforting. Approachable people get more information, know things earlier, and can get others to do more things. People just like to have them around.

Some Remedies

☐ **1. Not sure where to begin? Make the first move.** Being approachable means you have to initiate the transaction. You have to put out your hand first. Make first eye contact. Note the color of the person's eyes to ensure good eye contact. You have to ask the first question or share the first piece of information. You have to make the first three minutes comfortable for the other person or group so they can accomplish what they came to you to do.

☐ **2. Too quick to judge? Start listening.** Approachable people are very good at listening. They listen without interrupting. They ask clarifying questions. They don't instantly judge. They listen to understand. Judgment may come later. They restate what the other person has said to signal understanding. They nod. They may jot down notes. Listeners don't always offer advice or solutions unless it's obvious the person wants to know what they would do. *More help? – See #33 Listening.*

☐ **3. Are you overly private? Share more.** Approachable people share more information and get more in return. Confide your thinking on a business issue and invite the response of others. Pass on tidbits of information you think will help people do their jobs better or broaden their perspectives. Disclose some things about yourself. It's hard for people to relate to an enigma. Reveal things that people don't need to know to do their jobs, but which will be interesting to them—and help them feel valued. *More help? – See #44 Personal Disclosure.*

☐ **4. Not a fan of small talk? Make connections.** Approachable people work to know and remember important things about the people they work around, for, and with. Know three things about everybody—their interests or their children or something you can chat about other than the business agenda. Treat life as a small world. If you ask a few questions, you'll find you have something in common with virtually anyone. Establish things you can talk about with each person you work with that go beyond strictly work transactions. These need not be social, they could be issues of strategy, global events, market shifts. The point is to forge common ground and connections.

☐ **5. Appear to lack interest? Watch your non-verbals.** Approachable people appear and sound open and relaxed. They smile. They are calm. They keep eye contact. They nod while the other person is talking. They have an open body posture. They speak in a paced and pleasant tone. Eliminate any disruptive habits such as speaking too rapidly or forcefully, using strongly worded or loaded language, or going into too much detail. Watch out for signaling disinterest with actions like glancing at your watch, fiddling with paperwork or giving your impatient "I'm busy" look.

☐ **6. Think you've got all the answers? Ask lots of questions.** Many people don't ask enough curiosity questions when in their work mode. There are too many informational statements, conclusions, suggestions and solutions and not enough "what if," "what are you thinking," "how do you see that." In studies, statements outweighed questions eight to one. Ask more questions than others. Make fewer solution statements early in a discussion. Keep probing until you understand what they are trying to tell you.

☐ **7. Selective with your approachability? Be universally approachable.** Some people are approachable with some and not with others. Some might be approachable to direct reports and tense around senior management. List the people you can be approachable with and those you can't. What do the people you are comfortable around have in common? Not comfortable with? Is it level? Style? Gender? Race? Background? Of course, the principles of being approachable are the same regardless of the audience. Do what you do with the comfortable group with the uncomfortable groups. The results will be the same.

☐ **8. Need to get out of your shell? Overcome shyness.** Trouble with appearing vulnerable? Afraid of how people will react? Not sure of your social skills? Want to appear—while shaking inside—not shy? Hand first.

Consistent eye contact. Ask the first question. For low-risk practice, talk to strangers off-work. Set a goal of meeting 10 new people at a social gathering; find out what you have in common with them. Initiate contact at your place of worship, at PTA meetings, in the neighborhood, at the supermarket, on the plane and on the bus. See if any of the bad and scary things you think might happen to you if you initiate people contact actually happen. *More help? – See #31 Interpersonal Savvy.*

☐ **9. Make others uncomfortable? Put people at ease.** Arrogant people are seen as distant and impersonal loners who prefer their own ideas to anyone else's. They purposefully, or not, devalue others and their contributions. This usually results in people feeling diminished, rejected and angry. Why? Answers. Solutions. Conclusions. Statements. Dictates. That's the staple of arrogant people. Not listening. Instant output. Sharp reactions. Don't want to be that way? Read your audience. Do you know what people look like when they are uncomfortable with you? Do they back up? Stumble over words? Cringe? Stand at the door hoping not to get invited in? You should work doubly hard at observing others. Especially during the first three minutes of an important transaction, work to make the person or group comfortable with you before the real agenda starts. Ask a question unrelated to the topic. Offer them something to drink. Share something personal. *More help? – See #104 Arrogant.*

☐ **10. Difficulty serving as a sounding board? Prepare for conflict.** As you become more approachable, you will invite more conflict. If someone is angry, let him/her vent without saying anything other than you know he/she is upset. It's hard for most people to continue for very long with no encouragement or resistance. If someone is a chronic complainer, ask him/her to write down problems and solutions and then discuss it. This turns down the volume while hopefully moving him/her off complaining. If someone wants to complain about someone else, ask if he/she has talked to the person. Encourage him/her to do so. If that doesn't work, summarize what he/she has said without agreeing or disagreeing. *More help? – See #12 Conflict Management.* You'll also invite more contact along with the conflict, and you don't want to become the local coffee shop. Manage your time by gently interrupting to summarize or asking people to think about it more, then let's continue. Disclose things that can be said quickly. Defer extended conversations to other times. Approachability doesn't mean you have to give up control of your time.

Some Develop-in-Place Assignments

- ☐ Make peace with an enemy or someone you've disappointed with a product or service or someone you've had some trouble with or don't get along with very well.
- ☐ Manage the outplacement of a group of people.
- ☐ Manage a temporary group of "green," inexperienced people as their coach, teacher, guide, mentor, etc.
- ☐ Train customers in the use of the organization's products or services.
- ☐ Create employee involvement teams.

Small cheer and great welcome makes a merry feast.
William Shakespeare – English poet and playwright

Suggested Readings

Alessandra, T. (2002). *The 10 qualities of charismatic people: Secrets of personal magnetism*. Chicago: Nightingale-Conant Corp.

Bardwick, J. M. (2002). *Seeking the calm in the storm: Managing chaos in your business life*. Upper Saddle River, NJ: Financial Times/Prentice Hall.

Benton, D. A. (2003). *Executive charisma: Six steps to mastering the art of leadership*. New York: McGraw-Hill Trade.

DuBrin, A. (2006). *Human relations: Interpersonal job-oriented skills* (9th ed.). Upper Saddle River, NJ: Financial Times/Prentice Hall.

Elsdon, R. (2002). *Affiliation in the workplace: Value creation in the new organization*. Westport, CT: Praeger Publishers.

Fritz, S. M., Lunde, J. P., Brown, W., & Banset, E. A. (2004). *Interpersonal skills for leadership* (2nd ed.). Upper Saddle River, NJ: Prentice Hall.

Gilbert, M. (2002). *Communication miracles at work: Effective tools and tips for getting the most from your work relationships*. Berkeley, CA: Conari Press.

Goleman, D. (2007). *Social intelligence: The new science of human relationships*. New York: Bantam Books.

Goman, C. (2008). *The nonverbal advantage: Secrets and science of body language at work*. San Francisco: Berrett-Koehler Publishers.

Hayes, J. (2002). *Interpersonal skills at work*. New York: Routledge.

Klaus, P. (2007). *The hard truth about soft skills: Workplace lessons smart people wish they'd learned sooner*. New York: HarperCollins.

Lowndes, L. (2003). *How to talk to anyone: 92 Little tricks for big success in relationships*. New York: McGraw-Hill.

Maslow, A. H. (1998). *Maslow on management*. New York: John Wiley & Sons.

Oatey, H. S. (2000). *Culturally speaking: Managing rapport in talk across cultures*. New York: Continuum.

4 Boss Relationships

The person who knows 'how' will always have a job.
The person who knows 'why' will always be his boss.
Diane Ravitch – American author

Unskilled

- ☐ Not comfortable with bosses
- ☐ May be tense in boss's presence
- ☐ May not be open to coaching or direction from bosses
- ☐ Problems dealing comfortably with authority
- ☐ Poor boss relationships get in the way of working productively

Select one to three of the competencies listed below to use as a substitute for this competency if you decide not to work on it directly.

SUBSTITUTES: 3,11,12,15,21,27,29,33,37,41,48

Skilled

- ☐ Responds and relates well to bosses
- ☐ Would work harder for a good boss
- ☐ Is open to learning from bosses who are good coaches and who provide latitude
- ☐ Likes to learn from those who have been there before
- ☐ Easy to challenge and develop
- ☐ Is comfortably coachable

Overused Skill

- ☐ May be overdependent on bosses and high status figures for advice and counsel
- ☐ May shut out other sources of feedback and learning
- ☐ May pick the wrong boss to model

Select one to three of the competencies listed below to work on to compensate for an overuse of this skill.

COMPENSATORS: 1,17,34,38,45,51,53,54,57

Some Causes

- ☐ The boss doesn't think you're as good as you think you are
- ☐ Jealousy about the boss getting a job you think you should have had
- ☐ Large gap in skills leading to one undervaluing/not respecting the other; can be in either direction

- ☐ Mismatches in ethics, values and integrity
- ☐ Mismatches in management practices
- ☐ Mismatches in style, philosophy, pace and motivation

Leadership Architect® Factors and Clusters

This competency is in the Personal and Interpersonal Skills Factor (VI). This competency is in the Managing Diverse Relationships Cluster (P) with: 15, 21, 23, 42, 64. You may want to check other competencies in the same Factor/Cluster for related tips.

The Map

Most people have trouble with about 50% of their bosses, so you have lots of company. Remember, you never stay with one boss that long; either he/she will move on or you will. It may be best to try to wait it out; there will be a reorganization shortly. Try to learn from the experience.

Some Remedies

☐ **1. Unsure where to focus? Drive down the rocky road.** The key is to manage the rocky relationship so it leaves behind the least amount of long-term noise for you and the organization. Focus on the three key problems you need to work on with him or her and do them. Keep your head down. Keep your conversations with the boss directed at these core agenda. Focus on expectations; ask what results indicate success. Find out about your boss's job and what sorts of pressures he or she is under.

☐ **2. Loose lips? Keep it to yourself.** Unless the cause is related to breaches of ethics or integrity, don't gossip about it with your coworkers. Your boss has a right to expect your loyalty and support on issues of work and performance. If he/she gives you an assignment you view as unfair, how do you know it wasn't dumped on him/her? Even if it wasn't, this is hardly an unusual happening in organizations. Reset your priorities and get on with it. If you have to carry out an unpopular mission, this will hardly be the last time. Keep your eyes on the goal. While it's fine to discuss difficulties you're having in performing with others, it's not wise to question why you're having to perform it at all. All things you say have a way of coming around again. If there is an integrity issue involved, take it to the proper authorities. Remember that in a study of whistle-blowers, 100% of those with grand and general causes failed. People who go in with huge issues like integrity, philosophical differences, or the utter incompetence of a person usually fail to back up their charges. Go in with specifics and specific events. If they form a pattern, let others decide what that pattern is.

☐ **3. Don't like the boss? Learn to depersonalize and be neutral.** Try to separate the person from the boss role he/she is in; try to objectify the situation. Someone made her/him boss for a reason and you are never going to please everyone. Deal with him/her as your boss more than as a person. While you don't ever have to invite her/him to your home, you do have to deal with this person as a boss. Ask yourself why you dislike your boss so much or don't like to work with him/her. Write down everything you don't like on the left-hand side of a page. On the right-hand side write a strategy for dealing with it. Consider these strategies: Ask what strengths you can appeal to; ask what you can provide that the boss needs; ask what the boss would like for you to do to be more effective; design a project that you can do together so you can have a success experience; and consult with others for advice. What do people think who have a favorable impression of your boss? Do you share any common interests? Write down everything you've heard him/her say that was favorable. Play to the boss's good points. Whatever you do, don't signal what you think. Put your judgments on hold, nod, ask questions, summarize as you would with anyone else. A fly on the wall should not be able to tell whether you're talking to friend or foe. You can always talk less and ask more questions.

☐ **4. Think it's all the boss's fault? Try to learn from the situation.** Honestly, what part did you play in contributing to the rough relationship? What could you have done differently to make the situation more livable? What will you do next time when you see the first signs of trouble like this? Even if your boss would be condemned by many, you are responsible for your reactions. If you respond with anger and blame, you're not learning to do anything different. In fact, you may end up mirroring your boss!

☐ **5. Need a fresh perspective? Seek feedback from others.** Get some feedback from those you trust about who you are. What are your real strengths and weaknesses? You need to have the clearest possible view of the situation. Get advice about managing and improving on the relationship from a trusted mentor, colleague or someone in the Human Resources function. After all, maybe it's you as well. How are you at interpersonal reads? Do you know what drives your boss? Do you talk detail and he's a big picture person? Do you fight her style which is more action oriented than yours? Do you get in unproductive values debates? Do you use words that set the boss off? *More help? – See #31 Interpersonal Savvy.*

☐ **6. Easily irritated? Find your triggers.** Keep a journal on what the boss does to irritate or bother you to make sure that when you get promoted, you won't be guilty of the same behaviors. Once you know what triggers you, learn to manage these tense transactions better. If your boss blows up, for example, listen to the venting, but don't react directly. Remember that it's the person who hits back who usually gets in the most trouble. Listen. Nod. Ask "What could I do to help?" or "So you think I need to...." Restate his/her position periodically to signal you have understood. Even if the boss attacks, separate the person from the problem. Count to 10, then return to the problem, not you. *More help? – See #11 Composure and #12 Conflict Management.*

- ☐ **7. Confused by boss behavior? Assess boss motives.** Try to objectively describe the boss in terms of strengths and weaknesses. Even bad people have strengths. In confidence, get someone else to help you. Try to determine why the boss does what he/she does, even though you may not agree with the logic or wouldn't do it that way yourself. How would you act in the same circumstance?
- ☐ **8. Tempted to fight back? Seek some common ground.** Even if your boss is a bad one, research strongly indicates that confronting the situation directly usually fails. The best tactics are to view it as a conflict situation *(More help? – See #12 Conflict Management)*, see what you can learn from it and try to develop some common ground. If you can't, show some patience. Precipitous actions will probably reflect negatively on you more than on your boss. The book may have already been written on your boss; make sure it doesn't get written on you as well. For more help read *Coping with Difficult Bosses* by Robert Bramson or *How to Manage Your Boss* by Christopher Hegarty.
- ☐ **9. Want to improve the situation? Have solutions-based discussions with the boss.** If appropriate or possible, equipped with the insights you have come to in the previous steps, try to have a series of informal relaxed discussions with your boss about what the problem might be, leading with your contributions—we are seldom completely in the right—to the problem first; then give him/her an opportunity to add to the discussion. Make it easy for him/her by indicating, "You are doing me a favor. I need your help." In return for your boss's help, offer some in return. What are your boss's weakest areas or what can you do to make the job easier? Figure out what those are and pitch in. This is good practice because relationships don't often prosper unless there is some equity built in. Give to get or your boss may soon be uncomfortable with the one-way nature of the help. Some rules to follow. Describe. Say "I" not "you," focus on how to accomplish work better. (If you think the boss is blocking you, instead of saying this, say, "I need help in getting this done. I've tried the following things, but....") If your boss is reluctant to give criticism, help by making statements rather than asking questions. Saying "I think I focus too much on operations and miss some of the larger strategic connections" is easier for most people to reply to than a question which asks them to tell you this

point. If your manager is uninvolved, you will need to provide the structure and aim for a sign-off on your objectives. If you work for a detail-driven micromanager, ask what results you must achieve to be successful (and left alone more). If your manager is well-meaning, but a nuisance, ask if you can check in with him, because you are trying to be more autonomous. If you believe the boss is blocking you, access your network for performance help, think of five ways to accomplish anything and try them all. *More help? – See #43 Perseverance.*

☐ **10. Prepared to live with the situation? Strike a bargain with yourself.** Dedicate yourself to trying to please the boss in his/her role as boss in all legitimate requests by doing your best and not getting distracted by the noise of the relationship. Ask yourself, "What are the performance imperatives of this job?" Make the best of a bad situation. Your career will continue past this boss.

Some Develop-in-Place Assignments

☐ Prepare and present a proposal of some consequence to top management.

☐ Write a speech for someone higher up in the organization.

☐ Manage the interface between consultants and the organization on a critical assignment.

☐ Write a proposal for a new policy, process, mission, charter, product, service, or system, and present and sell it to top management.

☐ Plan an off-site meeting, conference, convention, trade show, event, etc.

If you think your teacher is tough, wait until you get a boss.
He doesn't have tenure.

Bill Gates – American business magnate and
Chairman and cofounder of Microsoft

Suggested Readings

Addesso, P. J. (2007). *The boss from outer space and other aliens at work: A down-to-earth guide for getting along with just about anyone.* New York: AMACOM.

Badowski, R. (with Gittines, R.). (2003). *Managing up: How to forge an effective relationship with those above you.* New York: Currency.

Bing, S. (2002). *Throwing the elephant: Zen and the art of managing up.* New York: HarperBusiness.

Bossidy, L. (2007). What your leader expects of you. *Harvard Business Review, 85*(4), 58-65.

Culbert, S. A., & Ullmen, J. B. (2001). *Don't kill the bosses: Escaping the hierarchy trap.* San Francisco: Berrett-Koehler Publishers.

Dobson, M., & Dobson, D. S. (2000). *Managing up! 59 Ways to build a career-advancing relationship with your boss.* New York: AMACOM.

Dominguez, L. R. (2003). *How to shine at work.* New York: McGraw-Hill.

Forsyth, P. (2007). *Manage your boss: 8 Steps to creating the ideal working relationship.* London: Cyan Communications.

Fox, J. J. (2002). *How to become a great boss: The rules for getting and keeping the best employees.* New York: Hyperion.

Gabarro, J. J., & Kotter, J. P. (2008). *Managing your boss.* Boston: Harvard Business School Press.

Haight, M. (2008). *Who's afraid of the big, bad boss? How to survive 13 types of dysfunctional, disrespectful, dishonest little dictators.* Peoria, AZ: Worded Write.

Hoover, J. (2003). *How to work for an idiot: Survive & thrive: Without killing your boss.* Hawthorne, NJ: Career Press.

Jay, R. (2002). *How to manage your boss: Developing the perfect working relationship.* London: Financial Times Management.

Lukaszewski, J. (2008). *Why should the boss listen to you? The seven disciplines of the trusted strategic advisor.* San Francisco: Jossey-Bass.

Sharpe, D. A., & Johnson, E. (2002). *Managing conflict with your boss.* Greensboro, NC: Center for Creative Leadership.

Useem, M. (2003). *Leading up: How to lead your boss so you both win.* New York: Three Rivers Press.

Weiner, D. L., & Lefton, R. E. (2002). *Power freaks: Dealing with them in the workplace or anyplace.* Amherst, NY: Prometheus Books.

5 Business Acumen

Management means, in the last analysis, the substitution of thought for brawn and muscle, of knowledge for folklore and superstition, and of cooperation for force.

Peter Drucker – Austrian-born American writer and management consultant

Unskilled

- ☐ Doesn't understand how businesses work
- ☐ Not knowledgeable and up-to-date about current and future policies, trends, technology, and information affecting his/her business and organization
- ☐ Doesn't know the competition
- ☐ Is unaware of how strategies and tactics work in the marketplace
- ☐ May be a very dedicated functional or professional expert
- ☐ May be narrowly tactical
- ☐ Lacks interest or experience in general business

Select one to three of the competencies listed below to use as a substitute for this competency if you decide not to work on it directly.

SUBSTITUTES: 8,15,24,30,32,38,46,52,58,61,65

Skilled

- ☐ Knows how businesses work
- ☐ Knowledgeable in current and possible future policies, practices, trends, technology, and information affecting his/her business and organization
- ☐ Knows the competition
- ☐ Is aware of how strategies and tactics work in the marketplace

Overused Skill

- ☐ May overdevelop or depend upon industry and business knowledge and skills at the expense of personal, interpersonal, managerial, and leadership skills

Select one to three of the competencies listed below to work on to compensate for an overuse of this skill.

COMPENSATORS: 14,24,30,32,45,46,54,57,58,61

Some Causes

- ☐ Inexperience; new to the organization
- ☐ Lack of interest in general business
- ☐ Narrow perspective
- ☐ No exposure outside the function
- ☐ Overly dedicated to a profession, not the organization
- ☐ Very tactical and here and now oriented

Leadership Architect® Factors and Clusters

This competency is in the Strategic Skills Factor (I). This competency is in the Understanding the Business Cluster (A) with: 24, 61. You may want to check other competencies in the same Factor/Cluster for related tips.

The Map

You gotta know the territory! Nothing beats knowing what's going on. When people get business savvy indicated as one of their needs, it usually comes in two flavors. The first is that you don't seem to know enough about business in general. This means some of the statements and suggestions you make don't pass the business practicality test. It may also mean what you're suggesting is known not to work and you are unaware of that. The second is that you don't know enough about this specific business and industry. That usually means you don't understand the agenda, issues and concerns of the people you serve inside your organization, and you make comments and have suggestions that don't match their priorities. Your contributions are limited because you don't see priorities as they do. You don't think in terms of the bigger picture. Unless you walk a mile in their shoes, they're not going to pay attention to you.

Some Remedies

☐ **1. Need to get informed? Read the right periodicals.** There are five publications that probably will teach you most of what you need to know about business in general on a continuous basis. They are the *Wall Street Journal, BusinessWeek, Fortune, Barron's,* and the *Harvard Business Review.* Subscribe and begin to scan those publications regularly. Try to see three items per issue that relate to your business. These will be parallels, trends that affect business now, emerging trends that may have a future impact, and general business savvy about how business works.

☐ **2. Not up to speed? Watch the right sources.** There are now three or more business channels on cable that carry business news and information full time. They have interviews with business leaders, reviews of industries by Wall Street experts, as well as general reviews of companies. Begin to watch one or two programs a week until you can zero in on what you specifically need to know.

- ☐ **3. Need access to expertise? Join national organizations.** The Conference Board is dedicated to creating and distributing information about business to its members. They have wonderful conferences where many top leaders of business come and share their thoughts about business in general and their business specifically. Attend one of the national Conference Board meetings. Join your national association. Your industry has a national association. Every function has a national organization. Join it and purchase a number of their publications about business in your specific industry. Attend the national conference.
- ☐ **4. Ready to educate yourself? Quick-study some business books.** Go to any business bookstore and pick three books on general business principles, one with a financial slant, one with a marketing slant and one about customer service. When you have scanned those, go back and get three more until you have the business knowledge you need. Attend a nighttime advanced business program or get an MBA at a local college or university. Subscribe to Soundview Executive Book Summaries (800-521-1227). They summarize in a few pages all the major business books that are on the best-seller lists.
- ☐ **5. Need a mental model? Figure out the rules of the game.** Reduce your understanding of how business operates to personal rules of thumb or insights. Write them down in your own words. An example would be, "What are the drivers in marketing anything?" One executive had 25 such drivers that he continually edited, scratched through and replaced with more up-to-date thinking. Use these rules of thumb to analyze a business that you know something about, possibly one of your hobbies or a sport you are enthusiastic about. Pick what you know. Then pick two businesses that have pulled off clever strategies—one related to yours and one not. Study what they did; talk to people who know what happened and see what you can learn. Then study two businesses that were not successful and see what they didn't do.
- ☐ **6. Superficial business understanding? Learn the specifics of your business.** Study your annual report and various financial reports. If you don't know how, the major investment firms have basic documents explaining how to read financial documents. After you've done this, consult a pro and ask him or her what he or she looks at and why. Ask for lunch or just a meeting with the person who is in charge of the strategic planning process in your company. Have him/her explain the strategic plan for the organization. Particularly have him or her point out the mission-critical functions and capabilities the organization needs to be on the leading edge in to win.

- ☐ **7. Feeling pigeon-holed? Try some broader tasks.** Volunteer for task forces that include people outside your area of expertise. Work on some Total Quality Management, Process Re-Engineering, Six Sigma, or ISO projects that cross functional or business unit boundaries to learn more about the business. Go talk with customers, work actually delivering the product or service, and write down five things you've learned about how the business works. Start up a mock business in something you know intimately. Write a business plan, complete the necessary forms, price equipment, and talk with people in this business about their problems.
- ☐ **8. Ready for a new perspective? Get close to customers.** Customer service is the best place to learn about the business. Arrange a meeting with a counterpart in customer service. Have him or her explain the function to you. If you can, listen in to customer service calls or even better handle a couple yourself.
- ☐ **9. Do you only think about your part of the business? Consider the integration points.** In order to be a well-running business, all of the pieces and parts need to work together. A business is a closed system. That means doing something in one area affects all of the other areas. Sunbeam decided to have an off-season discount in order to show more booked business in the fourth quarter. That was easy. Customers stocked up on the cheaper goods. Then plant production faltered in the next two quarters as orders decreased. Inventory prices went up for Sunbeam and its customers which led to dissatisfaction. Margins decreased as Sunbeam tried to fix the problem. What happens in one area always affects everything else. When you make decisions in your area, do you think about possible negative consequences for the other functions? Document your understanding of the drivers that run your business to a few key drivers organized around things like marketing, sales, operations, etc. Share your conclusions with others from other functions or units to see how your key drivers affect them. *More help? – See #38 Organizational Agility.*
- ☐ **10. Want to play with the pros? Learn to think as an expert in your business does.** Take problems to inside experts or external consultants and ask them what are the keys they look for; observe what they consider significant and not significant. Chunk up data into categories so you can remember it. Devise five key areas or questions you can consider each time a business issue comes up. Don't waste your time just learning facts; they won't be useful unless you have conceptual buckets to put them in. Then present your thinking to experts or write a strategic business plan for your unit and invite their review. There is no need to restrict your choices to just your organization; any astute business person should have some interesting insights.

Some Develop-in-Place Assignments

- ☐ Work on a team forming a joint venture or partnership.
- ☐ Work on a team studying a possible acquisition.
- ☐ Launch a new product, service, or process.
- ☐ Relaunch an existing product or service that's not doing well.
- ☐ Do a competitive analysis of your organization's products or services or position in the marketplace, and present it to the people involved.

Leaders are people who can discern the inevitable and act accordingly. When people talk about business acumen, discernment is a big part of it. It's a bit like gut instinct, but a little more developed.
Donald Trump – American businessman, Chairman and CEO of Trump Organization, and television personality

Suggested Readings

Alvesson, M. (2002). *Understanding organizational culture.* Thousand Oaks, CA: Sage.

Bazerman, M. H., & Watkins, M. (2008). *Predictable surprises: The disasters you should have seen coming and how to prevent them.* Boston: Harvard Business School Press.

Capon, C. (2003). *Understanding organisational context* (2nd ed.). London: Financial Times Management.

Charan, R. (2001). *What the CEO wants you to know: How your company really works.* New York: Crown Business.

Drucker, P. (2001). *Management: Tasks, responsibilities, practices.* Woburn, MA: Butterworth-Heinemann.

Fletcher, D. S. (2001). *Understanding organizational evolution: Its impact on management and performance.* Westport, CT: Quorum Books.

Fox, J. J. (2009). *Rain: What a paperboy learned about business.* San Francisco: Jossey-Bass.

Gundling, E. (2003). *Working GlobeSmart.* Palo Alto, CA: Davies-Black Publishing.

Harvard Business School Press. (2007). *Creating a business plan.* Boston: Harvard Business School Press.

Harvard Business School Press. (2007). *Understanding finance: Expert solutions to everyday challenges.* Boston: Harvard Business School Press.

Kanter, R. M. (1997). *On the frontiers of management.* Boston: Harvard Business School Press.

Keough, D. R. (2008). *The ten commandments for business failure.* New York: Penguin Group.

Lafley, A. G., & Charan, R. (2008). *The Game-changer: How you can drive revenue and profit growth with innovation*. New York: Crown Business.

McKee, S. (2009). When *growth stalls: How it happens, why you're stuck, and what to do about it*. San Francisco: Jossey-Bass.

Nickels, W. G., McHugh, J., & McHugh, S. (2006). *Understanding business* (8th ed.). New York: McGraw-Hill.

Prahalad, C. K., & Ramaswamy, V. (2004). *The future of competition: Co-creating unique value with customers*. Boston: Harvard Business School Press.

Sahlman, W. A. (2008). *How to write a great business plan*. Boston: Harvard Business School Press.

Slywotzky, A. (2003). *The art of profitability*. New York: Warner Business Books.

Slywotzky, A., Morrison, D., & Andelman, B. (2002). *The profit zone: How strategic business design will lead you to tomorrow's profits*. New York: Three Rivers Press.

Trout, J., & Rivkin, S. (2001). *Differentiate or die*. New York: John Wiley & Sons.

Webster, W. (2004). *Accounting for managers*. New York: McGraw-Hill.

Wheeler, A. (2006). *Designing brand identity: A complete guide to creating, building, and maintaining strong brands* (2nd ed.). New York: John Wiley & Sons.

6 Career Ambition

For me life is continuously being hungry.
The meaning of life is not simply to exist, to survive,
but to move ahead, to go up, to achieve, to conquer.
Arnold Schwarzenegger – Austrian-American bodybuilder, actor, businessman, and politician

Unskilled

- ☐ Unsure what he/she wants out of a career
- ☐ May be bored or in the wrong career or the wrong organization
- ☐ May not want to make sacrifices to get ahead
- ☐ May not understand how careers really work and how people get ahead
- ☐ A poor marketer of self; doesn't know how to get noticed
- ☐ Hesitant to speak up on career wants and needs
- ☐ Stuck in his/her career comfort zone; won't take a career risk

Select one to three of the competencies listed below to use as a substitute for this competency if you decide not to work on it directly.

SUBSTITUTES: 1,4,8,9,15,24,28,43,46,48,49,53,57

Skilled

- ☐ Knows what he/she wants from a career and actively works on it
- ☐ Is career knowledgeable
- ☐ Makes things happen for self
- ☐ Markets self for opportunities
- ☐ Doesn't wait for others to open doors

Overused Skill

- ☐ May make unwise career choices
- ☐ May only select jobs in the can-do comfort zone
- ☐ May be seen as excessively ambitious
- ☐ May not pay enough attention to the job at hand
- ☐ May not take career advice comfortably
- ☐ May not trust the career decisions others make for him/her

Select one to three of the competencies listed below to work on to compensate for an overuse of this skill.

COMPENSATORS: 16,17,30,32,33,42,46,48,50,51,53,55,58,63,66

Some Causes

- ☐ Bored
- ☐ Don't trust organization
- ☐ Don't want to make sacrifices
- ☐ Don't know how to market self
- ☐ Don't like to blow own horn
- ☐ Examine things to death
- ☐ Not career knowledgeable
- ☐ Too deep in your comfort zone
- ☐ Wait for things to happen
- ☐ Will only take a promotion
- ☐ Won't take a chance

Leadership Architect® Factors and Clusters

This competency is in the Organizational Positioning Skills Factor (V). This competency is in the Managing Up Cluster (M) with: 8. You may want to check other competencies in the same Factor/Cluster for related tips.

The Map

Being here on this page means someone or a number of people have told you that you are not ambitious enough. That means they think you have more going for you than you are aware of or want to sacrifice to get. They think you are undermanaging your career. The keys to career management are finding out how successful careers are built, figuring out how far you can and want to go, analyzing what's getting in your way, exposing yourself to new tasks that build your skills, and getting noticed by decision makers.

Some Remedies

☐ **1. How good are you? Take stock of your value.** How good could you be? Are you underselling yourself? You may be too critical of yourself. Get a good, confidential 360°. Are your ratings lower than those of others? Sit down with an experienced facilitator. The process should be, "How good could I be with this foundation of strengths? What do others think are my strengths that I don't see? What should I work on next to progress?" Build up your confidence. Take a course or work with a tutor to bolster your confidence in an area. Behave as if you were confident and successful. Reward yourself if you're a doubter. Master a skill. Prepare for meetings better than anyone else does. And learn how to cope with your mistakes. Acknowledge them, inform everyone affected, learn from them, and then move on. Remember you don't have to be good at everything or mistake free to succeed. *More help? – See #55 Self-Knowledge.*

- ☐ **2. Need a sounding board? Get and use a career Board of Directors.** Since you're not—at this time—your best career advisor, seek out one or more people who could be. A mentor. Boss you respect. Friend down the street. Spouse. Parent. Clergy. Consultant. Professional colleague. Periodically, pass your career thoughts, assumptions, concerns and opportunities by them for an objective opinion. Listen to them.
- ☐ **3. Bought into career myths? Learn the facts about successful careers.** Many people don't know how careers are built. Most are put off by the popular myth of getting ahead. All of us have seen *How to Succeed in Business Without Really Trying* or something like it. It's easy to get cynical and believe that successful people are political or sell out, suck up, knife people in the back, it's who you know, and so on. The facts are dramatically different from this. Those behaviors get people in trouble eventually. What has staying power is performing and problem solving on the current job, having a few notable strengths, and seeking new tasks you don't know how to do. It's solving every problem with tenacity while looking for what you haven't yet done and getting yourself in a position to do it. Read *The Lessons of Experience* by McCall, Lombardo and Morrison for the careers of men and *Breaking the Glass Ceiling* by Morrison, White and Van Velsor for the careers of women to see how successful careers really happen.
- ☐ **4. Doing the same old thing? Break out of your career comfort zone.** Maybe you haven't seen enough. Pick some activities you haven't done before but might find exciting. Take a course in a new area. Task trade—switch tasks with a peer. Volunteer for task forces and projects that are multi-functional or multi-business in nature. Read more broadly. *More help? – See #46 Perspective.*
- ☐ **5. Can't figure out the keys to success? Find out what it takes.** Think of five successful people in your organization/field whom you know well and ask what drives them? What sorts of jobs have they held? What are their technical skills? Behavioral skills? Use the Leadership Architect® Sort Cards to determine what the 10 key skills of each person are; compare this list with your own self-assessment and feedback. Ask Human Resources if they have a success profile for some of the jobs you may be interested in. Make a list of what you need to work on next. If you want to be a star, figure out what is important about your job to higher management. If you're an accountant, help management pinpoint high costs; if you're a chemist, find a cheaper way to do what you're now doing. Learn to love the details that affect your field. If your strengths are not technical, help out

coworkers or look for a management or organizational problem around you to solve.

- ☐ **6. Not comfortable marketing yourself? Create a successful career brand.** You don't know how to get promoted. You dislike people who blow their own horns. Here's how to do it. Build a performance track record of variety—start up things, fix things, innovate, make plans, come under budget. This is what will get you promoted. All organizations are looking for broad thinkers to give fresh opportunities to. Start by thinking more broadly.
- ☐ **7. Low profile? Get noticed by top decision makers.** Top managers aren't as interested in glitz as many would have you believe. They're interested in people who take care of problems, spot opportunities, ward off disaster, and have a broad repertoire of skills. They are looking for bold performers. But a better mousetrap alone is not enough. Volunteer for projects that will require interacting/presenting with higher management. Focus on activities that are the core of what your organization does. Find a business opportunity and make a reasoned case for it. Pick a big problem and work maniacally to solve it. You need to be seen and heard—but on substance not fluff.
- ☐ **8. Not willing to make sacrifices? Make the difficult moves.** Many people turn down career opportunities based upon current life comforts only to regret it later when they have been passed by. Studies indicate that the vast majority of moves successful general managers had to make during their careers were not seen as right for them at the time. They tried to turn them down. We all have the problems. Children in school. A house we like. A parent to take care of. A working spouse. A medical issue to manage. A good neighborhood. Most successful careers require moving around during the years that are the most inconvenient and painful—when we have kids in school, not much extra money, and aging parents to manage. Read *The Lessons of Experience* by McCall, Lombardo and Morrison for the careers of men and *Breaking the Glass Ceiling* by Morrison, White and Van Velsor for the careers of women to see how successful careers are really built. Set your mind to it. You must move to grow.
- ☐ **9. Waiting for your boss to retire so that you can get the big promotion? Take an alternate path.** It's hard to understand, but a promotion to your boss's job is about the least developmental promotion you can receive. Same issues. Same people. Same customers. Same products and services. Variety is the key to career building. Take laterals. Bury the ego. Work for the long term. Turn down a straight line promotion and ask for a like level job elsewhere.

☐ **10. Blindly following your passion? Diversify your talents.** Most of us make a very human error in career management. We pursue what we most like to do. Our parents and counselors told us to find something you like and that makes you happy, get really good at it, join a big company who will take care of you and provide you a nice pension. While that may have been good advice in the past, it doesn't fit today very well. Lifelong employment is dead. Layoffs. Virtual corporations. Chaos. Employability is the new term and concept. You have to be good at a lot of things. You will change organizations several times. You will have to move around to where the opportunities are.

Some Develop-in-Place Assignments

- ☐ Manage the outplacement of a group of people.
- ☐ Write a speech for someone higher up in the organization.
- ☐ Volunteer to fill an open management job temporarily until it's filled.
- ☐ Do a study of failed executives in your organization, including interviewing people still with the organization who knew or worked with them, and report the findings to top management.
- ☐ Do a study of successful executives in your organization, and report the findings to top management.

High expectations are the key to everything.
Sam Walton – American businessman
and founder of Wal-Mart and Sam's Club

Suggested Readings

Bolles, R. N. (2009). *What color is your parachute? 2009: A practical manual for job-hunters & career-changers.* Berkeley, CA: Ten Speed Press.

Brim, G. (2000). *Ambition: How we manage success and failure throughout our lives.* New York: Backinprint.com.

Butler, T. (2007). *Getting unstuck: How dead ends become new paths.* Boston: Harvard Business School Press.

Caesar, V. (2003). *Uncommon career success.* Seal Beach, CA: PCH Publishing.

Champy, J., & Nohria, N. (2000). *The arc of ambition.* Cambridge, MA: Perseus Publishing.

Christian, K. (2004). *Your own worst enemy: Breaking the habit of adult underachievement.* New York: Regan Books.

Darling, D. (2005). *Networking for career success.* New York: McGraw-Hill.

Dominguez, L. R. (2003). *How to shine at work.* New York: McGraw-Hill.

Fels, A. (2004). *Necessary dreams: Ambition in women's changing lives.* New York: Pantheon Books.

Goldsmith, M. (2007). *What got you here won't get you there: How successful people become even more successful.* New York: Hyperion.

Ibarra, H. (2003). *Working identity: Unconventional strategies for reinventing your career.* Boston: Harvard Business School Press.

Kaplan, R. S. (2008). Managing yourself. *Harvard Business Review, 86*, 45-49.

Kummerow, J. M. (2000). *New directions in career planning and the workplace: Practical strategies for career management professionals.* Palo Alto, CA: Davies-Black Publishing.

Mahan, B. J., & Coles, R. (2002). *Forgetting ourselves on purpose: Vocation and the ethics of ambition.* San Francisco: Jossey-Bass.

McCall, M. W., Lombardo, M. M., & Morrison, A. M. (1988). *The lessons of experience.* Lexington, MA: Lexington Books.

Morrison, A. M., White, R. P., & Van Velsor, E., & The Center for Creative Leadership. (1992). *Breaking the glass ceiling: Can women reach the top of America's largest corporations?* Reading, MA: Addison-Wesley Publishing Company.

Schweich, T. A. (2003). *Staying power: 30 Secrets invincible executives use for getting to the top: And staying there.* New York: McGraw-Hill.

Wendleton, K. (2006). *Navigating your career: Develop your plan, manage your boss, get another job inside.* New York: The Five O'clock Club.

7 Caring About Direct Reports

A little Consideration, a little Thought for Others, makes all the difference.
A.A. Milne – English writer, playwright, and poet

Unskilled

- ☐ May not care much about the personal needs of direct reports
- ☐ May be too busy to know much about direct reports
- ☐ May believe work and personal life should be separate
- ☐ May be more work and task oriented than most
- ☐ May be very tense and impersonal with direct reports
- ☐ May lack the listening skills or interest to know people's hopes and problems

Select one to three of the competencies listed below to use as a substitute for this competency if you decide not to work on it directly.

SUBSTITUTES: 3,10,11,18,19,23,27,31,33,36,39,41,60,64

Skilled

- ☐ Is interested in the work and non-work lives of direct reports
- ☐ Asks about their plans, problems, and desires
- ☐ Knows about their concerns and questions
- ☐ Is available for listening to personal problems
- ☐ Monitors workloads and appreciates extra effort

Overused Skill

- ☐ May have trouble being firm with direct reports
- ☐ May give them too much room for excuses
- ☐ May not challenge them to perform beyond their comfort zone
- ☐ May get too deep into their lives
- ☐ May not be able to make objective calls on performance and potential
- ☐ May not know when to stop showing care when efforts are rejected

Select one to three of the competencies listed below to work on to compensate for an overuse of this skill.

COMPENSATORS: 9,12,13,17,18,20,23,27,34,35,56,57,64

Some Causes

- ☐ Belief that work and personal life should be kept separate
- ☐ Care more for other things than people
- ☐ Fear being taken advantage of
- ☐ Fear of being placed in counselor role
- ☐ Low-priority activity
- ☐ Poor listener
- ☐ Too busy

Leadership Architect® Factors and Clusters

This competency is in the Personal and Interpersonal Skills Factor (VI). This competency is in the Caring about Others Cluster (O) with: 10. You may want to check other competencies in the same Factor/Cluster for related tips.

The Map

Caring for others is important on a number of levels. At the most basic is that people who are cared about return that care to others. People who are shown care work more effectively with and for the people who show that care. Cared-for people feel better and are more positive to be around and work with than people who are ignored. Caring about others doesn't have to be a soft or counselor activity—it simply means trying to show reasonable concern for direct reports in every way possible to help them perform and grow. People who care don't just smile and act friendly. At the mechanical level, good managers know more about their people than just the work they do. They know a little about their history, a little about their current situation, and a little about their dreams, preferences and wishes. They foster two-way information. They pick up the early warning signs for problems before they become serious, and are quick to help others perform better by removing obstacles. Long term they help by developing their direct reports and giving them critical feedback to help them grow. At the deeper level, good managers show care because they care. Either way, managing the whole person will always be rewarded with better performance and a better feeling for you, the manager.

Some Remedies

☐ **1. Impatient? Be a better listener.** Many bosses are marginal listeners. They are action oriented and more apt to cut off people mid-sentence than listen. They also are impatient and finish people's sentences for them when they hesitate. All of these impatient behaviors come across to others as a lack of caring. It's being insensitive to the needs and feelings of others. So step one in caring is listening longer. *More help? – See #33 Listening.*

- ☐ **2. Are you a closed book? Share and disclose.** Share your thinking on a business issue and invite the advice of direct reports. Pass on tidbits of information you think will help people do their jobs better or broaden their perspectives. Reveal things people don't need to know to do their jobs, but which will be interesting to them and help them feel valued. Disclose some things about yourself as well. It's hard for people to relate to a stone. Tell them how you arrive at decisions. Explain your intentions, your reasons, and your thinking when announcing decisions. If you offer solutions first, you invite resistance and feelings of not being cared about—"He/she just dumps things on us."
- ☐ **3. Think it's all about the work? Get to know your team.** Know three non-work things about everybody—their interests and hobbies or their children or something you can chat about. Life is a small world. If you ask your people a few personal questions, you'll find you have something in common with virtually anyone. Having something in common will help bond the relationship.
- ☐ **4. Lacking empathy? Be open and accepting.** Try to listen without judging initially. Turn off your "I agree; I don't agree" filter. You don't have to agree with it; just listen to understand. Assume when people tell you something they are looking for understanding; indicate that by being able to summarize what they said. Don't offer advice or solutions unless it's obvious the person wants to know what you would do. While offering instant solutions is a good thing to do in many circumstances, it's chilling where the goal is to get people to talk to you more freely.
- ☐ **5. Can't relate? Seek to understand.** Study the people you work with. Without judging them, collect evidence on how they think and what they do. What drives them to do what they do? Try to predict what they will do in given situations. Use this to understand how to relate to them. What are their hot buttons? What would they like for you to care about?
- ☐ **6. Prefer to give the answers? Be more curious.** Show you care what they think. Many people don't ask enough curiosity questions when they are in their work mode. There are too many probing or informational questions and not enough "what if," "what are you learning," "what would you change," questions. In studies, statements outweighed questions eight to one and few questions invited others to really think things through.
- ☐ **7. Think everyone is the same? Treat people equitably.** Caring is not treating people equally, it's treating people equitably. People are different. They have different needs. They respond differently to you. They have different dreams and concerns. Each person is unique and feels best when treated uniquely. *More help? – See #21 Managing Diversity.*

☐ **8. Afraid to get involved? Be concerned without becoming a therapist:**

- If someone brings you all his/her problems on a regular basis, pick one you think you can help with and ask him/her to seek counseling or employee assistance for the others.
- If someone is a rambler and repeats things, interrupt but summarize. This signals you heard him/her, but keeps him/her from consuming time.
- If someone is angry, let him/her vent without saying anything other than you know he/she is upset. It's hard for most people to continue very long with no encouragement or resistance. If he/she keeps on, invite him/her to talk with you outside of work hours.
- If someone is a chronic complainer, ask him/her to write down problems and solutions, and then discuss it. This turns down the volume while hopefully moving him/her off complaining.
- If someone wants to complain about someone else, ask if he/she has talked to the person. Encourage him/her to do so. If that doesn't work, summarize what he/she said without agreeing or disagreeing, which will add still more time to the discussion.
- If you have to criticize, avoid shoulds and rigid statements. Your role is to be helpful—the notion should be to help the person be more successful. Pick a good moment; focus on helping the person improve, not on making sure all your recommendations are written down and acted upon. Draw a picture of how the person will benefit.
- If someone is demotivated, focus on challenging job tasks and variety in his/her work. Ask what excitement on the job looks like to him/her. *More help? – See #19 Developing Direct Reports and Others, and #36 Motivating Others.*

☐ **9. Sending mixed messages? Signal that you care.** Watch out for unintentionally signaling to people that you don't care. A—"I leave the details to others"; B—"I'm not very organized"; C—"I've always believed in taking action then sorting it out later"; might mean A—"What I do isn't important"; B—"I'm left to pick up the pieces"; and C—"I have to deal with the havoc" to your direct reports. Think about impact on them when you speak.

☐ **10. Need examples on how to care for direct reports? List your last 10 bosses on a piece of paper.** Put five in the "he/she cared the least about me and other members of the team" and the other five in the "he/she cared the most about me and other members of the team." How did the low-care group act? What did they do that showed they didn't care? What didn't they do that showed they didn't care? What did the other group do and not do that showed they cared? Compare your analysis to how you behave as a manager.

Some Develop-in-Place Assignments

- ☐ Manage a project team of people who are older and more experienced than you.
- ☐ Help shut down a plant, regional office, product line, business, operation, etc.
- ☐ Manage a group of low-competence or low-performing people through a task they couldn't do by themselves.
- ☐ Manage a temporary group of "green," inexperienced people as their coach, teacher, guide, mentor, etc.
- ☐ Create employee involvement teams.

Kindness is in our power, even when fondness is not.
Samuel Johnson – 18th century English writer

Suggested Readings

Arthur, D. (2001). *The employee recruitment and retention handbook.* New York: AMACOM.

Ash, M. K. (2008). *The Mary Kay way: Timeless principles from America's greatest woman entrepreneur.* Hoboken, NJ: John Wiley & Sons.

Birx, E. (2002). *Healing Zen: Awakening to a life of wholeness and compassion while caring for yourself and others.* New York: Viking Press.

Cashman, K. (2008). *Leadership from the inside out: Becoming a leader for life* (2nd ed.). San Francisco: Berrett-Koehler Publishers.

De Waal, A. (2002). *Quest for balance: The human element in performance management systems.* New York: John Wiley & Sons.

Dotlich, D. L., Cairo, P. C., & Rhinesmith, S. H. (2006). *Head, heart and guts: How the world's best companies develop complete leaders.* San Francisco: Jossey-Bass.

Kaye, B., & Jordan-Evans, S. (2008). *Love 'em or lose 'em: Getting good people to stay* (4th ed.). San Francisco: Berrett-Koehler Publishers.

Kouzes, J. M., & Posner, B. Z. (2003). *Encouraging the heart: A leader's guide to rewarding and recognizing others.* San Francisco: Jossey-Bass.

Kouzes, J. M., & Posner, B. Z. (2006). *Encouraging the heart workbook.* San Francisco: Jossey-Bass.

Kouzes, J. M., & Posner, B. Z. (2007). *The leadership challenge* (4th ed.). San Francisco: Jossey-Bass.

Lewin, R., & Regine, B. (2001). *Weaving complexity and business: Engaging the soul at work.* New York: Texere.

Lloyd, K. L. (2002). *Be the boss your employees deserve.* Franklin Lakes, NJ: Career Press.

Mayo, A. (2001). *The human value of the enterprise: Valuing people as assets: Monitoring, measuring, managing.* Yarmouth, ME: Nicholas Brealey.

Ventrice, C. (2003). *Make their day! Employee recognition that works.* San Francisco: Berrett-Koehler Publishers.

8 Comfort Around Higher Management

Leadership is a two-way street, loyalty up and loyalty down.
Respect for one's superiors; care for one's crew.
Grace Murray Hopper – U.S. military leader, mathematician, educator

Unskilled

- ☐ Lacks self-confidence in front of more senior people
- ☐ May appear nervous and tense, not at his/her best
- ☐ May lose composure or get rattled when questioned by executives
- ☐ Doesn't know how to influence or impress more senior managers
- ☐ May not understand what top executives are looking for
- ☐ Says and does things that don't fit the situation

Select one to three of the competencies listed below to use as a substitute for this competency if you decide not to work on it directly.

SUBSTITUTES: 3,4,5,9,12,27,33,34,37,38,48,49,57

Skilled

- ☐ Can deal comfortably with more senior managers
- ☐ Can present to more senior managers without undue tension and nervousness
- ☐ Understands how senior managers think and work
- ☐ Can determine the best way to get things done with them by talking their language and responding to their needs
- ☐ Can craft approaches likely to be seen as appropriate and positive

Overused Skill

- ☐ May manage up too much
- ☐ May be seen as too political and ambitious
- ☐ May spend too much time with more senior managers, parrot their positions, overestimate the meaning and usefulness of the relationships
- ☐ Career may be too dependent on champions
- ☐ May be too free with confidential information

Select one to three of the competencies listed below to work on to compensate for an overuse of this skill.

COMPENSATORS: 5,9,12,17,22,24,29,30,45,51,53,57

Some Causes

- ☐ Lack of self-confidence in front of more powerful people
- ☐ Fear of making a mistake; slipping up and doing something dumb
- ☐ Perfectionism; the fear of not being perfect in the eyes of senior management
- ☐ Lack of proper preparation due to lack of knowledge or skills or a work style deficit
- ☐ Tendency to become more emotional under pressure and stress

Leadership Architect® Factors and Clusters

This competency is in the Organizational Positioning Skills Factor (V). This competency is in the Managing Up Cluster (M) with: 6. You may want to check other competencies in the same Factor/Cluster for related tips.

The Map

Performing in front of one or a number of higher level managers is usually tough; they are all highly skilled in something to get there; don't have much time; ask tough questions and expect answers; sometimes don't care how they make you feel. Many in your situation don't get through unscathed. Many higher level managers will test you to see what you are made of; some may ask tough questions just to see if you can handle them; some may intentionally want to push you to see what you are made of; they are not always going to be nice to you. It seems the higher up they get the less time they spend thinking about or making any effort to make others feel comfortable around them. They all made their share of mistakes when they were in your position. They learned through tough times. They stumbled once in a while. In fact, the research says successful higher level managers made more mistakes on the way up than the people who didn't get there.

Some Remedies

- ☐ **1. Nervous? Keep your cool.** Being nervous, anxious and uncomfortable around one or more higher-ups is fairly normal; the key is not allowing that to prevent you from doing your best. Being uncomfortable can sometimes lead to physical reactions like sweating, hesitating or stuttering speech, mispronounced words, flushing of the face, grumbling in the stomach, running out of breath while talking, etc. When that happens, stop a second or two, take a deep breath, compose yourself and continue what you were doing; they all have been there before. Remember, all you can do is the best you can do. You probably know more about this topic than they do. You're well-prepared—being anxious can prevent you from demonstrating your expertise. *More help? – See #11 Composure.*

☐ **2. Worried about mistakes? Worst-case it.** List all of your worst fears; what bad things do you think might happen; envision yourself in each of those situations; mentally practice how you would recover. Can't think of the right words? Pause, don't fill the void with "uhs." Refer to your notes. Feeling defensive? Ask a question. Running overtime? Go straight to the conclusion. Practice the more realistic recoveries live in front of a mirror or with a colleague playing the audience.

☐ **3. Unprepared? Practice, practice, practice.** Rehearse what you are going to do several times so you can do it as naturally as possible; this gives you time to deal with questions and unexpected reactions more comfortably. Record yourself on videotape. Did you speak no longer than five to 10 minutes per major point? Anything you went into with so much detail that you sounded like an almanac? Did you vary tone and volume or was it monotone? Will they remember your key points 15 minutes after the meeting ends? *More help? – See #49 Presentation Skills.*

☐ **4. Unfamiliar surroundings? Visit the setting.** If it's a presentation to a number of higher-ups, visit the setting of the event beforehand to get more comfortable in the actual setting; if you can, practice the event there. When you visit, consider the seating. Will people be able to hear you easily or should you speak up? Any spots where line of sight is restricted? Be sure not to stand there. Will your overheads be easy to read from the back? If not, go to fewer points and larger type.

☐ **5. Taking too much time? Be efficient.** Plan what you need to do and say carefully. Take as little time as necessary. Maybe bring more material than you need and will use. Since no one has ever run out of material, take 60 slides but show 40 and be prepared to show 30. Summary slides can help with this. Top managers are very busy; everyone loves someone who takes up less time than is planned or on the agenda. Let them ask for more detail; don't drown them.

☐ **6. Difficulty with questions? Be ready for Q&A.** Many people get in trouble during questions and answers. Don't fake answers; most high level managers will tolerate a "Don't know but I'll get back to you on that." Think of all the questions ahead of time; ask someone else to look at what you are going to say and do, and think of questions they would ask. Rehearse the answers to the questions. Another place people get in trouble when challenged is by retreating to a safe recitation of facts; executives are usually asking for logic and problem analysis, not a repackaging of what you've already said. The worst case of course is when an executive rejects your argument. If this happens, draw the person out to see if you've been misunderstood and clarify. If that's not the case, let the disagreement be as it is. Few executives respect someone who drops an argument as soon as challenged. You should listen carefully, and respond with logic in 30 seconds or less per point. Don't repeat the entire argument; long answers often backfire since people have already heard it and few may agree with the questioner. In haste to be thorough, you may just look defensive.

☐ **7. Need advice? Find a confidant.** Ask a member of top management you know well and trust for advice on how you could feel better and perform more effectively when you transact with him/her and the rest of the team. Share your anxieties with a trusted colleague and ask for suggestions and observations. Find someone who appears comfortable in the settings you find difficult and ask how to do it.

☐ **8. Annoyed? Consider who bothers you.** If only certain higher-ups bother you and others don't, take a piece of paper and list the styles of the two groups/individuals. What are the similarities? Why does one style bother you and the other doesn't? With the groups/individuals that bother you, how could you respond more comfortably and effectively? Perhaps you could use some of the techniques you use with the more comfortable groups. Probably you should prime yourself to take nothing in personal terms and no matter what happens, return to a discussion of the problem. *More help? – See #12 Conflict Management.*

☐ **9. Not acquainted? Get to know more top managers.** Try to meet and interact with higher-ups in informal settings like receptions, social or athletic events, charity events, off-sites, etc.; you will probably learn that higher-ups are just regular people who are older and therefore higher than you in the hierarchy. You may then feel more comfortable with them when back in the work setting.

☐ **10. Don't understand your audience? Find out how top managers think.** Read the biographies of five "great" people; see what is said about them and their view of people like you; read five autobiographies and see what they say about themselves and how they viewed people in your position. Write down five things you can do differently or better.

Some Develop-in-Place Assignments

☐ Manage a group through a significant business crisis.

☐ Prepare and present a proposal of some consequence to top management.

☐ Write a speech for someone higher up in the organization.

☐ Serve on a junior or shadow board.

☐ Write a proposal for a new policy, process, mission, charter, product, service, or system, and present and sell it to top management.

The greatest weakness of all is the great fear of appearing weak.
Jacques Bénigne Bousset – French bishop and theologian

Suggested Readings

Arredondo, L. (2000). *Communicating effectively*. New York: McGraw-Hill.

Bing, S. (2002). *Throwing the elephant: Zen and the art of managing up*. New York: HarperBusiness.

Chaleff, I. (2003). *The courageous follower: Standing up to and for our leaders*. San Francisco: Berrett-Koehler Publishers.

Charan, R. (2001). *What the CEO wants you to know: How your company really works*. New York: Crown Business.

Crowley, K., & Elster, K. (2006). *Working with you is killing me: Freeing yourself from emotional traps at work*. New York: Warner Business Books.

Dobson, M., & Dobson, D. S. (2000). *Managing up! 59 Ways to build a career-advancing relationship with your boss*. New York: AMACOM.

Gabarro, J. J., & Kotter, J. P. (2008). *Managing your boss*. Boston: Harvard Business School Press.

Harvard Business School Press. (2008). *Managing up*. Boston: Harvard Business School Press.

Hayes, J. (2002). *Interpersonal skills at work*. New York: Routledge.

Jay, R. (2002). *How to manage your boss: Developing the perfect working relationship*. London: Financial Times Management.

Mann, S. (2001). *Managing your boss*. Hauppauge, NY: Barron's Educational Series, Inc.

Useem, M. (2003). *Leading up: How to lead your boss so you both win*. New York: Three Rivers Press.

Weiner, D. L., & Lefton, R. E. (2002). *Power freaks: Dealing with them in the workplace or anyplace*. Amherst, NY: Prometheus Books.

9 Command Skills

A crisis is an opportunity riding the dangerous wind.
– Chinese proverb

Unskilled

- ☐ More comfortable following
- ☐ May avoid conflict and crises, be unwilling to take the heat, have problems with taking a tough stand
- ☐ Might be laid back and quiet
- ☐ Too concerned about what others may say or think
- ☐ May worry too much about being liked, correct or above criticism
- ☐ May be conflict shy or lack perseverance
- ☐ May not be cool under pressure
- ☐ May not display a sense of urgency

Select one to three of the competencies listed below to use as a substitute for this competency if you decide not to work on it directly.

SUBSTITUTES: 1,5,12,13,16,20,30,34,35,36,37,39,49,57,65

Skilled

- ☐ Relishes leading
- ☐ Takes unpopular stands if necessary
- ☐ Encourages direct and tough debate but isn't afraid to end it and move on
- ☐ Is looked to for direction in a crisis
- ☐ Faces adversity head on
- ☐ Energized by tough challenges

Overused Skill

- ☐ May not be a team player
- ☐ May not be tolerant of other people's ways of doing things
- ☐ May choose to strongly lead when other more team-based tactics would do as well or better
- ☐ May not develop other leaders
- ☐ May become controversial and be rejected by others

Select one to three of the competencies listed below to work on to compensate for an overuse of this skill.

COMPENSATORS: 3,7,10,19,31,33,36,38,41,47,52,59,60

Some Causes

- ☐ Avoid crises
- ☐ Can't set common cause
- ☐ Can't take a tough stand
- ☐ Can't take the heat of leading
- ☐ Fear of criticism/failure
- ☐ Getting others to believe
- ☐ Not cool under pressure
- ☐ Not credible leader
- ☐ Shy

Leadership Architect® Factors and Clusters

This competency is in the Courage Factor (III). This competency is in the Dealing with Trouble Cluster (H) with: 12, 13, 34, 57. You may want to check other competencies in the same Factor/Cluster for related tips.

The Map

Leading makes you more visible and more open to criticism. The heat is the hottest on the nose cone of the rocket. Leading is exciting and puts you in control. Leading in tough or crisis conditions is all about creating aligned and sustained motion. It involves keeping your eye on the goal, setting common causes, dealing with the inevitable heat, managing your emotions, being a role model, taking tough stands and getting others to believe in where you're headed.

Some Remedies

☐ **1. Taking heat? Face criticism with courage.** Leading is riskier than following. While there are a lot of personal rewards for leading, leading puts you in the limelight. Think about what happens to political leaders and the scrutiny they face. Leaders have to be internally secure. Do you feel good about yourself? They have to please themselves first that they are on the right track. Can you defend to a critical and impartial audience the wisdom of what you're doing? They have to accept lightning bolts from detractors. Can you take the heat? People will always say it should have been done differently. Listen to them, but be skeptical. Even great leaders are wrong sometimes. They accept personal responsibility for errors and move on to lead some more. Don't let criticism prevent you from taking the lead. Build up your heat shield. Conduct a postmortem immediately after finishing milestone efforts. This will indicate to all that you're open to continuous improvement whether the result was stellar or not.

☐ **2. Facing a difficult issue? Prepare to take tough stands against the grain.** Taking a tough stand demands utter confidence in what you're saying along with the humility that you might be wrong—one of life's paradoxes. To prepare to take the lead on a tough issue, work on your stand through mental interrogation until you can clearly state in a few sentences what your stand is and why you hold it. Build the business case. How do others win? People don't line up behind laundry lists or ambiguous objectives. Ask others for advice—scope the problem, consider options, pick one, develop a rationale, then go with it until proven wrong. Then redo the process. If this doesn't help, find out where the pain is for you. What have you been avoiding? Examine your past and see where taking-charge behavior has gotten you in trouble or you thought it would get you in trouble. Isolate the most troublesome elements, such as forgetting things under pressure, trouble with fierce debate, problems with unpopular stands, and things moving too fast. Devise counter strategies.

☐ **3. Need to win over detractors? Sell your leadership.** While some people may welcome what you say and want to do, others will go after you or even try to minimize the situation. Some will sabotage. To sell your leadership, keep your eyes on the prize but don't specify how to get there. Present the outcomes, targets and goals without the how to's. Welcome their ideas, good and bad. Any negative response is a positive if you learn from it. Allow them to fill in the blanks, ask questions, and disagree without appearing impatient with them. Allow others to save face; concede small points, invite criticism of your own. Help them figure out how to win. Keep to the facts and the problem before the group; stay away from personal clashes. *More help? – See #12 Conflict Management.*

☐ **4. Too emotional? Keep your cool.** Manage your emotional reactions. Sometimes your emotional reactions lead others to think you have problems with tough leadership situations. In the situations where this happens, what emotional reactions do you have? Do you show impatience or non-verbals like increasing voice volume or drumming your fingers? Learn to recognize those as soon as they start. Substitute something more neutral. If you tend to blurt out disagreement when uncomfortable or surprised by a point of view, ask a question instead to buy time. Or, ask the person to tell you more about his/her point of view. Don't go for the quick, obvious response. That's stress getting the better of you. Or, ask yourself questions. An angry activist group once demanded the microphone from a university chancellor during commencement. He handed it to them, said you've got five minutes, and stepped back. Asked about his move, he said, "I asked myself what's the worst that could happen? It's hard for people to remain angry when no one is resisting. So they talked for five minutes. It seemed a small price.

And they were awfully glad when their time was up." *More help? – See #11 Composure and #107 Lack of Composure.*

☐ **5. Making mistakes? Develop a philosophical stance toward failure/criticism.** After all, most innovations fail, most proposals fail, most efforts to lead change fail. Anything worth doing takes repeated effort. Anything could always have been done better. Research says that successful general managers have made more mistakes in their careers than the people they were promoted over. They got promoted because they had the guts to lead, not because they were always right. Other studies suggest really good general managers are right about 65% of the time. Put errors, mistakes and failures on your menu. Everyone has to have some spinach for a balanced diet.

☐ **6. Dealing with tough opponents? Practice the rules of one-on-one combat.** Leading always involves dealing with pure one-on-one confrontation. You want one thing, he/she wants something else. When that happens, keep it to the facts. You won't always win. Stay objective. Listen as long as he/she will talk. Ask a lot of questions. Sometimes he/she will talk him/herself to your point of view if you let him/her talk long enough. Always listen to understand first, not judge. Then restate his/her points until he/she says that's right. Then find something to agree with, however small that may be. Refute his/her points starting with the one you have the most objective information on. Then move down the line. You will always have points left that didn't get resolved. Document those and give a copy to your opponent. The objective is to get the list as small as possible. Then decide whether you are going to pull rank and go ahead. Delay and get more data. Go to a higher source for arbitration. *More help? – See #12 Conflict Management.*

☐ **7. Heard enough? Draw the line.** When all else fails, you may have to pull someone aside and say, "I have listened to all of your objections and have tried to understand them, but the train is moving on. Are you on or off?" Always follow the rules of dealing with conflict: Depersonalize; keep it on the problem not the person; try one last time to make your case; note the person's objections but don't concede anything; be clear; now is not the time for negotiation; give the person a day to think it over. Worst-case, if the person is a direct report, you may have to ask him/her to leave the unit. *More help? – See #13 Confronting Direct Reports.* If the person is a peer or colleague, inform your boss of the impasse and your intention to proceed without his/her support.

☐ **8. Caught off guard? Prepare for crises.** Studies say followers really appreciate sound leadership during a crisis. They want to know there is a firm hand on the tiller. During a crisis, time is the enemy, so be prepared. In a recent book, Mitroff and Anagnos say you must prepare for the seven types of crises: economic, loss of confidential information or computer records, physical/equipment, human resources (public embarrassment, crime, sabotage), reputational, psychopathic acts, and natural disasters. Their advice: Anticipate what hasn't occurred. Come up with signal detectors, such as increase in costs or threats for all potential crises. Collect all the data you can. Think through all of the worst-case consequences and assign a person or a team to prepare for them. When a crisis strikes, use the data you have and ask others for suggestions and thoughts. Then decide and execute the decision with an instant feedback loop. Make adjustments as you go. And communicate, communicate, communicate.

☐ **9. Haven't found your passion to lead? Lead outside the workplace.** Try small things. Try some leadership roles and tasks off-work. Volunteer for a leadership role in your place of worship, school, or the neighborhood. Volunteer to head a task force. Start up a credit union. Volunteer for the United Way drive. Start a softball league.

☐ **10. Not capturing enough attention? Enhance your leadership presence.** Leading takes presence. You have to look and sound like a leader. Voice is strong. Eye contact. Intensity. Confidence. A lot of leadership presence has to do with forceful presentation skills. Giving good presentations is a known technology. There are several books and workshops you can take. Look to workshops that use video taping. Join your local Toastmasters club for some low-risk training and practice. Look to small things such as do you look like a leader? What colors do you wear? Do you dress the part? Are your glasses right? Is your office configured right? Do you sound confident? Do you whine and complain or do you solve problems? If I met you for the first time in a group of 10, would I pick you as the leader?

Some Develop-in-Place Assignments

☐ Manage a group through a significant business crisis.

☐ Prepare and present a proposal of some consequence to top management.

☐ Manage a group of resistant people with low morale through an unpopular change or project.

☐ Assign a project with a tight deadline to a group.

☐ Manage a group of people involved in tackling a fix-it or turnaround project.

In really good companies, you have to lead. You have to come up with big ideas and express them forcefully. I have always been encouraged —or sometimes forced—to confront the very natural fear of being wrong. I was constantly pushed to find out what I really thought and then to speak up. Over time, I came to see that waiting to discover which way the wind was blowing is an excellent way to learn how to be a follower.

Roger Enrico – American business leader
and former CEO, PepsiCo

Suggested Readings

Argenti, P. (2002). Crisis communication: Lessons from 9/11. *Harvard Business Review 80*(12), 103-109.

Beck, J. D. W. (2001). *The leader's window: Mastering the four styles of leadership to build high-performing teams.* Palo Alto, CA: Davies-Black Publishing.

Cannon, J., & Cannon, J. (2003). *The leadership secrets of the U.S. Navy SEALS: Battle-tested strategies for creating successful organizations and inspiring extraordinary results.* New York: McGraw-Hill.

Caponigro, J. R. (2000). *The crisis counselor: A step-by-step guide to managing a business crisis.* Chicago: Contemporary Books.

Coombs, W. T. (2007). *Ongoing crisis communication: Planning, managing, and responding.* Thousand Oaks, CA: Sage.

Fink, S. (2002). *Crisis management: Planning for the inevitable.* Lincoln, NE: iUniverse, Inc.

Finkelstein, S. (2003). *Why smart executives fail: And what you can learn from their mistakes.* New York: Portfolio.

Gaines-Ross, L. (2003). *CEO capital: A guide to building CEO reputation and company success.* New York: John Wiley & Sons.

Gerstner, L. V. (2003). *Who says elephants can't dance? Leading a great enterprise through dramatic change.* New York: HarperBusiness.

Giuliani, R. W., & Kurson, K. (2002). *Leadership.* New York: Miramax.

Greenberg, J. W. (2002). September 11, 2001: A CEO's story. *Harvard Business Review 80*(10), 58-64.

Harvard Business School Press. (2004). *Crisis management: Master the skills to prevent disaster.* Boston: Harvard Business School Press.

Harvard Business School Press. (2008). *Managing crises.* Boston: Harvard Business School Press.

Kouzes, J. M., & Posner, B. Z. (2007). *The leadership challenge* (4th ed.). San Francisco: Jossey-Bass.

Krass, P. (Ed.). (1998). *The book of leadership wisdom.* New York: John Wiley & Sons.

Maginn, M. D. (2007). *Managing in times of change.* New York: McGraw-Hill.

Mitroff, I. I. (with Anagnos, G.). (2001). *Managing crises before they happen.* New York: AMACOM.

Sandys, C., & Littman, J. (2003). *We shall not fail: The inspiring leadership of Winston Churchill.* New York: Portfolio.

Ulmer, R. R., Sellnow, T. L., & Seeger, M. W. (2007). *Effective crisis communication: Moving from crisis to opportunity.* Thousand Oaks, CA: Sage.

10 Compassion

Compassion is the basis of all morality.
Arthur Schopenhauer – German philosopher

Unskilled

- ☐ May be less caring or empathic than most
- ☐ Doesn't ask personal questions; doesn't respond much when offered
- ☐ Results are all that matters; everything else gets in the way
- ☐ Believes in separation of personal life and business
- ☐ May find the plight of others an inappropriate topic at work
- ☐ Uncomfortable with people in stress and pain
- ☐ May not know how to show compassion or how to deal with people in trouble
- ☐ May have less sympathy than most for the imperfections and problems of others

Select one to three of the competencies listed below to use as a substitute for this competency if you decide not to work on it directly.

SUBSTITUTES: 3,7,12,21,22,27,29,33,36,41,64

Skilled

- ☐ Genuinely cares about people
- ☐ Is concerned about their work and non-work problems
- ☐ Is available and ready to help
- ☐ Is sympathetic to the plight of others not as fortunate
- ☐ Demonstrates real empathy with the joys and pains of others

Overused Skill

- ☐ May smooth over conflict in the interest of harmony
- ☐ May not be tough enough in the face of malingerers and may make too many concessions
- ☐ May get so close to people that objectivity is affected and they are able to get away with too much
- ☐ May have trouble with close calls on people

Select one to three of the competencies listed below to work on to compensate for an overuse of this skill.

COMPENSATORS: 12,13,16,18,20,34,35,37,50,53,57,59,62

Some Causes

- ☐ Fear of being consumed by non-work matters
- ☐ Fear of not being able to handle disagreements
- ☐ Hard to see the value at work
- ☐ Have trouble dealing with emotionally or politically charged issues
- ☐ See compassion as a weakness
- ☐ Trouble dealing with people/groups who are different
- ☐ Uncomfortable with feelings

Leadership Architect® Factors and Clusters

This competency is in the Personal and Interpersonal Skills Factor (VI). This competency is in the Caring about Others Cluster (O) with: 7. You may want to check other competencies in the same Factor/Cluster for related tips.

The Map

Genuinely cares. Empathizes and sympathizes. Hurts for others. Lends an open ear. Work and personal life flowing together. Sounds alien, painful and out of place to many managers. For most managers, compassion and work don't go together comfortably. Work can be a cold and bleak place. The road of life is bumpy and uneven. There is always rough water. There is probably more opportunity for pain and disappointment than pleasure and fulfillment. People need support and help to make it through. They look to family, religion, social friends and mentors for support but they also expect some compassion from bosses and coworkers. But if you don't show some compassion, you are quite likely to be seen as cold or impersonal. People who don't seem to care eventually run out of people to work with. Even when this isn't the case—you do show compassion—some people get into trouble because they don't handle situations involving compassion well.

Some Remedies

- ☐ **1. Difficulty dealing with strong emotions? Show understanding and empathy.** A primary reason for problems with compassion is that you don't know how to deal with strong feelings and appear distant or uninterested. You're uncomfortable with strong displays of emotion and calls for personal help. Simply imagine how you would feel in this situation and respond with that. Tell him/her how sorry you are this has happened or has to be dealt with. Offer whatever help is reasonable. A day off. A loan. A resource. If you can, offer hope of a better day. This is what the person can use most.
- ☐ **2. Tuning people out? Just listen.** Sometimes people just need to talk it out. Compassion is quiet listening. Nod and maintain eye contact to

indicate listening. When he/she pauses, respond with how he/she must feel, and suggest something you could do to help (e.g., if he/she needs to be gone for a while, you'll see that his/her work is covered).

☐ **3. Too quick to offer the answer? Delay advice-giving.** Don't offer advice unless asked. Indicate support through listening and a helpful gesture. There will be time for advice when the situation isn't so emotionally charged. Many times managers are too quick with advice before they really understand the problem. *More help? – See #7 Caring About Direct Reports.*

☐ **4. Want to learn from compassion experts? Study the three most compassionate people you know or know of.** Pick one at work, one off work, and one notable figure (such as Mother Teresa). What do they do that you don't? How do they show compassion? What words do they use; what gestures do they make? Do any of them, such as clergy, have to deal with compassion quickly? What does this person do? Can you translate any of these learnings into compassion for yourself?

☐ **5. Afraid of becoming a therapist? Set limits.** Another reason people have trouble with compassion is thinking that a counselor role isn't appropriate at work. You can be brief and compassionate by following three rules:

- Let people say what's on their mind without saying anything other than you know they're upset. Don't judge. Don't advise.
- Summarize when they start repeating. This signals that you heard them, but keeps them from consuming so much time that you begin to feel like a counselor.
- If someone overdoes it, invite him/her to talk with you outside of work hours or refer him/her to another resource like employee assistance.

This shows others that you cared, you listened and are willing to help if possible while not putting you in the counselor role that is making you uncomfortable.

☐ **6. Judgmental? Show compassion without bias.** Be candid with yourself. Is there a group or groups you don't like or are uncomfortable with? Do you judge individual members of that group without really knowing if your stereotype is true? Most of us do. Do you show compassion for one group's problems but not another's? To deal with this:

- Put yourself in their case. Why would you act that way? What do you think they're trying to achieve? Assume that however they act is rational to them; it must have paid off or they wouldn't be doing it. Don't use your internal standards.

- Avoid putting groups in buckets. Many of us bucket groups as friendly or unfriendly; good or bad; like me or not like me. Once we do, we generally don't show as much compassion towards them and may question their motives. Apply the logic of why people belong to the group in the first place. See if you can predict accurately what the group will say or do across situations to test your understanding of the group. Don't use your agreement program.
- Listen. Even though this tip may seem obvious, many of us tune out when dealing with difficult or not well-understood groups, or reject what they're saying before they say it. Just listen. Mentally summarize their views, and see if you can figure out what they want from what they say and mean. The true test is whether you can clearly figure it out even though you don't think that way.
- Many people who need your compassion most aren't the most pleasant people.
- For the cynical—delegate responsibility to them for what they are most cynical about.
- For the helpless and dependent—ask yourself what would make them feel the most powerful?
- For the truly resentful or hostile—don't encourage them to air all of their gripes in detail. This merely reinforces their views. Instead, find out what is bothering them the most at work, and give them something new to do where they have the authority to make a difference.

☐ **7. Insensitive? Tune in to people's needs.** You need to know what people's compassion hot buttons are because one mistake can get you labeled as insensitive with some people. The only cure here is to see what turns up the volume for them—either literally or what they're concerned about. Be careful of downplaying or demeaning someone else's cause (like the Native American community trying to remove Indian nicknames from athletic teams).

☐ **8. Emotions running high? Follow the rules of good listening.** If someone is clearly concerned about a lack of compassion related to something such as ethnic, gender concerns, level or status in the organization:

- Understanding and listening isn't the same thing as agreement.
- Don't argue if they're emotional about it. You'll lose no matter what you say. Discuss only that you've heard them, they acknowledge you've heard them, and indicate you want to discuss the problem from a rational point of view—what causes it, what it looks and feels like, and what can be done about it.

- ☐ **9. One-sided with compassion? Hear out the other side of the story in a compassion dispute.** Ask why—what are the principles behind the position, how do we know it's fair, what's the theory of the case. Play out what would happen if their position was accepted. Ask what they would do if they were in your shoes. Ask lots of questions, but make few statements.
- ☐ **10. On the defensive? Reframe charges of being non-compassionate.** Rephrase it as an attack on the problem/issue. In response to unreasonable proposals, attacks, or a non-answer to a question, you can always say nothing but acknowledge that you heard what they said. People will usually respond by saying more, coming off their position a bit, or at least revealing their interests. *More help? – See #12 Conflict Management.*

Some Develop-in-Place Assignments

- ☐ Manage the outplacement of a group of people.
- ☐ Work on a team that's deciding whom to keep and whom to let go in a layoff, shutdown, delayering, or merger.
- ☐ Represent to higher management the concerns of a group of nonexempt, clerical, or administrative employees to seek resolution of a difficult issue.
- ☐ Join a self-help or support group.
- ☐ Work for a year or more with a charitable organization.

The whole idea of compassion is based on a keen awareness of the interdependence of all these living beings, which are all part of one another, and all involved in one another.

Thomas Merton – French-born American Trappist monk, poet, social activist, and writer

Suggested Readings

Baker, W. F., & O'Malley, M. (2008). *Leading with kindness: How good people consistently get superior results.* New York: AMACOM.

Birx, E. (2002). *Healing Zen: Awakening to a life of wholeness and compassion while caring for yourself and others.* New York: Viking Press.

Boyatzis, R. E., & McKee, A. (2005). *Resonant leadership: Renewing yourself and connecting with others through mindfulness, hope, and compassion.* Boston: Harvard Business School Press.

The Dalai Lama. (2002). *An open heart: Practicing compassion in everyday life.* New York: Back Bay Books.

Goleman, D., & Boyatzis, R. (2008). Social intelligence and the biology of leadership. *Harvard Business Review, 86*(9), 74-81.

Hagen, S., & Carouba, M. (2002). *Women at ground zero: Stories of courage and compassion.* New York: Alpha Books.

Hopkins, J., & The Dalai Lama. (2002). *Cultivating compassion: A Buddhist perspective.* New York: Broadway Books.

Lewin, R., & Regine, B. (2001). *Weaving complexity and business: Engaging the soul at work.* New York: Texere.

Oliner, S. P. (2003). *Do unto others: Extraordinary acts of ordinary people.* Boulder, CO: Westview Press.

Patterson, K., Grenny, J., McMillan, R., Switzler, A., & Covey, S. R. (2002). *Crucial conversations: Tools for talking when stakes are high.* New York: McGraw-Hill.

Steinbrecher, S., & Bennett, J. B. (2003). *Heart-centered leadership: An invitation to lead from the inside out.* Memphis, TN: Black Pants.

Stone, D., Patton, B., & Heen, S. (2000). *Difficult conversations: How to discuss what matters most.* New York: Penguin Books.

Tutu, D. (2007). *Love: The words and inspiration of Mother Teresa.* Auckland, NZ: PQ Blackwell Ltd.

11 Composure

That is the happiest conversation where there is no competition, no vanity, but a calm, quiet interchange of sentiments.
Samuel Johnson – 18th century English writer

Unskilled

- ☐ Gets rattled and loses cool under pressure and stress
- ☐ May blow up, say things he/she shouldn't
- ☐ Gets easily overwhelmed and becomes emotional, defensive or withdrawn
- ☐ May be defensive and sensitive to criticism
- ☐ May be cynical or moody
- ☐ May be knocked off balance by surprises and get easily rattled
- ☐ May contribute to others losing composure or being unsettled
- ☐ May let anger, frustration and anxiety show

Select one to three of the competencies listed below to use as a substitute for this competency if you decide not to work on it directly.

SUBSTITUTES: 2,3,8,12,26,33,37,41,43,44,48,57

Skilled

- ☐ Is cool under pressure
- ☐ Does not become defensive or irritated when times are tough
- ☐ Is considered mature
- ☐ Can be counted on to hold things together during tough times
- ☐ Can handle stress
- ☐ Is not knocked off balance by the unexpected
- ☐ Doesn't show frustration when resisted or blocked
- ☐ Is a settling influence in a crisis

Overused Skill

- ☐ May not show appropriate emotion
- ☐ May be seen as cold and uncaring
- ☐ May seem flat in situations where others show feelings
- ☐ May be easily misinterpreted
- ☐ May not be able to relate well to those whose actions and decisions are based more on feelings than on thinking

Select one to three of the competencies listed below to work on to compensate for an overuse of this skill.

COMPENSATORS: 3,10,14,26,27,31,44,60,66

Some Causes

- ☐ Defensive
- ☐ Easily overwhelmed; very emotional
- ☐ Lack self-confidence
- ☐ Perfectionist
- ☐ Sensitive
- ☐ Too much going on
- ☐ Very control oriented
- ☐ Weak impulse control

Leadership Architect® Factors and Clusters

This competency is in the Personal and Interpersonal Skills Factor (VI). This competency is in the Being Open and Receptive Cluster (S) with: 26, 33, 41, 44. You may want to check other competencies in the same Factor/Cluster for related tips.

The Map

First about emotions. Emotions are electricity and chemistry. Emotions are designed to help you cope with emergencies and threats. Emotions trigger predictable body changes. Heart pumps faster and with greater pressure. Blood flows faster. Glucose is released into the bloodstream for increased energy and strength. Eyes dilate to take in more light. Breathing rate increases to get more oxygen. Why is that? To either fight or flee from saber-toothed tigers, of course. Emotions are designed to help us with the so-called fight or flight response. It makes the body faster and stronger temporarily. The price? In order to increase energy to the muscles, the emotional response decreases resources for the stomach (that's why we get upset stomachs under stress) and the thinking brain (that's why we say and do dumb things under stress). Even though we might be able to lift a heavy object off a trapped person, we can't think of the right thing to say in a tense meeting. Once the emotional response is triggered, it has to run its course. If no threat follows the initial trigger, it lasts from 45-60 seconds in most people. That's why your grandmother told you to count to 10. Trouble is, people have saber-toothed tigers in their heads. In modern times, thoughts can trigger this emotional response. Events which are certainly not physically threatening, like being criticized, can trigger the response. Even worse, today people have added a third "f" to the fight or flight response—freeze. Emotions can shut you down and leave you speechless, neither choosing to fight (argue, respond) or flee (calmly shut down the transaction and exit). You'll have to fight these reactions to learn to be cool under pressure.

Some Remedies

☐ **1. Do you know what sets you off? Identify your trigger points.** Write down the last 25 times you lost your composure. Most people who have composure problems have three to five repeating triggers. Criticism. Loss of control. A certain kind of person. An enemy. Being surprised. Spouse. Children. Money. Authority. Angry at yourself because you can't say no? Try to group 90% of the events into three to five categories. Once you have the groupings, ask yourself why these are a problem. Is it ego? Losing face? Being caught short? Being found out? Causing you more work? In each grouping, what would be a more mature response? Mentally and physically rehearse a better response. Try to decrease by 10% a month the number of times you lose your composure.

☐ **2. No filter? Increase your impulse control.** People say and do inappropriate things when they lose their composure. The problem is that they say or do the first thing that occurs to them. Research shows that generally somewhere between the second and third thing you think of to say or do is the best option. Practice holding back your first response long enough to think of a second. When you can do that, wait long enough to think of a third before you choose. By that time 50% of your composure problems should go away.

☐ **3. Need to regain composure? Count to 10.** Our thinking and judgment are not at their best during the emotional response. Create and practice delaying tactics. Go get a pencil out of your briefcase. Go get a cup of coffee. Ask a question and listen. Go up to the flip chart and write something. Take notes. See yourself in a setting you find calming. Go to the bathroom. You need about a minute to regain your composure after the emotional response is triggered. Don't do or say anything until the minute has passed.

☐ **4. Impatient? Delay gratification.** Are you impatient? Do you get upset when the plane is delayed? The food is late? The car isn't ready? Your spouse is behind schedule? For most of us, life is one big delay. We always seem to be waiting for someone else to do something so we can do our something. People with composure problems often can't accept delay of what they want, and think they deserve and have coming. When what they want is delayed, they get belligerent and demanding. Write down the last 25 delays that set you off. Group them into three to five categories. Create and rehearse a more mature response. Relax. Reward yourself with something enjoyable. Adopt a philosophical stance since there's little or nothing you can do about it. Think great thoughts while you're waiting. Force a smile or find something to laugh about. *More help? – See #41 Patience.*

☐ **5. Defensive? Deal constructively with criticism.** A lot of loss of composure starts with an intended or even an unintended criticism. There are a lot of perfect people in this world who cannot deal with a piece of negative information about themselves or about something they have or have not done. The rest of us have flaws that most around us know about and once in a while tell us about. We even know that once in a while unjust criticism is sent our way. Dealing constructively with criticism is a learnable skill. Learn to be an observer of defensiveness and anger around you. Many people with these problems have many shoulds, musts, and commandments about the behavior of others. *More help? – See #108 Defensiveness.*

☐ **6. Too controlling? Loosen your grip.** Are you somewhat of a perfectionist? Need to have everything just so? Create plans and expect them to be followed? Very jealous of your time? Another source of loss of composure is when things do not go exactly as planned. Put slack in your plans. Expect the unexpected. Lengthen the time line. Plan for delays. List worst-case scenarios. Most of the time you will be pleasantly surprised and the rest of the time you won't get so upset.

☐ **7. Feel a need to retaliate? Don't make it personal.** Do you feel a need to punish the people and groups that set you off? Do you become hostile, angry, sarcastic or vengeful? While all that may be temporarily satisfying to you, they will all backfire and you will lose in the long term. When someone attacks you, rephrase it as an attack on a problem. Reverse the argument—ask what they would do if they were in your shoes. When the other side takes a rigid position, don't reject it. Ask why—what are the principles behind the offer, how do we know it's fair, what's the theory of the case. Play out what would happen if their position was accepted. Let the other side vent frustration, blow off steam, but don't react.

☐ **8. Losing perspective? Be objective.** When you do reply to an attack, keep it to the facts and their impact on you. It's fine for you to draw conclusions about the impact on yourself ("I felt blindsided."). It's not fine for you to tell others their motives ("You blindsided me" means you did it, probably meant to, and I know the meaning of your behavior). So state the meaning for yourself; ask others what their actions meant.

☐ **9. Getting anxious and jumping to conclusions? Be deliberate.** Take quick action? Don't like ambiguity and uncertainty and act to wipe it out? Solutions first, understanding second? Take the time to really define the problem. Let people finish. Try not to interrupt. Don't finish others' sentences. Ask clarifying questions. Restate the problem in your own words to everyone's satisfaction. Ask them what they think. Throw out trial solutions for debate. Then decide.

- ☐ **10. Too much invested at work? Exercise for stress relief.** Find a release for your pent-up emotions. Get a physical hobby. Start an exercise routine. Jog. Walk. Chop wood. Sometimes people who have flair tempers hold it in too much, the pressure builds, and the teakettle blows. The body stores energy. It has to go somewhere. Work on releasing your work frustration off-work.
- ☐ **11. Letting it build up? Monitor your internal pressure gauge.** Maybe your fuse is too long. You may wait and wait, let the pressure build, keep your concerns to yourself, then explode as a pressure release. Write down what you're concerned about, then talk about the issues with confidantes and coworkers before you blow up. If the pressure interferes with your thought processes at work (you're supposed to be listening, but you're fretting instead), pick a time to worry. Say to yourself, "I'll write this down, then think about it on the way home." Train yourself to stay in the present.

Some Develop-in-Place Assignments

- ☐ Make peace with an enemy or someone you've disappointed with a product or service or someone you've had some trouble with or don't get along with very well.
- ☐ Manage a group through a significant business crisis.
- ☐ Handle a tough negotiation with an internal or external client or customer.
- ☐ Manage the assigning/allocating of office space in a contested situation.
- ☐ Manage a dissatisfied internal or external customer; troubleshoot a performance or quality problem with a product or service.

Every great player has learned the two Cs:
How to concentrate and how to maintain composure.
Byron Nelson – American golfing legend

Suggested Readings

Bradberry, T., & Greaves, J. (2005). *The emotional intelligence quick book: Everything you need to know to put your EQ to work.* New York: Fireside.

Carter, L. (2003). *The anger trap: Free yourself from the frustrations that sabotage your life.* New York: John Wiley & Sons.

Davies, W. (2001). *Overcoming anger and irritability.* New York: New York University Press.

Dinnocenzo, D. A., & Swegan, R. B. (2001). *Dot calm: The search for sanity in a wired world.* San Francisco: Berrett-Koehler Publishers.

Ellis, A. (2000). *How to control your anxiety before it controls you.* New York: Citadel Press.

Forni, P. M. (2002). *Choosing civility: The twenty-five rules of considerate conduct.* New York: St. Martin's Press.

Gibson, D., & Tulgan, B. (2002). *Managing anger in the workplace.* Amherst, MA: HRD Press.

Gonthier, G., & Morrissey, K. (2002). *Rude awakenings: Overcoming the civility crisis in the workplace.* Chicago: Dearborn Trade.

Lerner, H. (2002). *The dance of connection: How to talk to someone when you're mad, hurt, scared, frustrated, insulted, betrayed, or desperate.* New York: Quill/HarperCollins.

Lord, R. G., Klimoski, R. J., & Kanfer, R. (Eds.). (2002). *Emotions in the workplace: Understanding the structure and role of emotions in organizational behavior.* San Francisco: Jossey-Bass.

Losyk, B. (2004). *Get a grip! Overcoming stress and thriving in the workplace.* Hoboken, NJ: John Wiley & Sons.

Maravelas, A. (2005). *How to reduce workplace conflict and stress: How leaders and their employees can protect their sanity and productivity from tension and turf wars.* Franklin Lakes, NJ: Career Press.

Rogers, P., & McKay, M. (2000). *The anger control workbook.* Oakland, CA: New Harbinger Publications.

Semmelroth, C., & Smith, D. E. P. (2000). *The anger habit.* Lincoln, NE: Writer's Showcase Press.

12 Conflict Management

Conflict is inevitable, but combat is optional.
Max Lucado – American author

Unskilled

- ☐ Avoids conflict in situations and with people
- ☐ May accommodate, want everyone to get along
- ☐ May get upset as a reaction to conflict, takes it personally
- ☐ Can't operate under conflict long enough to get a good deal
- ☐ Gives in and says yes too soon
- ☐ Gets into conflict by accident; doesn't see it coming
- ☐ Will let things fester rather than dealing with them directly
- ☐ Will try to wait long enough for it to go away
- ☐ May be excessively competitive and have to win every dispute

Select one to three of the competencies listed below to use as a substitute for this competency if you decide not to work on it directly.

SUBSTITUTES: 2,3,4,8,9,11,13,16,31,33,34,36,37,41,50,51,52,57

Skilled

- ☐ Steps up to conflicts, seeing them as opportunities
- ☐ Reads situations quickly
- ☐ Good at focused listening
- ☐ Can hammer out tough agreements and settle disputes equitably
- ☐ Can find common ground and get cooperation with minimum noise

Overused Skill

- ☐ May be seen as overly aggressive and assertive
- ☐ May get in the middle of everyone else's problems
- ☐ May drive for a solution before others are ready
- ☐ May have a chilling effect on open debate
- ☐ May spend too much time with obstinate people and unsolvable problems

Select one to three of the competencies listed below to work on to compensate for an overuse of this skill.

COMPENSATORS: 2,3,31,33,34,36,37,40,41,51,52,56,60,64

Some Causes

- ☐ Avoid conflict
- ☐ Can't negotiate
- ☐ Get too emotional
- ☐ Slow to catch on
- ☐ Take things personally
- ☐ Too sensitive

Leadership Architect® Factors and Clusters

This competency is in the Courage Factor (III). This competency is in the Dealing with Trouble Cluster (H) with: 9, 13, 34, 57. You may want to check other competencies in the same Factor/Cluster for related tips.

The Map

One survey found that managers were spending 18% of their time dealing with direct face-to-face conflict. Most organizations are decentralized and compartmentalized which sets up natural conflict, group to group. Whenever you form two groups, conflict follows. Gender and race inroads have probably brought with them increased conflict. Competition has heated up, making speed and agility more important but also created more conflict and less relaxed reflection. There is data-based conflict—my numbers are better than your numbers. There is opinion conflict—my opinion has greater value than yours. There is power conflict—this is mine. And there is unnecessary conflict due to how people position themselves and protect their turf. Dealing with and resolving all these kinds of conflict is more important and frequent than it used to be.

Some Remedies

☐ **1. Caught in a win/lose predicament? Seek cooperative relations.** The opposite of conflict is cooperation. Developing cooperative relationships involves demonstrating real and perceived equity, the other side feeling understood and respected, and taking a problem oriented point of view. To do this more: increase the realities and perceptions of fairness—don't try to win every battle and take all the spoils; focus on the common-ground issues and interests of both sides—find wins on both sides, give in on little points; avoid starting with entrenched positions—show respect for them and their positions; and reduce any remaining conflicts to the smallest size possible.

☐ **2. Causing unnecessary conflict? Choose words appropriately.** Language, words and timing set the tone and can cause unnecessary conflict that has to be managed before you can get anything done. Do you use insensitive language? Do you raise your voice often? Do you use terms and phrases that challenge others? Do you use demeaning terms? Do you use negative humor? Do you offer conclusions, solutions, statements, dictates or answers early in the transaction? Give reasons first, solutions last. When you give solutions first, people often directly challenge the solutions instead of defining the problem. Pick words that are other-person neutral. Pick words that don't challenge or sound one-sided. Pick tentative and probabilistic words that give others a chance to maneuver and save face. Pick words that are about the problem and not the person. Avoid direct blaming remarks; describe the problem and its impact.

☐ **3. Tensions escalating? Practice Aikido.** Aikido is the ancient art of absorbing the energy of your opponent and using it to manage him/her. Let the other side vent frustration, blow off steam, but don't react. Listen. Nod. Ask clarifying questions. Ask open-ended questions like, "What one change could you make so we could achieve our objectives better?" "What could I do that would help the most?" Restate their position periodically to signal you have understood. But don't react. Keep them talking until they run out of venom. When the other side takes a rigid position, don't reject it. Ask why—what are the principles behind the position, how do we know it's fair, what's the theory of the case. Play out what would happen if their position was accepted. Then explore the concern underlying the answer. Separate the people from the problem. When someone attacks you, rephrase it as an attack on the problem. In response to threats, say you'll only negotiate on merit and fairness. If the other side won't play fair, surface their game—"It looks like you're playing good cop, bad cop. Why don't you settle your differences and tell me one thing?" In response to unreasonable proposals, attacks, or a non-answer to a question, you can always say nothing. People will usually respond by saying more, coming off their position a bit, or at least revealing their true interests. Many times, with unlimited venting and your understanding, the actual conflict shrinks.

☐ **4. Too focused on differences? Seize on common points of agreement.** Almost all conflicts have common points that get lost in the heat of the battle. After a conflict has been presented and understood, start by saying that it might be helpful to see if we agree on anything. Write them on the flip chart. Then write down the areas left open. Focus on common goals, priorities and problems. Keep the open conflicts as small as possible and concrete. The more abstract it gets, "We don't trust your unit," the more unmanageable it gets. To this respond, "Tell me your specific concern—why exactly don't you trust us, can you give me an example?" Usually after calm discussion, they don't trust your unit on this specific issue under these specific conditions. That's easier to deal with. Allow others to save face by conceding small points that are not central to the issue, don't try to hit a home run every time. If you can't agree on a solution, agree on a procedure to move forward. Collect more data. Appeal to a higher power. Get a third party arbitrator. Something. This creates some positive motion and breaks stalemates.

☐ **5. Too emotional? Keep your cool.** Sometimes our emotional reactions lead others to think we have problems with conflict. In conflict situations, what emotional reactions do you have (such as impatience or non-verbals like flushing or drumming your pen or fingers)? Learn to recognize those as soon as they start and substitute something more neutral. Most emotional responses to conflict come from personalizing the issue. Separate people issues from the problem at hand and deal with people issues separately and later if they persist. Always return to facts and the problem before the group; stay away from personal clashes. Attack the problem by looking at common interests and underlying concerns, not people and their positions. Try on their views for size, the emotion as well as the content. Ask yourself if you understand their feelings. Ask what they would do if they were in your shoes. See if you can restate each other's position and advocate it for a minute to get inside each other's place. If you get emotional, pause and collect yourself. You are not your best when you get emotional. Then return to the problem. *More help? – See #11 Composure and #107 Lack of Composure.*

☐ **6. Each possesses something the other wants? Seek opportunities to bargain and trade.** Since you can't absolutely win all conflicts unless you keep pulling rank, you have to learn to horse-trade and bargain. What do they need that I have? What could I do for them outside this conflict that could allow them to give up something I need now in return? How can we turn this into a win for both of us? *More help? – See #37 Negotiating.*

☐ **7. Not getting your message through? Deliver clear, problem-focused communication.** Follow the rule of equity: Explain your thinking and ask them to explain theirs. Be able to state their position as clearly as they do whether you agree or not; give it legitimacy. Separate facts from opinions and assumptions. Generate a variety of possibilities first rather than stake out positions. Keep your speaking to 30-60 second bursts. Try to get them to do the same. Don't give the other side the impression you're lecturing or criticizing them. Explain objectively why you hold a view; make the other side do the same. Ask lots of questions, make fewer statements. To identify interests behind positions, ask why they hold them or why they wouldn't want to do something. Always restate their position to their satisfaction before offering a response. *More help? – See #27 Informing.*

☐ **8. Hopelessly stuck? Go to arbitration.** When there is a true impasse, suggest a third equal-power party to resolve the remaining conflicts. Use a third party to write up each side's interests and keep suggesting solutions until you can agree. Or if time is an issue, pass it on to a higher authority. Present both sides calmly and objectively, and let the chips fall where they may.

☐ **9. Easily provoked? Identify conflict triggers.** Do specific people, issues, styles, or groups set you off and make you handle the conflict poorly? Write down the last 20 times when you handled conflict poorly. What's common in the situations? Are there three to five common themes? Are the same people involved? Different people but the same style? Certain kinds of issues? Once you have isolated the cause, mentally rehearse a better way of handling it when it comes up next time.

☐ **10. Committing blunders? Navigate the political terrain.** Organizations are a complex maze of constituencies, issues and rivalries peopled by strong egos, sensitives, and empire protectors. Political mistakes come in a variety of shapes and sizes. The most common is saying things you shouldn't. Next are actions that are politically out of line and not right for the context. Worst are politically unacceptable moves, initiatives, tactics and strategies. Last are unnecessary conflicts, tensions, misunderstandings and rivalries created because you took after a specific person or group. Work to understand the politics of the organization. Who are the movers and shakers in the organization? Who are the major gatekeepers who control the flow of resources, information and decisions? Who are the guides and the helpers? Get to know them better. Do lunch. Who are the major resisters and stoppers? Try to avoid or go around them or make peace with them. In the special case of dealing with top management, sensitivities are high, egos are big, sensitivity traps are set and tensions can be severe. There is a lot of room for making statements or acting in ways that would be seen as exhibiting your poor political judgment and causing conflict. *More help? – See #38 Organizational Agility, #48 Political Savvy and #119 Political Missteps.*

Some Develop-in-Place Assignments

☐ Make peace with an enemy or someone you've disappointed with a product or service or someone you've had some trouble with or don't get along with very well.

☐ Manage a cost-cutting project.

☐ Do a postmortem on a failed project, and present it to the people involved.

☐ Be a member of a union-negotiating or grievance-handling team.

☐ Coach a children's sports team.

Don't be afraid of opposition.
Remember, a kite rises against, not with, the wind.
Hamilton Mabie – American essayist

Suggested Readings

Blackard, K., & Gibson, J. W. (2002). *Capitalizing on conflict: Strategies and practices for turning conflict to synergy in organizations.* Palo Alto, CA: Davies-Black Publishing.

Cartwright, T. (2003). *Managing conflict with peers.* Greensboro, NC: Center for Creative Leadership.

Cloke, K., & Goldsmith, J. (2000). *Resolving conflicts at work: A complete guide for everyone on the job.* San Francisco: Jossey-Bass.

Crawley, J., & Graham, K. (2002). *Mediation for managers: Getting beyond conflict to performance.* Yarmouth, ME: Nicholas Brealey Publishing.

Dana, D. (2000). *Conflict resolution.* New York: McGraw-Hill Trade.

Deutsch, M., & Coleman, P. T. (Eds.). (2000). *The handbook of conflict resolution: Theory and practice.* San Francisco: Jossey-Bass.

Eadie, W. F., & Nelson, P. E. (Eds.). (2001). *The language of conflict and resolution.* Thousand Oaks, CA: Sage.

Furlong, G. T. (2005). *The conflict resolution toolbox: Models and maps for analyzing, diagnosing, and resolving conflict.* Mississauga, ON: John Wiley & Sons, Canada, Ltd.

Gerzon, M. (2006). *Leading through conflict: How successful leaders transform differences into opportunities.* Boston: Harvard Business School Press.

Guttman, H. M. (2003). *When goliaths clash: Managing executive conflict to build a more dynamic organization.* New York: AMACOM.

Harper, G. (2004). *The joy of conflict resolution: Transforming victims, villains, and heroes in the workplace and at home.* Gabriola Island, BC: New Society Publishers.

Harvard Business School Press. (2004). *Dealing with difficult people.* (The Results-Driven Manager Series.) Boston: Harvard Business School Press.

Kheel, T. W. (2001). *The keys to conflict resolution: Proven methods of resolving disputes voluntarily* (2nd ed.). New York: Four Walls Eight Windows.

Levine, S. (2000). *Getting to resolution: Turning conflict into collaboration.* San Francisco: Berrett-Koehler Publishers.

Masters, M. F., & Albright, R. R. (2002). *The complete guide to conflict resolution in the workplace.* New York: AMACOM.

Perlow, L. (2003). *When you say yes but mean no: How silencing conflict wrecks relationships and companies...and what you can do about it.* New York: Crown Business.

Popejoy, B., & McManigle, B. J. (2002). *Managing conflict with direct reports.* Greensboro, NC: Center for Creative Leadership.

13 Confronting Direct Reports

Harshness to me is giving somebody false hopes and not following through. That's harsh. Telling some guy or some girl who've got zero talent that they have zero talent actually is a kindness.
Simon Cowell – British television personality/producer

Unskilled

- ☐ Not comfortable delivering negative messages to direct reports
- ☐ Procrastinates and avoids problems until forced to act
- ☐ May not communicate clear standards or provide much feedback
- ☐ Lets problems fester hoping they will go away
- ☐ May give in too soon to excuses
- ☐ May give people too many chances
- ☐ Can't pull the trigger even when all else has failed
- ☐ Has low standards or plays favorites

Select one to three of the competencies listed below to use as a substitute for this competency if you decide not to work on it directly.

SUBSTITUTES: 1,9,12,16,20,27,34,35,36,37,53,56,57

Skilled

- ☐ Deals with problem direct reports firmly and in a timely manner
- ☐ Doesn't allow problems to fester
- ☐ Regularly reviews performance and holds timely discussions
- ☐ Can make negative decisions when all other efforts fail
- ☐ Deals effectively with troublemakers

Overused Skill

- ☐ May be too quick to act on problem direct reports
- ☐ May not put enough developmental effort toward the problem
- ☐ May expect turnarounds in too short a time
- ☐ May expect miracles

Select one to three of the competencies listed below to work on to compensate for an overuse of this skill.

COMPENSATORS: 3,7,12,19,20,21,23,31,33,36,41,56,60,64

Some Causes

- ☐ Can't deal with face-to-face conflict
- ☐ Can't turn around resistant people
- ☐ Don't give enough feedback
- ☐ Don't know how to draw the line
- ☐ Don't want the paperwork hassle of acting
- ☐ Don't follow up well
- ☐ Have unrealistic expectations
- ☐ Let problems fester
- ☐ Procrastinate or play favorites
- ☐ Won't make the ultimate call
- ☐ Won't take negative actions

Leadership Architect® Factors and Clusters

This competency is in the Courage Factor (III). This competency is in the Dealing with Trouble Cluster (H) with: 9, 12, 34, 57. You may want to check other competencies in the same Factor/Cluster for related tips.

The Map

Most organizations are running leaner today. With more rapid change and team-based efforts increasing, problem performers can't be hidden as they often were in the past. Overcoming your reluctance to deal with them is a key to your unit's performance and probably your career as well. Managers who excel at confronting direct reports are timely, consistent, focus on performance gaps, pitch in and help the person succeed, and are sensitive to how the person feels. But if the effort fails, taking timely but compassionate action to separate the person from the organization is the true test of management courage.

Some Remedies

- ☐ **1. Hesitant to deliver negative feedback? Let others know where they stand.** Most problem performers don't know it! Delivering bad news to people face-to-face came in number one in a survey of what managers hate to do. Survey after survey says employees do not get the feedback they need to correct performance problems. Women, minorities and older people get the least. Most people who are fired or take an honorary resignation have had satisfactory or high performance appraisals up to the point of leaving. It's tough to be the bearer of bad news. Emotions and defensiveness may flare. The consequences could be severe. You may have to defend your actions inside and outside the organization. Long term, it's cruel and unusual punishment not to deliver fair but direct feedback to someone who is struggling or failing. Otherwise he/she can't work on the problems and plan his/her career. The key to overcoming your reluctance is to focus on fairly applied and communicated standards and on gaps between expected and actual performance. Read *Becoming a Manager* by Linda A. Hill for case studies of managers applying standards to others for the first time. Make sure everyone under you knows what you expect of him/her and where he/she stands.

☐ **2. Employees not sure what to do? Create and communicate clear standards.** Are your problem performers confused? Do they know what's expected of them? You may not set clear enough performance standards, goals and objectives. You may be a seat-of-the-pants manager, and some people are struggling because they don't know what is expected or it changes. You may be a cryptic communicator. You may be too busy to communicate. You may communicate to some and not to others. You may have given up on some and stopped communicating. Or you may think they would know what to do if they're any good, but that's not really true because you have not properly communicated what you want. The first task is to outline the 5 to 10 key results areas and what indicators of success would be. Involve your problem direct reports on both ends, the standards and the indicators. Provide them with a fair way to measure their own progress. Employees with goals and standards are usually harder on themselves than you'll ever be. Often they set higher standards than you would. Sometimes the problem is behavioral, as in someone who can't control outbursts, and only affects performance on the back end in lost cooperation or sabotage. Then the best approach is to note the gap between behavior and expectations, and point out what some of the observed consequences are. If the person agrees, then coaching may suffice. If the person balks, then a 360° feedback process with follow-up may be needed to illuminate the depth of the problem before any help can be given. *More help? – See #35 Managing and Measuring Work.*

☐ **3. Impatient for improvements? Set realistic time frames for development.** Employees not performing up to standard? It's common to see 90-day improve-or-else plans that no one can accomplish. Be more strategic, improve your interpersonal skills, learn about the business, be less arrogant. Ask yourself how long did it take you to become proficient at what you are criticizing this person for. Because managers hesitate delivering negative messages, we get to people late. Sometimes the last five managers this person reported to saw the same difficulty, but none of them confronted the person. Get to people as soon as they do not meet agreed upon standards of performance. Don't wait. Early is the easiest time to do it with the highest return on investment for you, them and the organization.

Most people who have reached the problem performer status will take one to two years to turn around under the best of circumstances. It's cruel and unusual punishment to require a fixed-time turnaround or improvement plan. If your organization demands a 90-day wonder, fight it. Tell them that while a bit of improvement can be seen in that period, substantive change is not like producing a quarterly earnings statement.

☐ **4. Not sure when or how to deliver bad news? Plan the "improve or you're gone" process.** The first meeting. After you have made the assessment that a direct report just isn't making it, document your observations against the standards and arrange the first tough meeting. Experience directs that these first tough meetings should always be in the beginning of the week and in the mornings. They should not occur on Fridays or the day before holidays when most managers deliver them. They should not be at a time when the unit is on a bomb run getting ready for a big presentation. Start the meeting by saying "we" have a performance issue to talk about and fix. Be succinct. You have limited attention span in tough feedback situations. Don't waste time with a long preamble, just get to it. The recipient is likely to know the feedback is negative anyway so go ahead and say it first. They won't hear or remember anything positive you have to say anyway. Don't overwhelm the person, even if you have a lot to say. Pick the key areas and stick to them. Keep it to the facts and their impact on you, them and your unit. Talk about specific events and situations. Plan for enough time. This is not a process to rush.

☐ **5. Focusing on the problem, not the solution? Go in with an improvement plan.** Don't criticize without a solution and a plan. Tell the person what you want—paint a different outcome. Don't expect him/her to guess, and don't spend a lot of time rehashing the past. Suggest steps both of you can take to remedy the problem. Be positive but firm. Be constructive. Be optimistic in the beginning. Help him/her see the negative consequences and the potential timing—you can ask what he/she thinks and you can tell him/her what the consequences are from your side. Change starts with seeing an unacceptable consequence and a way out. Improve or else threats don't work. *More help? – See #19 Developing Direct Reports and Others.*

☐ **6. Caught off guard by disagreements and excuses? Manage the pushback.** Keep control of the discussion. Don't do fake listening—the obligatory "Now let's hear your side" if you don't think there is another side. Discussions like this will trigger most people's natural defense routines. Expect that. That's not necessarily a sign of true disagreement or denial; it's just a natural thing to do. Say something like, "I understand you have a different view, but the performance just isn't there in this area.

We've got to deal with this." The person may have 10 reasons why your appraisal isn't fair or accurate. Listen. Acknowledge that you understand what he/she has said. If the person persists, say "Let's talk about your view tomorrow after we've both had a chance to reflect on this discussion." Then, return to your agenda. Say, "I'm going to help you perform in this area." The best tack is to immediately schedule new work, trusting that the person will come through this time. You should discuss this as you would any other work assignment and not bring up the past. She/he has already heard what you said. (With a person who, in your opinion, lacks motivation not skill, raise the stakes. Sometimes a person who performs poorly at a C difficulty task performs well at an A difficulty task in exactly the same area.)

☐ **7. Emotions getting out of control? Prepare for defense condition four (defcon4).** Emotions can run high. This may truly be a surprise to the person. Even though this problem has been going on for years, this may be the first time a manager has dealt with it directly. Don't take too seriously what people say in that first meeting. He/she is running on emotion. Mentally rehearse for worst-case scenarios. Anticipate what the person might say and have responses prepared so as not to be caught off guard. Work on your stands through mental interrogation until you can clearly state in a few sentences what your stand is and why you hold it. Remain composed and don't use words you'll regret—communications killers such as "always" and "never." If he/she is not composed, don't respond. Just let him/her vent or even cry, then return to the problem at hand. Don't forget the pathos of the situation—even if you're totally right, feelings will run high. If you have to be critical, you can still empathize with how he/she feels, and you can help with encouragement later when the discussion turns more positive. Allow him/her to save face; concede some small points; don't rush the human process of grieving. *More help? – See #12 Conflict Management.*

☐ **8. Damaged relationships? Follow up on feedback the next day.** Go by and see the person the next day; don't have him/her come to your office. Ask him/her how he/she feels. Don't back off your points, just allow him/her to talk. Indicate you will pitch in and help, that you consider it your job to remove obstacles to performance, provide information and support, provide structure and advice on how, but not tell the person how to do it, and be available for trouble shooting. Consciously try to maintain the same or a closer relationship after the event. If the person feels written off, the situation can turn hopeless. Schedule regular checkpoints. Use a ruler you can both relate to. Track progress. If appropriate at some later time, ask the person for feedback on you as a manager. *More help? – See #7 Caring About Direct Reports.*

- ☐ **9. Last chance? Announce the two-minute warning.** The last chance for the person who isn't really trying. You may have to pull someone aside after a couple of months and say, "I understand all your issues and have tried to help you, but you aren't doing what we agreed. Are you committed or not?" If you have to do something like the above, follow the rules of dealing with conflict: depersonalize; keep it on the problem, not the person. Try one last time to help. Note the person's concerns or objections or description of what's getting in the way but don't concede anything. Be clear; now is not the time for negotiation. Give the person a day to think it over and come in with a believable performance improvement plan. At this point it's his/her problem. Be prepared to act immediately if the plan is insufficient. Obviously, you will have gotten any necessary clearances in advance and sought the help of Human Resources and Legal.
- ☐ **10. Time to part ways? Say good-bye with dignity and grace.** Just because the person can't do this job doesn't mean he/she is incompetent as a person or that he/she can't do 50 other things better than you can do them. Do nothing to generalize one performance failure to other situations, and point to the person's strengths in any way you can. Suggest what would be a better job match. Indicate what you can do to help; if you're willing to be a reference for certain types of work, say so. Make the meeting short. Go back to see the person later and talk about his/her feelings if he/she is willing. You don't have to respond, just listen. Come up with some sort of parting gesture that indicates to the person that you are not rejecting him or her; it was simply a matter of one job that wasn't a fit. A party, a note, a phone call—whatever you can do that's genuine. Even if he/she rejects you, if you meant it, that's all you can do.

Some Develop-in-Place Assignments

- ☐ Manage the outplacement of a group of people.
- ☐ Manage a group of resistant people with low morale through an unpopular change or project.
- ☐ Assign a project with a tight deadline to a group.
- ☐ Manage a group of people involved in tackling a fix-it or turnaround project.
- ☐ Hire and manage a temporary group of people to accomplish a tough or time-tight assignment.

It isn't the people you fire who will make your life miserable;
it's the people you don't fire.

Harvey Mackay– American author and business motivational speaker

Suggested Readings

Bernstein, A. J. (2001). *Emotional vampires: Dealing with people who drain you dry.* New York: McGraw-Hill.

Buron, R. J., & McDonald-Mann, D. (2003). *Giving feedback to subordinates* (Rev. ed.). Greensboro, NC: Center for Creative Leadership.

Crawley, J., & Graham, K. (2002). *Mediation for managers: Getting beyond conflict to performance.* Yarmouth, ME: Nicholas Brealey Publishing.

Grant, M. M. (2006). Six Sigma for people? The heart of performance management. *Human Resource Planning 29*(1), 10-11.

Grote, D. (2006). *Discipline without punishment* (2nd ed.). New York: AMACOM.

Harvard Business School Press. (2007). *Dismissing an employee.* Boston: Harvard Business School Press.

Hoover, J., & DiSilvestro, R. P. (2005). *The art of constructive confrontation: How to achieve more accountability with less conflict.* Hoboken, NJ: John Wiley & Sons.

Lang, M. D., & Taylor, A. (2000). *The making of a mediator: Developing artistry in practice.* San Francisco: Jossey-Bass.

Levin, R. A., & Rosse, J. G. (2001). *Talent flow: A strategic approach to keeping good employees, helping them grow, and letting them go.* New York: John Wiley & Sons.

Manzoni, J. (2002). A better way to deliver bad news. *Harvard Business Review 80*(9), 114-119.

McClure, L. F. (2000). *Anger and conflict in the workplace: Spot the signs, avoid the trauma.* Manassas Park, VA: Impact.

McKenna, P. J., & Maister, D. H. (2002). *First among equals: How to manage a group of professionals.* New York: Free Press.

Moss, S. E., & Sanchez, J. I. (2004). Are your employees avoiding you? Managerial strategies for closing the feedback gap. *Academy of Management Executive 18*(1), 32-44.

Patterson, K., Grenny, J., McMillan, R., & Switzler, A. (2005). *Crucial confrontations: Tools for talking about broken promises, violated expectations, and bad behavior.* New York: McGraw-Hill.

Patterson, K., Grenny, J., McMillan, R., Switzler, A., & Covey, S. R. (2002). *Crucial conversations: Tools for talking when stakes are high.* New York: McGraw-Hill/Contemporary Books.

Scott, G. G. (2004). *A survival guide for working with humans: Dealing with whiners, back-stabbers, know-it-alls, and other difficult people.* New York: AMACOM.

Scott, S. (2004). *Fierce conversations: Achieving success at work and in life, one conversation at a time* (Rev. ed.). New York: Viking Press.

Solomon, M. (2002). *Working with difficult people.* New York: Prentice Hall.

Stone, F. M. (1999). *Coaching, counseling and mentoring: How to choose and use the right technique to boost employee performance* (2nd ed.). New York: AMACOM.

Ursiny, T. (2003). *Coward's guide to conflict: Empowering solutions for those who would rather run than fight.* Naperville, IL: Sourcebook Trade.

14 Creativity

If you're going to create, create a lot. Creativity is not like playing the slot machines, where failure to win means you go home broke. With creativity, if you don't win, you're usually no worse off than if you hadn't played.
Scott Adams – American writer
and creator of the *Dilbert* comic strip

Unskilled

- ☐ Narrow, tactical, cautious and conservative
- ☐ May be more comfortable with the past, prefer the tried and true
- ☐ Narrow perspective may have resulted from narrow background
- ☐ Avoids risk and doesn't seek to be bold or different
- ☐ Doesn't connect with ideas from outside own area
- ☐ May have no idea how creativity works
- ☐ Uses old solutions for new problems
- ☐ May chill the creative initiatives of others

Select one to three of the competencies listed below to use as a substitute for this competency if you decide not to work on it directly.

SUBSTITUTES: 1,2,5,15,16,28,30,32,33,43,46,51,57,58,61

Skilled

- ☐ Comes up with a lot of new and unique ideas
- ☐ Easily makes connections among previously unrelated notions
- ☐ Tends to be seen as original and value-added in brainstorming settings

Overused Skill

- ☐ May get so infatuated with marginally productive ideas that he/she wastes time
- ☐ May get involved in too many things at once
- ☐ May not follow through after the idea
- ☐ May be disorganized or poor at detail
- ☐ May be a loner and not a good team player
- ☐ May not relate well to those less creative

Select one to three of the competencies listed below to work on to compensate for an overuse of this skill.

COMPENSATORS: 1,5,16,17,24,28,30,38,39,45,46,47,48,50,51,52,53,58,59,61,64

Some Causes

- ☐ Caught in the past
- ☐ Cautious
- ☐ Don't know what it is
- ☐ Limited ways to think
- ☐ Narrow
- ☐ Practical
- ☐ Reject creativity as fanciful
- ☐ Restrained
- ☐ Too focused
- ☐ Too good of a problem solver

Leadership Architect® Factors and Clusters

This competency is in the Strategic Skills Factor (I). This competency is in the Creating the New and Different Cluster (C) with: 2, 28, 46, 58. You may want to check other competencies in the same Factor/Cluster for related tips.

The Map

Being creative involves: (1) Immersing yourself in a problem; (2) Looking broadly for connections—in the past, what other organizations do, brainstorming with others; (3) Letting your ideas incubate; (4) The breakthrough which usually occurs when you are distracted or in a relaxed state; (5) Picking one or more to pilot. Most of us are capable of being more creative than we demonstrate. Upbringing, schooling and the narrowness of many jobs can have a chilling effect on creativity. Many of us are or have been taught to be restrained, narrow, focused, hesitant, cautious, conservative, afraid to err, and unwilling to make a fool of ourselves. All of that chills the creativity already inside us. One process is to lift those restraints. The other involves adding creative skills. There are research-based and experience-tested techniques that, if followed, will produce a more creative process from a person or a group. Creativity is a valued skill because most organizations need innovation in their products and services to succeed.

Some Remedies

- ☐ **1. Stuck? Remove the restraints.** What's preventing you from being more creative? Perfectionist? Being creative operates at well below having everything right. Cautious and reluctant to speculate? Being creative is the opposite. Worried about what people may think? Afraid you won't be able to defend your idea? By its very nature, being creative means throwing uncertain things up for review and critique. Narrow perspective; most comfortable with your technology and profession? Being creative is looking everywhere. More comfortable with what is very practical? Being creative begins as being impractical. Too busy to reflect and ruminate? Being creative takes time. Get out of your comfort zone. Many busy people rely too much on solutions from their own history. They rely on what has happened to them in the past. They see sameness in problems that isn't there. Beware of—"I have always..." or "Usually, I...." Always pause and look under rocks and ask yourself is this really like the problems you have solved in the past? You don't have to change who you are and what you're comfortable with other than when you need to be more creative. Then think and act differently; try new things; break free of your restraints.

☐ **2. Need a fresh approach? Use creative thinking strategies.** To be more personally creative, immerse yourself in the problem. Getting fresh ideas is not a speedboating process; it requires looking deeply.

- Carve out dedicated time—study it deeply, talk with others, look for parallels in other organizations and in remote areas totally outside your field. If your response to this is that you don't have the time, that also usually explains why you're not having any fresh ideas.
- Think out loud. Many people don't know what they know until they talk it out. Find a good sounding board and talk to him/her to increase your understanding of a problem or a technical area. Talk to an expert in an unrelated field. Talk to the most irreverent person you know. Your goal is not to get his/her input, but rather his/her help in figuring out what you know—what your principles and rules of thumb are.
- Practice picking out anomalies—unusual facts that don't quite fit, like sales going down when they should have gone up. What do these odd things imply for strategy? Naturally creative people are much more likely to think in opposite cases when confronted with a problem. Turn the problem upside down: Ask what is the least likely thing it could be, what the problem is not, what's missing from the problem, or what the mirror image of the problem is.
- Look for distant parallels. Don't fall into the mental trap of searching only in parallel organizations because "Only they would know." Back up and ask a broader question to aid in the search for solutions. When Motorola wanted to find out how to process orders more quickly, they went not to other electronics firms, but to Domino's Pizza and Federal Express. For more ideas, an interesting—and fun—book on the topic is *Take the Road to Creativity and Get Off Your Dead End* by David Campbell.

☐ **3. Trying to think outside the box? Break rules and invent new ones.** Creative thought processes do not follow the formal rules of logic, where one uses cause and effect to prove or solve something. Some rules of creative thought are:

- Not using concepts but changing them; imagining this were something else
- Move from one concept or way of looking at things to another, such as from economic to political
- Generate ideas without judging them initially
- Use information to restructure and come up with new patterns
- Jump from one idea to another without justifying the jump
- Look for the least likely and odd
- Look for parallels far from the problem, such as, how is an organization like a big oak tree?
- Ask what's missing or what's not here
- Fascination with mistakes and failure as learning devices

☐ **4. Need some creative solutions? Apply some standard problem-solving skills.** There are many different ways to think through and solve a problem more creatively.

- Ask more questions. In one study of problem solving, 7% of comments were questions and about half were answers. We jump to solutions based on what has worked in the past.
- Complex problems are hard to visualize. They tend to be either oversimplified or too complex to solve unless they are put in a visual format. Cut it up into its component pieces. Examine the pieces to see if a different order would help, or how you could combine three pieces into one.
- Another technique is a pictorial chart called a storyboard where a problem is illustrated by its components being depicted as pictures.
- A variation of this is to tell stories that illustrate the +'s and –'s of a problem, then flow chart those according to what's working and not working. Another is a fishbone diagram used in Total Quality Management.
- Sometimes going to extremes helps. Adding every condition, every worse case you can think of sometimes will suggest a different solution. Taking the present state of affairs and projecting into the future may indicate how and where the system will break down.

– Sleep on it. Take periodic breaks, whether stuck or not. This allows the brain to continue to work on the issue. Most breakthroughs come when we're "not thinking about it." Put it away; give it to someone else; sleep on it. Once you've come up with every idea you can think of, throw them all out and wait for more to occur to you. Force yourself to forget about the issue. For more techniques, read *The Art of Problem Solving* by Russell Ackoff and *Lateral Thinking* or *Serious Creativity* by Edward de Bono.

☐ **5. False starts? Define the problem.** Instant and early conclusions, solutions and how we solved it in the past are the enemies of creativity. Studies show that defining the problem and taking action occur almost simultaneously for most people, so the more effort you put on the front end, the easier it is to come up with a breakthrough solution. Stop and first define what the problem is and isn't. Since providing answers and solutions is so easy for everyone, it would be nice if they were offering solutions to the right problem. Figure out what causes it. Keep asking why, see how many causes you can come up with and how many organizing buckets you can put them in. This increases the chance of a more creative solution because you can see more connections. Be a chess master. Chess masters recognize thousands of patterns of chess pieces. Look for patterns in data, don't just collect information. Put it in categories that make sense to you. Ask lots of questions. Allot at least 50% of the time to defining the problem. Once you've defined the problem, studies have shown that on average, the most creative solution is somewhere between the second and third one generated. So if you tend to grab the first one, slow down. Discipline yourself to pause for enough time to define the problem better and always think of three solutions before you pick one.

☐ **6. Want to increase group creativity? Diversify.** During World War II it was discovered that teams of people with the widest diversity of backgrounds produced the most creative solutions to problems. The teams included people who knew absolutely nothing about the area (i.e., an English major working on a costing problem). When attacking a tough problem which has eluded attempts to solve it, get the broadest group you can. Involve different functions, levels, and disciplines. Pull in customers and colleagues from other organizations. Remember that you're looking for fresh approaches; you're not convening a work task force expected to implement or judge the practicality of the notions. Believe it or not, it doesn't matter if they know anything about the problem or the technology required to deal with it. That's your job.

☐ **7. Ready to brainstorm? Let the ideas fly.** A straightforward technique to enable creativity is brainstorming. Anything goes for an agreed upon time. Throw out ideas, record them all, no evaluation allowed. Many people have had bad experiences with brainstorming. Silly ideas. Nothing practical. A waste of time. This usually happens because the problem gets defined in the same old way. So define the problem well first (see tip 5). Allot hours to this, not two minutes to sketch the problem. Challenge your thinking—are you generalizing from one or two cases? How do you know the causes are really causes? They may simply be related. What is fact and what is assumption?

☐ **8. Want the most from a group? Facilitate the process.** Here are three methods commonly used:

- Brainstorming. Outline the problem for the group, tell them what you've tried and learned from the tries. Include things that may have happened only once. Invite the group to free-form respond, any idea is OK, no criticism allowed. Record all ideas on a flip chart. When the group has exhausted the possibilities, take the most interesting ones and ask the group to first name positive features of the ideas, then negative features, and finally what's interesting about the ideas. Follow this process until you've covered all the ideas that interest you. Then ask the group what else they would select as interesting ideas to do a plus, minus, interesting analysis. This process can usually be done in an hour or two.
- The nominal group. After the problem definition above, have the group write down as many ideas as occur to them. Record them all on a flip chart for freewheeling discussion. People can add, combine or clarify—"What were you thinking when you said...," but no criticism allowed. After this, follow the plus, minus, interesting process above.
- Analogies. Lots of creative solutions come from analogies to nature or other fields. Come up with a list (electrical engineering, cats, trees, the sea, biology, shipbuilding), any list will do, and insert it after you describe the problem to the group in the first or second option. Many times this will trigger novel ideas that no other process will.

☐ **9. Ready to take a risk? Experiment and learn.** Whether the ideas come from you or a brainstorming session, encourage yourself to do quick experiments and trials. Studies show that 80% of innovations occur in the wrong place, are created by the wrong people (dye makers developed detergent, Post-it® Notes was a failed glue experiment, Teflon® was created by mistake) and 30-50% of technical innovations fail in tests within the company. Even among those that make it to the marketplace, 70-90% fail. The bottom line on change is a 95% failure rate, and the most successful innovators try lots of quick inexpensive experiments to increase the chances of success. Watch several episodes of *Modern Marvels*, a cable program on the History Channel which answers the question "How did they do that?" You can buy the series.

- ☐ **10. Ready to select a solution? Put your ideas to the test.** Creativity relies on freedom early, but structure later. Once you come up with your best notion of what to do, subject it to all the logical tests and criticism that any other alternative is treated to. Testing out creative ideas is no different than any other problem-solving/evaluation process. The difference is in how the ideas originate.

Some Develop-in-Place Assignments

- ☐ Manage a dissatisfied internal or external customer; troubleshoot a performance or quality problem with a product or service.
- ☐ Take on a tough and undoable project, one where others who have tried it have failed.
- ☐ Launch a new product, service, or process.
- ☐ Relaunch an existing product or service that's not doing well.
- ☐ Help someone outside your unit or the organization solve a business problem.

The creative person wants to be a know-it-all. He wants to know about all kinds of things: ancient history, nineteenth-century mathematics, current manufacturing techniques, flower arranging, and hog futures. Because he never knows when these ideas might come together to form a new idea. It may happen six minutes later or six months, or six years down the road. But he has faith that it will happen.

Carl Ally – American advertising executive and founder Ally & Gargano

Suggested Readings

Axelrod, A. (2008). *Edison on innovation: 102 Lessons in creativity for business and beyond.* San Francisco: Jossey-Bass.

Berns, G. (2008). *Iconoclast: A neuroscientist reveals how to think differently.* Boston: Harvard Business School Press.

Bilton, C. (2007). *Management and creativity: From creative industries to creative management.* Malden, MA: Blackwell Publishing.

Birch, P., & Clegg, B. (2000). *Imagination engineering: The toolkit for business creativity* (2nd ed.). London: Pitman Publishing.

Ceserani, J. (2003). *Big ideas: Putting the zest into creativity and innovation at work.* London: Kogan Page.

Clegg, B., & Birch, P. (2007). *Instant creativity: Simple techniques to ignite innovation and problem solving.* London: Kogan Page.

D'Cruz, P. (2008). *Thinking creatively at work: A sourcebook.* New Delhi: Response Books.

DeGraff, J., & Lawrence, K. A. (2002). *Creativity at work: Developing the right practices to make innovation happen.* San Francisco: Jossey-Bass.

Gallagher Hateley, B. J., & Schmidt, W. H. (2001). *A peacock in the land of penguins: A fable about creativity and courage.* San Francisco: Berrett-Koehler Publishers.

Gelb, M., & Caldicott, S. M. (2007). *Innovate like Edison: The success system of America's greatest inventor.* New York: Dutton.

Goldenberg, J., & Mazursky, D. (2002). *Creativity in product innovation.* New York: Cambridge University Press.

Hesselbein, F., & Johnston, R. (Eds.). (2002). *On creativity, innovation, and renewal: A leader to leader guide.* San Francisco: Jossey-Bass.

Levesque, L. C. (2001). *Breakthrough creativity: Achieving top performance using the eight creative talents.* Mountain View, CA: Davies-Black Publishing.

Lucas, R. W. (2003). *The creative training idea book: Inspired tips and techniques for engaging and effective learning.* New York: AMACOM.

Michalko, M. (2006). *Thinkertoys: A handbook of creative-thinking techniques* (2nd ed.). Berkeley, CA: Ten Speed Press.

Nemiro, J. (2004). *Creativity in virtual teams: Key components for success.* San Francisco: Pfeiffer.

Pink, D. H. (2006). *A whole new mind: Why right-brainers will rule the future.* New York: Berkley Publishing Group.

Razeghi, A. (2008). *The riddle: Where ideas come from and how to have better ones.* San Francisco: Jossey-Bass.

Rich, J. R. (2003). *Brain storm: Tap into your creativity to generate awesome ideas and remarkable results.* Franklin Lakes, NJ: Career Press.

Saint-Exupéry, A. (2003). *The little prince* (R. Howard, Trans.). New York: Harcourt Brace. (Original work published 1943.)

Sawyer, K. (2008). *Group genius: The creative power of collaboration.* New York: Basic Books.

Von Oech, R. (2002). *Expect the unexpected or you won't find it: A creativity tool based on the ancient wisdom of Heraclitus.* San Francisco: Berrett-Koehler Publishers.

White, S. P. (with Patton Wright, G.). (2002). *New ideas about new ideas: Insights on creativity with the world's leading innovators.* Cambridge, MA: Perseus Publishing.

15 Customer Focus

Right or wrong, the customer is always right.
Marshall Field – American businessman and founder of Marshall Field and Company

Unskilled

- ☐ Doesn't think of the customer first
- ☐ May think he/she already knows what they need
- ☐ May focus on internal operations and get blindsided by customer problems
- ☐ May not make the first move—won't meet and get to know customers
- ☐ Uncomfortable with new people contacts
- ☐ May be unwilling to handle criticisms, complaints, and special requests
- ☐ May not listen well to customers, may be defensive
- ☐ May not make the time for customer contact

Select one to three of the competencies listed below to use as a substitute for this competency if you decide not to work on it directly.

SUBSTITUTES: 1,3,9,16,24,27,31,32,33,36,38,43,48,51,53,63,64

Skilled

- ☐ Is dedicated to meeting the expectations and requirements of internal and external customers
- ☐ Gets first-hand customer information and uses it for improvements in products and services
- ☐ Acts with customers in mind
- ☐ Establishes and maintains effective relationships with customers and gains their trust and respect

Overused Skill

- ☐ May be overly responsive to customer demands
- ☐ May be too willing to change established processes and timetables to respond to unreasonable customer requests
- ☐ May make too many exceptions and not form consistent policies, practices, and processes for others to learn and follow
- ☐ Sticks so close to current customer needs that breakthroughs are missed

Select one to three of the competencies listed below to work on to compensate for an overuse of this skill.

COMPENSATORS: 5,9,12,34,35,38,50,51,52,53,57,58,59,63,65

Some Causes

- ☐ Arrogant; know it all; want to do it yourself
- ☐ Defensive in the face of criticism
- ☐ Loner
- ☐ Poor listening skills
- ☐ Poor time management; too busy
- ☐ Self-centered
- ☐ Shy; afraid of transacting with new people; lack self-confidence

Leadership Architect® Factors and Clusters

This competency is in the Personal and Interpersonal Skills Factor (VI). This competency is in the Managing Diverse Relationships Cluster (P) with: 4, 21, 23, 42, 64. You may want to check other competencies in the same Factor/Cluster for related tips.

The Map

In a free-enterprise system, the customer is king. Those who please the customer best win. The same is true with internal customers. Those who please them the most will win. Winners are always customer-oriented and responsive.

Some Remedies

- ☐ **1. Disconnected from customers? Keep in high-quality touch.** Pleasing the reasonable needs of customers is fairly straightforward. First you need to know what they want and expect. The best way to do that is to ask them. Then deliver that in a timely way at a price/value that's justified. Find ways to keep in touch with a broad spectrum of your customers to get a balanced view: face-to-face, phone surveys, questionnaires, response cards with the products and services you render, etc. When customers get in touch with you, remember that too much job specialization sometimes irritates customers. All of us have experienced the utter frustration of being transferred four times by different people, or more likely today, computer routing, only to get no answer or get to the wrong person. Think through the number of transfers very carefully. Get customers to the right person in the minimum number of steps.
- ☐ **2. Defensive? Be prepared for customers' complaints.** Be ready for the good news and the bad news; don't be defensive; just listen and respond to legitimate criticisms and note the rest. Vocal customers will usually complain more than compliment; you need to not get overwhelmed by the negative comments; people who have positive opinions speak up less.

☐ **3. Looking to delight the customer? Anticipate customer needs.** Get in the habit of meeting with your internal or external customers on a regular basis to set up a dialogue; they need to feel free to contact you about problems and you need to be able to contact them for essential information. Use this understanding to get out in front of your customers; try to anticipate their needs for your products and services before they even know about them; provide your customers with positive surprises; features they weren't expecting; delivery in a shorter time; more than they ordered. Show your customer you're in it for the long run. One successful salesman says all he focuses on is interest in his customer's business. Period. Everything else follows from this.

☐ **4. Not sure what customers want or expect? Put yourself in your customer's shoes.** If you were a customer of yours, what would you expect; what kind of turnaround time would you tolerate; what price would you be willing to pay for the quality of product or service you provide; what would be the top three things you would complain about? Answer all calls from customers in a timely way; if you promise a response, do it; if the time frame stretches, inform them immediately; after you have responded, ask them if the problem is fixed.

☐ **5. Need a customer service process? Think customer in.** Always design your work and manage your time from the customer in, not from you out. Your best will always be determined by your customers, not you; try not to design and arrange what you do only from your own view; try to always know and take the viewpoint of your customer first; you will always win following that rule. Can you sell an experience, not just a product or service? A small firm took on larger firms through its easy access to no-charge expert information. Customers could turn to internal sources for free consulting, taking from a few minutes up to an hour.

☐ **6. Stuck in a customer service rut? Create an environment for experimentation and learning.** One principle of these techniques is to drive for continuous improvement. Never be satisfied. Always drive to improve all work processes so they deliver zero-defect goods and services the customers want. Don't be afraid to try and fail. *More help? – See #28 Innovation Management and #63 Total Work Systems (e.g., TQM/ISO/Six Sigma).*

☐ **7. Personal work style out of step with the customer? Look at your own personal work habits.** Are they designed for maximum effectiveness and efficiency for your customer or are they designed for your comfort? Is there room for some continuous improvement? Are you applying the principles you have learned to yourself? Remember, this is one of the major reasons why these efforts fail.

☐ **8. Want to know why customers leave? Think of yourself as a dissatisfied customer.** Write down all of the unsatisfactory things that have happened to you as a customer during the past month. Things like delays, orders not right, cost not as promised, phone calls not returned, cold food, bad service, inattentive clerks, out-of-stock items, etc. Are any of these things happening to your customers? Then do a study of your lost customers. Find out what the three key problems were and see how quickly you can eliminate 50% of the difficulties that caused them to depart. Study your competitor's foul-ups and see what you can do to both eliminate those and make your organization more attractive.

☐ **9. Want to know why customers stay? Think of yourself as a satisfied customer.** Write down all of the satisfactory things that have happened to you as a customer during the past month. What pleased you the most as a customer? Good value? On-time service? Courtesy? Returned phone calls? Are any of your customers experiencing any of these satisfactory transactions with you and your business? Study your successful customer transactions so they can be institutionalized. Then study what your competitors do well and see what you can also do to improve customer service.

☐ **10. Looking for opportunities to see customer service in action? Play detective.** Be a student of the work flows and processes around you at airports, restaurants, hotels, supermarkets, government services, etc. As a customer, how would you design those things differently to make them more effective and efficient? What principles did you follow? Apply those same principles to your own work.

☐ **11. Disconnect between employee and customer satisfaction? Construct a service-profit chain.** It's become fairly well known that employee satisfaction is linked to customer loyalty, satisfaction, and profits. A good example of this is how a fast food chain transformed itself. By asking customers, it found out they didn't care who made the food, or whether the décor was spiffy. All they wanted was hot, tasty and inexpensive. So the chain got rid of its restaurant kitchens, outsourcing or cooking at a central location, and drove down its costs. On the employee side, it set up a crew system without a manager. Working in teams proved to be more challenging and more motivating. They learned they could get better results for their customers. Happier employees—happier customers. More help? Read *Command Performance* (1994) by *The Harvard Business Review.*

☐ **12. Not focusing on the right customers? Nurture your most profitable customers.** Some customers may be unprofitable because of excess service requirements. You can require them to order in larger quantities, forego certain services or charge for them. Use activity-based accounting.

This method links purchasing data with cost data. It costs between 5 and 20 times as much to get a new customer than to keep an existing one. Old customers cost less over time and bring more revenue. How can you go from being a 20% supplier to a 50% one?

Some Develop-in-Place Assignments

- ☐ Manage a dissatisfied internal or external customer; troubleshoot a performance or quality problem with a product or service.
- ☐ Train customers in the use of the organization's products or services.
- ☐ Work a few shifts in the telemarketing or customer service department, handling complaints and inquiries from customers.
- ☐ Visit Malcolm Baldrige National Quality Award recipients or Deming Prize winners, and report how your findings would help your organization.
- ☐ Do a customer-satisfaction survey in person or by phone, and present the results to the people involved.

Touch your customer, and you're halfway there.
Estee Lauder – American entrepreneur
and cofounder, Estee Lauder Companies

Suggested Readings

Barlow, J., & Moller, C. (2008). *A complaint is a gift: Recovering customer loyalty when things go wrong* (2nd ed.). San Francisco: Berrett-Koehler Publishers.

Bell, C. R., & Bell, B. R. (2003). *Magnetic service.* San Francisco: Berrett-Koehler Publishers.

Berenbaum, D., & Larkin, T. (2007). *How to talk to customers: Create a great impression every time with MAGIC.* San Francisco: John Wiley & Sons.

Blacharski, D. W. (2006). *Superior customer service: How to keep customers racing back to your business: Time-tested examples from leading companies.* Ocala, FL: Atlantic Publishing Group.

Brock, R. (2003). *Inside the minds: Profitable customer relationships: The keys to maximizing acquisition, retention, and loyalty.* Boston: Aspatore Books.

Charan, R. (2007). *What the customer wants you to know: How everybody needs to think differently about sales.* New York: Penguin Group.

Evenson, R. (2007). *Award-winning customer service: 101 Ways to guarantee great performance.* New York: AMACOM.

Griffin, J., & Lowenstein, M. W. (2001). *Customer winback.* San Francisco: Jossey-Bass.

Gulati, R., & Oldroyd, J. B. (2005). The quest for customer focus. *Harvard Business Review, 83*(4), 92-101.

Keller, E., & Berry, J. (2003). *The influentials.* New York: Free Press.

Morgan, R. (2003). *Calming upset customers: Staying effective during unpleasant situations* (3rd ed.). Mississauga, ON: Crisp Publications, Inc.

Prahalad, C. K., & Ramaswamy, V. (2004). *The future of competition: Co-creating unique value with customers.* Boston: Harvard Business School Press.

Sobel, A. (2003). *Making rain: The secrets of building lifelong client loyalty.* Hoboken, NJ: John Wiley & Sons.

Solomon, M. R. (2003). *Conquering consumerspace.* New York: AMACOM.

Solomon, R. (2003). *The art of client service.* Chicago: Dearborn Financial Publishing.

Tate, R., & Stroup, J. (2003). *The service pro: Creating better, faster, and different customer experiences.* Amherst, MA: HRD Press.

Ulrich, D., & Smallwood, N. (2007). *Leadership brand: Developing customer-focused leaders to drive performance and build lasting value.* Boston: Harvard Business School Press.

Weber, L. (2007) *Marketing to the social web: How digital customer communities build your business.* San Francisco: John Wiley and Sons.

Zaltman, G. (2003). *How customers think.* Boston: Harvard Business School Press.

Zemke, R., & Bell, C. R. (2003). *Service magic: The art of amazing your customers.* Chicago: Dearborn Financial Publishing.

16 *Timely* Decision Making

The most difficult thing is the decision to act, the rest is merely tenacity.
The fears are paper tigers. You can do anything you decide to do.
You can act to change and control your life;
and the procedure, the process is its own reward.
Amelia Earhart – American aviation pioneer and author

Unskilled

- ☐ Slow to decide or to declare
- ☐ Conservative and cautious
- ☐ May procrastinate, seek more information to build confidence and avoid risk
- ☐ May be a perfectionist, needing to be right, protect strongly against criticism
- ☐ May be disorganized and always scrambling to meet decision deadlines
- ☐ May be slow to make decisions on more complex issues

Select one to three of the competencies listed below to use as a substitute for this competency if you decide not to work on it directly.

SUBSTITUTES: 1,2,12,27,32,37,39,40,43,47,50,51,52,53,62

Skilled

- ☐ Makes decisions in a timely manner, sometimes with incomplete information and under tight deadlines and pressure
- ☐ Able to make a quick decision

Overused Skill

- ☐ May jump to conclusions and take action before reasonable consideration of the information
- ☐ May get caught up in deciding for its own sake
- ☐ May have a chilling effect on getting everyone's input before deciding
- ☐ Might be considered impulsive and impatient
- ☐ Might have some trouble and freeze on issues and problems that are close calls
- ☐ May make decisions quickly to avoid debate and personal discomfort

Select one to three of the competencies listed below to work on to compensate for an overuse of this skill.

COMPENSATORS: 3,11,17,33,39,41,46,47,51,52,58,59,63,65

Some Causes

- ☐ Avoid conflict
- ☐ Avoid risk
- ☐ Disorganized
- ☐ Easily intimidated
- ☐ Need too much information
- ☐ Not focused
- ☐ Perfectionist
- ☐ Procrastinate
- ☐ Slow to make decisions
- ☐ Too busy
- ☐ Trouble meeting deadlines

Leadership Architect® Factors and Clusters

This competency is in the Operating Skills Factor (II). This competency is in the Keeping on Point Cluster (D) with: 50. You may want to check other competencies in the same Factor/Cluster for related tips.

The Map

Slow to act? Miss decision deadlines often? Have to scramble to get done? Still weighing the objections? Don't like to pull the trigger? Unless you're lucky and work in a very stable niche, this behavior will get you left behind. You won't respond quickly enough to change; you won't learn new things; people will be increasingly frustrated as you hold them up. The rewards are to the swift. David Ulrich, a top strategic business consultant, says that in the past there was a premium on being right. That is shifting to being first. In the past, organizations brought out no product until it was time; they worked to make sure it was right and it had a market. Now organizations put out products as fast as possible and fix them later after they get customer reaction. You may associate timely decisions with sloppy decisions, but this is not the case. Timely means sooner, as soon as possible or by a time-certain date but not sloppy. Timely, thoughtful decisions can be of high quality. It's quality incrementalism.

Some Remedies

☐ **1. Perfectionist? Learn to tolerate incomplete data.** Need or prefer or want to be 100% sure? Want to make sure that all or at least most of your decisions are right? A lot of people prefer that. Perfectionism is tough to let go of because most people see it as a positive trait for them. They pride themselves on never being wrong. Recognize perfectionism for what it might be—collecting more information than others do to improve confidence in making a fault-free decision and thereby avoiding the risk and criticism that would come from making decisions faster. Anyone with a brain, unlimited time and 100% of the data can make good decisions. The real test is who can act the soonest, being right the most, with less than all the data. Some studies suggest even successful general managers are about 65% correct. If you need to be more timely, you need to reduce your own internal need for data and the need to be perfect. Try to decrease your need for data and your need to be right all the time slightly every week until you reach a more reasonable balance between thinking it through and taking action. Try making some small decisions on little or no data. Trust your intuition more. Your experience won't let you stray too far. Let your brain do the calculations.

☐ **2. Procrastinator? Start early.** Are you a procrastinator? Get caught short on deadlines? Do it all at the last minute? Not only will you not be timely, your decision quality and accuracy will be poor. Procrastinators miss deadlines and performance targets. If you procrastinate, you might not produce consistent decisions. Start earlier. Always do 10% of thinking about the decision immediately after it is assigned so you can better gauge what it is going to take to finish the rest. Divide decisions into thirds or fourths and schedule time to work on them spaced over the delivery period. Remember one of Murphy's Laws: It takes 90% of the time to do 90% of the project, and another 90% of the time to finish the remaining 10%. Always leave more time than you think it's going to take. Set up checkpoints for yourself along the way. Schedule early data collection and analysis. Don't wait until the last moment. Set an internal deadline one week before the real one. *More help? – See #47 Planning.*

☐ **3. Disorganized? Organize with discipline.** Don't always get to everything on time? Forget deadlines? Lose requests for decisions? Under time pressure and increased uncertainty, you have to put the keel in the water yourself. You can't operate helter-skelter and make quality timely decisions. You need to set tighter priorities. Focus more on the mission-critical few decisions. Don't get diverted by trivial work and other decisions. Get better organized and disciplined. Keep a decision log. When a decision opportunity surfaces, immediately log it along with the ideal date it needs to be made. Plan backwards to the work necessary to make the decision on time. If you are not disciplined in how you work and are sometimes late making decisions and taking action because of it, buy books on TQM, ISO and Six Sigma. Go to one workshop on efficient and effective work design. *More help? – See #50 Priority Setting, #52 Process Management, #62 Time Management and #63 Total Work Systems (e.g., TQM/ISO/Six Sigma).*

☐ **4. Too cautious and conservative? Learn from mistakes.** Analysis paralysis? Break out of your examine-it-to-death and always-take-the-safest-path mode and just do it. Increasing timeliness will increase errors and mistakes but it also will get more done faster. Develop a more philosophical stance toward failure/criticism. After all, most innovations fail, most proposals fail, most change efforts fail, anything worth doing takes repeated effort. The best tack when confronted with a mistake is to say, "What can we learn from this?" Ask yourself if your need to be cautious matches the requirements for speed and timeliness of your job. *More help? – See #45 Personal Learning.*

☐ **5. Inconsistent timeliness? Choose when to be timely.** It's very common for people to be timely in some areas (budget decisions) and untimely in others (give an employee negative feedback). Sometimes we avoid certain areas. Create two columns. Left side are the areas where you seem to make timely and speedy decisions. What's common about those areas? Right side are the areas where you hold back, hesitate and wait too long to decide. What's common to that list? Money involved? People? Risk? Higher management's involved? Are you avoiding detail or strategy or a technical area you dislike or know little about? Since you already make timely decisions in at least one area, transfer your decision behaviors and practices to the other areas. You already have the skills. You just need to get over the barriers (most likely attitude barriers) in the more difficult areas. If you lack expertise, access your network. Go to the two wisest people you know on the decision, hire a consultant, convene a one-time problem-solving group. You don't have to be an expert in the area, but you do need to know how to access expertise to make timely decisions.

☐ **6. People issues getting in the way? Prepare for difficult conversations.** Sometimes we are timely with some people and not with others. Many times it relates to how they react to you. There are easy to approach people and difficult to deal with people. There are supportive people and punishing people. You may naturally adjust your decision-making style to match the decision customer. Sometimes we avoid hard to deal with people, leaving them to the last minute because we want to be right and not get punished or demeaned. Mentally rehearse for worst-case scenarios/hard-to-deal-with people. Anticipate what the person might say and have responses prepared so as not to be caught off guard. Focus on two or three key points in conflict situations and stick to those clearly and politely. Try not to bring up everything you can think of, but instead focus on essence. Try trial balloons with difficult people. Sometime before a decision is due, float up a small trial balloon on a direction you are thinking of. You'll take a little heat and maybe a little punishment, but you'll also get information to create a better decision later. *More help? – See #12 Conflict Management.*

☐ **7. Overwhelmed? Slice big decisions into bite-size chunks.** Think of a big decision as a series of smaller ones. The essence of timely decision making is the tolerance of increased errors and mistakes and absorbing the possible heat and criticism that follow. Acting on an ill-defined problem with no precedents to follow in a hurry means shooting in the dark with as informed a decision as you can make at the time. Incrementalists make a series of smaller decisions, get instant feedback, correct the course, get a little more data, move forward a little more, until the bigger decision gets made. They don't try to get it right the first time. They try their best educated guess now, and then correct as feedback comes in. Many problem-solving studies show that the second or third try is when we really understand the underlying dynamics of problems. So you need to work on two practices. Start smaller so you can recover more quickly. Do something as soon as you can and get used to heat.

☐ **8. Stressed? Manage stress and conflict under time pressure.** Some are energized by time pressure. Some are stressed with time pressure. It actually slows us down. We lose our anchor. We are not at our best when we are pushed. We get more anxious, frustrated, upset. What brings out your emotional response? Write down why you get anxious under time pressure. What fears does it surface? Don't want to make a mistake? Afraid of the unknown consequences? Don't have the confidence to decide? When you get stressed, drop the problem for a moment. Go do something else. Come back to it when you are under better control. Let your brain work on it while you do something safer. *More help? – See #11 Composure and #107 Lack of Composure.*

☐ **9. Holding back information? Inform people in a timely manner.** Another common pattern is for a person to have no problem making timely decisions inside one's head; the problem is holding back announcing the decisions until they become untimely. In this case, there is nothing wrong with your decision-making program; it's usually your courage and confidence programs. How soon did you come to the decision you are now finally making public? Two weeks ago? Why did you hold it back? Afraid of the reaction? Getting yourself emotionally prepared for the heat? Trying to find the safest time to declare? People like this don't usually change their minds once the decision is made; they just change their minds about when to tell people what they have decided. To check this out, write down the decisions you would make right now, then compare them with the decisions you actually make and announce later. Are the decisions more the same than different? If they are more the same, you may have this problem. Since the noise and the heat are the same, the simple solution is to declare as soon as you have made the decision. Better to be done with it. If there is any useful data in the noise and heat, you can adjust your decision sooner.

☐ **10. Hesitate in the face of resistance? Alleviate your hesitation by analyzing pros and cons.** Conflict slows you down? Shakes your confidence in your decision? Do you backpedal? Give in too soon? Try to make everyone happy? Do your homework first. Scope the problem, consider options, pick one, develop a rationale, then go to others. Be prepared to defend your selection; know what they will ask, what they will object to, how this decision will affect them. Listen carefully, invite criticism of your idea and revise accordingly in the face of real data. Otherwise, hold your ground. Are you a chronic worrier? What could happen? What might go wrong? Does it seem like an obsession? Try these two techniques. Write down everything you are worried about. It's usually hard to fill up a page. Divide your worries into whatever categories they fall under. Now write down a pro to each con (a worry). Worries are legitimate, but not if you don't consider the other side. All decision options have pros and cons.

Some Develop-in-Place Assignments

- ☐ Manage a group through a significant business crisis.
- ☐ Work on a crisis-management team.
- ☐ Manage liquidation/sale of a business, products, equipment, materials, furniture, overstock, etc.
- ☐ Launch a new product, service, or process.
- ☐ Become a referee for an athletic league or program.

Be willing to make decisions.
That's the most important quality in a good leader.
Don't fall victim to what I call the ready-aim-aim-aim-aim syndrome.
You must be willing to fire.
T. Boone Pickens – American businessman
Chair of the BP Capital Management Hedge Fund

Suggested Readings

Bruce, A., & Langdon, K. (2001). *Essential managers: Do it now!* London: DK Publishing.

Carrison, D. (2003). *Deadline! How premier organizations win the race against time.* New York: AMACOM.

Gladwell, M. (2005). *Blink: The power of thinking without thinking.* New York: Little, Brown and Company.

Harvard Business Essentials. (2006). *Decision making: 5 Steps to better results.* Boston: Harvard Business School Press.

Jennings, J., & Haughton, L. (2001). *It's not the big that eat the small...It's the fast that eat the slow.* New York: HarperCollins.

Kopeikina, L. (2005). Stop the indecision: How to eliminate bad habits that cloud your thinking. *Business West, 22.*

Malek, W. A., Morgan, M., & Levitt, R. E. (2008). *Executing your strategy: How to break it down and get it done.* Boston: Harvard Business School Press.

Martin, C. (2005). *Tough management: The 7 winning ways to make tough decisions easier, deliver the numbers, and grow the business in good times and bad.* New York: McGraw-Hill.

McGee, K. (2004). *Heads up: How to anticipate business surprises and seize opportunities first.* Boston: Harvard Business School Press.

Rogers, P., & Blenko, M. (2006). Who has the D? How clear decision roles enhance organizational performance. *Harvard Business Review, 84,* 52-61.

Russo, J. E., & Schoemaker, P. J. H. (with Hittleman, M.). (2002). *Winning decisions: Getting it right the first time.* New York: Currency.

Shaw, P. (2008). *Making difficult decisions: How to be decisive and get the business done.* Chichester, UK: Capstone Publishing Ltd.

Tichy, N. M., & Bennis, W. G. (2007). *Judgment: How winning leaders make great calls.* New York: Penguin Group.

Useem, M. (2006). *The go point: When it's time to decide—knowing what to do and when to do it.* New York: Crown Business.

Wall, S. J. (2004). *On the fly: Executing strategy in a changing world.* New York: John Wiley & Sons.

17 Decision Quality

No sensible decision can be made any longer without taking into account not only the world as it is, but the world as it will be....
Isaac Asimov – Russian-born American-Jewish author and biochemist

Unskilled

- ☐ Goes first with quick solutions, conclusions and statements before analysis
- ☐ May rely too much on self—doesn't ask for help
- ☐ Making decisions may trigger emotions and impatience
- ☐ May not use orderly decision methods, models or ways to think
- ☐ May jump to conclusions based on prejudices, historical solutions or narrow perspective
- ☐ Doesn't take the time to define the problem before deciding
- ☐ May have trouble with complexity
- ☐ May wait too long, agonize over every detail to avoid risk or error
- ☐ May go for the big elegant decision when five little ones would be better

Select one to three of the competencies listed below to use as a substitute for this competency if you decide not to work on it directly.

SUBSTITUTES: 5,12,24,30,32,46,47,50,51,53,58

Skilled

- ☐ Makes good decisions (without considering how much time it takes) based upon a mixture of analysis, wisdom, experience, and judgment
- ☐ Most of his/her solutions and suggestions turn out to be correct and accurate when judged over time
- ☐ Sought out by others for advice and solutions

Overused Skill

- ☐ May see him/herself as overly wise or close to perfect, as someone who can't or doesn't make mistakes
- ☐ May be seen as stubborn and not willing to negotiate or compromise
- ☐ May get frustrated when advice is rejected
- ☐ May not relate well to less data-based people

Select one to three of the competencies listed below to work on to compensate for an overuse of this skill.

COMPENSATORS: 2,5,12,16,30,32,33,37,45,51,52,58,61,63

Some Causes

- ☐ Arrogant
- ☐ Excessive emotionality; avoiding risk and exposure
- ☐ Faulty thinking
- ☐ Impatient; don't wait for the data
- ☐ Narrow perspective
- ☐ Perfectionist; wait too long for all of the data
- ☐ Prejudiced; preconceived solutions; rigid
- ☐ Want to do it all yourself; won't ask for help

Leadership Architect® Factors and Clusters

This competency is in the Strategic Skills Factor (I). This competency is in the Making Complex Decisions Cluster (B) with: 30, 32, 51. You may want to check other competencies in the same Factor/Cluster for related tips.

The Map

Life and work are just a series of big and small decisions followed by action in line with the decisions. Good decisions are based upon a mixture of data, analysis, intuition, wisdom, experience, and judgment. Making good decisions involves being patient enough to collect the available information, being humble enough to ask for other people's opinions and thoughts and then coldly making the decision. No one is ever right all the time; it's the percent correct over time that matters.

Some Remedies

☐ **1. Attitudes in play? Know your biases.** Be clear and honest with yourself about your attitudes, beliefs, biases, opinions and prejudices and your favorite solutions. We all have them. The key is not to let them affect your objective and cold decision making. Before making any sizable decision, ask yourself, are any of my biases affecting this decision? Do you play favorites, deciding quickly in one area, but holding off in another? Do you avoid certain topics, people, groups, functional areas because you're not comfortable or don't know? Do you drag out your favorite solutions often? Too often?

☐ **2. Making hasty assumptions? Check for common errors in thinking.** Do you state as facts things that are really opinions or assumptions? Are you sure these assertions are facts? State opinions and assumptions as that and don't present them as facts. Do you attribute cause and effect to relationships when you don't know if one causes the other? If sales are down, and we increase advertising and sales go up, this doesn't prove causality. They are simply related. Say we know that the relationship between sales/advertising is about the same as sales/number of employees. If sales go down, we probably wouldn't hire more people, so make sure one thing causes the other before acting on it. Do you generalize from a single example without knowing if that single example does generalize?

☐ **3. Do you do enough analysis? Thoroughly define the problem.** Figure out what causes it. Keep asking why. See how many causes you can come up with and how many organizing buckets you can put them in. This increases the chance of a better solution because you can see more connections. Look for patterns in data, don't just collect information. Put it in categories that make sense to you. A good rule of thumb is to analyze patterns and causes to come up with alternatives. Many of us just collect data, which numerous studies show increases our confidence but doesn't increase decision accuracy. Think out loud with others; see how they view the problem. Studies show that defining the problem and taking action usually occur simultaneously, so to break out of analysis paralysis, figure out what the problem is first. Then when a good alternative appears you're likely to recognize it immediately.

☐ **4. What's your track record? Consider your history.** Do an objective analysis of decisions you have made in the past and what the percentage correct was. Break the decisions into topics or areas of your life. For most of us, we make better decisions in some areas than others. Maybe your decision-making skills need help in one or two limited areas, like decisions about people, decisions about your career, political decisions, technical, etc.

☐ **5. Eager to act? Hold your horses.** Life is a balance between waiting and doing. Many in management put a premium on doing over waiting. Most could make close to 100% good decisions given all of the data and unlimited time. Life affords us neither the data nor the time. You may need to try to discipline yourself to wait just a little longer than you usually do for more, but not all, the data to come in. Push yourself to always get one more piece of data than you did before until your correct decision percent becomes more acceptable. Instead of just doing it, ask what questions would need to be answered before we'd know which way to go. In one study of problem solving, answers outnumbered questions 8 to 1. We jump to solutions based on what has worked in the past. So collect data to answer these questions, then shoot. *More help? – See #51 Problem Solving.*

☐ **6. Hesitant? Find one more alternative solution.** Play out the consequences in your head to see how the decision would play in real life. Test out a number of decisions. Some research says that the best decision isn't always the first or even the second solution you think of. The highest-quality decisions are somewhere between the second and third decision you come to. You may be hesitating because your little voice in your head is telling you something isn't right.

- ☐ **7. Can't decide? Sleep on it.** The brain works on things even when you are not thinking about them. Take some time, do something completely different, and get back to the decision later. Let a night's sleep go by and return to it in the morning.
- ☐ **8. Need input? Use others to help.** Delegate the decision. Sometime others above, aside, or below you may be in a better position to make the decision. Create a group or task force, present the decision and all you know about it, and let the group decide. Or set up competing groups or find a buddy group in another function or organization which faces a similar problem or consult history—surely this has happened before. Up your odds through others.
- ☐ **9. Have a guru in mind? Study decision makers.** Whom do you admire? Bill Gates? Winston Churchill? Read the biographies and autobiographies of a few people you respect, and pay attention to how they made decisions in their life and careers. Write down five things they did that you can do. For example, Churchill always slept on important decisions no matter what. He initially only asked questions and tried to understand the problem and argument as given. He kept his views to himself until later.
- ☐ **10. Know someone effective at making decisions? Go to a model decision maker.** Find someone around you who makes decisions in a way you think you ought to and ask how he/she does it. Go through several decision processes. Try to figure out with the person what questions he/she asks, and what principles are being followed. See how much he/she relies on advice, consults history for parallels, checks in with various constituencies and how she/he gets familiar with unfamiliar areas.

Some Develop-in-Place Assignments

- ☐ Manage a group through a significant business crisis.
- ☐ Prepare and present a proposal of some consequence to top management.
- ☐ Work on a team forming a joint venture or partnership.
- ☐ Hire/staff a team from outside your unit or organization.
- ☐ Manage the purchase of a major product, equipment, materials, program, or system.

When you approach a problem, strip yourself of preconceived opinions and prejudice, assemble and learn the facts of the situation, make the decision which seems to you to be the most honest, and then stick to it.
Chester Bowles – American diplomat and politician

Suggested Readings

Bazerman, H. (2002). *Judgment in managerial decision making*. New York: John Wiley & Sons.

Brousseau, K. R., Driver, M. J., Hourihan, G., & Larsson, R. (2006). The seasoned executive's decision-making style. *Harvard Business Review, 84,* 109-121.

Buchanan, L., & O'Connell, A. (2006). A brief history of decision making. *Harvard Business Review, 84*, 32-41.

Driver, M. J., Hunsaker, P., & Brousseau, K. R. (1998). *The dynamic decision maker*. New York: Harper & Row.

Drucker, P. F., Hammond, J., Keeney, R., Raiffa, H., & Hayashi, A.M. (2001). *Harvard Business Review on decision making*. Boston: Harvard Business School Press.

Gunther, R. E., Hoch, S. J., & Kunreuther, H. C. (2001). *Wharton on making decisions*. Hoboken, NJ: John Wiley & Sons.

Guy, A. K. (2004). *Balanced scorecard diagnostics: Maximizing performance through the dynamic decision framework*. New York: John Wiley & Sons.

Hammond, J. S., III., Keeney, R. L., & Raiffa, H. (2006). *The hidden traps in decision making*. Boston: Harvard Business School Press.

Harvard Business Essentials. (2006). *Decision making: 5 Steps to better results*. Boston: Harvard Business School Press.

Harvard Business School Press. (2007). *Harvard Business Review on making smarter decisions*. Boston: Harvard Business School Press.

Henderson, D. R., & Hooper, C. L. (2006). *Making great decisions in business and life*. Chicago Park, CA: Chicago Park Press.

Kaner, S., Lind, L., Toldi, C., & Fisk, S. (2007). *Facilitator's guide to participatory decision-making*. San Francisco: Jossey-Bass.

Klein, G. (2001). *The power of intuition: How to use your gut feelings to make better decisions at work*. New York: Currency.

Patton, B. R., & Downs, T. M. (2002). *Decision-making group interaction: Achieving quality*. Boston: Allyn & Bacon.

Rosenberger, L. E., & Nash, J. (with Graham, A.). (2009). *The deciding factor: The power of analytics to make every decision a winner*. San Francisco: Jossey-Bass.

Roth, B. M., & Mullen, J. D. (2002). *Decision making: Its logic and practice*. Lanham, MD: Rowman & Littlefield.

Snowden, D. J., & Boone, M. E. (2007). A leader's framework for decision making. *Harvard Business Review, 85*, 68-76.

Tichy, N. M., & Bennis, W. G. (2007). *Judgment: How winning leaders make great calls*. New York: Penguin Group.

Tichy, N. M., & Bennis, W. G. (2007). Making judgment calls. *Harvard Business Review, 85*, 94-102.

Yates, J. F. (2003). *Decision management: How to assure better decisions in your company*. San Francisco: Jossey-Bass.

18 Delegation

No man will make a great leader who wants to do it all himself or get all the credit for doing it.
Andrew Carnegie – Scottish-born industrialist, businessman, and philanthropist

Unskilled

- ☐ Doesn't believe in or trust delegation
- ☐ Lacks trust and respect in the talent of direct reports and others
- ☐ Does most things by him/herself or hoards, keeps the good stuff for him/herself
- ☐ Doesn't want or know how to empower others
- ☐ May delegate but micromanages and looks over shoulders
- ☐ Might delegate but not pass on the authority
- ☐ May lack a plan of how to work through others
- ☐ May just throw tasks at people; doesn't communicate the bigger picture

Select one to three of the competencies listed below to use as a substitute for this competency if you decide not to work on it directly.

SUBSTITUTES: 7,19,20,21,23,27,33,35,36,39,47,56,60,64

Skilled

- ☐ Clearly and comfortably delegates both routine and important tasks and decisions
- ☐ Broadly shares both responsibility and accountability
- ☐ Tends to trust people to perform
- ☐ Lets direct reports and others finish their own work

Overused Skill

- ☐ May overdelegate without providing enough direction or help
- ☐ May have unrealistic expectations for direct reports and others, or may overstructure tasks and decisions before delegating them to the point of limiting individual initiative
- ☐ May not do enough of the work him/herself

Select one to three of the competencies listed below to work on to compensate for an overuse of this skill.

COMPENSATORS: 7,19,20,21,23,33,35,36,57,60,63,64

Some Causes

- ☐ Delegate but don't follow up
- ☐ Delegate by throwing tasks at people
- ☐ Delegate little pieces
- ☐ Don't develop your people
- ☐ Hoard most things to self
- ☐ Not plan work
- ☐ Not trust others
- ☐ Overmanage people
- ☐ Too busy
- ☐ Too controlling

Leadership Architect® Factors and Clusters

This competency is in the Operating Skills Factor (II). This competency is in the Getting Work Done Through Others Cluster (F) with: 19, 20, 27, 35. You may want to check other competencies in the same Factor/Cluster for related tips.

The Map

Do you hoard tasks, keeping the good ones to yourself? Do you throw tasks at people without any overall plan or follow-up? Do you micromanage because you don't trust people will perform? Unless you can do the work of the unit all by yourself, both performance and morale will suffer until you learn to delegate.

Some Remedies

☐ **1. Need convincing? Learn the benefits of delegating.** How busy are you? Can't get everything done you would like to get to? Boss on your butt for more? No time for reflection? No time to get to long-range planning and strategy? Longer hours? Saturdays? Work at home? Family wondering if you still live there? Postpone vacations? If this sounds familiar, you join the majority of managers. Time is the most precious commodity. There is never enough. One of the main causes of this is that managers do too much themselves. The major fixes are better personal time management and organization, setting better priorities, designing better work flows and delegation. Delegation frees up time. Delegation motivates. Delegation develops people. Delegation gets more done. Learning to delegate is a major transition skill first-line supervisors are supposed to learn when they leave the personal contributor role early in their careers. Read *Becoming a Manager* by Linda A. Hill for how that's supposed to work. We say "supposed to" because there are many high level executives who still have not learned to delegate. They generally get to everything tactical and let everything strategic go until last. They also don't have the time to develop others, leading to their reluctance to delegate because their people aren't good enough! No wonder. You cannot fulfill your potential until you learn to delegate more and better.

☐ **2. How to delegate? Set expectations.** Communicate, set time frames and goals, and get out of the way. People need to know what it is you expect. What does the outcome look like? When do you need it by? What's the budget? What resources do they get? What decisions can they make? Do you want checkpoints along the way? How will we both know and measure how well the task is done? One of the most common problems with delegation is incomplete or cryptic up-front communication leading to frustration, a job not well done the first time, rework, and a reluctance to delegate next time. Poor communicators always have to take more time managing because of rework. Analyze recent projects that went well and didn't go well. How did you delegate? Too much? Not enough? Unwanted pieces? Major chunks of responsibility? Workload distributed properly? Did you set measures? Overmanage or abdicate? Find out what your best practices are. Set up a series of delegation practices that can be used as if you're not there. What do you have to be informed of? What feedback loops can people use for mid-course correction? What questions should be answered as the work proceeds? What steps should be followed? What are the criteria to be followed? When will you be available to help? *More help? – See #27 Informing and #35 Managing and Measuring Work.*

☐ **3. Providing the right amount of detail? Communicate the what and the why, leave the how up to them.** The best delegators are crystal clear on what and when, and more open on how. People are more motivated when they can determine the how for themselves. Inexperienced delegators include the hows which turns the people into task automatons instead of an empowered and energized staff. Tell them what and when and for how long and let them figure out how on their own. Give them leeway. Encourage them to try things. Besides being more motivating, it's also more developmental for them. Add the larger context. Although it is not necessary to get the task done, people are more motivated when they know where this task fits in the bigger picture. Take three extra minutes and tell them why this task needs to be done, where it fits in the grander scheme and its importance to the goals and objectives of the unit.

☐ **4. What to delegate? Figure out the best things to delegate.** Delegate as much as you can along with the authority to do it. Delegate more whole tasks than pieces and parts. People are more motivated by complete tasks. Delegate those things that others can do. Delegate those things that are not things you do well. Delegate tactical; keep strategic. Delegate short term; keep long term. One simple and effective way is to ask your people: "What do I do that you could help me with? What do I do that you could do with a little help from me? What do I do that you could do by yourself? What do you do that I could do faster and more effectively (re-delegation)?" You certainly won't agree to everything, but if you are now a poor delegator, they will help you improve by 50%. Pick one or a few things each time and let go.

☐ **5. Delegate to whom? Delegate to people who can be successful.** To those who can do it and those who can almost do it! The most common Catch-22 we hear from managers is that they can't delegate because their people are not good enough; they can't do the work. We ask, why is that? They say, because they inherited a weak staff from the previous manager. We say, why don't you get rid of the worst and get better people? They say they can't fire anyone because HR and Legal won't let them. (We ask HR and Legal if that's the case. They generally say no, as long as it's done properly.) Or they say they can't afford to have a position open at this time because there is so much to do. We say, but if they are truly poor performers, what's the difference? You can't and shouldn't delegate to poor performers unless it's for their development and motivation. On the other hand, you'll never get out of your bind until you bite the bullet and start releasing the poorest and replacing them with better. Read Covey's (*The Seven Habits of Highly Effective People*) point on sharpening your saw. A person comes upon a lumberjack sawing a large tree with a handsaw. He is sweating and breathing hard. It's going very, very slowly. The person asks why it's going so poorly. The lumberjack says because his saw isn't sharp. The person asks why he doesn't stop and sharpen the saw. The lumberjack says because there is no time. If your saws (direct reports) aren't sharp enough, switch to more of a teacher role. What are the first things you would tell them to help think about their work more productively, and to think about tasks as you think about them? Always explain your thinking. The role of a coach/teacher is to teach someone how to think/act as you do. Giving them solutions will make the person dependent at best. You may have to bubble your thinking to the surface first. To do this, work out loud with them on a task. What do you see as important? How do you know? What mental questions are you asking? What steps are you following? Why is this solution better than others? *More help? – See #13 Confronting Direct Reports and #25 Hiring and Staffing.*

☐ **6. Delegate for how long? Give a realistic time frame.** Allow more time than it would take you. Another common problem is that managers delegate and set time limits based upon their own capabilities and history. For many things, it is probably true that the manager could do the task faster and better. Remember when you started to learn how to do this task. How long did it take you? How did you feel about someone looking over your shoulder? Always allow more time in the schedule than it would take you to do it. Get the person to whom you are delegating to help you set a realistic time schedule. When you are going to delegate, start earlier in the project than you do now. *More help? – See #47 Planning.*

☐ **7. How much to delegate? Make the task fit the performer.** All of your people have differing skills and capacities. Good delegators match the size and complexity of the delegated task with the capacity of each person. Delegation is not an equal, one size fits all, activity. Equal opportunity delegators are not as successful as equitable delegators. Most people prefer stretching tasks to those they could do in their sleep; so it's OK to give each person a task slightly bigger than his/her current capabilities might dictate. Engage each person in the sizing task. Ask them. Most will select wisely. *More help? – See #56 Sizing Up People.*

☐ **8. Micromanaging? Monitor rather than obsess over delegated tasks.** Do you micromanage? If you're constantly looking over shoulders, you're not delegating. A properly communicated and delegated task doesn't need to be monitored. If you must monitor, set time-definite checkpoints by the calendar—every Monday; by percentage—after each 10% is complete; or by outcome—such as when you have the first draft. Be approachable for help, but not intrusive. Intervene only when agreed upon criteria are not being followed, or expectations are not being met. This focuses on the task, not the person. Let people finish their work.

☐ **9. Want to develop people? Delegate for development.** People grow by being assigned stretching complete tasks that contain elements they have not done before. Seventy percent of development in successful managers comes from doing stretch tasks and jobs. One bind of the poor delegator—my people aren't good enough—won't be solved until they are good enough. Doing most of the work yourself is a poor long-term development strategy and will never solve the problem.

☐ **10. Why aren't you delegating? Analyze what may be holding you back from delegating.** Are you hanging on to too much? Are you a perfectionist, wanting everything to be just so? Do you have unrealistic expectations of others? Someone made you leader because you are probably better at doing what the team does than some or most of the members. Do you feel guilty handing out tough work to do? Do you keep it yourself because you feel bad about giving them too much work? They would have to stay late or work on weekends to get it done. Most people enjoy being busy and on the move. If you think the workload is too much, ask. *More help? – See #36 Motivating Others.* Don't want to take the risk? If they don't perform, it will reflect on you. Poor delegation reflects on you, too. Are you really a personal contributor dressed in supervisor's clothes? Really prefer doing it yourself? People just get in the way? You need to examine whether management is the right career path for you. *More help? – See #6 Career Ambition.*

Some Develop-in-Place Assignments

- ☐ Manage a group of low-competence or low-performing people through a task they couldn't do by themselves.
- ☐ Manage a temporary group of "green," inexperienced people as their coach, teacher, guide, mentor, etc.
- ☐ Assign a project with a tight deadline to a group.
- ☐ Create employee involvement teams.
- ☐ Manage something "remote," away from your location.

Delegating work works, provided the one delegating works, too.
Robert Half – American businessman

Suggested Readings

Allen, D. (2003). *Getting things done: The art of stress-free productivity.* New York: Penguin Books.

Bossidy, L., & Charan, R. (with Burck, C.). (2002). *Execution: The discipline of getting things done.* New York: Crown Business.

Burns, R. (2001). *Making delegation happen: A simple and effective guide to implementing successful delegation.* Crows Nest, AU: Allen & Unwin.

Dittmer, R. E., & McFarland, S. (2008). *151 Quick ideas for delegating and decision making.* Franklin Lakes, NJ: Career Press.

Genett, D. M. (2004). *If you want it done right, you don't have to do it yourself! The power of effective delegation.* Sanger, CA: Quill/HarperCollins.

Ginnodo, B. (1997). *The power of empowerment.* Arlington Heights, IL: Pride Publications, Inc.

Harvard Business School Press. (2008). *Delegating work.* Boston: Harvard Business School Press.

McBee, S. (2003). *To lead is to empower: Leadership to empower your employees and yourself.* Shar McBee.

Murrell, K. L., & Meredith, M. (2000). *Empowering employees.* New York: McGraw-Hill.

Nelson, R. B. (1994). *Empowering employees through delegation.* Burr Ridge, IL: Irwin Professional Publishing.

Oncken, W., & Wass, D. L. (1999). Management time: Who's got the monkey? *Harvard Business Review, 77,* 178-186.

Truby, B., & Truby, J. (2000). *Successful delegation.* Mount Shasta, CA: Truby Achievement Center.

Tschohl, J. (2005). The importance of empowerment: If you want to keep customers, you must empower your employees. *The Canadian Manager, 28*(4), 25-26.

Ward, M. E., & Macphail-Wilcox, B. (1999). *Delegation and empowerment: Leading with and through others.* Larchmont, NY: Eye on Education.

19 Developing Direct Reports and Others

Tell me and I forget. Teach me and I remember. Involve me and I learn.
Benjamin Franklin – American scientist, author, inventor, statesman, and diplomat

Unskilled

- ☐ Not a people developer or builder
- ☐ Very results driven and tactical; no time for long-term development
- ☐ Doesn't see long-term development as his/her job
- ☐ Plays it safe—can't bring him/herself to assign really stretching (risky) work
- ☐ Thinks development is going to a course—doesn't know how development really happens
- ☐ May not know the aspirations of people, may not hold career discussions or provide coaching, may not push people to take their development seriously
- ☐ May prefer to select for talent rather than develop it
- ☐ Doesn't support or cooperate with the developmental system in the organization

Select one to three of the competencies listed below to use as a substitute for this competency if you decide not to work on it directly.

SUBSTITUTES: 7,10,13,18,20,27,33,35,36,56,60,64

Skilled

- ☐ Provides challenging and stretching tasks and assignments
- ☐ Holds frequent development discussions
- ☐ Is aware of each person's career goals
- ☐ Constructs compelling development plans and executes them
- ☐ Pushes people to accept developmental moves
- ☐ Will take on those who need help and further development
- ☐ Cooperates with the developmental system in the organization
- ☐ Is a people builder

Overused Skill

- ☐ May concentrate on the development of a few at the expense of many
- ☐ May create work inequities as challenging assignments are parceled out
- ☐ May be overly optimistic about how much people can grow
- ☐ May endorse the latest developmental fad within the organization and cooperate with the system even when it doesn't make sense for an individual

Select one to three of the competencies listed below to work on to compensate for an overuse of this skill.

COMPENSATORS: 7,12,18,20,21,23,25,35,36,47,54,56

Some Causes

- ☐ Don't believe people really develop
- ☐ Don't get paid to develop others
- ☐ Don't have the time for it
- ☐ Don't know how to develop people
- ☐ Think it's someone else's responsibility

Leadership Architect® Factors and Clusters

This competency is in the Operating Skills Factor (II). This competency is in the Getting Work Done Through Others Cluster (F) with: 18, 20, 27, 35. You may want to check other competencies in the same Factor/Cluster for related tips.

The Map

Most people want to grow and develop. Most people have aspirations to do well and be rewarded with more pay and higher positions. Most people have dreams and goals they want to achieve. Development and preparation for positions with greater responsibility is a three-part harmony. The person needs to be ambitious and willing to do what's required to grow and progress. The organization has to have a process in place to help those who want to grow. Those two are usually true in all organizations. The last part of the harmony is usually the problem: The boss has to be an active player in the three-part harmony or development won't happen. Without the boss's time, interest and effort, people will not grow much. People can't develop themselves without help. People won't grow if they don't want to. People won't grow if the organization shows no interest and offers no support. People won't grow if you don't make it a priority.

Some Remedies

☐ **1. Too busy? Take the time.** You have to invest some time. For most managers, time is what they have the least of to give. For the purposes of developing others beyond today's job, you need to allocate about eight hours per year per direct report. If you have a normal span of seven direct reports, that's 7 of 220 working days or 3% of your annual time. Two of the eight hours are for an annual in-depth appraisal of the person in terms of current strengths and weaknesses and of the competencies he/she needs to develop to move on to the next step. Two of the eight hours are for an in-depth career discussion with each person. What does he/she want? What will he/she sacrifice to get there? What is his/her own appraisal of his/her skills? Two of the eight hours are for creating a three- to five-year development plan and sharing it with the person. The last two hours are to present your findings and recommendations to the organization, usually in a succession planning process, and arranging for developmental events for each person. Start thinking of yourself as a coach or mentor. It's your job to help your people grow.

☐ **2. Do you know the current state? Start with an appraisal.** You can't help anyone develop if you can't or aren't willing to fairly and accurately appraise people. Sound appraisal starts with the best picture of current strengths and weaknesses. Then you need to know what competencies are going to be necessary going forward. You can find this out by looking at a success profile for the next possible job or two for the person. If there are no formal success profiles, you can ask the Human Resources group for assistance or ask someone you know and trust currently in that next job what he/she uses to be successful. *More help? – See #25 Hiring and Staffing and #56 Sizing Up People.*

☐ **3. Problems giving feedback? Learn the guidelines for providing effective feedback.** People need continuous feedback from you and others to grow. Some tips about feedback:

- Arrange for them to get feedback from multiple people, including yourself, on what matters for success in their future jobs; arrange for your direct reports to get 360° feedback about every two years.
- Give them progressively stretching tasks that are first-time and different for them so that they can give themselves feedback as they go.
- If they have direct reports and peers, another technique to recommend is to ask their associates for comments on what they should stop doing, start doing, and keep doing to be more successful.
- You have to be willing to be straight with your people and give them accurate but balanced feedback. Give as much real-time feedback as you have time for. Most people are motivated by process feedback against agreed-upon goals for three reasons. First, it helps them adjust what they are doing along the way in time to better achieve the goal—they can make midcourse corrections. Second, it shows them what they are doing is important and that you're there to help. Third, it's not the "gotcha" game of negative and critical feedback after the fact. If there are negatives, they need to know the negatives as soon as possible. *More help? – See #13 Confronting Direct Reports.*
- Set up a buddy system so people can get continuing feedback.

If your organization has a mentoring program, find out how it works. Best practices begin with those to be mentored writing down goals, objectives, and development needs. They are then carefully matched with mentors and the relationship is outlined. How often will the people meet? On what topics is the mentor to be helpful? What are the responsibilities of the person to be mentored? If your organization doesn't have such a program, look at setting one up within your unit or function.

☐ **4. Ready to put it on paper? Create a development plan.** You need to put together a development plan that, if followed, actually would work. At least 70% of reported skill development comes from having challenging, uncomfortable tasks/assignments. Development means that you do the new skill or fail at something important to you. Tasks that develop anything are those in which not doing it is not a viable option. Another 20% comes from studying and working with others to see useful behavior and get feedback. This can take the form of studying a role model, working with a developmental partner, keeping a written summary of what's working and not working, or preferably a formal assessment, like a 360° process. Without this continuous feedback, even the best developmental plans fail. About 10% of development comes from thinking differently or having new ways to think about things. Typically these come from coursework, books or mentors; the lion's share is learning from tough tasks and the learning from other people that comes from feedback. A good plan would have 70% job and task content; 20% people to study, listen to, and work with; and 10% courses and readings.

☐ **5. Struggling with equal opportunity? Tailor your effort to a person's unique needs.** If some of your people have limited or disadvantaged backgrounds, it is unrealistic to expect the same developmental procedures will work for them. According to research conducted by the Center for Creative Leadership (see *The New Leaders* by Ann Morrison), people from diverse backgrounds usually need additional support in the form of mentoring, information on how things work around here, greater access to formal organizational information, a critical mass of support from top management, and accountability/enforcement to make developing diversity a reality rather than a statistic. You may also be able to intern/apprentice those with limited backgrounds to begin to provide appropriate job experiences or provide necessary training. *More help? – See #21 Managing Diversity.*

☐ **6. Want to develop people? Delegate for development.** Brainstorm with your direct reports all the tasks that aren't being done, but are important to do. Ask them for a list of tasks that are no longer challenging for them. (You can also use parts of your own job to develop others. Take three tasks that are no longer developmental for you, but would be for others, and delegate them.) Trade tasks and assignments between two direct reports; have them do each other's work. Assign each of your direct reports an out-of-comfort-zone task that meets the following criteria: The task needs to be done, the person hasn't done it or isn't good at it, and the task calls for a skill the person needs to develop. Remember to focus on varied assignments—more of the same isn't developmental. *More help? – See #18 Delegation.*

☐ **7. Are you optimizing stress? Delegate real, challenging work.** Remember, meaningful development is not the stress-reduction business. It is not cozy or safe; it comes from varied, stressful, even adverse tasks that require we learn to do something new or different or fail. Real development involves real work the person largely hasn't done before. Real development is rewarding but scary. Be open with your people about this. Everyone won't want to be developed in new areas. Some are satisfied to do what they do, even if it limits their career options. While you should advise them of the consequences, all organizations need strong performers dedicated to skill building in their current area only. Don't imply that a pure tactician must become a strategist to be valued. Instead, create more ways for people to excel and get status recognition. For most of us this is a powerful need—some studies show that people in prestigious jobs are less likely to get seriously ill, regardless of their personal habits. If a person wants to be a customer service representative for life, recognize that as critical, and help the person develop in every way possible within that area—coaching, training, and networking with other experts.

☐ **8. Do you help your people learn by looking for repeating patterns? Encourage reflection.** Help them look for patterns in the situations and problems they deal with. What succeeded and what failed? What was common to each success or what was present in each failure but never present in a success? Focus on the successes; failures are easier to analyze but don't in themselves tell you what would work. Comparing successes, while less exciting, yields more information. The bottom line is help them reduce insights to principles or rules of thumb that might be repeatable. Ask them what they have learned to increase their skills and understanding, making them better managers or professionals. Ask them what they can do now that they couldn't do a year ago. Reinforce this and encourage more of it. Developing is learning in as many ways as possible. *More help? – See #32 Learning on the Fly.*

☐ **9. Can you influence people to take on a challenge? Sell development.** Part of developing others is convincing people that tough, new, challenging and different assignments are good for them. In follow-up studies of successful executives, more than 90% report that a boss in their past nearly forced them to take a scary job assignment they wanted to turn down. That assignment turned out to be the most developmental for them. The peculiar thing about long-term development is that even ambitious people turn down the very assignments they need to grow. They do not have the perspective to understand that. Your job is to help convince people on the way up to get out of their comfort zone and accept jobs they don't initially see as useful or leading anywhere.

- ☐ **10. Want to open their minds? Build perspective.** Give the people under you who have the potential for bigger and better things assignments that take them outside your function, unit or business. Help them expand their perspectives. Volunteer them for cross-boundary task forces. Have them attend meetings that include people from other areas. Open up the world for them so that they can better judge for themselves what's out there and what part of it they want.

Some Develop-in-Place Assignments

- ☐ Manage a group of resistant people with low morale through an unpopular change or project.
- ☐ Manage a group of low-competence or low-performing people through a task they couldn't do by themselves.
- ☐ Manage a temporary group of "green," inexperienced people as their coach, teacher, guide, mentor, etc.
- ☐ Manage a group of people in a rapidly expanding or growing operation.
- ☐ Manage a group of people where you are a towering expert and the people in the group are not.

All that is valuable in human society
depends upon the opportunity for development accorded the individual.
Albert Einstein – German-born Nobel Prize-winning physicist

Suggested Readings

Ahlrichs, N. S. (2003). *Manager of choice*. Palo Alto, CA: Davies-Black Publishing.

Andersen, E. (2006). *Growing great employees*. New York: Penguin Group.

Bell, C. R. (2002). *Managers as mentors: Building partnerships for learning*. San Francisco: Berrett-Koehler Publishers.

Broad, M. L. (2005). *Beyond transfer of training: Engaging systems to improve performance*. San Francisco: Pfeiffer.

Broad, M. L., & Newstrom, J. W. (2001). *Transfer of training: Action-packed strategies to ensure high payoff from training investments*. Jackson, TN: Perseus Books Group.

Byham, W. C., Smith, A. B., & Paese, M. J. (2002). *Grow your own leaders: How to identify, develop, and retain leadership talent*. Upper Saddle River, NJ: Prentice Hall, Inc.

Cashman, K. (2008). *Leadership from the inside out: Becoming a leader for life* (2nd ed.). San Francisco: Berrett-Koehler Publishers.

Cashman, K. (with Forem, J.). (2003). *Awakening the leader within: A story of transformation*. Hoboken, NJ: John Wiley & Sons.

Charan, R. (2007). *Know-how: The 8 skills that separate people who perform from those who don't*. New York: Crown Business.

Charan, R., Drotter, S., & Noel, J. (2000). *The leadership pipeline: How to build the leadership-powered company*. San Francisco: Jossey-Bass.

DeLong, T. J., Gabarro, J. J., & Lees, R. J. (2008, January). Why mentoring matters in a hypercompetitive world. *Harvard Business Review*.

Ensher, E. A., & Murphy, S. E. (2005). *Power mentoring: How successful mentors and protégés get the most out of their relationships*. San Francisco: Jossey-Bass Inc.

Fulmer, R. M., & Conger, J. A. (2004). *Growing your company's leaders*. New York: AMACOM.

Goldsmith, M., Kaye, B., & Shelton, K. (Eds.). (2000). *Learning journeys: Top management experts share hard-earned lessons on becoming great mentors and leaders*. Mountain View, CA: Davies-Black Publishing.

Goldsmith, M., & Reiter, M. (2007). *What got you here won't get you there: How successful people become even more successful*. New York: Hyperion.

Harvard Business Essentials. (2004). *Coaching and mentoring: How to develop top talent and achieve stronger performance*. Boston: Harvard Business School Press.

Holliday, M. (2001). *Coaching, mentoring, and managing: Breakthrough strategies to solve performance problems and build winning teams*. Franklin Lakes, NJ: Career Press.

Johnson, H. (2002). *Mentoring greatness: How to build a great business*. Irvine, CA: Griffin Trade Paperback.

Lawler, E. E., III. (2008). *Talent: Making people your competitive advantage.* San Francisco: Jossey-Bass.

Lencioni, P. M. (2007). *The three signs of a miserable job: A fable for managers (and their employees).* San Francisco: Jossey-Bass.

Levin, R. A., & Rosse, J. G. (2001). *Talent flow: A strategic approach to keeping good employees, helping them grow, and letting them go.* New York: John Wiley & Sons.

Lombardo, M. M., & Eichinger, R. W. (2004). *The leadership machine.* Minneapolis, MN: Lominger International: A Korn/Ferry Company.

Manzoni, J. F., & Barsoux, J. L. (2002). *The set-up-to-fail syndrome.* Boston: Harvard Business School Press.

Raelin, J. A. (2003). *Creating leaderful organizations: How to bring out leadership in everyone.* San Francisco: Berrett-Koehler Publishers.

Ready, D. A., & Conger, J. (2007, June). Make your company a talent factory. *Harvard Business Review.*

Reck, R. R. (2001). *The X-factor: Getting extraordinary results from ordinary people.* New York: John Wiley & Sons.

Rothwell, W. J., & Kazanas, H. C. (2003). *The strategic development of talent.* Amherst, MA: HRD Press, Inc.

Spear, S. J. (2004). Learning to lead at Toyota. *Harvard Business Review, 82,* 78-86.

Zachary, L. J. (2000). *The mentor's guide: Facilitating effective learning relationships.* San Francisco: Jossey-Bass.

Zenger, J. H., & Folkman, J. (2002). *The extraordinary leader: Turning good managers into great leaders.* New York: McGraw-Hill.

20 Directing Others

Good management consists in showing average people how to do the work of superior people.
John D. Rockefeller – American industrialist and philanthropist

Unskilled

- ☐ Unclear or cryptic communicator to direct reports
- ☐ Doesn't set goals, targets, mileposts and objectives
- ☐ Not very planful giving out work—just gives out tasks
- ☐ Mostly tells and sells; doesn't listen much
- ☐ Plays favorites and is tough on others
- ☐ May be too impatient to structure work for others
- ☐ Doesn't delegate well
- ☐ Doesn't take the time to manage
- ☐ May lack interest in managing and be more eager to work on own assignments

Select one to three of the competencies listed below to use as a substitute for this competency if you decide not to work on it directly.

SUBSTITUTES: 9,12,13,18,19,21,23,27,33,35,36,39,47,60

Skilled

- ☐ Is good at establishing clear directions
- ☐ Sets stretching objectives
- ☐ Distributes the workload appropriately
- ☐ Lays out work in a well-planned and organized manner
- ☐ Maintains two-way dialogue with others on work and results
- ☐ Brings out the best in people
- ☐ Is a clear communicator

Overused Skill

- ☐ May be overly controlling
- ☐ May have a chilling effect on others, discouraging input and ideas, intolerant of disagreements
- ☐ May only delegate pieces and not share the larger picture
- ☐ May be overly directive and stifle creativity and initiative

Select one to three of the competencies listed below to work on to compensate for an overuse of this skill.

COMPENSATORS: 3,7,14,18,19,21,23,28,31,33,35,36,60,64

Some Causes

- ☐ Impatient
- ☐ Inappropriate style or temperament
- ☐ Inexperienced; unskilled in managing
- ☐ Lack of interest in managing
- ☐ Major change in direction and mission
- ☐ New members on the team
- ☐ Time management, too busy to manage

Leadership Architect® Factors and Clusters

This competency is in the Operating Skills Factor (II). This competency is in the Getting Work Done Through Others Cluster (F) with: 18, 19, 27, 35. You may want to check other competencies in the same Factor/Cluster for related tips.

The Map

Managing others effectively and efficiently is a known technology. There are a number of research and experience verified techniques and practices that lead to groups performing well under a particular manager. There are also some personal styles and temperaments that work better than others.

Some Remedies

- ☐ **1. Do you know yourself? Assess your personal strengths and weaknesses.** Get some input from others. Ask your people what they appreciate about you as a person and as a manager and what they would prefer you change. What do you do well and what don't you do well personally and as a manager of others? Ask for help from the Human Resources function to get a list of the competencies most often related to managing others well. End up with a list of the good news and the bad news. Devise a development plan for the important things on your bad list. *More help? – See #55 Self-Knowledge.*
- ☐ **2. What's your approach? Assess your management practices.** Do an inventory of the common management techniques and practices you do well and those that you do not do so well or often enough. You can get a list of those techniques from any introductory text on management, from a course for first-time managers, or from the Human Resource function. Ask your people for input on those you do well and those you need to work on. Create a management practices skill-building plan for yourself.
- ☐ **3. Are you a good communicator? Check your communication skills.** Many times the breakdown in effectively managing others is related to poor, inadequate or inconsistent communication. How well do you inform? Listen? Explain? Get back to people? Give feedback? *More help? –*

See #27 Informing, #33 Listening, #49 Presentation Skills, and #67 Written Communications.

☐ **4. Do you delegate enough? Empower people.** Another common breakdown is in not delegating nor empowering. Do you give the people under you the authority to do their work? Do you over or under manage? Periodically, ask your people to give you a list of the things they think you are doing yourself that they believe they could do a good job on; delegate some of the things on everybody's list. *More help? – See #18 Delegation.*

☐ **5. Does your style chill or turn off others? Take stock of your management style.** Common styles that don't work well with others are impatience, devaluing others, public criticism, playing favorites, prejudice toward a class of people, disorganized, emotional, etc. Are you a poor time manager? Is there enough time left over to spend with your people? Are you any of those things? If yes, try to work on being less of that. *More help? – See #11 Composure, #21 Managing Diversity, #23 Fairness to Direct Reports, and #41 Patience.*

☐ **6. Are you organized and planful? Get organized and be clear.** Can people follow what you want? Do you lay out work and tasks to be done clearly? Do you set clear goals and objectives that can guide their work? *More help? – See #35 Managing and Measuring Work and #47 Planning.*

☐ **7. Do you share the credit? Celebrate people's success.** Do you use "we" more often than "I"? Do you celebrate successes with others? Do people want to work with you again? *More help? – See #36 Motivating Others.*

☐ **8. Do you confront problems quickly or let things fester? Address problems quickly.** The rest of the team suffers when a manager doesn't step up to problems quickly. *More help? – See #13 Confronting Direct Reports, #34 Managerial Courage, and #57 Standing Alone.*

☐ **9. Would you rather be on your own? Assess your desire to manage others.** Are you interested in getting work done through others or would you rather do it all yourself? Maybe management isn't for you. Maybe you would be better off being a senior personal contributor. Maybe you don't really care to relate to people very deeply. *More help? – See #7 Caring About Direct Reports, #10 Compassion, and #23 Fairness to Direct Reports.*

☐ **10. Whom could you learn from? Study models.** Seek out one or two people around you whom others consider to be good managers. Study them. What do they do that you don't? What do you do that they don't? Or, put your last 10 managers on a piece of paper. Create two lists; the five best and the five worst. What characteristics do the best share? The worst? How does that compare to you?

Some Develop-in-Place Assignments

- ☐ Build a multifunctional project team to tackle a common business issue or problem.
- ☐ Manage a group of resistant people with low morale through an unpopular change or project.
- ☐ Manage a group of low-competence or low-performing people through a task they couldn't do by themselves.
- ☐ Assign a project with a tight deadline to a group.
- ☐ Manage a group of people where you are a towering expert and the people in the group are not.

Look over your shoulder now and then
to be sure someone's following you.
Henry Gilmer – Gilmer's Law of Political Leadership

Suggested Readings

Bacal, R. (2007). *How to manage performance.* New York: McGraw-Hill.

Broom, M. F. (2002). *The infinite organization: Celebrating the positive use of power in organizations.* Mountain View, CA: Davies-Black Publishing.

Cashman, K. (2008). *Leadership from the inside out: Becoming a leader for life* (2nd ed.). San Francisco: Berrett-Koehler Publishers.

Cashman, K. (with Forem, J.). (2003). *Awakening the leader within: A story of transformation.* Hoboken, NJ: John Wiley & Sons.

Drucker, P. F. (2008). *Management* (Rev. ed.). New York: Collins Business.

Harvard Business School Press. (2006). *Leading teams: Expert solutions to everyday challenges.* Boston: Harvard Business School Press.

Hawkins, D. R. (2002). *Power vs. force: The hidden determinants of human behavior.* Carson, CA: Hay House.

McKenna, P. J., & Maister, D. H. (2002). *First among equals: How to manage a group of professionals.* New York: Free Press.

Pearman, R. R. (2005). *Hard wired leadership.* Jaico Publishing House.

Raelin, J. A. (2003). *Creating leaderful organizations: How to bring out leadership in everyone.* San Francisco: Berrett-Koehler Publishers.

Reck, R. R. (2001). *The X-factor: Getting extraordinary results from ordinary people.* New York: John Wiley & Sons.

Streibel, B. J. (2007). *Plan and conduct effective meetings: 24 Steps to generate meaningful results.* New York: McGraw-Hill.

Zenger, J. H., & Folkman, J. (2002). *The extraordinary leader: Turning good managers into great leaders.* New York: McGraw-Hill.

21 *Managing* Diversity

Differences challenge assumptions.
Anne Wilson Schaef – American writer and lecturer

Unskilled

- ☐ Not effective with groups much different from him/her
- ☐ May be uncomfortable with those not like him/her
- ☐ May act inappropriately with those different from him/her
- ☐ Defends turf from outsiders
- ☐ Avoids conflict and the noise of differing views and agendas
- ☐ Doesn't see the business value of diversity
- ☐ Treats everybody the same without regard to their differences
- ☐ Very narrow and ethnocentric; believes his/her group to be superior
- ☐ May carry around negative and demeaning stereotypes he/she has trouble getting rid of

Select one to three of the competencies listed below to use as a substitute for this competency if you decide not to work on it directly.

SUBSTITUTES: 7,10,18,22,23,29,33,35,40,41,46,53,56,60,64

Skilled

- ☐ Manages all kinds and classes of people equitably
- ☐ Deals effectively with all races, nationalities, cultures, disabilities, ages and both sexes
- ☐ Hires variety and diversity without regard to class
- ☐ Supports equal and fair treatment and opportunity for all

Overused Skill

- ☐ May make too many allowances for members of a particular class
- ☐ May not apply equal standards and criteria to all classes
- ☐ May show an inappropriate preference for a single class of people
- ☐ May compromise standards to achieve diversity

Select one to three of the competencies listed below to work on to compensate for an overuse of this skill.

COMPENSATORS: 9,12,13,18,19,20,25,34,35,36,37,56,57,60,64

Some Causes

- ☐ Are uncomfortable with different groups
- ☐ Believe in diversity, but don't know what to do
- ☐ Can't make the business case for diversity
- ☐ Don't see how diversity helps
- ☐ Narrow and rigid
- ☐ Think diversity means double standards
- ☐ Uncomfortable with the new and different

Leadership Architect® Factors and Clusters

This competency is in the Personal and Interpersonal Skills Factor (VI). This competency is in the Managing Diverse Relationships Cluster (P) with: 4, 15, 23, 42, 64. You may want to check other competencies in the same Factor/ Cluster for related tips.

The Map

In the new global world and economy (large, meaning worldwide) diversity is king. Markets are now more diverse. The labor pool is more diverse. And almost every global company's greatest opportunities are in cultures different and more diverse than its home country's. Those organizations that best manage large diversity will be the winners. Managing large diversity starts with managing small—home country—diversity. Managing diversity is basically deciding which differences make a difference and enrich, and which differences don't. Once you have figured that out, managing is managing. However, until you see the benefits of large and small diversity, little change is likely. To do this, you'll need to learn to understand without judging other groups, see people more as individuals and less as a member of a group, understand your own subtle stereotyping (if any), make the business case for diversity, make a personal case for diversity by seeing it work, and treat some people a bit differently due to their lack of opportunity in the past.

Some Remedies

☐ **1. Need to sell the importance of diversity? Make the business case.** Nothing much will happen until you have the business case in mind for increased diversity in the organization. Are your markets and customers more diverse than your employees? Where are your major new opportunities for volume and share? Are they in your home market? People just like you? Most likely not. Do you know a lot about the people and cultures inside and outside your home country who are going to buy your products and make you successful? As the population becomes more diverse, same-culture sales and marketing people have had more success selling (Hispanics to

Hispanics, for example). Innovation through diversity. Studies show that heterogeneous or diverse groups are more innovative than homogeneous groups. They view opportunities from different perspectives. The majority of the U.S. labor market will shortly be former minorities. Females and minorities collectively will be in the majority. Companies known in the marketplace for managing diversity well will get their pick of the best and the brightest. A broader talent pool means more to choose from; more effective managers tend to have a more diverse array of people around them. The rest will get the leftovers. Are you known for managing diversity well? Want increased motivation and productivity? There is a positive relationship between perceived equity/feeling valued and the performance of organizations. The business case boils down to more perspectives, more chances to learn, more ways to appeal to different market segments, and a more productive workforce where all employees think merit is what counts in an organization. Read "Making Differences Matter: A New Paradigm for Managing Diversity" by Thomas and Ely in the *Harvard Business Review* (HBR OnPoint Enhanced Edition), November 1, 2002. Also read "Diversity, Making the Business Case" by Michael L. Wheeler in *BusinessWeek*, Dec. 9, 1996.

☐ **2. Want to level the playing field? Provide equal opportunity to all.** If you don't buy this, you can't learn to be better at managing diversity. Equal opportunity means differential treatment. Equal opportunity does not mean equal treatment. In golf, do you object to handicaps? That's a system designed to even the playing field for golfers with different levels of expertise and experience. Do you object to veterans preference? That's a system of giving veterans a 10-point advantage on civil service tests to make up for the lost time and break in their business skill development while they were serving their four years in the military. What about handicap preferences? Do you mind that they have special bathroom stalls to adjust to their handicaps? Close-in parking? Ramps to get to work? Special buses? That's all unequal treatment to level the playing field. The same is true then for disadvantaged backgrounds. Never had a father role model at home. Never traveled out of town. Never was a student leader. Couldn't afford to belong to Scouts. Never went to camp. Never studied in Europe for a semester. Never knew anyone in the immediate family who had a regular job that lasted 20 years. Denied other opportunities due to what group they belonged to. But otherwise bright, ambitious and willing to learn. What adjustments would you have to or would you be willing to make to level the playing field? More orientation? More training? A little more patience? More understanding? Special exposures? Forming groups of like people to share common problems? The key is that all of this disadvantage was not the fault of the person sitting before you. He or she now wants to break free of that and have an equitable chance to learn and perform. You can provide the opportunity if you understand unequal treatment is necessary to reach equal opportunity. Read *The New Leaders* by Ann Morrison.

☐ **3. Double standards? Be consistent with performance standards.** This is tough. Are there double standards at entry? Probably. Due to whatever disadvantage (cultural, economic, physical, language) is at work, there is at entry probably a deficit in the past demonstration of needed skills and background. Are there double standards for treatment? Definitely yes. Should there be double standards long term? Definitely not. Once a person has been given preferential treatment—language training or problem-solving skills enhancement—to balance a disadvantage, the playing field should be equal and the same standards should apply to everyone. The whole point of this is the belief that when given equal opportunity, equal performance will be the result. If performance is not up to standard after some time, then the person will have to live with the consequences the same as anyone else in the same situation.

☐ **4. Think different groups perform differently? Acknowledge that people generally perform the same across groups.** What differences make a difference? Does gender make a difference in performance? Research says no. Some studies actually point to higher ratings for women, probably due to the pioneer effect. Also, research says that gender diverse teams are more creative and innovative. Age? Generally not. Some skills stay strong, others (memory) slowly decrease for some. Race? Not much research yet. Given equal opportunities, looks like not. Handicapped? Some studies show greater performance probably due to special motivation. Culture? Too many variables. Not much research. Certainly cultural background influences how you think about things but all cultures seem to have a sufficient work ethic and ambition to perform against reasonable standards. Some surveys on Asians in the U.S. say they outperform others in grades and academic and scientific achievement, again maybe because of the pioneer effect.

☐ **5. Clinging to stereotypes? Challenge your personal biases.** You have to understand your own subtle stereotyping. Helen Astin's research showed that both men and women rated women managers at the extremes (very high or very low) while they rate men on a normal curve. Do you think redheads have tempers? Blondes have more fun? Overweight people are lazy? Women are more emotional at work? Men can't show emotion? Find out your own pattern. Attend a course which delves into perception of others. Most stereotyping is false. Even if there are surface differences, they don't make a difference in performance.

☐ **6. Uncomfortable with certain groups? Deal with people equitably.** Try to see people more as individuals than members of a group. Avoid putting people in grouped buckets. Many of us bucket people as can or can't do this. We have good buckets and bad buckets. Buckets I like/am comfortable with and buckets that bother me. Once we bucket, we generally don't relate as well to the off-bucket people. Much of the time bucketing is based on like me—the good bucket; not like me—the bad bucket. Across time, the can do/like me bucket gets the majority of your attention, more feedback, stretching tasks, develops the most and performs the best, unfortunately proving your stereotyping again and again. To break this cycle, understand without judging. Be candid with yourself. Is there a group or groups you don't like or are uncomfortable with? Do you judge individual members of that group without really knowing if your stereotype is true? Most of us do. Try to see people as people.

☐ **7. Are you leaving people out? Balance people processes.** Women and people of color are less likely to get developmental feedback. Senior women haven't had the tough job assignments men have had on the way up. Women and minorities get less informal information. Sometimes women and minorities do not participate equally in off-work but organization-related socializing—where important business information is exchanged and decisions made in an informal and relaxed environment. Examine each of your people processes. Are there unintentional inequities? Drive special programming to make them more equal. Equal access to information, challenging jobs, relating, skill building and networking is equal opportunity.

☐ **8. Caught in a vicious cycle? Address legitimate concerns of dissatisfied groups.** If a group is inequitably treated, it will coalesce into a subgroup and fight back. It's natural. Misery loves company. People who are not in power tend to group together. They form special forums to discuss problems. They may eat together, socialize together and stand as a group united behind a position or a demand. All of this tends to irritate others (who steadfastly claim they have never discriminated against anyone), who may decide this just proves their negative assessments of the group in general. They then put the whole group and all its individual members back in the bad bucket. You have to relax. This is a human process. It happens all over the world at all levels when an identifiable group enters someone else's sandbox, like the Irish in the 1850's coming to New York. Help them form groups and attend and learn and listen. Address their legitimate demands and complaints. Help them out. Teach them to make the business or organizational case first, and to be more tentative and conditional than they actually are so others have room to get comfortable and negotiate and bargain. Figure out what they want and see if you can help them get it. *More help? – See #64 Understanding Others.*

- ☐ **9. Narrow sighted? Use diversity to broaden perspective.** Diversity of viewpoint, background, education, culture, experience, beliefs and attitudes matter, and all help produce a superior product in a diverse and global marketplace. Put diversity to the test yourself; attack problems with diverse task forces, pull in the widest array of thinking you can and see if you get broader, more inventive results. Assemble the most diverse team you can who have the skills to do the job but otherwise are different. Consciously spend more of your time with people around you who are different. Solicit the points of view of each person. How do those background differences lead to viewing problems differently?
- ☐ **10. Hampered by narrow experiences? Build your diversity experience:**
  - Stage one: Talk to people in your organization, neighborhood or place of worship who are different in some way than you. Do lunch. Go to a ballgame. Exchange views. House a foreign student from a country your organization is thinking about entering. Do volunteer work with a group not like you.
  - Stage two: Visit all ethnic festivals in your geography. Sample the foods. See the costumes and the crafts. Study their history. Talk to them.
  - Stage three: Vacation in Miami and spend time in the Cuban area. San Diego and San Antonio for Spanish. San Francisco and New York for Chinatown. Toronto for a number of ethnic areas within the city limits.
  - Stage four: Travel and stay for one week anywhere in the world where you are in the minority and most others do not speak your language. Get away from the tourist areas. See how that feels.

Some Develop-in-Place Assignments

- ☐ Be a member of a union-negotiating or grievance-handling team.
- ☐ Assemble a team of diverse people to accomplish a difficult task.
- ☐ Represent to higher management the concerns of a group of nonexempt, clerical, or administrative employees to seek resolution of a difficult issue.
- ☐ Serve for a year or more with a community agency.
- ☐ Work for a year or more with a charitable organization.

It is not best that we should all think alike;
it is difference of opinion that makes horse races.
Mark Twain – American humorist, satirist, lecturer, and writer

Suggested Readings

Barak, M. E. M. (2005). *Managing diversity: Toward a globally inclusive workplace.* Thousand Oaks, CA: Sage.

Bates-Ballard, P., & Smith, G. (2008). *Navigating diversity: An advocate's guide through the maze of race, gender, religion, and more.* Charleston, SC: BookSurge.

Bucher, R. D., & Bucher, P. L. (2003). *Diversity consciousness: Opening our minds to people, cultures, and opportunities.* New York: Prentice Hall.

Deresky, H. (2002). *Global management: Strategic and interpersonal.* Upper Saddle River, NJ: Prentice Hall.

Harvard Business School Press. (2002). *Harvard Business Review on managing diversity.* Boston: Harvard Business School Press.

Harvey, C. P., & Allard, M. J. (2008). *Understanding and managing diversity: Readings, cases, and exercises* (4th ed.). Upper Saddle River, NJ: Prentice Hall.

Hubbard, E. (2003). *The diversity scorecard: Evaluating the impact of diversity on organizational performance.* Boston: Butterworth-Heinemann.

Hubbard, E. (2004). *The manager's pocket guide to diversity management.* Amherst, MA: HRD Press.

Jacob, N. (2003). *Intercultural management.* London: Kogan Page.

Lancaster, L. C., Stillman, D., & MacKay, H. (2002). *When generations collide: Who they are. Why they clash. How to solve the generational puzzle at work.* New York: HarperCollins.

Livers, A. B., & Caver, K. A. (2003). *Leading in black and white: Working across the racial divide in corporate America.* San Francisco: Jossey-Bass.

Lustig, M. W., & Koester, J. (2005). *Intercultural competence: Interpersonal communication across cultures* (5th ed.). Boston: Allyn & Bacon.

Middleton, D. R. (2002). *The challenge of human diversity: Mirrors, bridges, and chasms.* Prospect Heights, IL: Waveland Press.

Miller, F. A., & Katz, J. H. (2002). *The inclusion breakthrough.* San Francisco: Berrett-Koehler Publishers.

Olver, K., Baugh, S., & Gurlides, D. (2006). *Leveraging diversity at work: How to hire, retain, and inspire a diverse workforce for peak performance and profit.* Country Club Hills, IL: Inside Out Press.

Ricucci, N. (2002). *Managing diversity in public sector workforces.* Boulder, CO: Westview Press.

Thiederman, S. (2008). *Making diversity work: Seven steps for defeating bias in the workplace.* New York: Kaplan Business.

Wilson, T., & Carswell, J. (2002). *Global diversity at work: Winning the war for talent.* New York: John Wiley & Sons.

22 Ethics and Values

We do not act rightly because we have virtue or excellence,
but we rather have those because we have acted rightly.
Aristotle (384-322 BCE) – Greek philosopher and scientist

Unskilled

- ☐ Values may be out of sync with those of the organization
- ☐ Strong individualist with low concern for values of others; may set his/her own rules; make others uncomfortable
- ☐ May play too close or over the edge for the organization
- ☐ May not think about own values much and have no idea how he/she comes across
- ☐ Behavior may vary too much across situations
- ☐ Values may be seen as too self-serving
- ☐ He/she doesn't walk the talk; says one thing, does another

Select one to three of the competencies listed below to use as a substitute for this competency if you decide not to work on it directly.

SUBSTITUTES: 5,7,10,21,24,29,40,46,47,50,52,53,58,63

Skilled

- ☐ Adheres to an appropriate (for the setting) and effective set of core values and beliefs during both good and bad times
- ☐ Acts in line with those values
- ☐ Rewards the right values and disapproves of others
- ☐ Practices what he/she preaches

Overused Skill

- ☐ May go to battle based on beliefs and values when not appropriate
- ☐ May be overly sensitive to situations he/she sees as litmus tests of principles, values, and beliefs
- ☐ May be seen as stubborn and insensitive to the need for change and compromise
- ☐ May be overly critical of those who do not hold the same values
- ☐ May use ethics statements to close off discussion

Select one to three of the competencies listed below to work on to compensate for an overuse of this skill.

COMPENSATORS: 10,11,12,17,21,32,33,37,41,45,46,48,55,56,58,64,65

Some Causes

- ☐ Inconsistent values/ethical stances
- ☐ Marginal values and ethics; operate close to the edge
- ☐ Old values/ethical stances
- ☐ Overly independent; set own rules
- ☐ Situational ethics
- ☐ Vague about values/ethics

Leadership Architect® Factors and Clusters

This competency is in the Personal and Interpersonal Skills Factor (VI). This competency is in the Acting with Honor and Character Cluster (R) with: 29. You may want to check other competencies in the same Factor/Cluster for related tips.

The Map

Values and ethics are shorthand statements of the core or underlying principles that guide what you say and do. Do unto others as you would have them do unto you. Although short and sometimes simple—"Quality is Job One" (Ford), "Our customers are always right" (Nordstrom), "Our employees are our most important asset"—values and ethics provide guidance on how we act and how we make choices. "We are an equal opportunity employer"—simple enough—covers behavior in hiring, firing, promotion, training, development, placement, and employee assistance programming. We all have a set of values and ethics but many times we haven't thought out our values/ethical stances well; we are on autopilot from childhood and our accumulated experience. All organizations have a set of reasonably consistent values and ethics they prefer to operate under. Organizations require reasonable conformity with those collective standards. People who are models of ethics and values have thought their values through, are clear about them, can deal with close calls by applying them, understand other value stances, speak up on these matters, and are reasonably consistent and in tune with those around them.

Some Remedies

☐ **1. Trouble with consistency? Align your words and actions.** Most of the evaluation of your ethics and values comes from people watching what you do. If they have not had the opportunity to see you in action, they will evaluate what you say. If they have both, they will take what you do over what you say. People are bothered by inconsistencies between what you say and what you do. If you tend to say one thing but do another, people will see that as inconsistent and will say of you that you don't walk your talk. Above all, align your actions and your mouth. Inconsistencies come in three kinds, outlined below in points two, three and four.

- ☐ **2. Sending mixed messages? Avoid "do as I say, not as I do" behavior.** The usual case is that there is a sizable gap between what you say about your ethics and values and what the ethics and values of others should be, and what you actually do in those same situations. We have worked with many who get themselves in trouble by making values and ethics speeches, high-toned, inspiring, lofty, passionate, charismatic, gives you goose bumps—until you watch that person do the opposite or something quite different in practice. Examine all the things you tend to say in speeches or in meetings or casual conversations that are values and ethics statements about you or what you think others should do. Write them down the left side of a legal pad. For each one, see if you can write three to five examples of when you acted exactly in line with that value or ethic. Can you write down any that are not exactly like that? If you can, it's the gap that's the problem. Either stop making values and ethics statements you can't or won't model or bring your stated values into alignment with your own actions.
- ☐ **3. Trouble finding the right words? Send clear messages.** Another, though more rare, possibility is that there is a sizable gap between what you say and the language you use, and what you actually think and do. We have worked with many who get themselves in trouble by using language and words that imply marginal values and ethics that make others uncomfortable that are not real. Do you shoot for effect? "Fire them all." Do you exaggerate? "There are no good vendors." Do you push your statements to the extreme to make a point? Do you overstate negative views? Do you trash talk to fit in? Do you use demeaning words? "All consultants are just mercenaries." What if I have never seen you in action? What would I think your values were if I listened to you talk and didn't know what you actually do? Examine the words and the language you tend to use in speeches or in meetings or casual conversations that are values and ethics based. Write them down the left side of a legal pad. For each one, see if you can write three to five examples of when you acted exactly in line with those words. Do you really act like that? Do you really think that way? If you don't, it's the gap that's the problem. Stop using words and language that are not in line with your real thoughts, values and actions.
- ☐ **4. Unpredictable? Be consistent across situations and groups.** Not everyone has a keel in the values water. You might just be inconsistent in your statements and actions across situations. You change your mind based on mood or who you talked with last or what your last experience was. You may express a pro people value in one instance (people you manage) and an anti people value in another (people from another unit). You may rigidly adhere to a high moral code in one transaction—with customers, and play it close to the acceptable margin in another—with

vendors. You may match your values with your audience when managing up and not when you're managing down. People are more comfortable with consistency and predictability. Do you do one thing with people you like and quite another with people you don't? Look for the three to five areas where you think these inconsistencies play out. Write down what you did with various people so you can compare. Did you do different things in parallel situations? Do you hold others to a different standard? Do you have so many values positions that they have to clash eventually? Try to balance your behavior so that you are more consistent across situations.

- ☐ **5. Misaligned? Check for alignment with the organization.** At the least, a low rating for ethics and values means the values and ethics you are operating under are not in line with the commonly held values and ethics of those around you. That's a common problem. You join an organization thinking it has the values you believe in and after you are there for a while, you find out they are something different. Or the organization makes a big shift in direction, gets acquired, or merges and changes its ethics and values overnight, out of your comfort zone. To some extent, that's life. It's hard to find a perfect match. If the gap is serious, leave. If the gap is just uncomfortable, try to affect it in any way you can by influencing the organization. Try not to challenge others with your discomfort. Maybe you're too independent? You set your own rules, smash through obstacles, see yourself as tough, action and results oriented. You get it done. The problem is you don't often worry about whether others think as you do. You operate from your inside out. What's important to you is what you think and what you judge to be right and just. In a sense, admirable. In a sense, not smart. You live in an organization that has both formal and informal commonly held standards, beliefs, ethics and values. You can't survive long without knowing what they are and bending yours to fit. Try to be a supporter of what you can and just be silent about the rest.
- ☐ **6. Lacking uniform standards? Avoid double standards.** Another common problem is one set of standards for you and a different set of standards for others. Or one set for you and the people you like and another for everyone else. Do you do what you expect others to do? Don't ask anyone to do what you wouldn't do. A common problem with higher level managers is telling the people below them to make tough people calls and fire those who don't meet standards. Then they give everyone reporting to them an above average rating and a bonus even though everyone knows one or two of these people are not up to standard. Do you do anything like this? Do you make close calls in favor of those you like or play favorites?
- ☐ **7. Muddled values? Get clarity about your values.** You may not think much in terms of ethics and values, and your statements may not clearly

represent your true values. Since you are having trouble in this area, it might be a good exercise to try to capture your value system on paper so you know what it is and are able to deliver a clear statement of it to others. Think about your past actions. How do you treat people? Think of the last 25 treatment events or opportunities. What did you do? Was it consistent? If it was, what values and ethics would you have shown to others: 25 honesty and straightforwardness opportunities; 25 opportunities to disclose; 25 opportunities to help others; 25 decisions about allocating resources; 25 spending opportunities; 25 hiring and 25 firing or layoff decisions; 25 delegation decisions, and so on. What are the values that underlie your actions? Are they the ones you want to be known for? Are they like the commonly held ethics and values of the organization you are in?

☐ **8. Stuck in the past? Adapt when it makes sense.** This is a tough one. Times change. Do values change? Some think not. That might be your stance. What about humor? Could you tell some ribald jokes 10 years ago that would get you in trouble today? Have dating practices and ages changed? Using the example of sexual harassment, what is it to you? What's the difference between poor taste, kidding, flirting and sexual harassment? Has the definition changed over your working career? Do you think your old values are better than today's? When did you form your current values? Over 20 years ago? Maybe it's time to examine your personal commandments in light of the new today to see whether you need to make any midcourse corrections. Others may view your stances as simplistic or rigid. List five common areas where values clash for you at work—quality/cost tradeoffs, work with someone or fire, treat different people differently or all the same. Can you describe how you deal with these situations? What are your tie-breakers? What wins out? Why? If you find yourself coming down on the same side in the same way almost every time, you need an update. Talk to people who would go the other way and begin to see more complexity in the issue. Turn off your judgment programming—listen to understand.

☐ **9. Lacking an ethics compass? Take corrective action.** On the more negative side, it could mean you have unacceptable values and ethics; that is, most would reject them. You may operate too close or over the edge for most people to feel comfortable with you. You hedge, sabotage others, play for advantage, set up others and make others look bad. You may be devious and scheming and overly political. You tell yourself it's OK because you're getting results. You really believe the end justifies the means. You tell people what they want to hear and then go off and do something else. If any of this is true, this criticism should be a repeat for you. This is not something that develops overnight. You need to find out if your career with this organization is salvageable. The best way to do this is to admit that you know your ethics and values are not the same as the people you work with and ask a boss or a mentor whether it's fixable. If they say yes, contact everyone you think you've alienated and see how they respond. Tell them the things you're going to do differently. Ask them if the situation can be repaired. Longer term, you need to seek some professional counsel on your values and ethics or find a place that has the same set as you do.

☐ **10. Time to change? Thoughtfully and intentionally adopt values and ethics.** Remember behavior is 10 times more important than words. What values do you want? What do you want your ethics to be? Write them down the left hand side of the page. I want to be known as a fair manager. Then down the right side, what would someone with that value do and not do? Wouldn't play favorites. Would offer everyone opportunities to grow and develop. Would listen to everyone's ideas. Would call for everyone's input in a staff meeting. Would apportion my time so everyone gets a piece of it. Hold everyone to the same standards. Have someone you trust check it over to see if you are on the right track. Then start to consistently do the things you have written on the right hand side.

Some Develop-in-Place Assignments

☐ Make peace with an enemy or someone you've disappointed with a product or service or someone you've had some trouble with or don't get along with very well.

☐ Handle a tough negotiation with an internal or external client or customer.

☐ Manage the assigning/allocating of office space in a contested situation.

☐ Manage a dissatisfied internal or external customer; troubleshoot a performance or quality problem with a product or service.

☐ Be a member of a union-negotiating or grievance-handling team.

Live in such a way that you would not be ashamed
to sell your parrot to the town gossip.

Will Rogers – American cowboy, comedian, social commentator, and actor

Suggested Readings

Badaracco, J. L., Jr. (2002). *Leading quietly*. Boston: Harvard Business School Press.

Badaracco, J. L., Jr. (2002). The discipline of building character. *Harvard Business Review*, 76, 114-124.

Badaracco, J. L., Jr. (2006). *Questions of character: Illuminating the heart of leadership through literature*. Boston: Harvard Business School Press.

Bellingham, R. (2003). *Ethical leadership: Rebuilding trust in corporations*. Amherst, MA: HRD Press.

Bennis, W. G., & Thomas, R. J. (2002). *Geeks and geezers*. Boston: Harvard Business School Press.

Boatright, J. R. (2006). *Ethics and the conduct of business* (5th ed.). Upper Saddle River, NJ: Prentice Hall.

Cloke, K., & Goldsmith, J. (2002). *The end of management and the rise of organizational democracy*. San Francisco: Jossey-Bass.

Dobrin, A. (2002). *Ethics for everyone: How to increase your moral intelligence*. New York: John Wiley & Sons.

Drucker, P. F. (2003). *The essential Drucker: The best of sixty years of Peter Drucker's essential writings on management*. New York: HarperBusiness.

Ferrell, O.C., Fraedrich, J., & Ferrell, L. (2006). *Business ethics: Ethical decision making and cases* (7th ed.). New York: Houghton Mifflin.

Gallagher, R. S. (2003). *The soul of an organization: Understanding the values that drive successful corporate cultures.* Chicago: Dearborn Financial Publishing.

Hartley, R. F. (2005). *Business ethics: Mistakes and successes*. Hoboken, NJ: John Wiley & Sons.

Heineman, B. W., Jr. (2008). *High performance with high integrity*. Boston: Harvard Business School Press.

Jennings, M. (2003). *A business tale: A story of ethics, choices, success and a very large rabbit*. New York: AMACOM.

Johnson, C. E. (2004). *Meeting the ethical challenges of leadership: Casting light or shadow* (2nd ed.). Thousand Oaks, CA: Sage.

Klein, A. (2003). *Stealing time: Steve Case, Jerry Levine, and the collapse of AOL Time Warner*. New York: Simon & Schuster.

McLean, B., & Elkind, P. (2003). *The smartest guys in the room: The amazing rise and scandalous fall of Enron*. New York: Portfolio.

Paine, L. S. (2003). *Value shift*. New York: McGraw-Hill.

Porter, M. E., & Kramer, M. R. (2006). Strategy and society: The link between competitive advantage and corporate social responsibility. *Harvard Business Review, 85*, 136-137.

Ruggiero, V. R. (2003). *Thinking critically about ethical issues.* New York: McGraw-Hill.

Seglin, J. L. (2000). *The good, the bad, and your business: Choosing right when ethical dilemmas pull you apart.* New York: John Wiley & Sons.

Spinello, R., & Tavani, H. T. (Eds.). (2001). *Readings in cyberethics* (2nd ed.). Sudbury, MA: Jones & Bartlett.

Trevino, L. K., & Nelson, K. A. (2006). *Managing business ethics: Straight talk about how to do it right* (4th ed.). Hoboken, NJ: John Wiley & Sons.

23 Fairness to Direct Reports

The way to get things done
is not to mind who gets the credit for doing them.
Benjamin Jowett – English scholar, classicist, and theologian

Unskilled

- ☐ Is not equitable toward direct reports
- ☐ Doesn't listen to direct reports' concerns and needs
- ☐ May not read people's needs well and not be able to tell how they are responding to his/her treatment
- ☐ Hides or keeps things from his/her people they have a right to know
- ☐ May be inconsistent and play favorites
- ☐ May not think about it or be too busy to pay attention to equity
- ☐ May bucket people into good and bad buckets and treat them accordingly

Select one to three of the competencies listed below to use as a substitute for this competency if you decide not to work on it directly.

SUBSTITUTES: 7,10,18,20,21,22,29,35,56,60,64

Skilled

- ☐ Treats direct reports equitably
- ☐ Acts fairly
- ☐ Has candid discussions
- ☐ Doesn't have hidden agenda
- ☐ Doesn't give preferential treatment

Overused Skill

- ☐ May spend too much time pleasing everyone
- ☐ May worry about distributing the work evenly and not using, challenging, or developing the best
- ☐ His/her need to be fair may mask real problems and differences

Select one to three of the competencies listed below to work on to compensate for an overuse of this skill.

COMPENSATORS: 9,12,13,18,19,20,21,25,34,35,36,37,51,52,56,57,64

Some Causes

- ☐ Believe strongly in a meritocracy; rewards to the winners
- ☐ Don't read people well
- ☐ Don't really care about people
- ☐ Inconsistent behavior toward others
- ☐ Play favorites
- ☐ Too busy to treat all equitably

Leadership Architect® Factors and Clusters

This competency is in the Personal and Interpersonal Skills Factor (VI). This competency is in the Managing Diverse Relationships Cluster (P) with: 4, 15, 21, 42, 64. You may want to check other competencies in the same Factor/ Cluster for related tips.

The Map

Fairness seems simple; treat all people the same. Lack of fairness plays out in many ways: Do you treat high performers differently than everyone else? Do you have favorite and less favorite groups? Do you develop some but not others? Do your ethics seem variable to direct reports? Does your candor vary? It's usually best to think of fairness as equity toward others and not signaling to others what your assessment is of them in your day-to-day behavior. A subtler way to think of fairness is to treat each person equitably, that is according to his or her needs. The treatment would actually differ somewhat from person to person but the outcome or effect would be the same; each person would feel fairly treated. A large part of each person's motivation will be determined by his/her feelings about fair treatment. Unfair treatment causes all kinds of noise in the relationship between a boss and a direct report and causes noise in the group. Unfair treatment leads to less productivity, less efficiency and wasted time seeking justice.

Some Remedies

- ☐ **1. Selective when sharing? Provide information equitably.** Follow the rule of equity of information with everyone: Explain your thinking and ask them to explain theirs. When discussing issues, give reasons first, solutions last. When you give solutions first, people often don't listen to your reasons. Some people get overly directive with some of their reports, and they in turn feel that you're not interested in what they think. Invite their thinking and their reasons before settling on solutions. Don't provide information selectively. Don't use information as a reward or a relationship builder with one or just a few and not others.

☐ **2. Selective with treatment? Treat all groups equitably.** Monitor yourself carefully to see if you treat different groups or people differently. Common patterns are to treat low performers, people with less status and people from outside your unit with less respect. Be candid with yourself. Is there a group or individuals you don't like or are uncomfortable with? Have you put them in your not very respected bucket? Many of us do. To break out of this, ask yourself why they behave the way they do and how you would like to be treated if you were in their position. Turn off your judgment program.

☐ **3. Double standards? Be equitable with standards of behavior.** Check to make sure you are not excusing a behavior in a high performer that you wouldn't tolerate in someone else. Does everyone have the same rules and get held to the same standard?

☐ **4. Treating groups differently? Leave behind personal biases.** Check to make sure you are not applying different standards based upon gender, age, nationality, ethnic origin, religion, etc. Do you treat groups more familiar and comfortable to you or like you differently than others? Does one group come in for more praise or criticism than the others? The best way to find out is to ask one or more from each group you work with for feedback. *More help? – See #21 Managing Diversity.*

☐ **5. Are some people not being heard? In meetings, make sure you include everyone.** Don't direct substantially more remarks toward one person or subgroup to the exclusion of others. Make sure you signal nothing negative to others; a neutral observer should not be able to tell from your demeanor who you like and don't like. Help the quiet, shy and reserved have their say. Quiet the loud, assertive and passionate. Give everyone a fair chance to be heard.

☐ **6. Fairness problems hard to nail down? Keep fairness conflicts small and concrete.** The more abstract it gets, the more unmanageable it becomes. Separate the people from the problem. Attack fairness problems by looking at the nature of the problem, not the particular positions people take. Try on their views of "what would have been fair" for size, the emotion as well as the content. Don't guess at their motives and intentions. Avoid direct blaming remarks; describe the problem and its impact. If you can't agree on a solution, agree on procedure; or agree on a few things, and agree that there are issues remaining. This creates some motion and breaks fairness stalemates.

☐ **7. Need a fairness measure? Create standards for fairness.** Install objective standards to determine the fairness of a treatment (pay, office choice, day off)—criteria, statistical models, professional standards, market value, cost models. Set standards anyone could independently measure and come up with the same conclusion.

☐ **8. Losing your cool? Maintain composure.** If you lose your composure with certain people, but not others, a good practice to follow is when your emotions rise to a challenge of your fairness, count to five in your head, then respond with a clarifying question. This serves the triple purpose of giving the person a second chance, allows you to compose yourself, and may prevent you from jumping to an incorrect conclusion and taking precipitous action.

☐ **9. Want to establish a fairness baseline? Involve others in developing fairness norms.** There are as many interpretations of what's fair as there are people in your world. Try to get the whole group involved in questions of fairness. Get everyone's opinion about how fair a particular program or treatment is. Let them tell you what's fair before you make that judgment for them without input. Everyone will feel better treated when they have had a hand in determining the rules.

☐ **10. Is a fairness issue hitting a core value of yours? Exercise restraint when core values are triggered.**

- Edit your actions before you act. Before you speak or act in problem situations, ask yourself if you would do the same thing in a parallel situation. Is your value really what should be operating here?
- Pick your battles. Make sure you only pull rank and impose your values on others in really mission-critical situations.

Some Develop-in-Place Assignments

☐ Manage a project team of people who are older and more experienced than you.

☐ Help shut down a plant, regional office, product line, business, operation, etc.

☐ Manage a group of low-competence or low-performing people through a task they couldn't do by themselves.

☐ Manage a group that includes former peers to accomplish a task.

☐ Represent to higher management the concerns of a group of nonexempt, clerical, or administrative employees to seek resolution of a difficult issue.

These men ask for just the same thing—fairness, and fairness only.
This, so far as in my power, they, and all others, shall have.
Abraham Lincoln – 16th President of the United States

Suggested Readings

Ahlrichs, N. S. (2003). *Manager of choice*. Palo Alto, CA: Davies-Black.

Benko, C., & Weisberg, A. (2007). *Mass career customization: Aligning the workplace with today's nontraditional workforce*. Boston: Harvard Business School Press.

Brockner, J. (2006). Why it's so hard to be fair. *Harvard Business Review, 84*, 122-129.

Finney, M. (2008). *The truth about getting the best from people*. Upper Saddle River, NJ: FT Press.

Genett, D. M. (2004). *If you want it done right, you don't have to do it yourself! The power of effective delegation*. Sanger, CA: Quill/HarperCollins.

Holliday, M. (2001). *Coaching, mentoring, and managing: Breakthrough strategies to solve performance problems and build winning teams*. Franklin Lakes, NJ: Career Press.

Katcher, B., & Snyder, A. (2007). *30 Reasons employees hate their managers: What your people may be thinking and what you can do about it*. New York: AMACOM.

Kim, W. C., & Mauborgne, R. (2003). Fair process: Managing in the knowledge economy. *Harvard Business Review, 81*(1), 127-136.

Lawler, E. E., III. (2008). *Talent: Making people your competitive advantage*. San Francisco: Jossey-Bass.

Manzoni, J. F., & Barsoux, J. L. (2002). *The set-up-to-fail syndrome*. Boston: Harvard Business School Press.

Maslow, A. H. (1998). *Maslow on management*. New York: John Wiley & Sons.

Mayo, A. (2001). *The human value of the enterprise: Valuing people as assets: Monitoring, measuring, managing*. Yarmouth, ME: Nicholas Brealey.

Raelin, J. A. (2003). *Creating leaderful organizations: How to bring out leadership in everyone*. San Francisco: Berrett-Koehler Publishers.

Reck, R. R. (2001). *The X-factor: Getting extraordinary results from ordinary people*. New York: John Wiley & Sons.

Weisinger, H. (2000). *Emotional intelligence at work*. San Francisco: Jossey-Bass.

Weiss, D. H. (2004). *Fair, square and legal: Safe hiring, managing and firing practices to keep you and your company out of court*. New York: AMACOM.

24 Functional/Technical Skills

If you want to be successful, it's just this simple.
Know what you are doing. Love what you are doing.
And believe in what you are doing.
Will Rogers – American cowboy, comedian,
social commentator, and actor

Unskilled

- ☐ Not up to functional or technical proficiency
- ☐ Makes technical/functional errors
- ☐ Judgment and decision making marginal because of lack of knowledge
- ☐ May be stuck in past skills and technologies
- ☐ May be inexperienced, new to the area, or lack interest in it
- ☐ Lack of detail orientation to go deep
- ☐ May not make the time to learn

Select one to three of the competencies listed below to use as a substitute for this competency if you decide not to work on it directly.

SUBSTITUTES: 5,18,20,30,32,33,46,50,61

Skilled

- ☐ Has the functional and technical knowledge and skills to do the job at a high level of accomplishment

Overused Skill

- ☐ May be seen as too narrow
- ☐ May overdevelop or depend upon technical and functional knowledge and skills at the expense of personal, interpersonal and managerial skills
- ☐ May use deep technical knowledge and skills to avoid ambiguity and risk

Select one to three of the competencies listed below to work on to compensate for an overuse of this skill.

COMPENSATORS: 14,28,30,32,45,46,51,57,58

Some Causes

- ☐ Inexperienced; new to the area
- ☐ Lack of detail orientation
- ☐ Lack of interest in the function
- ☐ Time management; haven't gotten around to it
- ☐ Stuck in a past technology

Leadership Architect® Factors and Clusters

This competency is in the Strategic Skills Factor (I). This competency is in the Understanding the Business Cluster (A) with: 5, 61. You may want to check other competencies in the same Factor/Cluster for related tips.

The Map

All areas of work have a single or sometimes a few sets of technologies behind doing them well. Doing the work of the function takes a higher level of technical/functional knowledge than managing it. In most functions or technical areas, there are a number of strong pros who know the technology in great depth. They are the experts. Most others have sufficient knowledge to do their jobs. Some have marginal skills and knowledge in the area and hurt the rest of the group.

Some Remedies

- ☐ **1. Need subject-matter expertise? Locate a pro.** Find the seasoned master professional in the technology or function and ask whether he/she would mind showing you the ropes and tutoring you. Most don't mind having a few "apprentices" around. Help him or her teach you. Ask, "How do you know what's important? What do you look at first? Second? What are the five keys you always look at or for? What do you read? Who do you go to for advice?"
- ☐ **2. Want to network? Sign up.** Almost all functions have national and sometimes regional professional associations made up of hundreds of people who do well what you need to learn every day. Sign up as a member. Buy some of the introductory literature. Go to some of their workshops. Go to the annual conference.
- ☐ **3. Need a good reference? Find the "bible" on your function/technology.** Almost every function and technology has a book people might call the "bible" in the area. It is the standard reference everyone looks to for knowledge. There is probably a journal in your technology or function. Subscribe for a year or more. See if they have back issues available.
- ☐ **4. Want to ask an expert? Meet the notables.** Identify some national leaders in your function/technology and buy their books, read their articles, and attend their lectures and workshops.
- ☐ **5. Ready to learn what matters most? Learn from those around you.** Ask others in your function/technology which skills and what knowledge is mission-critical and ask them how they learned it. Follow the same or a similar path.

☐ **6. Curious? Take a course.** Your local college or university might have some nighttime or weekend courses you could take in your technology. Your organization may have training classes in your technology.

☐ **7. What can be learned from history? Consult your past.** You might have been good in some previous function or technology. If this isn't the case, consider anything you know well such as a hobby. How did you learn it? *More help? – See #32 Learning on the Fly.*

☐ **8. Want to accelerate? Find a guru.** Find a consultant in your technology/function and hire him/her to provide a private tutorial to accelerate your learning.

☐ **9. Ready to organize your thinking? Learn to think as an expert in the technology does.** Take problems to him/her and ask what are the keys he/she looks for; observe what he/she considers significant and not significant. Chunk up data into categories so you can remember it. Devise five key areas or questions you can consider each time a technical issue comes up. Don't waste your time learning facts; they won't be useful unless you have conceptual buckets to put them in.

☐ **10. Want to solidify your learning? Teach others.** Form a study group and take turns presenting on new, different or unknown aspects of the technology. Having to teach it will force you to conceptualize and understand it more deeply. The relationships you form in such groups pay off in other ways as well. One company found its technicians learned more from coffee break conversations than from manuals.

Some Develop-in-Place Assignments

☐ Manage a cost-cutting project.

☐ Audit cost overruns to assess the problem, and present your findings to the person or people involved.

☐ Manage a group of people who are towering experts but you are not.

☐ Manage the purchase of a major product, equipment, materials, program, or system.

☐ Plan a new site for a building (plant, field office, headquarters, etc.).

In modern business it is not the crook who is to be feared most,
it is the honest man who doesn't know what he is doing.
Pablo Casals – Catalan cellist and conductor

Suggested Readings

Argyris, C. (2008). *Teaching smart people how to learn.* Boston: Harvard Business School Press.

Colvin, R. (2008). *Building expertise: Cognitive methods for training and performance improvement.* San Francisco: Pfeiffer.

Committee on Developments in the Science of Learning (with additional material from the Committee on Learning Research and Educational Practice), & National Research Council. (2000). *How people learn: Brain, mind, experience, and school.* Washington, DC: National Academies Press.

Committee on Developments in the Science of Learning, National Research Council, & Donovan, M. S., Bransford, J. D., & Pellegrino, J. W., (Eds.). (2000). *How people learn: Bridging research and practice.* National Academies Press.

Ericsson, K. A., Prietula, M. J., & Cokely, E. T. (2007). The making of an expert. *Harvard Business Review, 85*, 114-121.

Lizotte, K. (2007). *The expert's edge: Become the go-to authority people turn to every time.* New York: McGraw-Hill.

Rossiter, A. P. (2008). *Professional excellence: Beyond technical competence.* New York: John Wiley & Sons.

Waitzkin, J. (2008). *The art of learning: An inner journey to optimal performance.* New York: Free Press.

25 Hiring and Staffing

Hire people who are better than you are,
then leave them to get on with it.
Look for people who will aim for the remarkable,
who will not settle for the routine.
David Ogilvy – British-American advertising executive

Unskilled

- ☐ Doesn't have a good track record in hiring and/or staffing
- ☐ May clone him/herself or focus on one or two preferred characteristics
- ☐ May look narrowly for people who are similar to him/her
- ☐ May play it safe with selections
- ☐ Doesn't select much diversity
- ☐ May not know what competence looks like, lack criteria, or assume he/she just knows
- ☐ May lack the patience to wait for a better candidate

Select one to three of the competencies listed below to use as a substitute for this competency if you decide not to work on it directly.

SUBSTITUTES: 5,17,19,20,21,23,35,39,53,56,60,64

Skilled

- ☐ Has a nose for talent
- ☐ Hires the best people available from inside or outside
- ☐ Is not afraid of selecting strong people
- ☐ Assembles talented staffs

Overused Skill

- ☐ May overlook slow starters
- ☐ May select on surface characteristics
- ☐ May assemble a team of individual performers who aren't good team players
- ☐ May prefer currently talented people who aren't broad enough for further growth
- ☐ May be too quick to replace rather than work with a person

Select one to three of the competencies listed below to work on to compensate for an overuse of this skill.

COMPENSATORS: 21,30,33,41,52,56,60,64

Some Causes

- ☐ Fear of being shown up by a better person
- ☐ Inexperience with hiring people
- ☐ Lack of courage to do something different
- ☐ Lack of personal self-confidence
- ☐ Narrow perspective on what talent looks like
- ☐ Too impatient to wait for a better candidate

Leadership Architect® Factors and Clusters

This competency is in the Courage Factor (III). This competency is in the Making Tough People Calls Cluster (I) with: 56. You may want to check other competencies in the same Factor/Cluster for related tips.

The Map

The world runs on talent. The more talent you have personally and the more talented your team is the better. Talented people make big things happen. Working with and around talent is motivating and energizing. Talented people are competitive, most of the time friendly; sometimes not. Managing talented people is sometimes a challenge, albeit maybe a pleasant one. Lots of good things happen when there is talent around.

Some Remedies

☐ **1. Paying attention to the wrong things? Learn to spot talent.** Look around your environment and see who others think the very talented people are and who are not very talented. Do the talented have any common characteristics? Watch out for traps—it is rarely intelligence or pure personality that spells the difference in talent. Most people are smart enough and many personality characteristics don't matter that much for performance. Ask the second question. Look below surface descriptions of smart, approachable, technically skilled.

☐ **2. Difficulty identifying what you are looking for? Sharpen your interviewing skills.** There are commonly agreed upon methods to find talent in an interview. A couple of keys: Look for evidence of rapid learning, excitement about the kinds of tasks that are critical in the role, and a penchant for going into new situations. See the *Interview Architect®* or ask someone in the recruiting and staffing area in your organization for guidance on how to conduct a good interview. Research indicates that structured interviewing and biodata inventories are the best selection methods.

☐ **3. Can't tell okay from great? Identify talent differentiators.** Think back over your career. Make two lists—one, of the most talented people you have worked with, and the other of those who were so-so; although they may have had reasonable talents, they didn't really deliver. Do the people on each list have common characteristics? Why did you say one was talented and the other less so? What's the major difference between the two lists?

☐ **4. Trouble identifying good versus bad bosses? Conduct a boss audit.** List all of the bosses you have had. Divide them into the 33% most talented and the 33% least talented. Do the bosses on the most talented list have common characteristics. Why did you say one list was talented and the other not? What's the major difference between the two lists of bosses? Which list would you like to work for again?

☐ **5. Not sure what's important? Pinpoint organizational keys to success.** Ask your Human Resource person to share with you the success profile of successful and talented people in your organization.

☐ **6. Hiring people like yourself? Seek complementary talents.** When you make a hiring decision or are deciding who to work with on a problem or project, do you think you have a tendency to clone yourself too much? Do you have a preference for people who think and act as you do? What characteristics do you value too much? What downsides do you ignore or excuse away? This is a common human tendency. The key is to seek balance, variety and diversity. Shore up your weaknesses when hiring others. People good at this competency can comfortably surround themselves with people not like them.

☐ **7. Are your standards too high or too low? Identify and set reasonable standards.** Do you hire the first close candidate that comes along or do you wait for the perfect candidate and leave the position open too long? Either tendency will probably get you and the organization in trouble. Always try to wait long enough to have choices but not long enough to lose a very good candidate while you wait for the perfect one to come along. Learn how to set reasonable standards with the *Interview Architect®*.

☐ **8. Don't understand the role of talent? View talent strategically.** Do you have a long-term view of the talent it's going to take to produce both current and long-term results? Do you have a replacement plan for yourself? Do you use a success profile with the competencies you know you are going to need? Have you hired someone who now has or will have in a short period of time, the ability to take your job? Have you selected someone you would sponsor for promotion to another job at your level, possibly passing you up in time? The best managers surround themselves with talent and eventually some of the talent turns out to be better than the person who hired and trained them. That's a good thing and reason for a celebration.

☐ **9. Difficulty telling people apart? Become a student of people.** Read two or three books on personality or on how people differ from one another (such as *Gifts Differing* by Isabel Myers) or go to a class about how people differ. Check your people assessments with others you trust to give you their real opinion.

☐ **10. Hiring B players? Surround yourself with talent.** Some people feel insecure around talented people and are rightly afraid of being shown up. That's true. You will be, because no one has all possible strengths. Chances are everyone in your unit is better at something than you are. The key is to take this natural fear and use it as a positive—hire people for different talents, study how they think, watch how they go about exercising their strengths and use this knowledge to improve yourself.

☐ **11. Overlooking red flags? Think about outsourcing background checks.** You may need people expert in criminal investigation and how employers are protected from liability. They can often persuade a reluctant former employer to give out legally acceptable information. For example, they can explain that most states shield employers from liability when giving good-faith references. And the truth, of course, is always an absolute defense. When screening yourself, with all the online job services, you need to cull—use phone screening, ask prospects to supply a work sample on a task, use your Web site for assessment of prospects.

☐ **12. High turnover? Implement onboarding best practices.** Half or more of new employees quit within the first seven months. Critical steps are to welcome them, communicate how their job is important, and think through all the things veterans take for granted that mystify newcomers. How do they find out about this? What are the work expectations that aren't written down anywhere? The major reasons people quit are they feel isolated socially, left out of the stream of information, or stuck in depressing working conditions.

☐ **13. Revolving door of talent? Try working with whom you have.** Before firing and hiring, are you sure the problem isn't fixable with current staff? Perhaps the person is bored or needs a skills update. Retraining is generally cheaper and less disruptive, especially for lower-level jobs. *More help? – See #19, Developing Direct Reports and Others.*

Some Develop-in-Place Assignments

- ☐ Manage the outplacement of a group of people.
- ☐ Work on a team that's deciding whom to keep and whom to let go in a layoff, shutdown, delayering, or merger.
- ☐ Hire/staff a team from outside your unit or organization.
- ☐ Train and work as an assessor in an assessment center.
- ☐ Go to a campus as a recruiter.

I am convinced that nothing we do is more important
than hiring and developing people.
At the end of the day you bet on people,
not on strategies.
Larry Bossidy – American author and former CEO of Allied Signal

Suggested Readings

Adler, L. (2007). *Hire with your head: Using performance-based hiring to build great teams.* Hoboken, NJ: John Wiley & Sons.

Ashby, F. C., & Pell, A. R. (2001). *Embracing excellence.* New York: Prentice Hall.

Calvin, R. J. (2001). *Entrepreneurial management.* New York: McGraw-Hill.

Cooper, D., Robertson, I. T., & Tinline, G. (2003). *Recruitment and selection: A framework for success.* London: Thomson Learning.

Davila, L., & King, M. (2007). *Perfect phrases for perfect hiring: Hundreds of ready-to-use phrases for interviewing and hiring the best employees every time.* New York: McGraw-Hill.

Falcone, P. (2002). *The hiring and firing question and answer book.* New York: AMACOM.

Fields, M. R. A. (2001). *Indispensable employees: How to hire them, how to keep them.* Franklin Lakes, NJ: Career Press.

Hallenbeck, G. S., Jr., & Eichinger, R. W. (2006). *Interviewing right: How science can sharpen your interviewing accuracy.* Minneapolis, MN: Lominger International: A Korn/Ferry Company.

Harvard Business School Press. (2003). *Hiring and keeping the best people.* Boston: Harvard Business School Press.

Heneman, H. G., III, & Judge, T. A. (2008). *Staffing organizations* (6th ed.). New York: McGraw-Hill.

Levin, R. A., & Rosse, J. G. (2001). *Talent flow: A strategic approach to keeping good employees, helping them grow, and letting them go.* New York: John Wiley & Sons.

Menkes, J. (2005). Hiring for smarts. *Harvard Business Review 83*, 100-109.

Michaels, E., Handfield-Jones, H., & Axelrod, B. (2001). *The war for talent.* Boston: Harvard Business School Press.

Poundstone, W. (2003). *How would you move Mount Fuji? Microsoft's cult of the puzzle: How the world's smartest company selects the most creative thinkers.* Boston: Little, Brown and Co.

Sears, D. (2003). *Successful talent strategies: Achieving superior business results through market-focused staffing.* New York: AMACOM.

Smart, B. D. (2005). *Topgrading: How leading companies win: Hiring, coaching and keeping the best people* (Rev. ed.). New York: Prentice Hall.

Still, D. J. (2001). *High impact hiring: How to interview and select outstanding employees.* Dana Point, CA: Management Development Systems..

26 Humor

Laughter is the shortest distance between two people.
Victor Borge – Danish humorist and musician

Unskilled

- ☐ Appears humorless
- ☐ Doesn't know how or doesn't want to use humor in the workplace
- ☐ May have problems telling a joke
- ☐ May chill humor in others
- ☐ Thinks humor is out of place in the workplace
- ☐ May be too serious and want to avoid looking or sounding silly
- ☐ May lack a light touch
- ☐ May use sarcastic or politically offensive humor
- ☐ May use humor in the wrong time or wrong place or in the wrong way

Select one to three of the competencies listed below to use as a substitute for this competency if you decide not to work on it directly.

SUBSTITUTES: 3,14,31,44,49

Skilled

- ☐ Has a positive and constructive sense of humor
- ☐ Can laugh at him/herself and with others
- ☐ Is appropriately funny and can use humor to ease tension

Overused Skill

- ☐ May disrupt group process with untimely or inappropriate humor
- ☐ May use humor to deflect real issues and problems
- ☐ May use humor to criticize others and veil an attack
- ☐ May use humor to deliver sarcasm or cynicism
- ☐ May be perceived as immature or lacking in appropriate seriousness
- ☐ His/her humor may be misinterpreted

Select one to three of the competencies listed below to work on to compensate for an overuse of this skill.

COMPENSATORS: 7,10,11,22,31,33,41,43,48,52,55

Some Causes

- ☐ Can't tell a joke
- ☐ Don't think you're funny
- ☐ Think humor is out of place in business
- ☐ Avoid looking/sounding silly
- ☐ Too serious
- ☐ Avoid risk

Leadership Architect® Factors and Clusters

This competency is in the Personal and Interpersonal Skills Factor (VI). This competency is in the Being Open and Receptive Cluster (S) with: 11, 33, 41, 44. You may want to check other competencies in the same Factor/Cluster for related tips.

The Map

There's good humor and negative humor. There's constructive humor and destructive humor. There are humorous people. There are humorous stories that are funny regardless of who tells them. There are humorous situations that are funny regardless of who brings them to our attention. There are pictures and cartoons that are funny regardless of who shows them. Humor is an essential element to life and work. Properly used and delivered, it can be a constructive influence on those around you. It can increase a feeling of well-being and belonging, it can take the bite out of tension, and it can balance a negative situation for someone or the whole team.

Some Remedies

☐ **1. Need comic relief? Find humor in everyday life.** There are topics that can be near universally humorous. There are universal traits. Misers, bad drivers, absent-minded people, anything that is understood worldwide as the human condition. There are things that are funny about your life. Have funny kids, pets, hobbies? What's a ridiculous situation you've been caught in lately? There are funny things in the workplace. The jargon of it, memos, ironic rules. Stories from the picnic or the off-site. There is providing relief from our problems. The weather, taxes, any of life's little indignities and embarrassments. And there is always the news. Most programs have at least one humorous tale, and sometimes the news is funny enough as it is. There are cartoons that most find humorous in the work setting. There are funny jokes that most find funny. Humor that unites people rather than puts down people or groups is always safe. Begin to look for and remember the humor around you. Begin to pass on your observation to a few safe people to test your humor judgment.

- ☐ **2. Humor seen as offensive? Keep it in good taste.** Today, we live in a very politically sensitive world. Many people are turned off by political, sexist or ethnic humor. Humor that's out is anything ribald, sexist, religious or ethnic. Most gender and race humor is unacceptable. Humor that makes fun of entire groups (women) or cultures (Polish jokes) doesn't play well. Any humor about a handicap is out. Basically any humor that makes fun of others, makes others feel bad or diminished, or is at the expense of others is out.
- ☐ **3. Want respect? Laugh at yourself.** Self-humor is usually safe, seen as positive by others, and most of the time leads to increased respect. Funny and embarrassing things that happened to you (when the airline lost your luggage and you had to wash your underwear in an airport restroom and dry it under the hand dryer). Your flaws and foibles (when you were so stressed over your taxes that you locked the keys in your car with the motor running). Mistakes you've made. Blunders you've committed. Besides adding humor to the situation, it humanizes you and endears people to you. Anything can of course be overdone, so balance it with seriousness.
- ☐ **4. Sarcastic? Refrain from using humor to veil criticism.** Some people use humor to deliver negative messages. They are sarcastic and barbed in their humor. In a tense confrontation with an employee, to say, "I hope your resume is up-to-date," instead of saying, "Your performance is not what I expected. It has to improve or I will have to reconsider your continued employment," is not acceptable. There is a very simple rule. Do not use humor to deliver a critical point to a person or a group. Negative humor hurts more than direct statements and is basically chicken on your part. Say directly what you mean.
- ☐ **5. Feeling defensive? Don't use humor as a shield.** Some make light of things that make them uncomfortable. It's a very human defense technique. There is a difference between using unrelated humor for tension relief, which can be a good practice, and using direct humor to make light of the person or the issue. Better to say, "I'm uncomfortable with that" than to say through humor that it's less important than you're making it. This can also be seen as a subject change, in effect deflecting the topic.
- ☐ **6. Humor falling flat? Choose the right time for humor.** There is a time for everything and sometimes humor is not appropriate. Since you are reading this because you or others don't think you are good at using humor, the best technique is to follow the lead of others. Be second or third to be humorous in a setting until you find your funny legs. *More help? – See #48 Political Savvy.*
- ☐ **7. Need an expert opinion? Study the pros.** Read *How to Be Funny* by Jon Macks and *Laughing Matters* by Joel Goodman, Saratoga Springs, NY:

The HUMOR Project at Sagamore Institute, 1982. Go to three comedy performances at a local comedy club to study how the professionals do it. Study funny people in your organization. What do they do that you don't? Buy all the *Dilbert* and *Far Side* books. Cut out 10 from each that really are funny to you. Use them in your presentations and hang them in your office and see how others react.

☐ **8. Need help with your technique? Learn the basics.** There are some basic humor tactics. Use exaggeration, like when Bill Cosby exited the doctor's office in his new trifocals and began an odyssey through a mile-long elevator and across a newly terrifying street. Use reversal, where you turn the situation into its opposite—the paranoid who thinks the world's out to do her good; or the speaker who turned eight ways to help people succeed in their careers into eight ways to ruin the careers of your enemies. Physical or pratfall humor works, such as when your hand hits the microphone and lets out a loud boom and you say, "Sorry, Mike." Be brief. Cut out unnecessary words. Humor condenses the essential elements of a situation, just as good writing does. If the time of day or the color of the sky or city it happened in is not relevant, leave it out. Include touches, however, to set a mood. If heat is essential to the humor, let the listener see sweat pouring off people, flowers wilting, whatever it takes to set the stage. Be on the lookout for the ridiculous around you. Jot down funny things that happen around you so you can remember them.

☐ **9. Ready to humble yourself? Lose some inhibitions.** Play silly games (draw a picture with your eyes shut, play any of a number of board games devoted to laughter such as Pictionary®). Play with small children and let them take the lead. Be willing to make a fool of yourself at off-sites, picnics and parties. Volunteer to dress in the clown costume and have employees throw water balloons at you. Learn and demonstrate the latest dance craze at the company picnic!

☐ **10. Can't share the stage? Let others be humorous.** Sometimes people who aren't very humorous (or are very serious) chill and suppress humor in others. Even if you're not going to work on being more humorous or funny, at least let others be. That will actually help you be seen as at least more tolerant of humor than you were in the past. Eventually, you may even be tempted to join in.

Some Develop-in-Place Assignments

- ☐ Try to learn something frivolous and fun to see how good you can get (e.g., juggling, square dancing, magic).
- ☐ Study humor in business settings; read books on the nature of humor; collect cartoons you could use in presentations; study funny people around you; keep a log of funny jokes and sayings you hear; read famous speeches and study how humor was used; attend comedy clubs; ask a funny person to act as your tutor; practice funny lines and jokes with others.

A well-developed sense of humor is the pole that adds balance to your steps as you walk the tightrope of life.
William A. Ward – American author, editor, pastor, and teacher

Suggested Readings

Adams, S. (2002). *Dilbert and the way of the weasel.* New York: HarperBusiness.

Bing, S. (2002). *What would Machiavelli do? The ends justify the meanness.* New York: HarperBusiness.

DeGeneres, E. (2003). *The funny thing is...* New York: Simon & Schuster.

Drennan, M., & Anderson, J. (2002). *Soar above the madness: Surviving office politics without losing your mind, your job, or your lunch.* New York: Rutledge Hill Press.

Gostick, A., & Christopher, S. (2008). *The levity effect: Why it pays to lighten up.* Hoboken, NJ: John Wiley & Sons.

Hemsath, D., & Yerkes, L. (2001). *301 Ways to have fun at work.* San Francisco: Berrett-Koehler Publishers.

Kerr, M. (2001). *You can't be serious! Putting humor to work.* Canmore, AB: Speaking of Ideas.

Macks, J. (2003). *How to be funny.* New York: Simon & Schuster.

Marlatt, A. (2002). *Economy of errors: SatireWire gives business the business.* New York: Broadway Books.

O'Rourke, P. J. (2002). *The CEO of the sofa.* New York: Grove Press.

Rizzo, S. (2005). *Becoming a humor being: The power to choose a better way.* New Delhi: Full Circle Publishing.

Schwab, P. (2005). *Leave a mark, not a stain! What every manager needs to know about using humor in the workplace.* Seattle, WA: Rollingwood Press.

Tamblyn, D. (2002). *Laugh and learn: 95 Ways to use humor for more effective teaching and training.* New York: AMACOM.

Willis, E. E., & Weaver, R. L. (2005). *How to be funny on purpose.* Toronto, ON: Cybercom.

27 Informing

The mind revels in conjecture.
Where information is lacking, it will gladly fill in the gaps.
James Geary – American author and
former editor of *Time* magazine Europe

Unskilled

- ☐ Not a consistent communicator
- ☐ Tells too little or too much
- ☐ Tells too late; timing is off
- ☐ May be unclear, may inform some better than others
- ☐ May not think through who needs to know by when
- ☐ Doesn't seek or listen to the data needs of others
- ☐ May inform but lack follow-through
- ☐ May either hoard information or not see informing as important
- ☐ May only have one mode—written or oral or e-mail

Select one to three of the competencies listed below to use as a substitute for this competency if you decide not to work on it directly.

SUBSTITUTES: 1,3,13,18,20,31,33,34,35,44,60

Skilled

- ☐ Provides the information people need to know to do their jobs and to feel good about being a member of the team, unit, and/or the organization
- ☐ Provides individuals information so that they can make accurate decisions
- ☐ Is timely with information

Overused Skill

- ☐ May provide too much information
- ☐ May upset people by giving them information they can't handle or preliminary information that turns out not to be true

Select one to three of the competencies listed below to work on to compensate for an overuse of this skill.

COMPENSATORS: 2,8,11,12,22,29,33,38,41,47,48,50,52,64

Some Causes

- ☐ Don't think it's needed
- ☐ Inform some better than others
- ☐ Little informing
- ☐ Sporadic informing
- ☐ Too busy
- ☐ Too late in informing
- ☐ Unclear informing
- ☐ Use the wrong informing method

Leadership Architect® Factors and Clusters

This competency is in the Operating Skills Factor (II). This competency is in the Getting Work Done Through Others Cluster (F) with: 18, 19, 20, 35. You may want to check other competencies in the same Factor/Cluster for related tips.

The Map

Although it seems a simple skill, *Informing* ranks 52nd out of 67 (low) competencies in terms of skill proficiency in our research on the Leadership Architect®. Informing also has a very high return on investment. Things go better. People are more motivated. Are you too busy? A minimal communicator? Only inform to meet your needs? You don't package information or think through who needs to know what by when? This can lead to some bad consequences for others and you. Maybe that's why they rate Informing as 21st of 67 (high) in importance! It's a simple and important skill that many do not do well or enough of.

Some Remedies

☐ **1. Are you open? Share your thinking.** Do you think if they were any good they would figure it out themselves? You didn't need much information when you were in their jobs. To help those around you grow and learn from what you know, you have to sometimes think out loud. You have to share your thinking from the initial presentation of the issue through to conclusion. Most of us are on thinking autopilot. We don't think about thinking. When someone else has to or wants to understand how you came up with a decision, it's sometimes difficult to unravel it in your mind. You have to go step-by-step and recreate your thinking. Sometimes it helps if other people ask the questions. They can probably guide you through how you came up with an answer or a decision better than you can. Once in a while, you should document a decision or two. What was the issue? What were the pros and cons you considered? How did you weight things? Then you can use those examples to demonstrate to others how you make decisions. *More help? – See #17 Decision Quality.*

☐ **2. Don't inform enough? Paint a big picture.** Are you a minimalist? Do you tell people only what they need to know to do their little piece of the puzzle? People are motivated by being aware of the bigger picture. They want to know what to do in order to do their jobs and more. How does what they are doing fit into the larger picture? What are the other people working on and why? Many people think that's unnecessary information and that it would take too much time to do. They're wrong. The sense of doing something worthwhile is the number two motivator at work! It results in a high return on motivation and productivity. (Try to increase the amount of more-than-your-job information you share.) Focus on the impact on others by figuring out who information affects. Put five minutes on your meeting agenda. Ask people what they want to know and assuming it's not confidential information, tell them. Pick a topic each month to tell your people about.

☐ **3. Do you work alone? Freely share information.** Do you keep to yourself? Work alone or try to? Do you hold back information? Do you parcel out information on your schedule? Do you share information to get an advantage or to win favor? Do people around you know what you're doing and why? Are you aware of things others would benefit from but you don't take the time to communicate? In most organizations, these things and things like it will get you in trouble. Organizations function on the flow of information. Being on your own and preferring peace and privacy are OK as long as you communicate things to bosses, peers and teammates that they need to know and would feel better if they knew. Don't be the source of surprises.

☐ **4. Lacking the basics? Focus on fundamental communication principles.** Some people just aren't good at informing. Their communication styles are not effective. The most effective communicators, according to behavioral research studies: Speak often, but briefly (15-30 seconds); ask more questions than others; make fewer solution statements early in a discussion; headline their points in a sentence or two; summarize frequently, and make more frequent "here's where we are" statements; invite everyone to share their views; typically interject their views after others have had a chance to speak, unless they are passing on decisions. Compare these practices to yours. Work on those that are not up to standard.

☐ **5. Inconsistent informer? Get organized and be consistent.** Have an information checklist detailing what information should go to whom; pass on summaries or copies of important communications. Determine the information checklist by: keeping tabs on unpleasant surprises people report to you; ask direct reports what they'd like to know to do their jobs better; and check with boss, peers and customers to see if you pass along too little, enough, or too much of the right kinds of information. It's important to know what to pass, to whom to pass, and when to pass, to become an effective informer.

- ☐ **6. Need to get to the next level? Polish your technique.** Eliminate disruptive habits such as using the same words too often, hesitating, having frequent filler words like "you know" and "uh," speaking too rapidly or forcefully, using strongly judgmental words, or going into too much detail that leaves listeners bored or wondering what the point is. Are you a complexifier? Simplify and emphasize. Vary the volume and length of time spoken to emphasize key points and maintain the interest of others. Outline complex arguments/processes on paper or overheads or charts to make them easy to follow. Use visual aids. Use common action words, simple examples or visual catch phrases to cement information transfer. *More help? – See #49 Presentation Skills and #67 Written Communications.*

- ☐ **7. Selective informer? Inform up, down, and sideways.** The most common selective pattern is informing up and out but not down or sideways. When these people get their 360° feedback reports, there is a discrepancy among groups on informing. Some groups rate it high and others lower. That means there is not a skills block. You can inform. There is an attitude filter. I will inform some but not others. Why? What do you gain with one group that you lose with another? Is it personal? Are you gaining by sharing? At the expense of others? Why are you avoiding one group? Do you fear debate?
- ☐ **8. Time to blow the whistle? Inform thoughtfully and courageously.** A tough call. Do you know something others should but when they find out, there will be noise and trouble? Saying what needs to be said to the right person in a timely way takes courage. Everybody sees things, observes things, knows things or learns about things that others should know. Many times it's not positive information. Something is about to go wrong. Something is being covered up. Someone is holding back an important piece of information. Someone or something is going off in the wrong direction. It's good news and bad news. If you inform, the organization may gain. But a person or some people may lose. Generally, your best bet is to find the right person and inform. *More help? – See #34 Managerial Courage.*
- ☐ **9. Ready for the fallout? Deal with the heat.** Informing is not always benign and friendly. It many times generates heat. Defensiveness. Blame. Attacks. Threats. Many times they want to shoot the messenger. Separate

the passion from the message. Avoid direct blaming remarks. Deal with people issues directly but separately and maybe off line. If attacked for delivering bad news, you can always say nothing or ask a clarifying question. People will usually respond by saying more, coming off their position a bit, or at least revealing their interests. *More help? – See #12 Conflict Management.*

- ☐ **10. Too rigid in style? Adapt to your audience.** Unfortunately, one method or style of informing does not play equally well across audiences. Many times you will have to adjust the tone, pace, style and even the message and how you couch it for different audiences. If you are delivering the same message to multiple people or audiences, always ask yourself how are they different? Some differences among people or audiences include level of sophistication, friendly vs. unfriendly, time sensitivity, whether they prefer it in writing or not and whether a logical or emotional argument will play better. Write or tell? Writing is usually best for the extremes—complex descriptions complete with background and five or six progressive arguments, or on the other side, straightforward, unambiguous things people need to know. You should generally tell when it requires discussion or you are alerting them to a problem. Make a read on each person and each audience and adjust accordingly. *More help? – See #15 Customer Focus and #45 Personal Learning.*
- ☐ **11. Going overboard? Avoid bombarding.** Over informing can sometimes be worse than not informing enough. One study showed the average employee gets 2.3 million words over three months. Distinguish need-to-know from nice-to-know. Think twice before hitting cc:. Bombarded by overstimulation, the brain stops processing information to prevent psychological burnout. In that respect, too much is worse than too little.

Some Develop-in-Place Assignments

- ☐ Be a change agent; create a symbol for change; lead the rallying cry; champion a significant change and implementation.
- ☐ Write a proposal for a new policy, process, mission, charter, product, service, or system, and present and sell it to top management.
- ☐ Integrate diverse systems, processes, or procedures across decentralized and/or dispersed units.
- ☐ Manage something "remote," away from your location.
- ☐ Establish security procedures for a building or floor.

There must be a happy medium somewhere
between being totally informed and blissfully unaware.
Doug Larson – English middle-distance runner
and Gold Medal winner, 1924 Olympics

Suggested Readings

Allee, V. (2002). *The future of knowledge: Increasing prosperity through value networks.* Boston: Butterworth-Heinemann.

Baldoni, J. (2003). *Great communication secrets of great leaders.* New York: McGraw-Hill.

Bough, B., & Condrill, J. (2005). *101 Ways to improve your communication skills instantly.* San Antonio, TX: GoalMinds, Inc.

Bruck, B. (2003). *Taming the information tsunami.* Redmond, WA: Microsoft Press.

Davis and Company Staff, & Davis, A. (Ed.) (2005). *21 Strategies for improving employee communication.* Glen Rock, NJ: Davis & Company, Inc.

Holtz, S. (2004). *Corporate conversations: A guide to crafting effective and appropriate internal communications.* New York: AMACOM.

Keyton, J. (2002). *Communicating in groups: Building relationships for effective decision making.* New York: McGraw-Hill Higher Education.

Langford-Wood, N., & Salter, B. (2002). *Critical corporate communications: A best practice blueprint.* West Sussex, England: John Wiley & Sons, Ltd.

Matha, B., Boehm, M., & Silverman, M. (2008). *Beyond the babble: Leadership communication that drives results.* San Francisco: Jossey-Bass.

Patriotta, G. (2004). *Organizational knowledge in the making: How firms create, use, and institutionalize knowledge.* Oxford, UK: Oxford University Press.

Perlow, L. (2003). *When you say yes but mean no: How silencing conflict wrecks relationships and companies...and what you can do about it.* New York: Crown Business.

Probst, G. J. B., Raub, S., & Romhardt, K. (2000). *Managing knowledge: Building blocks for success.* New York: John Wiley & Sons.

Runion, M. (2004). *Perfect phrases for managers and supervisors: Hundreds of ready-to-use phrases for any management situation.* New York: McGraw-Hill.

Smith, L., & Mounter, P. (2008). *Effective international communication.* London: Kogan Page Limited.

Thatchenkery, T. (2004). *Appreciative sharing of knowledge: Leveraging knowledge management for strategic change.* Chagrin Falls, OH: Taos Institute.

Weeks, H. (2008). *Failure to communicate: How conversations go wrong and what you can do to right them.* Boston: Harvard Business School Press.

28 Innovation Management

Innovation distinguishes between a leader and a follower.
Steve Jobs – American entrepreneur
and cofounder of Apple and Pixar

Unskilled

- ☐ Not a good judge of what's creative
- ☐ Doesn't understand the marketplace for innovation
- ☐ Can't select from among creative ideas which one would work the best
- ☐ Doesn't innovate
- ☐ May not be open to the creative suggestions of others
- ☐ May be stuck in his/her comfort zone of tasks and methods of doing them
- ☐ May not understand creativity or the process of innovation
- ☐ May close too soon with solutions and conclusions
- ☐ May be a perfectionist avoiding risk and fearing failures and mistakes
- ☐ May not use experiments to learn and improve, and may block the innovations of others

Select one to three of the competencies listed below to use as a substitute for this competency if you decide not to work on it directly.

SUBSTITUTES: 2,5,12,14,16,24,30,32,34,37,38,46,48,51,53,57,58,61,63,65

Skilled

- ☐ Is good at bringing the creative ideas of others to market
- ☐ Has good judgment about which creative ideas and suggestions will work
- ☐ Has a sense about managing the creative process of others
- ☐ Can facilitate effective brainstorming
- ☐ Can project how potential ideas may play out in the marketplace

Overused Skill

- ☐ May err toward the new and reject the old
- ☐ May prefer creative people and undervalue those less creative
- ☐ May get too far out in front of others in thinking and planning

Select one to three of the competencies listed below to work on to compensate for an overuse of this skill.

COMPENSATORS: 16,17,24,27,33,47,50,52,53,59,61,64

Some Causes

- ☐ Don't understand the market
- ☐ Don't understand creativity
- ☐ Fear mistakes
- ☐ Get it right the first time
- ☐ Perfectionist
- ☐ Too comfortable

Leadership Architect® Factors and Clusters

This competency is in the Strategic Skills Factor (I). This competency is in the Creating the New and Different Cluster (C) with: 2, 14, 46, 58. You may want to check other competencies in the same Factor/Cluster for related tips.

The Map

Innovation involves three skills. The first is a total understanding of the marketplace for your products and services. That's knowing what sells and why. What more do your customers want? What features would be most attractive to them? And what do your non-customers want that they don't find in your products? The second is being able to select from among many possible creative ideas for new products and services, those which would have the highest likelihood of success in the marketplace. The third skill is taking the raw idea and managing its transition into a successful product in the marketplace.

Some Remedies

☐ **1. Have enough customer knowledge? Understand your markets.** Understand them historically, today, and most importantly tomorrow. What have your customers done in the past? Which new products succeeded and which failed? What do they buy today? Among your current customers, what more do they want and are willing to pay for? For those who did not buy your product or service, what was missing? What do your competitors have that you don't? What are the known future trends that will affect you? Aging of the population? Eating out? Electric cars? Green movement? What are some of the wilder possibilities? Fusion? Space travel? Subscribe to *THE FUTURIST* Magazine put out by the World Future Society. Talk to the strategic planners in your organization for their long-term forecasts. Talk to your key customers. What do they think their needs will be? *More help? – See #15 Customer Focus and #46 Perspective.*

☐ **2. Want to foster creativity? Manage the creative process.** You need raw creative ideas to be able to manage innovation. While you may not and don't need to be the source for the creative ideas, you need to understand the process. Creative thought processes do not follow the formal rules of logic where one uses cause and effect to prove or solve something. The rules of creative thought lie not in using existing concepts but in changing them—moving from one concept or way of looking at things to another. It involves challenging the status quo and generating ideas without judging them initially. Jumping from one idea to another without justifying the jump. Looking for the least likely and the odd. The creative process requires freedom and openness and a non-judgmental environment. The creative process can't be timed. Setting a goal and a time schedule to be creative will most likely chill creativity. *More help? – See #14 Creativity.*

☐ **3. Issues with creative types? Manage creative people differently.** Creative people have special gifts but special problems come along with the gifts. Many times you have to buffer and protect creative people from the normal processes and procedures of the organization. Creative people need rumination time undisturbed by the process expectations of others. They need to carve out some portion of their time to study problems deeply, talk with others, look for parallels in other organizations and in remote areas totally outside the field. Naturally creative people are much more likely to think in opposite cases when confronted with a problem. They turn problems upside down. They think differently. They ask what is the least likely thing it could be, what the problem is not, what's missing from the problem, or what the mirror image of the problem is. Creative people can be playful. Playfulness is highly related to coming up with new ideas. Anything goes. Most creative people are not detail oriented, get their expense reports in late and ignore deadlines they consider trivial compared with what they are doing. If you manage creative people, you have to give them room.

☐ **4. Can't brainstorm ideas on your own? Get creativity out of a group.** Many times the creative idea comes from a group, not single individuals. When working on a new idea for a product or service, have them come up with as many questions about it as you can. Often we think too quickly of solutions. In studies of problem-solving sessions, solutions outweigh questions eight to one. Asking more questions helps people rethink the problem and come to more and different solutions. Have the group take a current product you are dissatisfied with and represent it visually—a flow chart or a series of pictures. Cut it up into its component pieces and shuffle them. Examine the pieces to see if a different order would help, or how you could combine three pieces into one. Try many experiments or trials to find something that will work. Have the group think beyond current boundaries. What are some of the most sacred rules or practices in your organization? Unit? Think about smashing them—what would your unit be doing if you broke the rules? Talk to the most irreverent person you know about this. Buffer the group. It's difficult to work on something new if they are besieged with all the distractions you have to deal with, particularly if people are looking over your shoulder asking why isn't anything happening.

- ☐ **5. Reaching too far? Extend existing ideas into something new.** Very few innovations are pure breakthroughs. They are variations on a theme, borrowed ideas from other fields, or putting old ideas together in new ways. Knowledge and free flow of ideas increase the chance of novel connection, as when a Pizza Hut manager solved a time-to-bake problem by considering how to transfer heat using a child's Erector set as heat transfer probes. Many innovations are mistakes. Post-it® Notes was a glue experiment that failed. Creative ideas may be closer at hand than you think. Before you try for the grand idea, extend everything you now do 24 inches to see what you get.
- ☐ **6. Ready to decide? Select the idea.** Creativity relies on freedom early, but structure later. Once the unit comes up with its best notion of what to do, subject it to all the logical tests and criticism any other alternative is treated to. Testing out creative ideas is no different than any other problem-solving/evaluation process. The difference is in how the ideas originate.
- ☐ **7. No tolerance for mistakes? Develop a philosophical stance toward failure/criticism.** After all, most innovations fail, most new products fail, most change efforts fail, anything worth doing takes repeated effort, anything could always have been done better. To increase learning, build in immediate feedback loops. Look for something that is common to each failure and that is never present when there is a success. There will be many mistakes and failures in innovation; after all, no one knows what to do. The best tack is to ask what can we learn from this? What caused it? What do we need to do differently? Don't expect to get it right the first time. This leads to safe, less-than-innovative solutions. Many problem-solving studies show that the second or third try is when we come up with the best solution.
- ☐ **8. No traction for good ideas? Learn how to move ideas through the organization.** Once an idea has been selected, you need to manage it through to the marketplace. Designing processes to get the job done most efficiently and effectively is a known science. Look to the principles of TQM, ISO and Six Sigma. *More help? – See #63 Total Work Systems (e.g., TQM/ISO/Six Sigma).* Read a book on each. Go to a workshop. Ask for help from the Organizational Effectiveness group in your organization or hire a consultant. Have the team work with you to design the best way to proceed. Teams work better when they have a say in how things will be done.

☐ **9. Derailed by politics? Become a skilled politician.** Sometimes creative ideas are orphans until everyone is convinced they are going to work. Early in the process of turning the ideas into products, resources may be tight. You will also have to deal with many units outside your team to get it done. Organizations can be complex mazes with many turns, dead ends, quick routes and choices. In most organizations, the best path to get somewhere is almost never a straight line. There is a formal organization—the one on the organization chart—where the path may look straight, and then there is the informal organization where all paths are zigzagged. Since organizations are staffed with people, they become all that more complex. There are gatekeepers, expediters, stoppers, resisters, guides, Good Samaritans and influencers. All of these types live in the organizational maze. The key to being successful in maneuvering an innovation through complex organizations is to find your way through the maze in the least amount of time while making the least noise. *More help? – See #38 Organizational Agility.*

☐ **10. Curious? Become a student of innovation outside your field.** Look for and study new products you buy and use. Find out the process that was used to create it. Watch *Modern Marvels* on the History Channel. Read *The Soul of a New Machine* by Tracy Kidder to see how innovation happens from the inside. Write down five things from your research that you can model in your own behavior.

☐ **11. Want to reinvent the business? Innovate your business model.** Gary Hamel says the keys to doing this are to build a point of view of change and opportunity, inspire others with a manifesto, create a coalition, pick targets of opportunity, co-opt and neutralize the naysayers, find a translator to influence top management, go for small wins (demonstration projects), and infiltrate your innovation into ongoing projects.

Some Develop-in-Place Assignments

- ☐ Manage a group of people in a rapidly expanding or growing operation.
- ☐ Launch a new product, service, or process.
- ☐ Relaunch an existing product or service that's not doing well.
- ☐ Seek out and use a seed budget to create and pursue a personal idea, product, or service.
- ☐ Monitor and follow a new product or service through the entire idea, design, test market, and launch cycle.

I · C

There is no shortage of creativity or creative people in either academia or industry. The shortage is of innovators. All too often, people believe that creativity automatically leads to innovation. It doesn't. Creative people tend to pass the responsibility for getting down to brass tacks to others.

Ted Levitt – American marketing scholar and former *Harvard Business Review* editor

Suggested Readings

Anthony, S. D., Johnson, M. W., Sinfield, J. V., & Altman, E. J. (2008). *Innovator's guide to growth: Putting disruptive innovation to work.* Boston: Harvard Business School Press.

Berkun, S. (2007). *The myths of innovation.* Sebastopol, CA: O'Reilly Media.

Carlson, C. R., & Wilmot, W. W. (2006). *Innovation: The five disciplines for creating what customers want.* New York: Crown Business.

Chakravorti, B. (2003). *The slow pace of fast change: Bringing innovations to market in a connected world.* Boston: Harvard Business School Press.

Champy, J. (2008). *Outsmart! How to do what your competitors can't.* Upper Saddle River, NJ: FT Press.

Chesbrough, H. (2006). *Open business models: How to thrive in the new innovation landscape.* Boston: Harvard Business School Press.

Chesbrough, H., Vanhaverbeke, W., & West, J. (Eds.). (2006). *Open innovation: Researching a new paradigm.* New York: Oxford University Press.

Christensen, C. M. (2003). *The innovator's dilemma: The revolutionary book that will change the way you do business.* New York: HarperCollins.

Christensen, C. M., & Raynor, M. E. (2003). *The innovator's solution.* Boston: Harvard Business School Press.

Davila. T., Epstein, M. J., & Shelton, R. (2005). *Making innovation work: How to manage it, measure it, and profit from it.* Philadelphia: Wharton School Publishing.

Deschamp, J. P. (2008). *Innovation leaders: How senior executives stimulate, steer and sustain innovation.* West Sussex, England: John Wiley & Sons, Ltd.

Fenn, J., & Raskino, M. (2008). *Mastering the hype cycle: How to choose the right innovation at the right time.* Boston: Harvard Business School Press.

Gelb, M., & Caldicott, S. M. (2007). *Innovate like Edison: The success system of America's greatest inventor.* New York: Dutton.

Hamel, G. (2002). *Leading the revolution* (Rev. ed.). Boston: Harvard Business School Press.

Hamel, G. (2006). The why, what, and how of management innovation. *Harvard Business Review, 84,*140.

Hansen, M. T., & Birkinshaw, J. (2008). The innovation chain. *Harvard Business Review, 85,* 121-130.

28

Hargadon, A. (2003). *How breakthroughs happen: The surprising truth about how companies innovate.* Boston: Harvard Business School Press.

Horibe, F. (2008). *Creating the innovation culture: Leveraging visionaries, dissenters and other useful troublemakers.* Etobicoke, ON: John Wiley & Sons Canada, Ltd.

Hurson, T. (2007). *Think better: An innovator's guide to productive thinking.* New York: McGraw-Hill.

Jamrog, J., Vickers, M., & Bear, D. (2006). Building and sustaining a culture that supports innovation. *Human Resource Planning, 29*(3), 9-19.

Kanter, R. M. (2006). Innovation: The classic traps. *Harvard Business Review, 84*(11), 72-83.

Kao, J. (2007). *Innovation nation: How America is losing its innovation edge, why it matters, and what we can do to get it back.* New York: Free Press.

Kelley, T., & Littman, J. (2005). *The ten faces of innovation: IDEO's strategies for defeating the devil's advocate and driving creativity throughout your organization.* New York: Currency Doubleday.

Kemper, S. (2003). *Code name Ginger: The story behind Segway and Dean Kamen's quest to invent a new world.* Boston: Harvard Business School Press.

O'Sullivan, D., & Dooley, L. (2008). *Applying innovation.* Thousand Oaks, CA: Sage.

Peters, T. (1997). *The circle of innovation: You can't shrink your way to greatness.* New York: Alfred A. Knopf, Inc.

Phillips, J. (2008). *Make us more innovative: Critical factors for innovation success.* Bloomington, IN: iUniverse.

Prahalad, C. K., & Krishnan, M. S. (2008). *The new age of innovation: Driving co-created value through global networks.* New York: McGraw-Hill.

Rogers, E. (2003). *Diffusion of innovations* (5th ed.). New York: Free Press.

Sawyer, K. (2008). *Group genius: The creative power of collaboration.* New York: Basic Books.

Skarzynski, P., & Gibson, R. (2008). *Innovation to the core: A blueprint for transforming the way your company innovates.* Boston: Harvard Business School Press.

Taylor, W. C., & Labarre, P. G. (2008). *Mavericks at work: Why the most original minds in business win.* New York: HarperCollins.

Tidd, J., Bessant, J., & Pavitt, K. (2005). *Managing innovation: Integrating technological, market and organizational change* (3rd ed.). West Sussex, England: John Wiley & Sons, Ltd.

29 Integrity and Trust

Trust is the lubrication that makes it possible for organizations to work.
Warren G. Bennis – American scholar, organizational consultant, and author

Unskilled

- ☐ Is not widely trusted
- ☐ May hedge or not take a stand
- ☐ May treat others differently or indifferently at times
- ☐ May not walk his/her talk and be seen as inconsistent
- ☐ May have trouble keeping confidences and talks out of school
- ☐ Makes promises he/she doesn't or can't keep
- ☐ May lack follow-through and causes problems for others
- ☐ Blames others for own mistakes
- ☐ Seen as just out for him/herself

Select one to three of the competencies listed below to use as a substitute for this competency if you decide not to work on it directly.

SUBSTITUTES: 3,22,23,27,33,34,44,57

Skilled

- ☐ Is widely trusted
- ☐ Is seen as a direct, truthful individual
- ☐ Can present the unvarnished truth in an appropriate and helpful manner
- ☐ Keeps confidences
- ☐ Admits mistakes
- ☐ Doesn't misrepresent him/herself for personal gain

Overused Skill

- ☐ May be too direct at times, which may catch people off guard and make them uncomfortable
- ☐ May push openness and honesty to the point of being disruptive
- ☐ May be so "only the facts" driven as to omit drawing reasonable conclusions, rendering opinions, or fixing blame, even when it's reasonable

Select one to three of the competencies listed below to work on to compensate for an overuse of this skill.

COMPENSATORS: 2,5,14,22,26,31,33,38,40,42,46,48,52,54,56,64

Some Causes

- ☐ Avoid conflict
- ☐ Don't "walk your talk"
- ☐ Hedging; holding back
- ☐ Overly ambitious
- ☐ Problems with keeping confidences
- ☐ Spread too thin; can't say no
- ☐ Too anxious to make the sale
- ☐ Treat others differently
- ☐ Won't take a stand

Leadership Architect® Factors and Clusters

This competency is in the Personal and Interpersonal Skills Factor (VI). This competency is in the Acting with Honor and Character Cluster (R) with: 22. You may want to check other competencies in the same Factor/Cluster for related tips.

The Map

Integrity and trust are on almost every success profile we see. It is a basic threshold requirement to be a part of the team. Without it, almost nothing else matters. To think that people question our integrity or don't totally trust us is very difficult to accept. The more common causes are personal disorganization, inconsistencies and habits that get us into trouble. Many of us simply haven't thought through the impact of our actions and have little idea how we come across. It can also be a lack of integrity in the bigger sense; people just don't buy what you say.

Some Remedies

- ☐ **1. Are you a hedger? Say what needs to be said.** Do you hold back and qualify everything? Don't speak up when you should? Do you not know how to say what needs to be said so you go bland and qualify everything to death? Do you hesitate or slow down when you are sharing something that is difficult for you? Does your voice go up in volume? Freudian slips? Stumble over words? Even though it's not your intention, do people think you are not disclosing what you really know? Practice coming up with two or three clear statements you are prepared to defend. Test them with people you trust. Keep them on the facts and on the problems. Be specific and don't blame. Don't qualify or make your statements conditional. Just say it. *More help? – See #34 Managerial Courage.*
- ☐ **2. Trying too hard to make the sale? Don't exaggerate or overpromise.** Does your enthusiasm to make the sale or get your point across cause

you to commit to too many things in the heat of the transaction? Do you stretch the truth? Do you embellish? The customer you get by unrealistic commitments is the customer you will lose forever when he/she finds out you can't deliver. Can't say no to customers? Do you want to help so much that you put yourself in impossible situations? Afraid that people will think you're not helpful? Being helpful is not helpful when you don't deliver. If you goof on the time required, go back and tell him/her the problem; either renegotiate or ask what else you should move down his/her list of requests. Don't promise something unless you can deliver. If you don't know for sure, say, "I'll let you know when I do." Either promise or don't—don't say "I'll try." If you don't know, just say so and follow up when you do know. Try to reduce your sales pitches to the actual merits of the case.

☐ **3. Loose lips? Keep confidences.** Some people get into trust issues because they share information others intended to be kept confidential. Be clear on what keeping a confidence means. Some rules are:

- Keep personal information confidential.
- Don't agree too quickly to keep performance/ethical/legal matters confidential. Warn others up front, "Before you tell me, I can't promise confidentiality on matters that affect unit performance, ethics or legal matters."
- Ask up front, "Is this to be kept confidential?"
- If someone is complaining about a coworker's ethics, tell him/her you can do nothing since you know nothing directly. Have him/her confront the person or produce evidence before continuing the discussion.
- There is usually no guarantee of confidentiality on matters affecting performance, legal and ethical jeopardy.
- There is usually no guarantee of confidentiality on matters affecting personal safety. Even doctors and psychiatrists pass on warnings of harm to authorities even though they obtained the information in confidence.
- It doesn't take many slip-ups in an organization before people say you can't be trusted with confidential information.

☐ **4. Buying favor? Lose your agenda.** Do people think you disclose information and use your friendships for personal advantage? Being seen as taking advantage of friendships or using information for personal advantage is hard to deal with. There is a fine line between this and the normal way things get done in organizations: Friends tell each other things, deals get struck, people access their networks, and sharing information is part of the process. Some rules of thumb so as to not cross the line are:

– Make sure it is a business request for information, not a personal one.
– Make sure it improves performance or efficiency or adds value; any benefit to you is then a by-product.
– Make sure you would tell this or ask this of someone you didn't know well in your organization.

☐ **5. Trouble admitting mistakes? Take responsibility.** Look for others to blame? Do people get blindsided because you don't warn them? People who excel at dealing with their own mistakes usually do the following:

– Admit the mistake early and inform everyone affected what could occur because of it.
– Publicly acknowledge the mistake if necessary; take personal responsibility.
– Demonstrate what they have learned so the mistake does not happen again.
– Move on; don't dwell on it. In a report from Forum Corp, those who admit doubt, errors and mistakes are seen as more competent, just as people who solicit negative feedback are. "Never show weakness" is bad advice. People who show humility are seen as trustworthy because they are truthful.

☐ **6. Trying to avoid conflict? Step up to address issues.** Do you say what you need to say to get through the meeting or transaction? Do you say things just to go along and not cause trouble? Do you say what you need to say to avoid disagreement or an argument? All these behaviors will eventually backfire when people find out you said something different in another setting or to another person or they notice that you didn't actually follow through and do what you said. *More help? – See #12 Conflict Management.*

☐ **7. Too protective of information? Share information that others need.** Do you keep to yourself? Work alone or try to? Do you hold back information? Do you parcel out information on your schedule? Do you keep everything to yourself? Do people around you know what you're doing and why? Even though it may not be your intention, could people think you are holding things back? Do they think you are aware of things others would benefit from but you don't take the time or make the effort to communicate? In most organizations, these things and things like it will get you in trouble. Organizations function on the flow of information. Being on your own and preferring peace and privacy are OK as long as you communicate things to bosses, peers and teammates that they need to know and would feel better if they knew. Make the effort to find out from each group you interact with what it is that they want and need to know and try to comply. *More help? – See #27 Informing.*

☐ **8. Facing an ethical dilemma? Know when and how to sound an alarm.** Whistle-blowing. A tough call. Do you hesitate blowing the whistle? Do you know something others should but when they find out, there will be noise and trouble? Saying what needs to be said to the right person in a timely way takes courage, being direct and straightforward. Everybody sees things, observes things, knows things or learns about things that others should know. Many times it's not positive information. Something is about to go wrong. Something is being covered up. Someone is holding back an important piece of information. Someone or something is going off in the wrong direction. It's good news and bad news. If you inform, the organization may gain. But a person or some people may lose. Generally, your best bet is to find the right person and inform. *More help? – See #34 Managerial Courage.*

☐ **9. Failing to deliver? Follow through.** Do you follow up on simple commitments? Do you return phone calls in a timely manner? Do you forward material that you promised? Do you pass on information you promised to get? Do you carry through on tasks you promised someone you would take care of? Failing to do things like this damages relationships. If you don't follow through well, focus on the receiver. What does this person need to know to implement this change? If you tend to forget, write things down. If you are going to miss a deadline, let people know and give them a second date you will be sure to make. Always out of time? Do you intend to get to things but never have the time? Do you always estimate shorter times to get things done that then take longer? If you run out of time, set up a specific time each day to follow through on commitments. There is a well-established science and a set of best practices in time management. There are a number of books you can buy in any business bookstore, and there are a number of good courses you can attend. Delegating also helps use your time more effectively. *More help? – See #62 Time Management.*

☐ **10. Haunted by violations of trust? Repair damage caused by being untrustworthy.** You hedge, sabotage others, play for advantage, set up others, don't intend to follow up. You justify it by saying that things are tough, that you're just doing your job, getting results. After all, the end justifies the means. You use others to get your agenda accomplished. First, you need to examine whether this view of the world is really right and if that is the way you really want to be. Second, you need to find out if your career with this organization is salvageable. Have you burned too many bridges? The best way to do this is to admit you have regularly betrayed trusts and not followed through on your commitments. Talk with your boss or mentor to see if you can redeem yourself. If yes, meet with everyone you think you've alienated and see how they respond. Tell them what you're going to do differently. Ask them what you should stop doing. Ask them if the situation can be repaired. *More help? – See #105 Betrayal of Trust.*

- ☐ **11. Self-centered? Put the team first.** Use "we" instead of "I." Use "the team," "us," "together," more. Say "Let us." "Let's get together." "We can do it." "We're all in this together." Signal that you are thinking and acting "team." To the extent that you legitimately can, spread the credit throughout the team. Always try to share the credit and spread the rewards around. Do you promote the careers of others as well as your own? Do you help other people get ahead with the same vigor as you promote yourself? Be more of a mentor and coach to people with the right stuff who need help to grow and prosper. People will trust you more if they view the relationship as a long-term one rather than something you're just doing because you have to for a few years. *More help? – See #19 Developing Direct Reports and Others and #110 Failure to Build a Team.*
- ☐ **12. Perception problems? Do something about how you're seen.** Write down all the reasons people have for believing you aren't very trustworthy. ("People say I change my mind too much.") Beside this write down what you actually do or don't do to cause this impression. ("I jump to conclusions"; "I'm easily influenced when people complain about something.") Beside this write down the name of someone who does these well. What do they do that you don't? What do you do that they don't? What do you overdo or underdo that may be getting you in trouble? Finally, write down some counter strategies. ("I'll stop and ask questions, not give an immediate answer"; "I'll examine the situation and get back to them in a timely manner.")

Some Develop-in-Place Assignments

- ☐ Make peace with an enemy or someone you've disappointed with a product or service or someone you've had some trouble with or don't get along with very well.
- ☐ Handle a tough negotiation with an internal or external client or customer.
- ☐ Manage the assigning/allocating of office space in a contested situation.
- ☐ Manage the outplacement of a group of people.
- ☐ Be a member of a union-negotiating or grievance-handling team.

I never did give anybody hell.
I just told the truth and they thought it was hell.
Harry S. Truman – 33rd President of the United States

Suggested Readings

Bennis, W., Goleman, D., & O'Toole, J. (with Ward Biederman, P.). (2008). *Transparency: How leaders create a culture of candor.* San Francisco: Jossey-Bass.

Block, P. (2001). *The answer to how is yes: Acting on what matters.* San Francisco: Berrett-Koehler Publishers.

Boverie, P. E., & Kroth, M. (2001). *Transforming work: The five keys to achieving trust, commitment & passion in the workplace.* Cambridge, MA: Perseus Publishing.

Deems, R. S., & Deems, T. A. (2003). *Leading in tough times: The manager's guide to responsibility, trust, and motivation.* Amherst, MA: HRD Press.

Galford, R. M., & Siebold Drapeau, A. (2002). *The trusted leader: Bringing out the best in your people and your company.* New York: Free Press.

Golin, A. (2004). *Trust or consequences: Build trust today or lose your market tomorrow.* New York: AMACOM.

Hanson, T., & Hanson, B. Z. (2005). *Who will do what by when? How to improve performance, accountability and trust with integrity.* Longwood, FL: Power.

Johnson, L., & Phillips, B. (2003). *Absolute honesty: Building a corporate culture that values straight talk and rewards integrity.* New York: AMACOM.

Kaptein, M., & Wempe, J. (2002). *The balanced company: A corporate integrity theory.* Oxford, UK: Oxford University Press.

Maister, D. H., Green, C. H., & Galford, R. M. (2001). *The trusted advisor.* New York: Free Press.

McKay, Q. (2004). *The bottom line on integrity.* Layton, UT: Gibbs Smith.

O'Toole, J. (1996). *Leading change.* Boston: Harvard Business School Press.

Reina, D. S., & Reina, M. L. (2006). *Trust and betrayal in the workplace.* San Francisco: Berrett-Koehler Publishers.

Remick, N. T. (2002). *West Point: Character leadership education: A book developed from the readings and writings of Thomas Jefferson.* New York: RPR.

Seglin, J. L. (2006). *The right thing: Conscience, profit and personal responsibility in today's business.* Rollinsford, NH: Spiro Press.

Showkeir, J., & Showkeir, M. (2008). *Authentic conversations: Moving from manipulation to truth and commitment.* San Francisco: Berrett-Koehler Publishers.

Simons, T. (2008). *The integrity dividend: Leading by the power of your word.* San Francisco: Jossey-Bass.

Solomon, R. C., & Flores, F. (2001). *Building trust: In business, politics, relationships, and life.* Oxford, UK: Oxford University Press.

Tracy, D., & Morin, W. J. (2001). *Truth, trust, and the bottom line.* Chicago, IL: Dearborn Trade.

30 Intellectual Horsepower

The test of a first-rate intelligence is the ability to hold two opposed ideas in the mind at the same time, and still retain the ability to function.
F. Scott Fitzgerald – American writer of novels and short stories

Unskilled

- ☐ May be intellectually lazy or disorganized
- ☐ May not think things through carefully
- ☐ Always wants everything to be simple
- ☐ Emotions may get in the way of careful consideration
- ☐ Impatience may get in the way of careful consideration
- ☐ May be mentally inflexible or stale—believing that his/her way is the best and virtually only way to do things or solve problems
- ☐ May get frustrated when others are talking conceptually
- ☐ May be slow to catch on to things

Select one to three of the competencies listed below to use as a substitute for this competency if you decide not to work on it directly.

SUBSTITUTES: 1,5,14,17,24,32,33,46,51,58,61

Skilled

- ☐ Is bright and intelligent
- ☐ Deals with concepts and complexity comfortably
- ☐ Described as intellectually sharp, capable, and agile

Overused Skill

- ☐ May use intelligence to dominate and intimidate others
- ☐ May not be able to relate to those less intelligent
- ☐ May only accept own solutions
- ☐ May be impatient with due process

Select one to three of the competencies listed below to work on to compensate for an overuse of this skill.

COMPENSATORS: 3,4,7,10,15,18,19,26,31,33,36,41,42,44

Some Causes

- ☐ Disorganized
- ☐ Excessive emotionality
- ☐ Lack of patience, perseverance or self-confidence
- ☐ Lack of cognitive skills
- ☐ Lazy
- ☐ Rigid belief systems

Leadership Architect® Factors and Clusters

This competency is in the Strategic Skills Factor (I). This competency is in the Making Complex Decisions Cluster (B) with: 17, 32, 51. You may want to check other competencies in the same Factor/Cluster for related tips.

The Map

Much of success in life and work is based upon acquiring knowledge and skills and putting them to use solving life's problems and challenges. Although your level of basic intelligence is in a sense set at birth—you have as much as you are ever going to have—popular science writers commonly claim we use only 10% of the brain's capacity. Even though that number probably can't be specifically verified, it's safe to say we all have extra capacity we could put to use. Studies show that intelligence is a use it or lose it competence; those who stay mentally sharp show continuing though slight increases in intelligence throughout their lifetimes.

Some Remedies

- ☐ **1. Emotional? Cool down.** Excessive emotionality decreases the effective use of brain power. The emotional system hijacks the brain until the threat is removed. The brain works best under cool conditions. If you tend to get emotional about things, wait a minute or two to regain your composure and then try to solve the problem. Decision making under heat is unlikely to be correct over time. *More help? – See #11 Composure.*
- ☐ **2. Moving too fast? Take time to think.** Many of us are very action oriented. It's the famous fire-ready-aim. Many mistakes we make would not have happened if we had taken the time to think things through. Try to add one minute to your thinking time. Go through a mental checklist to see if you have thought about all of the ramifications of the problem or challenge. Go into any learning event with a goal. Ask questions about what you read. Chunk up what you learn. Put it in categories that make sense to you. Other research has shown that the first thing or solution you think of is seldom the best choice. Usually somewhere between the second and third choice turns out to be the most effective. If you are an action junkie and

jump at the first option, you will be wrong much of the time. *More help? – See #41 Patience and #43 Perseverance.*

☐ **3. Narrow belief system? Extend your horizon.** Much research from anthropology has shown that our brains are trapped inside our belief framework. The Hopi Indians in the Southwest have one word for snow whereas the Inuits of Alaska have 24 different words for 24 different kinds of snow conditions. A Hopi could not survive in Alaska with just one snow concept. Our experience unknowingly creates boundaries for our thinking. Try to think outside your belief boundaries. You don't have to give them up; just turn them off when you are thinking about a problem or challenge.

☐ **4. Need practice? Jump-start your mind.** There are all kinds of mental exercises to increase the use of whatever intellectual horsepower you have. You can create checklists so you don't forget anything. You can run scenarios. You can ask what's missing. You can do pro's and con's. You can visualize. You can diagram a problem. You can practice seeing how many patterns you can see in something or how many ways you can mentally organize it. These and many other practices will be in any text on problem solving. *More help? – See #51 Problem Solving and #52 Process Management.*

☐ **5. Too opinionated? Separate opinions from facts.** Help others do the same. Read Edward de Bono's *Six Thinking Hats* to learn more about this technique. Opinionated people are seldom clear thinkers and good problem solvers.

☐ **6. Preconceptions? Pause to consider the facts before rushing to a solution.** We all have a need to provide answers as soon as possible to questions and problems. We all have preconceived notions, favorite solutions, and prejudices that prevent our intellectual skills from dealing with the real facts of the problem. For one-half of the time you have to deal with an issue or a problem, shut off your solution machine and just take in the facts.

☐ **7. Want to know how things work? Think systems.** Subscribe to *The Systems Thinker®*, Pegasus Communications, Inc., Waltham, MA, 781-398-9700. This is a group dedicated to finding out how things work and why they work that way. They have a monthly publication as well as workshops, seminars and other materials available to help you see the world as a series of recurring systems or archetypes. They analyze everyday events and processes and try to see why they work the way they do. They take complex problems and try to show how almost all problems are some form of seven classic models.

- ☐ **8. Want to stay sharp? Exercise your brain.** Buy some beginning crossword puzzle books to do in your spare time. Buy other kinds of mental puzzle materials and practice on them. Get a book on "mind mapping" or better yet, attend a workshop. Mind mapping is a technique that teaches you how to organize concepts.
- ☐ **9. Can't picture it? Visualize.** Try to picture problems and challenges in the form of pictures or flows. Buy a flow charting software that does PERT and GANTT charts. Become an expert in its use. Use the output of the software to communicate the elements of a problem to others. Use the flow charts in your presentations to explain the problems you've solved.
- ☐ **10. Want a role model? Access great minds.** Study a few great thinkers and philosophers like John Stuart Mill who outlined the basic logic of problem solving. Read their biographies or autobiographies for clues into how they used their intellectual skills.

Some Develop-in-Place Assignments

- ☐ Do a postmortem on a failed project, and present it to the people involved.
- ☐ Audit cost overruns to assess the problem, and present your findings to the person or people involved.
- ☐ Teach a course, seminar, or workshop on something you don't know well.
- ☐ Teach/coach someone how to do something you're an expert in.
- ☐ Do a competitive analysis of your organization's products or services or position in the marketplace, and present it to the people involved.

When you know a thing, to hold that you know it;
and when you do not know a thing, to allow that you do not know it
—this is knowledge.
Confucius (551-479 BCE) – Chinese philosopher

Suggested Readings

Cooper, C. (1999). *Intelligence and abilities.* Wexford, Ireland: Creative, Print and Design.

Deary, I. J. (2001). *Intelligence: A very short introduction.* Oxford, UK: Oxford University Press, Inc.

Epstein, S., & Brodsky, A. (1993). *You're smarter than you think: How to develop your practical intelligence for success in living.* New York: Simon & Schuster.

Gardner, H. (1993). *Multiple intelligences: The theory in practice.* New York: Basic Books.

Gardner, H. (2004). *Changing minds: The art and science of changing our own and other people's minds.* Boston: Harvard Business School Press.

Macintosh, N.J. (2000). *IQ and human intelligence.* Oxford, UK: Oxford University Press.

Martin, R. (2007). How successful leaders think. *Harvard Business Review, 85*(6), 60-67.

Martin, R. (2007). *The opposable mind: How successful leaders win through integrative thinking.* Boston: Harvard Business School Press.

Maxwell, J. C. (2003). *Thinking for a change: 11 Ways highly successful people approach life and work.* New York: Warner Books.

Neisser, U., Boodoo, G., Bouchard, T., Boykin, A., Brody, N., & Ceci, S., (et al.). (1996). Intelligence: Knowns and unknowns. *American Psychologist, 51*(2), 77-101.

Roam, D. (2008). *The back of the napkin: Solving problems and selling ideas with pictures.* New York: Portfolio Hardcover.

Sofo, F. (2003). *Six myths of critical thinking: The 7 keys to thinking critically.* Crows Nest, Australia: Allen & Unwin Pty. Limited.

Sternberg, R. J. (2001). *Thinking styles.* Boston: Cambridge University Press.

Sternberg, R. J. (2004). *International handbook of intelligence.* Boston: Cambridge University Press.

Waitley, D. (2006). *Wordmaster: Improve your word power and improve your life!* Audio CD. LearnOutLoud.com.

Wellman, A. M. (2002). *The five faces of genius: Creative thinking styles to succeed at work.* New York: Penguin Books.

31 Interpersonal Savvy

The greatest compliment that was ever paid me
was when one asked me what I thought, and attended to my answer.
Henry David Thoreau – American author, poet, and philosopher

Unskilled

- ☐ Doesn't relate smoothly to a variety of people
- ☐ May not build relationships easily—may lack approachability or good listening skills
- ☐ Doesn't take the time to build rapport
- ☐ May be too raw and direct at times
- ☐ May be excessively work oriented or intense
- ☐ May be impatient to get on with the agenda; judgmental or arrogant toward others
- ☐ May not read others well
- ☐ May freeze or panic in the face of conflict, attack or criticism
- ☐ May be shy or lack confidence around others

Select one to three of the competencies listed below to use as a substitute for this competency if you decide not to work on it directly.

SUBSTITUTES: 1,3,7,10,12,15,21,27,33,37,39,41,42,49,60

Skilled

- ☐ Relates well to all kinds of people—up, down, and sideways, inside and outside the organization
- ☐ Builds appropriate rapport
- ☐ Builds constructive and effective relationships
- ☐ Uses diplomacy and tact
- ☐ Can defuse even high-tension situations comfortably

Overused Skill

- ☐ May be able to get by with smooth interpersonal skills
- ☐ May spend too much time building networks and glad-handing
- ☐ May not be taken as substantive by some
- ☐ May not be a credible take-charge leader when that's necessary
- ☐ May have some trouble and freeze when facing serious conflict

Select one to three of the competencies listed below to work on to compensate for an overuse of this skill.

COMPENSATORS: 1,5,9,12,13,20,24,34,36,50,51,52,57,62,65

Some Causes

- ☐ Arrogant, impatient, insensitive
- ☐ Can't handle disagreement and attacks
- ☐ Defensive in the face of criticism
- ☐ Don't know what to do in various interpersonal situations
- ☐ Judgmental, rigid
- ☐ Narrow
- ☐ Not self-confident
- ☐ Poor listening skills
- ☐ Poor time management; too busy
- ☐ Shy; afraid of transacting with new people; lack of self-confidence
- ☐ Too intense; can't relax

Leadership Architect® Factors and Clusters

This competency is in the Personal and Interpersonal Skills Factor (VI). This competency is in the Relating Skills Cluster (N) with: 3. You may want to check other competencies in the same Factor/Cluster for related tips.

The Map

The key to getting along with all kinds of people is to hold back or neutralize your personal reactions and focus on others first. Being savvy is working from the outside in. Then, interpersonal savvy becomes having a range of interpersonal skills and approaches and knowing when to use what with whom. The outcome is ease of transaction where you get what you need without damaging other parties unnecessarily and leave them wanting to work with you again.

Some Remedies

☐ **1. Not tuned in to people's styles? Be interpersonally flexible.** Except from a moral viewpoint (everyone is equal in the eyes of their creator), all people are different. There is a rich variety and diversity of people. Physical is easy to see. Height. Weight. Speed. Some personal characteristics are easy as well. Smart; not so smart. Articulate; not so articulate. Warm; cold. Composed; emotional. Good presenter; poor presenter. Other human characteristics are a little harder to read. Motivated; not so motivated. Good values; not so good values. Integrity? Decisive? Fair? To understand the differences, look to the obvious first. What do they do first? What do they emphasize in their speech? People focus on different things—taking action, details, concepts, feelings, other people. What's their interaction style? People come in different styles—pushy, tough, soft, matter-of-fact and so on. To figure these out, listen for the values behind their words and note what they have passion and emotion around. One key to getting anything of value done in the work world is the ability to see differences in people and to manage against and use those differences for everyone's benefit. Interpersonal savvy is meeting each person where he/she is to get done what you need to get done. Basically, people respond favorably to ease of transaction. If you make it easy by accepting their normal mode of doing things, not fighting their style, and neither defending your own nor letting style get in the way of performance, things will generally run smoothly. *More help? – See #56 Sizing Up People.*

☐ **2. Does your style chill the transaction? Tailor your approach to fit others' needs.** Arrogant? Insensitive? Distant? Too busy to pay attention? Too quick to get into the agenda? Do you devalue others and dismiss their contributions, resulting in people feeling diminished, rejected and angry? Do you offer answers, solutions, conclusions, statements, or dictates early in the transaction? That's the staple of people with a non-savvy style. Not listening. Instant output. Sharp reactions. Don't want to be that way? Read your audience. Do you know what people look like when they are uncomfortable with you? Do they back up? Stumble over words? Cringe? Stand at the door hoping not to get invited in? You should work doubly hard at observing others. Always select your interpersonal approach from the other person in, not from you out. Your best choice of approach will always be determined by the other person or group, not you. Think about each transaction as if the other person were a customer you wanted. How would you craft an approach? *More help? – See #45 Personal Learning and #112 Insensitive to Others.*

☐ **3. In a hurry to get down to business? Manage the first three minutes.** Managing the first three minutes is essential. The tone is set. First impressions are formed. Work on being open and approachable, and take in information during the beginning of a transaction. This means putting others at ease so that they feel OK about disclosing. It means initiating rapport, listening, sharing, understanding and comforting. Approachable people get more information, know things earlier, and can get others to do more things. The more you can get them to initiate and say early in the transaction, the more you'll know about where they are coming from, and the better you can tailor your approach. *More help? – See #3 Approachability.*

☐ **4. Quick to judge? Be a better listener.** Interpersonally skilled people are very good at listening. They listen to understand and take in information to select their response. They listen without interrupting. They ask clarifying questions. They don't instantly judge. Judgment might come later. They restate what the other person has said to signal understanding. They nod.

They might jot down notes. Listeners get more data. *More help? – See #33 Listening.*

- ☐ **5. Are you overly private? Share more.** Interpersonally skilled people share more information and get more in return. Confide your thinking on a business issue and invite the response of others. Pass on tidbits of information you think will help people do their jobs better or broaden their perspectives. Disclose more things about yourself. Reveal things people don't need to know to do their jobs, but which will be interesting to them, and help them feel valued. *More help? – See #44 Personal Disclosure.* Personalize. Work to know and remember important things about the people you work around, for, and with. Know three things about everybody—their interests or their children or something you can chat about other than the business agenda. Establish things you can talk about with each person you work with that go beyond strictly work transactions. These need not be social; they could also be issues of strategy, global events, market shifts. The point is to establish common ground and connections.
- ☐ **6. Are you demonstrating genuine interest? Manage your non-verbals.** Interpersonally savvy people understand the critical role of non-verbal communications, of appearing and sounding open and relaxed, smiling and calm. They keep consistent eye contact. They nod while the other person is talking. They speak in a paced and pleasant tone. Work to eliminate any disruptive habits such as speaking too rapidly or forcefully, using strongly worded or loaded language, or going into too much detail. Watch out for signaling disinterest with actions like glancing at your watch, fiddling with paperwork or giving your impatient "I'm busy" look.
- ☐ **7. Selective interpersonal skills? Accommodate differences.** Some people are interpersonally comfortable and effective with some and not others. Some might be interpersonally smooth with direct reports and tense around senior management. What do the people you are comfortable around have in common? What about those you're not comfortable with? Is it level? Style? Gender? Race? Background? The principles of interpersonal savvy are the same regardless of the audience. Do what you do with the comfortable group with the uncomfortable groups. The results will generally be the same.
- ☐ **8. Shy? Make the first move.** Lack self-confidence? Generally hold back and let others take the lead? Feelings of being too vulnerable? Afraid of how people will react? Not sure of your social skills? Want to appear—while shaking inside—not shy? Hand first. Consistent eye contact. Ask the first question. For low-risk practice, talk to strangers off-work. Set a goal of meeting new people at every social gathering; find out what you

have in common with them. Initiate contact at your place of worship, at PTA meetings, in the neighborhood, at the supermarket, on the plane and on the bus. See if any of the bad and scary things you think might happen to you if you initiate people contact actually happen. The only way people will know you are shy and nervous is if you tell them through your actions. Watch what non-shy people do that you don't do. Practice those behaviors.

☐ **9. Problems with troublesome people? Be savvy with people you don't like.** What do people see in them who do like them or can at least get along with them? What are their strengths? Do you have any common interests with them? Whatever you do, don't signal to them what you think. Put your judgments on hold, nod, ask questions, summarize as you would with anyone else. A fly on the wall should not be able to tell whether you're talking to friend or foe. You can always talk less and ask more questions; and neither apologize nor criticize. Even if they're contentious, you can respond neutrally by restating the problem you're working on.

☐ **10. Are you a target? Turn around tense transactions.** What if you're attacked? What if venom is flowing? What if someone doesn't like you very much? What if everyone is angry and upset? Practice interpersonal Aikido, the ancient art of absorbing the energy of your opponent and using it to manage him/her. Let the other side vent frustration, blow off steam, but don't react directly. Remember that it's the person who hits back who usually gets in the most trouble. Listen. Nod. Ask clarifying questions. Ask open-ended questions like, "Why is this particularly bothersome to you?" "What could I do to help?" "So you think I need to...." Restate his/her position periodically to signal you have understood. But don't react. Don't judge. Keep him/her talking until he/she runs out of venom. When the other side takes a rigid position, don't reject it. Ask why—what's behind the position, what's the theory of the case, what brought this about? Separate the people from the problem. When someone attacks you, rephrase it as an attack on a problem. Keep your cool even though he/she may have lost his/her cool. In response to unreasonable proposals, attacks, or a non-answer to a question, you can always say nothing. People will usually respond by saying more, coming off their position a bit, or at least revealing their true interests. Many times, with unlimited venting and your understanding, the actual conflict shrinks. *More help? – See #12 Conflict Management.*

Some Develop-in-Place Assignments

- ☐ Manage a dissatisfied internal or external customer; troubleshoot a performance or quality problem with a product or service.
- ☐ Manage a project team of people who are older and more experienced than you.
- ☐ Resolve an issue in conflict between two people, units, geographies, functions, etc.
- ☐ Manage a group that includes former peers to accomplish a task.
- ☐ Integrate diverse systems, processes, or procedures across decentralized and/or dispersed units.

The most important single ingredient in the formula of success is knowing how to get along with people.
Theodore Roosevelt – 26th President of the United States

Suggested Readings

Adler, R. B., & Elmhorst, J. M. (2005). *Communicating at work: Principles and practices for business and the professions* (8th ed.). New York: McGraw-Hill.

Baker, W. E. (2000). *Networking smart.* New York: Backinprint.com.

Bradberry, T., & Greaves, J. (2005). *The emotional intelligence quick book: Everything you need to know to put your EQ to work.* New York: Fireside.

Goleman, D., McKee, A., & Boyatzis, R. E. (2002). *Primal leadership: Realizing the power of emotional intelligence.* Boston: Harvard Business School Press.

Gudykunst, W. B., & Kim, Y. Y. (2002). *Communicating with strangers: An approach to intercultural communication.* New York: McGraw-Hill.

Gundry, L., & LaMantia, L. (2001). *Breakthrough teams for breakneck times: Unlocking the genius of creative collaboration.* Chicago: Dearborn Trade.

Hargrove, R. (1999). *Mastering the art of creative collaboration.* New York: McGraw-Hill.

Klaus, P. (2007). *The hard truth about soft skills: Workplace lessons smart people wish they'd learned sooner.* New York: HarperCollins.

Mai, R., & Akerson, A. (2003). *The leader as communicator: Strategies and tactics to build loyalty, focus effort, and spark creativity.* New York: AMACOM.

Maxwell, J. C. (2004). *Relationships 101.* London: Thomas Nelson.

Silberman, M. L. (with Hansburg, F.). (2005). *PeopleSmart: Developing your interpersonal intelligence.* Hoboken, NJ: John Wiley & Sons.

Thomas, D. C., & Inkson, K. (2004). *Cultural intelligence: People skills for global business.* San Francisco: Berrett-Koehler.

Vengel, A. A. (2000). *The influence edge: How to persuade others to help you achieve your goals.* San Francisco: Berrett-Koehler Publishers.

32 Learning on the Fly

It is not necessary to change. Survival is not mandatory.
W. Edwards Deming – American professor, author, and consultant

Unskilled

- ☐ Not agile or versatile in learning to deal with first-time or unusual problems
- ☐ May not analyze problems carefully or search for multiple clues and parallels
- ☐ May be afraid to take a chance on the unknown
- ☐ Learns new things slowly
- ☐ May be stuck in historical, tried-and-true methods, uncomfortable with ambiguity and quick to jump to a solution
- ☐ Doesn't look under rocks, just sticks to the obvious
- ☐ Looks for the simplest explanation too soon
- ☐ Gives up too soon and accepts a marginal solution
- ☐ Functions on the surface, doesn't go deep

Select one to three of the competencies listed below to use as a substitute for this competency if you decide not to work on it directly.

SUBSTITUTES: 1,2,5,14,16,17,24,28,30,33,43,45,46,50,51,61

Skilled

- ☐ Learns quickly when facing new problems
- ☐ A relentless and versatile learner
- ☐ Open to change
- ☐ Analyzes both successes and failures for clues to improvement
- ☐ Experiments and will try anything to find solutions
- ☐ Enjoys the challenge of unfamiliar tasks
- ☐ Quickly grasps the essence and the underlying structure of anything

Overused Skill

- ☐ May leave others behind
- ☐ May frustrate others with his/her need for change
- ☐ May tend to change things too often
- ☐ People may interpret openness as indecisiveness or being wishy-washy
- ☐ May seek out change for change's sake regardless of the situation
- ☐ May not be good at routine administration or unchallenging tasks or jobs

Select one to three of the competencies listed below to work on to compensate for an overuse of this skill.

COMPENSATORS: 27,33,39,41,43,47,52,59

Some Causes

- ☐ Don't analyze successes and failures for clues
- ☐ Historical problem solver
- ☐ Not a risk taker
- ☐ Not self-confident
- ☐ Perfectionist
- ☐ Stuck in the past
- ☐ Too narrow in search for parallels

Leadership Architect® Factors and Clusters

This competency is in the Strategic Skills Factor (I). This competency is in the Making Complex Decisions Cluster (B) with: 17, 30, 51. You may want to check other competencies in the same Factor/Cluster for related tips.

The Map

Most of us are good at applying what we have seen and done in the past. Most of us can apply solutions that have worked for us before. We are all pretty good at solving problems we've seen before. A rarer skill is doing things for the first time. Solving problems we've never seen before. Trying solutions we have never tried before. Analyzing problems in new contexts and in new ways. With the increasing pace of change, being quick to learn and apply first-time solutions is becoming a crucial skill. It involves taking risks, being less than perfect, discarding the past, going against the grain, and cutting new paths.

Some Remedies

- ☐ **1. Trouble making sense of the issues? Dig for root causes.** Keep asking why, see how many causes you can come up with, and how many organizing buckets you can put them in. This increases the chance of a better solution because you can see more connections. Chess masters recognize thousands of possible patterns of chess pieces. Look for patterns in data; don't just collect information. Put it in categories that make sense to you. To better understand new and difficult learning, read *The Future of Leadership* by White, Hodgson and Crainer.
- ☐ **2. Where to start? Locate the essence of the problem.** What are the key factors or elements in this problem? Experts usually solve problems by figuring out what the deep underlying principles are and working forward from there; the less adept focus on desired outcomes/solutions and either work backward or concentrate on the surface facts. What are the deep principles of what you're working on? Once you've done this, search the past for parallels—your past, the business past, the historical past. One common mistake here is to search in parallel organizations because

"only they would know." Backing up and asking a broader question will aid in the search for solutions. When Motorola wanted to find out how to process orders more quickly, they went not to other electronics firms, but to Domino's Pizza and Federal Express.

☐ **3. How to generalize? Look for patterns.** Look for patterns in personal, organization, or the world, in general successes and failures. What was common to each success or what was present in each failure but never present in a success? Focus on the successes; failures are easier to analyze but don't in themselves tell you what would work. Comparing successes, while less exciting, yields more information about underlying principles. The bottom line is to reduce your insights to principles or rules of thumb you think might be repeatable. When faced with the next new problem, those general underlying principles will apply again.

☐ **4. Want to speed up the learning cycle? Try different solutions and learn from the results.** Don't expect to get it right the first time. This leads to safe and stale solutions. Many studies show that the second or third try is when we really understand the underlying dynamics of problems. To increase learning, shorten your act and get feedback loops aiming to make them as immediate as possible. The more frequent the cycles, the more opportunities to learn; if we do something in each of three days instead of one thing every three days, we triple our learning opportunities and increase our chances of finding the right answer. Be more willing to experiment.

☐ **5. Need help? Use experts.** Find an expert or experts in your functional/technical/business area and go find out how they think and solve new problems. Ask them what are the critical principles/drivers/things they look for. Have them tell you how they thought through a new problem in this area; the major skills they look for in sizing up people's proficiency in this area; key questions they ask about a problem; how they would suggest you go about learning quickly in this area.

☐ **6. Need to change it up? Reverse your approach.** People who think in opposite cases when confronted with a problem tend to do better. Turn the problem upside down. Ask what is the least likely thing it could be, what the problem is not, what's missing from the problem, or what the mirror image of the problem is.

☐ **7. Want to learn from others? Assemble a team.** Teams of people with the widest diversity of backgrounds produce the most innovative solutions to problems. Get others with different backgrounds to analyze and make sense with you. When working together, come up with as many questions about it as you can. Set up a competition with another group or individual, asking them to work on exactly what you are working on. Set a certain time frame and have a postmortem to try to deduce some of the practices and procedures that work best. Find a team or individual that faces problems quite similar to what you face and set up dialogues on a number of specific topics.

- ☐ **8. Can't see the parallels? Use oddball tactics.** What is a direct analogy between something you are working on and a natural occurrence? Ask what in nature parallels your problem. When the terrible surfs and motion of the tide threatened to defeat their massive dam project, the Delta Works, the Dutch used the violence of the North Sea to drive in the pilings, ending the danger of the south of the Netherlands flooding. Practice picking out anomalies—unusual facts that don't quite fit, like sales going down when they should have gone up. What do these odd things imply for strategy?
- ☐ **9. Mistakes? Do quick experiments and trials.** Studies show that 80% of innovations occur in the wrong place, are created by the wrong people—dye makers developed detergent; Post-it® Notes was an error in a glue formula—and 30-50% of technical innovations fail in tests within the company. Even among those that make it to the marketplace, 70-90% fail. The bottom line on change is a 95% failure rate, and the most successful innovators try lots of quick, inexpensive experiments to increase the chances of success.
- ☐ **10. Too focused on a solution? Take time to ask questions and define the problem.** Too often we think first and only of solutions. In studies of problem-solving sessions, solutions outweigh questions eight to one. Most meetings on a problem start with people offering solutions. Early solutions are not likely to be the best. Set aside 50% of the time for questions and problem definition, and the last 50% for solutions. Asking more questions early helps you rethink the problem and come to more and different solutions.

Some Develop-in-Place Assignments

- ☐ Teach a course, seminar, or workshop on something you don't know well.
- ☐ Work on a project that involves travel and study of an international issue, acquisition, or joint venture and report back to management.
- ☐ Work short rotations in other units, functions, or geographies you've not been exposed to before.
- ☐ Benchmark innovative practices, processes, products, or services of competitors, vendors, suppliers, or customers, and present a report making recommendations for change.
- ☐ Manage a project team made up of nationals from a number of countries.

Only by being open to change will you have a true opportunity to get the most from your talent.
Nolan Ryan – American baseball pitcher

Suggested Readings

Chesbrough, H. (2006). *Open business models: How to thrive in the new innovation landscape.* Boston: Harvard Business School Press.

Chesbrough, H., Vanhaverbeke, W., & West, J. (Eds.). (2006). *Open innovation: Researching a new paradigm.* New York: Oxford University Press.

DuFour, R., DuFour, R., Eaker, R., & Many, T. (2006). *Learning by doing: A handbook for professional learning communities at work.* Bloomington, IN: Solution Tree.

Eichinger, R. W., & Lombardo, M. M. (2004). Learning agility as a prime indicator of potential. *Human Resource Planning, 27*(4), 12-15.

Hartley, D. (2000). *On-demand learning: Training in the new millennium.* Amherst, MA: HRD Press.

Honold, L. (2001). *Developing employees who love to learn: Tools, strategies, and programs for promoting learning at work.* Palo Alto, CA: Davies-Black Publishing.

Klein, G. A. (2002). *Intuition at work: Why developing your gut instincts will make you better at what you do.* New York: Doubleday.

Linsky, M., & Heifetz, R. A. (2002). *Leadership on the line: Staying alive through the dangers of leading.* Boston: Harvard Business School Press.

Manz, C. C. (2002). *The power of failure: 27 Ways to turn life's setbacks into success.* San Francisco: Berrett-Koehler Publishers.

McCall, M. W., Lombardo, M. M., & Morrison, A. M. (1988). *The lessons of experience.* Lexington, MA: Lexington Books.

Merriam, S. B., Caffarella, R. S., & Baumgartner, L. M. (2006). *Learning in adulthood: A comprehensive guide.* San Francisco: Jossey-Bass.

Mitroff, I. I. (2005). *Why some companies emerge stronger and better from a crisis: 7 Essential lessons for surviving disaster.* New York: AMACOM.

Sutton, R. I. (2007). *Weird ideas that work.* New York: Free Press.

Thomas, R. J. (2008). *Crucibles of leadership: How to learn from experience to become a great leader.* Boston: Harvard Business School Press.

Van der Heijden, K., Bardfield, R., Burt, G., Cairns, G., & Wright, G. (2002). *The sixth sense: Accelerating organisational learning with scenarios.* West Sussex, UK: John Wiley & Sons, Ltd.

Von Oech, R. (2002). *Expect the unexpected or you won't find it: A creativity tool based on the ancient wisdom of Heraclitus.* San Francisco: Berrett-Koehler Publishers.

Waitzkin, J. (2008). *The art of learning: An inner journey to optimal performance.* New York: Free Press.

Wall, S. J. (2004). *On the fly: Executing strategy in a changing world.* New York: John Wiley & Sons.

Wick, C. (1996). *The learning edge.* New York: McGraw-Hill.

Wick, C., Pollock, R., Jefferson, A., & Flanagan, R. (2006). *The six disciplines of breakthrough learning: How to turn training and development into business results.* San Francisco: Pfeiffer.

Yeung, A., Ulrich, D., Nason, S. W., & Von Glinow, M. A. (1999). *Organizational learning capability: Generating and generalizing ideas with impact.* New York: Oxford University Press.

33 Listening

I remind myself every morning: Nothing I say this day will teach me anything. So if I'm going to learn, I must do it by listening.
Larry King – American television/radio host

Unskilled

- ☐ Doesn't listen well
- ☐ Cuts people off and finishes their sentences if they hesitate
- ☐ Interrupts to make a pronouncement or render a solution or decision
- ☐ Doesn't learn much from interactions with others
- ☐ Appears not to listen or is too busy constructing his/her own response
- ☐ Many times misses the point others are trying to make
- ☐ May appear arrogant, impatient or uninterested
- ☐ May listen to some groups/people and not to others
- ☐ Inaccurate in restating the case of others

Select one to three of the competencies listed below to use as a substitute for this competency if you decide not to work on it directly.

SUBSTITUTES: 3,7,11,12,18,21,23,31,36,41,44,60

Skilled

- ☐ Practices attentive and active listening
- ☐ Has the patience to hear people out
- ☐ Can accurately restate the opinions of others even when he/she disagrees

Overused Skill

- ☐ May spend too much time listening
- ☐ May avoid necessary action
- ☐ Others may confuse listening with agreement

Select one to three of the competencies listed below to work on to compensate for an overuse of this skill.

COMPENSATORS: 1,9,12,13,16,17,27,34,37,38,50,57

Some Causes

- ☐ Arrogant
- ☐ Defensive
- ☐ Don't care
- ☐ Don't value others
- ☐ Impatient
- ☐ Insensitive
- ☐ Selective listening
- ☐ Too busy

Leadership Architect® Factors and Clusters

This competency is in the Personal and Interpersonal Skills Factor (VI). This competency is in the Being Open and Receptive Cluster (S) with: 11, 26, 41, 44. You may want to check other competencies in the same Factor/Cluster for related tips.

The Map

Listening means knowing what others have said and meant to say and leaving people comfortable that they have had their say. Most people know the techniques of good listening: Don't interrupt, be able to paraphrase, listen for underlying meaning, be accepting of other views. The problem is we all listen well only when we want to or have to. What most need to learn is how to listen when you don't want to. Remember, listening doesn't mean you accept what they have said or even that you have accepted them. It just means listening.

Some Remedies

☐ **1. Need to diagnose your listening problem? Identify the root cause:**

- The first is you don't know how to listen. That's the least likely problem.
- The second is that you know how to listen but you just don't do it with anyone. That's a little more likely.
- The third is that you listen intently to some, neutrally to others and not at all to yet others. That's the most likely problem. To test this out, do you listen to anyone? Boss? Chairperson? Mother? Children? Priest/minister/rabbi/clergy? Police officer? Best friend? Mentor? Spouse? Professional colleague outside of work? Has anyone ever complimented you or thanked you for listening? If the answer to any of those questions is yes, you have a selective listening problem. You know how to listen, you just turn it off and on.

☐ **2. Perceived as an uninterested non-listener? Focus on listening fundamentals.** First, remember the basics. You have your mouth closed. When your mouth is open, your ears automatically close. You have eye contact. You take notes. You don't frown or fidget. How do people know you've understood? You paraphrase what they have said to their satisfaction. How do people know if you have accepted or rejected what they said? You tell them. Hopefully in a tactful way if you reject what they have had to say. Give your reasons.

☐ **3. Shutting others down? Be patient.** Don't interrupt before they have finished. Don't suggest words when they hesitate or pause. Don't finish their sentences for them. Don't wave off any further input by saying, "Yes I know that," "Yes, I know where you're going," "Yes, I have heard that before." If time is really important, you can say, "Let me see if I know where this is going..." or "I wonder if we could summarize to save both of us some time?" Finally, early in a transaction answers, solutions, conclusions, statements, and dictates shut many people down. You've told them your mind's already made up. Listen first, solve second.

☐ **4. Trouble understanding what you're hearing? Ask more questions.** Good listeners ask lots of questions to get to a good understanding. Probing questions. Clarifying questions. Confirming—is this what you are saying—questions. Ask one more question than you do now and add to that until people signal you that they think you are truly listening.

☐ **5. Tuning some people out? Avoid selective listening.** Who do you listen to? Who don't you listen to? What factors account for the difference? Level? Age? Skills? Smarts? Like you/not like you? Gender? Direction (listen up but not down)? Setting? Situation? Your needs? Time available? Race? People I need/don't need? People who have something to offer/those who don't? Challenge yourself to practice listening to those you don't usually listen to. Listen for content. Separate the content from the person. Try to ferret out some value from everyone.

☐ **6. Need some structure? Manage the conversation flow.** With those you don't have time to listen to, switch to being a teacher. Try to help them craft their communications to you in a more acceptable way. Interrupt to summarize. Tell them to be shorter next time. Come with more/less data. Structure the conversation by helping them come up with categories and structures to stop their rambling. Good listeners don't signal to the "bad" people that they are not listening or are not interested. Don't signal to anyone what bucket they're in. Put your mind in neutral, nod, ask questions, be helpful.

☐ **7. Dealing with unpleasant information? Don't stop listening when it turns negative.** What if you're being criticized or attacked personally? What if people are wrong in what they are saying? The rules remain the same. You need to work on keeping yourself in a calm state when getting negative feedback. You need to shift your thinking. When getting the feedback, your only task is to accurately understand what the person is trying to tell you. It is not, at that point, to accept or refute. That comes later. Practice verbal Aikido, the ancient art of absorbing the energy of your opponent, and using it to manage him/her. Let the other side vent but don't react directly. Listen. Nod. Ask clarifying questions. But don't hit back. Don't judge. Keep him/her talking until he/she runs out of venom. Separate the person from the feedback. *More help? – See Tip #4 in #108 Defensiveness* for help on responding to negative attacks that aren't true. *More help? – See #12 Conflict Management.*

☐ **8. Sending the wrong signals? Work on your listening non-verbals.** Most people who are not in fact listening, have one or more non-verbals that signal that to others. It could be the washboard brow, blank stare, body agitation, finger or pencil drumming, interrupting, your impatient "I'm busy" look. Most around you know your signs. Do you? Ask someone you trust what it is you do when they think you are not listening. Work on eliminating those chilling non-verbals.

☐ **9. Judging instead of listening? Listen to people you don't like.** What do people see in them who do like them or can at least get along with them? What are their strengths? Do you have any common interests? Talk less and ask more questions to give them a second chance. Don't judge their motives and intentions—do that later.

☐ **10. Need to take the lead? Guide conversations with others when...**

- They are disorganized. Interrupt to summarize and keep the discussion focused. While interrupting is generally not a good tactic, it's necessary here.
- They just want to chat. Ask questions to focus them; don't respond to chatty remarks.
- They want to unload a problem. Assume when people tell you something they are looking for understanding; indicate that by being able to summarize what they said. Don't offer any advice.
- They are chronic complainers. Ask them to write down problems and solutions and then let's discuss it. This turns down the volume while hopefully moving them off complaining.
- They like to complain about others. Ask if they've talked to the person. Encourage them to do so. If that doesn't work, summarize what they have said without agreeing or disagreeing.

Some Develop-in-Place Assignments

- ☐ Benchmark innovative practices, processes, products, or services of competitors, vendors, suppliers, or customers, and present a report making recommendations for change.
- ☐ Work a few shifts in the telemarketing or customer service department, handling complaints and inquiries from customers.
- ☐ Do a customer-satisfaction survey in person or by phone, and present the results to the people involved.
- ☐ Attend a self-awareness/assessment course that includes feedback.
- ☐ Find and spend time with an expert to learn something in an area new to you.

No man has ever listened himself out of a job.
Calvin Coolidge – 30th President of the United States

Suggested Readings

Arredondo, L. (2000). *Communicating effectively*. New York: McGraw-Hill.

Barker, L., & Watson, K. (2001). *Listen up: At home, at work, in relationships: How to harness the power of effective listening*. Irvine, CA: Griffin Trade.

Donoghue, P. J., & Siegel, M. E. (2005). *Are you really listening? Keys to successful communication*. Notre Dame, IN: Sorin Books.

Harris, R. M. (2006). *The listening leader: Powerful new strategies for becoming an influential communicator*. Westport, CT: Praeger.

Hoppe, M. H. (2007). *Active listening: Improve your ability to listen and lead*. Greensboro, NC: Center for Creative Leadership.

Hybels, S., & Weaver, R. L. (2008). *Communicating effectively* (9th ed.). New York: McGraw-Hill.

Leeds, D. (2000). *Smart questions: The essential strategy for successful managers*. New York: Berkley Trade.

Loehr, J., & Schwartz, T. (2003). *The power of full engagement: Managing energy, not time, is the key to high performance and personal renewal*. New York: Free Press.

Lumsden, G., & Lumsden, D. L. (2003). *Communicating in groups and teams: Sharing leadership* (4th ed.). New York: Wadsworth Publishing Company.

Nichols, M. P. (2009). *The lost art of listening* (2nd ed.). New York: The Guilford Press.

Steil, L. K., & Bommelje, R. K. (2004). *Listening leaders: The ten golden rules to listen, lead, and succeed*. Edina, MN: Beaver's Pond Press.

34 Managerial Courage

Courage is resistance to fear, mastery of fear, not absence of fear.
Mark Twain – American humorist, satirist, lecturer, and writer

Unskilled

- ☐ Doesn't take tough stands with others
- ☐ Holds back in tough feedback situations
- ☐ Doesn't know how to present a tough position
- ☐ Knows but doesn't disclose
- ☐ Doesn't step up to issues
- ☐ Intimidated by others in power
- ☐ Hangs back and lets others take the lead
- ☐ Is a conflict avoider unwilling to take the heat of controversy
- ☐ Afraid to be wrong, get in a win/lose situation, or make a tough personnel call

Select one to three of the competencies listed below to use as a substitute for this competency if you decide not to work on it directly.

SUBSTITUTES: 1,4,8,9,12,13,27,37,38,43,48,57

Skilled

- ☐ Doesn't hold back anything that needs to be said
- ☐ Provides current, direct, complete, and "actionable" positive and corrective feedback to others
- ☐ Lets people know where they stand
- ☐ Faces up to people problems on any person or situation (not including direct reports) quickly and directly
- ☐ Is not afraid to take negative action when necessary

Overused Skill

- ☐ May be overly critical
- ☐ May be too direct and heavy-handed when providing feedback or addressing issues
- ☐ May provide too much negative and too little positive feedback
- ☐ May put too much emphasis on the dark side
- ☐ May fight too many battles

Select one to three of the competencies listed below to work on to compensate for an overuse of this skill.

COMPENSATORS: 3,7,10,11,12,19,23,26,31,33,36,41,56,60,64

Some Causes

- ☐ Avoid conflict
- ☐ Can't take the heat
- ☐ Fear of being wrong
- ☐ Fear of losing
- ☐ Get emotional
- ☐ Like to keep nose in own business

Leadership Architect® Factors and Clusters

This competency is in the Courage Factor (III). This competency is in the Dealing with Trouble Cluster (H) with: 9, 12, 13, 57. You may want to check other competencies in the same Factor/Cluster for related tips.

The Map

Saying what needs to be said at the right time, to the right person, in the right manner, is managerial courage. Everybody sees things, observes things, knows things or learns things that others need to hear. Many times it's not positive. Something went wrong. Something is being covered up or over. Something is not being done right. Someone isn't performing well. Someone is holding something back. Someone is going off on the wrong track. Some people speak up and maybe take some heat. They have managerial courage. Some people keep it to themselves. They do not.

Some Remedies

☐ **1. Heard a rumor? Check it out.** It's best to be right when presenting negative information about someone else or someone else's unit or process or mistake. Be careful with hearsay and gossip. Better that you've had direct contact with the data. If it doesn't put anyone else in jeopardy, check it out with other sources. Think of all the things it could be other than your interpretation. Check out those possibilities. Work on your message through mental interrogation until you can clearly state in a few sentences what your stand is and why you hold it. When you end up feeling or better yet knowing you're right, go with it.

☐ **2. Talking to the wrong people? Provide information to the right person.** The basic rule is to deliver it to the person who can do the most with it. Limit your passing of the information to one or as few people as possible. Consider telling the actual person involved and give him/her the opportunity to fix it without any further exposure to risk. If that's not possible, move up the chain of command. Don't pass indirect messages via messengers.

- ☐ **3. Not making your point effectively? Deliver a direct message.** Be succinct. You have limited attention span in tough feedback situations. Don't waste time with a long preamble, particularly if the feedback is negative. If your feedback is negative and the recipient is likely to know it, go ahead and say it directly. They won't hear anything positive you have to say anyway. Don't overwhelm the person/group, even if you have a lot to say. Go from specific to general points. Keep it to the facts. Don't embellish to make your point. No passion or inflammatory language. Don't do it to harm or out of vengeance. Don't do it in anger. If feelings are involved for you, wait until you can describe them, not show them. Managerial courage comes in search of a better outcome, not destroying others. Stay calm and cool. If others are not composed, don't respond. Just return to the message. *More help? – See #31 Interpersonal Savvy.*
- ☐ **4. Focusing on the negative? Bring a solution if you can.** Nobody likes a critic. Everybody appreciates a problem solver. Give people ways to improve; don't just dump and leave. Tell others what you think would be better—paint a different outcome. Help others see the consequences—you can ask them what they think and you can tell them what the consequences are from your side if you are personally involved ("I'd be reluctant to work with you on X again").
- ☐ **5. Upsetting others? Demonstrate tough concern.** Don't forget the pathos of the situation—even if you're totally right, feelings may run high. If you have to be critical, you can still empathize with how he/she feels or you can help with encouragement later when the discussion turns more positive. Mentally rehearse for worst-case scenarios. Anticipate what the person might say and have responses prepared so as not to be caught off guard. *More help? – See #12 Conflict Management.*
- ☐ **6. Catching others off guard? Choose the appropriate time and place.** Organizations are a complex maze of constituencies, issues and rivalries peopled by strong egos, sensitives and empire protectors. Worse yet, they are populated by people—which complicates organizations even further. Political savvy involves delivering negative messages in the maze, with the minimum of noise with the maximum effect. Tread boldly but carefully. Deliver messages in private. Cue the person what you are coming to talk about. "I have a concern over the way X is being treated and I would like to talk to you about it." Consider but don't be deterred by political considerations. Pick the right timing. A relaxed setting. With time to spare, don't try to fit it in the elevator. If possible let the person pick the timing and the setting. *More help? – See #38 Organizational Agility and #48 Political Savvy.*

☐ **7. Laid back? Step into the fray.** None of your business? Tend to shy away from managerial courage situations? Why? What's getting in your way? Are you prone to give up in tough situations, fear exposing yourself, don't like conflict, what? Ask yourself—what's the downside of delivering a message you think is right and will eventually help the organization but may cause someone short-term pain. What if it turns out you were wrong? Treat any misinterpretations as chances to learn. What if you were the target person or group? Even though it might hurt, would you appreciate it if someone brought the data to your attention in time for you to fix it with minimal damage? What would you think of a person you later found out knew about it and didn't come forward, and you had to spend inordinate amounts of time and political currency to fix it? Follow your convictions. Follow due process. Step up to the plate and be responsible, win or lose. People will think better of you in the long term. *More help? – See #12 Conflict Management and #57 Standing Alone.*

☐ **8. Is it personal? Focus on the behavior, not the person.** If you are personally involved and you are delivering a message to someone who didn't meet your expectations, stick to the facts and the consequences for you. Separate the event from the person. It's OK to be upset with the behavior, less so with the person, unless it's a repetitive transgression. Most of the time he/she won't accept it the first time you deliver the message. "I'm not happy with the way you presented my position in the staff meeting." Many people are defensive. Don't go for the close in every delivery situation. Just deliver the message enough so you are sure he/she understood it. Give him/her time to absorb it. Don't seek instant acceptance. Don't seek a kiss of your ring. Just deliver the message clearly and firmly. Don't threaten. *More help? – See #11 Composure.*

☐ **9. Not being heard? Go up the chain if you must.** Sometimes the seriousness of the situation calls for more drastic action. Keeping in mind you are doing this for the collective benefit of the organization and that personal gain or vengeance is not at stake, be prepared to go all the way, even if it pits you against a colleague or even a boss. If your initial message is rejected, covered, denied, hidden or glossed over and you are still convinced of its accuracy, go up the chain until it's dealt with or someone in power two levels or more above the event or person asks you to stop. If you have a mentor, seek his or her counsel along the way. A caution: In a study of whistle-blowers, 100% of the failures spoke in general terms, tying their message to lofty values such as integrity. All the successes dealt with the specific issue as it was—problem and consequences. They didn't generalize at all.

☐ **10. Reputation for being negative? Put balance in your messages.** Don't get the reputation of being the executioner or the official organization critic. Try to deliver as much positive information as negative over time. Keep track of the losers—if you have to work with these people again, do something later to show goodwill. Compliment them on a success, share something, help them achieve something. You have to balance the scales. Pick your battles. If you get the reputation of a Cassandra or a Don Quixote, anything you say will be discounted and you'll meet increasing resistance, even when you're clearly right.

Some Develop-in-Place Assignments

☐ Manage a group through a significant business crisis.

☐ Manage a cost-cutting project.

☐ Help shut down a plant, regional office, product line, business, operation, etc.

☐ Do a postmortem on a failed project, and present it to the people involved.

☐ Work on a team looking at a reorganization plan where there will be more people than positions.

Courage is rightly esteemed the first of human qualities . . .
because it is the quality which guarantees all others.
Winston Churchill – Former Prime Minister of the U.K.,
orator, historian, Nobel Prize-winning writer, and artist

Suggested Readings

Ackerman, L. D. (2000). *Identity is destiny.* San Francisco: Berrett-Koehler Publishers.

Bennis, W. G., & Nanus, B. (2007). *Leaders: Strategies for taking charge* (2nd ed.). New York: HarperBusiness.

Bossidy, L. A. (2002). The job no CEO should delegate (HBR OnPoint Enhanced Edition). Boston: *Harvard Business Review.*

Caponigro, J. R. (2000). *The crisis counselor: A step-by-step guide to managing a business crisis.* Chicago: Contemporary Books.

Chaleff, I. (2003). *The courageous follower: Standing up to and for our leaders.* San Francisco: Berrett-Koehler Publishers.

Collins, J. (2001). Level 5 leadership: The triumph of humility and fierce resolve (HBR OnPoint Enhanced Edition). Boston: *Harvard Business Review.*

Diffenderffer, B. (2005). *The Samurai leader: Winning business battles with the wisdom, honor and courage of the Samurai code.* Naperville, IL: Sourcebooks, Inc.

Dilenschneider, R. L. (2005). *A time for heroes: Business leaders, politicians, and other notables explore the nature of heroism.* Santa Monica, CA: Phoenix Books.

Downs, A. (2000). *The fearless executive: Finding the courage to trust your talents and be the leader you are meant to be.* New York: AMACOM.

George, B., & Sims, P. (2007). *True north: Discover your authentic leadership.* San Francisco: Jossey-Bass.

Goleman, D., McKee, A., & Boyatzis, R. E. (2002). *Primal leadership: Realizing the power of emotional intelligence.* Boston: Harvard Business School Press.

Klein, M., & Napier, R. (2003). *The courage to act: 5 Factors of courage to transform business.* Mountain View, CA: Davies-Black Publishing.

Kouzes, J. M., & Posner, B. Z. (2007). *The leadership challenge* (4th ed.). San Francisco: Jossey-Bass.

Lee, G., & Elliott-Lee, D. (2006). *Courage: The backbone of leadership.* San Francisco: Jossey-Bass.

Linsky, M., & Heifetz, R. A. (2002). *Leadership on the line: Staying alive through the dangers of leading.* Boston: Harvard Business School Press.

Reardon, K. K. (2007). Courage as a skill. *Harvard Business Review 85*(1), 58-64.

Thornton, P. B. (2002). *Be the leader, make the difference.* Irvine, CA: Griffin Trade Paperback.

Treasurer, B. (2008). *Courage goes to work: How to build backbones, boost performance, and get results.* San Francisco: Berrett-Koehler.

35 Managing and Measuring Work

The man who complains about the way the ball bounces is likely to be the one who dropped it.
Lou Holtz – American television commentator and former NCAA and NFL coach

Unskilled

- ☐ Doesn't use goals and objectives to manage self or others
- ☐ Not orderly in assigning and measuring work
- ☐ Isn't clear about who is responsible for what
- ☐ May be disorganized, just throw tasks at people, or lack goals or priorities
- ☐ May manage time poorly and not get around to managing in an orderly way
- ☐ Doesn't provide work-in-progress feedback
- ☐ Doesn't set up benchmarks and ways for people to measure themselves

Select one to three of the competencies listed below to use as a substitute for this competency if you decide not to work on it directly.

SUBSTITUTES: 5,9,12,13,18,20,24,27,39,47,52,53,63

Skilled

- ☐ Clearly assigns responsibility for tasks and decisions
- ☐ Sets clear objectives and measures
- ☐ Monitors process, progress, and results
- ☐ Designs feedback loops into work

Overused Skill

- ☐ May be overcontrolling
- ☐ May look over people's shoulders
- ☐ May prescribe too much and not empower people

Select one to three of the competencies listed below to work on to compensate for an overuse of this skill.

COMPENSATORS: 3,14,18,19,26,33,36,44,57,60,63,64,65

Some Causes

- ☐ Avoid the conflict that goes with setting tough goals
- ☐ Disorganized; not orderly thinking about work and tasks
- ☐ Inexperienced
- ☐ Not personally goal oriented; don't use goals
- ☐ Poor time management; don't get around to it

Leadership Architect® Factors and Clusters

This competency is in the Operating Skills Factor (II). This competency is in the Getting Work Done Through Others Cluster (F) with: 18, 19, 20, 27. You may want to check other competencies in the same Factor/Cluster for related tips.

The Map

Most people like to have goals. They like to measure themselves against a standard. They like to see who can run the fastest, score the most, jump the highest, and work the best. They like to be measured by people they respect and who make a difference to them in life and at work. They like goals to be realistic but stretching, goals that you don't know ahead of time you can really reach. Goals can make things fairer, an equitable way to measure one person against the other. People like it even better when they participate in a fair goal-setting process; it's even more motivating to them to have a hand in setting their own stretch goals.

Some Remedies

- ☐ **1. What's the target? Set clear goals.** You should set goals before assigning projects, work and tasks. Goals help focus people's time and efforts. It allows people to perform more effectively and efficiently. Most people don't want to waste time. Most people want to perform well. Learn about MBO—managing by objectives. Read a book about it. While you may not be interested in a full-blown application, all of the principles of setting goals will be in the book. Go to a course on goal setting.
- ☐ **2. What does success look like? Focus on metrics.** How would you tell if the goal was accomplished? If the things I asked others to do were done right, what outcomes could we all agree on as measures of success? Most groups can easily come up with success measures that are different from, and more important to them, than formal measures. Ask them to do so.
- ☐ **3. Seeking input? Engage your people in the goal-setting effort.** People are more motivated when they have a say in how goals are set and measured. Most won't sandbag the effort by lobbying for low goals. They are just as likely to set the goals higher than you might.

- ☐ **4. Struggling with equal opportunity? Match goals to the person.** People are different. You need to match the goals to each of the people you manage. They each respond differently to goals. Some like stretch goals; some perform better when they are assured of reaching the goal ahead of time. How do you like your goals? Did you ever work with someone who reacted to goals quite differently than you did? What was the difference? Try to relate the goals to everyone's hot button. Don't treat people alike when it comes to what goals you set and how you set them. If you let each person participate in the process, some of the matching will have already taken place.
- ☐ **5. Have enough clarity? Set crystal-clear expectations.** You need to be clear about goals, how they are going to be measured, and what the rewards and consequences will be for those who exceed, just make, or miss their goals. Communicate both verbally and in writing if you can.
- ☐ **6. Adequately tracking progress? Help people visualize progress.** Set up a process to monitor progress against the goals. People like running measures. They like to gauge their pace. It's like the United Way Thermometer in the lobby.
- ☐ **7. Problems giving feedback? Learn the guidelines for providing effective feedback.** Give as much in-process feedback as you have time for. Most people are motivated by process feedback against agreed upon goals for three reasons.
  - First, it helps them adjust what they are doing along the way in time to achieve the goal; they can make midcourse corrections.
  - Second, it shows them what they are doing is important and that you're eager to help.
  - Third, it's not the "gotcha" game of negative and critical feedback after the fact.
- ☐ **8. Ready to adjust your goals? Be flexible.** Things change all the time. Be ready to change goals midstream when faced with contrary information. Anticipate what could go wrong. *More help? – See #47 Planning.*
- ☐ **9. Do you follow through? Follow through with rewards and consequences.** Celebrate the exceeders, compliment the just made its, and sit down and discuss what happened with the missers. Actually deliver the reward or consequence you communicated. If you don't do what you said you were going to do, no one will pay attention to the next goal and consequence you set.

☐ **10. Are you taking control of your own destiny? Set goals for yourself in your job and your career.** Get used to measuring yourself. Ask your boss's help in setting goals and providing you continuous feedback. That way, you'll know better what effect goals have on others.

☐ **11. Want efficiency? Keep people focused.** Multitasking is wasteful. According to research, of all the time wasters, asking people to switch back and forth among three or more projects may be the worst. People have to reorient, switch gears, physically move, and go find their stuff. Studies back up common sense here. Multitasking doesn't always work. Few people can do it successfully. Most people should work on one project at a time.

☐ **12. How do you monitor productivity? Measure activity (in addition to measuring outcomes and results).** Say you bought some equipment. How many people are needed to run it? How much time will this take? Repairs? How much time? Activity-based accounting measures the cost of doing or not doing a task. By looking at work carefully in terms of time, core and non-core (those less important because the time spent isn't worth it) tasks can be determined. Using this method, a group of nurses doubled their productivity.

☐ **13. Can you marshal the resources? Balance time, cost, and resources.** Cost overruns are good sometimes. In a McKinsey study, for every 10% of expected product life you are late, there is a loss of about 30% in potential profit. McKinsey found, in contrast, that if a project is 50% over budget, yet the product is on time, the loss is 3% of potential profit. As the life cycle of most products is decreasing, don't manage yourself out of potential profit by rigidly sticking to cost data. If you have data on product life and the expected sales curve, you can determine the best strategy.

Some Develop-in-Place Assignments

- ☐ Manage a cost-cutting project.
- ☐ Audit cost overruns to assess the problem, and present your findings to the person or people involved.
- ☐ Manage a group of low-competence or low-performing people through a task they couldn't do by themselves.
- ☐ Assemble a team of diverse people to accomplish a difficult task.
- ☐ Manage a group of people in a rapidly expanding or growing operation.

Drive thy business or it will drive thee.

Benjamin Franklin – American scientist, author, inventor, statesman, and diplomat

Suggested Readings

Becker, B. E., Huselid, M. A., & Ulrich, D. (2001). *The HR scorecard: Linking people, strategy, and performance*. Boston: Harvard Business School Press.

Boudreau, J. W., & Ramstad, P. M. (2006). Talentship and HR measurement and analysis: From ROI to strategic organizational change. *Human Resource Planning, 29*(1), 25-33.

Cohen, D. J., & Graham, R. J. (2001). *The project manager's MBA: How to translate project decisions into business success.* New York: Jossey-Bass.

Eichinger, R. W., Ruyle, K. E., & Lombardo, M. M. (2007). *FYI for performance management™: Universal dimensions for success.* Minneapolis, MN: Lominger International: A Korn/Ferry Company.

Fitz-enz, J. (2000). *The ROI of human capital: Measuring the economic value of employee performance.* New York: AMACOM.

Fitz-enz, J. (2002). *How to measure human resources management* (3rd ed.). New York: McGraw-Hill.

Friedlob, G. T., Schleifer, L. L. F., & Plewa, F. J. (2002). *Essentials of corporate performance measurement.* New York: John Wiley & Sons.

Gerson, R. F., & Gerson, R. G. (2006). *Positive performance improvement: A new paradigm for optimizing your workforce.* Thousand Oaks, CA: Davies-Black Publishing.

Gupta, P., & Wiggenhorn, A. W. (2006). *Six Sigma business scorecard: Creating a comprehensive corporate performance measurement system* (2nd ed.). New York: McGraw-Hill.

Kirkpatrick, D. L., & Kirkpatrick, J. D. (2005). *Transferring learning to behavior: Using the four levels to improve performance.* San Francisco: Berrett-Koehler Publishers.

Luecke, R., & Hall, B. J. (2006). *Performance management: Measure and improve the effectiveness of your employees.* Boston: Harvard Business School Press.

Napier, R., & McDaniel, R. (2006). *Measuring what matters: Simplified tools for aligning teams and their stakeholders.* Thousand Oaks, CA: Davies-Black Publishing.

Niven, P. R. (2002). *Balanced scorecard step-by-step: Maximizing performance and maintaining results* (2nd ed.). Hoboken, NJ: John Wiley & Sons.

Rampersad, H. K. (2003). *Total performance scorecard: Redefining management to achieve performance with integrity.* Boston: Butterworth-Heinemann.

Schiemann, W. A. (2006). People equity: A new paradigm for measuring and managing human capital. *Human Resource Planning, 29*(1), 34-44.

Sullivan, J. (2003). *HR metrics the world-class way.* Peterborough, NH: Kennedy Information, Inc.

Wade, D., & Recardo, R. (2001). *Corporate performance management: How to build a better organization through measurement-driven, strategic alignment.* Boston: Butterworth-Heinemann.

Weiss, D. S., & Finn, R. (2005). HR metrics that count: Aligning human capital management to business results. *Human Resource Planning, 28*(1), 49-60.

36 Motivating Others

People often say that motivation doesn't last.
Well, neither does bathing...that's why we recommend it daily.
Zig Ziglar – American author, salesperson, and motivational speaker

Unskilled

- ☐ Doesn't know what motivates others or how to do it
- ☐ People under him/her don't do their best
- ☐ Not empowering and not a person many people want to work for, around or with
- ☐ May be a one-style-fits-all person, have simplistic models of motivation, or may not care as much as most others do; may be a driver just interested in getting the work out
- ☐ May have trouble with people not like him/her
- ☐ May be a poor reader of others, may not pick up on their needs and cues
- ☐ May be judgmental and put people in stereotypic categories
- ☐ Intentionally or unintentionally demotivates others

Select one to three of the competencies listed below to use as a substitute for this competency if you decide not to work on it directly.

SUBSTITUTES: 1,7,12,13,16,18,19,20,21,27,31,33,37,39,47,49,53,60,65

Skilled

- ☐ Creates a climate in which people want to do their best
- ☐ Can motivate many kinds of direct reports and team or project members
- ☐ Can assess each person's hot button and use it to get the best out of him/her
- ☐ Pushes tasks and decisions down
- ☐ Empowers others
- ☐ Invites input from each person and shares ownership and visibility
- ☐ Makes each individual feel his/her work is important
- ☐ Is someone people like working for and with

Overused Skill

- ☐ May not be good at building team spirit because of an emphasis on individuals
- ☐ May be seen as providing inequitable treatment by treating each person individually
- ☐ May not take tough stands when the situation calls for it
- ☐ May take too long getting input
- ☐ May be reluctant to assign work with tough deadlines

Select one to three of the competencies listed below to work on to compensate for an overuse of this skill.

COMPENSATORS: 9,12,13,18,19,20,34,35,37,50,52,56,57,60

Some Causes

- ☐ A one-style-fits-all
- ☐ Believe everyone should be naturally motivated
- ☐ Don't believe motivation is necessary or important
- ☐ Have trouble talking with people not like you
- ☐ Judgmental about others
- ☐ Prefer to treat everyone the same
- ☐ Too simple views of motivation

Leadership Architect® Factors and Clusters

This competency is in the Personal and Interpersonal Skills Factor (VI). This competency is in the Inspiring Others Cluster (Q) with: 37, 60, 65. You may want to check other competencies in the same Factor/Cluster for related tips.

The Map

Greater things can happen when people are motivated. Think of three accomplishments you're proud of, then ask yourself how motivated you were to accomplish them. Similarly, if you can figure out what motivates others, their accomplishments and yours will be greater. Some managers believe others should be automatically motivated, thinking motivation comes standard with the person. Some managers believe everyone should be as motivated as they are about the job and the organization. That's seldom the case. Fact is, people are different. Each person is different in the way he/she becomes and sustains being motivated. Being good in this area includes believing it's a manager's job to motivate—that all people are different, and that motivating each of them takes a little bit different approach.

Some Remedies

☐ **1. Confused by the process of motivating others? Read up on the subject.** Follow the basic rules of inspiring others as outlined in classic books like *People Skills* by Robert Bolton or *Thriving on Chaos* by Tom Peters. Communicate to people that what they do is important. Say thanks. Offer help and ask for it. Provide autonomy in how people do their work. Provide a variety of tasks. "Surprise" people with enriching, challenging assignments. Show an interest in their careers. Adopt a learning attitude toward mistakes. Celebrate successes, have visible accepted measures of achievement and so on. Too often, people behave correctly, but there are no consequences. Although it's easy to get too busy to acknowledge, celebrate, and occasionally criticize, don't forget to reinforce what you want. As a rule of thumb, 4 to 1 positive to negative is best.

☐ **2. Are you betting on the wrong motivators? Know and play the motivation odds.** According to research by Rewick and Lawler, the top motivators at work are: (1) Job challenge; (2) Accomplishing something worthwhile; (3) Learning new things; (4) Personal development; (5) Autonomy. Pay (12th), Friendliness (14th), Praise (15th) or Chance of promotion (17th) are not insignificant but are superficial compared with the more powerful motivators. Provide challenges, paint pictures of why this is worthwhile, create a common mindset, set up chances to learn and grow, and provide autonomy and you'll hit the vast majority of people's hot buttons.

☐ **3. Difficulty setting effective goals? Use stretch goals to motivate.** Most people are turned on by reasonable goals. They like to measure themselves against a standard. They like to see who can run the fastest, score the most, and work the best. They like goals to be realistic but stretching. People try hardest when they have somewhere between 1/2 and a 2/3 chance of success and some control over how they go about it. People are even more motivated when they participate in setting the goals. Set just out of reach challenges and tasks that will be first time for people—their first negotiation, their first solo presentation, etc. *More help? – See #35 Managing and Measuring Work.*

☐ **4. Trouble with non-verbals? Learn to read people's motivation signals.** What do they do first? What do they emphasize in their speech? What do they display emotion around? What values play out for them?

- First things. Does this person go to others first, hole up and study, complain, discuss feelings, or take action? These are the basic orientations of people that reveal what's important to them. Use these to motivate.
- Speech content. People might focus on details, concepts, feelings, or other people in their speech. This can tell you again how to appeal to them by mirroring their speech emphasis. Although most of us naturally adjust—we talk details with detail oriented people—chances are good that in problem relationships you're not finding the common ground. She talks detail and you talk people, for example.
- Emotion. You need to know what people's hot buttons are because one mistake can get you labeled as insensitive with some people. The only cure here is to see what turns up the volume for them—either literally or what they're concerned about.
- Values. Apply the same thinking to the values of others. Do they talk about money, recognition, integrity, efficiency in their normal work conversation?

Figuring out what their drivers are tells you another easy way to appeal to anyone. Once you have this basic understanding, you need to follow the basic rules of motivating others covered in this section.

☐ **5. Judgmental? Turn off your judgment program.** In trying to reach someone, work on not judging him/her. You don't have to agree, you just have to understand in order to motivate. The fact that you wouldn't be motivated that way isn't relevant.

☐ **6. Not relating? Be able to speak their language at their level.** It shows respect for their way of thinking. Speaking their language makes it easier for them to talk with you and give you the information you need to motivate.

☐ **7. Closed off from others? Bring him/her into your world.** Tell him/her your conceptual categories. To deal with you he/she needs to know how you think and why. Tell him/her your perspective—the questions you ask, the factors you're interested in. If you can't explain your thinking, he/she won't know how to deal with you effectively. It's easier to follow someone and something you understand.

☐ **8. All business? Get to know them on a personal level.** Know three non-work things about everybody—their interests and hobbies or their children or something you can chat about. Life is a small world. If you ask people a few personal questions, you'll find you have something in common with virtually anyone. Having something in common will help bond the relationship and allow you to individualize how you motivate.

☐ **9. Avoiding the tough cases? Turn a negative into a motivator.** If a person is touchy about something, he/she will respond to targeted help. If the person responds by being clannish, he/she may need your support to get more in the mainstream. If he/she is demotivated, look for both personal and work causes. This person may respond to job challenge. If the person is naive, help him/her see how things work.

☐ **10. Giving too much direction? Get people more involved in the work they are doing.** Delegate and empower as much as you can. Get him/her involved in setting goals and determining the work process to get there. Ask his/her opinion about decisions that have to be made. Have him/her help appraise the work of the unit. Share the successes. Debrief the failures together. Use his/her full tool set.

☐ **11. Trouble figuring out what drives people? Find out why people do what they do.** Follow the real consequences. One company had a million dollars of theft per year, both against the company and other employees. They brought in a renowned psychologist, Gary Latham, who asked a number of questions around the benefits and costs of being honest or stealing. Top management, of course, had originally wanted to install hidden cameras and hire detectives. They rejected this when Latham told them that the thieves had suggested this very solution! They wanted to steal the cameras to increase the thrill they got from theft. (They almost never sold or even used what they took.) Additionally, few people expected there would be any real penalty for getting caught (strong union protection). They did it because they could. Essentially, by asking why people do what they do rather than assuming it, the company hit upon a better solution: Create a library system where employees were allowed to borrow all that was previously stolen. Second, declare an amnesty day so the stolen goods could be returned. The outcome? Almost all the stolen goods were returned and theft dropped to near zero over the next three years.

This example has nothing to do with stopping theft. Setting up a library might be a disaster in many organizations. What it demonstrates is how to figure out why people do what they do:

- Absolute confidentiality, often using outsiders to collect information.
- Find out what the positive and negative consequences are for the person. In this case, what are the +'s and –'s of being honest or dishonest?
- Once you understand the anticipated consequences or outcomes, you understand the behavior.
- Change the consequences and you change the behavior.
- This same technique has been used to understand why customers choose a competitor and how to get the customer back. It has also been used in overcoming resistance to change. The logic is the same. What are the +'s and –'s of embracing change or resisting it? What are the +'s and –'s of staying with us versus going with a competitor?

Some Develop-in-Place Assignments

- ☐ Manage a temporary group of "green," inexperienced people as their coach, teacher, guide, mentor, etc.
- ☐ Manage a group of people who are older and/or more experienced to accomplish a task.
- ☐ Be a change agent; create a symbol for change; lead the rallying cry; champion a significant change and implementation.
- ☐ Create employee involvement teams.
- ☐ Integrate diverse systems, processes, or procedures across decentralized and/or dispersed units.

In motivating people, you've got to engage their minds and their hearts. I motivate people, I hope, by example—and perhaps by excitement, by having productive ideas to make others feel involved.
Rupert Murdoch – Australian-American global media mogul

Suggested Readings

Adair, J. (2003). *The inspirational leader.* London: Kogan Page.

Carlaw, M., Carlaw, P., Deming, V. K., & Friedmann, K. (2002). *Managing and motivating contact center employees: Tools and techniques for inspiring outstanding performance from your frontline staff.* New York: McGraw-Hill.

Charan, R. (2007). *Know-how: The 8 skills that separate people who perform from those who don't.* New York: Crown Business.

Cloke, K., & Goldsmith, J. (2003). *The art of waking people up: Cultivating awareness and authenticity at work.* San Francisco: Jossey-Bass.

Crainer, S. (2001). *Motivating the new generation: Modern motivation techniques.* New York: BrownHerron Publishing.

Deems, R. S., & Deems, T. A. (2003). *Leading in tough times: The manager's guide to responsibility, trust, and motivation.* Amherst, MA: HRD Press.

Deeprose, D. (2006). *How to recognize and reward employees: 150 Ways to inspire peak performance* (2nd ed.). New York: AMACOM.

Glanz, B. A. (2002). *Handle with CARE: Motivating and retaining employees.* New York: McGraw-Hill Trade.

Gostick, A., & Elton, C. (2007). *The carrot principle: How the best managers use recognition to engage their employees, retain talent, and drive performance.* New York: Free Press.

Grensing-Pophal, L. (2003). *Motivating today's employees.* Bellingham, WA: Self-Counsel Press.

Hiam, A. (2003). *Motivational management: Inspiring your people for maximum performance.* New York: AMACOM.

Karp, H. (2002). *Bridging the boomer-Xer gap: Creating authentic teams for high performance at work.* Palo Alto, CA: Davies-Black Publishing.

Kouzes, J. M., & Posner, B. Z. (2003). *Encouraging the heart: A leader's guide to rewarding and recognizing others.* San Francisco: Jossey-Bass.

Manville, B., & Kerr, S. (2003). *Harvard Business Review on motivating people.* Boston: Harvard Business School Press.

Manz, C. C., & Sims, H. P., Jr. (2001). *The new superleadership: Leading others to lead themselves.* San Francisco: Berrett-Koehler Publishers.

McKenna, P. J., & Maister, D. H. (2002). *First among equals: How to manage a group of professionals.* New York: Free Press.

Podmoroff, D. (2005). *365 Ways to motivate and reward your employees every day: With little or no money.* Ocala, FL: Atlantic Publishing Group.

Scott, W. J., Miller, T., III, & Scott, M. W. (2001). *Motivating others: Bringing out the best in people.* Bloomington, IN: 1stBooks Library.

37 Negotiating

Start out with an ideal and end up with a deal.
Karl Albrecht – German entrepreneur

Unskilled

- ☐ Not a good deal maker; doesn't come away with much
- ☐ May use ineffective tactics—too hard or too soft, may have to win every battle or gives away too much to get the agreement
- ☐ Poor conflict manager, trouble dealing with attack, contention or non-negotiable points
- ☐ May hold back and be afraid to take tough stands
- ☐ Poor listener
- ☐ May not seek or know how to find common ground
- ☐ May be too noisy and do too much damage to relationships
- ☐ May not know how to be diplomatic, direct and polite

Select one to three of the competencies listed below to use as a substitute for this competency if you decide not to work on it directly.

SUBSTITUTES: 2,9,11,12,16,27,30,32,33,36,38,48,50,51,52,56,57,64

Skilled

- ☐ Can negotiate skillfully in tough situations with both internal and external groups
- ☐ Can settle differences with minimum noise
- ☐ Can win concessions without damaging relationships
- ☐ Can be both direct and forceful as well as diplomatic
- ☐ Gains trust quickly of other parties to the negotiations
- ☐ Has a good sense of timing

Overused Skill

- ☐ May leave people-damage in his/her wake
- ☐ May walk over people's feelings
- ☐ May always need to win
- ☐ May hang on to a position too long
- ☐ May become overly accommodating and be reluctant to walk away
- ☐ May need to smooth over everything
- ☐ May take too long to get things decided

Select one to three of the competencies listed below to work on to compensate for an overuse of this skill.

COMPENSATORS: 2,12,16,17,30,38,41,48,50,51,52,53,56,57,63

Some Causes

- ☐ Can't take the heat
- ☐ Come on too hard/too soft
- ☐ Give in too much; too early
- ☐ Have to win every battle
- ☐ Have trouble reaching equitable agreements
- ☐ Have trouble when the other side is contentious
- ☐ Nervous about negotiating
- ☐ Not a good trader or bargainer
- ☐ Poor interpersonal skills
- ☐ Too serious and intense

Leadership Architect® Factors and Clusters

This competency is in the Personal and Interpersonal Skills Factor (VI). This competency is in the Inspiring Others Cluster (Q) with: 36, 60, 65. You may want to check other competencies in the same Factor/Cluster for related tips.

The Map

Negotiation is getting all you can at the least cost possible while leaving the other side intact and reasonably positive so that they will negotiate with you again. The best case is win-win where both sides go away with exactly what they wanted. A rare happening. More likely is that both sides got enough to feel good about the process. It is something-something. There are win-lose negotiations where one side wins a lot of concessions and the other side leaves with nothing or very little. That's usually only good for one-time events or buying cars. Losers are not happy people. Good win-win negotiators focus on the target, the issues and the underlying interests of both sides. They generally use commonly accepted ethical principles and fairness. They deal with personal issues separately if at all, deflect personal assaults, and stay away from early rigid positions.

Some Remedies

☐ **1. Impatient to get down to business? Set rapport and boundaries.** Start slow until you know where the other party is coming from. Pay attention to positioning. You and your team on one side and them on the other sets up a contest. Try to mix team members together on both sides. If you're the host, start with small talk unrelated to the subject of the negotiation. Give everyone time to settle in and get comfortable. When it's time, ask whether it would be useful for each side to lay out its goals, starting positions and any boundaries—such as, we aren't here to negotiate costs at this time. Volunteer to go first. Give reasons first, positions last. When you offer goals and positions, people often don't listen to your reasons. *More help? – See #3 Approachability and #31 Interpersonal Savvy.*

☐ **2. Trouble starting on the right foot? Avoid early rigid positions.** It's just physics. Action gets equal reaction. Strong statements. Strongly worded positions. Casting blame. Absolutes. Lines in the sand. Unnecessary passion. All of these will be responded to in kind, will waste time, cause ill will and possibly prevent a win-win or a something-something. It only has a place in one-time, either/or negotiations and even there it isn't recommended. Similarly, watch out for overcommitment to any need or course of action. Look for information that goes against your preferences. Be able to adjust your position and your wants. If you can't, your ego is getting the best of you. If you can't walk away until you get X, you'll probably either overpay or blow the negotiation. Don't negotiate around a single issue if you can add another. This is another situation which leads to rigidity.

☐ **3. Too focused on areas of disagreement? Downsize the negotiation.** Make the negotiations as small as possible. Even far apart initial positions will have something in common. Announce that you would first like to see if there are any points on which the two sides could tentatively agree. List those on a board or flip chart. Then ask if there are any tentative trades that could be made. I can give you this, if you could give me that. Document the possible trades, pending other things of course. Then list the seemingly far aparts, the deal stoppers each side has. Take each deal stopper one at a time and have the owner get as specific as possible as to the concessions they are asking for so time isn't wasted on assumed far aparts. See if you can move any of them off the far apart list. Have some things you can give away. Hold out some attractive concessions and giveaways. Release them as you need them during the negotiation process. (Better if you know ahead of time what they would be pleased with). To bring them out, state them in a proposition, "If I would give in on this point, could I have X in return?" Do this to generate a wider variety of possibilities.

☐ **4. Making faulty assumptions? Use questions to better understand positions.** In win-win and something-something negotiations, the more information about the other side you have, the more you will have to work with. What can you learn about what they know before going in? What will they do if they don't reach an agreement with you? In the negotiation, ask more questions, make fewer statements. Ask clarifying questions—"What did you mean by that?" Probes—"Why do you say that?" Motives—"What led you to that position?" Explain objectively why you hold a view; make the other side do the same. When the other side takes a rigid position, don't reject it. Ask why—what are the principles behind the offer, how will we know it's fair, what's the theory of the case. Play out what would happen if their position was accepted. Get everything out that you can. Don't negotiate assumptions, negotiate facts.

☐ **5. Caught off guard by tense negotiations? Be prepared for some heat.** Negotiations are not always benign and friendly. Many times they generate heat. Passion. Defensiveness. Blame. Attacks. Innuendoes. Threats. Separate the people from the heat they deliver and the people from the roles they play in the negotiations. Deal with people issues directly but separately and maybe off line during a break. Try to deal candidly with the toughest critic first. Avoid direct blaming remarks; describe the impasse and possible solutions. In response to unreasonable proposals, attacks, or a non-answer to a question, you can always say nothing. People will usually respond by saying more, coming off their position a bit, or at least revealing their interests. If the other side won't play fair, surface their game—"It looks like you're playing good cop, bad cop. Why don't you settle your differences and tell me one thing?" In response to threats, say you'll only negotiate on merit and fairness. Suggest objective standards or throw out ideas of what would be fair parameters for discussion. If someone makes a ridiculous offer, take it seriously. Ask him/her to explain it, then watch him/her squirm. Or generalize the demand. They offer 25% less. You say, "So you think this is worth less than our asking price?" When he/she engages in brinksmanship of the X dollars or nothing variety, treat the statement as a goal or wish or simply go on talking as if he/she hadn't said it. If someone yells at you, lower your voice or move closer to him/her. Beware the last minute add-on. This can happen when the negotiation is done, or when the final contract arrives. While it's tempting to get it over with, they have as much to lose as you do. Instead respond, "OK, I wasn't that happy with the deal anyway. Let's renegotiate all the issues." Hold back any threat of negative action until the impact will be the greatest. *More help? – See #12 Conflict Management.* Also read *Getting to Yes* by Fisher and Ury, and *Secrets of Power Negotiating for Salespeople* by Roger Dawson.

☐ **6. Can people read you like a book? Keep your cool.** Sometimes our emotional reactions lead others to think we are weak and have problems with tough situations. How do you show emotions? In negotiations, what emotional reactions do you have such as impatience, interrupting, denials or non-verbals like fidgeting or drumming your fingers? Learn to recognize those as soon as they start and ask a question instead to bide time, or ask the person to tell you more about his/her point of view. Let the other side vent frustration, blow off steam, but don't react. Return to facts, and the problem before the group, staying away from personal clashes. *More help? – See #11 Composure.*

☐ **7. Need to win on all points? Make small concessions.** Figure out ways to keep the other side intact. When they have to report back to their boss, what can they say they got? Allow others to save face; concede small points; don't try to hit a home run every time. Generally, you should hoard your larger concessions until last, however. Conceding any point early can set a bad precedent.

☐ **8. At an impasse? Find some common ground.** If you can't agree on everything, document the things both were able to agree upon, and delineate all the remaining issues. See if you can at least agree on process—design and agree upon definite time, certain follow-up steps. This creates some motion and breaks dead-in-the-water stalemates. *More help? – See #52 Process Management.*

☐ **9. Gone as far as you can alone? Arbitrate when necessary.** When there is a true impasse, suggest a third equal power and acceptable to both parties person, to help resolve the remaining conflicts. Use a third party to write up each side's interests and keep suggesting compromises until you can agree. Continue to move closer until each side can improve it no more. Or if time is an issue, pass it up to a higher authority. Present both sides calmly and objectively, and let the chips fall where they may.

☐ **10. Feeling trapped? Know when to walk away.** The most confident and focused negotiators are those who are comfortable walking away if necessary. Think it through ahead of time. Could you afford to walk away temporarily or permanently? How could you recoup? Do you have the time? Could you get what you need some other way? It's a real confidence builder to know you can say no. Be prepared to cut line and leave the negotiation. *More help? – See #57 Standing Alone.*

☐ **11. Can't close the deal? Reach a provisional agreement if needed.** You can also suggest a post-agreement agreement, meaning you agree to look for a better one, although still bound by the first agreement if a better one can't be reached. Sometimes you can trade time for price, or add an issue to make it even better.

Some Develop-in-Place Assignments

☐ Handle a tough negotiation with an internal or external client or customer.

☐ Be a member of a union-negotiating or grievance-handling team.

☐ Manage liquidation/sale of a business, products, equipment, materials, furniture, overstock, etc.

☐ Manage the interface between consultants and the organization on a critical assignment.

☐ Get involved with the negotiation of a contract or agreement with international consequences.

Allowing your opponent in a transaction to walk away with his dignity, his humor, and his hearing intact, and a pretty good deal in his pocket, is the right way to do business.

John Rutledge – American banker

Suggested Readings

Babcock, L., & Laschever, S. (2003). *Women don't ask: Negotiation and the gender divide*. Princeton, NJ: Princeton University Press.

Brett, J. M. (2007). *Negotiating globally: How to negotiate deals, resolve disputes, and make decisions across cultural boundaries* (2nd ed.). San Francisco: Jossey-Bass.

Dawson, R. (2001). *Secrets of power negotiating for salespeople: Inside secrets from a master negotiator.* Franklin Lakes, NJ: Career Press.

Fisher, R., Patton, B., & Ury, W. (1991). *Getting to yes: Negotiating agreement without giving in* (2nd ed.). New York: Penguin Books.

Fisher, R., & Shapiro, D. (2005). *Beyond reason: Using emotions as you negotiate.* New York: Penguin Group.

Gardner, H. (2004). *Changing minds: The art and science of changing our own and other people's minds.* Boston: Harvard Business School Press.

Harvard Business Essentials. (2003). *Negotiation.* Boston: Harvard Business School Press.

Levine, S. (2002). *The book of agreement: 10 Essential elements for getting the results you want.* San Francisco: Berrett-Koehler Publishers.

Macenka, M. J. (2001). *Inside the minds: Leading deal makers: Top venture capitalists and lawyers share their knowledge on negotiations, leveraging your position and the art of deal making.* Boston: Aspatore Books.

Miller, L. E., & Miller, J. (2002). *A woman's guide to successful negotiating: How to convince, collaborate, and create your way to agreement.* New York: McGraw-Hill.

Oliver, D. (2003). *How to negotiate effectively.* London: Kogan Page.

Patterson, K., Grenny, J., McMillan, R., Switzler, A., & Covey, S. R. (2002). *Crucial conversations: Tools for talking when stakes are high.* New York: McGraw-Hill.

Salacuse, J. (2003). *The global negotiator: Making, managing, and mending deals around the world in the twenty-first century.* New York: Palgrave Macmillan.

Shell, G. R. (2006). *Bargaining for advantage: Negotiation strategies for reasonable people* (2nd ed.). New York: Penguin Books.

Ury, W. (2007). *The power of a positive no: Save the deal save the relationship—and still say no.* New York: Bantam Books.

Watkins, M. (2002). *Breakthrough business negotiation.* San Francisco: Jossey-Bass.

38 Organizational Agility

More business decisions occur over lunch and dinner than at any other time, yet no MBA courses are given on the subject.
Peter Drucker – Austrian-born American writer and management consultant

Unskilled

- ☐ Doesn't get things done in organizations beyond his/her area
- ☐ May lack the interpersonal skills to get things done across boundaries
- ☐ May not negotiate well within organizations
- ☐ May be too timid and laid back to maneuver through organizations
- ☐ May reject the complexity of organizations
- ☐ May lack the experience or simply not know who and where to go
- ☐ May be too impatient to learn
- ☐ May neither know nor care to know the origins of how things work around the organization

Select one to three of the competencies listed below to use as a substitute for this competency if you decide not to work on it directly.

SUBSTITUTES: 5,8,32,39,48,52,59,64

Skilled

- ☐ Knowledgeable about how organizations work
- ☐ Knows how to get things done both through formal channels and the informal network
- ☐ Understands the origin and reasoning behind key policies, practices, and procedures
- ☐ Understands the cultures of organizations

Overused Skill

- ☐ May spend too much time maneuvering for advantage
- ☐ May spend too much time and energy working on issues that lack substance
- ☐ May be seen as too political

Select one to three of the competencies listed below to work on to compensate for an overuse of this skill.

COMPENSATORS: 4,5,8,12,17,22,27,29,51,52,53,57,63

Some Causes

- ☐ Don't see things in systems
- ☐ Impatient
- ☐ Inexperienced
- ☐ Poor interpersonal skills
- ☐ Resist the reality of complexity
- ☐ Weak negotiator

Leadership Architect® Factors and Clusters

This competency is in the Organizational Positioning Skills Factor (V). This competency is in the Being Organizationally Savvy Cluster (K) with: 48. You may want to check other competencies in the same Factor/Cluster for related tips.

The Map

Organizations can be complex mazes with many turns, dead ends, quick routes and choices. In most organizations, the best path to get somewhere is almost never a straight line. There is a formal organization—the one on the organization chart—where the path may look straight, and then there is the informal organization where all paths are zigzagged. Since organizations are staffed with people, they become all the more complex. There are gatekeepers, expediters, stoppers, resisters, guides, Good Samaritans and influencers. All of these types live in the organizational maze. The key to being successful in maneuvering through complex organizations is to find your way through the maze to your goal in the least amount of time while making the least noise. The best way to do that is to accept the complexity of organizations rather than fighting it and learn to be a maze-bright person.

Some Remedies

- ☐ **1. Not sure why you're having difficulty? Get an assessment.** Try to do the most honest self-assessment you can on why you aren't skilled at getting things done smoothly and effectively in the organization. Ask at least one person from each group you work with for feedback. *More help? – See #55 Self-Knowledge.*
- ☐ **2. Old approaches not working? Shake things up.** What you are doing now apparently isn't working. Do something different. Try things you generally don't do. Look to what others do who are more effective than you. Keep a log on what worked and what didn't.
- ☐ **3. Getting a poor response from others? Try to make a positive impression.** Personal style can get in the way. People differ in the impression they leave. Those who leave positive impressions get more things done

through the organization than those who leave a negative impression. Positive impressions include listening. *More help? – See #3 Approachability, #31 Interpersonally Savvy, #33 Listening, #37 Negotiating, #39 Organizing and #42 Peer Relationships.*

☐ **4. Taking more than you're giving? Think equity.** Relationships that work are built on equity and considering the impact on others. Don't just ask for things; find some common ground where you can provide help, not just ask for it. What does the unit you're contacting need in the way of problem solving or information? Do you really know how they see the issue? Is it even important to them? How does what you're working on affect them? If it affects them negatively and they are balky, can you trade something, appeal to the common good, figure out some way to minimize the work or other impact (volunteering staff help, for example)? *More help? – See #42 Peer Relationships.*

☐ **5. Others not coming through for you? Consider your sources of help.** Sometimes the problem is in assessing people. Who really wants to help? Who is going to get in the way? What do they really want? What price will they ask for helping? *More help? – See #56 Sizing Up People and #64 Understanding Others.*

☐ **6. Frustrated? Consider the nature of the organization.** Sometimes the problem is underestimating the complexity of organizations. Some people always want to think things are simpler than they are. While it's possible some organizations are simple, most are not. *More help? – See #48 Political Savvy and #59 Managing Through Systems.*

☐ **7. Scattered approach? Sharpen your focus.** Sometimes disorganization does you in. Understanding how organizations function takes some discipline. You have to look beyond what you see to what's really in the background. *More help? – See #47 Planning.*

☐ **8. Lost in the maze? Go with the flow.** Some people know the steps necessary to get things done but are too impatient to follow the process. Maneuvering through the maze includes stopping once in a while to let things run their course. It may mean waiting until a major gatekeeper has the time to pay attention to your needs. *More help? – See #41 Patience.* One additional problem might be in diagnosing the paths, turns, dead ends and zags. *More help? – See #32 Learning on the Fly, #48 Political Savvy and #51 Problem Solving.*

☐ **9. Getting rattled when what you try fails or gets rejected? Expect the unexpected.** If you tend to lose your cool and get frustrated, practice responses before the fact. What's the worst that could happen and what will you do? You can pause, count to 10, or ask why it can't be done. You can take in information and develop counter moves. So don't react, learn. *More help? – See #11 Composure.*

- ☐ **10. Don't know who are the movers and shakers in the organization? Identify the key players and their roles.** How do they get things done? Who do they rely on for expediting things through the maze? How do you compare to them? Who are the major gatekeepers who control the flow of resources, information and decisions? Who are the guides and the helpers? Get to know them better. Who are the major resisters and stoppers? Try to avoid or go around them.

Some Develop-in-Place Assignments

- ☐ Work on a team looking at a reorganization plan where there will be more people than positions.
- ☐ Launch a new product, service, or process.
- ☐ Be a change agent; create a symbol for change; lead the rallying cry; champion a significant change and implementation.
- ☐ Plan a new site for a building (plant, field office, headquarters, etc.).
- ☐ Integrate diverse systems, processes, or procedures across decentralized and/or dispersed units.

Every company has two organizational structures: The formal one is written on the charts; the other is the everyday relationship of the men and women in the organization.
Harold S. Geneen – American businessman

Suggested Readings

Anklam, P. (2007). *Net work: A practical guide to creating and sustaining networks at work and in the world.* Burlington, MA: Butterworth-Heinemann.

Ashkenas, R. N., Ulrich, D., Jick, T., & Kerr, S. (2002). *The boundaryless organization: Breaking the chains of organization structure* (Rev. ed.). San Francisco: Jossey-Bass.

Brache, A. P. (2002). *How organizations work: Taking a holistic approach to enterprise health.* Hoboken, NJ: John Wiley & Sons.

Cross, R. L., Parker, A., & Cross, R. (2004). *The hidden power of social networks: Understanding how work really gets done in organizations.* Boston: Harvard Business School Press.

Dominguez, L. R. (2003). *How to shine at work.* New York: McGraw-Hill.

Gobillot, E. (2007). *The connected leader: Creating agile organisations for people, performance, and profit.* London: Kogan Page.

Hall, K. (2007). *Speed lead: Faster, simpler ways to manage people, projects, and teams in complex companies.* London: Nicholas Brealey Publishing.

Honold, L., & Silverman, R. J. (2002). *Organizational DNA.* Palo Alto, CA: Davies-Black Publishing.

Marshak, R. J., & Schein, E. (2006). *Covert processes at work: Managing the five hidden dimensions of organizational change.* San Francisco: Berrett-Koehler Publishers.

Sathe, V. (2003). *Corporate entrepreneurship: Top managers and new business creation.* Boston: Cambridge University Press.

Segil, L., Goldsmith, M., & Belasco, J. (Eds.). (2003). *Partnering: The new face of leadership.* New York: AMACOM.

Wenger, E., McDermott, R., & Snyder, W. M. (2002). *Cultivating communities of practice: A guide to managing knowledge.* Boston: Harvard Business School Press.

39 Organizing

Organizing is what you do before you do something,
so that when you do it, it is not all mixed up.
A.A. Milne – American writer, playwright, and poet

Unskilled

- ☐ Doesn't pull resources together effectively
- ☐ May not know how to find and arrange people, materials, budget, etc.
- ☐ May be a poor delegator and planner and not very motivating to work with
- ☐ Performance decreases as the number of simultaneous activities increase
- ☐ May rely too much on self
- ☐ May scramble at the last minute and have to work long hours to finish
- ☐ May not anticipate or be able to see how multiple activities come together

Select one to three of the competencies listed below to use as a substitute for this competency if you decide not to work on it directly.

SUBSTITUTES: 9,18,20,25,36,47,52,60,62

Skilled

- ☐ Can marshal resources (people, funding, material, support) to get things done
- ☐ Can orchestrate multiple activities at once to accomplish a goal
- ☐ Uses resources effectively and efficiently
- ☐ Arranges information and files in a useful manner

Overused Skill

- ☐ May not be tolerant of normal chaos
- ☐ May too often want to do things his/her own way
- ☐ May not be open to suggestions and input
- ☐ May lose his/her effectiveness when things don't go as planned

Select one to three of the competencies listed below to work on to compensate for an overuse of this skill.

COMPENSATORS: 2,11,12,26,32,33,36,40,46,52,60

Some Causes

- ☐ Don't delegate
- ☐ Inexperienced
- ☐ Not motivating to work with
- ☐ Not resourceful
- ☐ Poor negotiator
- ☐ Poor planner
- ☐ Too self-centered

Leadership Architect® Factors and Clusters

This competency is in the Operating Skills Factor (II). This competency is in the Getting Organized Cluster (E) with: 47, 62. You may want to check other competencies in the same Factor/Cluster for related tips.

The Map

It is easier to get things done when everybody is pulling in the same direction. It is easier to perform when you have all the tools and resources you need. It is easier to get things done when everyone you need in your corner is supportive and pulling for you. It's fun to be able to work through others even when you don't have direct authority over them. Unless you prefer things to be hard and not much fun, organizing is an essential skill to have.

Some Remedies

☐ **1. Got a goal? Set goals and measures.** Nothing keeps projects on time and on budget like a goal and a measure. Set goals for the whole project and the sub-tasks. Set measures so you and others can track progress against the goals. *More help? – See #35 Managing and Measuring Work.*

☐ **2. Have a plan? Lay out the work.** Most resourcefulness starts out with a plan. What do I need to accomplish? What's the time line? What resources will I need? Who controls the resources—people, funding, tools, materials, support—I need? What's my currency? How can I pay for or repay the resources I need? Who wins if I win? Who might lose? Lay out the work from A to Z. Many people are seen as disorganized because they don't write the sequence or parts of the work and leave something out. Ask others to comment on ordering and what's missing.

☐ **3. Resources tight? Bargain for resources.** What do I have to trade? What can I buy? What can I borrow? What do I need to trade for? What do I need that I can't pay or trade for?

☐ **4. Shared your goals? Rally support.** Share your mission and goals with the people you need to support you. Try to get their input. People who are asked tend to cooperate more than people who are not asked. Figure out how the people who support your effort can win along with you.

- ☐ **5. Big projects? Delegate.** Getting long, complex or multi-tracked projects done involves accomplishing a series of tasks that lead up to the whole. One clear finding in the research is that empowered people work longer and harder. People like to have control over their work, determine how they are going to do it, and have the authority to make decisions. Give away as much as possible along with the authority that goes with it. Another clear finding is to pay attention to the weakest links—usually groups or elements you have the least interface with or control over—perhaps someone in a remote location, a consultant or supplier. Stay doubly in touch with the potential weak links.
- ☐ **6. Lots of complexity? Manage multiple tracks.** Many attempts to get complex things done involve managing parallel tracks or multiple tasks at the same time. It helps if you have a master plan. It helps if you delegate some of the work. *More help? – See #47 Planning.*
- ☐ **7. Limited resources? Manage efficiently.** Watch the budget. Plan spending carefully. Have a reserve if the unanticipated comes up. Set up a funding time line so you can track ongoing expenditures.
- ☐ **8. Flustered? Manage coolly.** Some get flustered when a lot of things are up in the air at the same time. A plan helps. Delegation helps. Goals and measures help. Getting frustrated seldom helps. *More help? – See #11 Composure.*
- ☐ **9. Experiencing success? Celebrate.** Get in the habit of sharing the successes and spreading the wealth. It will make it easier for you to go back to the well the next time you need resources.
- ☐ **10. Need a model? Seek help.** Find someone in your environment who is good at organizing people and things. Watch what he/she does. How does that compare to what you typically do?

Some Develop-in-Place Assignments

- ☐ Work on a team that's deciding whom to keep and whom to let go in a layoff, shutdown, delayering, or merger.
- ☐ Plan an off-site meeting, conference, convention, trade show, event, etc.
- ☐ Manage the purchase of a major product, equipment, materials, program, or system.
- ☐ Plan a new site for a building (plant, field office, headquarters, etc.).
- ☐ Manage the visit of a VIP (member of top management, government official, outside customer, foreign visitor, etc.).

Don't agonize. Organize.
Florynce Kennedy – American lawyer, activist,
Civil Rights advocate, and feminist

Suggested Readings

Allen, D. (2003). *Getting things done: The art of stress-free productivity.* New York: Penguin Books.

Byfield, M. (2003). *It's hard to make a difference when you can't find your keys: The seven-step path to becoming truly organized.* New York: Viking Press.

Cramer, K. D. (2002). *When faster harder smarter is not enough: Six steps for achieving what you want in a rapid-fire world.* New York: McGraw-Hill.

Crouch, C. (2005). *Getting organized: Improving focus, organization and productivity.* Memphis, TN: Dawson Publishing.

Davenport, L. (2001). *Order from chaos: A six-step plan for organizing yourself, your office, and your life.* New York: Three Rivers Press.

Hedrick, L. H. (2002). *Get organized in the digital age.* New York: New American Library Trade.

Hemphill, B. (2006). *Taming the office tiger.* Washington, DC: Kiplinger Books.

Herman, S. (Ed.). (2002). *Rewiring organizations for the networked economy: Organizing, managing, and leading in the information age.* San Francisco: Jossey-Bass/Pfeiffer.

Koch, R. (1998). *The 80/20 principle: The secret of achieving more with less.* New York: Currency/Doubleday.

Mann, S. (2006). *I hate filing: Everything you need to get organized for success and sanity at home, on the run, and in the office.* Deerfield Beach, FL: Health Communications, Inc.

Nelson, M. (2002). *Clutter-proof your business: Turn your mess into success.* Franklin Lakes, NJ: Career Press.

Sköldberg, K. (2002). *The poetic logic of administration: Styles and changes of style in the art of organizing.* London: Routledge.

Smallin, D. (2002). *Organizing plain and simple: A ready reference guide with hundreds of solutions to your everyday clutter challenges.* Pownal, VT: Storey Books.

Wheatley, M. J., & Kellner-Rogers, M. (1998). *A simpler way.* San Francisco: Berrett-Koehler Publishers.

Winston, S. (2001). *The organized executive: The classic program for productivity: New ways to manage time, people, and the digital office.* New York: Warner Business.

Winston, S. (2004). *Organized for success: Top executives and CEOs reveal the organizing principles that helped them reach the top.* New York: Crown Business.

40 *Dealing with* Paradox

The art of life is a constant readjustment to our surroundings.
Kakuzo Okakura – Japanese author and art critic

Unskilled

- ☐ Not very flexible
- ☐ Can't shift gears readily
- ☐ One-trick pony (although may be very good at that one trick)
- ☐ Believes strongly in personal consistency and following a few principles
- ☐ Tries to get everything done one way
- ☐ Doesn't take a balanced approach
- ☐ May be seen as rigidly following and overdoing his/her one best way
- ☐ May rely too much on personal strengths
- ☐ Has trouble shifting modes of behavior in the same meeting or situation

Select one to three of the competencies listed below to use as a substitute for this competency if you decide not to work on it directly.

SUBSTITUTES: 2,11,12,16,32,45,57

Skilled

- ☐ Can act in ways that seem contradictory
- ☐ Is very flexible and adaptable when facing tough calls
- ☐ Can combine seeming opposites like being compassionately tough, stand up for self without trampling others, set strong but flexible standards
- ☐ Can act differently depending upon the situation
- ☐ Is seen as balanced despite the conflicting demands of the situation

Overused Skill

- ☐ May be seen as two-faced or wishy-washy
- ☐ May change too easily from one style or mode to another
- ☐ May misread what skills are called for
- ☐ May confuse people who observe him/her across different settings
- ☐ May be misinterpreted

Select one to three of the competencies listed below to work on to compensate for an overuse of this skill.

COMPENSATORS: 5,9,12,17,29,30,34,37,38,47,50,51,52,53,58

Some Causes

- ☐ Abdicate or freeze when situations change quickly
- ☐ Don't read people
- ☐ Don't read situations
- ☐ Not very flexible
- ☐ One "me" fits all
- ☐ Rigid about values and beliefs
- ☐ Run over others
- ☐ Too much of a good thing

Leadership Architect® Factors and Clusters

This competency is in the Personal and Interpersonal Skills Factor (VI). This competency is in the Demonstrating Personal Flexibility Cluster (T) with: 45, 54, 55. You may want to check other competencies in the same Factor/Cluster for related tips.

The Map

Dealing with paradox involves attitudinal and behavioral flexibility—going from a planning discussion to customer complaints to administrative snafus and shifting gears accordingly. People who excel at this are versatile in situations and with others—they can lead and let others lead, know how to apply "tough love," or remain adaptable in the face of crises. They are able to think and act in seemingly contrary ways at the same time or when moving from one task to another. They are flexible and meet the needs of the moment. This requires having some flexibility in approach, tone and style, and then matching those to the demands of the situation.

Some Remedies

☐ **1. Not shifting gears? Learn to transition comfortably between situations.** As the song says, "I want to be me." Not many of us have that luxury. Each situation we deal with is a little bit, somewhat, or a lot different. In order to be truly effective across situations and people, we are called upon to act differently. In control at 9 a.m., following at 10 a.m., quiet at 11 a.m. and dominating at noon. It's all in a day's work. Respectful with the boss, critiquing with peers, caring for directs, and responding to customers. No trickery. No blowing with the wind. No Machiavellianism. Just adjusting flexibly to the demands of each situation. Work on first reading the situation and the people. Monitor your gear-shifting behavior for a week at work and at home. What switches give you the most trouble? The least? Why? Off-work, practice gear-shifting transitions. Go from a civic meeting to a water fight with your kids, for example. On the way between activities, if only for a few seconds, think about the transition you're making and the frame of mind needed to make it work well.

☐ **2. Trouble finding balance? Combine seemingly opposite behaviors.** Tough love is the best example. Deliver a tough message on layoffs but do it in a compassionate way. Dig into the details while trying to establish three basic conceptual drivers in the data. Take strong stands but listen and leave room for others to maneuver. Have a strong personal belief about an issue but loyally implement an organization plan which opposes your view. Being playful but firm. Being loose with parts of the budget but unyielding in others. Many situations in today's complex world call for mixed responses and behaviors. Doing two opposing things at once isn't comfortable for everyone. Many pride themselves on being just one person, believing and following one set of beliefs. Acting paradoxically doesn't really violate that. It just means within your normal range of behaviors and style, you use two of your extremes—as quiet as you can be in the first half of the meeting and as loud as you ever are in the last half—at once.

☐ **3. Got too much of a good thing? Pull back on overused skills.** A lot of us overdo some of our strengths. We push for results too hard. We analyze data too long. We try to be too nice. For those overdone behaviors, it's difficult for us to do the opposite. Find out what you overdo by getting feedback, either a 360° feedback instrument or by polling your closest associates. Find out how adaptable people think you are under pressure and how well you handle the fragmentation of a typical day. Try to balance your behavior against whatever you overdo. Don't replace what you do—add to it:

- If you get brusque under pressure, take three deep breaths and consciously slow down or use some humor.
- If you get frustrated easily, learn some pause strategies such as visualizing yourself in a more calming setting, asking a question, or asking yourself, "How should I act this instant?"
- If you're too tough, ask yourself how you'd like to be treated in this situation. Stop and ask how the other person is doing or responding.
- If you overmanage, work on setting standards, outcomes and delegating; let your team set the process.
- If you freeze under too much fragmentation, pause, walk around the building and ask yourself how you'd like to behave right now and what is most important. Then come back and start doing the task a piece at a time.

- If you get rigid, set a goal of understanding other people's views well enough that you can present them back to them without inaccuracy.
- If you habitually go into an action frenzy or grind to a halt, ask yourself what would be more effective right now.
- If you run over others, tell them what you're thinking about doing and ask them what they think should be done.

☐ **4. Selling someone else's vision? Get comfortable walking someone else's talk.** A common paradox is having to support someone else's program or idea when you don't really think that way or agree with it. You have to be a member of the loyal opposition. Most of the time, you may be delivering someone else's view of the future. Top management and a consultant created the mission, vision and strategy off somewhere in the woods. You may or may not have been asked for any input. You may even have some doubts about it yourself. Do not offer conditional statements to your audience. Don't let it be known to others that you are not fully on board. Your role is to manage this vision and mission, not your personal one. *More help? – See #22 Ethics and Values.* If you have strong contrary views, be sure to demand a voice next time around.

☐ **5. Stuck in the wrong mode? Tackle tough transitions.** Which transitions are the toughest for you? Write down the five toughest for you. What do you have a hard time switching to and from? Use this knowledge to assist you in making a list of discontinuities (tough transitions) you face such as:

- Confronting people vs. Being approachable and accepting.
- Leading vs. Following.
- Going from firing someone to a business-as-usual staff meeting.

Write down how each of these discontinuities makes you feel and what you may do that gets you in trouble. For example, you may not shift gears well after a confrontation or you may have trouble taking charge again after passively sitting in a meeting all day. Create a plan to attack each of the tough transitions.

☐ **6. Need to leave your comfort zone? Go for more variety at work.** Take a risk, then play it safe. Set tasks for yourself that force you to shift gears, such as being a spokesperson for your organization when tough questions are expected, making peace with an enemy, or managing people who are novices at a task. If you already have these tasks as part of your job, use them to observe yourself and try new behaviors.

☐ **7. Need a model or mentor? Study transition experts.** Interview people who are good at shifting gears, such as fix-it managers (tear down and build back up), shutdown managers (fire people yet support them and help them find other employment; motivating those who stay), or excellent parents. Talk to an actor or actress to see how he/she can play opposing roles back-to-back. Talk to people who have recently joined your organization from places quite different than yours. Talk to a therapist who hears a different problem or trauma every hour. See if you can figure out some rules for making comfortable transitions.

☐ **8. Too comfortable in the role of expert? Try becoming a novice.** Volunteer to teach others something you don't know well the next time a new procedure, policy or technology appears. This will force you to shift from experienced expert to novice.

☐ **9. Overreacting? Control your instant responses to shifts.** Many of us respond to the fragmentation and discontinuities of work as if they were threats instead of the way life is. Sometimes our emotions and fears are triggered by switching from active to passive or soft to tough. This initial anxious response lasts 45-60 seconds and we need to buy some time before we say or do something inappropriate. Research shows that generally somewhere between the second and third thing you think to say or do is the best option. Practice holding back your first response long enough to think of a second and a third. Manage your shifts, don't be a prisoner of them. *More help? – See #11 Composure.*

☐ **10. Searching for options? Use mental rehearsal to think about different ways you could carry out a transaction.** Try to see yourself acting in opposing ways to get the same thing done—when to be tough, when to let them decide, when to deflect the issue because it's not ready to decide. What cues would you look for to select an approach that matches? Practice trying to get the same thing done with two different groups with two different approaches. Did they both work?

Some Develop-in-Place Assignments

☐ Take on a tough and undoable project, one where others who have tried it have failed.

☐ Audit cost overruns to assess the problem, and present your findings to the person or people involved.

☐ Work on a team looking at a reorganization plan where there will be more people than positions.

☐ Manage a group of resistant people with low morale through an unpopular change or project.

☐ Manage a group of people involved in tackling a fix-it or turnaround project.

The executive exists to make sensible exceptions to general rules.
Elting E. Morison – American professor and historian of technology

Suggested Readings

Bellman, G. M. (2001). *Getting things done when you are not in charge.* San Francisco: Berrett-Koehler Publishers.

Fullan, M. (2007). *Leading in a culture of change* (Rev. ed.). San Francisco: Jossey-Bass.

Gilley, J. W., Quatro, S. A., Hoekstra, E., Whittle, D. D., & Maycunich, A. (2001). *The manager as change agent: A practical guide to developing high-performance people and organizations.* Cambridge, MA: Perseus Publishing.

Greenleaf, R. K., Spears, L. C., & Covey, S. R. (2002). *Servant leadership: A journey into the nature of legitimate power and greatness (25th Anniversary ed.).* Mahwah, NJ: Paulist Press.

Gurvis, J., & Calarco, A. (2007). *Adaptability: Responding effectively to change.* Greensboro, NC: Center for Creative Leadership.

Handy, C. (2003). *The elephant and the flea.* Boston: Harvard Business School Press.

Robinson, G., & Rose, M. (2004). *A leadership paradox: Influencing others by defining yourself.* Bloomington, IN: AuthorHouse.

Schwartz, B. (2004). *The paradox of choice: Why more is less.* Hopewell, NJ: Ecco Press.

Stone, D. A. (2001). *Policy paradox: The art of political decision making.* New York: W.W. Norton & Company.

Vandergriff, D. (2006). *Raising the bar: Creating and nurturing adaptability to deal with the changing face of war.* Washington DC: The Center for Defense Information.

Warren, R. A. (2002). *The achievement paradox: Test your personality and choose your behavior for success at work.* Novato, CA: New World Library.

41 Patience

The key to everything is patience. You get the chicken by hatching the egg, not by smashing it.
Arnold H. Glasgow – American humorist and writer

Unskilled

- ☐ Acts before it's time to act
- ☐ Intolerant of the slow pace and cumbersome processes of others
- ☐ May be seen as a self-centered do it my way and at my speed type
- ☐ Doesn't take the time to listen or understand
- ☐ Thinks almost everything needs to be faster and shorter
- ☐ Disrupts those facilitating meetings with his/her need to finish sooner
- ☐ Frequently interrupts and finishes other people's sentences
- ☐ Makes his/her own process rules; doesn't wait for others
- ☐ May appear to others as arrogant, uninterested or a know-it-all
- ☐ May be action oriented and resist process and problem complexity
- ☐ May just jump to conclusions rather than thinking things through

Select one to three of the competencies listed below to use as a substitute for this competency if you decide not to work on it directly.

SUBSTITUTES: 3,11,33,38,48,52

Skilled

- ☐ Is tolerant with people and processes
- ☐ Listens and checks before acting
- ☐ Tries to understand the people and the data before making judgments and acting
- ☐ Waits for others to catch up before acting
- ☐ Sensitive to due process and proper pacing
- ☐ Follows established process

Overused Skill

- ☐ May wait too long to act
- ☐ May try to please everyone
- ☐ Others may confuse attentive listening with acceptance of their position
- ☐ May waste time when faced with issues too close to a 50/50 proposition
- ☐ May let things fester without acting

Select one to three of the competencies listed below to work on to compensate for an overuse of this skill.

COMPENSATORS: 1,2,9,12,13,16,34,40,53,57

Some Causes

- ☐ Unrealistic standards
- ☐ Don't understand others well
- ☐ Action junkie
- ☐ Very intelligent
- ☐ Lack of composure
- ☐ Poor listener
- ☐ Poor tactical manager/disorganized
- ☐ Arrogant

Leadership Architect® Factors and Clusters

This competency is in the Personal and Interpersonal Skills Factor (VI). This competency is in the Being Open and Receptive Cluster (S) with: 11, 26, 33, 44. You may want to check other competencies in the same Factor/Cluster for related tips.

The Map

Many people pride themselves on impatience, thinking of it as high standards and a results orientation. This would be true sometimes, especially when the results just aren't there or standards are slack. In many situations though, impatience is a cover for other problems and has serious long-term consequences. It leads to overmanaging, not developing others, stacking the unit with your solutions, monitoring too much, and people shying away from you because you lack tolerance.

Some Remedies

- ☐ **1. Trouble listening? Be courteous.** Impatient people interrupt, finish other people's sentences when they hesitate, ask people to hurry, ask people to skip the next few transparencies and get to the last slide, urge people to finish and get to the point. All these behaviors of the impatient person intimidate, irritate, demotivate and frustrate others and lead to incomplete communications, damaged relationships, a feeling of injustice and leave others demeaned in the process. All for the sake of gaining a few minutes of your valuable time. Add five seconds to your average response/interrupt tolerance time until you stop doing these things most of the time. Learn to pause to give people a second chance. People often stumble on words with impatient people, hurrying to get through before their first or next interruption.
- ☐ **2. Sending the wrong signals? Watch the non-verbal signals.** Impatient people signal their impatience through speech and actions, of course, but they also signal non-verbally. The washboard brow, body shifting, finger

and pencil drumming, and glares. What do you do? Ask others you trust for your five most frequent impatience signals. Work to eliminate them.

☐ **3. Losing your composure? Keep cool.** Impatient people want it now. They are not good waiters. Sometimes impatience flowers into loss of composure. When things don't go as fast as they want, it triggers an emotional response. *More help? – See #11 Composure and #107 Lack of Composure.*

☐ **4. Know who sets you off? Identify who trips your impatience trigger.** Some people probably bring out your impatience more than others. Who are they? What is it about them that makes you more impatient? Pace? Language? Thought process? Accent? These people may include people you don't like, who ramble, who whine and complain, or who are repetitive advocates for things you have already rejected. Mentally rehearse some calming tactics before meeting with people who trigger your impatience. Work on understanding their positions without judging them—you can always judge later. In all cases, focus them on the issues or problems to be discussed, return them to the point, interrupt to summarize and state your position. Try to gently train them to be more efficient with you next time without damaging them in the process.

☐ **5. Arrogant? Keep arrogance in check.** People who have a towering strength or lots of success get less feedback and keep rolling along and over others until their careers get in trouble. If you are arrogant—you devalue the contributions of others—you should work doubly hard at reading and listening to others. You don't have to accept everything, just listen to understand before you react. You need to submerge your "what I want/think" demeanor and keep asking yourself, "What are they saying; how are they reacting?"

☐ **6. Being left out of the loop? Work on your openness and approachability.** Impatient people don't get as much information as patient listeners do. They are more often surprised by events when others knew they were coming. People are hesitant to talk to impatient people. It's too painful. People don't pass on hunches, unbaked thoughts, maybes, and possibilities to impatient people. You will be out of the information loop and miss important information you need to know to be effective. Suspend judgment on informal communications. Just take it in. Acknowledge that you understand. Ask a question or two. Follow up later.

☐ **7. Too quick? Rein in your horse.** Impatient people provide answers, conclusions, and solutions too early in the process. Others haven't even understood the problem yet. Providing solutions too quickly will make your people dependent and irritated. If you don't teach them how you think and how you can come up with solutions so fast, they will never learn. Take the time to really define the problem—not impatiently throw out a solution. Brainstorm what questions need to be answered in order to resolve it. Give your people the task to think about for a day and come back with some solutions. Be a teacher instead of a dictator of solutions. Study yourself. Keep a journal of what triggered your behavior and what the observed consequences were. Learn to detect and control your triggers before they get you in trouble. *More help? – See #11 Composure.*

☐ **8. Checking in too often? Follow a process.** Impatient people check in a lot. How's it coming. Is it done yet? When will it be finished? Let me see what you've done so far. That is disruptive to due process and wastes time. When you give out a task or assign a project, establish agreed upon time checkpoints. You can also assign percentage checkpoints. Check in with me when you are about 25% finished so we can make midcourse corrections and 75% so we can make final corrections. Let them figure out how to do the task. Hold back from checking in at other than the agreed upon times and percentages. *More help? – See #18 Delegation.*

☐ **9. Too dependent upon yourself? Let others bring solutions to you.** Look at others' solutions more. Invite discussion and disagreement, welcome bad news, ask that people come up with the second and third solution. A useful trick is to assign issues and questions before you have given them any thought. Two weeks before you are due to decide, ask your people to examine that issue and report to you two days before you have to deal with it. That way, you really don't have any solutions yet. This really motivates people and makes you look less impatient.

☐ **10. Lack of patience a hindrance to developing people? Read #19 Developing Direct Reports and Others.** Find out how people actually develop. Your impatience makes it less likely you will develop any deep skills in others since development doesn't operate on brief time frames and close monitoring. As you'll see, challenging tasks, feedback along the way, and encouraging learning are the keys. Impatient people seldom develop others.

Some Develop-in-Place Assignments

- ☐ Make peace with an enemy or someone you've disappointed with a product or service or someone you've had some trouble with or don't get along with very well.
- ☐ Manage the assigning/allocating of office space in a contested situation.
- ☐ Take on a task you dislike or hate to do.
- ☐ Manage a group of low-competence or low-performing people through a task they couldn't do by themselves.
- ☐ Teach a child a new skill (e.g., reading, operating a computer, a sport).

Good ideas are not adopted automatically.
They must be driven into practice with courageous patience.
Hyman Rickover – Four-star admiral, U.S. Navy

Suggested Readings

Bradberry, T., & Greaves, J. (2005). *The emotional intelligence quick book: Everything you need to know to put your EQ to work.* New York: Fireside.

Easwaran, E. (2006). *Take your time: How to find patience, peace, and meaning.* Tomales, CA: Nilgiri Press.

Gandhi, M., & Fischer, L. (Eds.). (2002). *The essential Gandhi: An anthology of his writings on his life, work, and ideas.* New York: Vintage Press.

Gonthier, G., & Morrissey, K. (2002). *Rude awakenings: Overcoming the civility crisis in the workplace.* Chicago: Dearborn Trade.

Losyk, B. (2004). *Get a grip! Overcoming stress and thriving in the workplace.* Hoboken, NJ: John Wiley & Sons.

Mehrotra, R. (2005). *The essential Dalai Lama: His important teachings.* New York: Penguin Group.

Plato. (H. Tarrant, Ed.). (2003). *The last days of Socrates* (H. Tredennick, Trans.). New York: Penguin Books.

Ryan, M. J. (2003). *The power of patience: How to slow the rush and enjoy more happiness, success, and peace of mind every day.* New York: Broadway Press.

Sellers, P., Harrington, A., & Wheat, A. (2001). Patient but not passive. *Fortune, 144*, 188-193.

Tutu, D. (2007). *Love: The words and inspiration of Mother Teresa.* Auckland, NZ: PQ Blackwell Ltd.

42 Peer Relationships

The path to greatness is along with others.
Baltasar Gracian – Spanish priest

Unskilled

- ☐ Not good at lateral cross-boundary relations
- ☐ Doesn't strike fair bargains or understand what peers expect or need
- ☐ Not open to negotiation
- ☐ A loner, not seen as a team player, doesn't have the greater good in mind
- ☐ May withhold resources from the other team members
- ☐ May not respect their functions or disciplines and somehow communicates that
- ☐ May be very competitive, play and maneuver for advantage and withhold information
- ☐ May have a chilling effect on the entire unit because he/she won't play
- ☐ May deal with lateral conflict noisily or uncooperatively

Select one to three of the competencies listed below to use as a substitute for this competency if you decide not to work on it directly.

SUBSTITUTES: 3,9,12,21,23,27,33,36,37,39,52,60,64

Skilled

- ☐ Can quickly find common ground and solve problems for the good of all
- ☐ Can represent his/her own interests and yet be fair to other groups
- ☐ Can solve problems with peers with a minimum of noise
- ☐ Is seen as a team player and is cooperative
- ☐ Easily gains trust and support of peers
- ☐ Encourages collaboration
- ☐ Can be candid with peers

Overused Skill

- ☐ May touch base with too many peers and be overly concerned with making everyone happy
- ☐ May be too accommodating
- ☐ May invest too much in peer relationships at the expense of others
- ☐ May be uncomfortable with relationships where everyone's not equal
- ☐ May share sensitive information inappropriately just to solidify a relationship
- ☐ May get in trouble by being too candid with peers

Select one to three of the competencies listed below to work on to compensate for an overuse of this skill.

COMPENSATORS: 4,8,9,12,16,23,29,34,37,43,50,53,57

Some Causes

- ☐ Bad experiences with peers in the past
- ☐ Competitive with peers
- ☐ Don't respect other groups
- ☐ Impersonal style
- ☐ Not a team player
- ☐ Not forthcoming with information
- ☐ Poor collegial skills
- ☐ Poor communication skills
- ☐ Poor time management
- ☐ Possessive

Leadership Architect® Factors and Clusters

This competency is in the Personal and Interpersonal Skills Factor (VI). This competency is in the Managing Diverse Relationships Cluster (P) with: 4, 15, 21, 23, 64. You may want to check other competencies in the same Factor/ Cluster for related tips.

The Map

Effective lateral or cross-boundary (peer) relationships are among the toughest to build in organizations. There is a strong not-invented-here mentality at work between units, businesses, functions, and geographies. There is natural competition between groups. Pay and reward systems many times pit one group against the other. If one group gets more, the other has to get less. One team likes to beat the other. Lots of messy political problems originate as turf disputes. Many people get their lowest scores on 360° feedback from peers because they are uncooperative. Quite often these problems are a result of not finding common ground with peers, failure to understand what they want and need, and failure to understand the nature of the relationship. There is high return on investment for the organization if lateral relationships are working. It leads to more efficient use of time and resources and the easy exchange of ideas and talent. There are wasted resources and suboptimization when they are not.

Some Remedies

☐ **1. Lack position power? Be an influencer.** Peers generally do not have power over each other. That means that influence skills, understanding, and trading are the currencies to use. Don't just ask for things; find some common ground where you can provide help. What do the peers you're contacting need? Do you really know how they see the issue? Is it even important to them? How does what you're working on affect them? If it affects them negatively, can you trade something, appeal to the common good, figure out some way to minimize the work (volunteering staff help, for example)? Go into peer relationships with a trading mentality.

☐ **2. Making the wrong impression? Pay attention to how your personal style is perceived.** Many times, negative personal styles get in the way of effective peer relationships. People differ in the impression they leave. Those who leave positive impressions get more things done with peers than those who leave cold, insensitive or impersonal negative impressions. *More help? – See #3 Approachability, #31 Interpersonal Savvy, and #33 Listening.*

☐ **3. Confused by behavior of peers? Assess your peers.** Do you really understand the peers you need to deal with? Which ones really want to help? Who is going to get in the way? What did they really want? What price will they ask for helping? *More help? – See #56 Sizing Up People and #64 Understanding Others.*

☐ **4. Overwhelmed by the complexity of the organization? Learn to maneuver through the organizational maze.** How do you get things done sideways? Who are the movers and shakers in the organization? How do they get things done? Who do they rely on for expediting things through the maze? Who are the major gatekeepers who control the flow of resources, information and decisions? Who are the guides and the helpers? Get to know them better. Who are the major resisters and stoppers? Try to avoid or go around them. *More help? – See #38 Organizational Agility and #39 Organizing.*

☐ **5. One-sided in your peer interactions? Be more cooperative.** If peers see you as excessively competitive, they will cut you out of the loop and may sabotage your cross-border attempts. To be seen as more cooperative, always explain your thinking and invite them to explain theirs. Generate a variety of possibilities first rather than stake out positions. Be tentative, allowing them room to customize the situation. Focus on common goals, priorities and problems. Invite criticism of your ideas.

☐ **6. Is your agenda getting in the way? Keep conflicts as small and concrete as possible.** Separate the people from the problem. Don't get personal. Don't give peers the impression you're trying to dominate or push something on them. Without agreeing or disagreeing, try on their views for size. Can you understand their viewpoint? When peers blow off steam, don't react; return to facts and the problem, staying away from personal clashes. Allow others to save face; concede small points; don't try to hit a home run every time. When a peer takes a rigid position, don't reject it. Ask why—what are the principles behind the position, how do we know it's fair, what's the theory of the case, play out what would happen if his/her position was accepted.

☐ **7. Getting competitive? Know the difference between healthy and unhealthy competition.** Separate working smoothly with peers from personal relationships, contests, competing for incentives, one-upsmanship, not-invented-here, pride and ego. Working well with peers over the long term helps everyone, makes sense for the organization and builds a capacity for the organization to do greater things. Usually the least-used resource in an organization is lateral exchanges of information and resources.

☐ **8. Is a peer out of line? Avoid telling others all about it if a peer doesn't play fair.** This often boomerangs. What goes around comes around. Confront the peer directly, politely and privately. Describe the unfair situation; explain the impact on you. Don't blame. Give the peer the chance to explain, ask questions, let him/her save some face and see if you can resolve the matter. Even if you don't totally accept what is said, it's better to solve the problem than win the argument.

☐ **9. Lacking self-awareness in peer conflicts? Monitor yourself in tough situations with peers.** What's the first thing you attend to? How often do you take a stand vs. make an accommodating gesture? What proportion of your comments deals with relationships vs. the issue to be addressed? Mentally rehearse for worst-case scenarios/hard-to-deal-with people. Anticipate what the person might say and have responses prepared so as not to be caught off guard. *More help? – See #12 Conflict Management.*

☐ **10. Too intent on winning? Make sure the winning and losing is balanced.** Watch out for winning concessions too often. If you win too much, how do the losers fare? Do you want them diminished or would you like them to work willingly with you again? The best tack is to balance the wins and losses. Make sure you are known in the organization as someone who is always ready to help and cooperate, and the favor will be returned.

Some Develop-in-Place Assignments

- ☐ Manage a cost-cutting project.
- ☐ Manage the assigning/allocating of office space in a contested situation.
- ☐ Resolve an issue in conflict between two people, units, geographies, functions, etc.
- ☐ Join a community board.
- ☐ Join a self-help or support group.

I'm not the smartest fellow in the world, but I can sure pick smart colleagues.
Franklin D. Roosevelt – 32nd President of the United States

Suggested Readings

Baker, W. E. (2000). *Networking smart.* New York: Backinprint.com.

Cartwright, T. (2003). *Managing conflict with peers.* Greensboro, NC: Center for Creative Leadership.

Cava, R. (2004). *Dealing with difficult people: How to deal with nasty customers, demanding bosses and annoying co-workers.* Toronto, ON: Firefly Books.

Chapman, E. N., & Wingfield, B. (2003). *Winning at human relations: How to keep from sabotaging yourself.* Mississauga, ON: Crisp Publications, Inc.

Crowley, K., & Elster, K. (2006). *Working with you is killing me: Freeing yourself from emotional traps at work.* New York: Warner Business Books.

Ferrazzi, K., & Raz, T. (2005). *Never eat alone: And other secrets to success, one relationship at a time.* New York: Doubleday.

Fritz, J. M. H., & Omdahl, B. L. (2006). *Problematic relationships in the workplace.* New York: Peter Lang Publishing, Inc.

Giovagnoli, M., & Carter-Miller, J. (2000). *Networlding: Building relationships and opportunities for success.* San Francisco: Jossey-Bass.

Juchnowski, J. A. (2004). *Know yourself, co-workers and your organization: Get focused on: Personality, careers and managing people.* Lincoln, NE: iUniverse Star.

Kottler, J. (2003). *Beyond blame: How to resolve conflicts with friends, lovers, and co-workers.* New York: MJF Books.

McKenna, P. J., & Maister, D. H. (2002). *First among equals: How to manage a group of professionals.* New York: Free Press.

Pascarella, P., & Frohman, M. (2000). *The collaborative leader: Mastering priorities.* San Francisco: Berrett-Koehler Publishers.

Patterson, K., Grenny, J., McMillan, R., Switzler, A., & Covey, S. R. (2002). *Crucial conversations: Tools for talking when stakes are high.* New York: McGraw-Hill.

Tamm, J. W., & Luyet, R. J. (2004). *Radical collaboration: Five essential skills to overcome defensiveness and build successful relationships.* New York: HarperCollins.

43 Perseverance

History has demonstrated that the most notable winners usually encountered heartbreaking obstacles before they triumphed. They won because they refused to become discouraged by their defeats.
B.C. Forbes – Scottish-born financial journalist and founder of *Forbes* magazine

Unskilled

- ☐ Gives up too soon or moves on to something that's going better
- ☐ Doesn't push hard enough to get things done
- ☐ Doesn't go back with different strategies for the third and fourth try
- ☐ May take rejection too personally
- ☐ May hesitate to push when met with conflict, disagreement or attacks
- ☐ May agree too early just to get it over with
- ☐ May compromise for less than the original goal or objective
- ☐ May simply not want to take charge and be out front

Select one to three of the competencies listed below to use as a substitute for this competency if you decide not to work on it directly.

SUBSTITUTES: 1,9,12,16,34,39,53

Skilled

- ☐ Pursues everything with energy, drive, and a need to finish
- ☐ Seldom gives up before finishing, especially in the face of resistance or setbacks

Overused Skill

- ☐ May stick to efforts beyond reason, in the face of overwhelming odds and evidence to the contrary
- ☐ May be seen as stubborn and unyielding
- ☐ May not set appropriate priorities
- ☐ May find it difficult to change course
- ☐ May confuse personal have-to-do's with what most needs to be done

Select one to three of the competencies listed below to work on to compensate for an overuse of this skill.

COMPENSATORS: 2,14,26,33,41,45,46,50,51,54,60

Some Causes

- ☐ Don't push hard enough
- ☐ Give up too soon
- ☐ Impatient
- ☐ Lost the passion
- ☐ Short span of attention
- ☐ Take things personally
- ☐ Uncomfortable with rejection
- ☐ Wilt in the face of resistance
- ☐ Won't take charge

Leadership Architect® Factors and Clusters

This competency is in the Energy and Drive Factor (IV). This competency is in the Focusing on the Bottom Line Cluster (J) with: 1, 53. You may want to check other competencies in the same Factor/Cluster for related tips.

The Map

The need for perseverance comes about because you weren't effective the first time, the thing you are trying to get done is being resisted, or your customers and the audience aren't ready to do what you need; it's not on their agenda. Sticking to the course, especially in the face of pushback, is what perseverance is all about. Going back a second and third time or however many tries are needed. Perseverance is also about using a variety of ways to get things done. Persevering people try it different ways when the first way isn't effective. Why don't people persevere? You may fear the rejection; the persevering don't take it personally even when people try to make it so. You may have trouble taking a stand; the persevering do it as a matter of course to accomplish something worthwhile. You may not be convinced of the worth of what you're doing. You may not be doing it the right way. All in all, persevering people get the job done.

Some Remedies

☐ **1. Giving up after one or two tries? Try something different.** If you have trouble going back the second or third time to get something done, then switch approaches. Sometimes people get stuck in a repeating groove that's not working. Do something different next time. If you visited the office of someone you have difficulties with, invite him/her to your office next time. Think about multiple ways to get the same outcome. For example, to push a decision through, you could meet with stakeholders first, go to a single key stakeholder, study and present the problem to a group, call a problem-solving session, or call in an outside expert. Be prepared to do them all when obstacles arise.

☐ **2. Meeting resistance? Put adverse reactions in perspective.** Don't persevere because you prefer to avoid conflict? Hesitate in the face of resistance and adverse reaction? Conflict slows you down? Shakes your confidence in your decision? Do you backpedal? Give in too soon? Try to make everyone happy? When your initiative hits resistance, keep it on the problem and the objectives. Depersonalize. If attacked, return to what you're trying to accomplish and invite people's criticisms and ideas. Listen. Correct if justified. Stick to your point. Push ahead again. Resistance is natural. Some of the time it's legitimate; most of the time it's just human nature. People push back until they understand. They are just protecting territory. *More help? – See #12 Conflict Management.*

☐ **3. Procrastinator? Start now.** You don't go back a second time until forced to by deadlines? Less motivated when your first attempt falls flat or meets resistance? Don't get back to people when you said you would? You might not produce results consistently. Some of your work will be marginal because you only had time for one or two attempts before the project was due. Start earlier. Reduce the time between attempts. Always start 10% of each attempt immediately after it is apparent it will be needed so you can better gauge what it is going to take to finish it. Always assume it will take more time than you think it's going to take. *More help? – See #47 Planning.*

☐ **4. Take resistance personally? Stay focused and take rejection in stride.** If you tend to take rejection or inattention or non-responsiveness personally, focus on why this isn't personal. Develop a philosophical stance toward rejection and failure. After all, most innovations fail, most proposals fail, the majority of efforts to change people fail and most attempts to change organizations fail. Anything really worth doing takes repeated effort, and everything could always be done better. Remember resistance is normal, not abnormal. Even resistance that looks and sounds personal may not be. Keep reminding yourself what you are there to do. Keep making the business case. How can everyone win? Don't get dragged down by personal concerns. Keep it objective. Listen. Absorb the heat. Look for quality feedback and respond appropriately. Always return to the facts and your agenda. The closer you get to success, the more the heat of the naysayers may increase. Work even harder, listen, answer all questions and objections—focus on the work, not yourself. Don't expect everyone to cheer your successes. Some will be jealous. *More help? – See #12 Conflict Management.*

☐ **5. Trouble taking tough stands? Prepare your case and present it with strength.** You may have to go back because you didn't make a strong enough case the first time. Do your homework. Be prepared. Don't make it sound like a trial balloon. Use more definite, direct language. Don't be vague or tentative. Don't throw things out without the air cover of the business case and the safety net of how everybody can gain. Prepare by rehearsing for tough questions, attacks, and countering views. Plan as if you're only going to have one shot. Match your style, tone, pace and volume with the feeling that you are right and that this thing must get done. Lead with strength.

☐ **6. Trying to do too much? Fight the right battles.** Maybe you're pushing on everything and getting tired and frustrated about your low batting average. Some persevere too much. Some persevere on the wrong things. Are you sure this is critical? What's mission-critical versus nice to get done versus not really in the mainstream? Be sure your priorities are right. *More help? – See #50 Priority Setting.*

☐ **7. Disorganized? Sharpen your focus.** Don't always get to everything on time? Forget deadlines? Lose requests for decisions? Forget to follow up on a request for more information? Lose interest in anything not right in front of you? Move from task to task until you find one that's working? Short attention span? You can't operate helter-skelter and persevere. Perseverance takes focus and continuity of effort. Get better organized and disciplined. Keep a task progress log. Keep a top 10 things I have to do list. Stick with tasks longer than you now do.

☐ **8. Path blocked at every turn? Learn to navigate the maze.** Organizations can be complex mazes with many turns and dead ends. Even worse, organizations are staffed with people which makes it more complex. Egos. Gatekeepers. Resisters. The best path to get something done may not be direct. The formal organization works only some of the time. Most of the time, the informal organization runs the show. To persevere efficiently, you have to know how to work the maze. You have to be patient with process. Things sometimes take time. People need to be ready to move. Maybe the best way to approach someone is through someone else. Maybe you have to work on your timing. When is the best time to approach someone for a decision or an action? Learn the informal organization. Identify the key players, especially the gatekeepers and the traffic controllers. Ask others the best way to get things done in this organization. Watch others. What path do they follow? *More help? – See #38 Organizational Agility and #52 Process Management.*

☐ **9. Trouble getting to the finish line? Commit to completing the last 20%.** While it's true that sometimes you get 80% of what you are pushing for with the first 20% of the effort, it unfortunately then takes another 80% of the time to finish the last 20%. It's not over until the gravity-challenged lady sings. In a fast-paced world, it's sometimes tough to pull the cart all the way to the finish line when the race is over. Not all tasks have to be completely finished. For some, 80% would be acceptable. For those who need all the i's dotted and the t's crossed, it will take perseverance. The devil is in the details. When you get caught in this situation, create a checklist with the 20% that remains to be done. Plan to do a little on it each day. Cross things off and celebrate each time you get to take something off the list. Remember, it's going to challenge your motivation and attention. Try to delegate finishing to someone who would see the 20% as a fresh challenge. Get a consultant to finish it. Task trade with someone else's 20% so you both would have something fresh to do.

☐ **10. Burned out? Rediscover what really matters.** Lost your passion? Run out of gas? Heart's not in it anymore? Not 100% committed? Maybe you don't persevere because deep down you don't care anymore—you're sick of doing this job or working for this organization or pushing against a particular person or group. Ask what is it that you want. Find your passion again. Prepare yourself for another job. To make the best of your current job, make a list of what you like and don't like to do. Concentrate on doing more liked activities each day. Work to delegate or task trade the things that are no longer motivating to you. Do your least preferred activities first to get them out of the way; focus not on the activity, but on your sense of accomplishment. Change your work activity to mirror your interests as much as you can. Volunteer for task forces and projects that would be motivating for you. *More help? – See #6 Career Ambition.*

Some Develop-in-Place Assignments

☐ Take on a task you dislike or hate to do.

☐ Take on a tough and undoable project, one where others who have tried it have failed.

☐ Resolve an issue in conflict between two people, units, geographies, functions, etc.

☐ Work on a crisis-management team.

☐ Be a change agent; create a symbol for change; lead the rallying cry; champion a significant change and implementation.

It's not that I'm so smart,
it's just that I stay with problems longer.
Albert Einstein – German-born Nobel Prize-winning physicist

Suggested Readings

Bossidy, L., & Charan, R. (with Burck, C.). (2002). *Execution: The discipline of getting things done.* New York: Crown Business.

Dumas, A. (2008). *Count of Monte Cristo* [sound recording]. Tantor Media (Audio CD).

Dumas, A. (2003). *Count of Monte Cristo.* New York: Penguin Classics. (Original work published 1844.)

Keller, H. (2000). *The story of my life* [unabridged sound recording]. Ashland, OR: Blackstone Audiobooks.

Keller, H. (2004). *The story of my life.* New York: Modern Library. (Original work published 1903.)

Klein, M. (2003). *The change makers: From Carnegie to Gates: How the great entrepreneurs transformed ideas into industries.* New York: Times Books.

Loehr, J., & Schwartz, T. (2003). *The power of full engagement: Managing energy, not time, is the key to high performance and personal renewal.* New York: Free Press.

Morrell, M., & Capparell, S. (2001). *Shackleton's way: Leadership lessons from the great Antarctic explorer.* New York: Viking Press.

Paris, D., Richards, M., & White, H. (2007). *High point of persistence: The Miriam Richards story.* Morrisville, NC: Lulu.com.

Schatzkin, P. (2004). *The boy who invented television: A story of inspiration, persistence, and quiet passion.* Terre Haute, IN: Tanglewood Books.

Thomas, R. J. (2008). *Crucibles of leadership: How to learn from experience to become a great leader.* Boston: Harvard Business School Press.

Troyat, H. (1987). *Peter the Great.* New York: Dutton.

44 Personal Disclosure

A man cannot utter two or three sentences, without disclosing to intelligent ears precisely where he stands in life and thought.
Ralph Waldo Emerson – American essayist, philosopher, and poet

Unskilled

- ☐ A private person who does not discuss personal information
- ☐ A closed book to most; hard to tell where he/she is coming from
- ☐ May not believe in sharing personal views and foibles
- ☐ Works to keep personal and business separate
- ☐ May fear what will happen if he/she discloses
- ☐ May be shy
- ☐ Doesn't ask others for personal information
- ☐ Doesn't know what is helpful to share or why people find it valuable
- ☐ May believe he/she has something to hide
- ☐ May be defensive and unwilling to share much

Select one to three of the competencies listed below to use as a substitute for this competency if you decide not to work on it directly.

SUBSTITUTES: 26,27,29,33,41,45,54,55

Skilled

- ☐ Shares his/her thoughts about personal strengths, weaknesses, and limitations
- ☐ Admits mistakes and shortcomings
- ☐ Is open about personal beliefs and feelings
- ☐ Is easy to get to know to those who interact with him/her regularly

Overused Skill

- ☐ May turn off some people by excessive directness
- ☐ May leave him/herself open for criticism because of his/her honesty
- ☐ Openness and directness may actually lead to a lack of trust
- ☐ Open style may lack credibility with some

Select one to three of the competencies listed below to work on to compensate for an overuse of this skill.

COMPENSATORS: 15,22,27,29,45,48,55,56,64

Some Causes

- ☐ Believe work and personal should not be mixed
- ☐ Don't have a good sense about what to disclose
- ☐ Don't see the point of disclosing
- ☐ Lack of self-confidence; others will find out the real me
- ☐ Perfectionist; don't want to show any weaknesses
- ☐ Seen it done very poorly by others
- ☐ Shy and uncomfortable being personal

Leadership Architect® Factors and Clusters

This competency is in the Personal and Interpersonal Skills Factor (VI). This competency is in the Being Open and Receptive Cluster (S) with: 11, 26, 33, 41. You may want to check other competencies in the same Factor/Cluster for related tips.

The Map

Personal relationships are give-and-take. Warmth is usually responded to with warmth, openness with openness, and coolness with coolness. You get what you give. Personal disclosure is one aspect of any job (like managing others; working on a team) that involves prolonged relationships. Many managers believe that keeping a proper distance from direct reports is the right practice. Their measure of proper is usually too distant and far. A balanced business plus personal relationship works best. People can't relate well to a cold role across time. Disclosing gives people a sense of where you're coming from and how to read you. When you disclose, most others will open up. It broadens the bandwidth of the relationship leading to working better together. Almost all working relationships benefit from reasonable personal disclosure.

Some Remedies

- ☐ **1. Unsure what to share? Disclose selectively.** The kinds of disclosure that people enjoy are the reasons behind why you do what you do, your self-appraisal, things you know behind what's happening in the business that they don't know—that you are at liberty to disclose, things both good and embarrassing that have happened to you in the past, commentary about what's going on around you—without being too negative about others, and things you are interested in and do outside of work. These are areas which you should learn to disclose more than you now do.
- ☐ **2. Unsure how to begin? Start with low-risk disclosures.** Start with three things you can talk about with almost anyone without risking uncomfortable personal disclosure. Vacations, hobbies, business interests, your thinking on business issues, children, etc. Decide what they are and make a

conscious effort to sprinkle them into some of your interactions with others you have generally had only a business relationship with before. Notice the reaction. Did they also share for the first time? Usually yes. And that's the point. Within limits, the more you know about each other, the better the working relationship will be.

☐ **3. Need to connect with coworkers? Try to get to know three non-work things about everybody.** Get to know their interests or their children or something you can chat about with them other than the weather or the weekend sports results.

☐ **4. Need a model or mentor? Observe someone who discloses a lot more than you do and does it well.** What do they disclose? What type of personal information do they share? How do they share? In what settings do they share? Then study someone who discloses less than you do. Which of the two do you work with the best?

☐ **5. Ready to try it out? Practice your disclosure skills with strangers on airplanes or at social gatherings.** Your goal is to disclose some things about yourself that you don't usually disclose in a work setting. Then see how many things you can get the other person to disclose. Test limits without irritating him/her. As he/she discloses more, you disclose more. After each event, ask yourself how that felt. What did the additional information about that person add to the temporary relationship? Would it be easier to work with that person now that you have some personal information?

☐ **6. Ready to go deeper? Get comfortable with disclosing personal strengths and weaknesses.** More serious personal disclosure involves talking about your self-appraisal. This involves talking about your personal strengths, weaknesses, limitations and beliefs. Most others are more comfortable with people who do reasonable disclosure. The funny thing about self-assessment disclosure is that most of the people around you already know what you're going to disclose! If you say, "I'm not the most organized person in the world," most around you will do a smiling nod because they suffer the consequences of your disorganization. But, that brief mention of a problem you have or a belief you hold will help the person feel more comfortable. This tells them they are not alone, that you have some of the same problems and worries they do.

☐ **7. Hesitant to admit errors? Disclose mistakes.** Learn to be more comfortable admitting your mistakes. This makes you more human, and it also establishes a routine of learning from our inevitable shortcomings. People who excel at dealing with their own mistakes usually do the following:

– Talk about mistakes matter-of-factly as quickly as possible.

– Volunteer the mistake and inform everyone affected what could occur.

- Publicly acknowledge the mistake if necessary.
- Demonstrate what they have learned so the mistake does not happen again.
- Move on; don't dwell on it.

☐ **8. Seen as overbearing and one-sided? Disclose the rationale behind your values.** When disclosing beliefs or values stances, always explain why you hold a belief—give reasons rather than just stating something. Statements cut off discussion and may make you look rigid or simplistic. Bold statements are those that are absolute and because of that limiting. There is no comeback to "never hire a friend" except to reject your disclosure. Saying "I had to fire someone once; this was the situation, my reasons, what I tried to do to help, and what I learned from it" sets up your belief statements. Making them first comes across as pronouncements ("Never hire a friend"). Try to start with moderate statements like, "This made me question how good an idea it is to hire a friend." That's a good disclosure. It invites discussion; it may even lead to some insights: under what conditions a friend should or shouldn't be hired.

☐ **9. Things getting awkward? Determine the disclosure comfort zone.** Try to balance your disclosure with what the other person is ready for. You start with a simple and short disclosure. What did the other person do? If he/she didn't respond with a disclosure, maybe the setting or situation isn't right for disclosure. If she/he acknowledged your disclosure and added one, then you disclose something else. Always check to see if your audience wants more.

☐ **10. Need boundaries? Set disclosure limits.** Avoid too much disclosure; it is probably worse than none. Set limits. Generally politics and religion are risky; ribald humor and anything ethnic or gender demeaning wouldn't be good and might end up in litigation. There are also people you can disclose to and some you shouldn't, since some people can't keep confidences. Be careful of putting someone in a counselor role or saying too much about an issue. Early in the process of disclosure, it's usually best for you to follow the lead of others and disclose about as much as they do.

Some Develop-in-Place Assignments

- ☐ Make peace with an enemy or someone you've disappointed with a product or service or someone you've had some trouble with or don't get along with very well.
- ☐ Join a self-help or support group.
- ☐ Try to learn something frivolous and fun to see how good you can get (e.g., juggling, square dancing, magic).
- ☐ Attend a self-awareness/assessment course that includes feedback.
- ☐ Attend a course or event which will push you personally beyond your usual limits or outside your comfort zone (e.g., Outward Bound, language immersion training, sensitivity group, public speaking).

You cannot collaborate with another person toward some common end unless you know him. How can you know him, and he you, unless you have engaged in enough mutual disclosure of self to be able to anticipate how he will react and what part he will play?
Sidney Jourard – Canadian-born Humanistic psychologist and author

Suggested Readings

Asacker, T., & Orloff, E. (2001). *The four sides of sandbox wisdom: Building relationships in an age of chaos, complexity and change.* Manchester, NH: Eastside Publishing.

Barron, L. A. (2006). *Openness works! Create personal, professional and financial growth in any organization.* Austin, TX: Hopeworks Publishing.

Giovagnoli, M., & Carter-Miller, J. (2000). *Networlding: Building relationships and opportunities for success.* San Francisco: Jossey-Bass.

Guber, P. (2007). The four truths of the storyteller. *Harvard Business Review, 85,* 52-59.

Gudykunst, W. B., & Kim, Y. Y. (2002). *Communicating with strangers: An approach to intercultural communication.* New York: McGraw-Hill.

Lencioni, P. M. (2002). *The five dysfunctions of a team: A leadership fable.* San Francisco: Jossey-Bass.

Lynn, A. B. (2007). *Quick emotional intelligence activities for busy managers: 50 Team exercises that get results in just 15 minutes.* New York: AMACOM.

Simmons, A. (2006). *The story factor.* Cambridge, MA: Perseus Publishing.

Stone, D., Patton, B., & Heen, S. (2000). *Difficult conversations: How to discuss what matters most.* New York: Penguin Books.

Tamm, J. W., & Luyet, R. J. (2004). *Radical collaboration: Five essential skills to overcome defensiveness and build successful relationships.* New York: HarperCollins.

45 Personal Learning

I present myself to you in a form suitable to the relationship
I wish to achieve with you.
Luigi Pirandello – Italian Nobel Prize-winning novelist

Unskilled

- ☐ Doesn't change or adapt to his/her surroundings or the situation
- ☐ May have a view that being true to oneself is all that matters
- ☐ May see adjusting to others as a sign of weakness
- ☐ May be a one-thing-at-a-time person or a person who only thinks about what he/she is doing, not how others are responding or what they need
- ☐ Doesn't pick up on the need for personal change
- ☐ Doesn't seek or listen to personal on-line feedback
- ☐ Not a people watcher or studier, doesn't see or understand their reactions to him/her
- ☐ May be arrogant or defensive

Select one to three of the competencies listed below to use as a substitute for this competency if you decide not to work on it directly.

SUBSTITUTE: 6,32,33,44,54,55

Skilled

- ☐ Picks up on the need to change personal, interpersonal, and managerial behavior quickly
- ☐ Watches others for their reactions to his/her attempts to influence and perform, and adjusts
- ☐ Seeks feedback
- ☐ Is sensitive to changing personal demands and requirements and changes accordingly

Overused Skill

- ☐ May be seen as too changeable
- ☐ May shift situationally too easily and leave the impression of being wishy-washy
- ☐ May err toward doing things differently rather than remaining the same
- ☐ May confuse people by experimenting and being so adaptable

Select one to three of the competencies listed below to work on to compensate for an overuse of this skill.

COMPENSATORS: 5,16,17,39,46,47,50,51,52,53,58,59,62,65

Some Causes

- ☐ Arrogant/defensive
- ☐ Can't do more than one thing at a time
- ☐ No role models
- ☐ Poor observer of others
- ☐ Being true to yourself is an overriding concern
- ☐ Think consistency is a virtue
- ☐ Think others should adjust to you

Leadership Architect® Factors and Clusters

This competency is in the Personal and Interpersonal Skills Factor (VI). This competency is in the Demonstrating Personal Flexibility Cluster (T) with: 40, 54, 55. You may want to check other competencies in the same Factor/Cluster for related tips.

The Map

We are all capable of a range of behaviors. Even a shy person can get up the courage and strength to be assertive once in a while. A loud person can be quiet. A smart person can act dumb. An action oriented person can reflect. How do you know where in your range of behaviors to be in any given situation? Observation and feedback. Ever watch people who always seem to know when to adjust their behavior and in what direction to adjust it? Just when a situation is about to turn bad, they change tactics. Such people are astute observers of the reactions of others to what they are doing. They select from their range of behaviors the tone and level that fits the situation. They are very customer and audience driven; they deliver what each customer wants. This competency is especially important in managing, developing and motivating others, and in tense situations like negotiating or political disputes.

Some Remedies

- ☐ **1. Clueless? Observe and listen to others.** You must watch the reactions of people to what you are doing while you are doing it to gauge their response. Are they bored? Change the pace. Are they confused? State it in a different way. Are they angry? Stop and ask what the problem is. Are they too quiet? Stop and get them involved in what you are doing. Are they fidgeting, scribbling on their pads or staring out the window? They may not be interested in what you are doing. Move to the end of your presentation or task, end it, and exit. Check in with your audience frequently and select a different tactic if necessary. *More help? – See #33 Listening.*
- ☐ **2. Not sure of your impact? Seek feedback.** Ask people for direct feedback on what you are doing while you are doing it and immediately after.

People are reluctant to give you feedback, especially negative or corrective information. Generally, to get it you must ask for it. If people are reluctant to give criticism, help by making self-appraisal statements rather than asking questions. Saying, "I think I talked too long on that topic in the meeting; what do you think?" is easier for most people to reply to than a question which asks them to volunteer this point. *More help? – See #55 Self-Knowledge.*

☐ **3. Need a model or mentor? Select three people to observe who are good in tense situations or good with interpersonal transactions and transitions.** Write down what they say or do when problems arise. What kinds of words do they use? How do they monitor what's happening? Do they ask questions or make statements? Do they state things in hard, moderate or soft ways? How much time do they talk vs. others? Compare this with what you do in these same situations. What differences do you see? Interview these people to see if they can take you inside their minds and explain why they did what they did and especially why they changed tactics midstream.

☐ **4. Only seeing it your way? Adopt another's point of view.** People who are good at this work from the outside (the customer, the audience, the person, the situation) in, not from the inside out ("What do I want to do in this situation; what would make me happy and feel good?"). Practice not thinking inside/out when you are around others. What are the demand characteristics of this situation? How does this person or audience best learn? Which of my approaches or styles would work best? How can I best accomplish my goals? How can I alter my approach and tactics to be the most effective? The one-trick pony can only perform once per show. If the audience doesn't like that particular trick, no oats for the pony.

☐ **5. Missing signals? Pay particular attention to non-verbal cues.** Common signals of trouble are changes in body posture (especially turning away), crossed arms, staring, or the telltale glancing at one's watch, scribbling on the pad, tapping fingers or the pencil, looking out the window, frowns and washboard foreheads. When this occurs, pause. Ask a question. Ask how we're doing. Do a live process check. Some people use the same body language to signal that they are done or not interested in what's going on. Get to know their signals. Construct an alternative plan for the five people you work with closely. When Bill begins to stare, I will... When Sally interrupts for the third time, I will....

☐ **6. Not getting a good read on others? Experiment with some new techniques.** Many excellent personal learners have a bag of techniques they use. They give reasons for everything they say, saving any solution statements for last. They ask lots of questions, speak briefly, summarize often, and when disagreeing they put it in conditional terms ("I don't think so, but what do you think?"). The point of these is to elicit as much information about the reactions of others as they can. They are loading their files so they can change behavior when needed.

☐ **7. Don't understand your audience? Become a better student of people.** Observe more than you do now. See if you can predict what people are going to say and do before they do it. See if their behavior shows a pattern. What do they do over and over again? By scoping out people better, you can better adjust to their responses. *More help? – See #56 Sizing Up People.*

☐ **8. Narrow range? Expand your repertoire of behavior.** Try to stretch yourself. Do things that are not characteristic of you. Go to your limits and beyond. By expanding the number of behaviors you have access to, you can become more effective across a larger number of situations. *More help? – See #54 Self-Development.*

☐ **9. Believe your ideas are best? Keep arrogance in check.** Many people who have a towering strength or lots of success get little feedback and roll along until their careers get in trouble. If you are arrogant (you devalue the contributions of others), you should work doubly hard at observing, reading about and interviewing others. You will need to submerge your "what I want/think" demeanor and keep asking yourself, "What do they want; how are they reacting?" Writing down your observations is a must, since in your normal mode you pay scant attention to your impact on others. *More help? – See #104 Arrogant.*

☐ **10. Rejecting what you hear? Avoid defensiveness.** If you are defensive, people will not offer course correction information. If you are defensive, the feedback won't get in. You will need to work on seeing yourself in a calm state prior to meetings, mentally rehearsing how you will react to tough situations before you go in, and developing automatic tactics to resist shutting down. Some useful tactics are to literally count to 10, tell yourself to think in slow motion (or see yourself doing it) or to temper the heat with stock questions like, "What do you think? Could you tell me more about that?" *More help? – See #108 Defensiveness.*

Some Develop-in-Place Assignments

- ☐ Go on a business trip to a foreign country you've not been to before.
- ☐ Join a self-help or support group.
- ☐ Try to learn something frivolous and fun to see how good you can get (e.g., juggling, square dancing, magic).
- ☐ Attend a course or event which will push you personally beyond your usual limits or outside your comfort zone (e.g., Outward Bound, language immersion training, sensitivity group, public speaking).
- ☐ Interview or work with a "tutor" or mentor on a skill you need to develop.

The weather-cock on the church spire, though made of iron,
would soon be broken by the storm-wind
if it did not understand the noble art of turning to every wind.
Heinrich Heine – German poet

Suggested Readings

Bardwick, J. M. (2002). *Seeking the calm in the storm: Managing chaos in your business life.* Upper Saddle River, NJ: Financial Times/Prentice Hall.

Caro, M. (2003). *Caro's book of poker tells.* New York: Cardoza Publishing.

Fulmer, R. M., & Conger, J. A. (2004). *Growing your company's leaders.* New York: AMACOM.

Glickman, R. (2002). *Optimal thinking: How to be your best self.* Hoboken, NJ: John Wiley & Sons.

Kouzes, J. M. (2003). *Credibility: How leaders gain and lose it, why people demand it.* San Francisco: Jossey-Bass.

Lombardo, M. M., & Eichinger., R. W. (2004). *The leadership machine.* Minneapolis, MN: Lominger International: A Korn/Ferry Company.

Marquardt, M. J. (2005). *Leading with questions: How leaders find the right solutions by knowing what to ask.* San Francisco: Jossey-Bass.

Niven, D. (2006). *The 100 simple secrets of successful people: What scientists have learned and how you can use it* (2nd ed.). New York: HarperBusiness.

Pearman, R. R., Lombardo, M. M., & Eichinger, R. W. (2005). *You: Being more effective in your MBTI type.* Minneapolis, MN: Lominger International: A Korn/Ferry Company.

Vandergriff, D. (2006). *Raising the bar: Creating and nurturing adaptability to deal with the changing face of war.* Washington DC: The Center for Defense Information.

Wainright, G. R. (2003). *Teach yourself body language.* New York: McGraw-Hill.

46 Perspective

The eye sees only what the mind is prepared to comprehend.
Henri-Louis Bergson – French philosopher

Unskilled

- ☐ Is narrow and parochial
- ☐ Has narrow views of issues and challenges
- ☐ Uses only one or a few lenses to view problems and opportunities
- ☐ Doesn't have far-ranging interests, not well-read
- ☐ Background may be narrow
- ☐ Isn't good at running "what if" scenarios
- ☐ Lacks interest in maybes and the future and how world events do and will affect his/her organization
- ☐ Won't be a good strategist or visionary
- ☐ A here-and-now person who is often surprised by unexpected change
- ☐ May be a single function/profession/technical area/skill person

Select one to three of the competencies listed below to use as a substitute for this competency if you decide not to work on it directly.

SUBSTITUTES: 2,5,15,21,28,32,38,48,58,61

Skilled

- ☐ Looks toward the broadest possible view of an issue/challenge
- ☐ Has broad-ranging personal and business interests and pursuits
- ☐ Can easily pose future scenarios
- ☐ Can think globally
- ☐ Can discuss multiple aspects and impacts of issues and project them into the future

Overused Skill

- ☐ Might have some trouble concentrating on the here and now
- ☐ May leave others behind when he/she speculates on the broad view of an issue
- ☐ May not set practical priorities
- ☐ May always be reaching for too much and/or the ideal
- ☐ May see connections that aren't there

Select one to three of the competencies listed below to work on to compensate for an overuse of this skill.

COMPENSATORS: 5,16,17,24,35,38,47,50,51,52,53,58,59,63,65

Some Causes

- ☐ Avoid risks
- ☐ Disadvantaged background
- ☐ Narrow interests
- ☐ Narrow upbringing
- ☐ Restricted experience base
- ☐ Tactically oriented
- ☐ Too comfortable
- ☐ Uncomfortable thinking/talking about future states

Leadership Architect® Factors and Clusters

This competency is in the Strategic Skills Factor (I). This competency is in the Creating the New and Different Cluster (C) with: 2, 14, 28, 58. You may want to check other competencies in the same Factor/Cluster for related tips.

The Map

Ideas, perspectives and strategies don't come from raw intelligence or creativity. They come from a prepared mind, one broadened by lots of varied but disconnected experiences, exposures and interests. The broadest people usually win because they have a greater repertoire to draw from and more chances to make unusual connections to new ideas, cultures, events, etc. In the Sears studies of effectiveness across 35 years, one of the best predictors of success was range of interests.

Some Remedies

☐ **1. Ready to expand your thinking? Do some reading.** Read *Management Challenges for the 21st Century* by Peter Drucker, any of the *Megatrends* books by John Naisbitt, *The Popcorn Report* by Faith Popcorn, or *THE FUTURIST*, the journal of the World Future Society. For example, Drucker raises issues such as what does it mean that the birth rate is collapsing in the developed world? By 2030 it is estimated that half of Japan's population will be 65 or older. Much the same is true in the rest of the developed world. Will the retirement age go up? Will we treat workers more like volunteers as they opt out of larger organizations? Leisure spending may go down since more time off is not likely. Education and health care will grow. Immigration? Even in the wake of terror attacks, we may have to import immigrants to maintain workforces. The average career of an employee will far outlive their employers (most corporations last about 30 years). Second and third "careers" will be standard. The means of production has largely become knowledge. Outsourcing is up—knowledge is increasingly specialized, expensive, and difficult to maintain. Is this a harbinger of more outsourcing and alliances? What are the trends at play and how do they affect your organization going forward?

☐ **2. Does history repeat itself? Learn from the past.** Study a few well-known inventions of the past, like the automobile (*The Machine That Changed the World* by James Womack and associates at MIT is an excellent source). See how they use the past to predict the future. See how several unrelated inventions came together to form a bigger one. There is a series on cable called *Modern Marvels*. Watch a few shows. Buy the series. How could you use the past of your organization—from 1960 to 1970; from 1970 to 1980, etc.—to predict the future?

☐ **3. See the interconnectedness? Observe what's happening in the world and how it links to your organization.** Read the *Wall Street Journal* and *BusinessWeek* and write down three to five interesting things that have a parallel or an effect on your organization. Learn to connect what's out there to what's in here.

☐ **4. Need a fresh approach? Tap into non-experts.** During World War II, the military discovered the most creative groups were those where the members had little or nothing in common, and knew little about the issue. Their freewheeling approach yielded fresher solutions. They were not trapped by the past. Take a current challenge to the most disparate group you can find (a historian, a college student, a theologian, a salesperson, a plumber, etc.) and see what insights they have into it. Find some problems outside of your area and see what you can add.

☐ **5. Curious? Dabble.** Study and dabble in three unrelated things that you have not yet paid much attention to—opera, romance novels, technical journals out of your area, MTV, learn a new language, take a magic course, study archeology. Connections can come from anywhere—your brain doesn't care where it gets perspectives. Try to think about how the principles of one tie into the other.

☐ **6. Need international perspective? Read widely.** Read international publications like the *Economist*, the *International Herald Tribune*, *Commentary*; autobiographies of people like Kissinger; pick a country and study it; read a book on the fall of the Soviet Union; or read "we present all sides" journals like the *Atlantic Monthly* to get the broadest possible view of issues. There are common underlying principles in everything. You need to expose yourself more broadly in order to find and apply those principles to what you're doing today.

☐ **7. Got vacation time? Go on adventures.** Travel to places you have not been before. Never vacation at the same place again. Eat at different theme restaurants. Go to events and meetings of groups you have never really met. Go to ethnic festivals and sample the cultures. Go to athletic events you've never attended before. Each week, you and your family should go on a perspectives adventure.

- ☐ **8. Ready to look beyond the workplace? Pick something you've never done, but which would broaden your perspective outside of work.** Serve with a community group, volunteer to be a Big Sister/Brother, travel to an unvisited country, follow a group of ten-year-olds around for a few days.
- ☐ **9. Ready for new experiences? At work, pick three tasks you've never done and go do them.** If you don't know much about customers, work in a store or handle customer complaints; if you don't know what engineering does, go find out; task trade with someone. Seek the broadest possible exposure inside the organization. Do lunch with counterparts of the organization and tell each other what you do.
- ☐ **10. Want a developmental experience? Serve on a task force.** Task forces/projects are a great opportunity. If the project is important, is multifunctional and has a real outcome which will be taken seriously (not a study group), it is one of the most common developmental events listed by successful executives. Such projects require learning other functions, businesses or nationalities well enough that in a tight time frame you can appreciate how they think and why their area/position is important. In so doing, you get out of your own experience and start to see connections to a broader world—how international trade works, or more at home, how the pieces of your organization fit together. You can build perspective.

Some Develop-in-Place Assignments

- ☐ Work on a project that involves travel and study of an international issue, acquisition, or joint venture and report back to management.
- ☐ Work short rotations in other units, functions, or geographies you've not been exposed to before.
- ☐ Manage a project team made up of nationals from a number of countries.
- ☐ Get involved with the negotiation of a contract or agreement with international consequences.
- ☐ Become a volunteer for a year or more for an outside organization.

The manager has a short-range view;
the leader has a long-range perspective.
Warren G. Bennis – American scholar, organizational consultant, and author

Suggested Readings

Bernstein, R.B. (2005). *Thomas Jefferson.* New York: Oxford University Press, Inc.

Chernow, R. (2004). *Titan: The life of John D. Rockefeller.* London: Vintage.

Collins, J. C. (2001). *Good to great: Why some companies make the leap...and others don't.* New York: HarperCollins.

De Kluyber, C. A., & Pearce, J. A. (2008). *Strategy: A view from the top.* Upper Saddle River, NJ: Prentice Hall.

Drucker, P. F. (2001). *Management challenges for the 21st century.* New York: HarperBusiness.

Drucker, P. F. (2008). *Classic Drucker: From the pages of Harvard Business Review.* Boston: Harvard Business School Press.

Duck, J. D. (2001). *The change monster.* New York: Crown Business.

Dudik, E. M. (2000). *Strategic renaissance: New thinking and innovative tools to create great corporate strategies using insights from history and science.* New York: AMACOM.

Durant, W., & Durant, A. (1968). *The lessons of history.* New York: Simon & Schuster.

Gladwell, M. (2002). *The tipping point: How little things can make a big difference.* New York: Back Bay Books.

Heleniak, R. J., Hyde, S. C., & Robison, W. B. (1999). *A broad perspective: Readings in western civilization from the ancient world to the present.* Sugarland, TX: American Heritage Custom Publishing.

Isaacson, W. (2004). *Benjamin Franklin: An American life.* New York: Simon & Schuster.

Kennedy, P. M. (1987). *The rise and fall of the great powers: Economic change and military conflict from 1500 to 2000.* New York: Random House.

Koch, R. (2001). *The natural laws of business: How to harness the power of evolution, physics, and economics to achieve business success.* New York: Doubleday.

Levinson, M. (2008). *The box: How the shipping container made the world smaller and the world economy bigger.* Princeton, NJ: Princeton University Press.

Nicholl, C. (2005). *Leonardo da Vinci: Flights of the mind.* New York: Penguin Group.

Nixon, R. M. (1982). *Leaders.* New York: Warner Books.

Ogilvy, J. A. (2002). *Creating better futures: Scenario planning as a tool for a better tomorrow.* New York: Oxford University Press, Inc.

Pinker, S. (2008). *The stuff of thought: Language as a window into human nature.* New York: Penguin Group.

Rabb, T. K. (2000). *Renaissance lives: Portraits of an age.* New York: Basic Books.

Smith, J. E. (2008). *FDR.* New York: Random House Trade Paperbacks.

Womack, J. P., & Jones, D. T. (2003). *Lean thinking: Banish waste and create wealth in your corporation.* New York: Free Press.

47 Planning

You can't overestimate the need to plan and prepare.
In most of the mistakes I've made, there has been
this common theme of inadequate planning beforehand.
You really can't over-prepare in business!
Chris Corrigan – Australian businessman

Unskilled

- ☐ Doesn't plan for much
- ☐ May be a seat-of-the-pants performer scratching it out at the last minute
- ☐ Doesn't follow an orderly method of setting goals and laying out work
- ☐ May be uncomfortable with structure and process flow
- ☐ May be disdainful of planning and come across to others as loose or too simple
- ☐ May not have the patience to establish goals and objectives, scope out difficulties, plan for task completion, develop schedules, and do roadblock management
- ☐ May be confusing to work for and with
- ☐ May be demotivating to others who work with him/her

Select one to three of the competencies listed below to use as a substitute for this competency if you decide not to work on it directly.

SUBSTITUTES: 18,20,24,35,39,51,52,62

Skilled

- ☐ Accurately scopes out length and difficulty of tasks and projects
- ☐ Sets objectives and goals
- ☐ Breaks down work into the process steps
- ☐ Develops schedules and task/people assignments
- ☐ Anticipates and adjusts for problems and roadblocks
- ☐ Measures performance against goals
- ☐ Evaluates results

Overused Skill

- ☐ May be overly dependent on rules, regulations, procedures, and structure
- ☐ May leave out the human element of the work
- ☐ May be inflexible and have trouble with rapid change

Select one to three of the competencies listed below to work on to compensate for an overuse of this skill.

COMPENSATORS: 2,3,10,14,15,26,31,32,33,40,46,57,60,64

Some Causes

- ☐ Arrogant; don't need it
- ☐ Impatient
- ☐ Low sense of structure and process
- ☐ Need for simplicity
- ☐ Time management; just don't get around to it

Leadership Architect® Factors and Clusters

This competency is in the Operating Skills Factor (II). This competency is in the Getting Organized Cluster (E) with: 39, 62. You may want to check other competencies in the same Factor/Cluster for related tips.

The Map

Nothing helps move things along better than a good plan. It helps the people who have to work under the plan. It leads to better use of resources. It gets things done faster. It helps anticipate problems before they occur. It is one of the aspects of managing others that universally receives a positive response. A good plan leaves more time to do other things secure in the knowledge that things are on track and proceeding as planned.

Some Remedies

- ☐ **1. Plans incomplete? Lay out tasks and work.** Most successful projects begin with a good plan. What do I need to accomplish? What are the goals? What's the time line? What resources will I need? How many of the resources do I control? Who controls the rest of the resources—people, funding, tools, materials, support—I need? Lay out the work from A to Z. Many people are seen as lacking a plan because they don't write down the sequence or parts of the work and leave something out. Ask others to comment on ordering and what's missing. *More help? – See #52 Process Management and #63 Total Work Systems (e.g., TQM/ISO/Six Sigma).*
- ☐ **2. Ready to get started? Set the plan.** Buy a flow charting and/or project planning software that does PERT and GANTT charts. Become an expert in its use. Use the output of the software to communicate your plans to others. Use the flow charts in your presentations.
- ☐ **3. Ready to track progress? Set goals and measures.** Nothing keeps projects on time and on budget like a goal, a plan and a measure. Set goals for the whole project and the sub-tasks. Plan for all. Set measures so you and others can track progress against the goals. *More help? – See #35 Managing and Measuring Work.*
- ☐ **4. Too much complexity? Manage multiple plans or aspects of big plans.** Many attempts to accomplish complex plans involve managing parallel tracks or

multiple tasks at the same time. It helps if you have a master plan. Good planning decreases the chances you will lose control by spreading yourself too thin.

☐ **5. Limited resources? Manage efficiently.** Plan the budget and manage against it. Spend carefully. Have a reserve if the unanticipated comes up. Set up a funding time line so you can track ongoing expenditures against plan.

☐ **6. Problems distributing the work? Match people and tasks.** People are different. They have different strengths and have differing levels of knowledge and experience. Instead of thinking of everyone as equal, think of them as different. Really equal treatment is giving people tasks to do that match their capacities. *More help? – See #56 Sizing Up People.*

☐ **7. Have you identified worst-case scenarios? Envision the plan in process.** What could go wrong? Run scenarios in your head. Think along several paths. Rank the potential problems from highest likelihood to lowest likelihood. Think about what you would do if the highest likelihood things were to occur. Create a contingency plan for each. Pay attention to the weakest links which are usually groups or elements you have the least interface with or control over (perhaps someone in a remote location, a consultant or supplier). Stay doubly in touch with the potential weak links. *More help? – See #51 Problem Solving.*

☐ **8. Unsure how progress will be monitored? Set up a process to monitor progress against the plan.** How would you know if the plan is on time? Could you estimate time to completion or percent finished at any time? Give people involved in implementing the plan progress feedback as you go.

☐ **9. Are you self-aware? Find role models and ask for feedback.** Find someone in your environment who is better at planning than you are to see how it's done. How does that compare against what you typically do? Try to increase doing the things he/she does. Ask for feedback from some people who have had to follow your plans. What did they like? What did they find difficult?

☐ **10. Need input? Get others to help.** Share your ideas about the project with others, possibly the people you need to support you later. Get their input on the plan. Delegate creating the plan to people who are better at it than you are. You provide the goals and what needs to be done, and let others create the detailed plan. *More help? – See #18 Delegation and #33 Listening.*

Some Develop-in-Place Assignments

☐ Plan an off-site meeting, conference, convention, trade show, event, etc.

☐ Manage the purchase of a major product, equipment, materials, program, or system.

☐ Manage the visit of a VIP (member of top management, government official, outside customer, foreign visitor, etc.).

- ☐ Integrate diverse systems, processes, or procedures across decentralized and/or dispersed units.
- ☐ Install a new process or system (computer system, new policies, new process, new procedures, etc.).

Luck is what happens when preparation meets opportunity.
Seneca (4 BCE-65 CE) – Roman philosopher, statesman, dramatist, and humorist

Suggested Readings

Angus, R. B., Gundersen, N. A., & Cullinane, T. P. (2002). *Planning, performing, and controlling projects.* Upper Saddle River, NJ: Prentice Hall.

Axson, D. A. J. (2003). *Best practices in planning and management reporting.* New York: John Wiley & Sons.

Bacon, T. R., & Pugh, D. G. (2003). *Winning behavior: What the smartest, most successful companies do differently.* New York: AMACOM.

Collins, J. C. (2001). *Good to great: Why some companies make the leap...and others don't.* New York: HarperCollins.

Devlin, E. S. (2007). *Crisis management planning and execution.* Boca Raton, FL: Auerbach Publications.

Hamel, G. (2002). *Leading the revolution* (Rev. ed.). Boston: Harvard Business School Press.

Harpst, G. (2008). *Six Disciplines® execution revolution: Solving the one business problem that makes solving all other problems easier.* Findlay, OH: Six Disciplines Publishing.

Jackson, P. Z., & McKergow, M. (2002). *The solutions focus.* Yarmouth, ME: Nicholas Brealey Publishing.

Kerzner, H. (2005). *Project management: A systems approach to planning, scheduling, and controlling* (9th ed.). Hoboken, NJ: John Wiley & Sons.

Lewis, J. P. (2005). *Project planning, scheduling and control.* Columbus, OH: McGraw-Hill.

Lewis, J. P. (2006). *Fundamentals of project management* (3rd ed.). New York: AMACOM.

Manas, J. (2006). *Napoleon on project management: Timeless lessons in planning, execution, and leadership.* Nashville, TN: Thomas Nelson.

Mitroff, I. I. (with Anagnos, G.). (2001). *Managing crises before they happen.* New York: AMACOM.

Perrin, R. (2008). *Real world project management: Beyond conventional wisdom, best practices and project methodologies.* Hoboken, NJ: John Wiley & Sons.

Tomczyk, C. A. (2005). *Project manager's spotlight on planning.* San Francisco: Jossey-Bass.

Vega, G. (2001). *A passion for planning: Financials, operations, marketing, management, and ethics.* Lanham, MD: University Press of America.

48 Political Savvy

Just because you do not take an interest in politics doesn't mean politics won't take an interest in you.
Pericles (495-429 BCE) – Greek statesman, orator, and general of Athens

Unskilled

- ☐ Doesn't know how to navigate smoothly and quietly through political waters
- ☐ Says and does things that cause political problems
- ☐ Doesn't understand how to deal with not-invented-here and territory protection
- ☐ Rejects politics and may view self as apolitical; others might see this as naïve
- ☐ May not deal with upper management persuasively
- ☐ May be impatient with political process and make procedural errors
- ☐ May be too direct and not consider impact on others
- ☐ May not project out consequences of his/her actions well

Select one to three of the competencies listed below to use as a substitute for this competency if you decide not to work on it directly.

SUBSTITUTES: 3,4,8,12,21,22,31,32,33,36,37,38,42,52,56,64

Skilled

- ☐ Can maneuver through complex political situations effectively and quietly
- ☐ Is sensitive to how people and organizations function
- ☐ Anticipates where the land mines are and plans his/her approach accordingly
- ☐ Views corporate politics as a necessary part of organizational life and works to adjust to that reality
- ☐ Is a maze-bright person

Overused Skill

- ☐ May be seen as excessively political
- ☐ May not be trusted
- ☐ May tell others what they are expecting to hear rather than what he/she knows to be true
- ☐ May overstate what he or she knows
- ☐ May be seen as manipulative and scheming

Select one to three of the competencies listed below to work on to compensate for an overuse of this skill.

COMPENSATORS: 4,8,12,17,22,27,29,30,34,38,44,51,53,57,63

Some Causes

- ☐ Don't read others or their interests well
- ☐ Excessively direct and straightforward
- ☐ Misunderstanding of what political savvy is
- ☐ No patience with due process
- ☐ Poor interpersonal skills
- ☐ Poor negotiator
- ☐ Reject the necessity of "playing politics"
- ☐ Seen as an advocate
- ☐ Very action oriented
- ☐ Very ego/ethnocentric

Leadership Architect® Factors and Clusters

This competency is in the Organizational Positioning Skills Factor (V). This competency is in the Being Organizationally Savvy Cluster (K) with: 38. You may want to check other competencies in the same Factor/Cluster for related tips.

The Map

Organizations are complex mazes of egos, constituencies, issues and rivalries. They are peopled with strong egos and empire-driven individuals. Everyone builds his or her own sandbox and defends it from attack and influence from outsiders. There are many traps and dead ends in organizations. More ways to turn wrong than right. People who are politically savvy accept this as the human condition and deal with it. Not to be confused with being "political" which is a polite term for not being trusted or lacking in substance, political savvy involves getting things done in the maze with the least noise for the maximum benefit.

Some Remedies

- ☐ **1. Not trusted? Identify how you rate on #22 Ethics and Values and #29 Integrity and Trust.** If high, then don't read this tip. If either is average or lower, you may be seen as not helpful to others. Your attempts to influence will not be trusted. Are you viewed as a loner? You might be cutting corners to look good. You may slap things together to look good when what's underneath wouldn't pass the test. You may be trying to blame others for things you should take responsibility for. You may be seen as pushing narrow or personal interests. You may be making up excuses that are not real to cover your butt. You may be trying to make your rivals look bad so you look better. You may hedge when asked a tough question. You may indicate little or no concern for others. If you do any of these things or things like it, you will eventually be found out. Being more politically savvy may actually backfire on you. Others will trust you less. Before you work on political savvy, work on yourself. *More help? – See #22 Ethics and Values and #29 Integrity and Trust.*

☐ **2. Stuck with a predictable approach? Adjust to the situation and the audience.** People who are politically savvy work from the outside (audience, person, group) in. They determine the demand characteristics or requirements of each situation and each person they face and select from among their various skills, tone, and styles to find the best approach to make things work. Practice not thinking inside/out when you are around others. *More help? – See #15 Customer Focus.*

☐ **3. Big presentations falling flat? Test things out with senior management.** In the special case of dealing with higher management, those who are best at it inform senior managers individually before the presentation/proposal. They often go to the toughest critic first to hone their ideas and get the worst-case out first. Using sound political tactics with senior managers is complicated by people's comfort around top management. Sound political moves require a cool and clear head. *More help? – See #8 Comfort Around Higher Management.*

☐ **4. Outmaneuvered? Learn to read the political landscape.** Organizations are politically complex. They are peopled with strong egos and empire-driven individuals. There are many political traps and dead ends. More ways to turn wrong than right. People who are politically savvy know the organization. They know how to get things done. They know who to rely on for expediting things. They know who the major gatekeepers are who control the flow of resources, information and decisions. *More help? – See #38 Organizational Agility.*

☐ **5. Right audience, wrong message? Understand what makes individuals and groups distinct.** Being politically sensitive includes being people sensitive. You have to be able to read people. You have to be able to predict how they are going to react to you and to what you are trying to get done. The magic and the complexity of life is that people are different. Each requires special consideration and treatment. If you are able to predict what individuals or groups will do, you will be able to select from among your various tactics, skills, and styles to get done what you need. *More help? – See #36 Motivating Others and #56 Sizing Up People.*

☐ **6. Missing signals? Pay attention to body language.** For close-in political savvy (live in a meeting) you need to learn how to read non-verbals. Common signals of trouble are changes in body posture (especially turning away), crossed arms, staring, or the telltale glancing at one's watch, scribbling on the note pad, tapping one's fingers or a pencil, looking out the window, frowns and washboard foreheads. When this occurs, pause. Ask a question. Ask how we're doing. Do a live process check.

- ☐ **7. Inviting opposition? Avoid the extremes.** Strong advocates for narrow views don't usually fare well politically in organizations. Initially be tentative. Give others some room to maneuver. Make the business or organizational case first. Be prepared to counter arguments that your objective is less important than theirs. A lot of political noise is caused by making extreme statements right out of the box.
- ☐ **8. Selectively savvy? Look at opposition groups objectively.** Is there a group or groups you have more trouble with politically than others? Is it because you don't like or are uncomfortable with them? To work better with problem groups, put yourself in their case. Turn off your "I like—I don't like; I agree—I don't agree" switch. Ask yourself why would you act that way? What do you think they're trying to achieve? Establish reciprocity. Relationships don't last unless you provide something and so do they. Find out what they want and tell them what you want. Strike a bargain.
- ☐ **9. Playing the blame game? Keep political conflicts small and concrete.** The more abstract it gets, the more unmanageable it becomes. Separate the people from the problem. Attack problems by looking at the nature of the problem, not the person presenting the problem. Avoid direct blaming remarks; describe the problem and its impact. If you can't agree on a solution, agree on procedure, or agree on a few things, and list all the issues remaining. This creates some motion and breaks political stalemates.
- ☐ **10. No plan B? Be process flexible.** Always have a plan of attack but also have a contingency plan. Be ready for instant change. Expect the unexpected. People who are politically savvy are personally flexible. They care more about accomplishing the objective than staying true to the one true "me." *More help? – See #32 Learning on the Fly and #45 Personal Learning.*

Some Develop-in-Place Assignments

- ☐ Prepare and present a proposal of some consequence to top management.
- ☐ Do a postmortem on a failed project, and present it to the people involved.
- ☐ Manage the interface between consultants and the organization on a critical assignment.
- ☐ Be a change agent; create a symbol for change; lead the rallying cry; champion a significant change and implementation.
- ☐ Write a proposal for a new policy, process, mission, charter, product, service, or system, and present and sell it to top management.

The political tradition of ancient thought, filtered in Italy by Machiavelli, says one thing clearly: every prince needs allies, and the bigger the responsibility, the more allies he needs.

Silvio Berlusconi – Italian Prime Minister, entrepreneur, real estate and insurance tycoon, bank and media proprietor, sports team owner, and songwriter

Suggested Readings

Ashkenas, R. N., Ulrich, D., Jick, T., & Kerr, S. (2002). *The boundaryless organization: Breaking the chains of organization structure* (Rev. ed.). San Francisco: Jossey-Bass.

Brandon, R., & Seldman, M. (2004). *Survival of the savvy: High-integrity political tactics for career and company success.* New York: Free Press.

Dobson, M. S., & Dobson, D. S. (2001). *Enlightened office politics: Understanding, coping with and winning the game: Without losing your soul.* New York: AMACOM.

Ferris, G. R., & Davidson, S. L., & Perrewé, P. L. (2005). *Political skill at work: Impact on work effectiveness.* Mountain View, CA: Davies-Black Publishing.

Finkelstein, S. (2003). *Why smart executives fail: And what you can learn from their mistakes.* New York: Portfolio.

Hawley, C. (2008). *100+ Tactics for office politics* (2nd ed.). New York: Barrons Educational Series.

Kissinger, H. (1994). *Diplomacy.* New York: Simon & Schuster.

Korten, D. C. (2001). *When corporations rule the world* (2nd ed.). San Francisco: Berrett-Koehler Publishers.

Linsky, M., & Heifetz, R. A. (2002). *Leadership on the line: Staying alive through the dangers of leading.* Boston: Harvard Business School Press.

Machiavelli, N. (2007). *The prince* (P. Constantine, Trans.). New York: Random House. (Original work published 1515.)

McIntyre, M. G. (2005). *Secrets to winning at office politics: How to achieve your goals and increase your influence at work.* New York: St. Martin's Press.

Puder-York, M. (2005). *The office survival guide.* New York: McGraw-Hill.

Ranker, G., Gautrey, C., & Phipps, M. (2008). *Political dilemmas at work: How to maintain your integrity and further your career.* Hoboken, NJ: John Wiley & Sons.

Reardon, K. K. (2002). *The secret handshake: Mastering the politics of the business inner circle.* New York: Doubleday.

Silberman, M. L. (with Hansburg, F.). (2005). *Peoplesmart: Developing your interpersonal intelligence.* Hoboken, NJ: John Wiley & Sons.

Walton, M. S. (2003). *Generating buy-in: Mastering the language of leadership.* New York: AMACOM.

49 Presentation Skills

It usually takes me more than three weeks to prepare a good impromptu speech.
Mark Twain – American humorist, satirist, lecturer, and writer

Unskilled

- ☐ Not a skilled presenter in varying situations
- ☐ May be shy
- ☐ May be disorganized, presentations lack focus
- ☐ May have a flat or grating style
- ☐ Doesn't listen to audience
- ☐ May have personal idiosyncrasies and habits that get in the way
- ☐ May be unprepared for or unable to handle tough questions
- ☐ May always present the same way, not adjusting to audiences
- ☐ May lose his/her cool during hot debate
- ☐ May be nervous, even scared when speaking

Select one to three of the competencies listed below to use as a substitute for this competency if you decide not to work on it directly.

SUBSTITUTES: 3,8,9,12,24,26,31,36,65,67

Skilled

- ☐ Is effective in a variety of formal presentation settings: one-on-one, small and large groups, with peers, direct reports, and bosses
- ☐ Is effective both inside and outside the organization, on both cool data and hot and controversial topics
- ☐ Commands attention and can manage group process during the presentation
- ☐ Can change tactics midstream when something isn't working

Overused Skill

- ☐ May try to win with style and presentation skills over fact and substance
- ☐ May be able to wing it and dance without really being prepared
- ☐ May be able to sell things that shouldn't be sold

Select one to three of the competencies listed below to work on to compensate for an overuse of this skill.

COMPENSATORS: 5,17,22,24,30,32,33,46,51,53,57,58,61,63,65

Some Causes

- ☐ Can't take the heat
- ☐ Disorganized
- ☐ Don't like open conflict
- ☐ Flat presenter
- ☐ Get nervous and emotional
- ☐ Scared to speak to larger groups
- ☐ Shy
- ☐ Intimidated by presentation technology
- ☐ Thrown by questions

Leadership Architect® Factors and Clusters

This competency is in the Organizational Positioning Skills Factor (V). This competency is in the Communicating Effectively Cluster (L) with: 67. You may want to check other competencies in the same Factor/Cluster for related tips.

The Map

There's presenting and being presentable presenting. Good presentations are those that achieve their objectives. Being presentable is being evaluated as being a good presenter with sufficient stage presence and audience sensitivity to give a good presentation.

Some Remedies

☐ **1. Unprepared? Make a checklist.** What's your objective? What's your point? What are five things you want them to remember? What would the ideal audience member say if interviewed 15 minutes after you finish? Who's your audience? How much do they know? What are five techniques you will use to hold their attention? What presentation technology would work best? What questions will the audience have? What's the setting? How much time do you have (always take a few minutes less, never more)? *More help? – See #47 Planning.*

☐ **2. Not making your point? Prepare the speech.** State your message or purpose in a single sentence. In other words, do the ending first. Then outline the three to five chunks of your argument to support your thesis. Any more and the audience won't follow it. Sometimes this can be accomplished by putting main concepts on index cards and shuffling them into order. A famous minister said, "No souls are saved after twenty minutes." Many speeches must be longer than this, but can still be divided into sections with clear conclusions and a hard bridge to the next related topic. What introduction will grab the audience and rivet them on your message? A story, a fact, a comparison, a quote, a photo, a cartoon?

For example, one speaker selected a comparison to introduce a series of research findings on career success by saying, "How can you take identical twins, hired for the same entry job in the same organization, and 20 years later, one of them succeeds and one of them doesn't?" She then returned to the twins periodically as she went through her argument on the different developmental experiences they had with the corporation. In organizing your talk, you should resist telling them all you know. What are your priority points, and how will you explain them? Some points are made better by example, some by the logic of the argument, some by facts or stories. You should vary how you drive home your point because you will reach more people. Use memory devices—state points in threes; repeat key words and phrases—"I have a dream"; use understatement and overstatement; use antithesis—"Ask not what your country can do for you; ask what you can do for your country." One nasty shock many learning presenters experience is that writing is different than speaking. A well-written speech is one that sounds right spoken, not read. Do not fall in love with what you have written until you record it on tape and listen to it. The cadence and pace is different in writing than in speaking. Writing doesn't take breathing into account. If your computer has a speech synthesizer, let the computer say your speech. Or have someone else read it to you. Never deliver a written speech until you have heard it spoken. Subscribe to *Presentations* magazine for tips, www.presentations.com.

☐ **3. Not connecting? Read the audience.** Unfortunately, one speech generally does not play equally well across audiences. Many times you will have to adjust the tone, pace, style and even the message and how you couch it for different audiences. If you are giving the same speech (or delivering the same message) to multiple audiences, always ask yourself how are they different? Some differences among audiences include level of sophistication, friendly vs. unfriendly, the time sensitivity of the audience, how much the audience expects to participate, how much entertainment they expect, and whether a logical or emotional argument will play better. Adjust accordingly. *More help? – See #15 Customer Focus.*

☐ **4. Uneven delivery? Rehearse.** If you are just building your presentation skills, rehearsals are very helpful. The best is to rehearse in the actual setting of the presentation. To get ready, practice in front of a video camera, in front of someone who can give you feedback, by using an audiotape, or worse case, in front of a mirror by yourself. Focus on time spent per major point—usually five to ten minutes. For your longest point, did you go into too much detail? Vary your volume and tone—sameness lulls the audience. Use your hands and body. Vary facial expression—if the words and the music don't match, people don't buy the message. Use pauses—

for effect, to drive in a point. Be careful of repeating the same words too often. If you're stumped for something to say, pause—uhs, ahs, and you knows distract and turn off some listeners. If you go blank, pause, then repeat your last statement in a paraphrasing of it. While you play for time, ask yourself what you can connect to that statement. Avoid speaking too forcefully or using loaded terms that will annoy some audience members. The best speech is the one that looks totally natural. It is usually the one that has been rehearsed a lot. If you can deliver the presentation on autopilot, you can scan the audience and adjust as you go.

☐ **5. Unable to respond? Prepare for questions.** Most fear being asked a question. There are infinite kinds of questions. Good questions and bad questions. Hot and cold questions. Good-intentioned questions and dark-intentioned questions. There are questions that come at a bad time and at good times. The ones we fear are the bad, hot, dark, at a bad time questions. Questions are all good because they tell you something about the audience and how successful you are being. In some settings, the arrangement is that questions are held until the end. In others, it's free speech. Think about the 10 most likely questions you could be asked. Rehearse what you would say. Some questions come out of nowhere. Some rules: If you are going to answer the question later, say, "Thanks for that great introduction to the next part of my talk; if you can hang on, I'll answer that in a minute or two." Don't disrupt your flow if you can help it. Practice 10- to 30-second answers. Then ask the questioner if that answered his/her question. Many new presenters spend too much time on the answers. Make sure you know what the question is. Many times presenters answer the wrong question. Ask one clarifying question before you answer—do you mean how would this product work in a foreign or domestic market? Only give two answers per question. The third time say, "I'm really sorry; I can't seem to give you the answer you're looking for; why don't you see me at the end and we can continue this exchange." If someone just won't let go, say, "We must really have different experiences. It's apparent we don't agree so let's just agree to disagree for now, but thanks for the debate." In rare situations, you can engage the audience. Say, "I'm stumped on that one; does anyone in the audience know?" If the question is hot, "Why are women so discriminated against in organizations?" extract the main issues and respond with, "Here are three things you can do about it." As a general rule, don't answer such questions as given because they are negative and stay away from classification—women, men, accountants—answers since they tend to split the audience into camps. Get it in your mind that questions are your friends. You just need five techniques to deal with them, including the dreaded "I don't know, but I'll find out and get back to you on that." Finally, Q & A sessions can be all over the place. Take a minute at the end to reinforce your key points only, or show an overhead which restates them.

☐ **6. Afraid? Conquer stage fright.** Nervous? Anxious? Didn't sleep well? Stomach's not working well? All normal. There is not a person in your audience who has not passed through that stage to become a competent presenter. Aside from death, speaking in front of large audiences is the most feared activity for adults. All of the things you think might happen don't. You won't pass out. You won't freeze and not be able to continue. You won't speak in tongues. You won't have to go to the bathroom midway through. You may run out of breath. Stop and breathe. Your mouth may get dry. Drink something. You may forget what you wanted to say. Refer to your notes. You may stumble on a word. Pause and repeat it. A sweat drop may run down your nose. Wipe it off. You may shake. Hold on to the podium. Look at three different people in the audience who are smiling and receptive. Avoid looking at frowners and head shakers.

☐ **7. Not holding others' attention? Consider staging and logistics.** Slides are nice but they lock you into a sequence you may want to change halfway through based upon audience reactions. Transparencies are good but they wed you to stand by the projector. Some rules of thumb. Ten lines only on slides and transparencies. Fewer lines if you can. Large type. Keep slides up for no more than 30 seconds. Don't read your slides. Don't put everything on the slide. Just put bullets and code or key words. There's nothing more boring than having someone present exactly what's on the slide. Have a handout for everyone if possible. Never give it out at the end, always before you start. The possible exception to this is detailed handouts. If they are too detailed, people will tend to read the notes and not listen to you. If you must hand out detail, give the audience a before (brief) and after (detailed) handout. Don't use slides that aren't in the handout unless they are cartoon or joke slides or proprietary slides (tell the audience before you put the slide up). Move around. Present left for a while, then right. Keep eye contact with a specific person in the audience each small time period. Smile. Try to look relaxed even if you're not. Don't stand and hold on to the podium unless you're shaking and need support. Pause here and there. There is nothing wrong with a little silence. If there are more than 25 people or there are poor acoustics in the room, always repeat questions before you answer them. Never say "in conclusion" or "in summary" or "to wrap it up" or "I'm almost finished" unless you are within 60 seconds of finishing. Don't turn off the projector between slides (besides being irritating, you may blow the bulb). Don't look at your watch. Find a wall clock or put your watch on the podium or have a friend signal you when there are five minutes left. Don't turn your back on the audience while you are speaking. If you have to look at the screen to remind you of something, stop talking for a moment and then continue after you have read the slide. Do thank the audience for their attention and questions if there were any.

☐ **8. Running out of time? Practice effective time management.** No one has ever run out of material. Everyone plans to get more in than they have time for. Always underplan. If that makes you nervous, bring along a slide or two for an encore. Don't go long. Everyone loves a person who is either right on time or even better, a few minutes short on the agenda. People don't appreciate you using more time than you have been allotted, especially if there are other speakers behind you or you are last on the agenda and are holding people who don't want to be there. You don't have to finish. There will always be another day. If you see that you're going to run over, go to your conclusion. Don't race through the rest of your slides. Or ask the audience for their preference. Say, "It's apparent I'm not going to get through all of this, what would you like in the time remaining?"

☐ **9. Difficult audience? Calmly deal with serious hecklers.** There are bad people who may want to embarrass you or anyone who presents to them. When heckled, bide time while asking the attacker to say more. If he or she gives you some data or opinion to work with, respond with something you both will agree on, paraphrase the person's argument and then respond, or simply acknowledge the disagreement. Generally, you won't win anyone over unless he or she truly misunderstood your argument. If that's the case, summarize it, then ask which part he/she disagrees with. If appropriate, you might ask others to respond to the attack if you can do it in a neutral problem oriented way. "That stumped me, does anyone have a response to that?" Don't take too much time responding to an attacker. The rule of 30 seconds, or two attempts, still applies. If you overdo your response, it may irritate others in the audience who have questions or who don't agree with the attacker. If the person persists, you should say that time is limited, you need to field other questions, and that the discussion can be continued later. If the person continues to be actively rude, you can ignore the insult and call for other questions.

☐ **10. Low impact? Make yourself presentable.** You are, after all, the one on stage. All eyes are on you. What is the impression they get by what you look like, how you carry yourself, how organized you appear to be, how prepared you are, how well you handle the presentation technology. All these may not be germane to the message but they are reflections of you. Part of presenting is marketing yourself as someone others should listen to. Watch what you wear. Match the audience. Don't come casual to a business dress affair and don't wear a suit to a casual setting. What do you carry on to the stage? Presentation in a three ring binder or loose? Old frayed briefcase? If I didn't know you and haven't yet heard your speech, have you led me to any impression of you? Is it the one you want? If you're just starting to build your presentation skills, join your local Toastmasters Club where you can comfortably learn the basics in a low-risk environment. Take a presentation skills course that uses video.

Some Develop-in-Place Assignments

- ☐ Train customers in the use of the organization's products or services.
- ☐ Present the strategy of your unit to others not familiar with your business.
- ☐ Be a change agent; create a symbol for change; lead the rallying cry; champion a significant change and implementation.
- ☐ Write a proposal for a new policy, process, mission, charter, product, service, or system, and present and sell it to top management.
- ☐ Represent the organization at a trade show, convention, exposition, etc.

It is not so much the content of what one says
as the way in which one says it.
However important the thing you say,
what's the good of it if not heard or, being heard, not felt.
Sylvia Ashton-Warner – New Zealand writer,
poet, and educator

Suggested Readings

Baldoni, J. (2003). *Great communication secrets of great leaders.* New York: McGraw-Hill.

Bates, S. (2005). *Speak like a CEO: Secrets for commanding attention and getting results.* New York: McGraw-Hill.

Booher, D. (2002). *Speak with confidence: Powerful presentations that inform, inspire, and persuade.* New York: McGraw-Hill.

Carnegie, D. (1962). *The quick and easy way to effective speaking.* New York: Association Press.

Davidson, J. (2002). *The complete guide to public speaking.* Hoboken, NJ: John Wiley & Sons.

Detz, J. (2002). *How to write and give a speech: A practical guide for executives, PR people, the military, fund-raisers, politicians, educators, and anyone who has to make every word count.* New York: St. Martin's Press.

Gallo, C. (2003). *10 Simple secrets of the world's greatest business communicators.* Naperville, IL: Sourcebooks, Inc.

Harvard Business School Press. (2004). *Presentations that persuade and motivate.* Boston: Harvard Business School Press.

Holliday, M. (1999). *Secrets of power presentations* (2nd ed.). Franklin Lakes, NJ: Career Press.

Humes, J. C. (2002). *Speak like Churchill, stand like Lincoln: 21 Powerful secrets of history's greatest speakers.* New York: Prima Publishing.

Hybels, S., & Weaver, R. L. (2008). *Communicating effectively* (9th ed.). New York: McGraw-Hill.

Koegel, T. J. (2007). *The exceptional presenter: A proven formula to OPEN UP! and own the room.* Austin, TX: Greenleaf Book Group Press.

Leeds, D. (2003). *Powerspeak: Engage, inspire, and stimulate your audience.* Franklin Lakes, NJ: Career Press.

Maxey, C., & O'Connor, K. E. (2006). *Present like a pro: The field guide to mastering the art of business, professional, and public speaking.* New York: St. Martin's Press.

Morgan, N. (2003). *Working the room: How to move people to action through audience-centered speaking.* Boston: Harvard Business School Press.

Pearce, T. (2003). *Leading out loud.* San Francisco: Jossey-Bass.

Uchida, T. (2005). Impression of speaker's personality and the naturalistic qualities of speech: Speech rate and pause duration. *Japanese Journal of Educational Psychology, 53*(1), 1-13.

Weissman, J. (2006). *Presenting to win: The art of telling your story.* New York: Prentice Hall.

Williams, R. G. (2002). *Voice power.* New York: AMACOM.

50 Priority Setting

I have to constantly juggle being a writer with being a wife and mother.
It's a matter of putting two different things first, simultaneously.
Madeleine L'Engle – American author

Unskilled

- ☐ Has little sense of what's mission-critical and what's just nice to do
- ☐ Doesn't identify the critical few well for self or others
- ☐ May believe that everything's equally important, may overwhelm others with unfocused activities
- ☐ May be addicted to action, do a little bit of everything quickly
- ☐ May be a poor time manager
- ☐ May not say no; wants to do everything
- ☐ Not good at figuring out how to eliminate a roadblock

Select one to three of the competencies listed below to use as a substitute for this competency if you decide not to work on it directly.

SUBSTITUTES: 16,17,24,33,39,40,47,51,52

Skilled

- ☐ Spends his/her time and the time of others on what's important
- ☐ Quickly zeros in on the critical few and puts the trivial many aside
- ☐ Can quickly sense what will help or hinder accomplishing a goal
- ☐ Eliminates roadblocks
- ☐ Creates focus

Overused Skill

- ☐ May let the trivial many accumulate into a critical problem
- ☐ May too quickly reject the priorities of others
- ☐ May have a chilling effect on necessary complexity by requiring everything to be reduced to the simple
- ☐ May confuse simple with simplistic
- ☐ May be too dominant a force on priorities for the team

Select one to three of the competencies listed below to work on to compensate for an overuse of this skill.

COMPENSATORS: 2,3,12,15,17,27,30,33,38,46,52,63,65

Some Causes

- ☐ Action junkie; always on the move
- ☐ Difficulty saying no
- ☐ Ego; overestimate capacity
- ☐ Perfectionist; need to do everything
- ☐ Short attention span; want to do a little bit of everything
- ☐ Time management; too busy to set priorities
- ☐ Trouble choosing

Leadership Architect® Factors and Clusters

This competency is in the Operating Skills Factor (II). This competency is in the Keeping on Point Cluster (D) with: 16. You may want to check other competencies in the same Factor/Cluster for related tips.

The Map

So much to do; so little time in which to do it. Finite resources; infinite needs. People to see, places to go, things to do. No time to say hello, good-bye, I'm late for a very important meeting. Sound familiar? That's life. Everyone has more to do than they can get to. Organizations have more opportunities than they have the resources to address. The higher up you go in the organization, the more you have to do and the less time you have to do it. Nobody can do it all. You have to set priorities to survive and prosper.

Some Remedies

- ☐ **1. Target out of focus? Be clear about your goals and objectives.** What exactly is it you need to accomplish? Use the annual plan and the strategic plan to understand the mission-critical things that must happen. *More help? – See #47 Planning and #58 Strategic Agility.*
- ☐ **2. Need clarity about what's mission critical? List goals in order of priority.** Using the goals, separate what you need to do into mission-critical, important to get done, nice if there is time left over, and not central to what we are trying to achieve. When faced with choices or multiple things to do, apply the scale and always choose the highest level.
- ☐ **3. Too much busy work? Watch out for the activity trap.** John Kotter, in *The General Managers*, found that effective managers spent about half their time working on one or two key priorities—priorities they described in their own terms, not in terms of what the business/organizational plan said. Further, they made no attempt to work as much on small but related issues that tend to add up to lots of activity. So rather than consuming themselves and others on 97 seemingly urgent and related smaller activities, they always returned to the few issues that would gain the most mileage long term.

☐ **4. Have a point of view? Get help from others.** When faced with multiple good things to do, pass them by a few others around you for their opinion. You don't have to do what they say but having other perspectives is always better than having only your opinion. *More help? – See #33 Listening.*

☐ **5. Need to get started? Take action.** Many times setting and operating on priorities isn't a reflective task. You may not have much time for ruminating. Most of life's choices have to be made on the spot, without all of the data. Nobody is ever right all the time under that kind of pressure. Perfectionists have a problem with this. Wait as long as you can and then shoot your best shot. *More help? – See #16 Timely Decision Making and #32 Learning on the Fly.*

☐ **6. Focused on what you like? Don't play favorites.** Be careful not to be guided by just what you like and what you don't like. That way of selecting priorities will probably not be successful over time. Use data, intuition and even feelings, but not feelings alone.

☐ **7. Time to choose? Weigh your options.** When you are stuck, write down the pros and cons for each option. Check what effect each would have both on the short and long term. Are there cost differences? Is one resource more efficient than the other? Is one apt to be more successful than the other? Think about the interaction of both short- and long-term goals. Sometimes what you decide to do today will hurt you or the organization downstream. When making either a short-term or long-term choice, stop for a second and ask what effect this might have on the other. Adjust as necessary. *More help? – See #65 Managing Vision and Purpose.*

☐ **8. No time? Be time sensitive.** Taking time to plan and set priorities actually frees up more time later than just diving into things hoping that you can get it done on time. Most people out of time claim they didn't have the time to plan their time. In the Stephen Covey *Seven Habits of Highly Effective People* sense, it's sharpening your saw. *More help? – See #62 Time Management.*

☐ **9. Avoiding something? Don't procrastinate.** Avoiding making choices actually leads to more choices downstream. Avoiding making choices actually makes life more difficult. You also miss opportunities. Basically, you can pay the price now or pay a bigger price tomorrow. *More help? – See #12 Conflict Management.*

☐ **10. Time waster? Be sensitive to the time of others.** Generally, the higher up you go or the higher up the person you are interacting with is, the less time you and he/she have. Be time efficient with others. Use as little of their time as possible. Get to it and get done with it. Give them an opportunity to open new avenues for discussion or to continue but if they don't, say your good-byes and leave.

Some Develop-in-Place Assignments

- ☐ Manage a cost-cutting project.
- ☐ Work on a crisis-management team.
- ☐ Assign a project with a tight deadline to a group.
- ☐ Manage the interface between consultants and the organization on a critical assignment.
- ☐ Manage the renovation of an office, floor, building, meeting room, warehouse, etc.

Decide what you want, decide what you are willing to exchange for it.
Establish your priorities and go to work.
H. L. Hunt – American oil tycoon

Suggested Readings

Birkinshaw, J., Bouquet, C., & Ambos, T. C. (2007). Managing executive attention in the global company. *MIT Sloan Management Review, 48*(4), 39-45.

Block, P. (2001). *The answer to how is yes: Acting on what matters.* San Francisco: Berrett-Koehler Publishers.

Bossidy, L., & Charan, R. (2004). *Confronting reality: Doing what matters to get things right.* New York: Crown Publishing Group.

Bossidy, L., & Charan, R. (with Burck, C.). (2002). *Execution: The discipline of getting things done.* New York: Crown Business.

Calhoon, J., & Bruce, J. (2005). *Prioritize! A system for leading your business and life on purpose.* Sevierville, TN: Insight Publishing.

Drucker, P. F. (2006). *The effective executive* (Rev. ed.). New York: HarperBusiness.

Goldratt, E. M., & Cox, J. (2004). *The goal: A process of ongoing improvement* (3rd ed.). Great Barrington, MA: North River Press.

Hammer, M. (2001). *The agenda: What every business must do to dominate the decade.* New York: Crown Business.

Hoover, J. (2007). *Time management: Set priorities to get the right things done.* New York: HarperCollins Business.

Le Blanc, R. (2008). *Achieving objectives made easy! Practical goal setting tools and proven time management techniques.* Maarheeze, NL: Cranendonck Coaching.

Stalk, G., Jr., & Hout, T. M. (2003). *Competing against time: How time-based competition is reshaping global markets.* New York: Free Press.

Tracy, B. (2007). *Time power: A proven system for getting more done in less time than you ever thought possible.* New York: AMACOM.

51 Problem Solving

Problems are only opportunities in work clothes.
Henry J. Kaiser – American industrialist and builder

Unskilled

- ☐ Not a disciplined problem solver; may be stuck in the past, wed to what worked before
- ☐ Many times has to come back and rework the problem a second time
- ☐ May be a fire-ready-aim type
- ☐ May get impatient and jump to conclusions too soon
- ☐ May not stop to define and analyze the problem; doesn't look under rocks
- ☐ May have a set bag of tricks and pull unfit solutions from it
- ☐ May miss the complexity of the issue and force-fit it to what he/she is most comfortable with
- ☐ Unlikely to come up with the second and better solution, ask penetrating questions, or see hidden patterns

Select one to three of the competencies listed below to use as a substitute for this competency if you decide not to work on it directly.

SUBSTITUTES: 5,14,17,24,30,32,33,46,50,52,58

Skilled

- ☐ Uses rigorous logic and methods to solve difficult problems with effective solutions
- ☐ Probes all fruitful sources for answers
- ☐ Can see hidden problems
- ☐ Is excellent at honest analysis
- ☐ Looks beyond the obvious and doesn't stop at the first answers

Overused Skill

- ☐ May tend toward analysis paralysis
- ☐ May wait too long to come to a conclusion
- ☐ May not set analysis priorities
- ☐ May get hung up in the process and miss the big picture
- ☐ May make things overly complex
- ☐ May do too much of the analysis personally

Select one to three of the competencies listed below to work on to compensate for an overuse of this skill.

COMPENSATORS: 1,16,18,20,35,36,50,52,55,60

Some Causes

- ☐ Disorganized
- ☐ Get emotional
- ☐ Impatient
- ☐ Jump to conclusions
- ☐ Perfectionist, need too much data
- ☐ Rely too much on historical solutions

Leadership Architect® Factors and Clusters

This competency is in the Strategic Skills Factor (I). This competency is in the Making Complex Decisions Cluster (B) with: 17, 30, 32. You may want to check other competencies in the same Factor/Cluster for related tips.

The Map

Most people are smart enough to solve problems effectively. Most people know how. Most people don't do it right, however. They don't define the problem and jump to conclusions, or they go to the other extreme and analyze it to death without trying out anything. They also rely too much on themselves when multiple people usually have a better chance of solving the problem.

Some Remedies

☐ **1. Where to start? Define the problem.** Instant and early conclusions, solutions, statements, suggestions, how we solved it in the past, are the enemies of good problem solving. Studies show that defining the problem and taking action occur almost simultaneously for most people, so the more effort you put on the front end, the easier it is to come up with a good solution. Stop and first define what the problem is and isn't. Since providing solutions is so easy for everyone, it would be nice if they were offering solutions to the right problem. Figure out what causes it. Keep asking why, see how many causes you can come up with and how many organizing buckets you can put them in. This increases the chance of a better solution because you can see more connections. Be a chess master. Chess masters recognize thousands of patterns of chess pieces. Look for patterns in data; don't just collect information. Put it in categories that make sense to you. Ask lots of questions. Allot at least 50% of the time to defining the problem.

☐ **2. Results driven? Show some patience.** The style that chills sound problem solving the most is the results-driven, time-short and impatient person. He/she does not take the time to define problems and tends to take the first close-enough solution that comes along. Studies have shown that on average, the solution somewhere between the second and third one generated is the best. Impatient people don't wait that long. Slow down. Discipline yourself to pause for enough time to define the problem better and always think of three solutions before you pick one.

☐ **3. Already made up your mind? Steer clear of biases.** Some people have solutions in search of problems. They have favorite solutions. They have biases. They have universal solutions to most situations. They pre-judge what the problem is without stopping to consider the nuances of this specific problem. Do honest and open analysis first. Did you state as facts things that are really assumptions or opinions? Are you sure these assertions are facts? Did you generalize from a single example? One of your solutions may in fact fit, but wait to see if you're right about the problem. *More help? – Read* Six Thinking Hats *by Edward de Bono.*

☐ **4. Always use the same solution? Get out of your comfort zone.** Many busy people rely too much on solutions from their own history. They rely on what has happened to them in the past. They see sameness in problems that isn't there. Beware of "I have always..." or "Usually I...." Always pause and look under rocks and ask yourself, is this really like the problems I have solved in the past?

☐ **5. Too self-reliant? Ask others for input.** Many try to do too much themselves. They don't delegate, listen or ask others for input. Even if you think you have the solution, ask some others for input just to make sure. Access your network. Find someone who makes a good sounding board and talk to her/him, not just for ideas, but to increase your understanding of the problem. Or do it more formally. Set up a competition between two teams, both acting as your advisors. Call a problem-solving meeting and give the group two hours to come up with something that will at least be tried. Find a buddy group in another function or organization that faces the same or a similar problem and both of you experiment.

☐ **6. Perfectionist? Balance perfection with action.** Need or prefer or want to be 100% sure? Want to wait for all of the information to come in. Lots might prefer that. Beware of analysis paralysis. A good rule of thumb is to analyze patterns and causes to come up with alternatives. Many of us just collect data, which numerous studies show increases our confidence but doesn't increase decision accuracy. Perfectionism is tough to let go of because most people see it as a positive trait for them. Recognize your perfectionism for what it might be—collecting more information than others do to improve your confidence in making a fault-free decision and thereby avoiding risk and criticism. Try to decrease your need for data and your need to be right all the time slightly every week until you reach a more reasonable balance between thinking it through and taking action.

☐ **7. Overwhelmed? Break it down.** Sometimes the key to bigger problem solving is to make them into a series of smaller problems. People who are good at this are incrementalists. They make a series of smaller decisions, get instant feedback, correct the course, get a little more data, move forward a little more, until the bigger problem is under control. They don't try to get it right the first time. Learn to break down problems into pieces and parts and solve them one at a time.

☐ **8. Need a new approach? Learn more problem-solving skills.** There are many different ways to think through and solve a problem.

- Ask more questions. In one study of problem solving, 7% of comments were questions and about half were answers. We jump to solutions based on what has worked in the past.
- To get fresh ideas, don't speedboat, look deeply instead. Tackle the most vexing problem of your job—carve out 20% of your time—study it deeply, talk with others, look for parallels in other organizations and in remote areas totally outside your field.
- Complex problems are hard to visualize. They tend to be either oversimplified or too complex to solve unless they are put in a visual format. Cut the problem up into its component pieces. Examine the pieces to see if a different order would help, or how you could combine three pieces into one.
- Another technique is a pictorial chart called a storyboard where a problem is illustrated by its components being depicted as pictures.
- A variation of this is to tell stories that illustrate the +'s and –'s of a problem, then flow chart those according to what's working and not working. Another is a fishbone diagram used in Total Quality Management.
- Sometimes going to extremes helps. Adding every condition, every worse case you can think of sometimes will suggest a different solution. Taking the present state of affairs and projecting into the future may indicate how and where the system will break down.
- Are you or others avoiding making the tough points? In almost any group, there are topics so hot they can't be mentioned, let alone discussed. A technique, pioneered by Chris Argyris, can bubble them to the surface. Everyone takes three index cards and writes down three undiscussables. (Names are not used; the assumption is that the position has an effect on behavior, and even if people think the issue is personal, they are asked to see it in system or group terms.) The cards are then shuffled and each person receives a different three back. The

cards are read, charted, and themes are arrayed for discussion. For more techniques, read *The Art of Problem Solving* by Russell Ackoff and *Lateral Thinking* by Edward de Bono.

☐ **9. Avoiding risks? Take calculated risks.** Develop a philosophical stance toward mistakes and failures in problem solving. After all, most innovations fail, most proposals fail, most change efforts fail, and the initial solutions to complex problems do not work. The best tack when a solution doesn't work is to say, "What can we learn from this?" and move on. The more tries, the more feedback and the more chances to find the best answer. *More help? – See #2 Dealing with Ambiguity.*

☐ **10. Disorganized? Get organized.** Problem solving involves using rigorous logic and disciplined methods. It involves going through checklists, looking under rocks, and probing all fruitful sources for answers. If you're disorganized, you need to set tight priorities. Focus on the mission-critical few. Don't get diverted by trivia. *More help? – See #47 Planning and #50 Priority Setting.*

Some Develop-in-Place Assignments

☐ Manage a group through a significant business crisis.

☐ Handle a tough negotiation with an internal or external client or customer.

☐ Take on a tough and undoable project, one where others who have tried it have failed.

☐ Assemble a team of diverse people to accomplish a difficult task.

☐ Relaunch an existing product or service that's not doing well.

Problems are to the mind what exercise is to the muscles,
they toughen and make strong.
Norman Vincent Peale – American preacher and author

Suggested Readings

Ben, D. (2002). *Advantage play: The manager's guide to creative problem solving.* Toronto: Key Porter Books.

Couzins, M., & Beagrie, S. (2003). How to...be an effective problem solver. *Personnel Today.* Retrieved July 16, 2008, from www.personneltoday.com/goto/20616.

Davidson, J. E., & Sternberg, R. J. (Eds.). (2003). *The psychology of problem solving.* New York: Cambridge University Press.

Dotlich, D. L., Cairo, P. C., & Rhinesmith, S. H. (2009). *Complexity and uncertainty: How to lead in turbulent times.* San Francisco: Jossey-Bass.

Haines, S. G. (2006). *The top 10 everyday tools for daily problem solving: Strategic thinking handbook #1.* San Diego: Systems Thinking Press.

Hoenig, C. W. (2000). *The problem-solving journey: Your guide for making decisions and getting results.* Cambridge, MA: Perseus Publishing.

Kourdi, J. (2007). *Think on your feet: 10 Steps to better decision making and problem solving at work.* London: Cyan Communications.

Nalebuff, B. J., & Ayers, I. (2003). *Why not? How to use everyday ingenuity to solve problems big and small.* Boston: Harvard Business School Press.

Robson, M. (2002). *Problem-solving in groups.* Hampshire, UK: Gower Publishing Limited.

Rosenhead, J., & Mingers, J. (2001). *Rational analysis for a problematic world: Problem structuring methods for complexity, uncertainty and conflict.* West Sussex, England: John Wiley & Sons, Ltd.

Straus, D. (2002). *How to make collaboration work: Powerful ways to build consensus, solve problems, and make decisions.* San Francisco: Berrett-Koehler Publishers.

Vaughn, R. H. (2007). *Decision making and problem solving in management.* Brunswick, OH: Crown Custom Publishing.

White, S. P. (with Patton Wright, G.). (2002). *New ideas about new ideas: Insights on creativity with the world's leading innovators.* Cambridge, MA: Perseus Publishing.

52 Process Management

The essential question is not, 'How busy are you?' but 'What are you busy at?'
Oprah Winfrey – American television host, media mogul, and philanthropist

Unskilled

- ☐ Not good at figuring out effective and efficient ways to get things done
- ☐ Works in a disorganized fashion
- ☐ Doesn't take advantage of opportunities for synergy and efficiency with others
- ☐ Can't visualize effective processes in his/her head
- ☐ Lays out tasks for self and others in a helter-skelter way
- ☐ Doesn't work to simplify things
- ☐ Uses more resources than others to get the same thing done
- ☐ Lacks attention to detail
- ☐ Doesn't anticipate the problems that will arise; not a systemic thinker

Select one to three of the competencies listed below to use as a substitute for this competency if you decide not to work on it directly.

SUBSTITUTES: 17,18,20,24,30,32,33,35,39,47,50,51,59,63

Skilled

- ☐ Good at figuring out the processes necessary to get things done
- ☐ Knows how to organize people and activities
- ☐ Understands how to separate and combine tasks into efficient work flow
- ☐ Knows what to measure and how to measure it
- ☐ Can see opportunities for synergy and integration where others can't
- ☐ Can simplify complex processes
- ☐ Gets more out of fewer resources

Overused Skill

- ☐ May always be tinkering and refining—nothing is ever the same for long
- ☐ May have trouble explaining his/her vision of a process
- ☐ May never finish anything
- ☐ May always be dissatisfied because of unreasonably high standards and expectations of self and others
- ☐ May attempt to put too much together at once
- ☐ May misjudge the capacity of others to absorb change

Select one to three of the competencies listed below to work on to compensate for an overuse of this skill.

COMPENSATORS: 3,14,15,19,27,33,36,41,46,47,50,56,57,58,60,63

Some Causes

- ☐ Don't see through things easily
- ☐ Don't view things in terms of systems
- ☐ Impatient
- ☐ Inexperienced
- ☐ Not interested in details
- ☐ Reject the emerging science of people and organizations

Leadership Architect® Factors and Clusters

This competency is in the Operating Skills Factor (II). This competency is in the Managing Work Processes Cluster (G) with: 59, 63. You may want to check other competencies in the same Factor/Cluster for related tips.

The Map

Most things happen in orderly ways. Aside from maybe chaos, all things follow orderly rules about what happens first and what happens next. There are predictable "action gets reaction" rules. There are best ways to get something done—best in the sense of the highest probability of success, fewest resources, lowest costs, minimum noise. Each area in life and work has a set of these best ways or known process rules. In the physical world, the laws of physics and chemistry will almost always, if followed, produce a known result; H2O will always be water. In the arena of people and organizations, the rules are a little more uncertain, but much is known. Those who know and follow the laws of due process almost always win and get what they need done.

Some Remedies

☐ **1. Curious about how things work? Read about it.** Subscribe to *The Systems Thinker®*, Pegasus Communications, Inc., Waltham, MA, 781-398-9700. This is a group dedicated to finding out how things work and why they work that way. They have a monthly publication as well as workshops, seminars and other materials available to help you see the world as a series of recurring systems or archetypes. They analyze everyday events and processes and try to see why they work the way they do.

☐ **2. Need to find your way through the organization?** Study how organizations work. Organizations can be complex mazes with many turns, dead ends, quick routes and choices. In most organizations, the best path to get somewhere is almost never a straight line. There is a formal organization—the one on the organization chart—where the path may look straight, and then there is the informal organization where all paths are zigzagged. Since organizations are staffed with people, they become all that more complex. There are gatekeepers, expediters, stoppers, resisters, guides, Good Samaritans and influencers. All of these types live in the maze. The key to successful maneuvering through complex organizations is to find your way through the maze in the least amount of time making the least noise. The best way to do that is to accept the complexity of organizations rather than fighting it, and learn to be a maze-bright person. *More help? – See #38 Organizational Agility.*

☐ **3. Have a plan? Lay out the process.** Most well-running processes start out with a plan. What do I need to accomplish? What's the time line? What resources will I need? Who controls the resources—people, funding, tools, materials, support—I need? What's my currency? How can I pay for or repay the resources I need? Who wins if I win? Who might lose? Buy a flow charting software that does PERT and GANTT charts. Become an expert in its use. Use the output of the software to communicate your plans to others. Use the flow charts in your presentations. Nothing helps move a process along better than a good plan. It helps the people who have to work under the plan. It leads to better use of resources. It gets things done faster. It helps anticipate problems before they occur. Lay out the work from A to Z. Many people are seen as lacking because they don't write the sequence or parts of the work and leave something out. Ask others to comment on ordering and what's missing. *More help? – See #47 Planning and #63 Total Work Systems (e.g., TQM/ISO/Six Sigma).*

☐ **4. Impatient? Follow a process, step-by-step.** Some people know the steps and the process necessary to get things done but they are too impatient to follow the process. Following a process to get things done includes stopping once in a while to let things run their course. It may mean waiting until a major gatekeeper has the time to pay attention to your needs. Due process takes time. *More help? – See #41 Patience.*

☐ **5. Need help? Rally support.** Share the goals of your process with the people you need to support you. Try to get their input. People who are asked tend to cooperate more than people who are not asked. Figure out how the people who support your process can win along with you. It's easier to get things done when everybody is pulling in the same direction. It's easier to perform when you have all the tools and resources you need. It's easier to get things done when everyone you need in your corner is supportive and pulling for you. *More help? – See #36 Motivating Others and #60 Building Effective Teams.*

☐ **6. What's the target? Set goals and measures.** Nothing keeps processes on time and on budget like a goal and a measure. Set goals for the whole project and the sub-tasks. Set measures so you and others can track progress against the goals. *More help? – See #35 Managing and Measuring Work.*

- ☐ **7. Struggling with equal opportunity? Match people to tasks.** You need to match people and tasks for processes to work well. People are different. They have different strengths and have differing levels of knowledge and experience. Instead of thinking of everyone as equal, think of them as different. Really equal treatment is giving each person tasks to do that match his/her capacities. *More help? – See #56 Sizing Up People.*
- ☐ **8. Have you considered the worst-case scenario? Envision the process unfolding.** What could go wrong? Run scenarios in your head. Think along several paths. Rank the potential problems from highest likelihood to lowest likelihood. Think about what you would do if the highest likelihood things were to occur. Create a contingency plan for each. Pay attention to the weakest links which are usually groups or elements you have the least interface with or control over—perhaps someone in a remote location, a consultant or supplier. Stay doubly in touch with the potential weak links. *More help? – See #51 Problem Solving.*
- ☐ **9. How are you tracking progress? Set up a plan to monitor progress of the process.** How would you know if the process is unfolding on time? Could you estimate time to completion or percent finished at any time? Give people involved in implementing the process feedback as you go.
- ☐ **10. Do you know someone who does this well? Find a mentor.** Find someone in your environment who appears to do this skill well. Study what he/she does that you don't do. Ask how he/she goes about figuring out how things work.

Some Develop-in-Place Assignments

- ☐ Manage a cost-cutting project.
- ☐ Work on a team that's deciding whom to keep and whom to let go in a layoff, shutdown, delayering, or merger.
- ☐ Monitor and follow a new product or service through the entire idea, design, test market, and launch cycle.
- ☐ Integrate diverse systems, processes, or procedures across decentralized and/or dispersed units.
- ☐ Install a new process or system (computer system, new policies, new process, new procedures, etc.).

I just wrap my arms around the whole backfield and peel 'em one by one until I get to the ball carrier. Him I keep.

Big Daddy Lipscomb – American football defensive lineman

Suggested Readings

Brown, T. (2008). Design thinking. *Harvard Business Review, 68*(6), 84-92.

Champy, J. A. (2002). *X-engineering the corporation: Reinventing your business in the digital age.* New York: Warner Books.

Gharajedaghi, J. (2006). *Systems thinking: Managing chaos and complexity: A platform for designing business architecture.* London: Butterworth-Heinemann.

Hammer, M., & Champy, J. A. (2003). *Reengineering the corporation: A manifesto for business revolution.* New York: HarperBusiness.

Jeston, J., & Nelis, J. (2008). *Business process management: Practical guidelines to successful implementations.* Oxford: Butterworth-Heinemann.

Juran, J. M. (2003). *Juran on leadership for quality.* New York: Free Press.

Lawler, E. E., III, Mohrman, S. A., & Benson, G. (2001). *Organizing for high performance: Employee involvement, TQM, reengineering, and knowledge management in the Fortune 1000: The CEO report.* San Francisco: Jossey-Bass.

Stewart, T. A. (2001). *The wealth of knowledge: Intellectual capital and the twenty-first century organization.* New York: Doubleday.

Strachan, D. (2008). *Process design: Making it work: A practical guide to what to do when and how for facilitators, consultants, managers and coaches.* San Francisco: Jossey-Bass.

Tan, A. (2007). *Business process reengineering in Asia: A practical approach.* Upper Saddle River, NJ: Prentice Hall.

53 *Drive for* Results

A business like an automobile, has to be driven, in order to get results.
B.C. Forbes – Scottish-born financial journalist
and founder of *Forbes* magazine

Unskilled

- ☐ Doesn't deliver results consistently
- ☐ Doesn't get things done on time
- ☐ Wastes time and resources pursuing non-essentials
- ☐ Something always gets in the way—personal disorganization, failure to set priorities, underestimating time frames, overcoming resistance
- ☐ Not bold or committed enough to push it through
- ☐ Procrastinates around whatever gets in his/her way
- ☐ Doesn't go all out to complete tasks
- ☐ Does the least to get by

Select one to three of the competencies listed below to use as a substitute for this competency if you decide not to work on it directly.

SUBSTITUTES: 1,5,9,16,18,20,24,28,35,36,39,43,50,52,60,63

Skilled

- ☐ Can be counted on to exceed goals successfully
- ☐ Is constantly and consistently one of the top performers
- ☐ Very bottom-line oriented
- ☐ Steadfastly pushes self and others for results

Overused Skill

- ☐ May go for results at all costs without appropriate concern for people, teams, due process, or possibly norms and ethics
- ☐ May have high turnover under him/her due to the pressure for results
- ☐ May not build team spirit
- ☐ May not celebrate and share successes
- ☐ May be very self-centered

Select one to three of the competencies listed below to work on to compensate for an overuse of this skill.

COMPENSATORS: 3,7,19,22,23,29,31,33,36,41,46,60,64

Some Causes

- ☐ Burned out
- ☐ Disorganized
- ☐ Inexperienced
- ☐ New to the job
- ☐ Not bold or innovative enough
- ☐ Not committed
- ☐ Not focused
- ☐ Perfectionist
- ☐ Procrastinate

Leadership Architect® Factors and Clusters

This competency is in the Energy and Drive Factor (IV). This competency is in the Focusing on the Bottom Line Cluster (J) with: 1, 43. You may want to check other competencies in the same Factor/Cluster for related tips.

The Map

Producing results means consistently hitting the goals and objectives set by you and others. It means pushing yourself and others to achieve stretch goals. It means keeping your eye on the ball and acting and talking as if you care about the bottom line.

Some Remedies

☐ **1. Trouble setting priorities? Focus on the important few.** What's mission-critical? What are the three to five things that most need to get done to achieve your goals? Effective performers typically spend about half their time on a few mission-critical priorities. Don't get diverted by trivia and things you like doing but that aren't tied to the bottom line. *More help? – See #50 Priority Setting.*

☐ **2. Not feeling committed? Set goals for yourself and others.** Most people work better if they have a set of goals and objectives to achieve and a standard everyone agrees to measure accomplishments against. Most people like stretch goals. They like them even better if they have had a hand in setting them. Set checkpoints along the way to be able to measure progress. Give yourself and others as much feedback as you can. *More help? – See #35 Managing and Measuring Work.*

☐ **3. Not sure how to get things done? Learn the most effective practices.** Some don't know the best way to produce results. There is a well-established set of best practices for producing results—TQM, ISO and Six Sigma. If you are not disciplined in how to design work flows and processes for yourself and others, buy one book on each of these topics. Go to one workshop on efficient and effective work design. Ask those responsible for total work systems in your organization for help. *More help? – See #52 Process Management and #63 Total Work Systems (e.g., TQM/ISO/Six Sigma).*

☐ **4. Difficulty organizing? Gather and manage critical resources.** Are you always short on resources? Always pulling things together on a shoe string? Getting results means getting and using resources. People. Money. Materials. Support. Time. Many times it involves getting resources you don't control. You have to beg, borrow, but hopefully not steal. That means negotiating, bargaining, trading, cajoling, and influencing. What's the business case for the resources you need? What do you have to trade? How can you make it a win for everyone? *More help? – See #37 Negotiating and #39 Organizing.*

☐ **5. Problems with getting work done through others? Focus on the fundamentals.** Some people are not good managers of others. They can produce results by themselves but do less well when the results have to come from the team. Are you having trouble getting your team to work with you to get the results you need? You have the resources and the people but things just don't run well. Maybe you do too much work yourself. You don't delegate or empower. You don't communicate well. You don't motivate well. You don't plan well. You don't set priorities and goals well. If you are a struggling manager or a first-time manager, there are well-known and documented principles and practices of good managing. Do you share credit? Do you paint a clear picture of why this is important? Is their work challenging? Do you inspire or just hand out work? Read *Becoming a Manager* by Linda A. Hill. Go to one course on management. *More help? – See #18 Delegation, #20 Directing Others, #36 Motivating Others, and #60 Building Effective Teams.*

☐ **6. Challenges with working across borders and boundaries? Leverage shared goals and interests.** Do you have trouble when you have to go outside your unit to reach your goals and objectives? This means that influence skills, understanding, and trading are the currencies to use. Don't just ask for things; find some common ground where you can provide help. What do the peers you're contacting need? Are your results important to them? How does what you're working on affect their results? If it affects them negatively, can you trade something, appeal to the common good, figure out some way to minimize the work—volunteering staff help, for example? Go into peer relationships with a trading mentality. To be seen as more cooperative, always explain your thinking and invite them to explain theirs. Generate a variety of possibilities first rather than stake out positions. Be tentative, allowing them room to customize the situation. Focus on common goals, priorities and problems. Invite criticism of your ideas. *More help? – See #42 Peer Relationships.*

☐ **7. Not bold enough? Learn to take calculated risks.** Won't take a risk? Sometimes producing results involves pushing the envelope, taking chances and trying bold new initiatives. Doing those things leads to more misfires and mistakes but also better results. Treat any mistakes or failures as chances to learn. Nothing ventured, nothing gained. Up your risk comfort. Start small so you can recover more quickly. See how creative and innovative you can be. Satisfy yourself; people will always say it should have been done differently. Listen to them, but be skeptical. Conduct a postmortem immediately after finishing. This will indicate to all that you're open to continuous improvement whether the result was stellar or not. *More help? – See #2 Dealing with Ambiguity, #14 Creativity, #28 Innovation Management, and #57 Standing Alone.*

☐ **8. Procrastinator? Start now.** Are you a lifelong procrastinator? Do you perform best in crises and impossible deadlines? Do you wait until the last possible moment? If you do, you will miss deadlines and performance targets. You might not produce consistent results. Some of your work will be marginal because you didn't have the time to do it right. You settled for a "B" when you could have gotten an "A" if you had one more day to work on it. Start earlier. Always do 10% of each task immediately after it is assigned so you can better gauge what it is going to take to finish the rest. Divide tasks and assignments into thirds and schedule time to do them spaced over the delivery period. Always leave more time than you think it's going to take. *More help? – See #47 Planning and #62 Time Management.*

☐ **9. Lacking persistence? Vary your approach.** Are you prone to give up on tough or repetitive tasks, have trouble going back the second and third time, lose motivation when you hit obstacles? Trouble making that last push to get it over the top? Attention span is shorter than it needs to be? Set mini-deadlines. Break down the task into smaller pieces so you can view your progress more clearly. Switch approaches. Do something totally different next time. Have five different ways to get the same outcome. Be prepared to do them all when obstacles arise. Task trade with someone who has your problem. Work on each other's tasks. *More help? – See #43 Perseverance.*

☐ **10. Under constant pressure? Learn to manage the stress and strain.** Producing results day after day, quarter after quarter, year after year is stressful. Some people are energized by moderate stress. They actually work better. Some people are debilitated by stress. They decrease in productivity as stress increases. Are you close to burnout? Dealing with stress and pressure is a known technology. Stress and pressure are actually in your head, not in the outside world. Some people are stressed by the same events others are energized by—losing a major account. Some people cry and some laugh at the same external event—someone slipping on a banana peel. Stress is how you look at events, not the events themselves. Dealing more effectively with stress involves reprogramming your interpretation of your work and about what you find stressful. There was a time in your life when spiders and snakes were life threatening and stressful to you. Are they now? Talk to your boss or mentor about getting some relief if you're about to crumble. Maybe this job isn't for you. Think about moving back to a less stressful job. *More help? – See #6 Career Ambition and #11 Composure.*

Some Develop-in-Place Assignments

- ☐ Work on a crisis-management team.
- ☐ Launch a new product, service, or process.
- ☐ Relaunch an existing product or service that's not doing well.
- ☐ Manage the purchase of a major product, equipment, materials, program, or system.
- ☐ Install a new process or system (computer system, new policies, new process, new procedures, etc.).

Excellence is the gradual result of always striving to do better.
Pat Riley – American National Basketball Association head coach

Suggested Readings

Aziza, B., & Fitts, J. (2008). *Drive business performance: Enabling a culture of intelligent execution.* Hoboken, NJ: John Wiley & Sons.

Baldoni, J. (2006). *How great leaders get great results.* New York: McGraw-Hill.

Bossidy, L., & Charan, R. (with Burck, C.). (2002). *Execution: The discipline of getting things done.* New York: Crown Business.

Carrison, D. (2003). *Deadline! How premier organizations win the race against time.* New York: AMACOM.

Collins, J. C. (2000). Turning goals into results: The power of catalytic mechanisms (HBR OnPoint Enhanced Edition). Boston: *Harvard Business Review.*

Drucker, P. F. (1993). *Managing for results.* New York: HarperCollins.

Goleman, D. (2001). Leadership that gets results (HBR OnPoint Enhanced Edition). Boston: *Harvard Business Review.*

Lefton, R. E., & Loeb, J. T. (2004). *Why can't we get anything done around here? The smart manager's guide to executing the work that delivers results.* New York: McGraw-Hill.

Locke, E. A., & Latham, G. P. (2002). Building a practically useful theory of goal setting and task motivation: A 35-year odyssey. *American Psychologist, 57,* 705-717.

Longenecker, C. O., & Simonetti, J. L. (2001). *Getting results: Five absolutes for high performance.* Hoboken, NJ: John Wiley & Sons.

Malhotra, D., Ku, G., & Murnighan, J. K. (2008). When winning is everything. *Harvard Business Review, 86*(5).

Stern, J. M., & Shiely, J. S. (2003). *The EVA challenge.* Hoboken, NJ: John Wiley & Sons.

Studer, Q. (2008). *Results that last: Hardwiring behaviors that will take your company to the top.* Hoboken, NJ: John Wiley & Sons.

Ulrich, D., & Smallwood, N. (2007). *Leadership brand: Developing customer-focused leaders to drive performance and build lasting value.* Boston: Harvard Business School Press.

Zook, C., & Allen, J. (2001). *Profit from the core: Growth strategy in an era of turbulence.* Boston: Harvard Business School Press.

54 Self-Development

Leadership and learning are indispensable to each other.
John F. Kennedy – 35th President of the United States

Unskilled

- ☐ Doesn't put in the effort to grow and change
- ☐ Doesn't do anything to act on constructive feedback
- ☐ May not know what to work on or how
- ☐ May know what but doesn't act on it
- ☐ Doesn't adjust approach to different audiences and situations
- ☐ May be immune to negative feedback—arrogant or defensive
- ☐ May fear failure and the risk of admitting shortcomings
- ☐ May not believe people really change, therefore it's not worth the effort
- ☐ May believe current skills will last
- ☐ May believe in development but is always too busy

Select one to three of the competencies listed below to use as a substitute for this competency if you decide not to work on it directly.

SUBSTITUTES: 1,6,19,32,33,44,45,55,61

Skilled

- ☐ Is personally committed to and actively works to continuously improve him/herself
- ☐ Understands that different situations and levels may call for different skills and approaches
- ☐ Works to deploy strengths
- ☐ Works on compensating for weakness and limits

Overused Skill

- ☐ May be a self-help development junkie
- ☐ Can lead to navel-gazing
- ☐ May confuse others with constant efforts to improve and change
- ☐ May be too self-centered
- ☐ May be susceptible to self-help fads
- ☐ May spend too much time improving and too little time acting and performing

Select one to three of the competencies listed below to work on to compensate for an overuse of this skill.

COMPENSATORS: 1,24,43,46,50,51,53,55,57,63

Some Causes

- ☐ Arrogant; don't have any weaknesses
- ☐ Defensiveness
- ☐ Don't know what I should be developing
- ☐ Don't know what to do
- ☐ Don't need any development; I can make it on what I have
- ☐ Don't think people really change
- ☐ Fear of failure or of admitting shortcomings
- ☐ Too busy getting the work out

Leadership Architect® Factors and Clusters

This competency is in the Personal and Interpersonal Skills Factor (VI). This competency is in the Demonstrating Personal Flexibility Cluster (T) with: 40, 45, 55. You may want to check other competencies in the same Factor/Cluster for related tips.

The Map

The bottom line is, those who learn, grow and change continuously across their careers are the most successful. Whatever skills you have now are unlikely to be enough in the future. Acquiring new skills is the best insurance you can get for an uncertain future. Some of us won't face our limitations; we make excuses, blame it on the boss or the job or the organization. Others are defensive and fight any corrective feedback. Some are just reluctant to do anything about our problems. Some of us want a quick fix; we don't have time for development. Some of us simply don't know what to do.

Some Remedies

☐ **1. Not sure where to start? Do a skills audit.** First, get a good multi-source assessment, a 360° questionnaire, or poll 10 people who know you well to give you detailed feedback on what you do well and not well, what they'd like to see you keep doing, start doing and stop doing. You don't want to waste time on developing things that turn out not to be needs.

☐ **2. Difficulty categorizing skills? Divide your skills into these categories:**

- Clear strengths—Me at my best.
- Overdone strengths—I do too much of a good thing—"I'm so confident that I'm seen as arrogant."
- Hidden strengths—Others rate me higher than I rate myself.
- Blind spots—I rate myself higher than others rate me.
- Weaknesses—I don't do it well.

- Untested areas—I've never been involved in strategy formulation.
- Don't knows—I need more feedback.

☐ **3. Trouble choosing the most productive path? Identify and develop what's important.** Find out what's important for your current job and the two or three next jobs you might have an opportunity to get. See if there are success profiles for those jobs. Compare the top requirements with your appraisal. If there are no success profiles, ask the Human Resources Department for help or ask one or two people who now have those jobs what skills they need and use to be successful.

☐ **4. Not applying your talents? Leverage your strengths.** A recent worldwide Gallup survey found that only 20% of employees thought their strengths were used every day. This is your greatest chance of success. What have you mastered? What do you learn quickly? What gives you the most satisfaction at work? If you are creative, what are three things you can start doing today? Where can you use your strengths to help others (so they will help you in return)? Can't use your strengths on your current job? How about a project, special assignment, or a task trade? So maintain the clear strengths you will need in the future by testing them in new task assignments. (You're good at conflict resolution—use this strength on a cross-functional problem-solving group while you learn about other functions.) Coach others in your strengths and ask for some help from them in their strengths.

☐ **5. Overusing strengths? Balance your overdone strengths in important areas.** If you're creative, telling yourself to do less of this won't work—it's the primary reason for your success to date. The key is to leave it alone and focus on the unintended consequences. (You're seen as lacking in detail orientation or disorganized.) Get the downside of your strength up to neutral; the goal is not to be good at it, but rather to see that it doesn't hurt you. Lominger's *FYI* lists the competencies that you can work on to balance your overused strengths.

☐ **6. Lacking critical skills? Build skill in weaker areas.** *More help? – See #19 Developing Direct Reports and Others for how to work on your weaknesses.* Weaknesses are best handled with a development plan which involves four keystones: stretching tasks in which you develop the skill or fail at the task (usually 70% of real development); continued feedback to help you understand how you're doing (usually 20% of learnings); building frameworks to understand through courses (about 10%); and ways to cement all your learning so you can repeat them next time.

☐ **7. Limited chance for improvement? Use existing skills to compensate for weaknesses.** We are all poor at something and beating on it is counterproductive. If you have failed repeatedly at sales, detail work or public speaking, find others who do this well, change jobs, or restructure your current job. Sometimes you can find indirect ways to compensate. Lincoln managed his temper by writing nasty letters, extracting the key points from the letters, tearing the letters up, then dealing with the key points contained in the letter when he regained composure.

- ☐ **8. Never tried it? Focus on untested areas.** Minimize weaknesses, but go after untested areas as well. In our research, we find that the profile of an individual contributor looks much like that of a manager, which in turn looks much like that of an executive. Nobody's developing much across time. Few managers are good at developing others, few executives at managing vision and purpose. But did they ever have a real chance to develop in these areas? The key is to find out the core demands of performance in a role, then work on these a level before they are necessary. Get involved in small versions of your untested areas—write a strategic plan for your unit, then show it to people; negotiate the purchase of office furniture. Write down what you did well and what you didn't. Then try a second bigger task and again write down the +'s and –'s of your performance. At this point, you may want to read a book or attend a course in this area. Keep upping the size and stakes until you have the skill at the level you need it to be.
- ☐ **9. Unaware of a need? Minimize blind spots.** Be very careful of blind spots, since you think you're much better at this than do others. Resist trying challenging tasks involving this skill until you clearly understand your behavior, have a target model of excellent behavior, and a plan so you don't get yourself into trouble. Collect more data. Ask someone you trust to monitor you and give you feedback each time. Study three people who are good at this and compare what you do with what they do. Don't rest until you have cleared up the blind spot.
- ☐ **10. Need support? Show others you take your development seriously.** State your developmental needs and ask for their help. Research shows that people are much more likely to help and give the benefit of the doubt to those who admit their shortcomings and try to do something about them. They know it takes courage. *More help? – See #44 Personal Disclosure.*

Some Develop-in-Place Assignments

- ☐ Make peace with an enemy or someone you've disappointed with a product or service or someone you've had some trouble with or don't get along with very well.
- ☐ Take on a task you dislike or hate to do.
- ☐ Teach/coach someone how to do something you're an expert in.
- ☐ Try to learn something frivolous and fun to see how good you can get (e.g., juggling, square dancing, magic).
- ☐ Attend a course or event which will push you personally beyond your usual limits or outside your comfort zone (e.g., Outward Bound, language immersion training, sensitivity group, public speaking).

If I am through learning, I am through.
John Wooden – American Hall of Fame basketball coach

Suggested Readings

Bell, A. H., & Smith, D. M. (2002). *Motivating yourself for achievement.* Upper Saddle River, NJ: Prentice Hall.

Bolles, R. N. (2009). *What color is your parachute? A practical manual for job-hunters & career-changers.* Berkeley, CA: Ten Speed Press.

Brim, G. (2000). *Ambition: How we manage success and failure throughout our lives.* New York: Backinprint.com.

Camarota, A. G. (2004). *Finding the leader in you: A practical guide to expanding your leadership skills.* Milwaukee, WI: American Society for Quality.

Cashman, K. (2008). *Leadership from the inside out: Becoming a leader for life* (2nd ed.). San Francisco: Berrett-Koehler Publishers.

Cashman, K. (with Forem, J.). (2003). *Awakening the leader within: A story of transformation.* Hoboken, NJ: John Wiley & Sons.

Christian, K. (2004). *Your own worst enemy: Breaking the habit of adult underachievement.* New York: Regan Books.

Edmondson, A. C. (2008). The competitive imperative of learning. *Harvard Business Review, 86*(7/8), 60-67.

Glickman, R. (2002). *Optimal thinking: How to be your best self.* Hoboken, NJ: John Wiley & Sons.

Lombardo, M. M., & Eichinger, R. W. (2004). *The leadership machine.* Minneapolis, MN: Lominger International: A Korn/Ferry Company.

Maslow, A. H., & Stephens, D. C. (Ed.). (2000). *The Maslow business reader.* Hoboken, NJ: John Wiley & Sons.

McCall, M. W., Lombardo, M. M., & Morrison, A. M. (1988). *The lessons of experience.* Lexington, MA: Lexington Books.

Morrison, A. M., White, R. P., Van Velsor, E., & The Center for Creative Leadership. (1992). *Breaking the glass ceiling: Can women reach the top of America's largest corporations?* Reading, MA: Addison-Wesley.

Niven, D. (2006). *The 100 simple secrets of successful people: What scientists have learned and how you can use it* (2nd ed.). New York: HarperBusiness.

Pedler, M., Burgoyne, J., & Boydell, T. (2007). *A manager's guide to self-development.* Berkshire, England: McGraw-Hill.

Rimanoczy, I., & Turner, E. (2008). *Action Reflection Learning™: Solving real business problems by connecting learning with earning.* Mountain View, CA: Davies-Black.

55 Self-Knowledge

Know thyself.
Socrates (469-399 BCE) – Greek philosopher

Unskilled

- ☐ Doesn't know him/herself well—strengths, weaknesses or limits
- ☐ Doesn't seek feedback—may be defensive or arrogant
- ☐ Doesn't listen to or learn from feedback
- ☐ May misestimate his/her performance—either too high or too low
- ☐ May rush in where he/she shouldn't, or not move when he/she should
- ☐ May be surprised by or not know own impact
- ☐ May know some shortcomings but will not share with others
- ☐ Avoids discussions about him/herself
- ☐ May assume he/she already knows when he/she doesn't
- ☐ May be an excuse maker and blamer; doesn't learn from mistakes
- ☐ Doesn't get much from personal insight exercises or performance discussions
- ☐ Is surprised by negative personal data

Select one to three of the competencies listed below to use as a substitute for this competency if you decide not to work on it directly.

SUBSTITUTES: 6,19,32,33,44,45,54,56,64

Skilled

- ☐ Knows personal strengths, weaknesses, opportunities, and limits
- ☐ Seeks feedback
- ☐ Gains insights from mistakes
- ☐ Is open to criticism
- ☐ Isn't defensive
- ☐ Is receptive to talking about shortcomings
- ☐ Looks forward to balanced (+'s and –'s) performance reviews and career discussions

Overused Skill

- ☐ May be too self-critical, too open about self
- ☐ May not move past knowledge to improvement and action
- ☐ May spend too much time in self-insight activities
- ☐ May be too dependent upon waiting for feedback
- ☐ May overly solicit feedback

Select one to three of the competencies listed below to work on to compensate for an overuse of this skill.

COMPENSATORS: 1,4,11,22,27,29,33,42,44,46,48,52,54,64

Some Causes

- ☐ Arrogant
- ☐ Assume you know but others think you don't
- ☐ Defensive
- ☐ Don't get any feedback
- ☐ Don't know how to get feedback
- ☐ The only perfect person on the planet
- ☐ Too much success

Leadership Architect® Factors and Clusters

This competency is in the Personal and Interpersonal Skills Factor (VI). This competency is in the Demonstrating Personal Flexibility Cluster (T) with: 40, 45, 54. You may want to check other competencies in the same Factor/Cluster for related tips.

The Map

Self-knowledge is strongly related to success in life and work. In one study, the best predictor of a high performance appraisal was seeing yourself as others see you; the best predictor of a low one was overrating your skills. Deploying yourself against life and work is greatly helped by really knowing what you're good, average and bad at, what you're untested in, and what you overdo or overuse. Known weaknesses don't get you in as much trouble as blind spots. You can loop around and compensate for a known weakness. A blind spot is the worst thing you can have. You can really get into performance or career trouble with a blind spot, because you don't know or are unwilling to admit you're not good at it. You will venture into areas that should make you cautious and humble, but you go in strutting and confident. Disaster soon follows. An important life and career goal is to have no blind spots.

Some Remedies

☐ **1. Not sure how others see you? Get feedback.** People are reluctant to give you feedback, especially negative or corrective information. Generally, to get it, you must ask for it. Seeking negative feedback increases both the accuracy of our understanding and people's evaluation of our overall effectiveness. A person who wants to know the bad must be pretty good. People will increase their estimation of you as you seek out and accept more feedback. If people are reluctant to give criticism, help by making self-appraisal statements rather than asking questions. Saying, "I think I focus too much on operations and miss some of the larger strategic connections; what do you think?" is easier for most people to reply to than a question which asks them to volunteer this point.

☐ **2. Want to get the real story? Keep it confidential.** Confidential feedback—a private discussion, a private 360°—tends to be more negative and more accurate than public—annual performance appraisal—feedback. Don't be lulled to sleep by your public feedback. For most of us, it's an excessively positive view. When the feedback giver knows results will be public, scores go up, accuracy goes down.

☐ **3. Want a broader view of yourself? Seek feedback from more than one source.** Different types of raters are likely to know more about and be more accurate about different competencies. Fruitful areas for bosses usually include: strategic grasp, selling-up skills, comfort around higher management, presentation of problems, solutions, clarity of thinking, team building, confronting and sizing up people skills. Customers generally know about responsiveness, listening, quality orientation, problem-solving skills, understanding of their business needs, persuasiveness. Peers know persuasion, selling, negotiation, listening to find common cause, keeping the interests of the organization in mind, follow-through on promises, and how well you maintain give-and-take in 50/50 relationships. Direct reports are best at the day-to-day behavior of leadership, management, team building, delegation, confronting, approachability, time use. When you get a piece of feedback, ask yourself if the person is in a position to know that about you. You may be the only one who doesn't know the truth about yourself. Other sources agree much more with one another about you than you will likely agree with any one of the sources. Even though your own view is important, don't accept it as fact until verified by more than one other person who should know.

☐ **4. Need a precise understanding? In choosing people to give you feedback, 360° or otherwise, focus on those who know you best to get the most accurate feedback.** Try not to stack the deck, picking either those you do best with or worst with. Both friend and foe tend to pick similar competencies as strengths and weaknesses. Friends will use higher scores than foes but their highest and lowest competencies will usually be the same.

☐ **5. Not sure what to do with your feedback results? When getting feedback, focus on the highest and lowest items or competency results from each group.** Spend less time worrying about whether your scores are high or low in an absolute sense. In development, you should worry about you relative to you, not you relative to anyone else. Your goal is simply to know yourself better. To do this, answer the following questions: Why am I this way? How did my strengths get to be strengths? What experiences shaped my pattern? Do I have strengths tipping over into weaknesses—"I'm intelligent but make others feel less so"; "I'm creative but disorganized." If you are clearly poor at something, what's getting in your way? Many times you'll find you don't like it and have a poor understanding of why and how it's done well. Think of tough situations for you where your strengths and weaknesses play out. *More help? – See #54 Self-Development.*

☐ **6. Is feedback intermittent? Work to get continuous feedback; don't wait for annual feedback events.** There are three ways to get better continued, high-quality feedback:

- Prepare specific areas you are concerned about and ask people to respond anonymously in writing. List the areas where you need feedback and ask them what they would like for you to keep doing, start doing, and stop doing to improve.
- Work with a development partner who knows what you're working on and gives up on-line feedback as you try new things.
- In areas you are working on, ask others who have watched you to debrief events with you shortly after they happen.

☐ **7. Screening out feedback? Consider all three kinds of feedback:**

- Things others see that you also see that are true about you.
- Things others see that you don't see that are true about you—these will be strengths you have that you sell yourself short on and weaknesses you have that you deny or are unaware of (blind spots).
- Things others think they see, but you don't agree and are not really true about you. The perceptions of others are facts to them, even though they may not be true about you. On just those incorrect observations that really matter, try to demonstrate by actions, not words, that their perceptions are wrong.

☐ **8. Attempting do-it-yourself feedback interpretation? Don't go it alone.** Regardless of how you get the feedback, get help in interpretation. Most 360° instruments can only be presented by a certified facilitator, but even if you get homegrown feedback, pick numerous people to talk with. Select people from each major constituency at work and people who know you best off-work. Don't ask them for general reactions. Select a few things from your feedback, state what you think the issue is, see if they agree and ask them what they would like to see you do differently in this area.

☐ **9. Arrogant? Adopt some humility.** Arrogance is a major blockage to self-knowledge. Many people who have a towering strength or lots of success get little feedback and roll along until their careers get in trouble. If you are viewed as arrogant, you may have to repeatedly ask for feedback, and when you get it, there may be some anger with it. Almost by definition, arrogant people overrate themselves in the eyes of others. Others who think you are arrogant might rate you lower than neutral observers. If you devalue others, they will return the insult.

☐ **10. Defensive? Let down your guard.** Defensiveness is the other major blockage to self-knowledge. Here people suspect you really can't take it, that you are defending against something, probably by blaming it on others or the job context. Defensive people get less feedback, thereby fulfilling their dream of being perfect. To break this cycle, you will need to follow the rules of good listening (*More help? – See #33 Listening*) and give examples of the behavior being described to validate what people are saying. While this may sound unfair, you should initially accept all feedback as accurate, even when you know it isn't. On those matters that really count, you can go back and fix it later. *More help? – See #108 Defensiveness.*

Some Develop-in-Place Assignments

- ☐ Make peace with an enemy or someone you've disappointed with a product or service or someone you've had some trouble with or don't get along with very well.
- ☐ Take on a task you dislike or hate to do.
- ☐ Manage a group of people who are towering experts but you are not.
- ☐ Join a self-help or support group.
- ☐ Attend a self-awareness/assessment course that includes feedback.

The unexamined life is not worth living.
Socrates (469-399 BCE) – Greek philosopher

Suggested Readings

Barth, F. D. (1997). *Daydreaming: Unlock the creative power of your mind.* New York: Viking Press.

Bennis, W. G. (2003). *On becoming a leader.* Cambridge, MA: Perseus Publishing.

Bennis, W. G., & Thomas, R. J. (2002). *Geeks and geezers.* Boston: Harvard Business School Press.

Branden, N. (1999). *The art of living consciously: The power of awareness to transform everyday life.* New York: Simon & Schuster.

Butler, G., & Hope, T. (2007). *Managing your mind.* New York: Oxford University Press.

Camarota, A. G. (2004). *Finding the leader in you: A practical guide to expanding your leadership skills.* Milwaukee, WI: American Society for Quality.

Cashman, K. (2008). *Leadership from the inside out: Becoming a leader for life* (2nd ed.). San Francisco: Berrett-Koehler Publishers.

Goldsmith, M., & Reiter, M. (2007). *What got you here won't get you there: How successful people become even more successful.* New York: Hyperion.

Leider, R. J., & Shapiro, D. A. (2001). *Whistle while you work: Heeding your life's calling.* San Francisco: Berrett-Koehler Publishers.

Lombardo, M. M., & Eichinger, R. W. (2004). *The leadership machine.* Minneapolis, MN: Lominger International: A Korn/Ferry Company.

Pearman, R. R., Lombardo, M. M., & Eichinger, R. W. (2005). *You: Being more effective in your MBTI type.* Minneapolis, MN: Lominger International: A Korn/Ferry Company.

Sheehan, J. K. (2007). *A leader becomes a leader: Inspiration stories of leadership for a new generation.* Belmont, MA: True Gifts.

56 Sizing Up People

Look at the means which a man employs, consider his motives, observe his pleasures. A man simply cannot conceal himself!
Confucius (551-479 BCE) – Chinese philosopher

Unskilled

- ☐ Isn't accurate in his/her appraisals of people
- ☐ Does not evaluate the strengths and weaknesses of others well
- ☐ Biases and stereotyping may play too much in his/her appraisals
- ☐ May have simplistic models of people
- ☐ May make instant judgments on almost no data
- ☐ Doesn't change after the initial appraisal
- ☐ His/her estimates and projections of what people will do in certain circumstances turn out to be wrong
- ☐ May be such a poor listener to and observer of others that he/she really doesn't know what they're like

Select one to three of the competencies listed below to use as a substitute for this competency if you decide not to work on it directly.

SUBSTITUTES: 7,21,23,25,32,33,35,46,51,55,64

Skilled

- ☐ Is a good judge of talent
- ☐ After reasonable exposure, can articulate the strengths and limitations of people inside or outside the organization
- ☐ Can accurately project what people are likely to do across a variety of situations

Overused Skill

- ☐ May be hypercritical of others
- ☐ May be unwilling to alter an initial judgment about others
- ☐ May not look for or be open to further evidence
- ☐ May miss on slow starters and quiet and less expressive people

Select one to three of the competencies listed below to work on to compensate for an overuse of this skill.

COMPENSATORS: 19,21,31,33,38,41,46,48,60,64

Some Causes

- ☐ Anti-elitist; want all people to be equal
- ☐ Avoid making tough calls on people
- ☐ Impatient
- ☐ Inexperienced
- ☐ Only accept the moral equality argument; all people are the same
- ☐ Poor listener/observer
- ☐ Reject a science of people
- ☐ Time management; don't have the time to study people

Leadership Architect® Factors and Clusters

This competency is in the Courage Factor (III). This competency is in the Making Tough People Calls Cluster (I) with: 25. You may want to check other competencies in the same Factor/Cluster for related tips.

The Map

Except from a moral viewpoint (everyone is equal in the eyes of their creator), all people are different. There is a rich variety and diversity of people. Physical is easy to see. Height. Weight. Speed. Strength. Some personal characteristics are easy as well. Smart; not so smart. Articulate; not so articulate. Warm; cold. Composed; emotional. Good presenter; poor presenter. Other human characteristics are harder. Motivated; not so motivated. Good values; not so good values. Integrity? Decisive? Fair? One key to getting anything of value done in the world of work is the ability to see differences in people and to manage against and use those differences for everyone's benefit.

Some Remedies

☐ **1. Biases getting in the way? Read three texts on how people differ.** Go to a college bookstore and get an introductory textbook on the theory of personality. Find a copy of *Gifts Differing* by Isabel Myers, a book about the background of the Myers-Briggs Type Indicator. (Ask someone in the Training or OD department.) It outlines 16 different types of people, why they are different, and what those differences mean in the world of work. Find *Competence at Work* by Spencer and Spencer which outlines 40 years of study on the differing characteristics people need to be successful in different jobs. Watch out for your personal biases—do you think you have a tendency to favor clones of yourself? Do you have a preference for people who think and act like you do? What characteristics do you value too much? What downsides do you ignore or excuse away? People good at this competency can see, describe and value the competencies of people not like them.

☐ **2. Lacking internal benchmarks for assessing others? Leverage self-awareness.** Understanding others starts with understanding self (see Socrates!). Learn all you can about yourself. Volunteer for a 360° feedback process. Ask others to help you get the best picture of yourself that you can. As honestly as you can, outline your strengths and weaknesses as others see them and how you see them. Once you complete your assessment, you can use the level of your competencies as a benchmark in understanding others. Do they have more than, about the same, or less of this than you do? What difference do the differences make in behavior or effectiveness? (How does poor listening play out, for example? How does it affect results? How about excellent listening?) Watch out for personal insecurities as well. Sometimes we don't size up people different from us well because we'd rather not face how much better they are at something than we are. This is true—since no one has all possible strengths, chances are everyone you work with is better at something than you are. The key is to take this natural fear and use it as a positive. Observe people for different talents, study how they think, watch how they go about exercising their strengths, and use this knowledge to improve yourself.

☐ **3. Surprised by others' actions? Become a student of the people around you.** First try to outline their strengths and weakness, their preferences and beliefs. Watch out for traps—it is rarely general intelligence or pure personality that spells the difference in people. Most people are smart enough, and many personality characteristics don't matter that much for performance. Ask a second question. Look below surface descriptions of smart, approachable, technically skilled people to describe specifics. Then try to predict ahead of time what they would do in specific circumstances. What percent of the time are your predictions correct? Try to increase the percent over time.

☐ **4. Not sure what differences make a difference? Identify differentiating competencies.** For each job, role, task or assignment, try to create a success profile of what would be required for success. What skills, knowledge, and competencies would be mission-critical to getting the job done? This means that they differentiate superior from average performance. Don't include competencies that, while important, most people on a job would be expected to already have. (For example, integrity is a must, but if people already have it, it can't predict success. Similarly, time management and planning are important, but most people have demonstrated a reasonable proficiency in those in order to be employable. They wouldn't distinguish superior from average performers often.) Go for the critical few, not the important many. Which competencies don't make a difference?

☐ **5. People out of alignment with their work? Match people to task requirements.** People are different; tasks are different. People have different strengths and have different levels of knowledge and experience. Instead of thinking of everyone as equal, think of them as different. Equal treatment is really giving each person tasks to do that match their capacities. Look at the success profile of each assignment and line it up with the capabilities of each person. Assign things based upon that match.

☐ **6. Difficulty delivering bad news? Recognize your responsibility to make tough calls when necessary.** All people have positive and negative qualities. People have the most trouble making public calls on the negative side. Most don't like giving people negative feedback. Negative reads on people have real-life consequences. People could miss out on promotions or could even be released from the organization based on your negative read. If you are a supervisor or a manager, part of why you get paid more is to make those calls. It's just part of the requirements of management.

☐ **7. Need to better align your perceptions with others? Volunteer to be part of an assessment center team.** You will be trained to observe and assess people as they are going through a number of tasks and assignments. As part of the process, you will compare your notes and assessments with others on the team. That way you will learn to calibrate your assessments.

☐ **8. Uncertain of how you are reading others? Find two or three people in your environment with whom you can trust to share your people assessments.** In what areas are you different? What did you miss? What areas of behavior do you tend to misjudge? Apply your insights to reading other people.

☐ **9. Missing out on obvious characteristics? Read a book and/or take a class on how to interview others.** That training will sharpen your observation skills and make you a more attentive listener for the signs of strengths and weaknesses in others.

☐ **10. Too quick to decide your view on others? Be cautious about early or rigid reads.** You may make a decent effort trying to read a person and form a reasonable judgment, but it may be wrong. Be willing to look at additional data. Be flexible; be willing to change as the information changes.

Some Develop-in-Place Assignments

- ☐ Work on a team that's deciding whom to keep and whom to let go in a layoff, shutdown, delayering, or merger.
- ☐ Hire/staff a team from outside your unit or organization.
- ☐ Train and work as an assessor in an assessment center.
- ☐ Go to a campus as a recruiter.
- ☐ Construct a success and derailment profile for a unit or the entire organization, and present it to decision makers for adoption.

When you hire people that are smarter than you are,
you prove you are smarter than they are.
R.H. Grant – American businessman
and former President and Chairman of the Board
of the Reynolds and Reynolds Company

Suggested Readings

Brinkman, R., & Kirschner, R. (2002). *Dealing with people you can't stand* (Rev. ed.). New York: McGraw-Hill.

Dimitrius, J., & Mazzarella, M. C. (2008). *Reading people: How to understand people and predict their behavior: Anytime, anyplace.* New York: Ballantine Books.

Fulmer, R. M., & Conger, J. A. (2004). *Growing your company's leaders.* New York: AMACOM.

Goman, C. K. (2008). *The nonverbal advantage: Secrets and science of body language at work.* San Francisco: Berrett-Koehler Publishers.

Greenhalgh, L. (2001). *Managing strategic relationships: The key to business success.* New York: Free Press.

Harvard Business School Press. (2003). *Hiring and keeping the best people.* Boston: Harvard Business School Press.

Lawrence, P. R., & Nohria, N. (2002). *Driven: How human nature shapes our choices.* San Francisco: Jossey-Bass.

Myers, I. B. (with Myers, P. B.). (1995). *Gifts differing: Understanding personality type.* Mountain View, CA: Davies-Black Publishing.

Navarro, J., & Karlins, M. (2008). *What every BODY is saying: An ex-FBI agent's guide to speed-reading people.* New York: Harper-Collins Publishers.

Pearman, R. R., & Albritton, S. (1997). *I'm not crazy, I'm just not you: The real meaning of the sixteen personality types.* Palo Alto, CA: Davies-Black Publishing.

Smart, B. D. (2005). *Topgrading: How leading companies win: Hiring, coaching and keeping the best people* (Rev. ed.). New York: Prentice Hall.

Wilson Learning Library. (2004). *The social styles handbook: Find your comfort zone and make people feel comfortable with you.* Herentals, Belgium: Nova Vista Publishing.

57 Standing Alone

Never, for the sake of peace and quiet,
deny your own experience or convictions.
Dag Hammarskjöld – Swedish diplomat and former
Secretary-General of the U.N.

Unskilled

- ☐ Isn't comfortable going it alone
- ☐ Prefers to be in the background
- ☐ May prefer to be one of many or be part of a team
- ☐ Doesn't take the lead on unpopular stands
- ☐ Doesn't take on controversial issues by him/herself
- ☐ May avoid and shrink from dispute and conflict
- ☐ May not have a passion, may be burned out

Select one to three of the competencies listed below to use as a substitute for this competency if you decide not to work on it directly.

SUBSTITUTES: 1,8,9,12,13,22,27,31,34,38,43,48,53

Skilled

- ☐ Will stand up and be counted
- ☐ Doesn't shirk personal responsibility
- ☐ Can be counted on when times are tough
- ☐ Willing to be the only champion for an idea or position
- ☐ Is comfortable working alone on a tough assignment

Overused Skill

- ☐ May be a loner and not a good team player or team builder
- ☐ May not give appropriate credit to others
- ☐ May be seen as too self-centered
- ☐ May not wear well over time

Select one to three of the competencies listed below to work on to compensate for an overuse of this skill.

COMPENSATORS: 3,4,7,15,19,27,33,36,42,60,64

Some Causes

- ☐ Can't take the heat
- ☐ Don't like to be out in front
- ☐ Don't relish working alone
- ☐ Laid back style
- ☐ Not identified strongly with any issue
- ☐ Not knowledgeable enough to take stands
- ☐ Not self-confident
- ☐ Shy away from conflict

Leadership Architect® Factors and Clusters

This competency is in the Courage Factor (III). This competency is in the Dealing with Trouble Cluster (H) with: 9, 12, 13, 34. You may want to check other competencies in the same Factor/Cluster for related tips.

The Map

Standing alone involves being comfortable with the conflict inherent with being an individual champion. It means staking out tough and lonely positions, speaking out as a lone voice, and taking the buffeting that comes with that. It requires a strong sense of self and a lot of self-confidence. Leading is many times standing alone.

Some Remedies

☐ **1. Not comfortable being out front? Face criticism with courage.** Leading is riskier than following. While there are a lot of personal rewards for taking tough stands, it puts you into the limelight. Look at what happens to political leaders and the scrutiny they face. People who choose to stand alone have to be internally secure. Do you feel good about yourself? Can you defend to a critical and impartial audience the wisdom of what you're doing? They have to please themselves first that they are on the right track. They have to accept lightning bolts from detractors. Can you take the heat? People will always say it should have been done differently. Even great leaders are wrong sometimes. They accept personal responsibility for errors and move on to lead some more. Don't let criticism prevent you from taking a stand. Build up your heat shield. If you know you're right, standing alone is well worth the heat. If it turns out you're wrong, admit it and move on.

☐ **2. Facing a challenging issue? Prepare for tough stands against the grain.** Taking a tough stand demands confidence in what you're saying along with the humility that you might be wrong—one of life's paradoxes. To prepare to take the lead on a tough issue, work on your stand through mental interrogation until you can clearly state in a few sentences what your stand is and why you hold it. Build the business case. How do others win? Ask others for advice. Scope the problem, consider options, pick one, develop a rationale, then go with it until proven wrong. Consider the opposing view. Develop a strong case against your stand. Prepare responses to it. Expect pushback.

☐ **3. Up against adversaries? Sell your stand.** While some people may welcome what you say and what you do, others will go after you or even try to minimize you or the situation your stand relates to. Some will sabotage. To sell your views, keep your eyes on the prize but don't specify everything about how to get there. Give others room to maneuver. Present the outcomes, targets and goals without the how to's. Welcome ideas, good and bad. Any negative response is a positive if you learn from it. Invite criticism of what you're doing. Even though you're going it alone, you need the advice and support of others to get there. Stay away from personal clashes. *More help? – See #12 Conflict Management.*

☐ **4. Too emotional? Keep your cool.** Manage your emotional reactions. Sometimes your emotional reactions lead others to think you have problems with taking tough positions and stands. When this happens, what emotional reactions do you have? Do you show nervousness or non-verbals like increasing or wavering voice volume or fidgeting? Learn to recognize those as soon as they start. Ask a question to buy time. Pause. Or ask the person to tell you more about his/her point of view. *More help? – See #11 Composure and #107 Lack of Composure.*

☐ **5. Afraid of failure? Develop a philosophical stance toward being wrong or losing.** After all, most innovations fail, most proposals fail, most efforts to lead change fail. Research says that successful general managers have made more mistakes in their careers than the people they were promoted over. They got promoted because they had the guts to stand alone, not because they were always right. Other studies suggest really good general managers are right about 65% of the time. Put errors, mistakes and failures on your menu. Everyone has to have some spinach for a balanced diet. Don't let the possibility of being wrong hold you back from standing alone when you believe it's right.

☐ **6. Engaged in a difficult fight? Practice the rules of one-on-one combat.** Standing alone usually involves dealing with pure hand-to-hand confrontations. You believe one thing, they want something else. When that happens, keep it to any facts that are available. You won't always win. Stay objective. Make the business case. Listen as long as they will talk. Ask a lot of clarifying questions. Sometimes they talk themselves to your point of view if you let them talk long enough. Always listen to understand first, not judge. Restate their points until they say that's right. Find something to agree with, however small that may be. Then refute their points starting with the one you have the most objective information for first. Move down the line. You will always have points left that didn't get resolved. Acknowledge those. The objective is to get the list as small as possible. Then decide whether you are going to continue your stand, modify it or withdraw. *More help? – See #12 Conflict Management.*

☐ **7. Afraid of nasty questions or ones you can't answer? Master the rules of responding.** Think about the 10 most likely questions you could be asked. Rehearse what you would say. Some rules. Practice 10- to 30-second answers. Ask the questioner if that answered his/her question. Many spend too much time on the answers. Make sure you know what the question is. Many answer the wrong question. Ask one clarifying question if you're unsure (do you mean how would this product work in a foreign or domestic market?). If someone just won't let go, say, "We must really have different experiences. It's apparent we don't agree so let's just agree to disagree for now, but thanks for the debate." If the question is hot, "Why are women so discriminated against in this organization?" extract the main issues and respond with, "Here are three things you can do about it." As a general rule, don't answer such questions as given because they are negative, and stay away from classification (women, men, accountants) answers. Get it in your mind that questions are your friends because they reveal opportunities to solve problems and headline the difficulties you face. You just need five techniques to deal with them including the dreaded "I don't know, but I'll find out and get back to you on that."

☐ **8. Don't like risk? Expand your comfort zone.** Standing alone involves pushing the envelope, taking chances and suggesting bold new initiatives. Doing those things leads to more misfires and mistakes. Treat any mistakes or failures as chances to learn. Nothing ventured, nothing gained. Up your risk comfort. Start small so you can recover more quickly. Go for small wins. Send up trial balloons. Don't blast into a major stand to prove your boldness. Break it down into smaller stands. Take the easiest one for you first. Then build up to the tougher ones. Review each one to see what you did well and not well, and set goals so you'll do something differently and better each time. Challenge yourself. See how inventive you can be in taking action a number of different ways. *More help? – See #2 Dealing with Ambiguity, #14 Creativity, and #28 Innovation Management.*

☐ **9. Blending in with the crowd? Tap into your passion.** Maybe there's nothing you care about deeply enough to stand alone on. You stay in the background or within your group. This is OK, but most likely won't get you recognized or promoted. Leaders lead and take tough stands. Look around you—what's your passion? What do you have enthusiasm for or what truly needs to be done? Identify it. Appoint yourself as champion. Throw out trial balloons to other units/groups to see if your notion strikes a chord or solves a common problem. Find an experimenter to go in with you. Bring in a heavy expert or someone with political clout to help you make your point. Plant seeds with others at every opportunity.

☐ **10. Afraid of the consequences? Take personal responsibility.** Standing alone means taking the consequences alone. Both the credit and the heat. You won't always be right so you need to just be as quick to take the blame as the credit. Just say, "Yes you're right, my stand was wrong, sorry about that." Make it a practice to conduct postmortems immediately after milestone efforts—win or lose. This will indicate to all that you're interested in improvement and excellence whether the results are stellar or not. Don't let your missteps chill your courage to speak up, step into the breach, and stake out tough stands.

Some Develop-in-Place Assignments

☐ Do a postmortem on a failed project, and present it to the people involved.

☐ Be a change agent; create a symbol for change; lead the rallying cry; champion a significant change and implementation.

☐ Write a proposal for a new policy, process, mission, charter, product, service, or system, and present and sell it to top management.

☐ Become a referee for an athletic league or program.

☐ Coach a children's sports team.

Even if I have to stand alone, I will not be afraid to stand alone.
I'm going to fight for you. I'm going to fight for what's right.
I'm going to fight to hold people accountable.
Barbara Boxer – U.S. Senator

Suggested Readings

Bennis, W. G., & Nanus, B. (2007). *Leaders: Strategies for taking charge* (2nd ed.). New York: HarperBusiness.

Chaleff, I. (2003). *The courageous follower: Standing up to and for our leaders.* San Francisco: Berrett-Koehler Publishers.

Cloud, H. (2006). *Integrity: The courage to meet the demands of reality.* New York: HarperCollins.

Cooper, C. (2008). *Extraordinary circumstances: The journey of a corporate whistleblower.* Hoboken, NJ: John Wiley & Sons.

Kolditz, T. A. (2007). *In extremis leadership: Leading as if your life depended on it.* Hoboken, NJ: John Wiley & Sons.

Kouzes, J. M., & Posner, B. Z. (2007). *The leadership challenge* (4th ed.). San Francisco: Jossey-Bass.

Lee, G., & Elliott-Lee, D. (2006). *Courage: The backbone of leadership.* San Francisco: Jossey-Bass.

Linsky, M., & Heifetz, R. A. (2002). *Leadership on the line: Staying alive through the dangers of leading.* Boston: Harvard Business School Press.

Maney, K. (2003). *The maverick and his machine: Thomas Watson, Sr. and the making of IBM.* Hoboken, NJ: John Wiley & Sons.

McPherson, J. M. (2009). *Abraham Lincoln: A presidential life.* New York: Oxford University Press.

Swartz, M., & Watkins, S. (2003). *Power failure: The inside story of the collapse of Enron.* New York: Doubleday.

Thornton, P. B. (2002). *Be the leader, make the difference.* Irvine, CA: Griffin Trade Paperback.

58 Strategic Agility

All men can see these tactics whereby I conquer,
but what none can see is the strategy out of which victory is evolved.
Sun Tzu (c. 500 BCE) – Chinese military strategist

Unskilled

- ☐ Doesn't think or talk strategy
- ☐ Can't put together a compelling strategic plan
- ☐ More comfortable in the tactical here and now
- ☐ Lacks the perspective to pull together varying elements into a coherent strategic view
- ☐ Can't weave a vision of the future
- ☐ May reject the usefulness of strategy, considering it pie in the sky
- ☐ May have narrow experience and not be knowledgeable of business and world events
- ☐ May try to simplify too much or be very tactical
- ☐ May lack the disciplined thought processes necessary to construct a strategic view

Select one to three of the competencies listed below to use as a substitute for this competency if you decide not to work on it directly.

SUBSTITUTES: 2,5,14,17,24,28,30,32,46,47,50,61,65

Skilled

- ☐ Sees ahead clearly
- ☐ Can anticipate future consequences and trends accurately
- ☐ Has broad knowledge and perspective
- ☐ Is future oriented
- ☐ Can articulately paint credible pictures and visions of possibilities and likelihoods
- ☐ Can create competitive and breakthrough strategies and plans

Overused Skill

- ☐ May be seen as too theoretical
- ☐ May not be tolerant of or have patience with day-to-day details
- ☐ May over-complicate plans
- ☐ May not be able to communicate with tactical or less complex people

Select one to three of the competencies listed below to work on to compensate for an overuse of this skill.

COMPENSATORS: 5,16,17,24,27,35,38,39,46,47,50,52,53,59,61,63

Some Causes

- ☐ Don't like complexity
- ☐ Don't think the future is knowable
- ☐ Inexperienced
- ☐ Aren't comfortable speculating
- ☐ Lack of perspective
- ☐ Low risk taker; don't like uncertainty
- ☐ Low-variety background
- ☐ New to the area
- ☐ Too busy with today's tasks
- ☐ Too laid back
- ☐ Too narrow
- ☐ Very tactical

Leadership Architect® Factors and Clusters

This competency is in the Strategic Skills Factor (I). This competency is in the Creating the New and Different Cluster (C) with: 2, 14, 28, 46. You may want to check other competencies in the same Factor/Cluster for related tips.

The Map

There are a lot more people who can take a hill than there are people who can accurately predict which hill it would be best to take. There are more people good at producing results in the short term than there are visionary strategists. Both have value but we don't have enough strategists. It is more likely that your organization will be outmaneuvered strategically than that it will be outproduced tactically. Most organizations do pretty well what they do today. It's what they need to be doing tomorrow that's the missing skill. Part of every manager's job is to be strategic. The higher you go, the more critical the requirement.

Some Remedies

☐ **1. Problems with presentation? Use strategic language.** In some rare cases, we have found people who could think strategically who were not identified as such because they either didn't know, rejected or chose not to use what they considered the latest strategic buzzwords. Strategy is an emerging and ever-changing field. At any time, there are gurus (at present probably Michael Porter, Ram Charan, C.K. Prahalad, Gary Hamel, Fred Wiersema and Vijay Govindarajan) in vogue, who create about 75 new words or concepts (values disciplines, strategic intent or destination, core capabilities, value migration, market oligarchy, co-evolution, strategic horizon) to describe strategic thinking. If you don't use these words, then I won't know you're being strategic. The words are to be found in books by these gurus, in the *Harvard Business Review* and *Strategy and Leadership*, a publication of the Strategic Leadership Forum. And yes, most of the words are bigger words for things we used to call something else before with smaller words. Nevertheless, if you want to be seen as more strategic, you have to talk more strategically. Every discipline has its lexicon. In order to be a member, you have to speak the code.

☐ **2. Rejecting strategy? Recognize the value of strategic planning.** There are people who reject strategic formulation as so much folly. They have never seen a five-year strategic plan actually happen as projected. They think the time they use to create and present strategic plans is wasted. They think it's where the rubber meets the sky. So much BS. While it's true that most strategic plans never work out as planned, that doesn't mean that it was a wasted effort. Strategic plans lead to choices about resources and deployment. They lead to different staffing actions and different financial plans. Without some strategic plans, it would be a total shot in the dark. Most failed companies got buried strategically, not tactically. They were still making high-quality buggy whips when they went under. They picked the wrong direction or too many. Not being able to produce a quality product or service today is generally not the problem.

☐ **3. Not curious? Be curious and imaginative.** Many managers are so wrapped up in today's problems that they aren't curious about tomorrow. They really don't care about the long-term future. They may not even be in the organization when the strategic plan is supposed to happen. They believe there won't be much of a future until we perform today. Being a visionary and a good strategist requires curiosity and imagination. It requires playing "what ifs." What are the implications of the growing gap between rich and poor? The collapse of retail pricing? The increasing influence of brand names? What if it turns out there is life on other planets, and we get the first message? What will that change? Will they need our products? What will happen when a larger percentage of the world's population is over the age of 65? The effects of terrorism? What if cancer is cured? Heart disease? AIDS? Obesity? What if the government outlaws or severely regulates some aspect of your business? True, nobody knows the answers, but good strategists know the questions. Work at developing broader interests outside your business. Subscribe to different magazines. Pick new shows to watch. Meet different people. Join a new organization. Look under some rocks. Think about tomorrow. Talk to others about what they think the future will bring.

☐ **4. Narrow perspective? Broaden your perspective.** Some are sharply focused on what they do and do it very well. They have prepared themselves for a narrow but satisfying career. Then someone tells them their job has changed, and they now have to be strategic. Being strategic requires a broad perspective. In addition to knowing one thing well, it requires that you know about a lot of things somewhat. You need to understand business. *More help? – See #5 Business Acumen.* You need to understand markets. *More help? – See #15 Customer Focus.* You need to understand how the world operates. *More help? – See #46 Perspective.* You need to put all that together and figure out what all that means to your organization. *More help? – See #32 Learning on the Fly and #51 Problem Solving.*

☐ **5. Too busy? Delegate the tactical and make time for strategy.** Strategy is always last on the list. Solving today's problems, of which there are many, is job one. You have to make time for strategy. A good strategy releases future time because it makes choices clear and leads to less wasted effort, but it takes time to do. Delegation is usually the main key. Give away as much tactical day-to-day stuff as you can. Ask your people what they think they could do to give you more time for strategic reflection. *More help? – See #18 Delegation.* Another key is better time management. Put an hour a week on your calendar for strategic reading and reflection throughout the year. Don't wait until one week before the strategic plan is due. *More help? – See #62 Time Management.* Keep a log of ideas you get from others, magazines, etc. Focus on how these impact your organization or function.

☐ **6. Avoiding ambiguity? Embrace the uncertainty.** Strategic planning is the most uncertain thing managers do next to managing people. It's speculating on the near unknown. It requires projections into foggy landscapes. It requires assumptions about the unknown. Many conflict avoiders and perfectionists don't like to make statements in public that they cannot back up with facts. Most strategies can be challenged and questioned. There are no clean ways to win a debate over strategy. It really comes down to one subjective estimate versus another. Sometimes it is the person who can talk the longest and loudest who wins. Join the World Future Society for a year and read their publication, *THE FUTURIST. More help? – See #2 Dealing with Ambiguity and #12 Conflict Management.*

☐ **7. Addicted to the simple? Embrace the complexity.** Strategy ends up sounding simple. Five clean, clear statements about where we want to go with a few tactics and decisions attached to each. Getting there is not simple. Good strategists are complexifiers. They extend everything to its extreme before they get down to the essence. Simplifiers close too early. They are impatient to get it done faster. They are very results oriented and want to get to the five simple statements before strategic due process has been followed. Be more tolerant of unlimited exploration and debate before you move to close.

- ☐ **8. Don't know how to be strategic? Become a student of strategy.** The simplest problem is someone who wants to be strategic and wants to learn. Strategy is a reasonably well-known field. Read the gurus (Michael Porter, Ram Charan, C.K. Prahalad, Gary Hamel, Fred Wiersema and Vijay Govindarajan). Scan the *Harvard Business Review* and *Sloan Review* regularly. Read the three to five strategic case studies in *BusinessWeek* every issue. Go to a three-day strategy course taught by one of the gurus. Get someone from the organization's strategic group to tutor you in strategy. Watch CEOs talk about their businesses on cable. Volunteer to serve on a task force on a strategic issue. Join the Strategic Leadership Forum for a year, read their publication, *Strategy and Leadership*, and attend one national convention. Attend The Conference Board's annual conference on strategy where CEOs talk about their companies. Read 10 annual reports a year outside your industry and study their strategies.
- ☐ **9. Can't think strategically? Practice strategic thinking.** Strategy is linking several variables together to come up with the most likely scenario. Think of it as the search for and application of relevant parallels. It involves making projections of several variables at once to see how they come together. These projections are in the context of shifting markets, international affairs, monetary movements and government interventions. It involves a lot of uncertainty, making risk assumptions, and understanding how things work together. How many reasons would account for sales going down? Up? How are advertising and sales linked? If the dollar is cheaper in Asia, what does that mean for our product in Japan? If the world population is aging and they have more money, how will that change buying patterns? Not everyone enjoys this kind of pie-in-the-sky thinking and not everyone is skilled at doing it. *More help? – See #32 Learning on the Fly, #46 Perspective and #51 Problem Solving.*
- ☐ **10. Don't want to be strategic? Get some help.** Some just don't feel they want to ramp up and learn to be strategic. But they like their job and want to be considered strategically responsible. Hire a strategic consultant once a year to sit with you and your team and help you work out your strategic plan. Accenture. The Boston Consulting Group. McKinsey. Booz Allen Hamilton. Strategos. Plus many more. Or delegate strategy to one or more in your unit who are more strategically capable. Or ask the strategic planning group to help. You don't have to be able to do everything to be a good manager. You like your nest? Some people are content in their narrow niche. They are not interested in being strategic. They just want to do their job and be left alone. They are interested in doing good work in

their specialty and want to get as high as they can. That's OK. Just inform the organization of your wishes and don't take jobs that have a heavy strategic requirement.

☐ **11. Ready to test it? Prove that your strategy is viable.** Beware of case-laden business books. Many of us look to them for tips on building successful strategies, but the cases are hand selected to "prove" the author's theory. Examples aren't proof. According to Evan Dudik, "If you want to prove the business strategy you want to pursue is right, you pose the question in a way intended to prove it wrong." The way to do this is an if-then statement: If we spend X on product development, we will beat (competitor) to market, and beat them on price by 5%. This will result in improved cash flow of Y and a Z reduction in inventory. The organization must then test each hypothesis by assigning people to gather confirming and disconfirming facts. Dudik says it is best to assign two teams to this task—one to advocate and one to oppose.

☐ **12. Got the talent? Get the right people working on the right strategy.** Sustainable competitive advantage may be going the way of non-digital electronics. Many experts say that a competitive advantage of a couple of months is the best you can hope for. The only solution is to constantly create opportunities, form lots of if-then hypotheses, and try many experiments. When something works, you'll know why. Then you can vary it to see how to make it better. Varying it depends on having trained staff ready to move into this area immediately to exploit an advantage. Ramping up won't work. You have to have a strike force ready.

☐ **13. Need a credible strategic activist? Take the lead on strategy.** Pick one distinctive competence or driving force. That's what the mediocre companies who became successful over time did in James Collins' latest research. Create a strategic plan for your unit around one distinctive competence—include breakthrough process and product improvements; justify your conclusions by pointing to hard data that points toward your conclusions. Have the plan reviewed by people you trust. Form a consortium with three other individuals or companies; each of you will present a strategic issue and a plan backed up with data and rationale. Agree to review your thinking every three months with this group and write down lessons learned. Analyze three business/organizational success stories in your area and the same number of failures. What did each have in common? How would these principles apply in your situation? What was common to the failures that was never present in the successes?

☐ **14. Aligned? Connect your work to the strategy.** Following the logic of the Balanced Scorecard and strategy mapping approaches of Kaplan and Norton, strategy should be everyone's daily job. If you can't demonstrate how a job aligns with the strategy, why do you have it? All teams should be able to answer what the implications are for daily work. As Gary Hamel and C.K. Prahalad have argued in their strategy work, most of what spells success needs to be found outside the organization one is in, and it must be hunted and used by as many people as possible. What they call the democratization of strategy is necessary in all jobs: Look outside the box, don't try to fit all knowledge into neat categories, and spend the head time necessary to come up with plans and visions to implement something new or different.

☐ **15. Unclear about time horizons? Focus on long-term strategy.** When Sunbeam needed short-term revenue to impress Wall Street, Dunlap created dealer incentives to warehouse more product than usual. This succeeded in pushing a lot of discounted product through the distribution system and made the year look good. Unfortunately, it also led to too much inventory. Motorola decided to develop the world's smallest analog phone when other competitors were working on digital. They were late to the market as Ericsson and Nokia moved in. In a fast-paced, quarter-by-quarter world, there is always the temptation to do something today that may have unintended consequences. So ask yourself some questions. Is this in line with our long-term strategy? What could a competitor reasonably do to blow this up in our faces? Is this sustainable? How could this good move become a bad move tomorrow?

Some Develop-in-Place Assignments

☐ Work on a team forming a joint venture or partnership.

☐ Work on a team studying a possible acquisition.

☐ Launch a new product, service, or process.

☐ Write a proposal for a new policy, process, mission, charter, product, service, or system, and present and sell it to top management.

☐ Study the history of a similar situation and draw parallels for a current business issue or problem, and present your findings to others for comment.

What do you want to achieve or avoid?
The answers to this question are objectives.
How will you go about achieving your desired results?
The answer to this you can call strategy.
William E. Rothschild – American businessman and author

Suggested Readings

Apgar, D. (2008). *Relevance: Hitting your goals by knowing what matters.* San Francisco: Jossey-Bass.

Breene, R. T. S., Nunes, P. F., & Shill, W. E. (2007, October). The chief strategy officer. *Harvard Business Review.*

Charan, R., & Tichy, N. M. (1998). *Every business is a growth business: How your company can prosper year after year.* New York: Times Business.

Collins, J. C. (2001). *Good to great: Why some companies make the leap...and others don't.* New York: HarperCollins.

Courtney, H. (2001). *20/20 Foresight: Crafting strategy in an uncertain world.* Boston: Harvard Business School Press.

Dranove, D., & Marciano, S. (2005). *Kellogg on strategy: Concepts, tools, and frameworks for practitioners.* Hoboken, NJ: John Wiley & Sons.

Drucker, P. F. (2001). *Management challenges for the 21st century.* New York: HarperBusiness.

Eigenhuis, A., & Van Dijk, R. (2007). *High performance business strategy: Inspiring success through effective human resource management.* Philadelphia: Kogan Page, Ltd.

Freedman, M. (with Tregoe, B. B.). (2003). *The art and discipline of strategic leadership.* New York: McGraw-Hill.

Gavetti, G., Levinthal, D. A., & Rivkin, J. W. (2005). Strategy making in novel and complex worlds: The power of analogy. *Strategic Management Journal, 26,* 691-712.

Ghemawat, P. (2007). *Redefining global strategy: Crossing borders in a world where differences still matter.* Boston: Harvard Business School Press.

Grant, R. M. (2002). *Contemporary strategy analysis: Concepts, techniques, applications* (4th ed.). Malden, MA: Blackwell Publishers Inc.

Hamel, G. (2002). *Leading the revolution* (Rev. ed.). Boston: Harvard Business School Press.

Hamel, G., & Prahalad, C. K. (1996). *Competing for the future.* Boston: Harvard Business School Press.

Hatch, M. J., & Schultz, M. (2008). *Taking brand initiative: How companies can align strategy, culture, and identity through corporate branding.* San Francisco: Jossey-Bass.

Hoffman, A. J., & Woody, J. G. (2008). *Climate change: What's your business strategy? (Memo to the CEO).* Boston: Harvard Business School Press.

Kaplan, R. S., & Norton, D. P. (2007). Using the balanced scorecard as a strategic management system (HBR OnPoint Enhanced Edition). *Harvard Business Review.*

Kim, W. C., & Mauborgne, R. (2005). *Blue ocean strategy: How to create uncontested market space and make competition irrelevant.* Boston: Harvard Business School Press.

Krames, J. A. (2003). *What the best CEOs know: 7 Exceptional leaders and their lessons for transforming any business.* New York: McGraw-Hill.

Montgomery, C. A. (2008). Putting leadership back into strategy. *Harvard Business Review, 86,* 124.

Morgan, M., Levitt, R. E., & Malek, W. A. (2008). *Executing your strategy: How to break it down and get it done.* Boston: Harvard Business School Press.

Pietersen, W. (2002). *Reinventing strategy: Using strategic learning to create and sustain breakthrough performance.* New York: John Wiley & Sons.

Porter, M. E. (1996). What is strategy? *Harvard Business Review, 74,* 61-78.

Porter, M. E. (1998). *Competitive strategy: Techniques for analyzing industries and competitors.* New York: Free Press.

Porter, M. E. (2008, January). The five competitive forces that shape strategy. *Harvard Business Review.*

Prahalad, C. K., & Ramaswamy, V. (2004). *The future of competition: Co-creating unique value with customers.* Boston: Harvard Business School Press.

Stalk, G. (2008). *Five future strategies you need right now (Memo to the CEO).* Boston: Harvard Business School Press.

Stern, C. W., & Deimler, M. S. (Eds.). (2006). *The Boston Consulting Group on strategies: Classic concepts and new perspectives.* Hoboken, NJ: John Wiley & Sons.

Sull, D. (2003). *Revival of the fittest: Why good companies go bad and how great managers remake them.* Boston: Harvard Business School Press.

Welborn, R., & Kasten, V. (2003). *The Jericho principle: How companies use strategic collaboration to find new sources of value.* New York: John Wiley & Sons.

59 *Managing Through Systems*

It's easy to cry 'bug' when the truth is that you've got a complex system and sometimes it takes a while to get all the components to co-exist peacefully.
Doug Vargas – CNET editor

Unskilled

- ☐ Prefers hands-on management
- ☐ Relies on personal intervention
- ☐ Has to physically be there for things to go well
- ☐ Doesn't think or manage in terms of policies, practices and systems
- ☐ Doesn't delegate much
- ☐ Doesn't really believe people can perform on their own
- ☐ Doesn't set up rules, procedures and tie breakers so people know what to do in his/her absence
- ☐ May be very controlling and a micromanager
- ☐ May not communicate clearly enough for people to know what to do without repeated inquiries of him/her

Select one to three of the competencies listed below to use as a substitute for this competency if you decide not to work on it directly.

SUBSTITUTES: 18,20,27,35,39,47,52,63

Skilled

- ☐ Can design practices, processes, and procedures which allow managing from a distance
- ☐ Is comfortable letting things manage themselves without intervening
- ☐ Can make things work through others without being there
- ☐ Can impact people and results remotely

Overused Skill

- ☐ May be too hard to reach and talk to, out of touch with the details
- ☐ May get too comfortable having things run on autopilot
- ☐ May get surprised by negative events
- ☐ May be slow to change existing systems

Select one to three of the competencies listed below to work on to compensate for an overuse of this skill.

COMPENSATORS: 3,10,12,14,15,21,23,31,33,36,44,60,64

Some Causes

- ☐ Don't delegate well
- ☐ Don't think in terms of systems
- ☐ Inexperienced
- ☐ Poor communicator
- ☐ Poor time management

Leadership Architect® Factors and Clusters

This competency is in the Operating Skills Factor (II). This competency is in the Managing Work Processes Cluster (G) with: 52, 63. You may want to check other competencies in the same Factor/Cluster for related tips.

The Map

For most managers, the quality of their impact on others and their work decreases as they become more remote. Most managers start as first-line supervisors where all of their people sit around them on the floor. As you progress in management, your people and the operations you manage become more remote. Your people may be in different parts of the building, different parts of the country, or even different parts of the world. The key to being a good systems-based manager is to have the qualities you bring to managing people and work remain when you are not physically there. That's done by having a vision, goals, processes and practices to follow, two-way communication, and policies to guide remote decision making.

Some Remedies

☐ **1. Curious about how things work? Read about it.** Subscribe to *The Systems Thinker®*, Pegasus Communications, Inc., Waltham, MA, 781-398-9700. This is a group dedicated to finding out how things work and why they work that way. They have a monthly publication as well as workshops, seminars and other materials available to help you see the world as a series of recurring systems or archetypes. They analyze everyday events and processes and try to see why they work the way they do. The material will help you view things in terms of whole systems.

☐ **2. Can't picture it? Create flow charts.** Try to picture things in the form of flows. Buy a flow charting and/or project planning software that does PERT and GANTT charts. Become an expert in its use. Use the output of the software to communicate the systems you manage to others. Use the flow charts in your presentations.

☐ **3. Need to find your way through the organization? Study how organizations work.** Organizations can be complex systems with many turns, dead ends, quick routes and choices. In most organizations, the best path to get somewhere is almost never a straight line. There is a formal organization—the one on the organization chart—where the path may look straight, and then there is the informal organization where all paths are zigzagged. Since organizations are staffed with people, they become all that more complex as systems. There are gatekeepers, expediters, stoppers, resisters, guides, Good Samaritans and influencers. *More help? – See #38 Organizational Agility.*

☐ **4. Know what works best? Study how to design rational and effective work flows and designs.** That technology can be found in *#35 Managing and Measuring Work, #47 Planning, #52 Process Management, and #63 Total Work Systems (e.g., TQM/ISO/Six Sigma).*

☐ **5. Need to impart the vision? Work on communicating.** Setting and communicating the vision creating a shared mindset is one key to remote management. *More help? – See #65 Managing Vision and Purpose.* Setting goals and establishing measures to guide decisions and work when you are not there is another key. *More help? – See #35 Managing and Measuring Work.* Being able to line up the resources you need to complete the work is the last key. *More help? – See #39 Organizing.*

☐ **6. Want to develop others remotely? Delegate.** Managing remotely is the true test of delegation and empowerment. It's impossible for you to do it all. Successful managers report high involvement in setting parameters, exceptions they want to be notified of, and expected outcomes. They detail what requires their involvement and what doesn't. When people call them for a decision, they always ask, "What do you think? What impact will it have on you—customers, etc.—if we do this?" rather than just render a judgment. If you don't, people will begin to delegate upward, and you'll be a close-in manager from a remote location. Help people think things through, and trust them to follow the plan. Delegation requires this clear communication about expectations and releasing the authority to decide and act. *More help? – See #18 Delegation.*

☐ **7. Need clarity? Write it down.** Effective remote management requires plans, policies, practices and procedures to be in writing. Verbal communication alone will seldom be sufficient. You need to write clearly and with as few words as you can. You may even have to write several versions of the same practice or policy to adapt to a remote location. Have someone else review your written work before you distribute it to check for clarity and purpose. *More help? – See #67 Written Communications.*

☐ **8. Need input? Involve others.** Another trick to effective remote management is involvement of those being managed in the creation of the system. You need to rally support. Share your mission and goals with the people you need to support you. Get their input. People who are asked tend to cooperate more than people who are not asked. Let the people who will have to work under the system help design it. *More help? – See #18 Delegation and #38 Organizational Agility.*

- ☐ **9. Need to understand what's working? Analyze your remote management technology.** How do you sound over the phone? Are you coming across like you want to? What do your e-mail messages look and sound like? Ask trusted others for feedback. What do your speeches sound like when you visit remote locations? Do you change your message to adjust for local conditions? Who do you spend time with when you travel remotely? What kind of message does that leave? Do you meet just with top management or do you also find time for others? What do your memos look and sound like? Are they leaving the kind of message you intended?
- ☐ **10. Are processes painful? Simplify processes.** Is it a constructive process or is it punishing or blame oriented? How accessible are you to your remote locations? Do you think they would report that it is easy or hard to access you?

Some Develop-in-Place Assignments

- ☐ Manage a group of people in a rapidly expanding or growing operation.
- ☐ Plan an off-site meeting, conference, convention, trade show, event, etc.
- ☐ Integrate diverse systems, processes, or procedures across decentralized and/or dispersed units.
- ☐ Install a new process or system (computer system, new policies, new process, new procedures, etc.).
- ☐ Manage something "remote," away from your location.

Chaos was the law of nature; Order was the dream of man.
Henry Adams – American historian

Suggested Readings

Bellingham, R. (2001). *The manager's pocket guide to virtual teams.* Amherst, MA: HRD Press.

Dennis, A. (2002). *Networking in the Internet age.* New York: John Wiley & Sons.

Dinnocenzo, D. A. (2006). *How to lead from a distance: Building bridges in the virtual workplace.* Flower Mound, TX: Walk the Talk Company.

Duarte, D. L., & Snyder, N. T. (2006). *Mastering virtual teams: Strategies, tools, and techniques that succeed* (3rd ed.). San Francisco: Jossey-Bass.

Fisher, K., & Fisher, M. (2001). *The distance manager: A hands-on guide to managing off-site employees and virtual teams.* New York: McGraw-Hill.

Fleming, J. H., & Asplund, J. (2007). *Human sigma: Managing the employee-customer encounter.* New York: Gallup Press.

Garton, C., & Wegryn, K. (2006). *Managing without walls: Maximize success with virtual, global, and cross-cultural teams.* Lewisville, TX: MC Press.

Gharajedaghi, J. (2006). *Systems thinking: Managing chaos and complexity: A platform for designing business architecture.* London: Butterworth-Heinemann.

Hildreth, P. M. (2004). *Going virtual: Distributed communities of practice.* Hershey, PA: Idea Group Publishing.

Hinds, P., & Kiesler, S. (2002). *Distributed work.* Boston: MIT Press.

Huotari, M., & Iivonen, M. (2004). *Trust in knowledge management and systems in organizations.* Hershey, PA: Idea Group Publishing.

LeBow, R., & Spitzer, R. (2002). *Accountability: Freedom and responsibility without control.* San Francisco: Berrett-Koehler Publishers.

Oshry, B. (2007). *Seeing systems: Unlocking the mysteries of organizational life.* San Francisco: Berrett-Koehler Publishers.

Van Ness, G., & Van Ness, K. (2003). *Being there without going there: Managing teams across time zones, locations and corporate boundaries.* Boston: Aspatore Books.

Whitman, M. E., & Woszczynski, A. B. (2004). *The handbook of information systems research.* Hershey, PA: Idea Group Publishing.

60 *Building Effective* Teams

Talent wins games, but teamwork and intelligence win championships.
Michael Jordan – U.S. basketball player

Unskilled

- ☐ Doesn't assemble, build or manage in a team fashion
- ☐ Manages people on a one-to-one basis
- ☐ Doesn't create a common mindset or common challenge
- ☐ Rewards and compliments individuals, not the team
- ☐ May not hold many team meetings
- ☐ Doesn't create any synergies in the team; everyone works on his/her own projects
- ☐ Doesn't manage in a way that builds team morale or energy
- ☐ Doesn't have the skills or interest to build a team
- ☐ May be very action and control oriented and won't trust a team to perform

Select one to three of the competencies listed below to use as a substitute for this competency if you decide not to work on it directly.

SUBSTITUTES: 3,7,18,36,37,39,42,52,63,64,65

Skilled

- ☐ Blends people into teams when needed
- ☐ Creates strong morale and spirit in his/her team
- ☐ Shares wins and successes
- ☐ Fosters open dialogue
- ☐ Lets people finish and be responsible for their work
- ☐ Defines success in terms of the whole team
- ☐ Creates a feeling of belonging in the team

Overused Skill

- ☐ May not treat others as unique individuals
- ☐ May slow down reasonable process by having everything open for debate
- ☐ May go too far in not hurting people's feelings and not making tough decisions
- ☐ May not develop individual leaders
- ☐ Might not provide take-charge leadership during tough times

Select one to three of the competencies listed below to work on to compensate for an overuse of this skill.

COMPENSATORS: 9,12,13,18,19,20,21,34,36,56,57,64

Some Causes

- ☐ A loner; an individual contributor
- ☐ Can't set common cause
- ☐ Control oriented manager
- ☐ Don't believe in or support teams
- ☐ Excessively action oriented
- ☐ Incentives are all based upon individual achievement
- ☐ Not a motivator
- ☐ Not a skilled process manager
- ☐ Poor time management
- ☐ The idea of a team is resisted by people
- ☐ Treat all people the same

Leadership Architect® Factors and Clusters

This competency is in the Personal and Interpersonal Skills Factor (VI). This competency is in the Inspiring Others Cluster (Q) with: 36, 37, 65. You may want to check other competencies in the same Factor/Cluster for related tips.

The Map

Everyone would enjoy being on the dream team. That's a group of performers each skilled in his/her own specialties, pulling together accomplishing greater things than the added total of each performing separately. Most organizations talk teams, but primarily reward individual achievement. They also attract and promote people who sometimes resist the idea of tying their performance to that of others. But teams, although uncomfortable to some, are the best way to accomplish integrated tasks like creating systems, producing complex products or sustained coordinated efforts. They are also useful in cutting across boundaries to get things done. The key to successful team building lies in identifying roles, jobs, tasks, rewards and objectives with the team, not with individuals.

Some Remedies

- ☐ **1. Team confused about its direction? Establish a common cause and a shared mindset.** A common thrust is what energizes dream teams. As in light lasers, alignment adds focus, power and efficiency. It's best to get each team member involved in setting the common vision. Establish goals and measures. Most people like to be measured. People like to have checkpoints along the way to chart their progress. Most people perform better with goals that are stretching. Again, letting the team participate in setting the goals is a plus. *More help? – See #35 Managing and Measuring Work.*

☐ **2. Need a clear course of action? Create a game plan.** Once mission and outcomes and goals are established, in order to be resource efficient, a plan is necessary to avoid duplicate work and things falling through the cracks. *More help? – See #47 Planning.*

☐ **3. Want to raise the odds that the team will excel? Inspire the team.** Follow the basic rules of inspiring team members as outlined in classic books like *People Skills* by Robert Bolton or *Thriving on Chaos* by Tom Peters. Tell people what they do is important, say thanks, offer help and ask for it, provide autonomy in how people do their work, provide a variety of tasks, "surprise" people with enriching, challenging assignments, show an interest in their work, adopt a learning attitude toward mistakes, celebrate successes, have visible accepted measures of achievement and so on. Each team member is different so good team managers deal with each person uniquely while being fair to all. *More help? – See #23 Fairness to Direct Reports and #36 Motivating Others.*

☐ **4. Team stuck in a rut? Create a climate of innovation and experimentation.** When how to do something is too rigidly specified, motivation and creativity decrease. How things are done should be as open as possible. Studies show that people work harder and are more effective when they have a sense of choice and ownership. Encourage quick, short-cycle experiments. Many will fail so communicate a learning attitude toward mistakes and failures. *More help? – See #28 Innovation Management.*

☐ **5. Not getting through to team members? Work on understanding people without judging them.** You don't have to agree; you just have to understand. To build a team, invest in their learning, education, trips to customers, and time to think problems through. Give them the benefit of your thinking and particularly what the key objectives of an effort are. The goal is to have them say, "We did it." *More help? – See #27 Informing.*

☐ **6. Too much individualism? Shift the focus from "me" to "we."** Resistance to the idea of a team is best overcome by focusing on common goals, priorities and problems, selling the logic of pulling together repeatedly, listening patiently to people's concerns, protecting people's feelings but also reinforcing the perspective of why the team is needed, inviting suggestions to reach the outcome, and showing patience toward the unconverted. Maintain a light touch. *More help? – See #13 Confronting Direct Reports.*

☐ **7. All work and no play? Build a sense of joy and fun for the team.** Even though some—including you—will resist it, parties, roasts, gag awards, picnics and outings build group cohesion. Working with the whole person tends to build better teams. Use humor and support it in others. Learn to celebrate wins.

☐ **8. Some team members underutilized? Leverage the variety of talent on the team.** Dream teams are usually made up of a variety of talent, not sameness. While dream teams have all of the talent they need to accomplish the task, not any one member has all of the talent. High-performing teams learn how to take advantage of each person's strengths and avoid unreasonable exposure to each person's weaknesses. High-performing teams have more disclosure to one another about their self-appraisal of strengths and weaknesses. A weakness is not considered bad. The team just adjusts to it and moves on. Successful teams specialize, cover for each other, and only sometimes demand that everyone participate in identical activities.

☐ **9. Unsure of how to assign team roles? Allow roles within the team to evolve naturally.** Some research indicates that in well-functioning teams people gravitate to eight roles. *More help? – See #64 Understanding Others.* Generally each of the eight roles needs to be played by someone on the team for the whole team to be effective. One member can play more than one role.

☐ **10. Not operating at peak performance? Learn how to operate effectively and efficiently.** Read *Overcoming Organizational Defenses* by Chris Argyris. Half of the book is about some of the common problems teams run into that block peak performance, and the other half offers strategies and tactics for undoing those chilling team behaviors.

☐ **11. Need an outside perspective? Engage a team coach.** Because a team coach is external to the team, he or she can objectively help you problem solve and provide you with feedback to avoid some of the temptations that can demotivate a team. The team coach could be a Human Resources partner or an external professional that specializes in coaching.

☐ **12. Slow to act as advocate for the team? Run interference.** Effective team leaders run interference for the team by eliminating obstacles that slow down or impede effectiveness. This may mean using the position power of the role to get the needed support from the organization, negotiating for resources, etc.

☐ **13. Struggling to build or lead a virtual team? Keep virtual teams motivated.** Virtual teams are everywhere now, so it's hard to avoid them. Use common-sense tactics to stay connected. Schedule frequent conference calls. Identify regular times when you can be available for mutual teamwork and communication (work out compromises for multiple time zones). Leverage multiple technologies (video conferencing, groupware, etc). And, be mindful of cultural differences, if the virtual team is global.

Some Develop-in-Place Assignments

- ☐ Manage a project team of people who are older and more experienced than you.
- ☐ Manage a group of resistant people with low morale through an unpopular change or project.
- ☐ Assemble a team of diverse people to accomplish a difficult task.
- ☐ Manage a group that includes former peers to accomplish a task.
- ☐ Create employee involvement teams.

No one can whistle a symphony. It takes an orchestra to play it.
Halford E. Luccock – Professor of Homiletics, Yale Divinity School

Suggested Readings

Ancona, D., & Bresman, H. (2007). *X-teams: How to build teams that lead, innovate, and succeed.* Boston: Harvard Business School Press.

Capretta Raymond, C., Eichinger, R. W., & Lombardo, M. M. (2004). *FYI for teams.* Minneapolis, MN: Lominger International: A Korn/Ferry Company.

Dyer, W., Dyer, W. G., Jr., & Dyer, J. H. (2007). *Team building: Proven strategies for improving team performance* (4th ed.). San Francisco: Jossey-Bass.

Guttman, H. M. (2008). *Great business teams: Cracking the code for standout performance.* Hoboken, NJ: John Wiley & Sons.

Hackman, J. R. (2002). *Leading teams: Setting the stage for great performances.* Boston: Harvard Business School Press.

Halverson, C. B., & Tirmizi, S. A. (Eds.). (2008). *Effective multicultural teams: Theory and practice* (Series: Advances in group decision and negotiation, Vol. 3.). New York: Springer.

Harvard Business School Press. (2004). *Creating teams with an edge.* Boston: Harvard Business School Press.

Harvard Business School Press. (2004). *Harvard Business Review on teams that succeed.* Boston: Harvard Business School Press.

Karp, H. (2002). *Bridging the boomer-Xer gap: Creating authentic teams for high performance at work.* Mountain View, CA: Davies-Black.

Katzenbach, J. R., Garvin, D. A., & Wenger, E. C. (2004). *Harvard Business Review on teams that succeed.* Boston: Harvard Business School Press.

Katzenbach, J. R., & Smith, D. K. (2003). *The wisdom of teams: Creating the high-performance organization.* New York: HarperBusiness.

Leigh, A., & Maynard, M. (2002). *Leading your team: How to involve and inspire teams.* Yarmouth, ME: Nicholas Brealey.

Lencioni, P. M. (2002). *The five dysfunctions of a team: A leadership fable.* San Francisco: Jossey-Bass.

Marquardt, M. (2001). *Global teams: How top multinationals span boundaries and cultures with high-speed teamwork.* Mountain View, CA: Davies-Black.

Nemiro, J., Beyerlein, M., Bradley, L., & Beyerlein, S. (2008). *The handbook of high performance virtual teams: A toolkit for collaborating across boundaries.* San Francisco: Jossey-Bass.

Parker, G. M. (2002). *Cross-functional teams: Working with allies, enemies, and other strangers.* San Francisco: Jossey-Bass.

Runde, C. E., & Flanagan, T. A. (2008). *Building conflict competent teams.* San Francisco: Jossey-Bass.

Schwarz, R. (2002). *The skilled facilitator.* San Francisco: Jossey-Bass.

Van Ness, G., & Van Ness, K. (2003). *Being there without going there: Managing teams across time zones, locations and corporate boundaries.* Boston: Aspatore Books.

Wysocki, R. K. (2001). *Building effective project teams.* New York: John Wiley & Sons.

61 Technical Learning

Science and technology multiply around us. To an increasing extent they dictate the languages in which we speak and think. Either we use those languages, or we remain mute.
J.G. Ballard – British novelist and short-story writer

Unskilled

- ☐ Doesn't learn new technical skills readily
- ☐ Is among the last to learn or adopt new technology—like Internet technology
- ☐ May be stuck and wed to past technologies and resist switching to new ones
- ☐ May be intimidated by technology
- ☐ May lack experience or exposure with new technologies
- ☐ May not be interested in things technical or areas involving lots of detail
- ☐ May not know how to or may reject using others to learn new technologies

Select one to three of the competencies listed below to use as a substitute for this competency if you decide not to work on it directly.

SUBSTITUTES: 5,14,24,28,30,32,46,51,58

Skilled

- ☐ Picks up on technical things quickly
- ☐ Can learn new skills and knowledge
- ☐ Is good at learning new industry, company, product, or technical knowledge—like Internet technology
- ☐ Does well in technical courses and seminars

Overused Skill

- ☐ May learn but not act
- ☐ May overdo learning at the expense of using it
- ☐ May be seen as too academic
- ☐ May not relate well to those who can't catch on as quickly

Select one to three of the competencies listed below to work on to compensate for an overuse of this skill.

COMPENSATORS: 1,3,5,15,26,33,36,41,45,46,53,54,57

Some Causes

- ☐ Inexperienced; new to the area
- ☐ Fear of computers
- ☐ Lack of interest in technology
- ☐ Time management; haven't gotten around to it
- ☐ Stuck in a past technology

Leadership Architect® Factors and Clusters

This competency is in the Strategic Skills Factor (I). This competency is in the Understanding the Business Cluster (A) with: 5, 24. You may want to check other competencies in the same Factor/Cluster for related tips.

The Map

All areas of work have new and emerging technologies that underlie doing them well. The pace of new technologies seems to be increasing as more people sign on the Internet. Computers, printers, cell phones and video cameras all seem to last only a year or two before they are replaced with fresh features and technology. Keeping up with new technology is becoming more important as the world is moving faster and competition increasing.

Some Remedies

☐ **1. Need someone to help? Find a tutor.** Find the master professional in the technology you need and ask whether he/she would mind showing you the ropes and tutoring you lightly. Most people good at something don't mind having a few "apprentices" around. They like to be asked for help.

☐ **2. Want to learn from experts in your field? Join professional associations.** Almost all technologies have national, and sometimes regional, professional associations made up of hundreds of people who do well every day the technology you need to learn. Sign up as a member. Buy some of the literature on emerging technologies. Go to some of their workshops featuring what's new. Go to the annual conference and attend those sessions featuring new technology.

☐ **3. Need a good reference? Find the "bible" on technology in your area.** Almost every technology has a book people might call the "bible" in the area. It is the standard reference everyone looks to for knowledge about the new technology. There is probably a journal in any new technology. Subscribe for a year or more. See if they have back issues available.

☐ **4. Need some direction? Follow the leader.** Identify some national leaders in your technology and buy their books, read their articles, and attend their lectures and workshops.

☐ **5. Curious? Take a class.** Your local college, university or trade school might have some nighttime or weekend courses you could take in the new technology. Also, your organization may have training classes in the technology.

- ☐ **6. Want to accelerate? Hire a consultant.** Find a consultant in the technology and hire him/her to provide a private tutorial for you to accelerate your learning.
- ☐ **7. Can't wait? Experiment.** Be an early tester of new and emerging technology. Don't wait until you have to hurry and catch up. Whenever a new technology surfaces, volunteer to learn and try it first. That gives you a head start and allows you to stumble a bit because you are the first.
- ☐ **8. Ready to explore? Go on a technology shopping spree.** Buy a computer for home. Get a cell phone. Buy a digital camera. Get on the Internet. Buy a personal digital assistant. Go to technical trade shows. Find out what's coming and be the first one to suggest it back at work.
- ☐ **9. Early adopter? Adapt new technology for the workplace.** Practice by picking some technology somewhat related to your work and quietly become an expert at it. Introduce it at work. Demonstrate it to your workmates. Market for others to learn it and adopt it for the business. Form a study group and take turns presenting on new, different or emerging technologies. Having to teach it will force you to conceptualize and understand it more deeply.
- ☐ **10. Ready to organize your thinking? Learn to think as experts in technology do.** Take problems to them and ask what are the keys they look for; observe what they consider significant and not significant. Chunk data into categories so you can remember it better. Devise five key areas or questions you can consider each time a technical issue comes up. Don't waste your time learning facts; they won't be useful unless you have conceptual buckets to put them in.
- ☐ **11. Got some time? Schedule time to browse on the Internet with no purpose.** Look for new things in and out of your specialty. Find some interesting item and see how it chains to others. Become an expert in something not directly related to what you are doing today.

Some Develop-in-Place Assignments

- ☐ Manage a cost-cutting project.
- ☐ Build a multifunctional project team to tackle a common business issue or problem.
- ☐ Manage the purchase of a major product, equipment, materials, program, or system.
- ☐ Plan a new site for a building (plant, field office, headquarters, etc.).
- ☐ Do a problem-prevention analysis on a product or service, and present it to the people involved.

Tame your technology...or it will become your master.
Lee J. Colan – American writer, executive advisor, and speaker

Suggested Readings

Beekman, G., & Beekman, B. (2008). *Tomorrow's technology and you* (10th ed.). Upper Saddle River, NJ: Prentice Hall.

Bennis, W. G., & Thomas, R. J. (2002). *Geeks and geezers*. Boston: Harvard Business School Press.

Burgelman, R. A., Christensen, C. M., & Wheelwright, S. C. (2008). *Strategic management of technology and innovation*. New York: McGraw-Hill/Irwin.

Davila, T., Epstein, M. J., & Shelton, R. (2005). *Making innovation work: How to manage it, measure it, and profit from it*. Philadelphia: Wharton School Publishing.

Glen, P. (2003). *Leading geeks: How to manage the people who deliver technology*. San Francisco: Jossey-Bass.

Holtsnider, B., & Jaffe, B. D. (2007). *IT manager's handbook: Getting your new job done*. Oxford, UK: Elsevier.

Li, C., & Bernoff, J. (2008). *Groundswell: Winning in a world transformed by social technologies*. Boston: Harvard Business School Press.

Pfleging, B., & Zetlin, M. (2006). *The geek gap: Why business and technology professionals don't understand each other and why they need each other to survive*. New York: Prometheus Books.

Reich, B., & Solomon, D. (2007). *Media rules! Mastering today's technology to connect with and keep your audience*. Hoboken, NJ: John Wiley & Sons.

Roam, D. (2008). *The back of the napkin: Solving problems and selling ideas with pictures*. New York: Portfolio Hardcover.

Scoble, R., & Israel, S. (2006). *Naked conversations: How blogs are changing the way businesses talk with customers*. Hoboken, NJ: John Wiley & Sons.

Stewart, T. A. (1997). *Intellectual capital: The new wealth of organizations*. New York: Doubleday.

Teten, D., & Allen, S. (2005). *The virtual handshake: Opening doors and closing deals online*. New York: AMACOM.

Tobin, D. R. (1996). *Transformational learning: Renewing your company through knowledge and skills*. New York: John Wiley & Sons.

62 Time Management

Time is the most valuable thing a man can spend.
Theophrastus – As quoted by Diogenes Laertius (372-287 BCE)
Greek botanist, humorist, and naturalist

Unskilled

- ☐ Is disorganized and wastes time and resources
- ☐ Flits from activity to activity with little rhyme or reason
- ☐ Doesn't set priorities
- ☐ Can't say no
- ☐ Can only concentrate on one thing at a time
- ☐ Is very easily distracted
- ☐ Mostly reactive to what's hot at the moment
- ☐ Doesn't have or follow a plan or method for his/her time
- ☐ Can't cut off transactions politely
- ☐ Doesn't have a clock in his/her head
- ☐ May do all right on important priorities and issues, but not good with the little things

Select one to three of the competencies listed below to use as a substitute for this competency if you decide not to work on it directly.

SUBSTITUTES: 17,39,47,50,52,63,66

Skilled

- ☐ Uses his/her time effectively and efficiently
- ☐ Values time
- ☐ Concentrates his/her efforts on the more important priorities
- ☐ Gets more done in less time than others
- ☐ Can attend to a broader range of activities

Overused Skill

- ☐ May be impatient with other people's agenda and pace
- ☐ May not take the time to stop and smell the roses
- ☐ May not give people rapport time with him/her to get comfortable

Select one to three of the competencies listed below to work on to compensate for an overuse of this skill.

COMPENSATORS: 2,3,7,12,14,17,26,27,31,33,36,41,46,51,60

Some Causes

- ☐ Can't say no
- ☐ Disorganized
- ☐ Don't take time to plan time
- ☐ Impatient
- ☐ Not a planner
- ☐ Not time aware; not a good judge of time
- ☐ Poor closing skills; can't say good-bye
- ☐ Poor delegator
- ☐ Procrastinate

Leadership Architect® Factors and Clusters

This competency is in the Operating Skills Factor (II). This competency is in the Getting Organized Cluster (E) with: 39, 47. You may want to check other competencies in the same Factor/Cluster for related tips.

The Map

Who ever has enough time? So much to do; so little time in which to do it. Finite resources; infinite needs. People to see, places to go, things to do. No time to say hello, good-bye, I'm late for a very important meeting. Sound familiar? That's life and work. Everyone has more to do than they can get to. The higher up you go in the organization, the more you have to do and the less time you have to do it. Nobody can do it all. You have to set priorities and manage your time well to survive and prosper.

Some Remedies

☐ **1. What's the target? Set goals.** Nothing manages time better than a goal, a plan and a measure. Set goals for yourself. These goals are essential for setting priorities. If you do not have goals, you can't set time priorities. Using the goals, separate what you need to do into mission-critical, important to get done, nice if there is time left over, and not central to what you are trying to achieve. When faced with choices or multiple things to do, apply the scale. *More help? – See #35 Managing and Measuring Work and #50 Priority Setting.*

☐ **2. What's the plan? Lay out tasks and work on a time line.** Most successful time managers begin with a good plan for time. What do I need to accomplish? What are the goals? What's mission-critical and what's trivial? What's the time line? How will I track it? Buy a flow charting software that does PERT and GANTT charts. Become an expert in its use. Use the output of the software to plan your time. Alternatively, write down your work plan. Many people are seen as lacking time management skills because they don't write down the sequence or parts of the work and leave something out. Ask others to comment on ordering and what's missing.

☐ **3. Do you value your time? Manage your time efficiently.** Plan your time and manage against it. Be time sensitive. Value time. Figure out what you are worth per hour and minute by taking your gross salary plus overhead and benefits. Attach a monetary value on your time. Then ask, is this worth $56 of my time? Review your calendar over the past 90 days to figure out what your three largest time wasters are and reduce them 50% by batching activities and using efficient communications like e-mail and voice mail for routine matters. Make a list of points to be covered in phone calls; set deadlines for yourself; use your best time of day for the toughest projects—if you're best in the morning, don't waste it on B and C level tasks.

☐ **4. Ready to make the up-front investment? Create more time for yourself.** Taking time to plan and set priorities actually frees up more time later than just diving into things, hoping that you can get it done on time. Most people out of time claim they didn't have the time to plan their time. In the Stephen Covey *Seven Habits of Highly Effective People* sense, it's sharpening your saw. *More Help – See #102 Poor Administrator.*

☐ **5. Can you delegate it? Give away as much time-consuming work as you can.** This can be done by a little planning and by delegating things you don't have to do yourself. Try to give away as much as possible to others. The win-win is that people enjoy being delegated to and empowered. You win; they win. *More help? – See #18 Delegation.*

☐ **6. Who does this well? Find someone in your environment who is better at time management than you are.** Watch what he/she does and compare against what you typically do. Try to increase doing the things he or she does and doesn't do. Ask for feedback from some people who have commented on your poor time management. What did they find difficult?

☐ **7. Focused on what you like? Be careful not to be guided by just what you like and what you don't like to do.** That way of using your time will probably not be successful over time. Use data, intuition and even feelings to apportion your time, but not feelings alone.

☐ **8. Time waster? Be sensitive to the time of others.** Generally, the higher up you go or the higher up the person you are interacting with is, the less time you and he/she has. Be time efficient with others. Use as little of their time as possible. Get to it and get done with it. Give them an opportunity to open new avenues for discussion or to continue, but if they don't, say your good-byes and leave.

- ☐ **9. Can't say no? Practice saying no.** Others will always ask you to do more than you can do. An important time saver is the ability to constructively say no. One technique people use is to ask the requester which of the other things they have asked you to do would they like to cancel or delay in order to do the most recent request. That way you say both yes and no and let the requester choose.
- ☐ **10. Do conversations drag on? Keep it brief.** Another common time waster is inadequate disengagement skills. Some poor time managers can't shut down transactions. Either they continue to talk beyond what would be necessary, or more commonly, they can't get the other party to quit talking. When it's time to move on, just say, "I have to get on to the next thing I have to do; we can pick this up some other time."

Some Develop-in-Place Assignments

- ☐ Work on a crisis-management team.
- ☐ Manage a group of resistant people with low morale through an unpopular change or project.
- ☐ Manage a group of people involved in tackling a fix-it or turnaround project.
- ☐ Plan an off-site meeting, conference, convention, trade show, event, etc.
- ☐ Plan a new site for a building (plant, field office, headquarters, etc.).

Time flies. It's up to you to be the navigator.
Robert Orben – American magician and comedy writer

Suggested Readings

Carrison, D. (2003). *Deadline! How premier organizations win the race against time.* New York: AMACOM.

Dodd, P., & Sundheim, D. (2005). *The 25 best time management tools and techniques: How to get more done without driving yourself crazy.* Windham, NH: Peak Performance Press.

Duncan, P. (2002). *Put time management to work: Get organized, streamline processes, use the right technology.* Atlanta: PSC Press.

Emmett, R. (2000). *The procrastinator's handbook: Mastering the art of doing it now.* New York: Walker & Company.

Forster, M. (2008). *Do it tomorrow and other secrets of time management.* London: Hodder & Stoughton.

Gleeson, K. (2003). *The personal efficiency program: How to get organized to do more work in less time* (3rd ed.). Hoboken, NJ: John Wiley & Sons.

Harvard Business School Press. (2006). *Managing time: Expert solutions to everyday challenges.* Boston: Harvard Business School Press.

Hutchings, P. J. (2002). *Managing workplace chaos: Solutions for managing information, paper, time, and stress.* New York: AMACOM.

Lencioni, P. M. (2004). *Death by meeting: A leadership fable...about solving the most painful problem in business.* San Francisco: Jossey-Bass.

MacKenzie, A. (2002). *The time trap: The classic book on time management* (3rd ed.). New York: AMACOM.

Mancini, M. (2007). *Time management: 24 Techniques to make each minute count at work.* Columbus, OH: McGraw-Hill.

Morgenstern, J. (2004). *Time management from the inside out: The foolproof system for taking control of your schedule—and your life* (2nd ed.). New York: Henry Holt.

Panella, V. (2002). *The 26-hour day: How to gain at least two hours a day with time control.* Franklin Lakes, NJ: Career Press.

Parker, G. M., & Hoffman, R. (2006). *Meeting excellence: 33 Tools to lead meetings that get results.* San Francisco: Jossey-Bass.

Pickering, P., & Clark, J. (2001). *How to make the most of your workday.* Franklin Lakes, NJ: Career Press.

Schwartz, T., & McCarthy, C. (2007). Manage your energy, not your time. *Harvard Business Review, 85*(10), 63-73.

Tracy, B. (2001). *Eat that frog! 21 Great ways to stop procrastinating and get more done in less time.* San Francisco: Berrett-Koehler Publishers.

Tracy, B. (2007). *Time power: A proven system for getting more done in less time than you ever thought possible.* New York: AMACOM.

Walsh, R. (2008). *Time management: Proven techniques for making every minute count.* Cincinnati, OH: Adams Media.

63 Total Work Systems
(E.G., TQM/ISO/SIX SIGMA)

We are what we repeatedly do. Excellence, then, is not an act, but a habit.
Aristotle (384-322 BCE) – Greek philosopher and scientist

Unskilled

- ☐ Doesn't think broadly regarding the impact of work processes
- ☐ Doesn't comply or work to build commonalities in processes
- ☐ Doesn't create effective and efficient work processes
- ☐ Isn't customer focused in how he/she designs and manages the work
- ☐ Isn't dedicated to continuous improvement of work processes
- ☐ Doesn't leverage technology to improve work processes
- ☐ Doesn't know the tools and techniques to improve work processes
- ☐ Sticks to the old and familiar rather than stepping back and seeing the larger pattern
- ☐ Isn't willing to scrap the past in favor of the new and improved
- ☐ Doesn't listen to employees about improving work design
- ☐ Doesn't empower others to design their own work processes
- ☐ Doesn't create an environment where the whole unit learns together how better to serve the customer

Select one to three of the competencies listed below to use as a substitute for this competency if you decide not to work on it directly.

SUBSTITUTES: 5,15,16,20,28,32,33,35,39,47,52,53,65

Skilled

- ☐ Is dedicated to providing organization or enterprise-wide common systems for designing and measuring work processes
- ☐ Seeks to reduce variances in organization processes
- ☐ Delivers the highest-quality products and services which meet the needs and requirements of internal and external customers
- ☐ Is committed to continuous improvement through empowerment and management by data
- ☐ Leverages technology to positively impact quality
- ☐ Is willing to re-engineer processes from scratch
- ☐ Is open to suggestions and experimentation
- ☐ Creates a learning environment leading to the most efficient and effective work processes

Overused Skill

- ☐ May become a work process or quality improvement missionary to the exclusion of everything else
- ☐ May make marginal incremental changes which are more disruptive than helpful
- ☐ May not deliver results because of extreme focus on process or rules
- ☐ May reject other approaches and non-believers

Select one to three of the competencies listed below to work on to compensate for an overuse of this skill.

COMPENSATORS: 2,32,33,40,46,57,58

Some Causes

- ☐ Don't delegate
- ☐ Don't listen
- ☐ Inexperienced
- ☐ Not a risk taker
- ☐ Not customer oriented
- ☐ Not planful and organized
- ☐ Not results oriented
- ☐ Stick to the old

Leadership Architect® Factors and Clusters

This competency is in the Operating Skills Factor (II). This competency is in the Managing Work Processes Cluster (G) with: 52, 59. You may want to check other competencies in the same Factor/Cluster for related tips.

The Map

There is a well-understood and accepted technology for producing products and services that work the first time and that meet or exceed customer requirements. Countless organizations have implemented these best practices which have led to increased success in the marketplace. For every successful implementation of these techniques, three more have failed. The number one cause for failure has been that management didn't really understand and support the effort and, even more important, they didn't change their behavior to align with the new practices. They didn't walk the talk. There is no better way to be personally successful and lead your organization to success than to learn and use the principles of TQM, ISO and Six Sigma.

Some Remedies

☐ **1. Need an overview? Learn the principles.** There are many sources available. Read about methods put forth by Deming, Juran, Crosby, Hammer and Champy and countless others. There are numerous conferences and workshops you can attend. It's best to get a sampling of what everybody thinks and then create your own version for your specific situation.

☐ **2. Want to exceed expectations? Be customer-driven.** In a free-enterprise system, the customer is king; those who please the customer best win. The same is true with internal customers; those who please them most will win. Winners are always customer oriented and responsive. Pleasing the reasonable needs of customers is fairly straightforward. First you need to know what they want and expect; the best way to do that is to ask them; then deliver that in a timely way at a price/value that's acceptable to them. Get in the habit of meeting with your internal or external customers on a regular basis to set up a dialogue; they need to feel free to contact you about problems and you need to be able to contact them for essential information. Also, get out in front of your customers; try to anticipate their needs for your products and services before they even know about them; provide your customers with positive surprises—features they weren't expecting; delivery in a shorter time; more than they ordered. *More help? – See #15 Customer Focus.*

☐ **3. Enough customer focus? Design work and manage time by starting with the customer.** Your best efforts will always be determined by your customers, not you. Try not to design and arrange what you do only from your own view; always try to know and take the viewpoint of your customer first; you will always win following that rule. What would you have to take care of so the phone wouldn't ring from outside? If you and your customer worked for the same business, what would you do differently?

☐ **4. Ready to empower your employees? Delegate and empower others to help design the best work flows.** Produce zero-defect products and services that meet the needs of your customers. This is a known process, well documented, and available to all who wish to implement its principles. *More help? – See #35 Managing and Measuring Work and #52 Process Management.*

☐ **5. Need ideas and suggestions? Be open and flexible.** Meeting customer needs with the best work designs possible involves a lot of people. You can never do it all yourself. You need to set up a process to solicit suggestions and comments from customers and the people working with you. You must set the tone for two-way dialogue. An idea missed is the one you didn't hear. The research is filled with examples of employee-driven work designs and suggestions that have big payoffs to the organization.

☐ **6. Afraid of failure? Create an environment for experimentation and learning.** One principle of these techniques is to drive for continuous improvement. Never be satisfied. Always drive to improve all work processes so that they deliver zero-defect goods and services the customers want. Don't be afraid to try and fail. *More help? – See #28 Innovation Management.*

- ☐ **7. Self-aware? Look at your own personal work habits.** Are they designed for maximum effectiveness and efficiency? Is there room for some continuous improvement? Are you applying the principles you have learned to yourself? Remember, this is one of the major reasons why these efforts fail.
- ☐ **8. Understand the customer's pain points? Think of yourself as a dissatisfied customer.** Write down all of the unsatisfactory things that have happened to you as a customer during the past month. Things like delays, orders not right, cost not as promised, phone calls not returned, cold food, bad service, inattentive clerks, out-of-stock items, etc. Would your customers report any of these problems? Then do a study of your lost customers. Find out what the three key problems were and see how quickly you can eliminate 50% of the difficulties that caused them to depart. Study your competitors' foul-ups and see what you can do to both eliminate those and make your organization more attractive. *More help? – See #15 Customer Focus.*
- ☐ **9. Understand the customer's favorable points of view? Think of yourself as a satisfied customer.** Write down all of the satisfactory things that have happened to you as a customer during the past month. What pleased you the most as a customer? Good value? On-time service? Courteousness? Returned phone calls? Are any of your customers experiencing any of these satisfactory transactions with you and your business? Study your successful customer transactions so they can be institutionalized. Then study what your competitors do well and see what you can also do to improve customer service. *More help? – See #15 Customer Focus.*
- ☐ **10. Understand best practices? Research work flows in other industries.** Be a student of the work flows and processes around you at airports, restaurants, hotels, supermarkets, government services, etc. As a customer, how would you design those things differently to make them more effective and efficient? What principles would you follow? Apply those same principles to your own work. Use Work-Out, an approach pioneered by GE to cut unnecessary work. In a typical application, Work-Out lasts three days with bosses attending only the last day. The first two days involve cutting down and eliminating work steps; the third day involves getting agreement on these proposals.

☐ **11. What does one expert say? According to Oren Harari, watch out for:**

- Focusing on processes rather than results.
- Driving for zero defects is just one small piece of the package. It's about products and services the customer wants.
- Creeping bureaucracy.
- Delegating quality to the experts rather than real people. This leads to discounting the importance of employee input and customer complaints.
- Cramming TQM into the same old structure. Quality improvement involves flattening, freeing up managers and employees, and the blasting away of functional silos. Empowered, cross-functional teams are the answer.
- Jerking your suppliers around. Suppliers must be treated as partners to improve quality.
- Using TQM as a substitute for innovation. Innovation requires risk and mistakes and putting out products that are not yet bug free, as Microsoft does.

Some Develop-in-Place Assignments

☐ Manage a cost-cutting project.

☐ Build a multifunctional project team to tackle a common business issue or problem.

☐ Benchmark innovative practices, processes, products, or services of competitors, vendors, suppliers, or customers, and present a report making recommendations for change.

☐ Work on a process-simplification team to take steps and costs out of a process.

☐ Do a problem-prevention analysis on a product or service, and present it to the people involved.

Quality in a product or service is not what the supplier puts in.
It is what the customer gets out and is willing to pay for.
A product is not quality because it is hard to make
and costs a lot of money, as manufacturers typically believe.
This is incompetence. Customers pay only for what is of use to them
and gives them value. Nothing else constitutes quality.
Peter Drucker – Austrian-born American writer
and management consultant

Suggested Readings

Bhote, K. (2002). *The ultimate Six Sigma: Beyond quality experience to total business excellence.* New York: AMACOM.

Brussee, W. (2004). *Statistics for Six Sigma made easy.* New York: McGraw-Hill.

Champy, J. A. (2002). *X-engineering the corporation: Reinventing your business in the digital age.* New York: Warner Books.

Chowdhury, S. (2003). *The power of design for Six Sigma.* Chicago: Dearborn Financial Publishing.

Dale, B. G., Van Der Wiele, T., & Van Iwaarden, J. (2007). *Managing quality* (5th ed.). Hoboken, NJ: John Wiley & Sons.

Eckes, G. (2001). *The Six Sigma revolution: How General Electric and others turned process into profits.* New York: John Wiley and Sons.

Eckes, G. (2003). *Six Sigma for everyone.* New York: John Wiley & Sons.

El-Haik, B., & Al-Aomar, R. (2006). *Simulation-based lean Six Sigma and design for Six Sigma.* Hoboken, NJ: John Wiley & Sons.

George, M. L. (2003). *Lean Six Sigma for service: How to use lean speed and Six Sigma quality to improve services and transactions.* New York: McGraw-Hill.

George, M. L., Maxey, J., Rowlands, D. T., & Price, M. (2005). *The lean Six Sigma pocket toolbook: A quick reference guide to 100 tools for improving quality and speed.* New York: McGraw-Hill.

Gitlow, H. S., & Levine, D. M. (2005). *Six Sigma for green belts and champions: Foundations, DMAIC, tools, cases, and certification.* Upper Saddle River, NJ: Pearson Education, Inc.

Goldratt, E. M., & Cox, J. (2004). *The goal: A process of ongoing improvement* (3rd ed.). Great Barrington, MA: North River Press.

Gourdin, K. (2006). *Global logistics management: A competitive advantage for the 21st century* (2nd ed.). Hoboken, NJ: John Wiley & Sons.

Greasley, A. (2007). *Operations management.* London: Sage Publications, Ltd.

Hammer, M., & Champy, J. A. (2003). *Reengineering the corporation: A manifesto for business revolution.* New York: HarperCollins.

Hodgetts, R. M. (1998). *Measures of quality and high performance.* New York: AMACOM.

Imai, M. (1997). *Gemba kaizen.* New York: McGraw-Hill.

Jugulum, R., & Samuel, P. (2008). *Design for lean Six Sigma: A holistic approach to design and innovation.* Hoboken, NJ: John Wiley & Sons.

Liker, J. (2004). *The Toyota way.* New York: McGraw-Hill.

Pyzdek, T. (2003). *The Six Sigma handbook: The complete guide for green belts, black belts, and managers at all levels.* New York: McGraw-Hill.

Watson, G. H. (2007). *Strategic benchmarking reloaded with Six Sigma: Improving your company's performance using global best practice.* Hoboken, NJ: John Wiley & Sons.

64 Understanding Others

Shallow understanding from people of good will is more frustrating than absolute misunderstanding from people of ill will.
Martin Luther King, Jr. – Clergyman, activist, and leader in American Civil Rights movement

Unskilled

- ☐ Doesn't read groups well
- ☐ Doesn't understand how groups operate or what purposes groups serve
- ☐ Can't predict what groups will do
- ☐ Stereotypes or pre-judges groups
- ☐ May only understand groups similar to him or her in purpose and characteristics
- ☐ Sees people as individuals only
- ☐ Doesn't understand how group membership affects people's views and behavior
- ☐ Prefers working one-on-one; can't reach or motivate groups
- ☐ May be a loner and not really a member of any voluntary groups

Select one to three of the competencies listed below to use as a substitute for this competency if you decide not to work on it directly.

SUBSTITUTES: 8,15,21,23,32,33,36,38,39,42,46,51,56

Skilled

- ☐ Understands why groups do what they do
- ☐ Picks up the sense of the group in terms of positions, intentions, and needs; what they value and how to motivate them
- ☐ Can predict what groups will do across different situations

Overused Skill

- ☐ May spend too much time trying to analyze what a group might or might not do
- ☐ May generalize from his/her group appraisal to individuals, letting personal impressions of a group cover individuals as well
- ☐ May discount variety of opinion
- ☐ May have trouble dealing with individuals when he/she is in conflict with the group the individual belongs to
- ☐ May spend too much energy understanding and analyzing group actions

Select one to three of the competencies listed below to work on to compensate for an overuse of this skill.

COMPENSATORS: 1,2,12,13,16,17,21,34,37,40,50,52,53,57,59

Some Causes

- ☐ A loner; not a joiner; hasn't experienced groups
- ☐ Dismiss the importance of groups
- ☐ Don't acknowledge groups
- ☐ Don't like people to form groups
- ☐ Don't understand how groups operate
- ☐ Judgmental about other groups
- ☐ Problems dealing with other functions/professions
- ☐ See groups as stereotypes

Leadership Architect® Factors and Clusters

This competency is in the Personal and Interpersonal Skills Factor (VI). This competency is in the Managing Diverse Relationships Cluster (P) with: 4, 15, 21, 23, 42. You may want to check other competencies in the same Factor/Cluster for related tips.

The Map

By knowing what group or groups a person belongs to, you can get a better handle on what the person believes, why, and what he or she might do in a given situation. Group members hold some but not all beliefs, assumptions about the world, habits and practices in common. Members of groups look alike because like-minded people form and join groups and because groups educate and orient new members into the norms and standards of the group.

Some Remedies

☐ **1. Need to understand volunteer groups? Study up on voluntary or advocacy groups.** If it is a voluntary/interest group, people usually belong for three reasons: The group fulfills social needs; provides a sense of belonging, gives emotional support and identification; and helps people achieve their goals by sharing information and helping each other. Groups are stronger than individuals and are natural to the human species. Being a loner is not. Belonging to voluntary groups is exceptionally important to most as they define our sense of what's worthwhile to a great degree. People go in and out of informal voluntary groups as their needs and interests change. Find out all you can about what groups people you need to deal with and manage belong to. It can help you deal with them and help them perform better.

☐ **2. Want to know why informal groups form? Study the history of group formation inside and outside the organization.** Voluntary groups generally form because of a common interest, challenge, threat, or goal individual members can't deal with by themselves. Unions were a reaction to oppressive management. Civil Rights groups were a reaction to a lack of equal opportunities. The AMA was formed to set standards for the medical profession and protect it from charlatans and snake oil salespersons. A group of minorities might form inside your organization because they think they are being held to a double standard and not being given enough opportunities. Especially inside your organization, watch what groups and cliques form on their own. Try to work backward and determine why they formed. What groups do you belong to? Why did you join?

☐ **3. Stereotyping group members? Don't automatically lump people into categories.** Some groups are forced by an involuntary category. There are gender and racial groups. There are country of origin groups. There is Mensa, limited by a high tested IQ. There is a national Bald Person's Club. Any individual may or may not choose to join and partake in the activities of the group. Other people, however, have a tendency to stereotype people into their categorical groups, whether the person buys into that or not. While some aspects of categorical groups might help you read people better, it is important not to lump people into categories. First find out if they buy into the interests and practices of their category before you begin to use that in your assessment of them.

☐ **4. Think all groups are the same? Know the difference between interest groups and functional/professional ones.** Other groups in organizations are not interest groups; they are nominal functional/professional ones. They are formed to define and maintain the boundaries between one group—accountants, and the other—marketers. Formal groups maintain entry standards and have membership criteria. They support the development of specialized skills and help individual members succeed, guard the group against attack from the outside, and lobby for beneficial legislation. Membership in these groups is defined by your job, your organization's method of organizing itself and your profession. If your job changes, if you move from division A to division B, you will change nominal groups as soon as you cross the border.

☐ **5. Looking for root causes of group behavior? Learn to be a cultural anthropologist.** In assessing groups, ask yourself what makes their blood boil? What do they believe? What are they trying to accomplish together? What do they smile at? What norms and customs do they have? What practices and behaviors do they share? Do they not like it if you stand too close? If you get right down to business? Do they like first names or are they more formal? If a Japanese manager presents his card, do you know what to do? Why do they have their cards printed in two languages and executives from the U.S. don't? Do you know what jokes are OK to tell? What do they believe about you and your group or groups? Positive? Neutral? Negative? What's been the history of their group and yours? Is this a first contact or a long history? Don't blunder in; nothing will kill you quicker with a group than showing utter disregard—read disrespect—for it and its norms or having no idea of how they view your group. Ask people who deal with this group often for insights. If it's an important group to you and your business, read about it. *More help? – See #21 Managing Diversity.*

☐ **6. Uncomfortable with some groups? Be candid with yourself.** Is there a group or groups you don't like or are uncomfortable with? Do you judge individual members of that group without really knowing if your impressions and stereotype is true? Most of us do. Avoid putting groups in good and bad buckets. Many of us bucket groups as friendly or unfriendly. Once we do, we generally don't talk to the unfriendliest as much and may question their motives. Don't generalize about individuals. A person might belong to a group for many reasons, yet not typify stereotypes of the group. All accountants aren't detail-driven introverts, for example. To deal with this put yourself in their shoes. Why would you act that way? What do you think they're trying to achieve? Assume that however they act is rational; it must have paid off or they wouldn't be doing it. Describe behavior and motives as neutrally as you can. Listen and observe to understand, not judge. If you are going to interact with a group you have trouble with, be on your guard and best behavior.

☐ **7. Unsure of who does what in groups? Identify the roles inside groups.** All groups share a common set of things that happen inside the group. Groups aren't undifferentiated masses. Many errors in dealing with groups involve failures in seeing groups as sets of roles. A commonly accepted typology of eight group roles was developed by Belbin. You should know about it because spotting the role played tells you whom to deal with as varying situations arise:

– *Leader.* Shapes the way in which group efforts are applied by focusing priorities and direction. Looked to when trouble comes.

– *Process Manager.* Focuses on process needed to reach team objectives.

– *Innovator.* Advances the new, challenges the old.

– *Evaluator.* The analyst; sifts through problems for the group.

– *Finisher.* Focuses on deadlines, commitments and urgency.

– *Work organizer.* Turns plans into procedures and sequences.

– *Internal negotiator.* Maintains relationships, builds team spirit.

– *External negotiator.* Scans outside for resources, ideas, contacts for deal making.

Additionally there are gatekeepers who protect and manage entry, clowns who manage tension relief, synergizers who bring disparate things together, enforcers who make sure members tow the line and so forth. So in addition to knowing what group or groups a person belongs to, you need to know what role or roles they play inside the group. Usually one person plays one role. Unless the group is very small or very hierarchical, you're better off going to the person who's most concerned with your issue or asking who that might be. Use the group's power. You will have little luck motivating a group by asking for something that asks them to go against a core reason for being in the group. Your best bet is to appeal to the person who plays the role you're interested in to exercise his/her power and influence. What role or roles do you usually play?

☐ **8. Want to effectively deal with groups? Interact with groups in ways with which they can relate.** To deal effectively with groups, establish reciprocity. Relationships don't last unless you provide something and so do they. Find out what they want and tell them what you want. Strike a bargain. If one group usually gets the benefit, the other group will eventually become uncooperative and balky. Learn their conceptual categories. People who went on to become successful executives often spoke of their first time dealing with another function. The most common tack for a marketing person dealing with finance for the first time was to show them something he/she was working on and ask them how they would analyze it. What questions would they ask? What are the key numbers and why? What were the four or five key factors they were looking at? Be able to speak their language. Speaking their language makes it easier for them to talk with you and shows respect. Tell them your conceptual categories. To deal with you they also need to know how you think and why. As in the tip above, tell them your perspective—the questions you ask, the factors you're interested in. If you can't explain your thinking, they won't know how to deal with you effectively.

☐ **9. Impatient to get your message across? Avoid early solution statements and extreme positions.** While the answer might be obvious to you, and might make perfect sense to someone in your field, it may either mean nothing or will be jarring to people in another function. Lay out your thinking, explain the alternatives, and keep them as maybes. Then invite them to apply their perspective to it. If you fire out solutions, you'll encourage them to reply in your terms. You'll never learn to understand them.

☐ **10. Is conflict between groups getting in the way? Get groups to work together.** The keys are to find the common ground, downsize the differences that will get in the way and use the differences that add value to form an alliance. Even groups seemingly far apart will have some things in common. Announce that you would first like to see if there are any points on which the two sides could tentatively agree. List those on a board or flip chart. Then list the seemingly far aparts, the real differences. Take each difference and list it as adding value—we can do that and you can't, and you can do something we are not good at—or getting in the way. Use the differences that add value and throw a plan around minimizing the troublesome differences. Based on the common ground and the value adding differences, form a common mindset about how these groups can work together more effectively. *More help? – See #12 Conflict Management.*

Some Develop-in-Place Assignments

- ☐ Handle a tough negotiation with an internal or external client or customer.
- ☐ Work on a team forming a joint venture or partnership.
- ☐ Create employee involvement teams.
- ☐ Go on a business trip to a foreign country you've not been to before.
- ☐ Do a study of failed executives in your organization, including interviewing people still with the organization who knew or worked with them, and report the findings to top management.

When you learn something from people, or from a culture,
you accept it as a gift,
and it is your lifelong commitment
to preserve it and build on it.
Yo-Yo Ma – French-born Chinese-American
cellist and Grammy Award winner

Suggested Readings

Ashkenas, R. N., Ulrich, D., Jick, T., & Kerr, S. (2002). *The boundaryless organization: Breaking the chains of organization structure* (Rev. ed.). San Francisco: Jossey-Bass.

Belbin, R. M. (2004). *Management teams* (2nd ed.). Boston: Butterworth-Heinemann.

Beyerlein, M. M., Freedman, S., McGee, C., & Moran, L. (2002). *Beyond teams: Building the collaborative organization*. San Francisco: Jossey-Bass.

Cohen, D., & Prusak, L. (2001). *In good company: How social capital makes organizations work*. Boston: Harvard Business School Press.

Deresky, H. (2002). *Global management: Strategic and interpersonal*. Upper Saddle River, NJ: Prentice Hall.

Greenhalgh, L. (2001). *Managing strategic relationships: The key to business success*. New York: Free Press.

Lancaster, L. C., Stillman, D., & MacKay, H. (2002). *When generations collide: Who they are. Why they clash. How to solve the generational puzzle at work*. New York: HarperCollins.

Lawrence, P. R., & Nohria, N. (2002). *Driven: How human nature shapes our choices*. San Francisco: Jossey-Bass.

Lee, Y. T., Jussim, L. J., & McCauley, C. R. (Eds.). (1995). *Stereotype accuracy: Toward appreciating group differences*. Washington, DC: American Psychological Association.

Lewis, R. D. (2006). *When cultures collide: Leading across cultures* (3rd ed.). Boston: Nicholas Brealey.

Maginn, M. (2004). *Making teams work: 24 Lessons for working together successfully*. New York: McGraw-Hill.

Maister, D. H. (2001). *Practice what you preach: What managers must do to create a high-achievement culture*. New York: Free Press.

Middleton, D. R. (2002). *The challenge of human diversity: Mirrors, bridges, and chasms*. Prospect Heights, IL: Waveland Press.

Miller, F. A., & Katz, J. H. (2002). *The inclusion breakthrough*. San Francisco: Berrett-Koehler Publishers.

Tomalin, B., & Nicks, M. (2007). *The world's business cultures and how to unlock them: Special chapters on China, USA, Germany, UK, Russia, India, Brazil, France, Italy, and Japan*. London: Thorogood.

Underwood, C. (2007). *The generational imperative: Understanding generational differences in the workplace, marketplace, and living room*. Charleston, SC: BookSurge.

65 *Managing* Vision and Purpose

Good business leaders create a vision, articulate the vision, passionately own the vision, and relentlessly drive it to completion.
Thomas Hardy – English author

Unskilled

- ☐ Can't communicate or sell a vision
- ☐ Not a good presenter
- ☐ Can't turn a good phrase or create compelling one-liners
- ☐ Uncomfortable speculating on the unknown future
- ☐ Isn't charismatic or passionate enough to excite and energize others
- ☐ Can't simplify enough to help people understand complex strategy
- ☐ May not understand how change happens
- ☐ Doesn't act like he/she really believes in the vision
- ☐ More comfortable in the here and now

Select one to three of the competencies listed below to use as a substitute for this competency if you decide not to work on it directly.

SUBSTITUTES: 5,9,15,24,28,36,46,49,59,60,63

Skilled

- ☐ Communicates a compelling and inspired vision or sense of core purpose
- ☐ Talks beyond today
- ☐ Talks about possibilities
- ☐ Is optimistic
- ☐ Creates mileposts and symbols to rally support behind the vision
- ☐ Makes the vision sharable by everyone
- ☐ Can inspire and motivate entire units or organizations

Overused Skill

- ☐ May leave people behind
- ☐ May lack patience with those who don't understand or share his/her vision and sense of purpose
- ☐ May lack appropriate detail-orientation and concern for administrative routine
- ☐ May lack follow-through on the day-to-day tasks

Select one to three of the competencies listed below to work on to compensate for an overuse of this skill.

COMPENSATORS: 3,5,24,27,33,35,41,52,64,67

NOTE: This competency deals with communicating and implementing an existing vision; for creating a vision, see #58 Strategic Agility.

Some Causes

- ☐ Can't create simple messages
- ☐ Can't deal with conflict
- ☐ Don't understand change
- ☐ Don't walk the talk
- ☐ Not committed
- ☐ Poor presenter
- ☐ Talk too long

Leadership Architect® Factors and Clusters

This competency is in the Personal and Interpersonal Skills Factor (VI). This competency is in the Inspiring Others Cluster (Q) with: 36, 37, 60. You may want to check other competencies in the same Factor/Cluster for related tips.

The Map

Much research has shown that organizations with sound and inspiring missions and visions do better in the marketplace. Sound missions and visions motivate and guide people on how to allot their time and how to make choices. As important as the vision, mission and strategy might be, communicating and managing them is even more critical.

Some Remedies

☐ **1. Confusion about what's mission critical? Craft the message.** C.K. Prahalad, one of the leading strategic consultants, believes that in order to qualify as a mission statement, it should take less than three minutes to explain it clearly to an audience. Really effective mission statements are simple, compelling and capable of capturing people's imagination. Mission statements should help everyone allot his/her time. They should signal what's mission-critical and explain what's rewarded in the organization and what's not. Create a simple obvious symbol, visual or slogan to make the cause come alive. Ford's "Quality is Job One" seems clear enough. Nordstrom's "The Customer is Always Right" tells employees how they should do their jobs. Although the actual mission and vision document would be longer, the message needs to be finely crafted to capture the essence of what's important around here. *More help? – See #27 Informing.*

☐ **2. Individuals confused about how they fit in? Build a common mindset.** The power of a mission and vision communication is providing everyone in the organization with a road map on how they are going to be part of something grand and exciting. Establish common cause. Imagine what the change would look like if fully implemented, then describe the outcome often—how things will look in the future. Help people see how their efforts fit in by creating simple, obvious measures of achievement like bar or thermometer charts. Be succinct. People don't line up behind laundry lists or ambiguous objectives. Missions and visions should be more about where we are going and less about how we are going to get there. Keep your eyes on the prize.

☐ **3. Facing change management challenges? Be a change leader.** Most significant vision and mission statements represent a deviation from the past. They represent a rallying call for a departure from business as usual. They require that people are going to have to think, talk and act differently. For that reason, underneath the excitement will be apprehension, anxiety and fear of the unknown. All of the principles of change management apply to communicating a mission. Expect trouble and admit that 20-40% of time will be spent debugging, fixing mistakes and figuring out what went wrong. Treat each one as a chance to learn—document difficulties and learn from them. Without sounding like you're hedging, present it as a work-in-progress to be improved over time. How changes are made should be as open as possible. Studies show that people work harder and are more effective when they have a sense of choice over how they accomplish stretch goals and objectives. Invite multiple attacks, encourage experimentation, talk with people who have successfully pulled off changes. *More help? – See #28 Innovation Management.*

☐ **4. Sending mixed messages? Walk your talk.** Many times employees listen more to what you do than to what you say. The largest reason change efforts fail is that the messenger does not act in line with the new vision and mission. Words are wonderful. Actions are stronger. If you want to be credible, make sure you incorporate the new thinking and behavior into your repertoire. Otherwise it will be gone as soon as the echoes of your words are gone. *More help? – See #22 Ethics and Values.*

☐ **5. Message not compelling? Tailor the message to the audience.** Learn to adjust to your audience. Unfortunately, one vision and mission speech generally does not play equally well across audiences. Many times you will have to adjust the tone, pace, style and even the message and how you couch it for different audiences. If you are giving the mission speech—or delivering the same message—to multiple audiences, always ask yourself how are they different. The union? Managers? Individual producers? Already stressed out from the last mission that fizzled? Merged team? Adjust accordingly. *More help? – See #15 Customer Focus.*

☐ **6. Need people to rally behind the plan? Deliver an inspiring message.** Missions and visions are meant to motivate. Don't threaten. Don't say this is our last chance. Don't blame the past. Visions are optimistic, inspirational, about possibilities, about getting to a grand place in the market. Paint a positive, "we can do it" picture. You have to blow a little smoke and use fairy dust. It's a performance. You have to get people to see what you see. This is all about how to present well (*More help? – See #49 Presentation Skills*) and motivate (*More help? – See #36 Motivating Others*). Always rehearse. Use a test group before you go public. See it yourself on video. Would you understand and be motivated?

☐ **7. Meeting unexpected resistance? Be prepared for detractors and resisters.** There will always be those who don't buy it, have seen it all before, haven't yet seen a mission or vision come true. They may be private about it or come at you in public. Before you communicate the mission and vision, think about the 10 critical questions that might come up. "What happened to last year's brand-new mission that we've already abandoned? I don't think that will work. Our customers won't go for it." Be prepared for the most likely criticisms. Mentally rehearse how you might respond to questions. Listen patiently to people's concerns, protecting their feelings, but also reinforcing the perspective of why the change is needed. Attack positions, not the people. Show patience toward the unconverted; maintain a light touch. Remember, there was a time during the crafting of this vision that you were not convinced. Invite alternative suggestions to reach the same outcome. In the end, thank everyone for their time and input and just say the train is leaving. Rarely, you may have to pull a specific person aside and say, "I understand all your worries and have tried to respond to them, but the train is moving on. Are you on or off?" *More help? – See #12 Conflict Management.*

☐ **8. Need to close the deal? Think like a salesperson.** Managing vision and mission is a lot like selling. You have a product you think others would buy if they knew about it. Each customer is a little different. What features and benefits would they be looking for? What would they be willing to pay in terms of time and commitment? What are their objections likely to be? How will you answer them? How are you going to ask for the order?

☐ **9. Too focused on short-term priorities? Become future oriented.** The very nature of missions and visions is that they are statements about the future. A good manager of visions and purpose would have to be able to talk the future. The future in general. The future of the industry and the market. The future of this organization. Futuring is a series of educated "what ifs." What if there is life on other planets? Will they need our products? What if fusion is possible? Will cheaper energy impact us? When over 50% of the wealth in the U.S. is held by retired baby boomers, will that change anything we are doing? Will the green movement cause any opportunities for us? In order to get good at futuring, you need to read widely, especially outside of your industry. Read *THE FUTURIST,* a magazine of the World Future Society. Watch *Modern Marvels* on cable. Try to attend one meeting a year to hear futurists speculate on what they see. *More help? – See #46 Perspective.*

☐ **10. Conflicted about the vision and purpose? Own the message.** Most of the time, you may be delivering someone else's view of the future. Top management and a consultant created the mission, vision and strategy off somewhere in the woods all by themselves. You may or may not have been asked for any input. You may even have some doubts about it yourself. Your role is to manage this vision and mission, not your personal one. Do not offer conditional statements to your audience, "I've got some concerns myself." Don't let it be known to others that you are not fully on board. Your job is to deliver and manage the message. While it's okay to admit your problems in dealing with change, it's not okay to admit them in dealing with this change. If you have better ideas, try to get them to the people who form missions in your organization. *More help? – See #22 Ethics and Values.*

Some Develop-in-Place Assignments

☐ Build a multifunctional project team to tackle a common business issue or problem.

☐ Manage a temporary group of "green," inexperienced people as their coach, teacher, guide, mentor, etc.

☐ Launch a new product, service, or process.

☐ Be a change agent; create a symbol for change; lead the rallying cry; champion a significant change and implementation.

☐ Work on a project that involves travel and study of an international issue, acquisition, or joint venture and report back to management.

People buy into the leader before they buy into the vision.
John C. Maxwell – American leadership expert, speaker, and author

Suggested Readings

Adair, J. (2003). *The inspirational leader.* London: Kogan Page.

Angelica, E. (2001). *The Fieldstone Alliance guide to crafting effective mission and vision statements.* St. Paul, MN: Amherst H. Wilder Foundation.

Bacon, T. R., & Pugh, D. G. (2003). *Winning behavior: What the smartest, most successful companies do differently.* New York: AMACOM.

Black, J. S., & Gregersen, H. B. (2002). *Leading strategic change: Breaking through the brain barrier.* Upper Saddle River, NJ: Financial Times/Prentice Hall.

Bossidy, L., & Charan, R. (with Burck, C.). (2002). *Execution: The discipline of getting things done.* New York: Crown Business.

Center for Creative Leadership, Cartwright, T., & Baldwin, D. (2007). *Communicating your vision.* Hoboken, NJ: Pfeiffer.

Collins, J. C., & Porras, J. I. (2002). *Built to last.* New York: HarperBusiness.

Davidson, H. (2004). *The committed enterprise: How to make vision and values work* (2nd ed.). Boston: Butterworth-Heinemann.

Futurist Magazine. http://www.wfs.org.

Hamel, G. (2002). *Leading the revolution.* Boston: Harvard Business School Press.

Heath, C., & Heath, D. (2007). *Made to stick: Why some ideas survive and others die.* New York: Random House.

Kotter, J. (2008). *A sense of urgency.* Boston: Harvard Business School Press.

Kotter, J. P., & Cohen, D. S. (2002). *The heart of change: Real-life stories of how people change their organizations.* Boston: Harvard Business School Press.

Lasley, M. (2004). *Courageous visions: How to unleash passionate energy in your life and your organization.* Burlington, PA: Discovery Press.

Mortensen, K., & Allen, R. (2004). *Maximum influence: The 12 universal laws of power persuasion.* New York: AMACOM.

Reed, P. J. (2001). *Extraordinary leadership: Creating strategies for change.* London: Kogan Page.

Tellis, G. J., & Golder, P. N. (2001). *Will and vision.* New York: McGraw-Hill.

Thornton, P. B. (2002). *Be the leader, make the difference.* Irvine, CA: Griffin Trade Paperback.

Welch, J., & Byrne, J. A. (2002). *Jack: Straight from the gut.* New York: Warner Books.

66 Work/Life Balance

Knowing when not to work hard is as important as knowing when to.
Harvey Mackay – American author and business motivational speaker

Unskilled

- ☐ Lacks balance between work and personal life
- ☐ Overdoes one at the harmful expense of the other
- ☐ May be a workaholic
- ☐ May be bored off-work or can't relax
- ☐ May be a poor time manager and priority setter; may just react
- ☐ Can't turn off one area of life and fully concentrate on the other
- ☐ Can't keep multiple and mixed priorities going at one time
- ☐ Carries troubles from one area of life into the other
- ☐ Can only seem to manage one or the other

Select one to three of the competencies listed below to use as a substitute for this competency if you decide not to work on it directly.

SUBSTITUTES: 1,39,45,47,50,54,55,62

Skilled

- ☐ Maintains a conscious balance between work and personal life so that one doesn't dominate the other
- ☐ Is not one-dimensional
- ☐ Knows how to attend to both
- ☐ Gets what he/she wants from both

Overused Skill

- ☐ May not be flexible enough when work or personal life demands change dramatically
- ☐ May not be willing to adjust one at the expense of the other
- ☐ May value balance over temporary discomfort
- ☐ May try to force his/her view of balance on others

Select one to three of the competencies listed below to work on to compensate for an overuse of this skill.

COMPENSATORS: 2,6,11,12,17,22,23,32,40,45,46,50,54,55

Some Causes

- ☐ A worrier
- ☐ Can't relax
- ☐ Off-work is not exciting
- ☐ Overly ambitious
- ☐ Poor priority setting
- ☐ Time management
- ☐ Too intense
- ☐ Workaholic

Leadership Architect® Factors and Clusters

This competency is in the Personal and Interpersonal Skills Factor (VI). This competency is in the Balancing Work/Life Cluster (U). You may want to check other competencies in the same Factor/Cluster for related tips.

The Map

Research on well-being shows that the best adjusted people are generally the busiest people, on- and off-work. Balance is not achieved only by people who are not busy and have the time. It's the off-work part of balance that gives most people problems. With downsizing, wondering if you'll be in the next layoff, and 60 hour work weeks, many people are too exhausted to do much more than refuel off-work. Nonetheless, frustration and feeling unidimensional are often the result of not forcing the issue of balance in one's life. There is special pressure on those with full dual responsibilities—they have full-time jobs and they have full-time care giver and home management duties.

Some Remedies

- ☐ **1. Overcommitting? Don't put all your eggs in one basket.** Add things to your off-work life. This was a major finding of a stress study at AT&T of busy, high-potential women and men. It may seem counterintuitive, but the best adjusted people forced themselves to structure off-work activities just as much as on-work activities. Otherwise work drives everything else out. Those with dual responsibilities (primary care giver and home manager and a full-time job holder) need to use their management strengths and skills more at home. What makes your work life successful? Batch tasks, bundle similar activities together, delegate to children or set up pools with coworkers or neighbors to share tasks such as car pooling, soccer games, Scouts, etc. Pay to have some things done that are not mission-critical to your home needs. Organize and manage efficiently. Have a schedule. Set up goals and plans. Use some of your work skills more off-work.

☐ **2. Not sure how to define balance? Learn what works for you.** Balance has nothing to do with 50/50 or clock time. It has to do with how we use the time we have. It doesn't mean for every hour of work, you must have an hour off-work. It means finding what is a reasonable balance for you. Is it a few hours a week unencumbered by work worries? Is it four breaks a day? Is it some solitude before bedtime? Is it playing with your kids more? Is it having an actual (rather than "Did you remember the dry cleaning?") conversation with your spouse (partner) each day? Is it a community, religious or sports activity that you're passionate about? Schedule them; structure them into your life. Negotiate with your partner; don't just accept your life as a given. Define what balance is for you and include your spouse or friends or family in the definition.

☐ **3. Weighed down? Concentrate on the present.** There's time and there's focused time. Busy people with not much time learn to get into the present tense without carrying the rest of their burdens, concerns and deadlines with them. When you have only one hour to read or play with the kids or play racquetball or sew—be there. Have fun. You won't solve any problems during the 60 minutes anyway. Train your mind to be where you are. Focus on the moment.

☐ **4. Leaving your strengths behind? Create deadlines, urgencies, and structures off-work.** One tactic that helps is for people to use their strengths from work off-work. If you are organized, organize something. If you are very personable, get together a regular group. If you are competitive, set up a regular match. As common-sensical as this seems, AT&T found that people with poor off-work lives did not use their strengths off-work. They truly left them at the office.

☐ **5. Can't say no? Recognize you can't do it all.** What are your NOs? If you don't have any, chances are you'll be frustrated on both sides of your life. Part of maturity is letting go of nice, even fun and probably valuable, activities. What are you hanging on to? What can't you say no to at the office that really isn't a priority? Where do you make yourself a patsy? If your saying no irritates people initially, this may be the price. You can usually soften it, however, by explaining what you are trying to do. Most people won't take it personally if you say you're going to pick up your child or maybe coach his/her soccer team or you can't help with this project because of an explicit priority which is critical to your unit. Give reasons that don't downgrade the activity you're giving up. It's not that it's insignificant; it just didn't quite make the cut.

☐ **6. Bored? Make your off-work life more exciting.** Many of us want as little stress as we can get off-work and seeking this comfort ends up as boredom. What are three really exciting things you and/or your family could do? Work will always be exciting or at least full of activity. Combating this stimulus overload means finding something you can be passionate about off the job.

☐ **7. Can't get your mind off work? If you can't relax once you leave work, schedule breakpoints or boundaries.** One of the great things about the human brain is that it responds to change; signal it that work is over—play music in your car, immediately play with your children, go for a walk, swim for 20 minutes—give your mind a clear and repetitious breakpoint. Try to focus all your energy where you are. At work, worry about work things and not life things. When you hit the driveway, worry about life things and leave work things at the office. Schedule a time every week for financial management and worries. Try to concentrate your worry time where it will do some good.

☐ **8. Unable to let go? Compartmentalize.** If your problem goes beyond that—you're three days into vacation and still can't relax—write down what you're worried about, which is almost always unresolved problems. Write down everything you can think of. Don't worry about complete sentences—just get it down. You'll usually find it's hard to fill a page and there will be only three topics—work problems, problems with people, and a to-do list. Note any ideas that come up for dealing with them. This will usually shut off your worry response, which is nothing but a mental reminder of things unresolved. Since we're all creatures of habit, though, the same worries will pop up again. Then you have to say to yourself (as silly as this seems), "I've done everything I can do on that right now," or "That's right, I remember, I'll do it later." Obviously, this tactic works when we're not on vacation as well.

☐ **9. Do you truly live to work? If you love work, and you're really a happy but unbalanced workaholic, try tip #4.** If that doesn't work, you need to see yourself 20 years from now. Find three people who remind you of you but are 20 years older. Are they happy? How are their personal lives? Any problems with stress or depression? If this is OK with you, protect yourself with #7. If you don't do something to refresh yourself, your effectiveness will eventually suffer or you'll burn out.

☐ **10. Not sure what to do? Talk to people who have your best interests at heart.** Seek counsel from those who accept you for who you are and with whom you can be candid. What do they want for you? Ask them how they would change your balance.

Some Develop-in-Place Assignments

- ☐ Manage the outplacement of a group of people.
- ☐ Seek out and use a seed budget to create and pursue a personal idea, product, or service.
- ☐ Join a self-help or support group.
- ☐ Serve for a year or more with a community agency.
- ☐ Attend a self-awareness/assessment course that includes feedback.

If A is a success in life, then A equals x plus y plus z.
Work is x; y is play; and z is keeping your mouth shut.
Albert Einstein – German-born Nobel Prize-winning physicist

Suggested Readings

Alboher, M. (2007). *One person/multiple careers: A new model for work/life success.* Boston: Business Plus.

Cohen, D., & Prusak, L. (2001). *In good company: How social capital makes organizations work.* Boston: Harvard Business School Press.

Deering, A., Dilts, R., & Russell, J. (2002). *Alpha leadership: Tools for business leaders who want more from life.* West Sussex, England: John Wiley & Sons.

Ferriss, T. (2007). *The 4-hour workweek: Escape 9–5, live anywhere, and join the new rich.* New York: Crown Publishing Group.

Germer, F. (2001). *Hard won wisdom: More than 50 extraordinary women mentor you to find self-awareness, perspective, and balance.* New York: Perigee.

Glanz, B. (2003). *Balancing acts.* Chicago: Dearborn Trade.

Gordon, G. E. (2001). *Turn it off: How to unplug from the anytime-anywhere office without disconnecting your career.* New York: Three Rivers Press.

Hakim, C. (2000). *Work-lifestyle choices in the 21st century: Preference theory.* Oxford, UK: Oxford University Press.

Harvard Business School Press. (2000). *Harvard Business Review on work and life balance.* Boston: Harvard Business School Press.

Jackson, M. (2002). *What's happening to home: Balancing work, life and refuge in the information age.* Notre Dame, IN: Sorin Books.

Johnson, T., & Spizman, R. F. (2008). *Will work from home: Earn the cash—without the commute.* New York: Berkley Publishing Group.

Lewis, S., & Cooper, C. L. (2005). *Work-life integration: Case studies of organizational change.* West Sussex, England: John Wiley & Sons.

Mainiero, L. A., & Sullivan, S. E. (2006). *The opt-out revolt: Why people are leaving companies to create kaleidoscope careers.* Mountain View, CA: Davies-Black.

Matthews, J., & Dennis, J. (2003). *Lessons from the edge: Survival skills for starting and growing a company.* New York: Oxford University Press.

Merrill, A. R., & Merrill, R. R. (2003). *Life matters: Creating a dynamic balance of work, family, time and money.* New York: McGraw-Hill.

Sawi, B. (2000). *Coming up for air: How to build a balanced life in a workaholic world.* New York: Hyperion.

St. James, E. (2001). *Simplify your work life: Ways to change the way you work so you have more time to live.* New York: Hyperion.

Williams, J. (2000). *Unbending gender: Why family and work conflict and what to do about it.* Oxford, UK: Oxford University Press.

67 Written Communications

Writing is a lot easier if you have something to say.
Sholem Asch – Polish-born American Jewish novelist

Unskilled

- ☐ Not a clear communicator in writing
- ☐ May be hard to tell what the point is
- ☐ May be too wordy or too terse or have grammar/usage problems
- ☐ May not construct a logical argument well
- ☐ May not adjust to different audiences; may have a single style of writing

Select one to three of the competencies listed below to use as a substitute for this competency if you decide not to work on it directly.

SUBSTITUTES: 5,15,27,37,47,49,51,65

Skilled

- ☐ Is able to write clearly and succinctly in a variety of communication settings and styles
- ☐ Can get messages across that have the desired effect

Overused Skill

- ☐ May invest too much time crafting communications
- ☐ May too often try for perfection when something less would do the job
- ☐ May be overly critical of the written work of others

Select one to three of the competencies listed below to work on to compensate for an overuse of this skill.

COMPENSATORS: 1,2,3,12,15,17,27,32,38,44,46,48,50,51,53,57,62

Some Causes

- ☐ Dull writing
- ☐ Too busy
- ☐ Too wordy; too long
- ☐ Hard to tell what your point is
- ☐ Disorganized
- ☐ Grammar/usage problems
- ☐ Don't write for the audience

Leadership Architect® Factors and Clusters

This competency is in the Organizational Positioning Skills Factor (V). This competency is in the Communicating Effectively Cluster (L) with: 49. You may want to check other competencies in the same Factor/Cluster for related tips.

The Map

You are what you write. Good writing is that which efficiently and effectively communicates to readers the points and messages you want them to know. No more. No less. It respects the time and the intelligence of the reader. Learn to write as if you had three minutes to present an argument to a group whose opinion is important to you. The border patrol has stopped you, drawn weapons and asked why you are there. What would you do? You would probably speak their language, make it clear what you want, use as few words as you could, sound plaintive, and reinforce key points that argue in your favor. Think of what you wouldn't do. You wouldn't ramble, expect them to guess your point or use vague words or jargon that would baffle them. Good writing is the same. Use the least amount of print possible to communicate your message.

Some Remedies

- ☐ **1. Lacking focus or clarity? Prepare an outline before you write.** Too many people write without a plan. Go through a checklist. What's your objective? What are your main points? Outline your main points in logical support of the objective. What are five things you want them to know and remember about each point? When you write, any sentence that does not relate to the objective and the points shouldn't be there. What would the ideal reader say if interviewed 15 minutes after he/she finishes reading your piece? Who's your audience? How much do they know that you don't have to repeat? How much background should you include? What questions will the audience have when they read your piece? Are they covered? What's the setting for readers? How much time will they spend? How long can it be? Pick up something you've written lately and take a test. Does it have a thesis? Does each paragraph have a topic sentence—a subject? If you state one sentence per paragraph, do the statements follow logically? *More help? – See #47 Planning.*
- ☐ **2. Losing the reader's attention? Keep to the plan.** Follow your outline. State your message or purpose in a lead single sentence or two early in the document. Any reader should immediately know why he/she is reading the piece. Then outline the three to five chunks of your argument to support your thesis. Any more and the readers won't follow it. What in the introduction will grab the reader and rivet him/her on your message? A story, a fact, a comparison, a quote, a photo, a cartoon? What are five

techniques you will use to get and hold his/her attention? What style would work best? What are your priority points, and how will you explain them? Some points are made better by example, some by the logic of the argument, some by facts or stories. You should vary how you drive home your point because you will reach more people.

☐ **3. Not connecting? Write for a targeted audience.** Unfortunately, one document generally does not play equally well across differing audiences. Many times you will have to adjust the length, tone, pace, style, and even the message and how you couch it for different audiences. If you are writing a single message to multiple audiences, always ask yourself how are they different? Adjust accordingly. Writing for a higher level manager? Use an executive summary. One page. Just like your outline. At the end, tell the person what decision you are asking him or her to make. If the executive indicates interest, follow with the longer document. A support group? What resources will you need to support this activity? They probably need detail to line up their schedules. Legal? They need why, the history, parallels in the marketplace, legal potholes. Direct reports? They need implementation detail to understand the goals and outcomes you are considering. In one sense, you need to write the entire document and then chunk it up for the various audiences. Don't try to make one document stretch. *More help? – See #15 Customer Focus.*

☐ **4. Too much information? Don't drown the reader in detail he/she doesn't need or can't use.** Use detail only when it's essential to understanding your argument/thesis. What are five facts that show your point? Even if writing a lengthy report, those five facts should be highlighted in a paragraph or two, not revealed slowly. Readers will forget why they are reading about each problem since problems usually have more than one cause, and they will become distracted thinking about other matters. Few people read an almanac; if your argument is data driven, use the few; put the many in appendices.

☐ **5. Too dense? Provide headlines and checkpoints for the reader, just as a newspaper does.** If the communication is more than two or three pages, break it into headings such as "The Purchasing Problem," "Why the Purchasing System Is Breaking Down," "Purchasing Options," "Questions to Answer," etc.

☐ **6. Difficult to understand? Don't lose your readers with poor use of words.** Eliminate embellishing words such as very, great, exciting, etc. Most adjectives and adverbs add nothing, cause the reader to pause, or come across as overstatements. Arguments are carried by logic and facts, not filler. Avoid stringing abstract words together—usually nouns—such as "optimal personnel interface." Substitute common equivalents for these words. The numbing string of nouns above actually means "the best way for people to talk to each other." Since all word processing systems have a thesaurus embedded in them, use this if stumped. Use Spell Check to correct misspellings and to spot commonly misused words such as irregardless (for regardless), or orientate (for orient). Poor usage is more difficult to spot. Perhaps the easiest method is to have someone check your grammar. Another more difficult but longer-term strategy is to get a copy of *The Elements of Style* by Strunk and White, a simple guide to the most common problems in grammar and what to do about them.

☐ **7. Not capturing attention? Use action and visuals.** Pep up your writing. Use words that call up pictures whenever possible. Vivid, visual arguments are best remembered. (Can you make the reader see the purchasing problem? "The boxes were stacked to the ceiling, blocking two rows.") Vary sentence length and type. Too many writers fall into the trap of "The quick brown fox jumped over the lazy dog's back"—a string of simple sentences made long with lots of filler. Turning verbs into nouns makes writing dull—say, "X organized," not, "the organization was accomplished by...." Use action—or active—words. Avoid "is" and "are," double negatives like "not bad" or veiled insults like "not very good." Say what you mean with active words: If a sentence has multiple commas, or multiple clauses, it may be too long. Say it out loud. Could you say it in half the words? Long, tortuous sentences usually come from turning the subject into the object of the sentence. In "Employees are inspired by X, Y, and Z," the employees are passive recipients of X, Y, and Z, which comprise the point of the sentence. Decide what inspires employees and put it first. Try a little drama. In contrast to the above point, if you want to emphasize something, put it last: "In conclusion, doing X increased profit 14%" is more likely to make the point than "Profit increased 14% by...."

☐ **8. Redundant? Reduce repetition.** If your writing is repetitious, usually your second or third statement or qualifier will be the best. Often we write something, decide it needs clarification, and write another sentence or two to explain the first. In reading it over, we notice this and scratch out the later sentences, making the problem worse. First, check the later statements to see if they are better statements; if not, combine the sentences into one.

☐ **9. Difficulty conveying your point in writing? Write like you speak.** Most people who don't write well, speak better than they write. Use this to your advantage. Talk out your argument with a friend, say it out loud, use a tape recorder, buy one of the new word recognition software programs. Then reduce your argument to the logical format required by writing.

☐ **10. Come across better when you say it? Don't always write like you speak.** Watch out for cute and humorous remarks. What is funny in person often seems cynical on paper. Watch out for strongly worded statements. While you may get away with them in person because you have a soft voice, they will come across as hard and uncompromising in writing. Watch out for jargon and other $1,000 words that bore readers or confuse them. This might be fine in person because you can gauge reactions and clear up any furrowed-brow responses; in writing, you can't see your audience. And don't ever, ever, write when you're angry. If you do, put it away overnight. Read it the next day, extract the points, rewrite it, then throw the original missile away. That's what Lincoln did and he was pretty successful.

Some Develop-in-Place Assignments

- ☐ Write a speech for someone higher up in the organization.
- ☐ Work on a team writing a proposal to obtain significant government or foundation grants or funding of an activity.
- ☐ Write a proposal for a new policy, process, mission, charter, product, service, or system, and present and sell it to top management.
- ☐ Draft a mission statement, policy proposal, charter, or goal statement and get feedback from others.
- ☐ Write public press releases for the organization.

Do but take care to express yourself in a plain, easy manner,
in well-chosen, significant and decent terms, and to give a harmonious
and pleasing turn to your periods: study to explain your thoughts,
and set them in the truest light, labouring as much as possible,
not to leave them dark nor intricate, but clear and intelligible.
Miguel de Cervantes – Spanish dramatist, poet, and author

Suggested Readings

Abell, A. (2003). *Business grammar, style & usage: The most used desk reference for articulate and polished business writing and speaking by executives worldwide*. Boston, MA: Aspatore, Inc.

Alred, G. J., Brusaw, C. T., & Oliu, W. E. (2006). *The business writer's handbook* (8th ed.). New York: St. Martin's Press.

Appleman, J. E. (2008). *10 Steps to successful business writing*. Alexandria, VA: ASTD Press.

Bailey, E. P., Jr. (2007). *Writing and speaking at work* (4th ed.). Upper Saddle River, NJ: Prentice Hall.

Baldoni, J. (2003). *Great communication secrets of great leaders*. New York: McGraw-Hill.

Bond, A. (2005). *300+ Successful business letters for all occasions* (2nd ed.). Hauppauge, NY: Barron's Educational Series.

Booher, D. (2001). *E writing: 21st Century tools for effective communication*. New York: Pocket Books.

Bovée, C. L., & Thill, J. V. (2007). *Business communication today* (9th ed.). Upper Saddle River, NJ: Prentice Hall.

Cunningham, H., & Greene, B. (2002). *The business style handbook: An A-to-Z guide for writing on the job with tips from communications experts at the Fortune 500*. Chicago: McGraw-Hill.

Davis, K. (2005). *The McGraw-Hill 36-hour course in business writing and communication*. New York: McGraw-Hill.

Dumaine, D. (2004). *Write to the top: Writing for corporate success*. New York: Random House Trade Paperbacks.

Ellison, P. T., & Barry, R. E. (2006). *Business English for the 21st century* (4th ed.). Upper Saddle River, NJ: Prentice Hall.

Harvard Business School Press. (2003). *Business communication*. Boston: Harvard Business School Press.

Iacone, S. J. (2003). *Write to the point: How to communicate in business with style and purpose*. Franklin Lakes, NJ: Career Press.

Lindsell-Roberts, S. (2004). *Strategic business letters and e-mail*. Boston: Houghton Mifflin Company.

Meyer, V., Sebranek, P., & Van Rys, J. (2004). *Write for business*. Burlington, WI: UpWrite Press.

O'Quinn, K. (2006). *Perfect phrases for business letters*. New York: McGraw-Hill.

Picardi, R. P. (2001). *Skills of workplace communication: A handbook for T & D specialists and their organizations*. Westport, CT: Quorum Books.

Ryan, K. (2003). *Write up the corporate ladder: Successful writers reveal the techniques that help you write with ease and get ahead*. New York: AMACOM.

The 19 Career Stallers and Stoppers

There are no competencies 68-80 or 91-100.
Those numbers are reserved for future additions.

Performance Dimensions (numbered 81-90)
can be found in FYI for Performance Management.™

101 *Unable to* Adapt to Differences

The world hates change, yet it is the only thing that has brought progress.
Charles F. Kettering – American inventor

A Problem

- ☐ Has trouble working with and adapting to new or different bosses, strategies, plans and programs, cultures, philosophies or technical developments
- ☐ Might disagree inappropriately or too vocally with top management on mission, values, strategies, and tactics
- ☐ Would not do well with a person he/she disagreed with

Not A Problem

- ☐ Comfortable with change
- ☐ Challenges constructively but then goes along with change
- ☐ Can support things he/she doesn't totally agree with
- ☐ Easily makes transitions to the new and different
- ☐ Relates well to bosses
- ☐ Can deal with bad bosses reasonably well
- ☐ Can handle conflict evenhandedly
- ☐ Open to the views of others

Some Causes

- ☐ Arrogant
- ☐ Can't handle conflicting views
- ☐ Defensive
- ☐ Hangs on hoping to make it without changing
- ☐ Like own ideas too much
- ☐ Low risk taker
- ☐ Narrow in scope and interests
- ☐ Not open to new approaches
- ☐ Not strategic
- ☐ Perfectionist
- ☐ Poor interpersonal skills
- ☐ Prefer the tried and true

- ☐ Problems with authority figures
- ☐ Problems with diversity
- ☐ Rigid values
- ☐ Too busy to change
- ☐ Too comfortable
- ☐ Very smart and successful

Other Causes

BEING UNSKILLED AT: 2,4,8,11,16,21,32,33,40,45,46,48,55,56,58,61,64

OVERUSING: 9,16,22,29,32,35,39,47,52

Leadership Architect® Factors and Clusters

This competency is in the Trouble with People Factor (VII) (S1). This competency is in the Doesn't Relate Well to Others Cluster (V) with: 106, 108, 112. You may want to check other competencies in the same Factor/Cluster for related tips.

The Map

This has become one of, if not the most common reason promising people get in trouble. While you may be performing well now, people say you're inflexible or can't handle disagreement. You may have gotten in your comfort zone and be uncomfortable with change; there may be certain types of authority figures you have trouble dealing with. You are not updating and keeping yourself fresh.

Some Remedies

☐ **1. Defensive? Ask for feedback and input.** Defensiveness and arrogance are major blockages to adapting to change. Defensive and arrogant people get less feedback from others. They don't listen. Interrupt. See change as a personal threat and an indictment of their current thinking and practices. People don't like working with or around defensive and arrogant people. Defensive and arrogant people are typically out of the information loop so they hear about the change late, which increases their defensive reaction. Even though it may not be true, defensiveness and arrogance are seen as resistance to input and therefore change. *More help? – See #104 Arrogant and #108 Defensiveness.*

☐ **2. Resisting new ideas? Try something new and give it a chance.** People say you're stuck in the past. For some reason, you resist anything or anybody new or different. You're the last to get on board a new initiative. You're from Missouri (the "Show Me" state); we have to prove it to you before you'll move. Surveys done with a major outplacement firm show that those most likely to be let go during a downsizing have good technical, individual skills, but are seen as not learning to do anything new or different, and resisting change. You can't survive today without keeping you and your skills fresh. There's not much room anymore for someone stuck in the past. In your day-to-day interactions with people, your style may make you appear closed or blocked to new or different points of view. Your first job is to turn off your evaluator/rejector program and learn to listen more. *More help? – See #33 Listening.* Ask more questions—"How did you conclude a change is necessary? Do you prefer the change to what we're now doing?" If you disagree, give your reasons first. Then invite criticism of your response. Turn the disagreement back to the nature of the problem or strategy the change is aimed at—"What are we trying to solve? What causes it? What questions should be asked and answered? What objective standards could we use to measure success?"

☐ **3. Think you know it all? Pause to listen, ask questions, and consider alternative viewpoints.** Answers. Solutions. Conclusions. Statements. Dictates. That's the staple of resisters and dismissers. Instant output. Sharp reactions. This may be getting you in trouble. You jump to conclusions, categorically dismiss what others say about the need for change, use challenging words in an absolute tone. People then see you as closed or combative. More negatively, they may believe you think they're stupid or ill-informed because they suggested change. Use gentler words—"Another factor is...," "I see this a bit differently," "I think the problem is more one of...." People usually respond well to qualifiers; then you can state your point directly. Give people a chance to talk without interruption. If you're seen as intolerant or closed, people will often stumble over words in their haste to talk with you or shortcut their argument since they assume you're not listening anyway. Ask a question, invite them to disagree with you, present their argument back to them softly, let them save face no matter what. Add a 15-second pause into your transactions before you say anything and add two clarifying questions per transaction to signal you're listening and want to understand the need for change. *More help? – See #33 Listening and #41 Patience.*

☐ **4. Too rigid? Articulate your values in an enlightened way.** You may be seen as rigid in your values stances and unwilling to accept, or even see, those of others. *See Overdoing #22 Ethics and Values.* Rigid stances often come from childhood and early adult experiences. You need to know why you hold these values and critically examine if they are appropriate here. Statements of belief are pronouncements—a true value holds up to action scrutiny; you can say why you hold it, how it plays out in different situations, and what happens when it conflicts with other values. You may have reduced your beliefs to rigid commandments.

☐ **5. Selectively resistant? Evaluate ideas, not people.** Do you adapt to some and not to others? You probably have good people buckets and bad people buckets and signal your disagreement with them to the bad bucket groups or individuals. You may have good group buckets and bad group buckets—gender, race, age, origin. Learn to understand without accepting or judging. Listen, take notes, ask questions, and be able to make their case as well as they can. Pick something in their argument you agree with. Present your argument in terms of the problem only—why you think this is the best manner to deal with a mutually agreed upon problem. A careful observer should not be able to tell your assessment of people or their arguments at the time. Find someone who is a fair observer and get a critique. Was I fair? Did I treat everyone the same? Were my objections based on reasoning against standards and not directed at people?

☐ **6. Too comfortable? Find new solutions.** You may be caught in your comfort zone. You rely on historical, tried-and-true solutions. You use what you know and have seen or done before—so you naturally resist anything you yet don't know or understand. When faced with a new issue, challenge or problem, first figure out what causes it. Don't go to your past for the solution or conclusion first. Keep asking why, see how many causes you can come up with and how many organizing buckets you can put them in. This increases the chance of a better solution because you can see more connections. Look for patterns in data, don't just collect information. *More help? – See #51 Problem Solving.*

☐ **7. Need a fresh perspective? Rely on novices for valuable perspectives.** You may be highly intelligent and quite skilled in your area. You may work around people who aren't as informed or educated as you are. You may be in a position of essentially dictating what should be done. When others less experienced than you suggest change, you may quickly dismiss it. But you don't have to make it demeaning or painful. Studies of creativity show that people less familiar with an area can contribute some unique and valuable suggestions because they are not trapped in the knowledge. You need to switch to an idea facilitator—tell him/her how you think about the need for change, don't just fire out solutions. Tell him/her what you think the problem is, what questions need to be asked and answered, how you would go about finding out, what you think some likely solutions might be. Listen to what he/she has to say.

☐ **8. Lack perspective? Broaden your horizons.** First, *see #5 Business Acumen, #46 Perspective, and #58 Strategic Agility.* Then do an independent study of the issues in disagreement and come up with your own perspective. Do others the courtesy of analyzing their proposed solution as if it were valid as well.

- ☐ **9. Ready to experience something new? Be an early adopter of a change.** Find some new thing, technique, software, tool, system, process or skill relevant to your activity. Privately become an expert in it. Read the books. Get certified. Visit somewhere where it's already being done. Then surprise everyone and be the first to introduce the change into your world. Sell it. Train others. Integrate it into your work.
- ☐ **10. Ready to commit to being open? Fix the root cause.** Whatever applies in Some Causes, you will have to work on *#3 Approachability, and #31 Interpersonal Savvy.* Until you signal repeatedly that you are open to others, interested in what they have to say, share things you don't have to share, invite people to talk with you and then listen, little will come of this effort. You will have to persevere, endure some rejection, and perhaps some angry or dismissive remarks in order to balance the situation. Mentally rehearse so you're not blindsided by this. It would be a rare group of people who would respond to your overtures without making you squirm a bit because you have caused them pain in the past.

Some Develop-in-Place Assignments

- ☐ Make peace with an enemy or someone you've disappointed with a product or service or someone you've had some trouble with or don't get along with very well.
- ☐ Handle a tough negotiation with an internal or external client or customer.
- ☐ Manage a group of resistant people with low morale through an unpopular change or project.
- ☐ Work on a project that involves travel and study of an international issue, acquisition, or joint venture and report back to management.
- ☐ Go on a business trip to a foreign country you've not been to before.

It is not our differences that divide us. It is our inability to recognize, accept, and celebrate those differences.
Audre Lorde – American poet, teacher, and activist

Suggested Readings

Badowski, R. (with Gittines, R.). (2003). *Managing up: How to forge an effective relationship with those above you.* New York: Currency.

Beyerlein, M. M., Freedman, S., McGee, C., & Moran, L. (2002). *Beyond teams: Building the collaborative organization.* San Francisco: Jossey-Bass.

Calzada, L. (2007). *180 Ways to effectively deal with change: Get over it! Get with it! Get to it!* Flower Mound, TX: Walk the Talk Company.

Cartwright, T. (2003). *Managing conflict with peers.* Greensboro, NC: Center for Creative Leadership.

Cloke, K., & Goldsmith, J. (2000). *Resolving conflicts at work: A complete guide for everyone on the job.* San Francisco: Jossey-Bass.

Cloke, K., & Goldsmith, J. (2005). *Resolving conflicts at work: Eight strategies for everyone on the job* (Rev. ed.). San Francisco: Jossey-Bass.

Forsyth, P. (2007). *Manage your boss: 8 Steps to creating the ideal working relationship.* London: Cyan Communications.

Fullan, M. (2004). *Leading in a culture of change: Personal action guide and workbook.* San Francisco: Jossey-Bass.

Gerzon, M. (2006). *Leading through conflict: How successful leaders transform differences into opportunities.* Boston: Harvard Business School Press.

Goldsmith, M., & Reiter, M. (2007). *What got you here won't get you there: How successful people become even more successful.* New York: Hyperion.

Harvard Business School Press. (2007). *Managing stress* (Pocket Mentor). Boston: Harvard Business School Press.

Harvey, C. P., & Allard, M. J. (2008). *Understanding and managing diversity: Readings, cases, and exercises* (4th ed.). Upper Saddle River, NJ: Prentice Hall.

Kantor, S., Kram, K. E., & Sala, F. (2008). Change factor: Making the case for executive adaptability. *Leadership in Action, 27*(6), 8-12.

Lukaszewski, J. (2008). *Why should the boss listen to you? The seven disciplines of the trusted strategic advisor.* San Francisco: Jossey-Bass.

Moran, R. T., Harris, P. R., & Moran, S. V. (2007). *Managing cultural differences: Global leadership strategies for the 21st century* (7th ed.). Burlington, MA: Butterworth-Heinemann.

Pascale, R. T., Millemann, M., & Gioja, L. (2001). *Surfing the edge of chaos: The laws of nature and the new laws of business.* New York: Three Rivers Press.

Popejoy, B., & McManigle, B. J. (2002). *Managing conflict with direct reports.* Greensboro, NC: Center for Creative Leadership.

Salkowitz, R. (2008). *Generation blend: Managing across the technology age gap.* Hoboken, NJ: John Wiley & Sons.

Scott, S. (2004). *Fierce conversations: Achieving success at work and in life, one conversation at a time* (Rev. ed.). New York: Viking Press.

Sharpe, D. A., & Johnson, E. (2002). *Managing conflict with your boss.* Greensboro, NC: Center for Creative Leadership.

Sindell, M., & Sindell, T. (2006). *Sink or swim: New job. New boss. 12 Weeks to get it right.* Avon, MA: Adams Media.

Waitzkin, J. (2008). *The art of learning: An inner journey to optimal performance.* New York: Free Press.

Wall, S. J. (2004). *On the fly: Executing strategy in a changing world.* New York: John Wiley & Sons.

Wilkinson, D. (2006). *The ambiguity advantage: What great leaders are great at.* Hampshire, England: Palgrave Macmillan.

102 *Poor* Administrator

The triumph over anything is a matter of organization.
Kurt Vonnegut – American novelist and essayist

A Problem

- ☐ Has low detail-orientation
- ☐ Lets things fall through the cracks
- ☐ Overcommits and underdelivers
- ☐ Misses key details
- ☐ Forgets undocumented commitments
- ☐ Has to scramble to pull things together at the last minute
- ☐ Moves on without completing the task

Not A Problem

- ☐ Well organized and detail skilled
- ☐ Reliable—keeps tabs on work in process; remembers commitments
- ☐ Good administrator; keeps things on track
- ☐ Sets tight priorities
- ☐ Uses time well
- ☐ Says no if he/she can't get to it
- ☐ Completes most things on time and in time

Some Causes

- ☐ Can't say no to people; get overloaded
- ☐ Impatient
- ☐ Poor grasp of due process as seen by others
- ☐ Poor mental organization
- ☐ Poor sense of time
- ☐ Procrastinate
- ☐ Too busy to get organized

Other Causes

BEING UNSKILLED AT: 12,13,16,18,20,23,24,27,34,35,36,39,41,47,50,52,59,62,67
OVERUSING: 1,9,14,24,28,46,58,65

Leadership Architect® Factors and Clusters

This competency is in the Trouble with Results Factor (VIII) (S2). This competency is in the Doesn't Deliver Results Cluster (Z) with: 118. You may want to check other competencies in the same Factor/Cluster for related tips.

The Map

People differ widely on personal organization, ranging from the perfectionist with everything having to be just so, to the disorganized absent-minded professor never knowing where things are and never being on time with anything. There are really two issues. The first is personal disorganization. The fallout is having too much to do, being late on commitments, having to work longer hours to keep up, losing key documents, forgetting appointments, not doing things completely that have to be redone later, etc. It leads to personal inefficiency and ineffective use of personal time and resources. The second issue is many times worse than the first. It's the disruption your personal disorganization has on the processes managed by others. When your reports are late, others get delayed. When you're late, others have to wait. When the form isn't completed properly, someone else has to take the time to get it corrected. Many people go through life happily disorganized and disheveled. The key is its impact on the people around you.

Some Remedies

- ☐ **1. Unsure where to start? Make a list of things to fix.** Do an upstream and downstream check on the people you work for, work around and those who work for you, to create a list of the administrative slip-ups you do that give them the most trouble. Be sure to ask them for help creating the list. That way you have a focused list of the things you need to fix first. If you fix the top 10, maybe that will do and the rest of your habits can stay the same.
- ☐ **2. Overbooked? Practice good time management.** Personal time management is a known technology. There are a number of books on the topic as well as a number of good personal time management courses you could attend. There are also personal organizer products on the market. Many of the courses include training in how to use the personal organizing books and software to be better organized. *More help? – See #62 Time Management.*
- ☐ **3. Disorganized? Get organized.** Put the things you have to do in two piles—things I have to do that are for me, and things I have to do that are for others or that will affect others. Do the second pile first. Further divide the other pile into the mission-critical, important, and things that can wait. Do them in that order.

☐ **4. Need more help? Hire people with organization skills.** If you have the luxury of an assistant or a secretary, select on the ability to organize him/herself and you. Pick someone who is candid, who will stand up to you and help you be successful.

☐ **5. Messy work environment? Contain the clutter.** Make your personal disorganization less obvious to others. Get a roll top desk so you can close it when you have guests in your office or cubicle. If you are a pile manager, get shelving that has addressable cubbyholes so you can get your piles out of the way. Get an L-shaped desk, one for your piles and one that you keep clean for only the project you are working on at the moment. Put the pile table in back of you toward the wall. Have an area of your office, a couple of chairs and a table that you never put anything on, that you can use for visitors. Frame this saying and put it on your wall so others know you are not very organized: "If a cluttered desk is the sign of a cluttered mind, what is an empty desk the sign of?"

☐ **6. Personal preferences getting in the way? Focus on priorities.** Don't work based upon your feelings. Don't organize your work around what you like to do and put off what you don't like to do. That's one reason people get into organization problems. Use priorities of what needs to be done instead. *More help? – See #50 Priority Setting.*

☐ **7. Failing to keep your commitments? Let others help you prioritize.** Ask your internal and external customers for the order in which they need things. If there is going to be a delay beyond the commitment you've made, send an e-mail, memo or card, or call and tell them when to expect what you've promised. You can only do this once.

☐ **8. Trouble meeting deadlines? Set your own deadline.** Set false deadlines for yourself that are ahead of the real deadlines. Delegate any of the things you have trouble getting done. *More help? – See #18 Delegation.*

☐ **9. Don't care? Check your attitude toward administrative tasks.** Some people ignore this need as not that important; administration has a trivial sound to it. The problem is, what else does it say about you? Most likely it tells people what you overdo. You're an action junkie and leave a trail of problems around you; you're creative and have your fingers in too many pies; or you're a strategist or a visionary and show disdain for details which tells others that what they do isn't very important. People rightly see this as a sort of arrogance. To find the cause, look to your strengths and learn to temper the criticism by developing in this area.

☐ **10. Not dependable? Build trust.** The bottom line for this need is that people don't trust people who are disorganized, particularly if you indicate you don't much care. They feel they can't count on you, that your actions may wreak havoc for them. Behaving as a consistently responsible administrator will eliminate this problem.

Some Develop-in-Place Assignments

- ☐ Manage a cost-cutting project.
- ☐ Help shut down a plant, regional office, product line, business, operation, etc.
- ☐ Plan an off-site meeting, conference, convention, trade show, event, etc.
- ☐ Manage the purchase of a major product, equipment, materials, program, or system.
- ☐ Work on a process-simplification team to take steps and costs out of a process.

It is vain to do with more what can be done with less.
William of Occam – English Franciscan friar
and scholastic philosopher

Suggested Readings

Allen, D. (2003). *Getting things done: The art of stress-free productivity.* New York: Penguin Books.

Bossidy, L., & Charan, R. (with Burck, C.). (2002). *Execution: The discipline of getting things done.* New York: Crown Business.

Byfield, M. (2003). *It's hard to make a difference when you can't find your keys: The seven-step path to becoming truly organized.* New York: Viking Press.

Charan, R. (2007). *Know-how: The 8 skills that separate people who perform from those who don't.* New York: Crown Business.

Cramer, K. D. (2002). *When faster harder smarter is not enough: Six steps for achieving what you want in a rapid-fire world.* New York: McGraw-Hill.

Crouch, C. (2005). *Getting organized: Improving focus, organization, and productivity.* Memphis, TN: Dawson Publishing.

Cunningham, M. J. (2006). *Finish what you start: 10 Surefire ways to deliver your projects on time and on budget.* Chicago: Kaplan Business.

Dittmer, R. E., & McFarland, S. (2008). *151 Quick ideas for delegating and decision making.* Franklin Lakes, NJ: Career Press.

Dodd, P., & Sundheim, D. (2005). *The 25 best time management tools and techniques: How to get more done without driving yourself crazy.* Windham, NH: Peak Performance Press.

Dotlich, D. L., Cairo, P. C., & Rhinesmith, S. H. (2006). *Head, heart, and guts: How the world's best companies develop complete leaders.* San Francisco: Jossey-Bass.

Drucker, P. F. (2006). *The effective executive* (Rev. ed.). New York: HarperBusiness.

Emmett, R. (2000). *The procrastinator's handbook: Mastering the art of doing it now.* New York: Walker & Company.

Herman, S. (Ed.). (2002). *Rewiring organizations for the networked economy: Organizing, managing, and leading in the information age.* San Francisco: Jossey-Bass/Pfeiffer.

Hoover, J. (2007). *Time management: Set priorities to get the right things done.* New York: HarperCollins Business.

Hutchings, P. J. (2002). *Managing workplace chaos: Solutions for handling information, paper, time, and stress.* New York: AMACOM.

Kaplan, R. S., & Norton, D. P. (2008). *Execution premium: Linking strategy to operations for competitive advantage.* Boston: Harvard Business School Press.

Limoncelli, T. A. (2005). *Time management for system administrators.* Sebastopol, CA: O'Reilly Media.

Whipp, R., Adam, B., & Sabelis, I. (Eds.). (2002). *Making time: Time and management in modern organizations.* Oxford, UK: Oxford University Press.

Winston, S. (2001). *The organized executive: The classic program for productivity: New ways to manage time, people, and the digital office.* New York: Warner Business.

103 *Overly* Ambitious

It is better to deserve honours and not have them
than to have them and not to deserve them.
Mark Twain – American humorist, satirist, lecturer, and writer

A Problem

- ☐ Is focused excessively on self and on upward career movement, sometimes at the expense of others
- ☐ Is willing to politic for promotion and step on people on the way up
- ☐ Primarily manages up in order to market and position him/herself with management

Not A Problem

- ☐ Takes career advancement in stride
- ☐ Concentrates on performing well
- ☐ Lets results do the marketing
- ☐ Helps others advance
- ☐ Spreads credit for successes around
- ☐ Humble about his/her accomplishments

Some Causes

- ☐ Loner
- ☐ Overly aggressive
- ☐ Poor political skills
- ☐ Problems with trust
- ☐ Unrealistic self-assessment

Other Causes

BEING UNSKILLED AT: 19,22,29,42,60,66

OVERUSING: 1,4,6,8,21,27,38,42,43,48,53,54,57,66

Leadership Architect® Factors and Clusters

This competency is in the Trouble with People Factor (VII) (S1). This competency is in the Self-Centered Cluster (W) with: 104, 105, 107, 109, 119. You may want to check other competencies in the same Factor/Cluster for related tips.

The Map

Most people you and I know are ambitious. Ambition is good. It drives people to do well and want to improve themselves. Being overly ambitious means you make too big a deal out of it. You market yourself too actively. You make political mistakes in terms of whom you approach to inquire about being promoted. At the extremes, people wonder if you care about today's job at all because you are always talking about moving on. They wonder if you make yourself look good at the expense of others. They wonder if you position yourself on the class picture to cover your rival behind you. They wonder if you cut corners to get ahead. They wonder if you really care about others or are you just using people for your own purposes. Others may or may not agree on your overall worth, but they think you spend too much time and effort promoting yourself.

Some Remedies

☐ **1. Eager to move up? Focus on performance.** The cream rises to the top. Build a better mouse trap and the world will beat a path to your door. Maybe not, but good solid work will always attract attention. People who get ahead have two things going for them: They consistently perform well, and they market themselves enough to be noticed. The research is clear—over the long term, people who succeed are seen first and foremost as tenacious problem solvers in whatever job they're in. They pay far more attention to the present than the future. Their performance makes them visible, more than their words. Make sure your performance is stellar before you talk about or ask about your next job or complain about a promotion you think you missed. Also, make sure it won't be the view of others that almost anyone could have accomplished this. Make sure your achievements are unusual before you say anything—nothing will hurt you more than having managers think you don't know performance as usual from something exemplary.

☐ **2. Overpromoting yourself? Engage in selective self-promotion.** Pick your battles carefully. Self-marketing needs to be done with great political care. Don't wear out your welcome. While people are usually positive about moderate self-promotion, they turn off quickly to what they consider too much or self-promotion that's too loud. Who really matters? Approach them once or twice carefully and with moderation. Don't share your ambitions with people who don't play a part in your future. And never, never bad-mouth competitors for a promotion. This will say far more about you than it says about them. *More help? – See #38 Organizational Agility and #48 Political Savvy.*

- ☐ **3. Cutting corners? Take responsibility.** How were, or what would be, your ratings on *#22 Ethics and Values and #29 Integrity and Trust?* If they were or would be high, then don't read on. If they are average, you may be seen as not helpful enough to others. How much time do you spend helping others solve problems vs. pushing your own agenda? Are you viewed as a loner? Do you help peers, help direct reports develop, visibly work to build a team? If your ratings are low, you may be cutting corners to look good. You may be trying to blame others for things you should take responsibility for. You may be making up excuses that are not real to cover your butt. You may be trying to make your rivals look bad so that you look better. You may hedge when asked a tough question. You may slap things together to look good when what's underneath wouldn't pass the test. You may be disorganized and your actions cause problems for others. You may indicate little or no concern for others. If you do any of these things or things like it, you will eventually be found out and you will lose the future you have been marketing yourself for. Stop them all.
- ☐ **4. Unsure of what you're selling? Ask for feedback and a reality check.** Get some real feedback. Volunteer for a 360° feedback process. Ask people you trust. Talk to a confidant in the Human Resources Department. Make sure you have the strengths you think you have. Make sure you do not deny your weaknesses. Generally, overly ambitious people overestimate their worth to the organization, and research indicates this is a primary cause of poor performance ratings. So don't rush into a negotiation believing yourself to be a superb negotiator unless you know that's true. *More help? – See #55 Self-Knowledge.*
- ☐ **5. Need some counsel? Find a mentor.** If you don't have a mentor or confidant higher up in the organization, work to get one. A mentor can offer unfiltered advice and counsel about you and your prospects in the organization.
- ☐ **6. Need some perspective? Read and reflect.** The best two books on this subject are *Career Mastery* by Harry Levinson and *What Color is Your Parachute?* by Richard Bolles. Get both and read them repeatedly until this problem goes away.
- ☐ **7. Focused on managing up? Work on peer relationships.** Overly ambitious people generally manage up more than down and sideways. That leaves others to feel they are second-class citizens. You may well feel that way but you must never show that side of you. Make sure you make time for others. Make sure you don't position or peacock in front of others. Make sure you're not always the one who picks up the boss from the airport and gives the tour. Make sure you're not always seated at the boss's table.

- ☐ **8. Ready to lend a hand? Promote other people's careers, too.** Do you promote the careers of others as well as your own? Do you help other people solve their problems or do they only help you solve yours? People will tolerate more ambition from you if you have a demonstrated track record of helping others get ahead as well. *More help? – See #19 Developing Direct Reports and Others.*
- ☐ **9. Hogging opportunities to get in front of top management? Share the spotlight.** Sometimes that's a sign of being overly ambitious. Let others present sometimes. Try to gain stature with top management through the success of your people. Usually that's just as fast a track to a career as is doing everything yourself. Executives quickly notice people builders, those who surround themselves with high performers. *More help? – See #18 Delegation.*
- ☐ **10. Not listening? Strike a balance between listening and talking.** How much time do you spend talking about yourself and marketing yourself versus listening to others about what you need to improve to get ahead? The ratio should be at least 75% listening and 25% promoting. If it's not, work to get the ratio in line.

Some Develop-in-Place Assignments

- ☐ Teach/coach someone how to do something you are not an expert in.
- ☐ Serve for a year or more with a community agency.
- ☐ Become a volunteer for a year or more for an outside organization.
- ☐ Do a study of failed executives in your organization, including interviewing people still with the organization who knew or worked with them, and report the findings to top management.
- ☐ Attend a self-awareness/assessment course that includes feedback.

It is a good idea to be ambitious, to have goals, to want to be good at what you do, but it is a terrible mistake to let drive and ambition get in the way of treating people with kindness and decency. The point is not that they will then be nice to you. It is that you will feel better about yourself.
Robert Merton Solow – American economist

Suggested Readings

Bennis, W., Goleman, D., & O'Toole, J. (with Ward Biederman, P.). (2008). *Transparency: How leaders create a culture of candor.* San Francisco: Jossey-Bass.

Bolles, R. N. (2009). *What color is your parachute? A practical manual for job-hunters & career-changers.* Berkeley, CA: Ten Speed Press.

Brandon, R., & Seldman, M. (2004). *Survival of the savvy: High integrity political tactics for career and company success.* New York: Free Press.

Buchanan, D. A., & Badham, R. J. (2008). *Power, politics, and organizational change: Winning the turf game.* Thousand Oaks, CA: Sage.

Champy, J., & Nohria, N. (2000). *The arc of ambition.* Cambridge, MA: Perseus Publishing.

Chapman, E. N., & Wingfield, B. (2003). *Winning at human relations: How to keep from sabotaging yourself.* Mississauga, ON: Crisp Publications, Inc.

Christian, K. (2004). *Your own worst enemy: Breaking the habit of adult underachievement.* New York: Regan Books.

Deering, A., Dilts, R., & Russell, J. (2002). *Alpha leadership: Tools for business leaders who want more from life.* Hoboken, NJ: John Wiley & Sons.

Donald, R. (2006). *Successful career management: Strategies beyond technical preparation.* Bloomington, IN: AuthorHouse.

Faulkner, R. (2008). *The case for greatness: Honorable ambition and its critics.* New Haven, CT: Yale University Press.

Fels, A. (2004). *Necessary dreams: Ambition in women's changing lives.* New York: Pantheon Books.

Ferrazzi, K., & Raz, T. (2005) *Never eat alone: And other secrets to success, one relationship at a time.* New York: Doubleday.

Goldsmith, M. (2007). *What got you here won't get you there: How successful people become even more successful.* New York: Hyperion.

Goleman, D. (2001). Leadership that gets results. *Harvard Business Review, 78*(2), 78-90.

Heineman, B. W., Jr. (2008). *High performance with high integrity.* Boston: Harvard Business School Press.

Kaplan, B., & Kaiser, R. (2006). *The versatile leader: Make the most of your strengths—without overdoing it.* San Francisco: Pfeiffer.

Lombardo, M. M., & Eichinger, R. W. (1989). *Preventing derailment: What to do before it's too late.* Minneapolis, MN: Lominger International: A Korn/Ferry Company.

Mahan, B. J., & Coles, R. (2002). *Forgetting ourselves on purpose: Vocation and the ethics of ambition.* San Francisco: Jossey-Bass.

McCall, M. W., Lombardo, M. M., & Morrison, A. M. (1988). *The lessons of experience.* Lexington, MA: Lexington Books.

Morrison, A. M., White, R. P., Van Velsor, E., & The Center for Creative Leadership. (1992). *Breaking the glass ceiling: Can women reach the top of America's largest corporations?* Reading, MA: Addison-Wesley.

Pfeffer, J. (1994). *Managing with power: Politics and influence in organizations.* Boston: Harvard Business School Press.

Sawi, B. (2000). *Coming up for air: How to build a balanced life in a workaholic world.* New York: Hyperion.

Schweich, T. A. (2003). *Staying power: 30 Secrets invincible executives use for getting to the top: And staying there.* New York: McGraw-Hill.

Scott, G. G. (2006). *A survival guide for working with bad bosses: Dealing with bullies, idiots, back-stabbers, and other managers from hell.* New York: AMACOM.

Shepard, G. (2005). *How to manage problem employees: A step-by-step guide for turning difficult employees into high performers.* Hoboken, NJ: John Wiley & Sons.

104 Arrogant

It's much easier to be critical than to be correct.
Benjamin Disraeli – British Conservative, statesman, literary figure, and former Prime Minister

A Problem

- ☐ Always thinks he/she has the right and only answer
- ☐ Discounts or dismisses the input of others
- ☐ Can be cold and aloof, makes others feel inferior
- ☐ May detach him/herself from others unless on his/her own terms
- ☐ Keeps distance between him/herself and others

Not A Problem

- ☐ Listens and responds to others
- ☐ Is approachable and warm
- ☐ Interested in others' views even if they counter his/hers
- ☐ Includes and builds others up
- ☐ Values the opinions of others
- ☐ Treats others as equal partners
- ☐ Shares credit with others
- ☐ Seldom pulls rank or tries to overpower others
- ☐ Gets close to some people and interacts with many more

Some Causes

- ☐ Don't appear to like others much
- ☐ Lack of feedback
- ☐ Like own ideas too much
- ☐ Low personal disclosure
- ☐ Not very comfortable with people
- ☐ Poor interpersonal skills
- ☐ Poor reader of others
- ☐ Very smart and successful

Other Causes

BEING UNSKILLED AT: 3,4,7,10,12,21,26,31,32,33,36,41,42,44,54,55,60
OVERUSING: 5,9,11,13,14,20,26,29,30,45,59,61,65

Leadership Architect® Factors and Clusters

This competency is in the Trouble with People Factor (VII) (S1). This competency is in the Self-Centered Cluster (W) with: 103, 105, 107, 109, 119. You may want to check other competencies in the same Factor/Cluster for related tips.

The Map

Arrogant people are usually seen as distant loners who prefer their own ideas to anyone else's. Formally, being arrogant means to devalue others and the contributions of others. It usually results in people feeling diminished, rejected and angry. Arrogance is hard to fix for two reasons: It's hard to get feedback on what the problem specifically is since people hesitate giving arrogant people any feedback, and it's hard to change since you don't listen or read the reactions of others well. Nevertheless, people seen as arrogant usually get their expressed if not intended wish in the long term—they end up isolated and alone.

Some Remedies

- ☐ **1. Lacking self-awareness? Ask for feedback.** Arrogance is a major blockage to building self-knowledge. *More help? – See #55 Self-Knowledge.* Research says that successful people know themselves better. Many people who have a towering strength or lots of success get less feedback and roll along thinking they are perfect until their careers get in trouble. If you are viewed as arrogant, your best chance of understanding it is to get facilitated 360° feedback where the respondents can remain anonymous. It is unlikely you could get useful data from people directly since they don't think you listen and it has been painful in the past to try to influence you. Arrogant people typically overrate themselves. Their ratings from others may be lower than they should be because people believe they need to make it look worse than it is to get through your defiance shield. If you are seen as devaluing others, they will return the favor.
- ☐ **2. Acting like you're perfect? Work on being more approachable.** There are two possibilities: You are really talented and near perfect and people just have had a hard time getting used to you mostly being right, or you're not perfect but you act as if you are. If you are in fact really, really bright and successful and knowledgeable and right most of the time, you have to stop making people feel bad and rejected because of your special gifts. If you're not almost perfect, there is no reason to act as if you are. In either case, you have to work on being more behaviorally open and approachable and help people deal with you comfortably.
- ☐ **3. Sending the wrong signals? Watch your non-verbals.** Arrogant people look, talk and act arrogantly. As you try to become less arrogant, you need to find out what your non-verbals are. All arrogant people do a series of

things that can be viewed by a neutral party and judged to give off the signals of arrogance. Washboard brow. Facial expressions. Body shifting, especially turning away. Impatient finger or pencil tapping. False smile. Tight lips. Looking away. Find out from a trusted friend what you do and try to eliminate those behaviors.

☐ **4. Think you know it all? Take time to listen and ask questions.** Answers. Solutions. Conclusions. Statements. Dictates. That's the staple of arrogant people. Instant output. Sharp reactions. This may be getting you in trouble. You jump to conclusions, categorically dismiss what others say, use challenging words in an absolute tone. People then see you as closed or combative. More negatively, they may believe you think they're stupid or ill-informed. Give people a chance to talk without interruption. If you're seen as intolerant or closed, people will often stumble over words in their haste to talk with you or shortcut their argument since they assume you're not listening anyway. Ask a question, invite them to disagree with you, present their argument back to them softly, let them save face no matter what. Add a 15-second pause into your transactions before you say anything and add two clarifying questions per transaction to signal you're listening and want to understand. *More help? – See #33 Listening and #41 Patience.*

☐ **5. Out of touch? Read your audience.** Do you know what people look like when they are uncomfortable with your arrogance? Do they back up? Frown? Flush? Stumble over words? Shut down? Cringe? Stand at the door hoping not to get invited in? You should work doubly hard at observing others. Especially during the first three minutes of an important transaction, work to make one person or group comfortable with you before the agenda starts. Ask a question unrelated to the topic. Offer them something to drink. Tell them something you did last weekend that you found interesting.

☐ **6. Afraid to open up? Get personal.** Arrogant people keep their distance and don't share much personal data. You may believe you shouldn't mix personal with business. You may believe it's wise to keep distance between you and others you work around and with. Since it's hard for others to relate to an arrogant person in the first place, your reputation may be based on only short unsatisfactory transactions. The kinds of disclosures people enjoy are: The reasons behind why you do and decide what you do; your self-appraisal; things you know behind what's happening in the business that they don't know—that you are at liberty to disclose; things both good and embarrassing that have happened to you in the past; comments about what's going on around you—without being too negative about others; and things you are interested in and do outside of work. These are areas which you should learn to disclose more than you now do. *More help? – See #44 Personal Disclosure.*

- ☐ **7. Too critical? Evaluate the problem, not the person.** You probably have good people buckets and bad people buckets and signal to the bad bucket groups or individuals your disagreement with them. Learn to understand without either accepting or judging. Listen, take notes, ask questions, and be able to make their case as well as they can even though you don't agree. Pick something in their argument you agree with. Present your argument in terms of the problem only—why you think this is the best manner to deal with a mutually agreed upon problem.
- ☐ **8. Too directive? Be a teacher, not a director.** You may be highly intelligent and quite skilled in your area. You may work around people who aren't as informed or educated as you are. You may be in a position of essentially dictating what should be done. But you don't have to make it demeaning or painful. You need to switch to a teacher/guru role—tell them how you think about an issue, don't just fire out solutions. Tell them what you think the problem is, what questions need to be asked and answered, how you would go about finding out, what you think some likely solutions might be. Work to pass on your knowledge and skills.
- ☐ **9. Need affirmation? Find affirmation by building others up.** Do you really want to leave the majority of people you deal with feeling stupid, inferior and unintelligent? Most don't but that's what you do. Arrogant people may be looking for feedback that they are really superior, smart and knowledgeable. But they are looking for that affirmation in the wrong place. If you crave reinforcement of your excellence, perform better. Help others perform better. Produce tangible results. If your results don't measure up to your self-view, your words and arrogant behavior certainly won't help you any. Don't try to feel good on the backs of others who are not your equal. Look at three people whom you consider excellent performers, talented people, but who are not arrogant. What do they do and not do? Contrast this with your behavior.
- ☐ **10. Ready to fix it? Show your commitment by being open to others.** Whatever applies in Some Causes, you will have to work on *#3 Approachability and #31 Interpersonal Savvy.* Until you signal repeatedly that you are open to others, interested in what they have to say, share things you don't have to share, invite people to talk with you and then listen, little will come of this effort. You will have to persevere, endure some rejection, and perhaps some angry or dismissive remarks in order to balance the situation. Mentally rehearse so you're not blindsided by this. It would be a rare group of people who would respond to your overtures without making you squirm a bit because you have caused them pain in the past.

Some Develop-in-Place Assignments

- ☐ Make peace with an enemy or someone you've disappointed with a product or service or someone you've had some trouble with or don't get along with very well.
- ☐ Manage the outplacement of a group of people.
- ☐ Take on a task you dislike or hate to do.
- ☐ Manage a group of people who are older and/or more experienced to accomplish a task.
- ☐ Try to learn something frivolous and fun to see how good you can get (e.g., juggling, square dancing, magic).

The challenge of leadership is to be strong, but not rude;
be kind, but not weak; be bold, but not bully;
be thoughtful, but not lazy; be humble, but not timid;
be proud, but not arrogant; have humor, but without folly.
Jim Rohn – American speaker and author

Suggested Readings

Barker, L., & Watson, K. (2001). *Listen up: At home, at work, in relationships: How to harness the power of effective listening.* Irvine, CA: Griffin Trade.

Barron, L. A. (2006). *Openness works! Create personal, professional and financial growth in any organization.* Austin, TX: Hopeworks Publishing.

The Dalai Lama. (2002). *An open heart: Practicing compassion in everyday life.* New York: Back Bay Books.

Donoghue, P. J., & Siegel, M. E. (2005). *Are you really listening? Keys to successful communication.* Notre Dame, IN: Sorin Books.

Dotlich, D. L., & Cairo, P. C. (2003). *Why CEOs fail: The 11 behaviors that can derail your climb to the top and how to manage them.* San Francisco: Jossey-Bass.

Fritz, J. M. H., & Omdahl, B. L. (2006). *Problematic relationships in the workplace.* New York: Peter Lang Publishing, Inc.

Goldsmith, M., & Reiter, M. (2007). *What got you here won't get you there: How successful people become even more successful.* New York: Hyperion.

Goleman, D. (2007). *Social intelligence: The new science of human relationships.* New York: Bantam Books.

Goman, C. (2008). *The nonverbal advantage: Secrets and science of body language at work.* San Francisco: Berrett-Koehler Publishers.

Gonthier, G., & Morrissey, K. (2002). *Rude awakenings: Overcoming the civility crisis in the workplace.* Chicago: Dearborn Trade.

Gostick, A., & Christopher, S. (2008). *The levity effect: Why it pays to lighten up.* Hoboken, NJ: John Wiley & Sons.

Haight, M. (2005). *Who's afraid of the big bad boss? 13 Types and how to survive them.* West Conshohocken, PA: Infinity Publishing.

Kaplan, B., & Kaiser, R. (2006). *The versatile leader: Make the most of your strengths—without overdoing it.* San Francisco: Pfeiffer.

Lieberman, D. J. (2002). *Make peace with anyone: Breakthrough strategies to quickly end any conflict, feud, or estrangement.* New York: St. Martin's Press.

Lubit, R. H. (2003). *Coping with toxic managers, subordinates...and other difficult people: Using emotional intelligence to survive and prosper.* Upper Saddle River, NJ: Financial Times Prentice Hall.

Maxwell, J. C. (2006). *The difference maker: Making your attitude your greatest asset.* Nashville, TN: Thomas Nelson.

Maxwell, J. C. (2008). *Leadership gold: Lessons I've learned from a lifetime of leading.* Nashville, TN: Thomas Nelson.

Perlow, L. (2003). *When you say yes but mean no: How silencing conflict wrecks relationships and companies...and what you can do about it.* New York: Crown Business.

Showkeir, J., & Showkeir, M. (2008). *Authentic conversations: Moving from manipulation to truth and commitment.* San Francisco: Berrett-Koehler Publishers.

Tamm, J. W., & Luyet, R. J. (2004). *Radical collaboration: Five essential skills to overcome defensiveness and build successful relationships.* New York: HarperCollins.

Waitzkin, J. (2008). *The art of learning: An inner journey to optimal performance.* New York: Free Press.

Waldroop, J., & Butler, T. (2000). *Maximum success: Changing the 12 behavior patterns that keep you from getting ahead.* New York: Doubleday.

105 Betrayal of Trust

The glue that holds all relationships together—including the relationship between the leader and the led is trust, and trust is based on integrity.
Brian Tracy – American TV host

A Problem

- ☐ Says one thing and means or does another
- ☐ Is inconsistent and unpredictable at times
- ☐ Fails to follow through on commitments

Not A Problem

- ☐ Always follows through
- ☐ Keeps confidences
- ☐ Walks his/her talk
- ☐ Does what he/she says he/she will do
- ☐ Finishes what he/she starts
- ☐ Is steady and predictable
- ☐ Checks back if there is going to be a problem

Some Causes

- ☐ Avoid conflict
- ☐ Devious
- ☐ Disorganized/unpredictable
- ☐ Forgetful
- ☐ Not customer oriented
- ☐ Poor political skills
- ☐ Poor time management
- ☐ Spread too thin; can't say no
- ☐ Too anxious to make the sale
- ☐ Overly ambitious

Other Causes

BEING UNSKILLED AT: 10,11,12,13,22,23,29,34,57
OVERUSING: 6,8,21,27,31,38,48

Leadership Architect® Factors and Clusters

This competency is in the Trouble with People Factor (VII) (S1). This competency is in the Self-Centered Cluster (W) with: 103, 104, 107, 109, 119. You may want to check other competencies in the same Factor/Cluster for related tips.

The Map

Trust that you will do what you committed to and what is expected drives the world. Anything less than that leads to damaged or severed relationships, lost customers, unfinished projects, re-work and wasted time, and lots of noise. There is no up-side to betraying a trust.

Some Remedies

- ☐ **1. Unreliable? Follow through.** Do you return phone calls in a timely manner? Do you forward material you promised? Did you pass on information you promised to get? Did you carry through on a task you promised someone you would take care of? Failing to do things like this damages relationships. If you tend to forget things, write them down. If you run out of time, set up a specific time each day to follow through on commitments. If you are going to miss a deadline, let them know and give them a second date you will be sure to make.
- ☐ **2. Overcommitted? Learn to say no.** A lot of trouble follows over-committing. Overcommitting usually comes from wanting to please everyone or not wanting to face the conflict if you say no. You can only do so much. Only commit to that which you can actually do. Commit to a specific time for delivery. Write it down. Learn to say "no," pleasantly. Learn to pass it off to someone else who has the time—"Gee no, but I'm sure Susan could help you with that." Learn to say, "Yes, but it will take longer than you might want to wait," and give them the option of withdrawing the request. Learn to say, "Yes, but what else that I have already committed to do for you would you like to delay to get this done?" *More help? – See #50 Priority Setting.*
- ☐ **3. Unrealistic? Don't exaggerate or overpromise.** Trying too hard to make the sale? Does your enthusiasm to make the sale or get your point across cause you to commit to too many things in the heat of the transaction? The customers you get by unrealistic commitments are the customers you will lose forever when they find out you can't deliver.
- ☐ **4. Trying too hard to impress? Prove yourself by your results.** It's common for people to promise too much so others will be impressed. It's also common that people who do that repeatedly lose in the long term because others will learn to discount promises and only measure results.

☐ **5. Trying to avoid conflict? Say what you intend to do and do what you say.** Do you say what you need to say to get through the meeting or transaction but have little intention of doing what you said? Do you say things just to go along and not cause trouble? Do you say what you need to say to avoid disagreement or an argument? All these behaviors will eventually backfire when people find out you said something different in another setting or to another person, or they notice you didn't actually follow through and do what you said.

☐ **6. Intentionally saying things to gain an advantage? Lose your agenda.** Do you actually know ahead of time that what you are saying is not really true or that you really don't think that? Do you say things you don't mean to gain an advantage or forward a relationship or get some resources? Do you forward your personal agenda ahead of that of the team or organization? Any of these will eventually catch up to you and cause you career disruption. *More help? – See #22 Ethics and Values and #29 Integrity and Trust.*

☐ **7. Unpredictable? Be consistent.** Many people are inconsistent in at least some of the things they do. Many follow through some days and weeks and not others. Some follow through up but not down in the organization. Some follow through with individuals they like and not with people they don't like. While all this is human nature, it's a losing strategy. Basically, if you can do it once, do it with one person, do it on one day, you should be able to do it much more often. *More help? – See #43 Perseverance.*

☐ **8. Leave things undone? Finish what you start.** Very action oriented? Impatient? Fingers in many pies? Interest wanes if it takes too long? All of these result in unmet commitments. Try to discipline yourself to finish what you've started. Don't move on until it's done. Delegate finishing it to someone you trust. Check back to see that it was done. If you are not going to finish it, inform those concerned that you do not intend to complete the task with the reasons for your decision.

☐ **9. Always out of time? Manage your time.** Do you intend to get to things but never have the time? Do you always estimate shorter times to get things done that then take longer? There is a well-established science and a set of best practices in time management. There are a number of books you can buy in any business bookstore, and there are a number of good courses you can attend. Delegating also helps you use your time more effectively. *More help? – See #62 Time Management.*

☐ **10. Not trustworthy? Reconsider your worldview.** Perhaps you really aren't very trustworthy. You hedge, sabotage others, play for advantage, set up others, don't intend to follow up. You justify it by saying that things are tough, that you're just doing your job, getting results. After all, the end justifies the means. You use others to get your agenda accomplished. First, you need to examine whether this view of the world is really right and whether it is the way you really want to be. Second, you need to find out if your career with this organization is salvageable. Have you burned too many bridges? The best way to do this is to admit you have regularly betrayed trusts and not followed through on your commitments. Talk with your boss or mentor to see if you can redeem yourself. If yes, meet with everyone you think you've alienated and see how they respond. Tell them what you're going to do differently. Ask them what you should stop doing. Ask them if the situation can be repaired.

Some Develop-in-Place Assignments

- ☐ Make peace with an enemy or someone you've disappointed with a product or service or someone you've had some trouble with or don't get along with very well.
- ☐ Manage a group through a significant business crisis.
- ☐ Handle a tough negotiation with an internal or external client or customer.
- ☐ Manage the assigning/allocating of office space in a contested situation.
- ☐ Manage a dissatisfied internal or external customer; troubleshoot a performance or quality problem with a product or service.

To be persuasive, we must be believable;
to be believable, we must be credible;
to be credible, we must be truthful.
Edward R. Murrow – American journalist

Suggested Readings

Bellingham, R. (2003). *Ethical leadership: Rebuilding trust in corporations.* Amherst, MA: HRD Press.

Branham, L. (2005). *The 7 hidden reasons employees leave: How to recognize the subtle signs and act before it's too late.* New York: AMACOM.

Bunker, K. A., & Wakefield, M. (2005). *Leading with authenticity in times of transition.* Greensboro, NC: Center for Creative Leadership.

Cooper, C. (2008). *Extraordinary circumstances: The journey of a corporate whistleblower.* Hoboken, NJ: John Wiley & Sons.

Covey, S. M. R. (with Merrill, R. R.). (2006). *The speed of trust: The one thing that changes everything.* New York: Free Press.

Csorba, L. T. (2004). *Trust: The one thing that makes or breaks a leader.* Nashville, TN: Thomas Nelson.

Deems, R. S., & Deems, T. A. (2003). *Leading in tough times: The manager's guide to responsibility, trust, and motivation.* Amherst, MA: HRD Press.

Forni, P.M. (2002). *Choosing civility: The twenty-five rules of considerate conduct.* New York: St. Martin's Press.

Geisler, N. L., & Douglass, R. (2007). *Integrity at work: Finding your ethical compass in a post-Enron world.* Grand Rapids, MI: Baker Books.

Golin, A. (2004). *Trust or consequences: Build trust today or lose your market tomorrow.* New York: AMACOM.

Hanson, T., & Hanson, B. Z. (2005). *Who will do what by when? How to improve performance, accountability and trust with integrity.* Sydney, Australia: Power.

Johnson, L., & Phillips, B. (2003). *Absolute honesty: Building a corporate culture that values straight talk and rewards integrity.* New York: AMACOM.

Kaptein, M., & Wempe, J. (2002). *The balanced company: A corporate integrity theory.* Oxford, UK: Oxford University Press.

Kouzes, J. M., & Posner, B. Z. (2003). *The five practices of exemplary leadership.* San Francisco: John Wiley & Sons.

Lee, G., & Elliott-Lee, D. (2006). *Courage: The backbone of leadership.* San Francisco: Jossey-Bass.

Mishra, A. K., & Mishra, K. E. (2008). *Trust is everything: Become the leader others will follow.* Durham, NC: Aneil K. Mishra and Karen E. Mishra.

Patterson, K., Grenny, J., McMillan, R., & Switzler, A. (2004). *Crucial confrontations: Tools for talking about broken promises, violated expectations, and bad behavior.* New York: McGraw-Hill.

Perlow, L. (2003). *When you say yes but mean no: How silencing conflict wrecks relationships and companies...and what you can do about it.* New York: Crown Business.

Seglin, J. L. (2006). *The right thing: Conscience, profit, and personal responsibility in today's business.* Rollinsford, NH: Spiro Press.

Solomon, R. C., & Flores, F. (2001). *Building trust: In business, politics, relationships, and life.* Oxford, UK: Oxford University Press.

Stroh, L. K. (2007). *Trust rules: How to tell the good guys from the bad guys in work and life.* Westport, CT: Praeger.

Telford, D., & Gostick, A. (2005). *Integrity works: Strategies for becoming a trusted, respected, and admired leader.* Layton, UT: Gibbs Smith.

106 Blocked Personal Learner

The only person who is educated
is the one who has learned how to learn—and change.
Carl Rogers – American psychologist

A Problem

- ☐ Is closed to learning new personal, interpersonal, managerial, and leadership skills, approaches, and tactics
- ☐ Prefers staying the same, even when faced with new and different challenges
- ☐ Is narrow in interests and scope
- ☐ Uses few learning tactics
- ☐ Doesn't seek input
- ☐ Lacks curiosity
- ☐ Is not insightful about him/herself

Not A Problem

- ☐ Eager to learn; interested in what's new or better
- ☐ Has broad interests and perspective
- ☐ Seeks and listens to feedback
- ☐ Takes criticism to heart
- ☐ Always looking to improve him/herself
- ☐ Carefully observes others for their reactions and adjusts accordingly
- ☐ Reads people and groups well
- ☐ Picks up on subtle corrective cues from others
- ☐ Is sensitive to different challenges and changes accordingly

Some Causes

- ☐ Hang on hoping to make it without changing
- ☐ Low risk taker
- ☐ May block change for others
- ☐ Narrow in scope and interests
- ☐ Not open to new approaches
- ☐ Perfectionist
- ☐ Prefer the tried and true
- ☐ Self-learning/development interest is low
- ☐ Too busy to learn anything new
- ☐ Too comfortable

Other Causes

BEING UNSKILLED AT: 2,11,32,33,41,44,45,46,47,51,54,55,58,61,64

OVERUSING: 9,11,22,24,29,30,39,44,47,53,57,62

Leadership Architect® Factors and Clusters

This competency is in the Trouble with People Factor (VII) (S1). This competency is in the Doesn't Relate Well to Others Cluster (V) with: 101, 108, 112. You may want to check other competencies in the same Factor/Cluster for related tips.

The Map

People say you're stuck in the past. For some reason, you resist learning new personal and managerial behaviors. You're the last to get on board a new initiative. You're from Missouri (the "Show Me" state); we have to prove it to you before you'll move. Surveys done with a major outplacement firm show that those most likely to be let go during a downsizing have good technical and individual skills, but poor learning to do anything new or different skills. You can't survive today without keeping you and your skills fresh. There's not much room anymore for someone stuck in the past.

Some Remedies

☐ **1. Need a defined approach? Work from the outside in.** People who are good at this work from the outside—the customer, the audience, the person, the situation—in, not from the inside—What do I want to do in this situation? What would make me happy and feel good?—out. Practice not thinking inside/out when you are around others. What are the demand characteristics of this situation? How does this person or audience best learn? Which of my approaches or styles or skills or knowledge would work best? How can I best accomplish my goals? How can I alter my approach and tactics to be the most effective? The one-trick pony can only perform once per show. If the audience doesn't like that particular trick, no oats for the pony, no encore. *More help? – See #15 Customer Focus.*

☐ **2. Caught in your comfort zone? Find new solutions.** You're probably caught in your comfort zone. You rely on historical, tried-and-true solutions. You use what you know and have seen or done before. So when faced with a new issue, challenge or problem, first figure out what causes it. Don't go to the solution or conclusion first. Keep asking why, see how many causes you can come up with and how many organizing buckets you can put them in. This increases the chance of a better solution because you can see more connections. Look for patterns in data, don't just collect information or assume that you know what to do. People are telling you that you often don't. *More help? – See #51 Problem Solving.*

☐ **3. Failing to connect with others? Adjust to your audience.** You must constantly observe others' reactions to you to be good at adjusting to others. You must watch the reactions of people to what you are saying and doing while you are doing it in order to gauge their response. Are they bored? Change the pace. Are they confused? State it in a different way. Are they angry? Stop and ask what the problem is. Are they too quiet? Stop and get them involved in what you are doing. Are they fidgeting, scribbling on their pads or staring out the window? They may not be interested in what you are doing. Move to the end of your presentation or task, end it, and exit. Check in with your audience frequently and select a different tactic if necessary. *More help? – See #33 Listening and #45 Personal Learning.*

☐ **4. Not open to learning? Make repeated efforts to learn from others.** Whatever the causes are, people view you as not open to learning. Until you signal repeatedly that you are open to others, interested in what they have to say, share things you don't have to share, invite people to talk with you and then listen, little will come of this effort. You will have to persevere, endure some rejection, and perhaps some angry or dismissive remarks in order to balance the situation. Mentally rehearse so you're not blindsided by this. It would be a rare group of people who would respond to your new overtures without making you squirm a bit because they have seen you as closed up to this point. *More help? – See #3 Approachability and #31 Interpersonal Savvy.*

☐ **5. Need a new bag of tricks? Experiment with some new techniques with people.** Many excellent personal learners have a bag of engaging techniques they use: They give reasons for everything they say, saving any solution statements or conclusions for last. They ask more questions than make statements, speak briefly, summarize often, and when disagreeing they put it in conditional terms: "I don't think so, but what do you think?" The point of these is to elicit as much information about the reactions of others as they can. They are loading their files so they can change behavior when needed.

☐ **6. Stuck in a rut? Expand your repertoire.** Stretch yourself. Do things that are not characteristic of you. Go to your limits and beyond. By expanding the number of behaviors you have access to, you can become more effective across a larger number of situations. *More help? – See #54 Self-Development.*

☐ **7. Ready to try something new? Be an early adopter of something.** Find some new thing, technique, software, tool, system, process or skill relevant to your activity. Privately become an expert in it. Read the books. Get certified. Visit a location where it's being done. Then surprise everyone and be the first to introduce it into your world. Sell it. Train others. Integrate it into your work.

☐ **8. Don't know where to start? Pick three tasks you've never done before and go do them.** If you don't know much about customers, work in a store or handle customer complaints; if you don't know what engineering does, go find out; task trade with someone. Meet with your colleagues from other areas and tell each other what, and more importantly, how you do what you do.

☐ **9. Need a broader perspective? Volunteer for task forces.** Task forces/projects are a great opportunity to learn new things in a low-risk environment. Task forces are one of the most common developmental events listed by successful executives. Such projects require learning other functions, businesses or nationalities well enough that in a tight time frame you can appreciate how they think and why their area/position is important. In so doing, you get out of your own experience and start to see connections to a broader world—how international trade works, or more at home, how the pieces of your organization fit together.

☐ **10. Need to also stretch in your personal life? Expand your horizons.** Do you eat at the same restaurants? Vacation at the same places? Holidays are always done the same as in the past? Buy the same make or type car over and over again? Have the same insurance agent your father had? Expand yourself. Go on adventures with the family. Travel to places you have not been before. Never vacation at the same place again. Eat at different theme restaurants. Go to events and meetings of groups you have never really met. Go to ethnic festivals and sample the cultures. Go to athletic events you've never attended before. Each week, you and your family should go on a personal learning adventure. See how many different perspectives you can add to your knowledge.

Some Develop-in-Place Assignments

☐ Make peace with an enemy or someone you've disappointed with a product or service or someone you've had some trouble with or don't get along with very well.

☐ Attend a self-awareness/assessment course that includes feedback.

☐ Find and spend time with an expert to learn something in an area new to you.

☐ Interview or work with a "tutor" or mentor on a skill you need to develop.

☐ Study an admired person who has a skill you need.

No matter how one may think himself accomplished,
when he sets out to learn a new language, science,
or the bicycle, he has entered a new realm
as truly as if he were a child newly born into the world.
Frances Willard – American educator and women's suffragist

Suggested Readings

Bell, A. H., & Smith, D. M. (2002). *Motivating yourself for achievement.* Upper Saddle River, NJ: Prentice Hall.

Bennis, W. G., & Thomas, R. J. (2007). *Leading for a lifetime: How defining moments shape leaders of today and tomorrow.* Boston, MA: Harvard Business School Press.

Blakeley, K. (2007). *Leadership blind spots and what to do about them.* Chichester, England: John Wiley & Sons.

Cashman, K. (2008). *Leadership from the inside out: Becoming a leader for life* (2nd ed.). San Francisco: Berrett-Koehler Publishers.

Christian, K. (2004). *Your own worst enemy: Breaking the habit of adult underachievement.* New York: Regan Books.

Eichinger, R. W., & Lombardo, M. M. (2004). Learning agility as a prime indicator of potential. *Human Resource Planning, 27*(4), 12-15.

Eichinger, R. W., Lombardo, M. M., & Stiber, A. (2005). *Broadband talent management: Paths to improvement.* Minneapolis, MN: Lominger International: A Korn/Ferry Company.

Fulmer, R. M., & Conger, J. A. (2004). *Growing your company's leaders.* New York: AMACOM.

Gardner, H. (2006). *Five minds for the future.* Boston, MA: Harvard Business School Press.

Kotter, J., & Rathgeber, H. (2006). *Our iceberg is melting: Changing and succeeding under any conditions.* New York: St. Martin's Press.

Kourdi, J. (2007). *Think on your feet: 10 Steps to better decision making and problem solving at work.* London: Cyan Communications.

Lee, R. J., & King, S. N. (2000). *Discovering the leader in you: A guide to realizing your personal leadership potential.* San Francisco: Jossey-Bass.

Lucas, B. (2001). *Power up your mind: Learn faster, work smarter.* Yarmouth, ME: Nicholas Brealey Publishing.

Malone, A. J. (2003). *Managing your greatest assets: An effective and practical guide to "real life" people management.* Victoria, Canada: Trafford.

McCall, M. W., Lombardo, M. M., & Morrison, A. M. (1988). *The lessons of experience.* Lexington, MA: Lexington Books.

Merriam, S. B., Caffarella, R. S., & Baumgartner, L. M. (2006). *Learning in adulthood: A comprehensive guide.* San Francisco: Jossey-Bass.

Rimanoczy, I., & Turner, E. (2008). *Action Reflection Learning™: Solving real business problems by connecting learning with earning*. Mountain View, CA: Davies-Black Publishing.

Thomas, R. J. (2008). *Crucibles of leadership: How to learn from experience to become a great leader*. Boston, MA: Harvard Business School Press.

Waitzkin, J. (2008). *The art of learning: An inner journey to optimal performance*. New York: Free Press.

Wick, C., Pollock, R., Jefferson, A., & Flanagan, R. (2006). *The six disciplines of breakthrough learning: How to turn training and development into business results*. San Francisco: Pfeiffer.

Wilkinson, D. (2006). *The ambiguity advantage: What great leaders are great at*. Hampshire, England: Palgrave Macmillan.

107 *Lack of* Composure

Forego your anger for a moment
and save yourself a hundred days of trouble.
– Chinese proverb

A Problem

- ☐ Does not handle pressure and stress well
- ☐ Gets emotional, subjective, and unpredictable when things don't go as planned
- ☐ May become hostile or sarcastic or withdraw from people as stress increases
- ☐ May make snap or poor decisions under pressure
- ☐ Performance degrades when things get tough

Not A Problem

- ☐ Cool under stress and pressure
- ☐ Can take conflict in stride
- ☐ Can absorb criticism and sarcasm without losing control
- ☐ Stays steady under pressure
- ☐ Keeps to the issues
- ☐ Doesn't fly off the handle when things don't go as expected
- ☐ Just tries harder when blocked
- ☐ Expects surprises
- ☐ Helps keep others calm in the storm

Some Causes

- ☐ Defensive
- ☐ Easily overwhelmed
- ☐ In a bad set of circumstances you can't get out of
- ☐ Lack of self-confidence
- ☐ Over your head
- ☐ Overly sensitive
- ☐ Perfectionist
- ☐ Too much going on
- ☐ Very control oriented
- ☐ Weak impulse control

Other Causes

BEING UNSKILLED AT: 2,11,12,13,16,30,33,34,40,41,43,48,51,58,66

OVERUSING: 11,52,59,66

Leadership Architect® Factors and Clusters

This competency is in the Trouble with People Factor (VII) (S1). This competency is in the Self-Centered Cluster (W) with: 103, 104, 105, 109, 119. You may want to check other competencies in the same Factor/Cluster for related tips.

The Map

Life is rough water. There are a lot of things that don't go right and are upsetting. There's lots to pay attention to. There are bad people. There are impossible situations. There are sad, catastrophic events. There is conflict and tension. There are contests and tests to win and pass. Sometimes you lose and it hurts. All unfortunately normal. On the other hand, losing one's cool and getting unduly upset isn't conducive to a successful career. Being able to function normally under stress and pressure is one of the mission-critical requirements for most managerial jobs. Impulse control and delay of gratification are skills that can be improved.

Some Remedies

☐ **1. Losing your cool? Deal with emotions.** Emotions are electricity and chemistry. Emotions are designed to help you cope with emergencies and threats. Emotions trigger predictable body changes. Heart pumps faster and with greater pressure. Blood flows faster. Glucose is released into the bloodstream for increased energy and strength. Eyes dilate to take in more light. Breathing rate increases to get more oxygen. Why is that? To either fight or flee from saber-toothed tigers, of course. Emotions are designed to help us with the so-called fight or flight response. They make the body faster and stronger temporarily. The price? In order to increase energy to the muscles, the emotional response decreases resources for the stomach—that's why we get upset stomachs under stress, and the thinking brain—that's why we say and do dumb things under stress. Even though we may be able to lift a heavy object off a trapped person, we can't think of the right thing to say in a tense meeting. Once the emotional response is triggered, it has to run its course. If no threat follows the initial trigger, it lasts from 45-60 seconds in most people. That's why your grandmother told you to count to 10. Trouble is, people have saber-toothed tigers in their heads. In modern times, thoughts can trigger this emotional response. Events which are certainly not physically threatening, like being criticized, can trigger the response. Even worse, people today have added a third "f" to the fight or flight response—freeze. Emotions can shut you down and leave you speechless, neither choosing to fight—argue, respond, nor flee—calmly shut down the transaction and exit.

☐ **2. Do you know what sets you off? Identify your trigger points.** Write down on 3" x 5" note cards or Post-it® Notes the last 25 times you lost your composure. Most people who have composure problems have three to five repeating triggers. Criticism. Loss of control. A certain kind of person. An enemy. Being surprised. Spouse. Children. Money. Authority. Try to group 90% of the events into three to five categories. Once you have the groupings, ask yourself why these are problems. Is it ego? Losing face? Being caught short? Being found out? Causing you more work? In each grouping, what would be a more mature response? Mentally and physically rehearse a better response. Try to decrease by 10% a month the number of times you lose your composure.

☐ **3. No filter? Increase your impulse control.** People say and do dumb and inappropriate things when they lose their composure. The problem is that they say the first thing that occurs to them to say. They do the first thing that occurs to them to do. Research shows that generally somewhere between the second and third thing you think of to say or do is the best option. Practice holding back your first response long enough to think of a second. When you can do that, wait long enough to think of a third before you choose. By that time 50% of your composure problems should go away.

☐ **4. Need to regain composure? Count to 10.** Our thinking and judgment is not at its best during the emotional response. Create and practice delaying tactics. Go get a pencil out of your briefcase. Go get a cup of coffee. Ask a question and listen. Go up to the flip chart and write something. Take notes. Think of something you like. See yourself in a setting you find calming. Go to the bathroom. You need about a minute to regain your composure after the emotional response is triggered. Don't do or say anything until the minute has passed. *More help? – See #11 Composure.*

☐ **5. Impatient? Delay gratification.** Are you impatient? Do you get upset when the plane is delayed? The food is late? The car isn't ready? Your spouse is behind schedule? For most of us, life is one big delay. We always seem to be waiting for someone else to do something so we can do our something. People with composure problems often can't accept delay of what they want and think they deserve and have coming. When what they want is delayed, they get belligerent and demanding. They get emotional. Voice gets louder. Criticism of the blocking person or group goes up. Write down the last 25 delays that set you off. Group them into three to five categories. Create and rehearse a more mature response. Relax. Reward yourself with something enjoyable. Adopt a philosophical stance since there's little or nothing you can do about it. Think great thoughts while you're waiting. *More help? – See #41 Patience.*

- ☐ **6. Defensive? Deal constructively with criticism.** A lot of loss of composure starts with an intended or even an unintended criticism. There are a lot of perfect people in this world who cannot deal with a piece of negative information about themselves or about something they have or have not done. You might be one of these perfect people. The rest of us have flaws that most around us know about and once in a while tell us about. We even know that once in a while unjust criticism is sent our way. Dealing constructively with criticism is a learnable skill. *More help? – See #108 Defensiveness.*
- ☐ **7. Too controlling? Loosen your grip.** Are you somewhat of a perfectionist? Need to have everything just so? Create plans and expect them to be followed? Very jealous of your time? Another source of loss of composure is when things do not go exactly as planned. Put slack in your plans. Expect the unexpected. Lengthen the time line. Plan for delays. List worst-case scenarios. Most of the time you will be pleasantly surprised and the rest of the time you won't get so upset.
- ☐ **8. Feel a need to retaliate? Don't make it personal.** Do you feel a need to punish the people and groups that set you off? Do you become hostile, angry, sarcastic or vengeful? While all that may be temporarily satisfying to you they will all backfire and you will lose in the long term. When someone attacks you, rephrase it as an attack on a problem. Reverse the argument—ask what they would do if they were in your shoes. When the other side takes a rigid position, don't reject it. Ask why—what are the principles behind the offer, how do we know it's fair, what's the theory of the case, play out what would happen if their position was accepted. Let the other side vent frustration, blow off steam, but don't react. When you do reply to an attack, keep it to the facts and their impact on you. It's fine for you to draw conclusions about the impact on yourself—"I felt blindsided"; it's not fine for you to tell others their motives—"You blindsided me" means you did it, probably meant to, and I know the meaning of your behavior. So state the meaning for yourself; ask others what their actions meant.
- ☐ **9. Getting anxious and jumping to conclusions? Be deliberate.** Take quick action? Don't like ambiguity and uncertainty and act to wipe it out? Solutions first, understanding second? Take the time to really define the problem. Let people finish. Try not to interrupt. Don't finish others' sentences. Ask clarifying questions. Restate the problem in your own words to everyone's satisfaction. Ask them what they think. Throw out trial solutions for debate. Then decide.

- ☐ **10. Too much invested at work? Exercise for stress relief.** Find a release for your pent-up emotions. Get a physical hobby. Start an exercise routine. Jog. Walk. Chop wood. Sometimes people who have flare tempers hold it in too much, the pressure builds, and the teakettle blows. The body stores energy. It has to go somewhere. Work on releasing your work frustration off-work.

Some Develop-in-Place Assignments

- ☐ Make peace with an enemy or someone you've disappointed with a product or service or someone you've had some trouble with or don't get along with very well.
- ☐ Manage a group through a significant business crisis.
- ☐ Handle a tough negotiation with an internal or external client or customer.
- ☐ Manage the assigning/allocating of office space in a contested situation.
- ☐ Take on a task you dislike or hate to do.

Genuine good taste consists in saying much in few words,
in choosing among our thoughts, in having order and arrangement
in what we say, and in speaking with composure.
François Fénelon – French Roman Catholic theologian, poet, and writer

Suggested Readings

Berry, D. M., & Berry, T. J. (2008). *A peace of my mind: A therapist's guide to handling anger and other difficult emotions.* Manitowoc, WI: Blue Water.

Brantley, J., Millstine, W., & Matik, W. O. (2005). *Five good minutes: 100 Morning practices to help you stay calm and focused all day long.* Oakland, CA: New Harbinger.

Calzada, L. (2007). *180 Ways to effectively deal with change: Get over it! Get with it! Get to it!* Flower Mound, TX: Walk the Talk Company.

Carter, L. (2003). *The anger trap: Free yourself from the frustrations that sabotage your life.* New York: John Wiley & Sons.

Carter, L. (2007). *Getting the best of your anger: Before it gets the best of you.* Grand Rapids, MI: Fleming H. Revell.

Cloke, K., & Goldsmith, J. (2005). *Resolving conflicts at work: Eight strategies for everyone on the job* (Rev. ed.). San Francisco: Jossey-Bass.

Dotlich, D. L., & Cairo, P. C. (2003). *Why CEOs fail: The 11 behaviors that can derail your climb to the top and how to manage them.* San Francisco: Jossey-Bass.

Eifert, G. H., McKay, M., & Forsyth, J. P. (2006). *Act on life, not on anger: The new acceptance and commitment therapy guide to problem anger.* Oakland, CA: New Harbinger.

Ellis, A. (2000). *How to control your anxiety before it controls you.* New York: Citadel Press.

Forsyth, J. P., & Eifert, G. H. (2007). *The mindfulness and acceptance workbook for anxiety: A guide to breaking free from anxiety, phobias, and worry using acceptance and commitment therapy.* Oakland, CA: New Harbinger.

Freedman, M. (with Tregoe, B. B.). (2003). *The art and discipline of strategic leadership.* New York: McGraw-Hill.

Gibson, D., & Tulgan, B. (2002). *Managing anger in the workplace.* Amherst, MA: HRD Press.

Gonthier, G., & Morrissey, K. (2002). *Rude awakenings: Overcoming the civility crisis in the workplace.* Chicago: Dearborn Trade.

Greenleaf, R. K., Spears, L. C., & Covey, S. R. (2002). *Servant leadership: A journey into the nature of legitimate power and greatness (25th Anniversary ed.).* Mahwah, NJ: Paulist Press.

Harris, R. M. (2006). *The listening leader: Powerful new strategies for becoming an influential communicator.* Westport, CT: Praeger.

Hershatter, A. (2007). *Business at the speed of molasses: How patience produces profits.* New York: Crown Business.

Krames, J. A. (2003). *What the best CEOs know: 7 Exceptional leaders and their lessons for transforming any business.* New York: McGraw-Hill.

Lerner, H. (2002). *The dance of connection: How to talk to someone when you're mad, hurt, scared, frustrated, insulted, betrayed, or desperate.* New York: Quill/HarperCollins.

Lord, R. G., Klimoski, R. J., & Kanfer, R. (Eds.). (2002). *Emotions in the workplace: Understanding the structure and role of emotions in organizational behavior.* San Francisco: Jossey-Bass.

Newman, J. (2007). *How to stay cool, calm, and collected when the pressure's on: A stress control plan for business people.* New York: AMACOM.

Straus, D. (2002). *How to make collaboration work: Powerful ways to build consensus, solve problems, and make decisions.* San Francisco: Berrett-Koehler Publishers.

108 Defensiveness

I've learned I can make a mistake and the whole world doesn't end.
I had to learn to allow myself to make a mistake
without becoming defensive and unforgiving.
Lisa Kudrow – American actress

A Problem

- ☐ Is not open to criticism
- ☐ Denies mistakes and faults
- ☐ Rationalizes away failures
- ☐ Gets upset at the messenger who brings bad news
- ☐ Blames others for his/her own problems
- ☐ Doesn't listen to and doesn't hear negative feedback
- ☐ Doesn't share views of personal limitations with others
- ☐ Doesn't benefit much from formal feedback events or workshops

Not A Problem

- ☐ Takes criticism as a chance to learn
- ☐ Listens attentively to negative feedback
- ☐ Learns from feedback
- ☐ Admits flaws and mistakes
- ☐ Takes personal responsibility when things don't go well
- ☐ Learns from personal growth workshops and plans
- ☐ Thanks people for feedback

Some Causes

- ☐ Blame others
- ☐ Can't read others
- ☐ Combative style
- ☐ Deny faults
- ☐ Don't seek feedback
- ☐ Don't share much
- ☐ Not approachable
- ☐ Perfectionist
- ☐ Rigid
- ☐ Shut down in the face of criticism

Other Causes

BEING UNSKILLED AT: 3,11,12,29,33,40,44,45,46,54,55,57,64

OVERUSING: 5,6,10,14,21,22,24,30,39,47,52,53,62

Leadership Architect® Factors and Clusters

This competency is in the Trouble with People Factor (VII) (S1). This competency is in the Doesn't Relate Well to Others Cluster (V) with: 101, 106, 112. You may want to check other competencies in the same Factor/Cluster for related tips.

The Map

Self-knowledge is a mission-critical key to success and defensiveness takes away that key. People will give you less and less feedback and you'll rely increasingly on inaccurate self-perception. Your blind spots—things they know about you that you deny or are unaware of—will multiply and eventually one of them will stall your career. The fix is to signal to others that you are open to listening to feedback, accurate or not, justified or not, and you'll take it all under advisement. Some of it you'll respond to with developmental efforts, some you will discard, and some you will refute. You can't do those three very constructive things until after you have taken it in.

Some Remedies

- ☐ **1. Need honest feedback? Get 360° feedback.** Defensiveness is a major blockage to accurate and comprehensive self-knowledge. *More help? – See #55 Self-Knowledge.* Defensive people overrate themselves in the eyes of others. If you are seen as denying your faults, you may get jumped on when people finally get the chance to give you feedback. Their evaluations of you have to be lower than justified because they think the message has to be louder to get through your defense shields. Your best chance of getting real feedback as a defensive person is to get facilitated 360° feedback where the respondents remain anonymous or get a Human Resources professional to collect information for you and interpret it with you. If you ask for feedback directly, you are unlikely to find truth because of your history of being defensive in the face of negative criticism. Nobody enjoys giving even truthful and helpful criticism and feedback to a defensive person. It's just too painful.
- ☐ **2. Getting ruffled? Manage your defensive response.** You will need to work on keeping yourself in a calm state when getting negative feedback. You need to change your thinking. When getting the feedback, your only task is to accurately understand what people are trying to tell you. It is not your task at that point to accept or reject. That comes later. Mentally rehearse how you will calmly react to tough feedback situations before

they happen. Develop automatic tactics to shut down or delay your usual emotional response. Some useful tactics are to slow down, take notes, ask clarifying questions, ask them for concrete examples, and thank them for telling you since you know it's not easy for them.

☐ **3. Can't take feedback? Listen to feedback without worrying about its accuracy.** Remember, people suspect you really can't take feedback, that you believe yourself to be perfect, that you are defending against any suggestion to the contrary, and probably blaming the messenger of the feedback for the bad data. They expect the transaction to be painful for them and you. To break this cycle, you need to follow the rules of good listening. *More help? – See #33 Listening.* While this may sound unfair, you should initially accept all feedback as accurate, even when you know it isn't. You have to help others give you feedback in the beginning to overcome their fear of your defensiveness. On those matters that really count, you can go back and fix it later.

☐ **4. Can't make sense of it? Reflect on and analyze the feedback.** Once you have understood the feedback, and after the event, write down all of the criticisms on 3" x 5" cards or Post-it® Notes. Create two piles. These criticisms are probably true of me and these are probably not. Ask someone you trust who knows you well to help you so you don't delude yourself. For those that are true, signal the people who gave you the feedback that you have understood, think it was accurate, and will try to do something about it. For those that are not true, resort the pile into criticisms that are important to you and those that are small and trivial or unimportant. Throw the unimportant pile away. With those that are probably not true but important, re-sort the pile into career threatening—if people above me really thought this was true about me, my career would be damaged, and not career stopping. Throw the not-career-stopping away. With the remaining pile, review them with your boss and/or mentor to see what the general opinion is about you. This leaves you with two piles: those that people do believe—even though they are not true—and those they don't. Throw the don't-believe pile away. With the remaining pile, plot a strategy to convince people around you by deeds, not words, that those criticisms are untrue of you.

☐ **5. Courageous enough to admit it? Show others you take your development seriously.** Share your developmental needs and ask for their help. One of the best ways to avoid criticism is to bring it up yourself first and let others just fill in the details. Research shows that people are much more likely to help and give the benefit of the doubt to those who admit their shortcomings and try to do something about them. They know it takes courage. *More help? – See #44 Personal Disclosure.*

☐ **6. Resisting new ideas? Focus on the problem and invite criticism of your ideas.** A corollary to personal defensiveness is resistance to anything new or different. In your day-to-day interactions with people, your defensiveness may make you appear closed or blocked to new or different points of view. Your first job is to turn off your evaluator/rejector program and learn to listen more. *More help? – See #33 Listening.* Ask more questions—"How did you get there?" "Do you prefer this to that or to what we're now doing?" If you disagree, give your reasons first. Then invite criticism of your response. Turn the disagreement back to the nature of the problem or strategy—"What are we trying to solve? What causes it? What questions should be answered? What objective standards could we use to measure success?" Get the discussion off your view versus whomever and onto the criteria for making a decision. *More help? – See #12 Conflict Management.* Develop a more open style. You should work on *#3 Approachability and #31 Interpersonal Savvy.* Until you signal repeatedly that you are open to others, interested in what they have to say, share personal things you don't have to share, invite people to talk with you and then listen, little will come of this effort. You will have to persevere, endure some rejection, and perhaps some angry or dismissive remarks in order to balance the situation. Mentally rehearse so you're not blindsided by this. Since others think they will get a defensive reaction if they offer some criticism, you have to open the conversation.

☐ **7. Got blind spots? Turn blind spots into known weaknesses.** The thing that gets us in the most career trouble is a blind spot that matters. Blind spots are weaknesses we really have that we deny or reject. That means we go about performing as if we were very good at it when in fact we're not. Better to have a known and admitted weakness. We know we are not good at it so we try harder, ask for help, delegate it, get a consultant, get a tutor, read a book or loop around it. Your new life task is to have no blind spots. Turn all of your blind spots into known weaknesses and then the known weaknesses into skills. Make it a quest to find out what everybody really thinks about you. *More help? – See #55 Self-Knowledge.*

☐ **8. Afraid to open up? Disclose more.** Defensive people tend to be shy or not very forthcoming with personal data, especially about possible weaknesses and mistakes. *More help? – See #44 Personal Disclosure.* The kinds of disclosures that people enjoy are the reasons behind why you do and decide what you do, your self-appraisal, things you know behind what's happening in the business that they don't know—that you are at liberty to disclose, things both good and embarrassing that have happened to you in the past, comment about what's going on around you—without being too negative about others, and things you are interested in and do outside of work. These are areas which you should learn to disclose more than you now do. If you share your self-appraisal of your possible weaknesses and shortcomings, that decreases the number of times you need to be defensive. These icebreakers open the door to the kind of relationships where you can get more feedback.

☐ **9. Making knee-jerk responses? Avoid sharp and instant reactions.** This is very likely getting you into trouble. You may jump to conclusions, categorically dismiss what others say, use aggressive or inflammatory language or are quick to deny or blame. People then see you as closed or combative. More negatively, they may believe you think they're stupid or ill-informed. If you're seen as intolerant or closed or quick to jump, people will often stumble over words in their haste to talk with you or short-cut their argument since they assume you're not listening anyway. The key is always to ask a clarifying question first to get you more information and to prepare a measured and calmer response.

☐ **10. Sending the wrong signals? Watch your non-verbals.** Most defensive people have one or more non-verbals that signal to others they don't accept what the person is saying. It could be the washboard brow, blank stare, flushing, body agitation, finger or pencil drumming, pointing, etc. Most around you know the signs. Do you? Ask someone you trust what it is that you do. Work on eliminating those chilling non-verbals.

Some Develop-in-Place Assignments

☐ Make peace with an enemy or someone you've disappointed with a product or service or someone you've had some trouble with or don't get along with very well.

☐ Manage a dissatisfied internal or external customer; troubleshoot a performance or quality problem with a product or service.

☐ Manage a group of people who are towering experts but you are not.

☐ Try to learn something frivolous and fun to see how good you can get (e.g., juggling, square dancing, magic).

☐ Attend a self-awareness/assessment course that includes feedback.

When you become defensive, blame others, and do not accept
and surrender to the moment, your life meets resistance.
Any time you encounter resistance, recognize that
if you force the situation, the resistance will only increase.
You don't want to stand rigid like a tall oak
that cracks and collapses in the storm. Instead, you want
to be flexible, like a reed that bends with the storm and survives.
Deepak Chopra – Indian physician and writer

Suggested Readings

Berry, D. M., & Berry, T. J. (2008). *A peace of my mind: A therapist's guide to handling anger and other difficult emotions.* Manitowoc, WI: Blue Water.

Blakeley, K. (2007). *Leadership blind spots and what to do about them.* Chichester, England: John Wiley & Sons.

Brantley, J., Millstine, W., & Matik, W. O. (2005). *Five good minutes: 100 Morning practices to help you stay calm and focused all day long.* Oakland, CA: New Harbinger.

Buron, R. J., & McDonald-Mann, D. (2003). *Giving feedback to subordinates* (Rev. ed.). Greensboro, NC: Center for Creative Leadership.

Calzada, L. (2007). *180 Ways to effectively deal with change: Get over it! Get with it! Get to it!* Flower Mound, TX: Walk the Talk Company.

Cox, D., & Hoover, J. (2002). *Leadership when the heat's on.* New York: McGraw-Hill.

Donoghue, P. J., & Siegel, M. E. (2005). *Are you really listening? Keys to successful communication.* Notre Dame, IN: Sorin Books.

Dotlich, D. L., & Cairo, P. C. (2003). *Why CEOs fail: The 11 behaviors that can derail your climb to the top and how to manage them.* San Francisco: Jossey-Bass.

Folkman, J. R. (2006). *The power of feedback: 35 Principles for turning feedback from others into personal and professional change.* Hoboken, NJ: John Wiley & Sons.

Garner, R. (2006). *Criticism management: How to more effectively give, receive, and seek criticism in our lives.* The Woodlands, TX: Prescient Press.

Goman, C. (2008). *The nonverbal advantage: Secrets and science of body language at work.* San Francisco: Berrett-Koehler Publishers.

Hershorn, M. (2002). *:60 Second anger management: Quick tips to handle explosive feelings.* New Jersey: New Horizon Press.

Lerner, H. (2002). *The dance of connection: How to talk to someone when you're mad, hurt, scared, frustrated, insulted, betrayed, or desperate.* New York: HarperCollins.

Levine, S. (2000). *Getting to resolution: Turning conflict into collaboration.* San Francisco: Berrett-Koehler Publishers.

Lord, R. G., Klimoski, R. J., & Kanfer, R. (Eds.). (2002). *Emotions in the workplace: Understanding the structure and role of emotions in organizational behavior.* San Francisco: Jossey-Bass.

Nichols, M. P. (2009). *The lost art of listening* (2nd ed.). New York: The Guilford Press.

Patterson, K., Grenny, J., McMillan, R., Switzler, A., & Covey, S. R. (2002). *Crucial conversations: Tools for talking when stakes are high.* New York: McGraw-Hill.

Pearman, R. R., Lombardo, M. M., & Eichinger, R. W. (2005). *You: Being more effective in your MBTI type.* Minneapolis, MN: Lominger International: A Korn/Ferry Company.

Scott, S. (2004). *Fierce conversations: Achieving success at work and in life, one conversation at a time* (Rev. ed.). New York: Viking Press.

Tamm, J. W., & Luyet, R. J. (2004). *Radical collaboration: Five essential skills to overcome defensiveness and build successful relationships.* New York: HarperCollins.

Weisinger, H. (2000). *The power of positive criticism.* New York: AMACOM.

109 *Lack of* Ethics and Values

Ethics, too, is nothing but reverence for life.
This is what gives me the fundamental principle of morality,
namely, that good consists in maintaining, promoting, and enhancing life,
and that destroying, injuring, and limiting life are evil.
Albert Schweitzer – Alsatian theologian, physician, and philosopher

A Problem

- ☐ Lacks the necessary sensitivity to the operating ethics and values of the organization
- ☐ Operates too close to the margins
- ☐ Pushes the limits of tolerance
- ☐ Doesn't operate within the norms

Not A Problem

- ☐ Values and ethics are generally aligned with the organization's
- ☐ Operates within boundaries most others would agree to
- ☐ Looked to for guidance on standards and norms
- ☐ Stays steady through crises involving close calls on ethics
- ☐ Can articulate own and others' values
- ☐ Helpful to others in making close calls on values/ethical matters
- ☐ Projects a consistent set of values

Some Causes

- ☐ Inconsistent
- ☐ Operate close to the edge
- ☐ Overly ambitious
- ☐ Overly independent
- ☐ Pragmatic to a fault
- ☐ Set own rules of conduct
- ☐ Situational ethics

Other Causes

BEING UNSKILLED AT: 7,10,11,21,22,29,40,48,57

OVERUSING: 6,16,21,27,37,38,49,52,53,66

Leadership Architect® Factors and Clusters

This competency is in the Trouble with People Factor (VII) (S1). This competency is in the Self-Centered Cluster (W) with: 103, 104, 105, 107, 119. You may want to check other competencies in the same Factor/Cluster for related tips.

The Map

Being seen as having questionable ethics is a category killer. At the least it means the values and ethics you are operating under are not in line with the commonly held values and ethics of those around you. On the more negative side, it could mean you have unacceptable values and ethics in a more absolute sense; that is, most would reject them. You may hedge or operate too close to the edge for people to feel comfortable with you. Most of us haven't thought out our values/ethical stances well; we are on autopilot from childhood and our collective experience. People deduce your values and ethics by listening to what you say and more importantly watching what you do. Unless you address this issue now, your career with this organization might be in jeopardy.

Some Remedies

☐ **1. Unsure of the real issues? Diagnose the problem.** Make sure you know exactly what your problem is. The range of possibilities is great. Get 360° feedback on this specific issue by having a Human Resource professional or outside consultant poll people to find out what your difficulty is. As a less severe problem, you may be just stubborn and rigid, tied to the values of the past, out of tune with the times, pragmatic to a fault, be seen as not helpful enough to others, pushing your own agenda, playing favorites, or being reluctant to speak up. As a more severe problem, you might be cutting corners to look good, setting your own rules, blaming others for things you should take responsibility for, sabotaging your rivals, hedging the truth, or showing little concern for others. *More help? – See #55 Self-Knowledge.*

☐ **2. Ready to admit it? Take corrective action.** The worst case—your ethics really are questionable. You hedge, sabotage others, play for advantage, set up others and make others look bad. You may be devious and scheming and overly political. You tell yourself it's OK because you are getting the results out on time. You really believe the end justifies the means. If any of this is true, this criticism should have also happened to you in the past. This is not something that develops overnight. You need to find out if your career with this organization is salvageable. The best way to do this is to admit that you know your ethics and values are not the same as the people you work with and ask a boss or a mentor whether it's fixable. If they say yes, contact everyone you think you've alienated and see how they respond. Tell them the things you're going to do differently. Ask them if the situation can be repaired. Longer term, you need to seek some professional counsel on your values and ethics.

☐ **3. Unpredictable? Be consistent across situations and groups.** You might just be inconsistent in your value stances and actions. You change your mind based on mood or who you talked with last. That may confuse and bother people. You may express a pro people value in one instance—people you manage, and an anti people value in another—people from another unit. You may rigidly adhere to a high moral code in one transaction—with customers, and play it close to the acceptable margin in another—with vendors. You may match your values with your audience when managing up and not when you're managing down. You may play favorites. People are more comfortable with consistency and predictability. Look for the three to five areas where you think these inconsistencies play out. Write down what you did with various people so you can compare. Did you do different things in parallel situations? Do you hold others to a different standard? Do you have so many values positions that they have to clash? Do you state so few that people have to fill in the blanks with guesses? Try to balance your behavior so that you are more consistent across situations.

☐ **4. Sending mixed messages? Avoid "do as I say, not as I do" behavior.** Another possibility is that there is a sizable gap between what you say about your ethics and values and what the ethics and values of others should be and what you actually do in those same situations. We have worked with many who get themselves in trouble by giving motivating values and ethics speeches, high-toned, passionate, charismatic, gives you goose bumps—until you watch that person do the opposite or something quite different in practice. Examine all the things you tend to say in speeches or in meetings or casual conversations that are values and ethics based. Write them down the left side of a legal pad. For each one, see if you can write three to five examples of when you acted exactly in line with that value or ethic. Can you write down any that are not exactly like that? If you can, it's the gap that's the problem. Either stop making values and ethics statements you can't model or bring your values into alignment with your own statements.

☐ **5. Trouble finding the right words? Send clear messages.** Another possibility is that there is a sizable gap between what you say and the language you use and what you actually think and do. We have worked with many who get themselves in trouble by using language and words that imply marginal values and ethics that are not real. Do you shoot for effect? Do you exaggerate? Do you push your statements to the extreme to make a point? Do you overstate negative views? Do you trash talk to fit in?

Do you use demeaning words? What would others think your values were if they listened to you talk and didn't know what you actually do? Examine the words and the language you tend to use in speeches or in meetings or casual conversations that are values and ethics based. Write them down the left side of a legal pad. For each one, see if you can write three to five examples of when you acted exactly in line with those words. Do you really act like that? Do you really think that way? If you don't, it's the gap that's the problem. Stop using words and language that are not in line with your real thoughts and values.

☐ **6. Muddled values? Get clarity about your values.** You may not think in terms of values much, and your statements may not clearly state your values. To pass the test of a thoughtfully held value, you should be able to state it in a sentence, give five examples of how it plays out, both the situation and consequences; state what is the opposite of the value—what is dishonesty, for example, and demonstrate how you follow the value. Since you are having trouble in this area, it may be a good exercise to try to capture your value system on paper so you can practice delivering a clear statement of it to others. If you ignore obvious values implications, people may assume you don't care.

☐ **7. Struggling with close calls? Bring focus and clarity to the gray areas.** Sometimes people get in trouble because they don't understand the underlying mismatch between values. Few people have any trouble with clear-cut value clashes; it's the close calls where ill-thought-through positions get us in trouble. You should be able to pro and con various values. You should be able to help people think through when to break a confidence or when loyalty to the organization supersedes loyalty to an individual. What are the common values clashes you deal with? In these situations, you need to be able to argue both sides of the question. Hedging on your tax return and padding of an expense account; is that the same or different? Working with or firing a marginal performer? Cutting quality or raising the price? Firing someone for drug abuse and serving alcohol at company functions? *More help? – See #12 Conflict Management.*

☐ **8. Too independent? Recognize that you don't operate in a vacuum.** You set your own rules, smash through obstacles, see yourself as tough, action and results oriented. You get it done. The problem is, you wreak havoc for others; they don't know which of your actions will create headaches for them in their own unit or with customers. You don't often worry about whether others think like you do. You operate from the inside out. What's important to you is what you think and what you judge to be right and just. In a sense, admirable. In a sense, not smart. You live in an organization that has both formal and informal commonly held standards, beliefs, ethics and values. You can't survive long without knowing what they are and bending yours to fit. To find out, focus on the impact on others and how they see the issue. This will be hard at first since you spend your energy justifying your own actions.

☐ **9. Constrained by your own point of view? Go beyond the facts to consider the values of others.** You may be a fact-based person. Since to you the facts dictate everything, you may be baffled as to why people would see it any differently than you do. The reason they see it differently is that there is a higher order of values at work. People compare across situations to check for common themes, equity and parity. They ask questions like who wins and loses here, who is being favored, is this a play for advantage? Since you are a here-and-now person, you will look inconsistent to them across slightly different situations. You need to drop back and ask what will others hear, not what you want to say. Go below the surface. Tell them why you're saying something. Ask them what they think.

☐ **10. Stuck in the past? Adapt when it makes sense.** This is a tough one. Times change. Do values change? Some think not. That may be your stance. What about humor? Could you tell some ribald jokes 10 years ago that would get you in trouble today? Have dating practices and ages changed? Has television and 24-hour news changed our world view? Is there still lifelong employment? How long does a college education last today versus 20 years ago? Values run pretty deep. They don't change easily. When did you form your current values? Over 20 years ago? Maybe it's time to examine them in light of the new today to see whether you need to make any midcourse corrections.

Some Develop-in-Place Assignments

☐ Make peace with an enemy or someone you've disappointed with a product or service or someone you've had some trouble with or don't get along with very well.

☐ Manage a group through a significant business crisis.

☐ Handle a tough negotiation with an internal or external client or customer.

☐ Manage the assigning/allocating of office space in a contested situation.

☐ Manage a dissatisfied internal or external customer; troubleshoot a performance or quality problem with a product or service.

The most exhausting thing in life is being insincere.
Anne Morrow Lindbergh – American aviator and author

Suggested Readings

Bellingham, R. (2003). *Ethical leadership: Rebuilding trust in corporations.* Amherst, MA: HRD Press.

Bennis, W., Goleman, D., & O'Toole, J. (with Ward Biederman, P.). (2008). *Transparency: How leaders create a culture of candor.* San Francisco: Jossey-Bass.

Boatright, J. R. (2006). *Ethics and the conduct of business* (5th ed.). Upper Saddle River, NJ: Prentice Hall.

Brown, M. T. (2005). *Corporate integrity: Rethinking organizational ethics and leadership.* New York: Cambridge University Press.

Buckner, M. L. (2007). *The ABCs of ethics: A resource for leaders, managers, and professionals.* Lincoln, NE: iUniverse.

Ciulla, J. B. (Ed.). (2004). *Ethics, the heart of leadership* (2nd ed.).Westport, CT: Praeger.

Cooper, C. (2008). *Extraordinary circumstances: The journey of a corporate whistleblower.* Hoboken, NJ: John Wiley & Sons.

Dobrin, A. (2002). *Ethics for everyone: How to increase your moral intelligence.* New York: John Wiley & Sons.

Ferrell, O. C., Fraedrich, J., & Ferrell, L. (2006). *Business ethics: Ethical decision making and cases* (7th ed.). Boston: Houghton Mifflin.

Heineman, B. W., Jr. (2008). *High performance with high integrity.* Boston: Harvard Business School Press.

Johnson, C. E. (2005). *Meeting the ethical challenges of leadership: Casting light or shadow* (2nd ed.). Thousand Oaks, CA: Sage.

Klann, G. (2007). *Building character: Strengthening the heart of good leadership.* San Francisco: Jossey-Bass.

Knapp, J. C. (Ed.). (2007). *Leaders on ethics: Real-world perspectives on today's business challenges.* Westport, CT: Praeger.

Lubit, R. H. (2003). *Coping with toxic managers, subordinates...and other difficult people: Using emotional intelligence to survive and prosper.* Upper Saddle River, NJ: Financial Times Prentice Hall.

McLean, B., & Elkind, P. (2003). *The smartest guys in the room: The amazing rise and scandalous fall of Enron.* New York: Portfolio.

Porter, M. E., & Kramer, M. R. (2006). Strategy and society: The link between competitive advantage and corporate social responsibility. *Harvard Business Review, 85*, 136-137.

Ruggiero, V. R. (2003). *Thinking critically about ethical issues.* New York: McGraw-Hill.

Seglin, J. L. (2000). *The good, the bad, and your business: Choosing right when ethical dilemmas pull you apart.* New York: John Wiley & Sons.

Showkeir, J., & Showkeir, M. (2008). *Authentic conversations: Moving from manipulation to truth and commitment.* San Francisco: Berrett-Koehler Publishers.

Spinello, R., & Tavani, H. T. (Eds.). (2004). *Readings in cyberethics* (2nd ed.). Sudbury, MA: Jones & Bartlett.

Terris, D. (2005). *Ethics at work: Creating virtue at an American corporation.* Waltham, MA: Brandeis University Press.

110 Failure to Build a Team

Build for your team a feeling of oneness, of dependence on one another, and of strength to be derived by unity.
Vince Lombardi – American football coach

A Problem

- ☐ Doesn't believe much in the value of teams
- ☐ Doesn't pull the group together to accomplish the task
- ☐ Delegates pieces and parts
- ☐ Doesn't resolve problems within the team
- ☐ Doesn't share credit for successes
- ☐ Doesn't celebrate
- ☐ Doesn't build team spirit
- ☐ Treats people more as a collection of individuals than as a team

Not A Problem

- ☐ Usually operates in a team format
- ☐ Talks "we," "us" and "the team" versus "I"
- ☐ Gets the whole team motivated and enthused
- ☐ Runs participative meetings and processes
- ☐ Shares credit with the team for successes
- ☐ Adds people to strengthen the team
- ☐ Team performance doesn't suffer when a key person moves on
- ☐ Trusts the team to perform

Some Causes

- ☐ Can't set common cause
- ☐ Can't resolve conflict among direct reports
- ☐ Don't believe in teams
- ☐ Don't have the time
- ☐ Don't want to deal with the conflict
- ☐ More comfortable one-on-one
- ☐ The idea of a team is resisted by people
- ☐ Time management; too busy
- ☐ Too serious and heavy

Other Causes

BEING UNSKILLED AT: 3,7,9,10,11,13,16,19,20,21,23,27,31,33,34,35,36,39,41, 44,47,52,55,57,58,59,60,63,64

OVERUSING: 9,12,14,16,20,21,26,30,33,35,39,47,52,53,57,59,65

Leadership Architect® Factors and Clusters

This competency is in the Trouble with People Factor (VII) (S1). This competency is in the Doesn't Inspire or Build Talent Cluster (X) with: 111, 117. You may want to check other competencies in the same Factor/Cluster for related tips.

The Map

There is more talk of teams than there are well-functioning teams. Most managers grow up as strong individual contributors. That's why they get promoted. They weren't like the rest of the members of the team. They were not raised in teams. They owe little of their success to teams. As a matter of fact, most of them could tell you stories about how some past team held them back from getting things done. But teams, although strange and uncomfortable to many, are the best way to accomplish some tasks such as creating systems that cross boundaries, producing complex products, or sustained coordinated efforts. It's really rewarding to be a member of a well-functioning, high-performance team. Well-functioning teams can outproduce the collective of what each individual could do on his/her own. Most individuals would choose to work for a boss who was able to build a well-functioning team.

Some Remedies

- ☐ **1. Prefer an individualistic approach? Find the value in teams.** If you don't believe in teams, you are probably a strong individual achiever who doesn't like the mess and sometimes the slowness of due-process relationships and team processes. You are very results oriented and truly believe the best way to do that is manage one person at a time. To balance this thinking, observe and talk with three excellent team builders and ask them why they manage that way. What do they consider rewarding about building teams? What advantages do they get from using the team format? Read *The Wisdom of Teams* by Katzenbach and Smith. If you can't see the value in teams, none of the following tips will help much.
- ☐ **2. No time? Make the time and reap the benefits.** Don't have the time; teaming takes longer. That's true and not true. While building a team takes longer than managing one person at a time, having a well-functioning team increases results, builds in a sustaining capability to perform, maximizes collective strengths and covers individual weaknesses, and actually releases more time for the manager because the team members help each other. Many managers get caught in the trap of thinking it takes up too much time to build a team and end up taking more time managing one-on-one. *More help? – See #62 Time Management.*
- ☐ **3. Not a people person? Focus on basic people skills.** Many managers are better with things, ideas, and projects than they are with people. They may be

driven and very focused on producing results and have little time left to develop their people skills. It really doesn't take too much. There is communicating. People are more motivated and do better work when they know what's going on. They want to know more than just their little piece. *More help? – See #27 Informing.* There is listening. Nothing motivates more than a boss who will listen, not interrupt, not finish your sentences, and not complete your thoughts. Increase your listening time 30 seconds in each transaction. *More help? – See #33 Listening.* There is caring. Caring is questions. Caring is asking about me and what I think and what I feel. Ask one more question per transaction than you do now. *More help? – See #7 Caring About Direct Reports.*

☐ **4. Want to optimize team performance? Study the characteristics of high-performing teams.** High-performance teams have four common characteristics: (1) They have a shared mindset. They have a common vision. Everyone knows the goals and measures. *More help? – See #35 Managing and Measuring Work.* (2) They trust one another. They know you will cover me if I get in trouble. They know you will pitch in and help even though it may be difficult for you. They know you will be honest with them. They know you will bring problems to them directly and won't go behind their backs. *More help? – See #29 Integrity and Trust.* (3) They have the talent collectively to do the job. While not any one member may have it all, collectively they have every task covered. *More help? – See #25 Hiring and Staffing.* (4) They know how to operate efficiently and effectively. They have good team skills. They run effective meetings. They have efficient ways to communicate. They have ways to deal with internal conflict. *More help? – See #52 Process Management and #63 Total Work Systems (e.g., TQM/ISO/Six Sigma).*

☐ **5. Want to raise the odds that the team will excel? Inspire the team.** Follow the basic rules of inspiring others as outlined in classic books like *People Skills* by Robert Bolton or *Thriving on Chaos* by Tom Peters. Communicate to people that what they do is important, say thanks, offer help and ask for it, provide autonomy in how people do their work, provide a variety of tasks, "surprise" people with enriching, challenging assignments, show an interest in their careers, adopt a learning attitude toward mistakes, celebrate successes, have visible accepted measures of achievement and so on. Try to get everyone to participate in the building of the team so they have a stake in the outcome. *More help? – See #36 Motivating Others.*

☐ **6. Unsure of how to assign team roles? Allow roles within the team to evolve naturally.** Cement relationships. Even though some—maybe including you—will resist it, parties, roasts, gag awards, picnics and outings help build group cohesion. Allow roles to evolve naturally rather than being specified by job descriptions. Some research indicates that people gravitate naturally to eight roles—*See #64 Understanding Others*, and that successful teams are not those where everyone does the same thing. Successful teams specialize, cover for each other, and only sometimes demand that everyone participate in identical activities.

☐ **7. Are you betting on the wrong motivators? Know and play the motivation odds.** According to research by Rewick and Lawler, the top motivators at work are: (1) Job challenge; (2) Accomplishing something worthwhile; (3) Learning new things; (4) Personal development; (5) Autonomy. Pay (12th), Friendliness (14th), Praise (15th) or Chance of promotion (17th) are not insignificant but are superficial compared with the five top motivators. Provide challenges, paint pictures of why this is worthwhile, set up chances to learn and grow, and provide autonomy and you'll hit the vast majority of people's hot buttons.

☐ **8. Want to know the secret to team building? Delegate and empower others.** One true team builder is giving people tough tasks to do, the resources to do them and the authority to make decisions about it. Delegating increases motivation, releases your time to move on to other things, and gets more work done. Delegating is scary at first. They probably can't do it the first time as well as you can. But with coaching and support they will learn, and eventually either do it as well as you can or even better yet, do it better. *More help? – See #18 Delegation.*

☐ **9. Focused on the individual? Leverage the power of words and rewards.** Use we instead of I. Use the team, us, together, more. Say let us. Let's get together. We can do it. We're all in this together. Signal that you are thinking team. Do you talk teams and reward individuals? To the extent that you can, reward the team more. Take some incentive money and divide it equally among the team members. Set team goals and line up team rewards.

☐ **10. Team stuck in a rut? Create a climate of innovation and experimentation.** Don't prescribe how to do everything. How things are done should be as open as possible. Studies show that people work harder and are more effective when they have a sense of choice. Encourage quick experiments. Most innovations and experiments will fail so communicate a learning attitude toward mistakes and failures.

☐ **11. Need an outside perspective? Engage a team coach.** Because a team coach is external to the team, he or she can objectively help you problem solve and provide you with feedback to avoid some of the temptations that can demotivate a team. The team coach could be a Human Resources partner or an external professional that specializes in coaching.

☐ **12. All work and no play? Build a sense of joy and fun for the team.** Research noted in *The Wisdom of Teams* by Jon R. Katzenbach and Douglas K. Smith found there were several common threads among high-performing teams, including having fun. Fun is a by-product of the team's sense of commitment to each other and performance. If your team doesn't seem to be having fun, look for likely causes. Are the team members committed to the goals of the team? Are the team members committed to one another? Fixing one or both of these issues might result in more fun.

☐ **13. Ready to lead? Set the standard by modeling it.** Use your behavior to shape the behavior and performance of others. You have an opportunity to set the standard for the team. Many people resist developing new behaviors if they don't see those behaviors rewarded or demonstrated by more senior people. If behavior changes are required to improve team performance, they must start with you.

☐ **14. Team in a downward spiral? Study the characteristics of low-performing teams.** Much research has been done on why teams fail. Your team is probably not unique. Read *Why Teams Don't Work* and determine if your team has fallen into one of the common team traps and work to create a strategy to get the team back on track.

Some Develop-in-Place Assignments

☐ Manage a project team of people who are older and more experienced than you.

☐ Manage a group of resistant people with low morale through an unpopular change or project.

☐ Manage a group of low-competence or low-performing people through a task they couldn't do by themselves.

☐ Assemble a team of diverse people to accomplish a difficult task.

☐ Manage a group that includes former peers to accomplish a task.

The leaders who work most effectively, it seems to me, never say 'I.'
And that's not because they have trained themselves not to say 'I.'
They don't think 'I.' They think 'we'; they think 'team.'
They understand their job to be to make the team function.
They accept responsibility and don't sidestep it, but 'we' gets the credit.
This is what creates trust, what enables you to get the task done.
Peter Drucker – Austrian-born American writer
and management consultant

Suggested Readings

Barner, R. W. (2000). *Team troubleshooter.* Palo Alto, CA: Davies-Black.

Capretta Raymond, C., Eichinger, R. W., & Lombardo, M. M. (2004). *FYI for teams.* Minneapolis, MN: Lominger International: A Korn/Ferry Company.

Duarte, D. L., & Snyder, N. T. (2006). *Mastering virtual teams: Strategies, tools, and techniques that succeed* (3rd ed.). San Francisco: Jossey-Bass.

Dyer, W. G., Dyer, W. G., Jr., & Dyer, J. H. (2007). *Team building: Proven strategies for improving team performance* (4th ed.). San Francisco: Jossey-Bass.

Gibson, C. B., & Cohen, S. G. (Eds.). (2003). *Virtual teams that work: Creating conditions for virtual team effectiveness.* San Francisco: Jossey-Bass.

Guttman, H. M. (2008). *Great business teams: Cracking the code for standout performance.* Hoboken, NJ: John Wiley & Sons.

Hackman, J. R. (2002). *Leading teams: Setting the stage for great performances.* Boston: Harvard Business School Press.

Halverson, C. B., & Tirmizi, S. A. (Eds.). (2008). *Effective multicultural teams: Theory and practice* (Series: Advances in group decision and negotiation, Vol. 3.). New York: Springer.

Holliday, M. (2001). *Coaching, mentoring, and managing: Breakthrough strategies to solve performance problems and build winning teams.* Franklin Lakes, NJ: Career Press.

Jones, S. D., & Schilling, D. J. (2000). *Measuring team performance: A step-by-step, customizable approach for managers, facilitators, and team leaders.* San Francisco: Jossey-Bass.

Katzenbach, J. R., & Smith, D. K. (2003). *The wisdom of teams: Creating the high-performance organization.* New York: HarperBusiness.

Klann, G. (2004). *Building your team's morale, pride, and spirit.* Greensboro, NC: Center for Creative Leadership.

Leigh, A., & Maynard, M. (2002). *Leading your team: How to involve and inspire teams.* Yarmouth, ME: Nicholas Brealey.

Lencioni, P. (2005). *Overcoming the five dysfunctions of a team: A field guide for leaders, managers, and facilitators.* San Francisco: Jossey-Bass.

Parker, G. M. (2002). *Cross-functional teams: Working with allies, enemies, and other strangers.* San Francisco: Jossey-Bass.

Parker, G. M. (2008). *Team players and teamwork: New strategies for the competitive enterprise* (2nd ed.). San Francisco: Jossey-Bass.

Robbins, H., & Finley, M. (2000). *The new why teams don't work: What goes wrong and how to make it right.* San Francisco: Berrett-Koehler Publishers.

Straus, D. (2002). *How to make collaboration work: Powerful ways to build consensus, solve problems, and make decisions.* San Francisco: Berrett-Koehler Publishers.

Thompson, L. L. (2004). *Making the team: A guide for managers* (2nd ed.). Upper Saddle River, NJ: Pearson.

Van Ness, G., & Van Ness, K. (2003). *Being there without going there: Managing teams across time zones, locations, and corporate boundaries.* Boston: Aspatore Books.

111 Failure to Staff Effectively

The toughest decisions in organizations are people decisions—hiring, firing, promotion, etc. These are the decisions that receive the least attention and the hardest to 'unmake.'

Peter Drucker – Austrian-born American writer and management consultant

A Problem

- ☐ Does not assemble skilled staff either from inside or outside the organization
- ☐ Uses inappropriate criteria and standards
- ☐ May select people too much like him/herself
- ☐ Is not a good judge of people
- ☐ Is consistently wrong on estimates of what others may do or become

Not A Problem

- ☐ Good judge of people
- ☐ Hires for diversity and balance of skills
- ☐ Describes people in a textured manner
- ☐ Uses a broad set of criteria in staffing
- ☐ Objective track record better than most on selections
- ☐ Takes his/her time to find the right person

Some Causes

- ☐ Impatient
- ☐ Narrow perspective
- ☐ Non-strategic
- ☐ Poor people reading skills
- ☐ Unfocused
- ☐ Unwilling to take negative people actions

Other Causes

BEING UNSKILLED AT: 3,7,12,13,17,21,25,31,32,33,34,41,55,56,64

OVERUSING: 2,16,22,25,55,56,60,64

Leadership Architect® Factors and Clusters

This competency is in the Trouble with People Factor (VII) (S1). This competency is in the Doesn't Inspire or Build Talent Cluster (X) with: 110, 117. You may want to check other competencies in the same Factor/Cluster for related tips.

The Map

There is no substitute for a talented team all pulling in one direction accomplishing great things. Anything less than that is inefficient and ineffective. Getting there is a combination of hiring people against both a short-term and long-term staffing plan and having people with the necessary variety of skills and talents to do today's job with reserve to tackle tomorrow. You need the variety because no single profile or person is going to have it all.

Some Remedies

☐ **1. Need a process? Use an established and proven process for sizing up people.** You try to hire good people but you keep getting negatively surprised when they come on board. You need to develop one or more models of people to use in reading and sizing up others. There are a number of acceptable models available. *More help? – See #56 Sizing Up People and #64 Understanding Others.* Use the Leadership Architect® Sort Cards to learn how to think in terms of competencies.

☐ **2. Going with your gut? Use proven interview techniques.** You just can't seem to make accurate appraisals based upon interviews and reference checks. Sound interviewing is a known technology. Read a book on interviewing techniques and successful practices and go to a course that teaches interviewing skills, preferably one with videotaped practice and feedback. Also, have others interview the candidates using standard competency rating scales and seek their counsel.

☐ **3. Not sure what you're looking for? Define the skills that are required for success.** You don't have a feel for what skills and talents are required. Ask someone from Human Resources for help. Ask other bosses of units like yours what they look for. Benchmark with peers in other firms to see what they look for. *More help? – See #25 Hiring and Staffing.*

☐ **4. Shortsighted? Make sure your success profile takes a long-term view.** Your people choices work out in the short term but become less effective longer term. This usually means you are using a success profile that is too narrow over time. *More help? – See #46 Perspective and #58 Strategic Agility.* It could also be that your organization only pays for current skills and you have trouble hiring the best people. In this case, try to hire people who have the current skills needed and are eager to learn new skills. *More help? – See #32 Learning on the Fly.* Add "What did you learn?" and "How have you applied that?" questions to your interviews to try to hire current doers and future learners.

☐ **5. Hesitant to take action? Address people problems promptly.** You inherited the team and some of the people are just not up to standard and you don't want to pull the trigger. If you don't, it just means more work for you and the rest of the team. The sooner you address people problems, the better off everyone will be, even the people involved. *More help? – See #13 Confronting Direct Reports and #16 Timely Decision Making.*

☐ **6. Impatient? Give yourself a choice of candidates.** You are impatient to fill empty spots on your team and tend to take the first acceptable or near acceptable candidate that comes along. That means you will make compromises and probably never meet the best candidate. Always try to wait long enough for multiple candidates and a real choice. *More help? – See #41 Patience.*

☐ **7. Need diversity? Avoid hiring clones.** You tend to hire too much in your own image. You prefer working with people who think and act as you do so the team ends up skilled in only a few areas. You may load up on friends, people you have worked with in the past, or favorites. If you clone yourself in terms of skills, beliefs, background, or orientation, you and your team will not have the variety and diversity for truly great performance. *More help? – See #25 Hiring and Staffing.*

☐ **8. Ready to learn the best practices? Study high-performing teams.** Look to teams around you that you feel are the best-performing teams. What does the talent look like? What does the hiring model look like? Are the team members more the same or are they different from one another? Do they have the same background or come from a variety of situations? How do those team managers hire? Ask them what they do when filling an opening.

☐ **9. Not challenged? Stretch yourself and your team.** You spend too little time worrying about improving the team. You may as well just do the important things yourself and let the team fend for itself. This is a very short-term strategy—one that will usually get you in more trouble as the situation continues. A good rule of thumb to follow is that your team should spend 20% of its time working outside its, and perhaps your, comfort zone. Stretching assignments are the prime source or reason for improvement. *More help? – See #18 Delegation, #19 Developing Direct Reports and Others, #50 Priority Setting, and #62 Time Management.*

☐ **10. Trouble saying no? Stick to your criteria for candidates.** You take the easy way out and are hesitant to go against the grain and reject internal candidates. You can't say no to higher-ups. You will be better able to do this if you have criteria for success for the job, ones that you can discuss easily. It's far easier to take a stand if you can say, "This candidate is strong in these competencies but not in these; we need someone who can do these as well." Discussions of criteria get discussions off individuals and on to what it takes to do the job. Beyond this, you have to take a stand. Prepare a brief list of what you are looking for and stick to it calmly. Invite input on criteria, not people. *More help? – See #34 Managerial Courage and #57 Standing Alone.*

Some Develop-in-Place Assignments

☐ Work on a team that's deciding whom to keep and whom to let go in a layoff, shutdown, delayering, or merger.

☐ Hire/staff a team from outside your unit or organization.

☐ Train and work as an assessor in an assessment center.

☐ Go to a campus as a recruiter.

☐ Construct a success and derailment profile for a unit or the entire organization, and present it to decision makers for adoption.

Get the right people on the bus, get the wrong people off the bus,
and put the right people in the right seats in the bus.
Jim Collins – American business consultant and author

Suggested Readings

Adler, L. (2007). *Hire with your head: Using performance-based hiring to build great teams.* Hoboken, NJ: John Wiley & Sons.

Charan, R., Lorsch, J. W., Khurana, R., Sorcher, M., Brant, J., Bennis, W., & O'Toole, J. (2005). Hire the right CEO (HBR OnPoint Collection). Boston: *Harvard Business Review.*

Dimitrius, J., & Mazzarella, M. C. (2008). *Reading people: How to understand people and predict their behavior: Anytime, anyplace.* New York: Ballantine Books.

Fields, M. R. A. (2001). *Indispensable employees: How to hire them, how to keep them.* Franklin Lakes, NJ: Career Press.

Guion, R. M., & Highhouse, S. (2006). *Essentials of personnel assessment and selection.* Mahwah, NJ: Lawrence Erlbaum Associates.

Hallenbeck, G. S., Jr., & Eichinger, R. W. (2006). *Interviewing right: How science can sharpen your interviewing accuracy.* Minneapolis, MN: Lominger International: A Korn/Ferry Company.

Harvard Business Essentials. (2002). *Hiring and keeping the best people.* Boston: Harvard Business School Press.

Harvey, M., Novicevic, M. M., & Garrison, G. (2004). Challenges to staffing global virtual teams. *Human Resource Management, 14,* 275-294.

Levin, R. A., & Rosse, J. G. (2001). *Talent flow: A strategic approach to keeping good employees, helping them grow, and letting them go.* New York: John Wiley & Sons.

Michaels, E., Handfield-Jones, H., & Axelrod, B. (2001). *The war for talent.* Boston: Harvard Business School Press.

Rosenberger, L. E., & Nash, J. (with Graham, A.). (2009). *The deciding factor: The power of analytics to make every decision a winner.* San Francisco: Jossey-Bass.

Sears, D. (2003). *Successful talent strategies: Achieving superior business results through market-focused staffing.* New York: AMACOM.

Smart, B. D. (2005). *Topgrading: How leading companies win: Hiring, coaching and keeping the best people* (Rev. ed.). New York: Prentice Hall.

Still, D. J. (2001). *High impact hiring: How to interview and select outstanding employees.* Dana Point, CA: Management Development Systems.

Wylie, K. (2005). *Hiring the right candidate: Forms, FAQs, and resources for every employer.* Port Orchard, WA: Windstorm Creative.

112 Insensitive to Others

Too often we underestimate the power of a touch, a smile, a kind word, a listening ear, an honest compliment, or the smallest act of caring, all of which have the potential to turn a life around.
Leo F. Buscaglia – American professor and author

A Problem

- ☐ Has an intimidating style
- ☐ Makes others feel bad
- ☐ Doesn't care or doesn't think about how he/she affects others
- ☐ Doesn't follow interpersonal due process
- ☐ Doesn't care about the needs of others
- ☐ Doesn't ask and doesn't listen

Not A Problem

- ☐ Has a smooth and approachable style
- ☐ Shows empathy and caring
- ☐ Can tell when people are hurting
- ☐ Good at reading other people's hot buttons
- ☐ Listens
- ☐ Allows others to play out their agenda without interrupting
- ☐ Helpful toward others
- ☐ Asks others what they are feeling and thinking
- ☐ Sensitive to how he/she is coming across

Some Causes

- ☐ Abuse others
- ☐ Action junkie
- ☐ Aggressive, results oriented
- ☐ Blow up under pressure
- ☐ Don't care
- ☐ No idea of impact
- ☐ Run over people
- ☐ Unrealistic standards
- ☐ Very successful

Other Causes

BEING UNSKILLED AT: 3,4,7,10,15,21,23,27,31,33,36,41,42,48,60,64
OVERUSING: 5,9,12,13,20,26,27,34,39,47,52,62

Leadership Architect® Factors and Clusters

This competency is in the Trouble with People Factor (VII) (S1). This competency is in the Doesn't Relate Well to Others Cluster (V) with: 101, 106, 108. You may want to check other competencies in the same Factor/Cluster for related tips.

The Map

This evaluation may have been shocking for you, since few of us like to think of ourselves as insensitive. Chances are you see yourself as candid and forthright. Results oriented and matter-of-fact. Business oriented. Mostly right. Tough on slackers. Demanding manager. Focused and jealous of your time. Whatever your perception, others feel discounted and ignored. They don't find you pleasant to work with or for. You can get away with this only as long as your results are stellar. One stumble, and the sharks will be circling.

Some Remedies

- ☐ **1. Perceived as insensitive? Find out why people think you are insensitive.** Insensitivity is a catch-all term. The authors have found 29 reasons why people might say this about you. Before you react to this evaluation and certainly before you try to do something about it, invest in 360° feedback or get a Human Resource specialist to talk with people and find out exactly why you are seen as insensitive, or talk to a mentor or someone you really trust will tell you the truth. It's unlikely that people will tell you directly, and even if they do, it's likely to be too general or too much based on one situation to do you much good. Of all needs, this one is probably the most complex to specify. Get a complete textured view of yourself. *More help? – See #55 Self-Knowledge*. The good news is that most people get this negative rating due only to a few aspects of insensitivity. It's also common to have some people view you as insensitive and others not. That makes it easier to address. Few are truly insensitive in 29 ways!
- ☐ **2. Making knee-jerk responses? Maintain your composure.** It may be that you blow up and are especially bullying or pressuring under stress. Avoid instant and sharp reactions. This is most likely what's getting you in trouble. You jump to conclusions, categorically dismiss what others say, use inflammatory words or something of the sort. People then see you as closed or combative when you probably want them to see you as reasonable. More negatively, they may believe you think they're stupid or ill-informed. Give people second chances. If you're seen as intolerant or closed, people will often stumble over words in their haste to talk with you or short cut their argument since they assume you're not listening anyway. Ask a question, invite them to disagree with you, present their argument back to them, let them save face no matter what. *More help? – See #11 Composure.*

- ☐ **3. Failing to adapt your delivery? Be sensitive to your audience.** In any situation, there are always multiple ways you can deliver messages and get things done. You could use a direct attack—candor and instant assessment. You could send a surrogate to deliver the message. You could wait until the next meeting to react. Some of these tactics are more effective and acceptable than others. Some people get into trouble because they act the same in all situations. They don't take the time to think about the most effective ways to get things done for each event and person. People who are seen as sensitive operate from the outside—audience, person, group, organization—in. They pick their pace, style, tone, timing and tactics based upon an evaluation of what would work best in each situation. It's the one-trick ponies that get into sensitivity trouble because they don't adjust what they say and do to each audience. *More help? – See #15 Customer Focus, #36 Motivating Others, and #45 Personal Learning.*
- ☐ **4. Stubborn? Open up to different points of view.** You may either be or may be signaling being stubborn, rigid and closed to new or different points of view. You must learn to turn off your instant evaluator/rejector filter and listen. Your first task is to understand, your second is to let the other person know you understand by repeating or rephrasing, and your third task can be to reject, with a fuller explanation of why than you now do. Ask more questions—"How did you get there?" "Do you prefer this to that or to what we're now doing?" If you disagree, give your reasons first. Then invite criticism. Turn the disagreement back to the nature of the problem or strategy—"What are we trying to solve? What causes it? What questions should be answered? What objective standards could we use to measure success?" *More help? – See #12 Conflict Management and #33 Listening.*
- ☐ **5. No rapport? Get personal.** A lot of insensitivity is due to not taking the time to let others get more comfortable with you. Many insensitive people are very action oriented, results oriented and very agenda driven. There's not much rapport building. One third of the people who work around you prefer people like you. "Just the facts, ma'am. Let's get down to it." Two thirds need a little up front time to adjust to the situation before getting down to work. Usually three minutes is sufficient. You have to start by opening the discussion on a non-business topic. What did you do this weekend? How are the kids? Which college did your daughter pick? Did you see the Olympics? How do you like the new car? And then let them talk for a while to give them time to get comfortable. *More help? – See #3 Approachability.*

☐ **6. Jumping to conclusions? Seek to understand before you seek a solution.** You might be seen as someone who jumps to conclusions and solutions before others have had a chance to finish their statement of the problem. Take the time to really define the problem. Let people finish. Try not to interrupt. Don't finish others' sentences. Ask clarifying questions. Restate the problem in your own words to everyone's satisfaction. Then decide.

☐ **7. Interpersonally challenged? Open up to other people.** You have to go first, no matter how shy you may be. Until you signal that you are open to others—listening with eye contact, interested in what they have to say—let them finish, share things you don't have to share—get personal, invite people to talk with you—ask questions—and then listen, little will come of this effort to be seen as more sensitive. You will have to persevere, endure some rejection and embarrassment to improve. *More help? – See #3 Approachability and #31 Interpersonal Savvy.*

☐ **8. Too directive? Be a teacher, not a director.** You may be highly intelligent and quite skilled in your area. You may work around people who aren't as informed or skilled as you are. You may be in a position of essentially dictating what should be done because they don't know. In this case, you need to switch to a teacher role—tell them how you think about an issue, don't just fire out solutions. Tell them what you think the problem is, what questions need be asked, how you would go about finding out, what you think some likely solutions might be. Most important, invite their thinking. If you're the expert and they aren't, help them think better by showing them how you think. Be open to the fact that uninformed people in studies of creative problem solving usually come up with the most inventive solutions. Once immersed in the problem they bring a new perspective to it. Use that power. *More help? – See #18 Delegation.*

☐ **9. Fail to see the importance of sensitivity? Figure out why it matters.** Some hard-charging managers just don't think it matters what people think of them. They think getting the results out on time and on budget is job one. They think good people can take it and those who are too sensitive aren't going to make it anyway and are not worth the time. Studies show that the vast majority of senior managers who fail do not fail because they can't get the work out. They fail because they damage people in the process. Think of the last 10 people who were forced to leave your organization. Why were they fired or asked to leave? What were the real reasons? Most likely, the problem was in relationships with others. You really need to rethink your priorities.

☐ **10. Good intentions not enough? Make time for others.** Some insensitivity is benign neglect. Usually it hits direct reports most. You manage your boss first. Your customers second. Issues and problems third. Your peers next. And your direct reports last. But it's now Friday at 4:50 p.m. Sensitivity takes time. Since insensitivity causes noise, unproductive transactions, a de-motivated team, and reworking communications and issues, increased sensitivity would actually buy you more time. Each week allot five additional minutes per direct report for just general conversation, their nickel. No agenda. No business. Just be there for them.

Some Develop-in-Place Assignments

- ☐ Make peace with an enemy or someone you've disappointed with a product or service or someone you've had some trouble with or don't get along with very well.
- ☐ Handle a tough negotiation with an internal or external client or customer.
- ☐ Manage the outplacement of a group of people.
- ☐ Manage a project team of people who are older and more experienced than you.
- ☐ Resolve an issue in conflict between two people, units, geographies, functions, etc.

All cruel people describe themselves as paragons of frankness!
Tennessee Williams – American playwright

Suggested Readings

Barlow, J., & Moller, C. (2008). *A complaint is a gift: Recovering customer loyalty when things go wrong* (2nd ed.). San Francisco: Berrett-Koehler Publishers.

Beyerlein, M. M., Freedman, S., McGee, C., & Moran, L. (2002). *Beyond teams: Building the collaborative organization.* San Francisco: Jossey-Bass.

Boyatzis, R. E., & McKee, A. (2005). *Resonant leadership: Renewing yourself and connecting with others through mindfulness, hope, and compassion.* Boston: Harvard Business School Press.

Bradberry, T., & Greaves, J. (2005). *The emotional intelligence quick book: Everything you need to know to put your EQ to work.* New York: Fireside.

Donoghue, P. J., & Siegel, M. E. (2005). *Are you really listening? Key to successful communication.* Notre Dame, IN: Sorin Books.

Dotlich, D. L., & Cairo, P. C. (2003). *Why CEOs fail: The 11 behaviors that can derail your climb to the top and how to manage them.* San Francisco: Jossey-Bass.

Fineman, S. (2003). *Understanding emotion at work.* London: Sage.

Frazier, T., & Frazier, D. (2006). *Boss: 21 Simple rules to make your business grow and keep your people happy.* Abilene, TX: McWhiney Foundation Press.

Goleman, D. (2007). *Social intelligence: The new science of human relationships.* New York: Bantam Books.

Hoppe, M. H. (2007) *Active listening: Improve your ability to listen and lead.* Greensboro, NC: Center for Creative Leadership.

Kaye, B., & Jordan-Evans, S. (2008). *Love 'em or lose 'em: Getting good people to stay* (4th ed.). San Francisco: Berrett-Koehler Publishers.

Kouzes, J. M., & Posner, B. Z. (2003). *Encouraging the heart: A leader's guide to rewarding and recognizing others.* San Francisco: Jossey-Bass.

Mayo, A. (2001). *The human value of the enterprise: Valuing people as assets: Monitoring, measuring, managing.* Yarmouth, ME: Nicholas Brealey.

Moran, R. T., Harris, P. R., & Moran, S. V. (2007). *Managing cultural differences: Global leadership strategies for the 21st century* (7th ed.). Burlington, MA: Butterworth-Heinemann.

Morgan, R. (2003). *Calming upset customers: Staying effective during unpleasant situations* (3rd ed.). Mississauga, ON: Crisp Publications, Inc.

Pellicer, L. O. (2008). *Caring enough to lead: How reflective practice leads to moral leadership* (3rd ed.). Thousand Oaks, CA: Corwin Press.

Zenger, J. H., & Folkman, J. (2002). *The extraordinary leader: Turning good managers into great leaders.* New York: McGraw-Hill.

113 Key Skill Deficiencies

Today, many companies are reporting that their number one constraint on growth is the inability to hire workers with the necessary skills.
Bill Clinton – 42nd President of the United States

A Problem

- ☐ Lacks one or more key job-required talents or skills needed to perform effectively

Not A Problem

- ☐ Skilled in most if not all of the mission-critical areas of the job
- ☐ Scopes out what skills are required to perform
- ☐ Works to improve and expand skill set
- ☐ Open to tutors, courses, any learning mode to improve proficiency

Some Causes

- ☐ Counting backwards to retirement
- ☐ Inexperienced
- ☐ Lack of technical/functional skills
- ☐ Narrow perspective
- ☐ New to the job or function
- ☐ Not interested in self-development

Other Causes

BEING UNSKILLED AT: 32,44,45,54,55,61
OVERUSING: NONE APPLY

Leadership Architect® Factors and Clusters

This competency is in the Trouble with Results Factor (VIII) (S2). This competency is in the Too Narrow Cluster (Y) with: 114, 115, 116. You may want to check other competencies in the same Factor/Cluster for related tips.

The Map

New and different jobs, roles, geographies, business units, and organizations require new and different skills and abilities. Many times as we move up, in, out, down and sideways, we are caught without the requisite skills needed to perform well. Some go about the business of learning the new skills and others wait to see if they can get through without building new skills. Most of the time you can't wait. Those who wait too long get rated as having Key Skill Deficiencies.

Some Remedies

☐ **1. Unsure about your needs? Ask for feedback.** You need to find out what it is that people think you are missing. The best way to do that is to volunteer for a 360° feedback process. Find out what skills others think are important to do the job and compare your feedback against that standard. You can also simply ask your boss for that gap information. *More help? – See #55 Self-Knowledge.*

☐ **2. Unreceptive? Listen to feedback.** Sometimes you miss essential feedback about what you need to build because you didn't listen. Turn off your evaluator and listen to what you're being told. *More help? – See #33 Listening.*

☐ **3. Need to take action? Act on feedback.** Sometimes you hear the feedback but you choose not to do anything about it. *More help? – See #45 Personal Learning and #54 Self-Development.*

☐ **4. Resisting? Stop being defensive.** Sometimes people try to deliver feedback to help you and you fight it. *More help? – See #108 Defensiveness.*

☐ **5. No time? Prioritize and manage your time.** Sometimes you know what you need to develop or build but you don't have the time. *More help? – See #50 Priority Setting and #62 Time Management.*

☐ **6. Don't know how? Work on continuous improvement.** Sometimes you know what you need and don't know how to go about building it. *More help? – See #54 Self-Development.*

☐ **7. Ready to learn from a master performer? Identify and observe experts in your area.** Look to what others in your role or job have that you don't have. What skills do they apply to the job that you don't as yet have? Talk to your mentor and ask him/her for information about what you are missing.

☐ **8. Curious? Make a commitment to learning.** Learn how to become a learner. *More help? – See #32 Learning on the Fly and #45 Personal Learning.*

☐ **9. Need functional expertise? Identify functional skills required.** Sometimes the missing skills are functional. *More help? – See #24 Functional/Technical Skills.*

☐ **10. Need new technical skills? Identify technical skills required.** Sometimes the missing skills are technical. *More help? – See #24 Functional/Technical Skills and #61 Technical Learning.*

Some Develop-in-Place Assignments

- ☐ Take on a task you dislike or hate to do.
- ☐ Find and spend time with an expert to learn something in an area new to you.
- ☐ Interview or work with a "tutor" or mentor on a skill you need to develop.
- ☐ Study some aspect of your job or a new technical area you haven't studied before that you need in order to be more effective.
- ☐ Study an admired person who has a skill you need.

Public education is the key civil rights issue of the 21st century. Our nation's knowledge-based economy demands that we provide young people from all backgrounds and circumstances with the education and skills necessary to become knowledge workers. If we don't, we run the risk of creating an even larger gap between the middle class and the poor. This gap threatens our democracy, our society and the economic future of America.

Eli Broad – American businessman
and former CEO of SunAmerica

Suggested Readings

Argyris, C. (2008). *Teaching smart people how to learn.* Boston: Harvard Business School Press.

Bell, A. H., & Smith, D. M. (2002). *Motivating yourself for achievement.* Upper Saddle River, NJ: Prentice Hall.

Bunker, K. A., Kram, K. E., & Ting, S. (2002). The young and the clueless. *Harvard Business Review, 80*(12), 80-89.

Colvin, R. (2008). *Building expertise: Cognitive methods for training and performance improvement.* San Francisco: Pfeiffer.

Eichinger, R. W., Lombardo, M. M., & Capretta Raymond, C. (2004). *FYI for talent management™: The talent development handbook.* Minneapolis, MN: Lominger International: A Korn/Ferry Company.

Finkelstein, S. (2003). *Why smart executives fail: And what you can learn from their mistakes.* New York: Portfolio.

Furnham, A. (2005). *The incompetent manager: The causes, consequences, and cures of management failure.* London: John Wiley & Sons.

Goldsmith, M., & Reiter, M. (2007). *What got you here won't get you there: How successful people become even more successful.* New York: Hyperion.

Lizotte, K. (2007). *The expert's edge: Become the go-to authority people turn to every time.* New York: McGraw-Hill.

Lombardo, M. M., & Eichinger, R. W. (2004). *The leadership machine.* Minneapolis, MN: Lominger International: A Korn/Ferry Company.

Rossiter, A. P. (2008). *Professional excellence: Beyond technical competence.* New York: John Wiley & Sons.

Waitzkin, J. (2008). *The art of learning: An inner journey to optimal performance.* New York: Free Press.

Wick, C., Pollock, R., Jefferson, A., & Flanagan, R. (2006). *The six disciplines of breakthrough learning: How to turn training and development into business results.* San Francisco: Pfeiffer.

Woller, L., & Woller, J. (2008). *The skill: The most critical tool needed to increase your potential, performance, and promotability.* Victoria, Canada: Trafford Publishing.

114 Non-Strategic

So companies have to be very schizophrenic.
On one hand, they have to maintain continuity of strategy.
But they also have to be good at continuously improving.
Michael Porter – American writer and University Professor, Harvard

A Problem

- ☐ Can't create effective strategies
- ☐ Can't deal effectively with assignments that require strategic thinking
- ☐ Gets mired in tactics and details
- ☐ Prefers the tactical over the strategic, simple versus complex
- ☐ Isn't a visionary
- ☐ Lacks broad perspective

Not A Problem

- ☐ Can think and talk strategy with the best
- ☐ Intrigued and challenged by the complexity of the future
- ☐ Likes to run multiple "what if" scenarios
- ☐ Very broad perspective
- ☐ Counsels others on strategic issues
- ☐ Can juggle a lot of mental balls
- ☐ Isn't afraid to engage in wild speculation about the future
- ☐ Can bring several unrelated streams of information together to form a compelling vision
- ☐ Good at meaning making
- ☐ Produces distinctive and winning strategies

Some Causes

- ☐ Don't like complexity
- ☐ Don't think the future is knowable
- ☐ Inexperienced
- ☐ Lack of perspective
- ☐ Low-variety background
- ☐ Low risk taker; don't like uncertainty
- ☐ New to the area
- ☐ Too busy with today's tasks
- ☐ Too narrow
- ☐ Very tactical

Other Causes

BEING UNSKILLED AT: 2,5,14,21,28,30,32,40,41,46,50,51,58,61,65
OVERUSING: 1,52,53,59

Leadership Architect® Factors and Clusters

This competency is in the Trouble with Results Factor (VIII) (S2). This competency is in the Too Narrow Cluster (Y) with: 113, 115, 116. You may want to check other competencies in the same Factor/Cluster for related tips.

The Map

There are a lot more people who can take a hill than there are people who can accurately predict which hill it would be best to take. There are more people good at producing results in the short term than there are visionary strategists. Both have value but we don't have enough strategists. It is more likely that your organization will be outmaneuvered strategically than that it will be outproduced tactically. Most organizations do pretty well what they do today. It's what they need to be doing tomorrow that's the missing skill. Part of every manager's job is to be strategic. The higher you go, the more critical the requirement.

Some Remedies

- ☐ **1. Problems with presentation? Use strategic language.** In some rare cases, we have found strategic thinkers who were not identified as such because they either didn't know, rejected or chose not to use what they considered the latest strategic buzzwords. Strategy is an emerging field. At any time, there are a small number of gurus (at present probably Michael Porter, Ram Charan, C.K. Prahalad, Gary Hamel, Fred Wiersema and Vijay Govindarajan) in vogue, who have created about 75 new words or concepts—values disciplines, strategic intent, value migration, co-evolution, market oligarchies, core capabilities, strategic horizon—to describe strategic thinking. If you don't use those words others won't know you're being strategic. The words are to be found in books by the gurus and in the *Harvard Business Review*. And yes, most of the words are bigger words for things we used to call something else before with smaller words. Nevertheless, if you want to be seen as strategic, you have to talk strategic. Every discipline has its lexicon. In order to be a member, you have to speak the code.
- ☐ **2. Rejecting strategy? Recognize the value of strategic planning.** There are people who reject strategic formulation as so much folly. They have never seen a five-year strategic plan actually happen as projected. They think the time they use to create and present strategic plans is wasted.

They think it's where the rubber meets the sky. So much BS. While it's true that most strategic plans never work out as planned, that doesn't mean that it was a wasted effort. Strategic plans lead to choices about resources and deployment. They lead to different staffing actions and different financial plans. Without some strategic plans, it would be a total shot in the dark. Most failed companies got buried strategically. They picked the wrong direction or too many. Not being able to produce a quality product or service today is generally not the problem.

☐ **3. Not curious? Be curious and imaginative.** Many managers are so wrapped up in today's problems they aren't curious about tomorrow. They really don't care about the future. They believe there won't be much of a future until we perform today. Being a visionary and a good strategist requires curiosity and imagination. It requires playing "what ifs." What if there is life on other planets and we get the first message? What will that change? What will happen when a larger percentage of the world's population is over the age of 65? What if cancer is cured? Heart disease? Obesity? What if the government outlaws or severely regulates some aspect of your business? True, nobody knows the answers, but good strategists know the questions. Work at developing eclectic interests outside your business. Subscribe to different magazines, pick new shows to watch, meet different people, join a new organization. Look under some rocks.

☐ **4. Narrow perspective? Broaden your perspective.** Some are sharply focused on what they do and do it very well. They have prepared themselves for a narrow but satisfying career. Then someone tells them their job has changed and they now have to be strategic. Being strategic requires a broad perspective. In addition to knowing one thing well, it requires that you know about a lot of things somewhat. You need to understand business. *More help? – See #5 Business Acumen.* You need to understand markets. *More help? – See #15 Customer Focus.* You need to understand how the world operates. *More help? – See #46 Perspective.* You need to put all that together and figure out what it means to your organization. *More help? – See #32 Learning on the Fly and #51 Problem Solving.* And then you have to create a strategy. *More help? – See #58 Strategic Agility.*

☐ **5. Too busy? Delegate the tactical and make time for strategy.** Strategy is always last on the list. Solving today's problems, of which there are many, is job one. You have to make time for strategy. A good strategy releases future time because it makes choices clear and leads to less wasted effort, but it takes time to do. Delegation is usually the key. Give away as much tactical day-to-day stuff as you can. Ask your people what they think they could do to give you more time for strategic reflection. *More help? – See #18 Delegation.* Another key is better time management. Put an hour a week on your calendar for strategic reading and reflection throughout the year. Don't wait until one week before the plan is due. *More help? – See #62 Time Management.* Keep a log of ideas you get from others, magazines, etc. Focus on how these impact your organization or function.

☐ **6. Avoiding ambiguity? Embrace the uncertainty.** Strategic planning is the most uncertain thing managers do. It's speculating on the near unknown. It requires projections into foggy landscapes. It requires assumptions about the unknown. Many conflict avoiders don't like to make statements in public that they cannot back up with facts. Most strategies can be questioned. There are no clean ways to win a debate over strategy. It really comes down to one subjective estimate versus another. *More help? – See #2 Dealing with Ambiguity.*

☐ **7. Addicted to the simple? Embrace the complexity.** Strategy ends up sounding simple—five clean, clear statements about where we want to go with a few tactics and decisions attached to each. Getting there is not simple. Good strategists are complexifiers. They extend everything to its extreme before they get down to the essence. Simplifiers close too early. They are impatient to get it done faster. They are very results oriented and want to get to the five simple statements before strategic due process has been followed. Be more tolerant of unlimited exploration and debate before you move to close.

☐ **8. Don't know how to be strategic? Become a student of strategy.** The simplest problem is someone who wants to be strategic and wants to learn. Strategy is a reasonably well-known field. Read the gurus—Michael Porter, Ram Charan, C.K. Prahalad, Gary Hamel, Fred Wiersema and Vijay Govindarajan. Scan the *Harvard Business Review* regularly. Read the three to five strategic case studies in *BusinessWeek*. Go to a three-day strategy course hopefully taught by one of the gurus. Get someone from the organization's strategic group to tutor you in strategy. Watch CEOs talk about their businesses on cable. Volunteer to serve on a task force on a strategic issue.

☐ **9. Can't think strategically? Practice strategic thinking.** Strategy is linking several variables together to come up with the most likely scenario. It involves making projections of several variables at once to see how they come together. These projections are in the context of shifting markets, international affairs, monetary movements and government interventions. It involves a lot of uncertainty, making risk assumptions, and understanding how things work together. How many reasons would account for sales going down? Up? How are advertising and sales linked? If the dollar is cheaper in Asia, what does that mean for our product in Japan? If the world population is aging and they have more money, how will that change buying patterns? Not everyone enjoys this kind of pie-in-the-sky thinking and not everyone is skilled at doing it. *More help? – See #32 Learning on the Fly, #46 Perspective, and #51 Problem Solving.*

☐ **10. Don't want to be strategic? Get some help.** Some just don't feel they want to ramp up and learn to be strategic. But they like their job and want to be considered strategically responsible. Hire a strategic consultant once a year to sit with you and your team and help you work out your strategic plan. Accenture. The Boston Consulting Group. McKinsey. Booz Allen Hamilton. Plus many more. Or delegate strategy to one or more in your unit who are more strategically capable. Or ask the strategic planning group to help. You don't have to be able to do everything to be a good manager. You like your nest? Some people are content in their narrow niche. They are not interested in being strategic. They just want to do their job and be left alone. They are interested in doing good work in their specialty and want to get as high as they can. That's OK. Just inform the organization of your wishes and don't take jobs that have a heavy strategic requirement.

Some Develop-in-Place Assignments

- ☐ Work on a team forming a joint venture or partnership.
- ☐ Work on a project that involves travel and study of an international issue, acquisition, or joint venture and report back to management.
- ☐ Study and summarize a new trend, product, service, technique, or process, and present and sell it to others.
- ☐ Do a competitive analysis of your organization's products or services or position in the marketplace, and present it to the people involved.
- ☐ Do a feasibility study on an important opportunity and make recommendations to those who will decide.

Do not repeat the tactics which have gained you one victory,
but let your methods be regulated by the infinite variety of circumstances.
Sun Tzu (c. 500 BCE) – Chinese military strategist

Suggested Readings

Apgar, D. (2008). *Relevance: Hitting your goals by knowing what matters.* San Francisco: Jossey-Bass.

Barney, J., & Hesterly, W. S. (2007). *Strategic management and competitive advantage: Concepts and cases* (2nd ed.). Upper Saddle River, NJ: Prentice Hall.

Camillus, J. C. (2008). Strategy as a wicked problem. *Harvard Business Review, 86*(5), 98-107.

Charan, R. (2005). *Boards that deliver: Advancing corporate governance from compliance to competitive advantage.* San Francisco: John Wiley & Sons.

Collins, J. C. (2001). *Good to great: Why some companies make the leap...and others don't.* New York: HarperCollins.

Eichinger, R. W., Ruyle, K. E., & Ulrich, D. O. (2007). *FYI for strategic effectiveness™: Aligning people and operational practices to strategy.* Minneapolis, MN: Lominger International: A Korn/Ferry Company.

Freedman, M. (with Tregoe, B. B.). (2003). *The art and discipline of strategic leadership.* New York: McGraw-Hill.

Ghemawat, P. (2007). *Redefining global strategy: Crossing borders in a world where differences still matter.* Boston: Harvard Business School Press.

Hughes, R. L., & Beatty, K. M. (2005). *Becoming a strategic leader: Your role in your organization's enduring success.* San Francisco: John Wiley & Sons.

Hunger, J. D., & Wheelen, T. (2006). *Essentials of strategic management* (4th ed.). Upper Saddle River, NJ: Prentice Hall.

Kaplan, R. S., & Norton, D. P. (2000). *The strategy-focused organization: How balanced scorecard companies thrive in the new business environment.* Boston: Harvard Business School Press.

Krames, J. A. (2003). *What the best CEOs know: 7 Exceptional leaders and their lessons for transforming any business.* New York: McGraw-Hill.

Nolan, T. N., Goodstein, L. D., & Goodstein, J. (2008). *Applied strategic planning: An introduction* (2nd ed.). San Francisco: Pfeiffer.

Ohmae, K. (1982). *The mind of the strategist.* New York: McGraw-Hill.

Pearce, J. A., & Robbins, D. K. (2008). Strategic transformation as the essential last step in the process of business turnaround. *Business Horizons, 51,* 121-130.

Pietersen, W. (2002). *Reinventing strategy: Using strategic learning to create and sustain breakthrough performance.* New York: John Wiley & Sons.

Porter, M. E. (1998). *Competitive strategy: Techniques for analyzing industries and competitors.* New York: Free Press.

Prahalad, C. K., & Ramaswamy, V. (2004). *The future of competition: Co-creating unique value with customers.* Boston: Harvard Business School Press.

Stalk, G. (2008). *Five future strategies you need right now (Memo to the CEO).* Boston: Harvard Business School Press.

Thompson, A. A., Jr., Strickland, A. J., III., & Gamble, J. E. (2007). *Crafting and executing strategy* (16th ed.). New York: McGraw-Hill.

Welborn, R., & Kasten, V. (2003). *The Jericho principle: How companies use strategic collaboration to find new sources of value.* New York: John Wiley & Sons.

115 Overdependence on an Advocate

There is no dependence that can be sure
but a dependence upon one's self.
John Gay – English poet and dramatist

A Problem

- ☐ Has been with the same boss, champion, mentor, advocate too long
- ☐ Isn't seen as independent
- ☐ Others question whether he/she could stand up to a tough assignment or situation without help
- ☐ Might not do well in the organization if the advocate lost interest, lost out him/herself, or left the organization

Not A Problem

- ☐ Has largely done it on his/her own
- ☐ Has multiple advocates and champions
- ☐ No one questions whether he/she could go it alone
- ☐ Independent, resourceful person
- ☐ Doesn't use a champion's influence to get things done
- ☐ Has moved around a lot; has not been with one boss very long
- ☐ Has survived an advocate or two leaving the organization

Some Causes

- ☐ Dependent
- ☐ Don't get results alone
- ☐ Has gotten lazy
- ☐ Narrow experience base
- ☐ Not tough
- ☐ Overly loyal

Other Causes

BEING UNSKILLED AT: 6,42,53,57

OVERUSING: 4,6,8,48

Leadership Architect® Factors and Clusters

This competency is in the Trouble with Results Factor (VIII) (S2). This competency is in the Too Narrow Cluster (Y) with: 113, 114, 116. You may want to check other competencies in the same Factor/Cluster for related tips.

The Map

The most successful men in studies of managerial success usually didn't have a single long-term mentor or advocate. They were more likely to have multiple advocates at various stages of their careers. Women have reported a higher incidence of having single mentors because of being pioneers into a new arena. They needed one to get into the "Club." There's good news and bad news. Having an advocate/mentor is a great way to get into the mainstream of an organization, be privy to fresh information and get advantages—promotions, choice assignments, invitations to events, etc. Having a strong advocate is also one of the best ways to stall your career long term. People wonder if you can do it on your own; can you stand alone without the advocate and be successful? How much of your success was windfall? What would happen to you if your advocate/mentor left or fell from grace?

Some Remedies

☐ **1. In a rut? Determine how long is too long.** Being trapped with an advocate/mentor starts innocently enough. Two people take a liking to each other. They respect each other. A bond is formed. One helps the other break in. The other works hard to reward the advocate/mentor. The advocate/mentor gets promoted. He/she takes you along. You pass up other opportunities to stay with this positive and supportive person. The advocate/mentor doesn't put you up for other jobs because he or she really appreciates what you can do. And it's so easy working for each other. Each of you is in the groove and in your comfort zone. How long is too long? When others begin to question whether you could perform alone. When your advocate/mentor turns down opportunities for you. When your advocate/mentor keeps you for his or her own comfort. When you aren't learning anything new. When you don't have to push yourself to please him or her. Then it's time to break free. Volunteer for a job change. Ask your advocate/mentor for help in getting another assignment. Ask Human Resources how to market yourself for another opportunity.

☐ **2. Can't change jobs? Spread your wings.** Volunteer for task forces/projects your advocate/mentor is not involved in. If the project is important, is multifunctional and has a real outcome which will be taken seriously, it is one of the most common developmental events listed by successful executives. Such projects require learning other functions, businesses or nationalities. You can get out of your own experience and start to see connections to a broader world—how international trade works or how the pieces of your organization fit together. Your performance will also be seen as yours and part of the project's and not connected with your advocate/mentor. *More help? – See #46 Perspective.*

☐ **3. Ready to explore? Try something new.** Do things in your job that you have not done before. Broaden your experience base. In your unit there are things to start up or fix, problems to confront, etc. Pick three tasks you've never done and volunteer to do them. If you don't know much about customers, work in a store or handle customer complaints; if you don't know what engineering does, go find out; task trade with someone; write a strategic plan for your unit. *More help? – See #54 Self-Development.*

☐ **4. Need variety? Locate some additional role models.** You have learned great stuff from your advocate/mentor but it's time to add some new stuff. Pick a person in the organization who is different in some aspects from your advocate/mentor. Observe what he/she does and how he/she does it. He/she is as successful as your advocate/mentor but does it in other ways. If possible, ask for a meeting/lunch to discuss his/her success and the things he/she has learned. See if he/she has any interest in teaching you something and being a temporary coach. Get to know other potential advocates on- and off-work. Go for maximum variety in the towering strengths they possess.

☐ **5. Ready to take on more responsibility? Perform more independently.** What do you take for granted that your advocate/mentor does for you? How is he/she helpful? Helps you make final decisions? Start making the decisions yourself. Gets you invitations to special events? Get them on your own. Shares interesting information? Get it from other sources. Helps you prepare important presentations? Do a few by yourself. Covers your mistakes? Fix them yourself. Passes on feedback from others to you? Go talk to the originators on your own. Try to think about all the things you rely on your advocate/mentor for and try to begin to perform more independently from him or her.

☐ **6. Seen as a proxy for your manager? Avoid overusing your advocate/ mentor.** One common problem of being with a boss or advocate too long is that you might get in the habit of acting in his/her absence or on his/her behalf. You may take on his/her authority. You might even get in the lazy habit of saying "Larry" would like it this way or "Larry" would approve or not approve of this when that isn't literally true. People may get in the habit of passing information to you because they know it will get to Larry. People may pass things by you and ask you how you think Larry would react to it. People may ask you what Larry is really like because they are having some difficulty with him. All of these types of things are natural consequences of your special relationship with Larry, but they can just as well backfire longer term in your career. Don't use Larry's name, use your own.

☐ **7. Need to develop courage? Take more risks.** If you have trouble standing alone because you have been overly dependent upon an advocate/mentor, increase the risks you take on your own. Stake out a position on an issue that will require some courage and where you know there will be some detractors. Prepare by rehearsing for tough questions, attacks, and countering views. Don't use your advocate/mentor. Talk to yourself. Pump yourself up by focusing on your strengths. *More help? – See #34 Managerial Courage and #57 Standing Alone.*

☐ **8. Need to break a habit? Try new approaches.** Stuck in the ways the advocate/mentor passed on to you? Do you approach situations much the same every time? Then switch approaches. Do something totally different next time. If you visited the office of someone you have difficulties with, invite him/her to your office next time. Compare the situations and see which was more valuable. Develop three different ways to get the same outcome. For example, to push a decision through, you could meet with stakeholders first, go to a key stakeholder, study and present the problem to a group, call a problem-solving session, or call in an outside expert. Be prepared to do them all when obstacles arise.

☐ **9. Need an advocate? Once you're in, establish your independence.** Here's the Catch-22. If you are different or new or a first-timer or a member of any minority, you need a mentor, guide, orienter or advocate to get invited in. That's the only way you are going to get the information you need to be effective. That's the only way you can get invited to attend important meetings. It's the only way, aside from stellar performance, you will be considered for career progression. The trick is to take advantage of this special relationship long enough to get plugged in and comfortable and not long enough to question whether you could have done it on your own. That usually means unplugging before you want to. Before you become too comfortable. Before the mentor has taught you everything you need to know. Before you get evaluated as being overdependent on an advocate. Start early to find multiple models, multiple advocates. Make sure at least five key figures know who you are and what you can do.

☐ **10. Ready to say good-bye? Know when to move on.** One situation involves what to do when your advocate/mentor stumbles, falls, fails or leaves. Many times the person may ask you to join him or her in the next company. Think very carefully about that. There are many cases of entourages of people following a general manager from company to company. You will be an outsider. Your career will be closely tied to the person you are following. The same thing will happen to you in the next company, only faster. If he/she falls out of favor but stays, be supportive but keep out of it. It's not your problem. Don't go around defending your advocate/mentor. You will get tainted, too. The other situation occurs when you decide to change jobs within your organization. Advocate/mentors may not buy the fact that you have to establish a performance track on your own to be truly successful. They may think or say that they can counsel you to the top. You don't need to take another job. You don't need to work for someone else. Remember that these kinds of wonderful relationships have advantages for both sides. They get things they need from you also. You are in no way rejecting or devaluing your advocate/mentor by breaking free. In a sense it's a celebration of the success the advocate/mentor has had with you. You are now fully prepared to go it on your own. Be appreciative. Keep a light in the window. And move on to new vistas.

Some Develop-in-Place Assignments

- ☐ Make peace with an enemy or someone you've disappointed with a product or service or someone you've had some trouble with or don't get along with very well.
- ☐ Launch a new product, service, or process.
- ☐ Be a change agent; create a symbol for change; lead the rallying cry; champion a significant change and implementation.
- ☐ Become a referee for an athletic league or program.
- ☐ Plan an off-site meeting, conference, convention, trade show, event, etc.

A simple and independent mind does not toil at the bidding of any prince.
Henry David Thoreau – American author, poet, and philosopher

Suggested Readings

Badowski, R. (with Gittines, R.). (2003). *Managing up: How to forge an effective relationship with those above you.* New York: Currency.

Baker, W. E. (2000). *Networking smart.* New York: Backinprint.com.

Bell, C. R. (2002). *Managers as mentors: Building partnerships for learning.* San Francisco: Berrett-Koehler Publishers.

Butler, T. (2007). *Getting unstuck: How dead ends become new paths.* Boston: Harvard Business School Press.

Chaleff, I. (2003). *The courageous follower: Standing up to and for our leaders.* San Francisco: Berrett-Koehler Publishers.

Champy, J., & Nohria, N. (2000). *The arc of ambition.* Cambridge, MA: Perseus Publishing.

Darling, D. (2005). *Networking for career success.* New York: McGraw-Hill.

Ensher, E. A., & Murphy, S. E. (2005). *Power mentoring: How successful mentors and protégés get the most out of their relationships.* San Francisco: Jossey-Bass.

Ferrazzi, K., & Raz, T. (2005). *Never eat alone: And other secrets to success, one relationship at a time.* New York: Doubleday.

Gardner, H. (2006). *Five minds for the future.* Boston, MA: Harvard Business School Press.

Ibarra, H. (2003). *Working identity: Unconventional strategies for reinventing your career.* Boston: Harvard Business School Press.

Kouzes, J. M., & Posner, B. Z. (2007). *The leadership challenge* (4th ed.). San Francisco: Jossey-Bass.

Warrell, M. (2007). *Find your courage! Unleash your full potential and live the life you really want.* Austin, TX: Synergy Books.

Wendleton, K. (2006). *Navigating your career: Develop your plan, manage your boss, get another job inside.* New York: The Five O'clock Club.

Zigarmi, D., Blanchard, K., O'Connor, M., & Edeburn, C. (2005). *The leader within: Learning enough about yourself to lead others.* Upper Saddle River, NJ: Prentice Hall.

116 Overdependence on a Single Skill

CONNOISSEUR, n. A specialist who knows everything about something and nothing about anything else.
Ambrose Bierce – American journalist, short-story writer

A Problem

- ☐ Relies too much on a single strength for performance and career progression
- ☐ Uses the same core talent, function, or technology to leverage him/herself
- ☐ Acts as if he/she can make it all the way on one strength

Not A Problem

- ☐ Has a broad and varied background
- ☐ Has moved around a lot
- ☐ Relies on several different skills to get the job done
- ☐ Has multiple functional exposures
- ☐ Has worked in different business units
- ☐ Always looking to learn more
- ☐ Works on adding more skills

Some Causes

- ☐ Counting backwards to retirement
- ☐ Inexperienced
- ☐ Lazy
- ☐ Lives in the glory of the past
- ☐ Narrow perspective
- ☐ Not interested in broadening or self-development
- ☐ Too comfortable

Other Causes

BEING UNSKILLED AT: 46

OVERUSING: 14,26,30,31,48,61

Leadership Architect® Factors and Clusters

This competency is in the Trouble with Results Factor (VIII) (S2). This competency is in the Too Narrow Cluster (Y) with: 113, 114, 115. You may want to check other competencies in the same Factor/Cluster for related tips.

The Map

We are comfort zone creatures. We build nests. We go where it feels safe and good. Most of us don't like taking chances. Most of us don't venture on to alien ground comfortably. For those reasons, many of us take the safe career track, we think, of learning one thing and doing that well. In our early careers, that gets us good pay and promotions up the career ladder. We pass up people who are not as deeply skilled as we. We play the one skill, one technology, one business, one function or one talent (e.g., selling) all the way. Trouble is, it doesn't go all the way. All things change. One of the requirements for higher level management and career fulfillment is broadness and diversity. If you succeed long enough, you'll manage or work closely with new functions and businesses. A single skill is never enough.

Some Remedies

- ☐ **1. Need a change? Plan your next assignment.** Think carefully about your next natural point for an assignment change. This time, press your boss, business unit or organization for something different. Could be different geography, same job but different business unit, same job but different assignments, or a completely different job. Sometimes if you have been in something too long, you may have to take a lateral or even a short-term downgrading to get on a different track.
- ☐ **2. Want to see alternatives? Broaden your perspective.** Volunteer for task forces and study teams outside your area.
- ☐ **3. Ready to learn from others? Learn from other functions.** Attend off-sites and meetings of functions and units other than yours.
- ☐ **4. Reading narrowly? Expand your reading selections.** In addition to the literature you now read in your specialty, expand to a broader selection of journals and magazines.
- ☐ **5. Curious? Take a class.** Take a seminar or workshop outside your area just for the fun of it.
- ☐ **6. Need a vacation? Explore new destinations.** Vacation more broadly than you now do. Get out of your comfort zone and explore new places. If you can arrange it, vacation outside of your home country.
- ☐ **7. Ready to teach in order to learn? Organize a knowledge exchange.** Find someone who is as specialized as you are who also is seeking expansion

and teach your specialties to each other. Get together a small group; have each person agree to present a new technology or business topic each month to the group. Teaching something new for you is one of the best ways to learn it yourself.

- ☐ **8. Got what it takes? Observe higher-level general managers.** Look to some people in your area who are in higher-level jobs than you are. Are they as specialized as you are? Are they struggling in their new roles because they are as specialized as you are? Read *Career Mastery* by Harry Levinson. *More help? – See #6 Career Ambition and #54 Self-Development.*
- ☐ **9. Want to learn the field? Interview an expert.** Find some experts in what you need to learn. Interview them; find out how they think about their area. Take something to them in their area and ask them how they figure it out. What are the five key things they look for?
- ☐ **10. Want to learn about alternatives? Interview a generalist.** Pick three people who are broadly skilled. Ask them how they got to be that way. What job experiences have they had? What do they read? Watch on TV? Who do they like to learn from?

Some Develop-in-Place Assignments

- ☐ Manage a group through a significant business crisis.
- ☐ Find and spend time with an expert to learn something in an area new to you.
- ☐ Interview or work with a "tutor" or mentor on a skill you need to develop.
- ☐ Study some aspect of your job or a new technical area you haven't studied before that you need in order to be more effective.
- ☐ Volunteer to do a special project for and with a person you admire and who has a skill you need to develop.

Anyone who keeps learning stays young.
The greatest thing in life is to keep your mind young.
Moshe Arens – Israeli politician

Suggested Readings

Cashman, K. (2008). *Leadership from the inside out: Becoming a leader for life* (2nd ed.). San Francisco: Berrett-Koehler Publishers.

Champy, J., & Nohria, N. (2000). *The arc of ambition*. Cambridge, MA: Perseus Publishing.

Charan, R., Drotter, S., & Noel, J. (2000). *The leadership pipeline: How to build the leadership-powered company*. San Francisco: Jossey-Bass.

DuFour, R., DuFour, R., Eaker, R., & Many, T. (2006). *Learning by doing: A handbook for professional learning communities at work*. Bloomington, IN: Solution Tree.

Friedman, T. L. (2006). *The world is flat 3.0: A brief history of the twenty-first century* (Updated ed.). New York: Farrar, Straus and Giroux.

Goldsmith, M., & Reiter, M. (2007). *What got you here won't get you there: How successful people become even more successful*. New York: Hyperion.

Kaplan, B., & Kaiser, R. (2006). *The versatile leader: Make the most of your strengths—without overdoing it*. San Francisco: Pfeiffer.

Lombardo, M. M., & Eichinger, R. W. (2004). *The leadership machine*. Minneapolis, MN: Lominger International: A Korn/Ferry Company.

McCall, M. W., Lombardo, M. M., & Morrison, A. M. (1988). *The lessons of experience*. Lexington, MA: Lexington Books.

Morrison, A. M., White, R. P., Van Velsor, E., & The Center for Creative Leadership. (1992). *Breaking the glass ceiling: Can women reach the top of America's largest corporations?* Reading, MA: Addison-Wesley.

Rothwell, W. J., Jackson, R. D., Knight, S. C., & Lindholm, J. E. (2005). *Career planning and succession management: Developing your organization's talent—for today and tomorrow*. Westport, CT: Praeger.

Waitzkin, J. (2008). *The art of learning: An inner journey to optimal performance*. New York: Free Press.

117 Overmanaging

If you allow staff to own a project, you must trust in their capacity and avoid micromanagement... Be there to provide support when needed, but don't force yourself into the picture.
Barbara Moses – Canadian organizational consultant, author, and speaker

A Problem

- ☐ Overcontrols and meddles
- ☐ Doesn't empower others
- ☐ Doesn't get the most out of people
- ☐ Doesn't develop direct reports well
- ☐ Does too much of the work him/herself
- ☐ Is a poor delegator

Not A Problem

- ☐ Delegates and empowers
- ☐ Lets others finish their work once assigned
- ☐ Checks in infrequently unless there is a problem
- ☐ Assigns enough authority for people to make their own decisions
- ☐ Lets others contribute to how the work is to be done
- ☐ Works to do less personally and trust others more
- ☐ Usually helps only when needed or asked

Some Causes

- ☐ Don't have any good people
- ☐ Excessively action oriented
- ☐ Impatient
- ☐ Isn't willing to trust others
- ☐ Know too much about the work
- ☐ Perfectionist
- ☐ Very control driven

Other Causes

BEING UNSKILLED AT: 2,7,18,19,20,33,40,41,50,60,63

OVERUSING: 1,5,9,13,14,16,20,24,34,36,38,47,51,53,57,61,62,65

Leadership Architect® Factors and Clusters

This competency is in the Trouble with People Factor (VII) (S1). This competency is in the Doesn't Inspire or Build Talent Cluster (X) with: 110, 111. You may want to check other competencies in the same Factor/Cluster for related tips.

The Map

Most of us really prefer depending upon ourselves to get important things done. It's probably more uncommon to comfortably delegate and empower. Overmanaging means you don't trust your people to perform against standards and on time. You may feel they are not qualified or that they are not motivated. Both of those, of course, are your responsibilities. The Catch-22 is that the more time you spend managing and re-managing, the less time you will have left to do what you need to do and the less they will develop.

Some Remedies

☐ **1. Need to raise the bar? Upgrade your team's skill level.** If you are overmanaging because you don't think your people are good enough to do what you need doing, look to the plan for *#25 Hiring and Staffing* and *#56 Sizing Up People* for tips on upgrading the selections you make. Look to *#13 Confronting Direct Reports* for help on making tough calls and taking actions, and look to *#19 Developing Direct Reports and Others* for help in upgrading the skills level of your team. Any manager of a marginal team would have to overmanage to survive but that's a very poor long-term strategy.

☐ **2. Poor communicator? Improve your informing skills.** If you are overmanaging because you are too busy to communicate with your people about what you need and would rather do it yourself or delegate it and then monitor it to death, read *#18 Delegation, #27 Informing* and *#62 Time Management.* Poor communicators always have to take up more time managing.

☐ **3. Need assistance? Let your team help you.** Periodically, send out a memo asking each person whether there is anything he or she thinks he/she could do that you are now doing or monitoring too closely. Pick one or two things per person and empower them to do it on their own. Make sure the up-front communication is adequate for them to perform well. Explain your standards—what the outcome should be, the key things that need to be taken care of, then ask them to figure out how to do it themselves.

☐ **4. Impatient? Agree on a schedule for progress checks.** If you are impatient and find yourself checking in too frequently, set up a timetable with your people with agreed upon checkpoints and in-progress checks. Let them initiate this on a schedule you are comfortable with. Ask yourself who your most motivating bosses were. Chances are they gave you a lot of leeway, encouraged you to try things, were good sounding boards, and cheered your successes. Do what they did with you. *More help? – See #41 Patience.*

- ☐ **5. Reaching too far? Set realistic and achievable goals with your team.** Are you hanging on to too much? Are you a perfectionist, wanting everything to be just so? Do you have unrealistic expectations of others? Someone made you leader because you are probably better at doing what the team does than some or most of the members. Be careful to set the goals and objectives in a realistic and motivating manner. *More help? – See #35 Managing and Measuring Work.*
- ☐ **6. Delegating without empowerment? Delegate the task and the authority.** Delegating the work without the authority to make process or how-to decisions is demotivating. People grow if they have a chance to decide and succeed or fail on their own. *More help? – See #18 Delegation.*
- ☐ **7. Have a skill you can transfer? Coach and mentor others.** Ask yourself why this is a strength for you. What are the first items you would teach as the keys to help others form umbrellas for understanding? Watch others carefully for their reactions when teaching and coaching. What works and doesn't for you as a coach? Reveal things that people don't need to know to do their jobs, but which will be interesting to them—and help them feel valued.
- ☐ **8. Feeling guilty about assigning too much? Check in about workload.** Do you keep it yourself because you feel bad about giving them too much work? They would have to stay late or work on weekends to get it done. Most people enjoy being busy and on the move. If you think the workload is too much, ask. *More help? – See #36 Motivating Others.*
- ☐ **9. Do things go better when you are there than when you are on a trip, at a meeting, or on vacation? Step away from giving day-to-day guidance.** It should be the same. You should have informed and delegated in such a way that the work can be completed without any further guidance from you. *More help? – See #59 Managing Through Systems.* It could also be that you are a one-on-one, face-to-face manager. You focus your attention on single tasks and on individuals one at a time. That means there is not a feeling of team or a greater purpose or shared mindset. In your absence, there are no left-behind principles to follow and the team members can't help each other. *More help? – See #60 Building Effective Teams.*
- ☐ **10. Not sharing your knowledge? Focus on being a teacher.** Read this only if your ratings would be—or are—OK to high on most of the preceding tips and reference competencies. Sometimes good managers overmanage, too. Are you so good and know so much that you overwhelm others and make them dependent on you? Have you become arrogant? Have you given up on passing on your knowledge and skills to your people? In this, switch to a teacher role and pay particular attention to *#18 Delegation* and *#19 Developing Direct Reports and Others.*

Some Develop-in-Place Assignments

- ☐ Manage a project team of people who are older and more experienced than you.
- ☐ Manage a group that includes former peers to accomplish a task.
- ☐ Manage a group of people who are towering experts but you are not.
- ☐ Create employee involvement teams.
- ☐ Manage something "remote," away from your location.

A good manager is best when people barely know that he exists.
Not so good when people obey and acclaim him.
Worse when they despise him.
Lao Tzu (c. 600 BCE) – Chinese philosopher

Suggested Readings

Bacal, R. (2007). *How to manage performance: 24 Lessons for improving performance.* New York: McGraw-Hill.

Belker, L. B. (2005). *The first-time manager* (5th ed.). New York: AMACOM.

Bielaszka-DuVernay, C. (2007). Essentials: Micromanage at your peril. *Harvard Management Update, 12*(2), 3.

Bossidy, L., & Charan, R. (with Burck, C.). (2002). *Execution: The discipline of getting things done.* New York: Crown Business.

Branham, L. (2005). *The 7 hidden reasons employees leave: How to recognize the subtle signs and act before it's too late.* New York: AMACOM.

Daniels, A. C. (2000). *Bringing out the best in people: How to apply the astonishing power of positive reinforcement.* New York: McGraw-Hill.

Dyer, W., Dyer, W. G., Jr., & Dyer, J. H. (2007). *Team building: Proven strategies for improving team performance* (4th ed.). San Francisco: Jossey-Bass.

Genett, D. M. (2004). *If you want it done right, you don't have to do it yourself! The power of effective delegation.* Sanger, CA: Quill/HarperCollins.

Harvard Business School Press. (2008). *Delegating work.* Boston: Harvard Business School Press.

Johnson, H. T., & Bröms, A. (2000). *Profit beyond measure: Extraordinary results through attention to work and people.* New York: Free Press.

Kaye, B., & Jordan-Evans, S. (2008). *Love 'em or lose 'em: Getting good people to stay* (4th ed.). San Francisco: Berrett-Koehler Publishers.

Logan, D., & King, J. (2001). *The coaching revolution: How visionary managers are using coaching to empower people and unlock their full potential.* Avon, MA: Adams Media Corporation.

Manville, B., & Kerr, S. (2003). *Harvard Business Review on motivating people.* Boston: Harvard Business School Press.

Manzoni, J., & Barsoux, J. (2002). *The set-up-to-fail syndrome: How good managers cause great people to fail.* Boston: Harvard Business School Press.

Selden, B. (2008). *What to do when you become the boss: How new managers become successful managers.* Parker, CO: Outskirt Press.

Swindall, C. (2007). *Engaged leadership: Building a culture to overcome employee disengagement.* Hoboken, NJ: John Wiley & Sons.

118 Performance Problems

Do not waste a minute, not a second in trying to demonstrate to others the merits of your performance. If your work does not vindicate itself, you cannot vindicate it.
Thomas W. Higginson – American minister, author, soldier, and abolitionist

A Problem

- ☐ Does not consistently hit targets and objectives
- ☐ Doesn't produce results across a variety of situations

Not A Problem

- ☐ Consistently produces results
- ☐ Meets all goals and targets
- ☐ Plans and sets priorities well
- ☐ Is organized and gets things done on time and in time
- ☐ Has produced results under a variety of conditions

Some Causes

- ☐ Don't deliver consistently
- ☐ Inexperienced
- ☐ New to the job
- ☐ Not bold or innovative
- ☐ Procrastinate
- ☐ Scramble at the last minute

Other Causes

BEING UNSKILLED AT: 1,2,5,9,13,15,16,17,20,21,24,34,35,36,39,43,47,50,52,53,54, 58,59,61,62,63,65

OVERUSING: 14,24,35,46,53,58,66

Leadership Architect® Factors and Clusters

This competency is in the Trouble with Results Factor (VIII) (S2). This competency is in the Doesn't Deliver Results Cluster (Z) with: 102. You may want to check other competencies in the same Factor/Cluster for related tips.

The Map

Performance problems can come from a number of causes. Exactly what is getting in your way must be determined before you can do much about this. Something in the situation, the people dealt with or yourself, causes you not to deliver as expected and on time. People think you're not doing enough to get results.

Some Remedies

☐ **1. Trouble setting priorities? Prioritize the three to five most important things.** You don't have a correct set of priorities. Some people get results, but on the wrong things. Effective managers typically spend about half their time on two or three key priorities. What should you spend half your time on? Can you name five things that are less critical? If you can't, you're not differentiating well. Or even if you know the priorities, your team doesn't. You communicate that everything's important and has a deadline of yesterday. They see their jobs as 97 things that need to be done right now. To deal with this: Ask yourself what would happen if they only did four or five things today? What would they be? Ask what the three things they spend the most time on are, and what they would be if we were doing things better? Find out what the 10-20% most time-consuming activities are and either eliminate them or structure them through processes and policies to take less time. *More help? – See #50 Priority Setting.*

☐ **2. Procrastinator? Get an early start.** Are you a lifelong procrastinator? Do you perform best in crises and impossible deadlines? Do you wait until the last possible moment? If you do, you will miss some deadlines and performance targets. You might not produce consistent results. Some of your work will be marginal because you didn't have the time to do it right. You settled for a "B" when you could have gotten an "A" if you had one more day to work on it. Start earlier. Always do 10% of each task immediately after it is assigned so you can better gauge what it is going to take to finish the rest. Divide tasks and assignments into thirds or fourths and schedule time to do them spaced over the delivery period. Remember Murphy's Law: It takes 90% of the time to do 90% of the project, and another 90% of the time to finish the remaining 10%. Always leave more time than you think it's going to take. *More help? – See #47 Planning.*

☐ **3. Not sure how to get things done? Learn the most effective practices.** Some don't know the best way to get things done. There is a well-established set of best practices for getting work done efficiently and effectively—TQM/ISO/Six Sigma. If you are not disciplined in how you design work for yourself and others, buy one book on each of these topics. Go to one workshop on efficient and effective work design. *More help? – See #52 Process Management and #63 Total Work Systems (e.g., TQM/ISO/Six Sigma).*

☐ **4. Difficulty organizing? Gather and manage critical resources.** Are you always short resources? Always pulling things together on a shoe string? Getting results means getting and using resources. People. Money. Materials. Support. Time. Many times it involves getting resources you don't control. You have to beg, borrow but hopefully not steal. That means negotiating, bargaining, trading, cajoling, and influencing. What's the business case for the resources? What do I have to trade? How can I make it a win for everyone? *More help? – See #37 Negotiating and #38 Organizational Agility.*

☐ **5. Doing too much yourself? Get work done through others.** Some people are not good managers. Are you having trouble getting your team to work with you to get the results you need? You have the resources and the people but things just don't run well. You do too much work yourself. You don't delegate or empower. You don't communicate well. You don't motivate well. You don't plan well. You don't set priorities and goals well. If you are a struggling manager, there are well-known and documented principles and practices of good managing. Do you share credit? Do you paint a clear picture of why this is important? Is their work challenging? Do you inspire or just hand out work? Read two books on managing. Go to one course on management. Get 360° feedback on your current management skills. Pick a few to work on. *More help? – See #18 Delegation, #20 Directing Others, #36 Motivating Others, and #60 Building Effective Teams.*

☐ **6. New to the job? Learn your business.** Sometimes you can't produce results because you keep moving around from job to job and never have the time to get smart in the business of the unit. How about general business principles that would go across all jobs? Do you understand how businesses operate? Do you know what causes what in organizations? Do you know what's going on in the market? Do you know what future trends might be? If you are shaky on any of these, read *BusinessWeek* regularly. Scan the *Harvard Business Review*. Subscribe to the *Wall Street Journal*. Watch a show or two on a cable business channel each week. *More help? – See #5 Business Acumen.* Never quite up to speed in the functional skills? Work on your ability to learn more quickly. Use seasoned pros in the technology to tutor you from the start. Hire a consultant. Delegate more. *More help? – See #24 Functional/Technical Skills, #32 Learning on the Fly, and #61 Technical Learning.*

☐ **7. Not bold enough? Take some calculated risks.** Won't take a risk? Sometimes producing results involves pushing the envelope, taking chances and trying bold new initiatives. Doing those things leads to more misfires and mistakes. Treat any mistakes or failures as chances to learn.

Nothing ventured, nothing gained. Up your risk comfort. Start small so you can recover quickly. Make it fun. Challenge yourself. See how creative and innovative you can be. *More help? – See #2 Dealing with Ambiguity, #14 Creativity, and #28 Innovation Management.*

☐ **8. Stuck in old habits and comfortable ways? Change things up.** You're a creature of habit. You do things too much the same way. You're not very flexible. Just as you use the same style, you gravitate toward the same tasks again and again. You've gotten stale. Shake things up. Off-work, force yourself to shift gears. Go from a civic meeting to a water fight with your kids, for example. Go for maximum variety at work. Take a risk, play it safe. Set yourself tasks that force you to shift gears, such as being a spokesperson for your organization when tough questions are expected, making peace with an enemy or managing people who are novices at a task. If you already have these tasks as part of your job, use them to observe yourself and try new behavior. Switch approaches. Do something totally different next time. Have five different ways to get the same outcome. For example, to push a decision through, you could meet with stakeholders first, go to a key stakeholder, study and present the problem to a group, call a problem-solving session, or call in an outside expert. Be prepared to do them all when obstacles arise. Whatever you are doing, it doesn't seem to be working. It may have worked in the past but it's now time to change. *More help? – See #45 Personal Learning.*

☐ **9. Working across borders and boundaries? Find common ground with others outside your area.** You have trouble when you have to go outside your unit. This means that influence skills, understanding, and trading are the currencies to use. Don't just ask for things; find some common ground where you can provide help, not just ask for it. What do the peers you're contacting need? Do you really know how they see the issue? Is it even important to them? How does what you're working on affect them? If it affects them negatively, can you trade something, appeal to the common good, figure out some way to minimize the work—volunteering staff help, for example? Go into peer relationships with a trading mentality. To be seen as more cooperative, always explain your thinking and invite them to explain theirs. Generate a variety of possibilities first rather than stake out positions. Be tentative, allowing them room to customize the situation. Focus on common goals, priorities and problems. Invite criticism of your ideas. *More help? – See #42 Peer Relationships.*

☐ **10. Under constant pressure? Learn to manage the stress and strain.** Producing results day after day, quarter after quarter, year after year, is pressureful. Nothing is ever good enough. Bar is always rising. Goals are set higher. Have to learn new ways and new methods. Lots of stress. Some people are energized by moderate stress. They actually work better. Some people are debilitated by stress. They decrease in productivity as stress increases. Dealing with stress and pressure is a known technology. Stress and pressure are actually in your head, not in the outside world. Some people are stressed by the same events others are energized about—losing a major account. Some people cry and some laugh at the same external event—someone slipping on a banana peel. Stress is how you look at events, not the events themselves. Dealing more effectively with stress involves reprogramming your interpretation of your work and about what you find stressful. There was a time in your life where spiders and snakes were life threatening and stressful to you. Are they now? *More help? – See #11 Composure and #107 Lack of Composure.*

Some Develop-in-Place Assignments

- ☐ Manage a group through a significant business crisis.
- ☐ Manage a cost-cutting project.
- ☐ Take on a tough and undoable project, one where others who have tried it have failed.
- ☐ Plan for and start up something small (secretarial pool, athletic program, suggestion system, program, etc.).
- ☐ Plan an off-site meeting, conference, convention, trade show, event, etc.

*Wanting to be better in performance is like wanting
to be happy—it is very difficult to get there directly.
It is much wiser, first, to focus on the building blocks,
and in the case of performance,
the building blocks are commitment, resilience,
and ruthless disregard for distractions.*
Laura Teresa Marquez – American author

Suggested Readings

Allen, D. (2003). *Ready for anything: 52 Productivity principals for work and life.* New York: Penguin Group.

Baldoni, J. (2006). *How great leaders get great results.* New York: McGraw-Hill.

Bereaux, E. (2007). *The complete guide to project management for new managers and management assistants: How to get things done in less time.* Ocala, FL: Atlantic Publishing.

Bossidy, L., & Charan, R. (with Burck, C.). (2002). *Execution: The discipline of getting things done.* New York: Crown Business.

Carrison, D. (2003). *Deadline! How premier organizations win the race against time.* New York: AMACOM, 2003.

Charan, R. (2007). *Know-how: The 8 skills that separate people who perform from those who don't.* New York: Crown Business.

Collins, J. C. (2000). Turning goals into results: The power of catalytic mechanisms (HBR OnPoint Enhanced Edition). Boston: *Harvard Business Review.*

Daniels, A. C., & Daniels, J. E. (2004). *Performance management: Changing behavior that drives organizational effectiveness* (4th ed.). Tucker, GA: Performance Management Publications.

Eichinger, R. W., Ruyle, K. E., & Lombardo, M. M. (2007). *FYI for performance management™: Universal dimensions for success.* Minneapolis, MN: Lominger International: A Korn/Ferry Company.

Lefton, R. E., & Loeb, J. T. (2004). *Why can't we get anything done around here? The smart manager's guide to executing the work that delivers results.* New York: McGraw-Hill.

Linsky, M., & Heifetz, R. A. (2002). *Leadership on the line: Staying alive through the dangers of leading.* Boston: Harvard Business School Press.

Luecke, R., & Hall, B. J. (2006). *Performance management: Measure and improve the effectiveness of your employees.* Boston: Harvard Business School Press.

Shepard, G. (2005). *How to manage problem employees: A step-by-step guide for turning difficult employees into high performers.* Hoboken, NJ: John Wiley & Sons.

Ulrich, D., & Smallwood, N. (2007). *Leadership brand: Developing customer-focused leaders to drive performance and build lasting value.* Boston: Harvard Business School Press.

Ulrich, D., Zenger, J., & Smallwood, N. (1999). *Results-based leadership.* Boston: Harvard Business School Press.

119 Political Missteps

Politics is how interests and influence play out in an institution.
Benjamin Franklin – American scientist, author, inventor, statesman, and diplomat

A Problem

- ☐ Can't get things done in complex political settings and environments
- ☐ Lacks sensitivity to people and organizational politics
- ☐ Doesn't recognize political due process requirements
- ☐ Says and does the wrong things
- ☐ Shares sensitive information and opinions with the wrong people

Not A Problem

- ☐ Is politically smooth and noiseless
- ☐ Reads individuals and groups well; knows how they are affected
- ☐ Modifies approach when resistance is met
- ☐ Keeps confidences
- ☐ Can maneuver through rough water without getting wet
- ☐ Uses multiple ways to get things done
- ☐ Adjusts to the realities of the political situation
- ☐ Counsels others on political approaches
- ☐ Usually knows the right thing to do and say

Some Causes

- ☐ Competitive with peers
- ☐ Don't read others or their interests well
- ☐ May be too candid to curry favor
- ☐ May share wrong/sensitive information
- ☐ Misunderstanding of what political savvy is
- ☐ No patience with due process
- ☐ Poor impulse control
- ☐ Poor interpersonal skills
- ☐ Poor negotiator
- ☐ Seen as a strident advocate

Other Causes

BEING UNSKILLED AT: 2,3,4,8,11,21,22,29,31,32,33,41,42,45,48,52,55,56,58,60,64
OVERUSING: 6,22,27,38,44,49,52,67

Leadership Architect® Factors and Clusters

This competency is in the Trouble with People Factor (VII) (S1). This competency is in the Self-Centered Cluster (W) with: 103, 104, 105, 107, 109. You may want to check other competencies in the same Factor/Cluster for related tips.

The Map

Organizations are a complex maze of constituencies, issues and rivalries peopled by strong egos, sensitivities and empire protectors. People who are politically savvy accept this as the human condition and deal with it by considering the impact of what they say and do on others. This is not to be confused with "political," which is a polite term for not being trusted or lacking in substance; political savvy involves getting things done in the maze with the minimum of noise. Political mistakes come in a variety of shapes and sizes. The most common is saying things that you shouldn't. This comes in two shapes—you knew it was wrong but you couldn't hold it back, or you didn't know it was wrong to say and were surprised at the reaction. Next are actions that are politically out of line and not right for the context. Worst are politically unacceptable moves, initiatives, tactics and strategies. You tried to get something done in the organization and went about it in the wrong way. Last are unnecessary conflicts, tensions, misunderstandings and rivalries created because you took after a specific person or group.

Some Remedies

☐ **1. Can't hold back? Work on impulse control.** Many people get into political trouble because they have a lot of trouble holding things back. It's not that they didn't know what they were about to say was going to cause noise, they just have weak impulse control. They say almost everything that occurs to them to say. It's even possible that others in the room or in the meeting were thinking the same thing; the difference is that they kept it to themselves. When you dump everything before you put it through a political filter, much of what you say will cause noise and will be seen as poor political judgment by others. One rule is to let others speak first and follow their lead before you dump. *More help? – See #11 Composure and #41 Patience.*

☐ **2. Humor seen as offensive? Keep it in good taste.** Many people get into political trouble with their humor. Times have changed drastically in the past decade. Humor that was seen as positive 10 years ago in organizations is now politically unacceptable. The rules now are real simple. Any humor that hurts others, demeans others, or makes fun of the difficulties others are having is out. No humor that is critical or sarcastic is acceptable. No ribald or off-color humor. No ethnic humor. No gender humor. No religious humor. No humor about people's disabilities. No humor about people in other countries. What's left? You can tell clean jokes, make fun of yourself, tell funny stories, and laugh with others. *More help? – See #26 Humor.*

☐ **3. Want to avoid politics? Evaluate your attitude toward politics.** Many people confuse the terms political savvy and being political. When someone criticizes you for not being political, you might interpret it as the bad political. Being bad political means that your motives should not be trusted. Being bad political means saying one thing and meaning another. It means being devious and scheming. Being politically savvy means saying and doing things that fit into the commonly held beliefs people have around you about what's appropriate and wise and what is not. It's about a set of standards most around you would agree to. Being politically savvy means you can transact with others and get things done in the maze with minimum noise and without triggering an unnecessary negative reaction from others.

☐ **4. Stuck with a predictable approach? Adjust to the situation and the audience.** In any culture or organization, there are multiple ways you can get things done. You could use a direct attack. You could get an ally first. You could send in a more acceptable substitute for yourself. Some of these tactics are more effective and acceptable than others. Some people get into trouble because they treat all situations the same. They don't do any research about the most effective ways to get things done for each event. People who are politically savvy operate from the outside—audience, person, group, organization—in. They pick their pace, style, tone and tactics based upon an evaluation of what would work best in each situation. We all have a number of ways in which we can behave if we want to. It's the one-trick ponies that get into political trouble because they don't adjust what they say and do to each audience. *More help? – See #15 Customer Focus and #45 Personal Learning.*

☐ **5. Too honest? Decide whether candor is appropriate.** Candor can be a mission-critical requirement in a 9 a.m. meeting and politically unwise and unacceptable in a 10 a.m. meeting. Many people get themselves in political trouble with either too much candor that ends up hurting others and causing noise, or too little candor seen as holding back something important. Many often say, "I just say what I think. I've always believed in saying exactly what I mean. Consequences be damned. If they don't like it, they shouldn't have asked me about it." While that might get good marks for integrity, it would fail the political savvy test. Each situation must be examined on the candor scale. Are the right people here? Is this the best time for candor? Should I let someone else start before I do? Did the speaker who asked for candor really mean it? *More help? – See #56 Sizing Up People and #64 Understanding Others.*

☐ **6. Don't know the key players? Navigate the politics of the organization.** Who are the movers and shakers in the organization? Who are the major gatekeepers who control the flow of resources, information and decisions? Who are the guides and the helpers? Get to know them better. Do lunch. Who are the major resisters and stoppers? Try to avoid or go around them or make peace with them. Every maze has its solution. Being politically savvy means finding that least distant path through the organizational maze. *More help? – See #38 Organizational Agility.*

☐ **7. Sharing too much? Make sure comments are relevant and proper.** Are you sharing things inappropriately to cement a relationship, to get something you need, to feel like an important insider, or because you just don't think it through? Monitor yourself closely and ask these questions: "Why am I sharing this? Does it move a problem along? Do people really need to know this? Will this make someone else look bad or will it be obvious where I got it? Am I name dropping? Have I labeled facts as facts and opinions as opinions? Will this be considered grousing, gossiping or cutting down another person or group? In the worst case how could this person use this information in a way that would reflect badly on me?" A general rule of thumb is you can be as candid as you like as long as comments refer to specific problems/issues and you're not violating confidences and the person you are giving the information to can be trusted.

☐ **8. Talking about people? Refrain from gossiping.** A lot of political noise comes from sharing private views of others in the wrong settings and with the wrong people. All things come around that go around. In closed organizations, people quickly find out what you have said about them. If you are having trouble with this, the simplest rule is never to share any negative information about another person unless it is a formal evaluation process in the organization.

☐ **9. Dealing with executives? Approach top management with extra care.** In the special case of dealing with top management, sensitivities are high, egos are big, sensitivity traps are set and tensions can be severe. There is a lot of room for making statements or acting in ways that would be seen as exhibiting poor political judgment. There usually isn't a second chance to make a good first impression. *More help? – See #8 Comfort Around Higher Management.*

☐ **10. Strong point of view? Temper your advocacy and make the business case.** Strident advocates don't usually fare well in organizations because their perspectives are seen as rigid and narrow. To avoid being seen this way, make the business or organizational case first. Be more tentative than you actually are so others have room to get comfortable and negotiate and bargain. People who have trouble with this state things in such an extreme that others are turned off and can't save face even if they agree with more than 50% of what you are pushing for. *More help? – See #37 Negotiating.*

Some Develop-in-Place Assignments

- ☐ Manage a group through a significant business crisis.
- ☐ Manage the assigning/allocating of office space in a contested situation.
- ☐ Prepare and present a proposal of some consequence to top management.
- ☐ Manage the interface between consultants and the organization on a critical assignment.
- ☐ Integrate diverse systems, processes, or procedures across decentralized and/or dispersed units.

Important changes that are shaping the nature of work in today's complex organizations demand that we become more sophisticated with respect to issues of leadership, power, and influence.
John P. Kotter – American professor and author

Suggested Readings

Ashkenas, R. N., Ulrich, D., Jick, T., & Kerr, S. (2002). *The boundaryless organization: Breaking the chains of organization structure* (Rev. ed.). San Francisco: Jossey-Bass.

Bradberry, T., & Greaves, J. (2005). *The emotional intelligence quick book: Everything you need to know to put your EQ to work.* New York: Fireside.

Brandon, R., & Seldman, M. (2004) *Survival of the savvy: High-integrity political tactics for career and company success.* New York: Free Press.

Buchanan, D. A. (2008). You stab my back, I'll stab yours: Management experience and perceptions of organizational political behavior. *British Journal of Management, 19,* 49-65.

Buchanan, D. A., & Badham, R. J. (2008). *Power, politics, and organizational change: Winning the turf game.* London: Sage.

Cashman, K. (2008). *Leadership from the inside out: Becoming a leader for life* (2nd ed.). San Francisco: Berrett-Koehler Publishers.

Cohen, D., & Prusak, L. (2001). *In good company: How social capital makes organizations work.* Boston: Harvard Business School Press.

de Janasz, S. C., Dowd, K. O., & Schneider, B. Z. (2008). *Interpersonal skills in organizations* (3rd ed.). New York: McGraw-Hill.

Dimitrius, J., & Mazzarella, M. C. (2008). *Reading people: How to understand people and predict their behavior: Anytime, anyplace.* New York: Ballantine Books.

Douglas, C., & Ammeter, A. P. (2004). An examination of leader political skill and its effect on ratings of leader effectiveness. *Leadership Quarterly, 15,* 537-551.

Fritz, S. M., Lunde, J. P., Brown, W., & Banset, E. A. (2004). *Interpersonal skills for leadership* (2nd ed.). Upper Saddle River, NJ: Prentice Hall.

Harvard Business School Press. (2008). *Managing up.* Boston: Harvard Business School Press.

Hawley, C. F. (2008). *100+ Tactics for office politics* (2nd ed.). New York: Barrons Educational Series.

Kissinger, H. (1994). *Diplomacy.* New York: Simon & Schuster.

Klaus, P. (2007). *The hard truth about soft skills: Workplace lessons smart people wish they'd learned sooner.* New York: HarperCollins.

Lerner, H. (2002). *The dance of connection: How to talk to someone when you're mad, hurt, scared, frustrated, insulted, betrayed, or desperate.* New York: HarperCollins.

Linsky, M., & Heifetz, R. A. (2002). *Leadership on the line: Staying alive through the dangers of leading.* Boston: Harvard Business School Press.

McIntyre, M. G. (2005). *Secrets to winning at office politics: How to achieve your goals and increase your influence at work.* New York: St. Martin's Press.

Parekh, B. (1989). *Gandhi's political philosophy.* Notre Dame, IN: University of Notre Dame Press.

Pfeffer, J. (1994). *Managing with power: Politics and influence in organizations.* Boston: Harvard Business School Press.

Ranker, G., Gautrey, C., & Phipps, M. (2008). *Political dilemmas at work: How to maintain your integrity and further your career.* Hoboken, NJ: John Wiley & Sons.

Reardon, K. K. (2001). *The secret handshake: Mastering the politics of the business inner circle.* New York: Currency/Doubleday.

Walton, M. S. (2003). *Generating buy-in: Mastering the language of leadership.* New York: AMACOM.

Global Focus Areas

Many clients and users of this handbook for development operate in a global environment. Some manage people and operations outside their home country while residing in their own. Some reside and operate outside their home country. Others travel extensively across countries and regions. Many have asked us whether there are any unique competencies involved with operating globally. Our general response after scanning the relevant literature is that, at least for companies doing business globally, the competencies are basically the same as they would be in a one-country or domestic business. Most major competency models are used worldwide. Competencies are competencies. Listening skills are needed throughout the world.

At the same time, the way competencies are applied, described, or emphasized may differ from culture to culture. For example, what is described as action oriented in Japan or India may not be described the same way as it is in the United States or China. From our reading of the global management literature, we think there are seven areas that deserve special attention and emphasis. These seven areas are based on both supporting research and the experiences of the authors. Over time, as more research is available, this list most likely will change. It is also expected that future research will allow a more culturally specific framework for all of the Lominger Competencies.

It is interesting to note that the international research mirrors our mostly North American and European results. When you look at the special focus areas the international studies identify, they look a lot like the Lominger Leadership Library Structure. The seven key Global Focus Areas are roughly parallel to and grounded in the Factors in the Lominger Library Structure. So it's basically the same concept but in a global context. The eight Factors from the Lominger Library Structure and their Global Equivalents are shown on the next page.

FACTOR	GLOBAL EQUIVALENT
Factor I: Strategic Skills	161. Global Business Knowledge
Factor II: Operating Skills	162. Cross-Cultural Resourcefulness*
Factor III: Courage	163. Cross-Cultural Agility
Factor IV: Energy and Drive	164. Assignment Hardiness
Factor V: Organizational Positioning Skills	165. Organizational Positioning Skills
Factor VI: Personal and Interpersonal Skills	166. Cross-Cultural Sensitivity
Factor VII: Trouble with People	167. Humility
Factor VIII: Trouble with Results	162. Cross-Cultural Resourcefulness*

**Listed twice—once in the positive and once in the negative*

There are no competencies numbered 120-160.
Those numbers are reserved for future additions.

161 Global Business Knowledge

Some Leadership Architect® Equivalents
2,5,28,32,46,51,58,64

The knowledge of the world is only to be acquired in the world, and not in a closet.
Philip Dormer Stanhope – British statesman and man of letters

Unskilled

- ☐ Doesn't understand global business
- ☐ Sees business issues in terms of a one-country experience
- ☐ Is rigid about doing things only one way
- ☐ Does not learn new ways of doing things
- ☐ Has a narrow perspective
- ☐ Does not accept novel ways of approaching problems

Skilled

- ☐ Understands business on a global scale
- ☐ Understands what works in many countries
- ☐ Understands what's different from country to country
- ☐ Understands global differences in customers
- ☐ Knows how capital flows and operates internationally
- ☐ Understands that different laws and regulations govern global business
- ☐ Is learning agile
- ☐ Understands that different approaches work in different places

Overuse

- ☐ Unnecessarily complicates things
- ☐ Overthinks challenges and opportunities
- ☐ Not patient with those who do not know as much
- ☐ Can't settle on a course of action
- ☐ Thinks of too many options
- ☐ Has difficulty prioritizing a course of action
- ☐ Changes strategic and tactical course too quickly

Select one to three of the competencies listed below to work on to compensate for an overuse of this skill.

COMPENSATORS: 3,31,33,41,50,51

Some Causes

- ☐ Not curious
- ☐ Too eager to get to an answer
- ☐ Very ethnocentric
- ☐ Very narrow background
- ☐ Uncomfortable with ambiguity
- ☐ Difficulty in accepting different ways of doing things
- ☐ Rigid about selecting a course of action and staying with it

The Map

The world is a big and small place simultaneously. In some sense, business is business. Someone has a product or service someone needs or wants. A customer buys it. If enough customers buy it, it becomes a profitable venture. On the other hand, rules, regulations, laws, customs, and preferred ways of operating can be quite different country to country. In order to be successful, you have to know how things work differently in different countries. Being flexible in the face of different rules for doing global business is essential. Successful internationalists can understand the complexity of global business and simplify that complexity for others in a way that leads to the successful execution of strategies, tactics, and business plans.

Some Remedies

☐ **1. Need to get informed? Read the right periodicals.** There are five publications that probably will teach you most of what you need to know about business in general as well as about international business issues. These publications are the *Wall Street Journal, BusinessWeek, Fortune, Barron's,* and the *Harvard Business Review*. Subscribe and begin to scan those publications regularly with particular attention to global business knowledge and concepts. Try to identify at least three international items per issue. There are other publications that are more specifically international in nature. Read international publications like the *Economist,* the *International Herald Tribune* or *Commentary*. Also look at autobiographies of people like Henry Kissinger; pick a country and study it; read a book on the fall of the Soviet Union; or read "we present all sides" journals like the *Atlantic Monthly* to get the broadest possible view of global issues like trade and currency management. There are common underlying principles in everything. You need to expose yourself more broadly in order to find and apply those principles to what you're doing today. Also get copies of local newspapers (hopefully in your native language) and see what they cover and what's important. Read and compare a U.S. paper with a non-U.S. paper and look for the very different perspectives on key issues.

☐ **2. Ready to learn more? Study and understand global trends.** Read *Management Challenges for the 21st Century* by Peter Drucker, any of the *Megatrends* books by John Naisbitt, *The Popcorn Report* by Faith Popcorn, or *THE FUTURIST*, the journal of the World Future Society. For example, Drucker raises issues such as what does it mean that the birth rate is collapsing in the developed world? By 2030 it is estimated that half of Japan's population will be 65 or older. Much the same is true in the rest of the developed world. Will the retirement age go up? Will we treat workers more like volunteers as they opt out of larger organizations? Leisure spending may go down since more time off is not likely. Education and health care will grow. Immigration? Increasingly, developing countries will import immigrants to maintain workforces. The average career of an employee will far outlive their employers (most corporations last about 30 years). Second and third "careers" will be standard. The means of production has largely become knowledge. Outsourcing of HR is up 30%—knowledge is increasingly specialized, expensive, and difficult to maintain. Is this a harbinger of more outsourcing and alliances? Become a student of global trends.

☐ **3. Falling behind? Stay current with international business and current events.** There are now many domestic and foreign and global business channels on cable that carry business news and information full time. They have interviews with business leaders, reviews of industries by experts, as well as general reviews of specific companies. Begin to watch one or two programs a week until you can zero in on what you specifically need to know. If you know the countries you will be working in or visiting, start watching the broadcasts that originate in those countries. Subscribe to a Web-based service that flags events in countries, industries, or companies of interest.

☐ **4. Ready to learn from others? Join an international organization.** The Conference Board is dedicated to creating and distributing information about business to its members, including global issues. They have wonderful global-themed conferences where many top leaders come and share their thoughts about business in general and their business specifically. Use universities with international programs (e.g., Thunderbird, INSEAD, IMEDE, The London Business School) and find out what organizations or contacts these programs have that might be useful.

☐ **5. Need to understand emerging trends? Read books on global business.** Go to any business bookstore and pick three books on global business principles—one with a financial slant, one with a cultural slant, and one about customer behavior. When you have scanned those, go back and get three more until you have the global business knowledge you need. Read about emerging global trends such as in Thomas Friedman's book, *The Lexus and the Olive Tree*. Check the *New York Times* best-selling book list for titles of international interest. Review works on international/global business published by the Harvard Business School Press. Do a search on Amazon.com.

- ☐ **6. Don't understand global business? Figure out the rules of the global business game.** Reduce your understanding of how global business operates to personal rules of thumb or insights. Write them down in your own words. An example would be, "What are the drivers in marketing across countries and cultures?" One executive had 25 such drivers that was continually edited, scratched through, and replaced as more up-to-date thinking emerged. Use these rules of thumb to analyze a business that you know something about. Then pick two businesses that have pulled off clever global strategies, one related to yours and one not. Study what they did, talk to people who know what happened and see what you can learn. Pick a particular business function such as foreign exchange hedging or logistics and develop an understanding of how these functions work internationally or impact the country in which you are interested.
- ☐ **7. Narrow perspective? Try some globally broadening tasks.** Volunteer for task forces that include people outside your country of origin. Talk with customers outside of your home country; work actually delivering a product or service. Write down things you've learned about how global business works. Have lunch with fellow employees from outside your home country. Volunteer for a project dealing with issues outside of your home country. Plan a vacation to a region of the world you have never seen. Be a guest lecturer in a university where there is a wide diversity of nationality and ask questions about what these students think about key issues.
- ☐ **8. Disconnected from the customer? Get closer to your global customers.** Customer service is the best place to learn about the business. Arrange a meeting with a counterpart in customer service. Have him or her explain the function to you. If you can, listen in on customer service calls or, even better, handle a couple yourself. Ask lots of questions about what customers like or don't like about your company's products or services. Take a market tour in a different country with a key member of your marketing staff. Look at what competitors are doing and how they are similar, different, priced. Work hard at understanding how product preferences change from culture to culture.
- ☐ **9. Curious? Take a course.** Attend a workshop or seminar on a topic of interest at Thunderbird University in Arizona, the London School of Economics, or INSEAD in France. Those events are attended by people from around the globe and taught by international experts on global

issues. Pay special attention to those participants from countries of special interest to you. Spend as much time as possible with them. Be active in breakouts and work groups. Listen. Ask questions.

- ☐ **10. Want to wrap your head around it? Do your own case study.** Pick a global company or competitor of interest and read everything you can get your hands on from news sources or business news services and build a picture of what they have done well or not so well, and try to determine where they might be vulnerable. Do a comparison with your company. Look at specific functional areas such as marketing, and build a case study around that discipline. Ask yourself what you would do differently from your competitors. Do a case study from the standpoint of a competitor and attempt to determine where your company is vulnerable.

Some Develop-in-Place Assignments

- ☐ Work on a project that involves travel and study of an international issue, acquisition, or joint venture and report back to management.
- ☐ Manage a project team made up of nationals from a number of countries.
- ☐ Build or work on a multinational project team to tackle a common international business issue or problem.
- ☐ Prepare and present a proposal of some consequence to top management in the international sector of your business.
- ☐ Work short rotations in other countries you've not been exposed to before.

I find that because of modern technological evolution
and our global economy, and as a result of the great increase
in population, our world has greatly changed. It has become much smaller.
However, our perceptions have not evolved at the same pace.
We continue to cling to old national demarcations
and the old feelings of 'us' and 'them.'
The Dalai Lama – Spiritual leader of the Tibetan people
and Nobel Peace Prize winner

Suggested Readings

Bartlett, C. A., & Ghoshal, S. (2002). *Managing across borders: The transnational solution* (2nd ed.). Boston: Harvard Business School Press.

Cavusgil, T., Knight, G., & Riesenberger, J. (2007). *International business: Strategy, management, and the new realities.* Upper Saddle River, NJ: Prentice Hall.

Cohen, E. (2007). *Leadership without borders: Successful strategies from world-class leaders.* Singapore: John Wiley & Sons.

Deresky, H. (2006). *International management: Managing across borders and cultures* (5th ed.). Upper Saddle River, NJ: Prentice Hall.

Friedman, T. L. (2000). *The Lexus and the olive tree: Understanding globalization.* Landover Hills, MD: Anchor Books.

Hill, C. W. L. (2004). *Global business today* (3rd ed.). New York: McGraw-Hill/Irwin.

Issenberg, S. (2007). *The sushi economy: Globalization and the making of a modern delicacy.* New York: Penguin Group.

McCall, M. W., Jr., & Hollenbeck, G. P. (2001). *Developing global executives: The lessons of international experience.* Boston: Harvard Business School Press.

Meredith, R. (2007). *The elephant and the dragon: The rise of India and China and what it means for all of us.* New York: W. W. Norton & Company.

Rakocy, B., Reuss, A., & Sturr, C. (Eds.). (2007). *Real world globalization: A reader in business, economics, and politics* (9th ed.). Boston, MA: Dollars & Sense: Economic Affairs Bureau.

Travis, T. (2007). *Doing business anywhere: The essential guide to going global.* Hoboken, NJ: John Wiley & Sons.

Trompenaars, F., & Hampden-Turner, C. (2002). *21 Leaders for the 21st century: How innovative leaders manage in the digital age.* New York: McGraw-Hill.

Wild, J. J., & Wild, K. L. (2007). *International business: The challenges of globalization* (4th ed.). Upper Saddle River, NJ: Prentice Hall.

Williamson, P. J., & Zeng, M. (2007). *Dragons at your door: How Chinese cost innovation is disrupting global competition.* Boston: Harvard Business School Press.

162 Cross-Cultural Resourcefulness

Some Leadership Architect® Equivalents:
2,20,21,27,32,39,50,52,53,59

The greatest achievement of the human spirit is to live up to one's opportunities and make the most of one's resources.
Marquis de Vauvenargues – French moralist, essayist, and writer

Unskilled

- ☐ Only has one way of doing things
- ☐ Too rigid
- ☐ Doesn't adjust swiftly enough
- ☐ Has trouble with transitions
- ☐ Doesn't negotiate well
- ☐ Can't stay focused on outcomes
- ☐ Tries to impose one way of doing things
- ☐ Takes a long time to build relationships
- ☐ Has difficulty relating to people with different ways of doing things

Skilled

- ☐ Gets things done across varied and different international conditions
- ☐ Can make do without having everything they need
- ☐ Gets rare resources others can't get
- ☐ Is a skilled negotiator
- ☐ Operates effectively under ambiguous, uncertain conditions
- ☐ Tries to learn the local language
- ☐ Can figure out what's important
- ☐ Listens to and acts on advice of local managers
- ☐ Builds relationships quickly
- ☐ Relates well to a wide spectrum of people
- ☐ Effectively leverages local skills to get things done

Overuse

- ☐ Cuts corners
- ☐ Tries to impose complex standards
- ☐ Delegates too many details
- ☐ Is too loose about standards
- ☐ Avoids close direction of others
- ☐ Overly creative and drives staff crazy with options
- ☐ Avoids metrics and measures
- ☐ Overplans and overorganizes

Select one to three of the competencies listed below to work on to compensate for an overuse of this skill.

COMPENSATORS: 3,17,31,33,41,46,48,50,52

Some Causes

- ☐ Very strong values, beliefs, and preferred ways of doing things
- ☐ Impatient with due process
- ☐ Not a good delegator
- ☐ Doesn't trust people who are different
- ☐ Lacks confidence
- ☐ Lacks flexibility
- ☐ Doesn't listen to others
- ☐ Tries to force local process into home country methods

The Map

Getting things done in new settings is always a challenge. Internationally, it can be really challenging. Phones don't work. There are no deliveries on Wednesdays. Suppliers can't provide what you need. Corporate support is eight thousand miles away and in another time zone. The country has a holiday that doesn't match with home office needs or requirements. Government regulators take their time responding to your requests. Locals simply do not understand what needs to be done differently even though you have explained it many times. In these tough situations, resourcefulness and scrappiness is essential. Finding a way is key—sometimes any way. A willingness to flex to local operating conditions while keeping a critical eye on the needed results is critical. Always remember there is rarely only one way of getting something done. Let innovation and creativity be your focus. A true measure of globalization is the extent to which ideas are developed outside of a headquarters market and then retrofitted to work "at home."

Some Remedies

☐ **1. Need direction? Clarify your goals and objectives.** What exactly is it you need to accomplish? Use the annual business plan and the strategic plan to understand the mission-critical things that must happen. *More help? – See #58 Strategic Agility and #47 Planning.* Using the goals, separate what you need to do into mission-critical, important to get done, nice if there is time left over, and not central to what you are trying to achieve. When faced with choices or multiple things to do, apply the scale and always focus most on the highest priorities. Be very careful about thinking out loud. In some cultures, a simple thought will be taken by the staff as a directive to get something done. Give people just the right amount of direction—not too much or too little.

☐ **2. Unsure how to start? Lay out the work carefully.** Most resourcefulness starts out with a plan. What do I need to accomplish? What's the time line? What resources will I need? Who controls the resources—people, funding, tools, materials, support—I need? What's my currency? How can I pay for or repay the resources I need? Who wins if I win? Who might lose? Lay out the work from A to Z. Many people are seen as disorganized because they don't fully understand a work sequence or leave something out. Ask others to comment on ordering and what's missing. Break down the work into chunks that the local staff can execute. Be careful to not make assignments that are beyond the capability of the local staff.

☐ **3. Operating on a shoestring? Bargain for resources.** International business is often short on resources. Always pulling things together on a shoestring? Getting results means getting and using resources. People. Money. Materials. Support. Time. Many times it involves getting resources you don't control. You may have to beg, borrow, but within the boundaries of acceptable practices. That means negotiating, bargaining, trading, cajoling, and influencing. What do you have to trade? How can you make it a win for everyone? What do I have to trade? What can I buy? What can I borrow? What do I need to trade for? What do I need that I can't pay or trade for? Being effective in many international settings requires creative resourcefulness. Many times the tools and information you need to move forward are not as readily available as you might be used to in your home country. You are usually separated from headquarters or home office support systems and basically on your own. You have to make do. You may have to learn to barter and bargain. Is what I need anywhere around? What do I need that they have? What could I do for them that could allow them to give up something I need now in return? How can we turn this into a win for both of us? Understand what is accepted and ethical in the local culture. Understand the United States Foreign Corrupt Practices Act and how that may influence or limit what you can do. If you are operating in a questionable area, get help from legal or others who have worked in similar situations. Relationships help. Who do you know who could help? What could you provide in return? Could a colleague in a contiguous country help? Could someone from a non-competitive company help? *More help? – See #37 Negotiating and #39 Organizing.*

☐ **4. Faced with complexity? Manage along multiple tracks.** Getting things done internationally is almost always more difficult. Many attempts to get complex things done involve managing parallel tracks or multiple tasks at the same time. It helps if you have a master plan. It helps if you delegate some of the work. *More help? – See #47 Planning and #39 Organizing.* Use other expatriates or social contacts in the local economy to provide advice and counsel. Understand how government and regulatory agencies can help or hinder your agenda. Try to anticipate what could go wrong and be prepared with contingency plans. Work multiple agendas, for example, with government regulators, customs, and third-party distributors in order to get your product to market.

☐ **5. Ready to leverage a team? Get more work done through others.** Being resourceful internationally usually includes using and trusting others. Some people are not good managers of others. They can produce results by themselves but do less well when the results have to come from the team. This is particularly true in a culture you do not fully understand. Are you having trouble getting others to work with you to get the results you need? Maybe you do too much work yourself. You don't delegate or empower. You don't communicate well. You don't motivate well. You don't plan well. You don't set priorities and goals well. If you are a struggling delegator, there are well-known and documented principles and practices of good delegating. Do you share credit? Do you paint a clear picture of why this is important? Is their work challenging? Do you inspire or just hand out work? Teams of people with the widest diversity of backgrounds produce the most innovative solutions to problems. Get others with different backgrounds to analyze and make sense with you. When working together, come up with as many questions about it as you can. Find individuals who have faced problems quite similar to what you face in the same country and set up dialogues to learn more about specific topics of interest.

☐ **6. Working across boundaries? Work collaboratively for mutual benefit.** Develop a facility for working across multiple borders and boundaries. Do you have trouble when you have to go outside your unit to reach your goals and objectives? This means that influence skills, understanding, and trading are the currencies to use. Don't just ask for things; find some common ground where you can provide help. What do the peers you're contacting need? Are your results important to them? How does what you're working on affect their results? If it affects them negatively, can you trade something, appeal to the common good, figure out some way to minimize the work—volunteering staff help, for example? Go into peer relationships with a trading mentality. To be seen as more cooperative, always explain your thinking and invite them to explain theirs. Generate a variety of possibilities first rather than stake out positions. Be tentative, allowing others the opportunity to customize the situation. Focus on common goals, priorities and problems. Invite criticism of your ideas. *More help? – See #42 Peer Relationships.*

☐ **7. Want to speed up the learning process? Experiment, get feedback, and make progress.** Don't expect to get it right the first time. In most international assignments, the way is not clear and "you must build the airplane while flying it." Many studies show that the second or third try is when we really understand the underlying dynamics of problems. To increase learning, get fast feedback loops. The more frequent the cycles, the more opportunities to learn; if we do something in each of three days instead of one thing every three days, we triple our learning opportunities and increase our chances of finding the right answer. Be more willing to experiment. Movement and steady progress is more important than being perfect, particularly in emerging markets.

☐ **8. Struggling with communication? Overcommunicate and engage in dialogue.** Building a shared understanding of an operating agenda is very difficult outside of one's own culture. There can rarely be enough communication and dialogue about what needs to be done. In an international environment, it is essential to check for understanding with the local staff. In some cultures, yes does not mean yes. Ask for input from multiple sources and check these sources against each other. Ask lots of questions. As much as possible, be consistent. If others perceive you to be inconsistent, they may take actions that are counterproductive. Pay attention to what others say or don't respond to. Constantly encourage your staff to offer points of view. Be patient if dialogue does not come all at once, and keep encouraging it.

☐ **9. Dealing with hierarchy? Respect the role and limits of authority or power in a given culture.** Listen to little messages or suggestions coming from your local staff. In some cultures, offending the manager is a major no-no and your staff may be very reluctant to speak up or confront you. Read and understand the principles surrounding authority in the culture. Some cultures are very driven by a collective or relationship mind-set, and simply giving orders in those cultures will not lead to positive actions and likely lead to passive resistance. Other cultures are so hierarchical they will do almost anything the manager suggests. Know your audience. Learn what the reactions will likely be to your particular style of driving an agenda, and adjust your agenda accordingly. Across cultures, your natural mode of operation isn't enough to be effective. *More help? – See #45 Personal Learning.*

☐ **10. Making assumptions about what works? Adjust your leadership approach.** Carefully examine your management principles/practices for their appropriate applicability. Carefully examine the practices you take for granted in your home country. For example, if you believe in delegation and you delegate an important process or project to an unskilled workforce, the result could be a disaster. Never assume that the principles of leadership you have learned are transferable and immediately applicable in a new country environment. Find a trusted local advisor who can help explain how the locals view your leadership approach and what they expect of a leader. At the same time, global business education is producing a class of business leaders and managers who understand how differences in principles and practices impact results. Ask some of the more junior staff how things will play.

Some Develop-in-Place Assignments

☐ Build or work on a multinational project team to tackle a common international business issue or problem.

☐ Assemble a team of internationally diverse people to accomplish a difficult task.

☐ Manage a group of people in a rapidly expanding or growing market in another country.

☐ Integrate diverse systems, processes, or procedures across decentralized and/or dispersed international units.

☐ Launch a new product, service, or process in another country or across countries.

It isn't always about adding resources,
it's about ensuring your resources are appropriately allocated.
Cathy Allen – American political consultant

Suggested Readings

Adekola, A., & Sergi, B. S. (2007). *Global business management: A cross-cultural perspective.* Hampshire, UK: Ashgate.

Bartlett, C. A., & Ghoshal, S. (2002). *Managing across borders: The transnational solution* (2nd ed.). Boston: Harvard Business School Press.

Brett, J. M. (2007). *Negotiating globally: How to negotiate deals, resolve disputes, and make decisions across cultural boundaries* (2nd ed.). San Francisco: John Wiley & Sons.

Cavusgil, T., Knight, G., & Riesenberger, J. (2007). *International business: Strategy, management, and the new realities.* Upper Saddle River, NJ: Prentice Hall.

Cox, T., Jr. (2001). *Creating the multicultural organization: A strategy for capturing the power of diversity.* San Francisco: Jossey-Bass.

Dalton, M., Ernst, C., Deal, J., & Leslie, J. (2002). *Success for the new global manager: How to work across distances, countries, and cultures.* San Francisco: Jossey-Bass.

Deresky, H. (2006). *International management: Managing across borders and cultures* (5th ed.). Upper Saddle River, NJ: Prentice Hall.

Fulkerson, J. R., & Tucker, M. F. (1999). Diversity: Lessons from global human resource practices. In A. I. Kraut & A. K. Korman (Eds.), *Evolving practices in human resources management* (pp. 249–274). San Francisco: Jossey-Bass.

House, R. J., Hanges, P. J., Javidan, M., Dorfman, P., & Gupta, V. (Eds.). (2004). *Culture, leadership, and organizations: The GLOBE study of 62 societies.* Thousand Oaks, CA: Sage.

Konopaske, R., & Ivancevich, J. M. (2004). *Global management and organizational behavior: Text, readings, cases, and exercises.* New York: McGraw-Hill/Irwin.

Law, W. K. (Ed.). (2007). *Information resources management: Global challenges.* Hershey, PA: Idea Group.

Losey, M., Meisinger, S., & Ulrich, D. (Eds.). (2005). *The future of human resource management: 64 Thought leaders explore the critical HR issues of today and tomorrow.* Hoboken, NJ: John Wiley & Sons.

Taggart, J. H., Berry, M., & McDermott, M. (Eds.). (2001). *Multinationals in a new era: International strategy and management.* Hampshire, UK: Academy of International Business.

Walker, D., Walker, T., & Schmitz, J. (2003). *Doing business internationally: The guide to cross-cultural success* (2nd ed.). New York: McGraw-Hill.

Wild, J. J., & Wild, K. L. (2007). *International business: The challenges of globalization* (4th ed.). Upper Saddle River, NJ: Prentice Hall.

163 Cross-Cultural Agility

Some Leadership Architect® Equivalents:
12,13,25,34,56,57

People can only live fully by helping others to live.
When you give life to friends you truly live.
Cultures can only realize their further richness by honoring other traditions.
And only by respecting natural life can humanity continue to exist.
Daisaku Ikeda – Japanese peace activist and Buddhist leader

Unskilled

- ☐ Has difficulty taking on tough situations
- ☐ Does not understand the local culture
- ☐ Lets others deal with conflict
- ☐ Won't take charge in difficult situations
- ☐ Won't confront performance issues
- ☐ Doesn't adjust to local conditions
- ☐ Needs support and approval before acting
- ☐ Makes bad hiring decisions
- ☐ Will not fire someone for fear of offending cultural sensitivities
- ☐ Won't take a business stand when cultural clashes occur

Skilled

- ☐ Knows how to work the local culture
- ☐ Is not afraid of committing to a course of action to get started
- ☐ Has the courage of his/her convictions
- ☐ Understands the need for flexibility
- ☐ Won't let unresolved issues drift
- ☐ Engages in-country locals in dialogue about how to get things done
- ☐ Is willing to start something and make adjustments along the way
- ☐ Is not afraid to try something never done before
- ☐ Will advocate with the home office for a locally driven initiative

Overuse

- ☐ Uses cultural differences as an excuse for not taking action
- ☐ Relies on locals or in-country practices too much
- ☐ Discusses cultural-difference impact on every action
- ☐ Overadapts to local way of doing things and loses perspective
- ☐ Lets issues drift
- ☐ Appears indecisive
- ☐ Uses lack of cultural comfort as an excuse for not hiring someone

Select one to three of the competencies listed below to work on to compensate for an overuse of this skill.

COMPENSATORS: 1,8,9,20,36,39,57

Some Causes

- ☐ Lacks confidence
- ☐ Overthinks cultural issues
- ☐ Is uncomfortable taking action in culturally ambiguous situations
- ☐ Needs to understand nuances of a culture before taking action
- ☐ Has a fear of offending cultural norms
- ☐ Does not understand the local culture
- ☐ Does not know how to handle conflict

The Map

There is always an element of uncertainty when working in a culture different from one's own. Cultural differences can be used as an excuse for not taking action. In the end, business is still business and the product or service is generally still the same even across borders. People will always have excuses for not doing things, and you will have to stand alone and push for action. Many times, new business practices are required for progress. You need both the courage and conviction that, even when there is resistance, progress is made only by pushing the edge of the envelope. Not confronting performance problems or other difficult issues always leads to more problems down the road. Successful internationalists learn how to recognize the competencies of others in any culture and do not use a lack of cultural comfort as an excuse for not taking action.

Some Remedies

- ☐ **1. Facing conflict? Cooperate.** The opposite of conflict is cooperation. Developing cooperative relationships involves demonstrating real and perceived equity, the other side feeling understood and respected, and taking a problem-oriented point of view. To do this more: Increase the realities and perceptions of fairness—don't try to win every battle and take all the spoils; focus on the common-ground issues and interests of both sides—find wins on both sides, give in on little points; avoid starting with entrenched positions—show respect for others and their positions; and, reduce any remaining conflicts to the smallest size possible. Getting things done in international settings must include an operational understanding of where others are coming from and why they think like they do. The beginning point of cooperation is mutual understanding. The rest is mutual problem solving coupled with flexibility about exactly how things are to get done.

☐ **2. Dealing with uncertainty? Stay focused on the end result but flexible on the methods.** In any international assignment, there will be uncertainty around what is the right thing to do. More often than not, by staying focused on the end result, a solution will present itself. For example, a product delivery system does not necessarily need hand-held computers and a zero-defects product replenishment system. Products can be delivered by bicycle, on foot, by canoe, or by handcart just as they can by a truck. At the end of the day, the product must be delivered. Don't let your experience limit your creativity, and let local conditions help lead you to the solution. Look for and take advantage of what another culture offers.

☐ **3. Communication style creating issues? Avoid creating unnecessary conflict.** Language, words, and timing set a tone that can be positive or negative. You can cause unnecessary conflict with the wrong or culturally insensitive approach. Do you use insensitive language in a different culture? Do you raise your voice when frustrated? Do you use terms and phrases that unnecessarily challenge others? Do you use terms that are considered demeaning in that culture? Do you use humor inappropriate for that country or culture? Do you offer conclusions, solutions, statements, dictates, or answer too early in discussions? Give reasons first, solutions last. When you give solutions first, people often challenge the solutions instead of defining the problem. Pick words that are culturally sensitive and neutral. Pick words that don't challenge or sound one-sided or culturally arrogant. Pick tentative and probabilistic words that give others a chance to maneuver and save face. Pick words that are about the problem and not the person. Avoid direct blaming remarks; describe the problem and its impact. Don't inadvertently introduce conflict with inappropriate or insensitive language or non-verbals. Until you learn the culture, use a degree of caution in your approach. Do not criticize the practices of other cultures until you fully understand the implications of your remarks.

☐ **4. Need to find common ground? Downsize the conflict.** Almost all conflicts have common points that get lost in the heat of the battle. After a conflict has been presented and understood, start by saying that it might be helpful to see what can be agreed upon. Focus on common goals, priorities, and problems. Keep open conflicts as small and as concrete as possible. The more abstract a conflict gets, "We don't trust your unit," the more unmanageable it becomes. Respond with "Tell me your specific concern—why exactly don't you trust us; can you give me an example?" Usually after calm discussion, actual concerns will surface and they are easier to deal with. Allow others to save face by conceding small points that are not central to the issue; don't try to hit a home run every time. If you can't agree on a solution, agree on a procedure to move forward. Collect more data. Appeal to a higher power. Get a third-party arbitrator. Work hard at being seen as reasonable and keep everyone focused on the end result. Stay positive and optimistic.

☐ **5. On your own? Bargain and trade to reach your objectives.** Being effective in many international settings requires creative resourcefulness. Many times the tools and information you need to move forward are not as readily available as you might be used to in your home country. You are usually separated from headquarters or home office support systems and people. You are often on your own. You have to make do. You have to learn to barter and bargain. Is what I need anywhere around? What do I need that they have? What could I do for them that could allow them to give up something I need now in return? How can we turn this into a win for both of us? Relationships help. Who do you know that would help? What could you provide in return? Could a colleague in a contiguous country help? Could someone from a non-competitive company help? *More help? – See #37 Negotiating.*

☐ **6. Ready to lead? Stand up and take a risk.** Learn to be comfortable being out front. Leading and making things happen in tough international settings is much riskier than just following standard or home country procedures. While there may be personal rewards for taking tough stands, tough stands put you into the limelight. Look at what happens to political leaders and the scrutiny they face. People who choose to stand alone have to be internally secure. Do you feel good about yourself? Can you defend to a critical and impartial audience the wisdom of what you're doing? You must please yourself and be very secure that you are on the right track. You have to accept lightning bolts from detractors. Can you take the heat? People will always say it should have been done differently. Even great leaders are wrong sometimes. They accept personal responsibility for errors and move on to lead some more. Don't let criticism prevent you from taking a stand. Build up your heat shield. If you know you're right, standing alone is well worth the heat. If it turns out you're wrong, admit it and move on. You are more alone and on your own in international settings.

International managers and executives have to make more decisions by themselves. Many times, the people who may be critical either don't know the local situation or have never had to do what you have to do. Even a bad plan or action is many times better than taking no action at all. If you do something and it doesn't work, you can always adjust and move forward again. At least you now know one thing that doesn't work. Taking a tough stand demands confidence in what you're saying along with the humility that you might be wrong—one of life's paradoxes. To prepare to take the lead on a tough issue, work on your stand through mental interrogation until you can clearly state in a few sentences what your stand is and why you hold it. Build the business case. How do others win? Ask others for advice. Scope the problem, consider options, pick one, develop a rationale, then go with it until proven wrong. Consider the opposing view. Develop a strong case against your stand. Prepare responses to it. Expect pushback.

☐ **7. Ready to take a risk? Learn from mistakes.** Develop more comfort with the inherent risks of international business. Successful international executives are often alone, pushing the envelope, taking chances, and taking bold new initiatives. Doing those things leads to more misfires and mistakes. Treat any mistakes or failures as chances to learn. Nothing ventured, nothing gained. Up your risk comfort. Start small so you can recover more quickly. Go for small wins. Send up trial balloons. Don't blast into a major stand to prove your boldness. Break it down into smaller stands. Take the easiest one for you first. Then build up to the tougher ones. Review each one to see what you did well and not so well. Set a goal to do something differently and better each time. Challenge yourself. See how inventive you can be in taking action a number of different ways. *More help? – See #14 Creativity, #28 Innovation Management, and #2 Dealing with Ambiguity.*

☐ **8. Need advice? Get the counsel of others.** Being effective across cultures requires leaning on others for advice and counsel. Spend time building working relationships with those in a position to help. Find people who know and who have experience. Find people experienced in the culture and country. Test out what you want to do and say ahead of time. Have a trusted local write out what you should do and say to get the result you want. Talk to other heads of non-competitive businesses for advice. Call your predecessor. *More help? – See #36 Motivating Others.*

☐ **9. In a tough situation? Watch and do as the locals do.** Most cultures have a unique way of handling difficult situations. In some cultures, direct confrontation is a no-no, while in others confrontation is expected and accepted. In some cultures, an intermediary is used to deliver tough messages. It is important to know and understand both local practices as well as understand that individuals also react according to general cultural norms for tough situations. Watch and learn and, as a rule of thumb, move with caution until there is a full understanding of what locals do and what the cultural context may be.

☐ **10. Not getting results? Trust your judgment, take action, and actively learn.** At the end of the day, poor performance is still poor performance, and if things are not getting done, don't let a fear of offending local cultural norms keep you from taking action. At the same time, learn as you go and experiment with different ways of doing things. In most cultures, unless there is a major cultural offense, locals are more tolerant of non-locals who "just don't understand how things are done around here." The worst thing that you can do is let issues slide. If you are uncertain about the best way to handle something, ask a local advisor for counsel. Trust what you have learned from past experiences and build on that.

Some Develop-in-Place Assignments

☐ Build or work on a multinational project team to tackle a common international business issue or problem.

☐ Assemble a team of internationally diverse people to accomplish a difficult task.

☐ Resolve an issue in conflict between two people, units, geographies, functions, etc. in two different countries.

☐ Work with a national team out of your home country looking at a reorganization plan where there will be more people than positions.

☐ Manage a group through a significant international business crisis that is outside your home country.

International business has always existed in some form.
But because of advances in technology and travel, we can
do business with India as well as Indiana. In fact, it might even be
cheaper to do business with India than Indiana. And that's true whether
you're a large multinational corporation, or a mom-and-pop business.
There are new cross-cultural markets you can expand into.
You've got to know how to work well with other cultures.
Dean Foster – American writer

Suggested Readings

Aziza, B., & Fitts, J. (2008). *Drive business performance: Enabling a culture of intelligent execution.* Hoboken, NJ: John Wiley & Sons.

Bartlett, C. A., & Ghoshal, S. (2002). *Managing across borders: The transnational solution* (2nd ed.). Boston: Harvard Business School Press.

Brett, J. M. (2007). *Negotiating globally: How to negotiate deals, resolve disputes, and make decisions across cultural boundaries* (2nd ed.). San Francisco: John Wiley & Sons.

Cohen, E. (2007). *Leadership without borders: Successful strategies from world-class leaders.* Singapore: John Wiley & Sons.

Dalton, M., Ernst, C., Deal, J., & Leslie, J. (2002). *Success for the new global manager: How to work across distances, countries, and cultures.* San Francisco: Jossey-Bass.

Halverson, C. B., & Tirmizi, S. A. (Eds.). (2008). *Effective multicultural teams: Theory and practice* (Series: Advances in group decision and negotiation, Vol. 3.). New York: Springer.

House, R. J., Hanges, P. J., Javidan, M., Dorfman, P., & Gupta, V. (Eds.). (2004). *Culture, leadership, and organizations: The GLOBE study of 62 societies.* Thousand Oaks, CA: Sage.

Konopaske, R., & Ivancevich, J. M. (2004). *Global management and organizational behavior: Text, readings, cases, and exercises.* New York: McGraw-Hill/Irwin.

Lewis, R. D. (2006). *When cultures collide: Leading across cultures* (3rd ed.). Boston: Nicholas Brealey International.

Moodian, M. A. (2008). *Contemporary leadership and intercultural competence: Exploring the cross-cultural dynamics within organizations.* Thousand Oaks, CA: Sage.

Smith, P. B., Peterson, M. F., & Thomas, D. C. (2008). *The handbook of cross-cultural management research.* Thousand Oaks, CA: Sage.

Warner, M., & Witzel, M. (2004). *Managing in virtual organizations.* London: Thomson Learning.

164 Assignment Hardiness

Some Leadership Architect® Equivalents:
1,2,11,12,43,50,52,53,55,62

*The very greatest things—great thoughts, discoveries, inventions—
have usually been nurtured in hardship, often pondered over in sorrow,
and at length established with difficulty.*
Samuel Smiles – Scottish author and reformer

Unskilled

- ☐ Gets travel weary
- ☐ Does not know how to manage the rigors of international travel
- ☐ Takes a while to adjust to new international locations
- ☐ Gets out of sorts under the pressure of constant travel and changes in living conditions
- ☐ Is disorganized
- ☐ Not a good time manager
- ☐ Not resourceful enough to bargain for personal accommodation and comfort
- ☐ Not a fast starter when traveling
- ☐ Continually misses transportation connections

Skilled

- ☐ Adjusts quickly to new international locations and conditions
- ☐ Travels comfortably
- ☐ Maintains health and spirit under adverse living conditions
- ☐ Gets up to speed rapidly where resources are sparse
- ☐ Able to function under extreme hardship and difficulty
- ☐ Well organized
- ☐ Good time manager
- ☐ Good negotiator and a resourceful traveler
- ☐ Seems to be motivated by challenge
- ☐ Curious about the unknown
- ☐ Can relax and sleep on airplanes
- ☐ Maintains a positive attitude

Overuse

- ☐ Adapts to the local way of doing things too soon
- ☐ Appears to others as trying too hard to fit in
- ☐ Expects others to match his/her stamina
- ☐ Does not listen
- ☐ Does not know when a battle is lost
- ☐ Acts too quickly without considering all the facts

Select one to three of the competencies listed below to work on to compensate for an overuse of this skill.

COMPENSATORS: 41,48

Some Causes

- ☐ Not physically fit
- ☐ Not a good time manager
- ☐ Doesn't set priorities
- ☐ Can't relax in new and strange situations
- ☐ Very strong personal beliefs and values
- ☐ Not good with uncertainty
- ☐ Doesn't switch gears comfortably
- ☐ Disorganized
- ☐ Slow to figure out new ways of doing things
- ☐ Needs a routine to be comfortable

The Map

International service can extract quite a toll. Long flights. Marginal living conditions. Rapid change. Different rules and standards of conduct. Time zone stress. Transportation delays and challenges. Language problems. The key is to be able to function effectively under extreme physical and mental difficulty and strain. The international traveler is many times at a disadvantage against local colleagues who are well-rested and sleep in their own beds. International service can, for most, be exciting and challenging, as well as trying. Maintaining balance and sharpness is one key to international success. Reacting to every international event or circumstance can be exhausting. Learning how to relax and go with the flow are important aspects of mental, emotional, and physical well-being, and in turn lead to business effectiveness.

Some Remedies

☐ **1. Feeling uncertain? Know what to expect.** Read about the countries to be visited. Know what to expect in terms of living conditions, tipping, restaurants, laws, dress, and standards of conduct. Talk with those who have been there. Is business just like in your home country? More formal? Long lead times to get anything done or more transactional and quick? Lots of socializing expected or none? Are you supposed to talk about your family or is that a faux pas? Be prepared for what you may experience.

☐ **2. Fighting fatigue? Figure out how to get enough sleep.** Read the research about adjusting to different time zones. Work with your doctor to find safe but effective medications if necessary. Being rested while traveling internationally is a rare gift. When you travel, get on local time as soon as possible. Adjust your internal clock and eating/sleeping times to be close to or the same as your destination. A rule of thumb for many international travelers is: Don't stand when you can sit; don't sit when you can recline; don't recline when you can lie down; and don't lie down when you can also catch a nap. Save your energy for what is important.

☐ **3. Need more energy? Stay in shape.** Comfortable international travel takes more stamina. People in better physical shape generally do better. Try to maintain part of your exercise routine even while traveling. Focusing while tired is a special skill. Go to a bookstore and find a book on handling the rigors of international travel. Have a routine that works for you. Try to remain physically active while traveling. Exercising after a long flight helps many restart their batteries and energy levels.

☐ **4. Dietary concerns? Eat well.** Great eating around the world is a mixed blessing. Great food. Great cuisines. But different than you are used to. Eating times are different. Eating durations are different. The temptation is to try it all. Be politically sensitive to the expectations of your hosts, but take care of yourself as well. If you are going to an area for the first time, sample the cuisine ahead of time. Become knowledgeable about the cuisine and typical menu. In today's global environment, almost every global cuisine is available in the larger cities. Learn the 20 foreign words for chicken, fish, beef, vegetables, and soups. Stay within your dietary preferences.

☐ **5. Dealing with demanding flight schedules? Learn the guidelines to travel well.** Many times, you will be in the air for long periods of time. Managing that flight time will be essential. When to sleep? How to sleep? What class of service? What to eat? When to eat? Should you drink alcoholic beverages? Do you know how to get some exercise while on a plane? There are various books and guides on how to travel healthy. Get two of them from your local bookstore and plan a personalized program for yourself.

☐ **6. Ready for the change? Plan ahead to avoid unnecessary hassles.** Different is a hassle for many. Every international location presents a new challenge. Study the process ahead of time. Talk to people who have been there. One key is what to do in the airport to be safe. Should you give your bags to anyone? Are the cabs legitimate? What currency do you need to carry? Is it cheaper to convert currency in your home country or wait until you get to your destination? How do you reserve a room if you land at 8:00 in the morning? (In many cases, you need to reserve and pay for the room the night before or you will be sitting in the lobby for hours waiting for a room to be available.) Customs. What can you carry? What should you declare? Are there some code words you should and shouldn't use. Immigration. Do you have the necessary documentation? In summary, just be as prepared as possible.

☐ **7. Considered worst-case scenarios? Create contingency plans.** Be ready for the unexpected. What if you lose your travel documents or papers? What if you lose your cash? What if you get ill? What if your transportation plans get disrupted? How do you get up-to-date information? Think and plan ahead. Know how to contact a local embassy. What might they do for you? Check with your doctor about medical contingency plans. Check with your bank or financial provider on ways to get money. Know how to contact the local staff in case of an emergency.

☐ **8. Stressed? Let the little things go.** Learn when to relax and when to react. In any new and unfamiliar environment, it is easy to overreact. As you gain more international experience, you will have enhanced judgment about what requires a response and what can either be ignored or delegated. It is important to find a pace of action and maintain a longer-term perspective on the issues you will likely encounter. Stay focused on what is really important to the success of the business and learn to let other (little) things go. Maintain a sense of humor and don't be afraid to laugh at yourself.

☐ **9. Clear on expectations? Overcommunicate with headquarters.** Learn how to manage home office communication and expectations. A great deal of stress is experienced by international managers who are not certain what the home office expects and do not know how to maintain effective lines of open and candid communication. At the same time, one of the primary sources of stress is a lack of understanding from the home office regarding local circumstances and operating conditions. A large dose of overcommunication is essential to taking off the pressure of uncertainty about how headquarters will react to a particular initiative. If you are uncertain about how your boss or headquarters will react to an initiative, communicate whenever time permits.

☐ **10. Narrow-minded? Develop a non-judgmental attitude about things that are different.** One of the most powerful tools for an effective international manger is to view events and circumstances as simply different from what is expected or normal in their home country environment—as opposed to labeling and comparing events in terms of good or bad. Avoiding the bad-good label while applying the simply different label permits a more objective and balanced view of an event. It is this attitude that helps keep things on a more even keel. One international manager claims that, on average, three bad things happen on every trip; so when the number of critical events is fewer, it was a really good trip, and if the number of events was more, it was simply off the average. Accept differences and learn why things are the way they are before trying to change them.

Some Develop-in-Place Assignments

- ☐ Manage a group through a significant international business crisis that is outside your home country.
- ☐ Work on a project team working on an international topic which includes traveling to several countries or locations that are new to you.
- ☐ Help shut down a plant, regional office, product line, business, operation, etc. in another country.
- ☐ Manage a group of resistant people with low morale through an unpopular change or project that has global reach or implications.
- ☐ Take on a tough and undoable international project, one where others who have tried it have failed.

The gentle reader will never, never know
what a consummate ass he can become, until he goes abroad.
Mark Twain – American humorist, satirist, lecturer, and writer

Suggested Readings

Black, J. S., Gregersen, H. B., Mendenhall, M. E., & Stroh, L. K. (1999). *Globalizing people through international assignments.* New York: Addison-Wesley Longman.

Dalton, M., Ernst, C., Deal, J., & Leslie, J. (2002). *Success for the new global manager: How to work across distances, countries, and cultures.* San Francisco: Jossey-Bass.

Hess, M. B., & Linderman, P. (2002). *The expert expatriate: Your guide to successful relocation abroad: Moving, living, and thriving.* Yarmouth, ME: Intercultural Press.

Lewis, R. D. (2006). *When cultures collide: Leading across cultures* (3rd ed.). Boston: Nicholas Brealey International.

McCall, M. W., Jr., & Hollenbeck, G. P. (2001). *Developing global executives: The lessons of international experience.* Boston: Harvard Business School Press.

Moodian, M. A. (2008). *Contemporary leadership and intercultural competence: Exploring the cross-cultural dynamics within organizations.* Thousand Oaks, CA: Sage.

Moran, R. T., Harris, P. R., & Moran, S. V. (2007). *Managing cultural differences: Global leadership strategies for the 21st century* (7th ed.). Burlington, MA: Butterworth-Heinemann.

Reuvid, J. (2006). *Working abroad: The complete guide to overseas employment* (27th ed.). London: Kogan Page.

Stroh, L. K., Black, J. S., Mendenhall, M. E., & Gregersen, H. B. (2004). *International assignments: An integration of strategy, research, and practice.* Mahwah, NJ: Lawrence Erlbaum Associates.

Walker, D., Walker, T., & Schmitz, J. (2003). *Doing business internationally: The guide to cross-cultural success* (2nd ed.). New York: McGraw-Hill.

Wennersten, J. R. (2007). *Leaving America: The new expatriate generation.* Westport, CT: Praeger Publishers.

Wilson, M. S., & Dalton, M. A. (1998). *International success: Selecting, developing, and supporting expatriate managers.* Greensboro, NC: Center for Creative Leadership.

165 Organizational Positioning Skills

Some Leadership Architect® Equivalents:
3,8,31,33,38,39,48,49,59,61,65,67

The single biggest problem in communication
is the illusion that it has taken place.
George Bernard Shaw – Irish essayist, playwright, and literary critic

Unskilled

- ☐ Does not keep headquarters informed of key actions
- ☐ Believes only they know best
- ☐ Ignores requests or suggestions from management
- ☐ Does not share important information in a timely fashion
- ☐ Does not ask for help when things get tough
- ☐ Does not take the time to explain in-country issues to headquarters

Skilled

- ☐ Is skilled politically
- ☐ Can explain headquarters' actions to in-country staff
- ☐ Teaches in-country staff and headquarters about each other's perspectives
- ☐ Knows when to stop on a battle
- ☐ Is an outstanding communicator
- ☐ Works the informal network well
- ☐ Never misses an opportunity to explain or sell a position

Overuse

- ☐ Is always traveling back to headquarters
- ☐ Spends so much time communicating that time is lost before an action is taken
- ☐ Spends an inordinate amount of time on presentations
- ☐ Is seen as attempting to curry favor with superiors
- ☐ Level of communication is often seen as self-serving
- ☐ Is always asking how this will play at headquarters/in-country

Select one to three of the competencies listed below to work on to compensate for an overuse of this skill.

COMPENSATORS: 47,50,53,57,62

Some Causes

- ☐ Overemphasizes need for headquarters' approval
- ☐ Lacks self-confidence
- ☐ Is afraid of making a mistake
- ☐ Is too detail oriented
- ☐ Wants a great deal of support before taking action
- ☐ Avoids confrontations

The Map

Being a long way from headquarters can be both lonely and a challenge. On the one hand, headquarters may have a parochial view of how an in-country business should work without having first-hand knowledge of the culture or business climate. The challenge is to communicate thoroughly and get as much buy-in as possible from superiors. On the other hand, global business is by its very nature risky. There comes a time when action, independent of headquarters (a fire at the plant in the middle of the night for headquarters but high noon in-country), must be taken. There is a fine balance that must be struck between keeping headquarters informed and taking actions that appear much more risky to headquarters than to the in-country staff and business. Successful international managers know how to keep the lines of communication open as well as respect the views of others. In one sense, the effective international manager is always willing to look for and listen to good ideas regardless of the source. The effective international manager uses headquarters to help when appropriate.

Some Remedies

☐ **1. Equipped for communication? Leverage technology to communicate across time zones.** Staying in touch internationally is a challenge because of differences in time zones. There are unique challenges and advantages for both e-mail and video conferencing. Flash fly-in-and-fly-out visits with little time for chitchat limit time for quality conversation. Language differences present their own unique problems. Communicating when you are not fresh and awake is always tough. Issue positioning takes discipline and effective time management. Written communication skills for most managers are rarely as effective as face-to-face, particularly when the topic is complicated (*see #67 – Written Communication*). Become an agile user of available technology. Get help from an expert. Practice. Get feedback. Customize to the receiver of your communications. Negotiate with the receivers what they need and when they need it. When in doubt, overcommunicate. Headquarters communication is always a balancing act.

- ☐ **2. Informing sufficiently? Hone your communication skills.** Are you a minimalist communicator? Do you tell people only what you think they need to know? People are motivated by being aware of the bigger picture. What are other people working on and why? Many people think that simply informing others is unnecessary and takes too much time to do. They're wrong. The sense of doing something worthwhile is the number two motivator at work! It results in a high return on motivation and productivity. Try to increase the amount of more-than-what-I-think-you-need-to-know information you share. Focus on the impact on others by figuring out who information affects. Ask people what they want to know and, assuming the information is not confidential information, tell them. Treat staff with as much respect as you would a customer.
- ☐ **3. Like being on your own? Stay connected with people around you.** Don't be a loner. Do you keep to yourself? Work alone or try to? Do you hold back information? Do you parcel out information on your schedule? Do you share information to get an advantage or to win favor? Do people around you know what you're doing and why? Are you aware of things others would benefit from but you don't take the time to communicate? In most organizations, these things and things like it will get you in trouble. Organizations function on the flow of information. Being on your own and preferring peace and privacy are OK as long as you communicate things to bosses, peers, and teammates. Don't be the source of surprises.
- ☐ **4. Ineffective informer? Tailor your communication style.** Don't be a cryptic informer. Some people just aren't good at fully informing. Their communication styles are not effective. The most effective communicators, according to studies: speak often, but briefly (15–30 seconds); ask more questions than others; make fewer solution statements early in a discussion; headline their points in a sentence or two; summarize frequently and make more frequent "here's where we are" statements; invite everyone to share their views; typically interject their views after others have had a chance to speak, unless they are passing on decisions. Compare these practices to yours. Work on those communication practices that are not up to standard.
- ☐ **5. Inconsistent informer? Inform the right people of the right things.** Have an information checklist detailing what information should go to whom; pass on summaries or copies of important communications. Determine the information checklist by: keeping tabs on unpleasant surprises that people report to you; ask direct reports what they'd like to know to do their jobs better; check with boss, peers, and customers to see if you pass along too little, enough, or too much of the right kinds of information; and check with headquarters on their information

requirements. It's important to know what to pass, to whom to pass, and when to pass, to become an effective informer. Some managers keep a list of hot topics by the phone and always share information at every available opportunity.

☐ **6. Selective informer? Inform more openly.** Be inclusive and a broadband informer. Avoid being a selective informer. The most common selective pattern is informing up and out but not down or sideways. Make certain you include all relevant parties in your communications. Avoid an attitude filter about informing some but not others. Why? What do you gain with one group or person that you lose with another? Is it personal? Are you gaining by sharing? At the expense of others? Why are you avoiding one group? Do you fear debate?

☐ **7. Need advice? Get to know more of the top managers.** Try to meet and interact with higher-ups in informal settings like receptions, social or athletic events, charity events, off-sites, etc. Find out what they think. Find out what kind of information they like and need. Find out their preferred ways of receiving information. Customize your approach to each recipient. Ask questions and ask for advice. Ask them how they handle certain situations.

☐ **8. Stuck in the organizational maze? Study how your organization works.** Organizations can be complex systems with many ways of getting things done. There can also be many turns, dead ends, and more/less efficient routes for getting things done. In most organizations, the best path to get somewhere is almost never a straight line. There is a formal organization—the one on the organization chart—where the path may look straight, and then there is the informal organization where all paths are zigzagged. Since organizations are staffed with people, they become all that more complex as systems. There are gatekeepers, expediters, stoppers, resisters, guides, Good Samaritans, and influencers. *More help? – See #38 Organizational Agility.*

☐ **9. Out of touch? Keep up with trends at corporate headquarters.** Being in a headquarters environment means having more of an opportunity to know where the action is and what's the hottest and latest action plan. The successful international manager keeps the pipeline working in both directions and knows how to stay on top of the latest decision or plan. Keep in regular contact with your headquarters counterparts and ask them to help you stay informed on what's new or different. Ask to be put on distribution lists for key information and make sure you are the recipient of key e-mails. When you visit headquarters or regional offices, make certain to allow sufficient time to visit with your colleagues in other functions.

☐ **10. Ready to be transparent? Maintain an open agenda.** One of the best tools for avoiding trouble and maintaining a pipeline of information is to share your agenda with as many people as possible. Of course, confidential information remains confidential, but transparency will make you more likely to get an early "heads up" on critical information. An open agenda will also lead others to trust you as one who does not hold back information. Always offer more than you are asked, and ask others if you can tell them more than was required. Work hard to be perceived as an open executive who asks for help and is always open to ideas about how to improve.

Some Develop-in-Place Assignments

☐ Plan an off-site meeting, conference, convention, trade show, event, etc.

☐ Build or work on a multinational project team to tackle a common international business issue or problem.

☐ Prepare and present a proposal of some consequence to top management in the international sector of your business.

☐ Relaunch an existing product or service that's not doing well in another country or across countries.

☐ Integrate diverse systems, processes, or procedures across decentralized and/or dispersed international units.

The one who figures on victory at headquarters before even doing battle is the one who has the most strategic factors on his side.
Sun Tzu (c. 500 BCE) – Chinese military strategist

Suggested Readings

Bartlett, C. A., & Ghoshal, S. (2002). *Managing across borders: The transnational solution* (2nd ed.). Boston: Harvard Business School Press.

Brett, J. M. (2007). *Negotiating globally: How to negotiate deals, resolve disputes, and make decisions across cultural boundaries* (2nd ed.). San Francisco: John Wiley & Sons.

Cavusgil, T., Knight, G., & Riesenberger, J. (2007). *International business: Strategy, management, and the new realities.* Upper Saddle River, NJ: Prentice Hall.

Cullen, J. B., & Parboteeah, K. P. (2008). *Multinational management: A strategic approach* (4th ed.). Mason, OH: Thomson/South-Western.

Dalton, M., Ernst, C., Deal, J., & Leslie, J. (2002). *Success for the new global manager: How to work across distances, countries, and cultures.* San Francisco: Jossey-Bass.

Deal, J. J., & Prince, D. W. (2003). *Developing cultural adaptability: How to work across differences.* Greensboro, NC: Center for Creative Leadership.

Fisher, K., & Fisher, M. (2001). *The distance manager: A hands-on guide to managing off-site employees and virtual teams.* New York: McGraw-Hill.

Konopaske, R., & Ivancevich, J. M. (2004). *Global management and organizational behavior: Text, readings, cases, and exercises.* New York: McGraw-Hill/Irwin.

Morgan, G., Kristensen, P. H., & Whitley, R. (Eds.). (2001). *The multinational firm: Organizing across institutional and national divides.* New York: Oxford University Press.

Schmidt, W. V., Conaway, R. N., Easton, S. S., & Wardrope, W. J. (2007). *Communicating globally: Intercultural communication and international business.* Thousand Oaks, CA: Sage.

Stahl, G. K., & Björkman, I. (2006). *Handbook of research in international human resource management.* Cheltenham, UK: Edward Elgar.

Steger, U., Amann, W., & Maznevski, M. (Eds.). (2007). *Managing complexity in global organizations.* West Sussex, England: John Wiley & Sons.

Walker, D., Walker, T., & Schmitz, J. (2003). *Doing business internationally: The guide to cross-cultural success* (2nd ed.). New York: McGraw-Hill.

166 Cross-Cultural Sensitivity

Some Leadership Architect® Equivalents:
3,21,29,31,33,40,41,45,54,55,56,60,64,65

We learned to know each other and know our differences.
This is the way to build the culture of peace.
Valentino Castellani – Italian professor, author, and politician

Unskilled

- ☐ Judges differences from a personal point of view
- ☐ Uncomfortable with differences
- ☐ Dismisses differences
- ☐ Doesn't make an effort to understand differences
- ☐ Turns down invitations to participate in local events
- ☐ Makes value judgments about goodness/badness as opposed to just different
- ☐ Is rigid
- ☐ Lacks personal flexibility

Skilled

- ☐ Understands and can empathize with differences in people and cultures
- ☐ Is not judgmental about differences
- ☐ Respects differences
- ☐ Operates at a minimal noise level
- ☐ Tries to learn the local language
- ☐ Dutifully participates in local rituals and ceremonies
- ☐ Understands nuances of local culture
- ☐ Respects different value sets
- ☐ Handles and is comfortable with diversity

Overuse

- ☐ Doesn't make decisions about differences even when appropriate
- ☐ Waits too long to act in the face of cultural differences or resistance
- ☐ Overadapts to the local way of doing things
- ☐ Overly sensitive to local culture in the face of business urgency
- ☐ Doesn't do the right thing for fear of offending someone
- ☐ Loses time due to overthinking cultural implications of an action

Select one to three of the competencies listed below to work on to compensate for an overuse of this skill.

COMPENSATORS: 1,9,12,17,39,40,50,51,53,57,62

Some Causes

- ☐ Very strong beliefs and values
- ☐ Very judgmental
- ☐ Narrow background
- ☐ Ethnocentric
- ☐ Shy and quiet
- ☐ Not learning agile
- ☐ Lacks openness to new ideas

The Map

There is always more than one way to do anything. Differences abound internationally. Religious. Cultural. History. Philosophy. Beliefs. Political foundations. Economic systems. While there are some universal similarities among peoples, countries, and cultures, it's the differences that matter most. It's all too easy to judge a cultural difference in negative terms. Dietary practices vary widely from culture to culture. Some countries do not allow mentioning a competitor's product in advertising. Some have female executives and others don't allow women to work. Alcohol is freely available in some cultures and not allowed in others. Some cultures have open and free debate while others may arrest you for talking negatively about those in power. To be successful internationally, accepting and working with the differences is truly a key difference between success and failure. The successful international executive is able to accept differences and work within the parameters established by a particular culture.

Some Remedies

☐ **1. Curious? Ask the right questions.** Begin by asking yourself the right questions. Among them, according to McCall and Hollenbeck in *Developing Global Executives*:

- How narrow vs. how worldly is the culture?
- How open vs. closed, guarded, or subtle is communication?
- What does it mean to treat people with respect?
- What does it take to gain trust?
- Are business relationships more personal vs. more formal?
- What are the prime motivators in this culture?
- Fast vs. slow in action?
- What are the predominant ways of thinking?
- What is the attitude toward a "good day's work"?
- How is a leader expected to act?

- What are relationships with customers like?
- What are the lessons of history for this culture, especially their attitudes toward other cultures?
- What is the general state of the culture (economically, politically, and socially)?

☐ **2. Dismissive of cultural characteristics? Recognize cultural differences.** Be aware that cultural differences truly exist and often have a significant influence on our actions. Recognize and accept that you may not be aware that differences exist on leadership or management practices you take for granted. Because we all grow up and learn in the context of a given culture, much of what we learn is simply taken as part of the natural order of the world. We who take our world view for granted are often surprised when others do not understand or share our point of view. We may wrongly assume others think and act like we do. After asking the right questions (*see Remedy #1 above*), understand how the differences highlighted in the answers to the questions translate into thought and action. Imagine if you had grown up in a culture other than your own how you might think differently about such issues as gender, history, religion, food preferences, age, education, race, work ethic, value of education, etc. It is not enough to just know that preferences and attitudes are different; you must also understand how those differences impact how things get done. Expose your thinking to different views. Purchase several international newspapers or magazines and compare articles on a common issue. You will find very different perspectives that are often founded in the experience and culture of the country where the newspaper or magazine was written. Literally put yourself in the shoes of someone from another culture with vastly different life experiences from your own. Think about significant experiences in your own life, and reflect on how these have changed or influenced you. Consider how being reared as a Muslim, a Jew, a Christian, a Catholic, a Hindu, a Buddhist, an Atheist, or as an Animist has an impact, often unconscious, on how you see the world and what you believe. Actively ask questions and discuss various business or management practices with trusted local counterpoints and listen carefully to their perspectives. Try to avoid being judgmental about points of view that differ from yours. Above all, listen and accept differences before taking a critical action. So in each situation, ask what cultural differences there are and which ones make a difference and why?

☐ **3. Prone to stereotype? Acknowledge cultural stereotypes and your own in particular.** You have to understand your own subtle stereotyping. Helen Astin's research showed that both men and women rated women managers at the extremes (very high or very low), while they rated men on a normal curve. Do you think the Irish drink more? Swiss citizens can make better watches? Germans make better engineers? The Dutch have no emotions? People who eat dogs are disgusting? The Mexicans are lazy? Most cultural stereotyping is false. Even if there are surface differences, there is probably equal variance inside every culture. There will always be individuals who are significantly different than the general cultural norm in any country. Look to the person as an individual before you jump to conclusions using country or origin or culture as a base.

☐ **4. Categorizing people unnecessarily? Deal with people equitably.** Try to see people more as individuals than members of a country or culture. Avoid putting people in grouped buckets. Many of us bucket people as can or can't do this. We have good buckets and bad buckets. Buckets "I like/am comfortable with" and buckets "that bother me." Once we bucket, we generally don't relate as well to the off-bucket people. Much of the time bucketing is based on "like me—the good bucket; not like me—the bad bucket." Across time, the can do/like me bucket gets the majority of your attention, more feedback, stretching tasks, develops the most, and performs the best—unfortunately proving your stereotyping again and again. To break this cycle, understand without judging. Be candid with yourself. Is there a country or culture you don't like or are uncomfortable with? Do you judge individual members of that country or culture without really knowing if your stereotype is true? Most of us do. Try to see people as people.

☐ **5. Skeptical of differences? Accept that diversity can add value.** Diversity of viewpoint, background, education, culture, experience, beliefs, and attitudes matter, and all help produce a superior product in a diverse and global marketplace. During World War II, the military discovered the most creative groups were those where the members had little or nothing in common and knew little about the issue. Their freewheeling approach yielded fresher solutions. They were not trapped by the past. Take a current challenge to the most disparate group you can find (a historian, a college student, a theologian, a salesperson, a plumber, etc.) and see what insights they have into it. Find some problems outside of your area and see what you can add. Put cultural diversity to the test yourself; attack problems with diverse task forces, pull in the widest array of thinking you can, and see if you get broader, more inventive results. Assemble the most culturally diverse team you can who have the skills to do the job but otherwise are different. Consciously spend more of your time with people who are different. Solicit the points of view of each person. Examine how background differences lead to viewing problems differently.

☐ **6. Need more exposure? Increase your experience of cultural diversity.** Not much cultural diversity in your background but want to increase it?

- Stage one: Talk to people in your organization, neighborhood, or place of worship who are culturally different in some way than you. Do lunch. Go to a ball game. Exchange views. House a foreign student from a country you are thinking about entering or working in.
- Stage two: Visit cultural festivals in your geography. Sample the foods. See the costumes and the crafts. Study their history. Watch the customs. Talk to them.
- Stage three: Vacation in Miami and spend time in the Cuban area. San Diego and San Antonio for the Mexican influence. San Francisco and New York for Chinatown. New York City has over 140 distinct cultural neighborhoods. Toronto for a number of ethnic and cultural areas within the city limits. Quebec for a taste of the French ambiance.
- Stage four: Travel and stay for one week anywhere in the world where you are in the minority and most others do not speak your language. Get away from the tourist areas. See how that feels.

☐ **7. Want to understand differences? Develop an understanding of cultural anthropology.** Become a student of cultures. Pick up a few books in your local bookstore or at your local university bookstore about the study of cultures. What are the ways in which cultures differ? How did they get that way? Are there similarities across all of most cultures? What's the role of religion? Geography? History? Economics? Natural resources? Read Will and Ariel Durant's *The Lessons of History* (1968) to get a great picture of how countries and cultures formed.

☐ **8. Want to learn more? Take an intercultural class or learn a language.** Take a course or go to a workshop or seminar on a topic of interest at Thunderbird University in Arizona, the London School of Economics, or INSEAD in France. Those events are attended by people from around the globe and taught by international experts. Pay special attention to those participants from countries of special interest to you. Spend as much time as possible with them. Try to get in the same breakouts and work groups. Listen. Ask questions. Build relationships that might come in handy later when you travel to those countries. One of the best ways to understand a culture is to study its language and history. Develop an understanding of how language is used, and pay particular attention to slang that has hidden meanings.

☐ **9. Need to build self-knowledge? Do an international service self-assessment.** Maxine Dalton's (et al.) book, *Success for the New Global Manager* (chapter 4), contains a self-assessment. The assessment includes: Do I have the core competencies for managing in another country? What do I need to learn? What is my personality type? You can compare your results against others and form a development plan for international service. Contact ITAP International (www.itapintl.com) for another assessment tool to help you understand how your individual world view contrasts with that from other cultures. Also look to Tucker International (www.tuckerintl.com) for information about developing cross-cultural skills.

☐ **10. Need a reference point? Build a framework for understanding cultures different from your own.** An excellent framework for understanding the dimensions that differentiate between cultures may be found in Fons Trompenaars' *Riding the Waves of Culture*. These dimensions are based on research that indicates that cultures differ along seven major dimensions. Cultures may be placed somewhere on each dimension and compared with other cultures in terms of the behaviors likely to be exhibited or in terms of the relative value placed on a particular competency by a given culture. The dimensions and a short definition are as follows:

- Universalistic vs. Particularistic Cultures
  - In a more universalistic culture (Canada, United States) rules apply to everyone, while in a more particularistic culture (Russia, South Korea) rules are more dependent on relationships and special circumstances.
- Individualistic vs. Collectivistic Cultures
  - In a more individualistic culture (Canada, United States) the individual is primarily responsible for their actions, while in a more collectivistic culture (China, Japan) the group is more important than the individual.
- Neutral vs. Affective Cultures
  - In a more neutral culture (United Kingdom, Japan) self-control is prized and emotions are more closely guarded, while in a more affective culture (Italy, France) emotions are more likely to be expressed with little or no filtering.
- Specific vs. Diffuse Cultures
  - In a more specific culture (Sweden, Switzerland) relationships are based on a specific purpose (you are my finance director) and personal issues or relationships are rarely mixed into the business relationship. In a more diffuse culture (Indonesia, Thailand) the boundaries between personal or business issues are often mixed and very important.

- Ascriptive vs. Achievement Cultures
  - In a more ascriptive culture (Austria, Nigeria) status is more often based on family status or wealth, while in an achievement culture (United States, Australia) hard work and personal achievement have more value.
- Internal Control vs. External Control Cultures
  - In a more internal control culture (West Germany prior to reunification or South Korea today) the individual is expected to be the source of action, while in a more external control culture (East Germany prior to reunification or North Korea today) the individual is more likely to be influenced by external forces and have fewer personal options. Don't we have a better example? Western democracies on one side and China, the Middle East on the other?
- Past, Present, and Future Cultures
  - Past-focused cultures are more focused on tradition and protocol (Russia); present-focused cultures are more focused on the here and now (Venezuela); while future-focused cultures are more focused on what will be the vision for tomorrow (United States).

Some Develop-in-Place Assignments

- ☐ Build or work on a multinational project team to tackle a common international business issue or problem.
- ☐ Assemble a team of internationally diverse people to accomplish a difficult task.
- ☐ Resolve an issue in conflict between two people, units, geographies, functions, etc. in two different countries.
- ☐ Attend a course with diverse international participants.
- ☐ Work as an assessor in an assessment center with internationally diverse people.

The rapprochement of peoples is only possible
when differences of culture and outlook are respected and
appreciated rather than feared and condemned, when the common bond
of human dignity is recognized as the essential bond for a peaceful world.
J. William Fulbright – American politician

Suggested Readings

Barak, M. E. M. (2005). *Managing diversity: Toward a globally inclusive workplace.* Thousand Oaks, CA: Sage.

Bennett, J. J. (2004). Becoming interculturally competent. In J. Wurzel (Ed.), *Towards multiculturalism: A reader in multicultural education* (2nd ed., pp. 62-77). Newton, MA: Intercultural Resource Corporation.

Dalton, M., Ernst, C., Deal, J., & Leslie, J. (2002). *Success for the new global manager: How to work across distances, countries, and cultures.* San Francisco: Jossey-Bass.

Deal, J. J., & Prince, D. W. (2003). *Developing cultural adaptability: How to work across differences.* Greensboro, NC: Center for Creative Leadership.

Halverson, C. B., & Tirmizi, S. A. (Eds.). (2008). *Effective multicultural teams: Theory and practice* (Series: Advances in group decision and negotiation, Vol. 3.). New York: Springer.

Hampden-Turner, C., & Trompenaars, F. (2000). *Building cross-cultural competence.* New Haven: Yale University Press.

Hofstede, G. J., Pedersen, P. B., & Hofstede, G. (2002). *Exploring culture: Exercises, stories, and synthetic cultures.* Yarmouth, ME: Intercultural Press.

Konopaske, R., & Ivancevich, J. M. (2004). *Global management and organizational behavior: Text, readings, cases, and exercises.* New York: McGraw-Hill/Irwin.

Landis, D., Bennett, J. M., & Bennett, M. J. (2004). *Handbook of intercultural training* (3rd ed.). Thousand Oaks, CA: Sage.

Lewis, R. D. (2006). *When cultures collide: Leading across cultures* (3rd ed.). Boston: Nicholas Brealey International.

McCall, M. W., Jr., & Hollenbeck, G. P. (2001). *Developing global executives: The lessons of international experience.* Boston: Harvard Business School Press.

Meredith, R. (2007). *The elephant and the dragon: The rise of India and China and what it means for all of us.* New York: W. W. Norton & Company.

Moran, R. T., Harris, P. R., & Moran, S. V. (2007). *Managing cultural differences: Global leadership strategies for the 21st century* (7th ed.). Burlington, MA: Butterworth-Heinemann.

Morrison, T., & Conaway, W. A. (2006). *Kiss, bow, or shake hands: The bestselling guide to doing business in more than 60 countries* (2nd ed.). Avon, MA: Adams Media.

Peterson, B. (2004). *Cultural intelligence: A guide to working with people from other cultures.* Yarmouth, ME: Intercultural Press.

Schmidt, W. V., Conaway, R. N., Easton, S. S., & Wardrope, W. J. (2007). *Communicating globally: Intercultural communication and international business.* Thousand Oaks, CA: Sage.

Thomas, D. C., & Inkson, K. (2004). *Cultural intelligence: People skills for global business.* San Francisco: Berrett-Koehler Publishers.

Tomalin, B., & Nicks, M. (2007). *The world's business cultures and how to unlock them: Special chapters on China, USA, Germany, UK, Russia, India, Brazil, France, Italy, and Japan.* London: Thorogood.

167 Humility

Some Leadership Architect® Equivalents:
7,11,21,23,104,108,112,119

Humility does not mean thinking less of yourself than of other people,
nor does it mean having a low opinion of your own gifts.
It means freedom from thinking about yourself at all.
William Temple – Archbishop of Canterbury

Unskilled

- ☐ Is loud, dominating, and very self-centered
- ☐ Exhibits bravado
- ☐ Demeans others
- ☐ Is an unwelcome center of attention
- ☐ Does not give credit to others
- ☐ Individual recognition is more important than group accomplishment
- ☐ Does not listen

Skilled

- ☐ Can get things done quietly without unnecessary noise
- ☐ Quickly admits flaws and mistakes
- ☐ Is careful to make others comfortable
- ☐ Is authentic
- ☐ Helps others save face in difficult situations
- ☐ Maximizes the contribution of all
- ☐ Encourages the expression of viewpoints from all concerned
- ☐ Is modest and self-effacing
- ☐ Respects the views of others

Overuse

- ☐ Hesitant to make decisions
- ☐ Waits too long to make decisions
- ☐ Doesn't address people problems in a timely enough fashion
- ☐ Can't hold sway with others from outside their culture
- ☐ Is too demanding

Select one to three of the competencies listed below to work on to compensate for an overuse of this skill.

COMPENSATORS: 1,9,12,13,16,50,53,56,57

Some Causes

- ☐ Self-centered
- ☐ Needs to dominate
- ☐ Overly ambitious
- ☐ Arrogance
- ☐ Insensitive to others
- ☐ Unaware of personal impact

The Map

Lack of humility is an easy way to get into trouble with people in specific cultures and possibly in general. Humility may also be seen as a special case of the Trompenaars' dimensions of: (a) individualistic vs. collectivistic cultures, and (b) neutral vs. affective cultures. In some cultures (mostly Asian or Northern European), humility in leaders is seen as a positive and in some cases a necessary requirement for effective leadership. Saving face is important in many cultures and the leader has to be careful not to put others on the spot in public settings. It is also important to admit mistakes and take the blame as captain of the ship. In high-value humility cultures, a leader is most likely to be a servant leader as opposed to the celebrity leader who is constantly in the news. A lack of humility may lead to ignoring important input from others and setting a course or direction that will run into trouble because of political miscalculations. Lack of humility often shows up and is described as a lack of cultural sensitivity coupled with a huge overemphasis on one's personal views as being the correct views.

Some Remedies

- ☐ **1. Arrogant? Ask for feedback.** Arrogance is a major blockage to effective relationships in many cultures. Many people who have a towering strength or lots of success get less feedback and roll along thinking and signaling others that they are perfect until their relationships get in trouble. If you are viewed as arrogant (not being humble), your best chance of understanding your issues is to get a facilitated 360° feedback where respondents can remain anonymous. It is unlikely you will get useful data from people directly because they don't think you listen and it has been painful for them to try to influence you in the past. Arrogant people or people lacking appropriate humility typically overrate themselves. The ratings of arrogant individuals are often lower than they should be because people believe they need to give very low ratings in order to make a point. If you are seen as lacking humility and undervaluing others, they will return the favor. Research says that successful people know themselves better and rate more in line with others or slightly lower. Your goal should be to get to know how others see you and get your views more in line with theirs.

☐ **2. Sending the wrong signals? Watch your non-verbals.** People lacking humility look, talk, and act arrogantly. As you try to become more humble, you need to find out what your non-verbals are. All arrogant people do a series of things that can be viewed by a neutral party and judged to give off the signals of arrogance. Washboard forehead. Facial expressions. Body shifting, especially turning away. Impatient finger or pencil tapping. False smile. Tight lips. Looking away. Find out from a trusted friend what you do and try to eliminate those behaviors. The non-verbals are also culture specific. What signals a lack of productive humility in one setting will have less or no impact in another. Lacking in humility will block finding out how to act with sensitivity across cultures.

☐ **3. Interrupting? Take time to listen and ask questions.** Answers. Solutions. Conclusions. Statements. Dictates. Solutions first, understanding second? You might be seen as someone who jumps to conclusions and solutions before others have had a chance to finish their statement of the problem. Humility includes giving others a fair chance to have their say, participate, and provide input. Let others speak early. Let people finish. Try not to interrupt. Don't finish other's sentences. Ask clarifying questions. Restate the problem in your own words to everyone's satisfaction. Then decide together. Add a 15-second pause into your transactions before you say anything, and add two clarifying questions per transaction to signal you're listening and want to understand. *More help? – See #33 Listening and #41 Patience.*

☐ **4. Know your audience? Read the needs of your audience.** Do you know what people look like when they are uncomfortable with your lack of humility? Do they back up? Frown? Flush? Stumble over words? Shut down? Cringe? Stand at the door hoping not to get invited in? You should work doubly hard at observing others for their reactions to you and your style. Especially during the first three minutes of an important transaction, work to make the person or group comfortable with you before the agenda starts. Ask a question unrelated to the topic. Offer them a beverage. Tell them something you did last weekend that you found interesting. Audience sensitivity. In any situation, there are always multiple ways you can deliver messages and get things done. You could use a direct attack—candor and instant assessment. You could send a surrogate to deliver the message. You could wait until the next meeting to react. Some of these tactics are more effective and acceptable than others depending upon the culture. Some people get into trouble because they act the same in all situations across cultures. They don't take the time to think about the most effective ways to get things done for each event and person and culture. People who are seen as sensitive operate from the outside—audience, person, group, organization—in. They pick their pace, style, tone, timing, and tactics based upon an evaluation of what would work best in each culture. It's the one-trick ponies that get into sensitivity trouble because they don't adjust what they say and do to each audience. *More help? – See #36 Motivating Others, #45 Personal Learning, and #15 Customer Focus.*

☐ **5. Promoting yourself at the expense of others? Affirm your ability without demeaning other people.** Do you really want to leave the majority of people you deal with feeling stupid, inferior, unintelligent, and losing face? Most don't but that's what you might be doing. Arrogant people may be looking for feedback that they are really superior, smart, and knowledgeable. But they are looking for that affirmation in the wrong place. If you crave reinforcement of your excellence, perform better. Help others perform better. Produce tangible results together. If your results don't measure up to your self-view, your words and arrogant behavior certainly won't help you any. Don't try to feel good on the backs of others who are not your equal. Look at three people whom you consider excellent performers, talented people, but have more humility than you do. What do they do and not do? Contrast this with your behavior.

☐ **6. Serious about connecting with others? Be open and approachable.** Until you signal repeatedly that you are open to others, interested in what they have to say, share things you don't have to share, invite people to talk with you and then listen, little will come of this effort. You will have to persevere, endure some rejection and perhaps some angry or dismissive remarks in order to balance the situation.

☐ **7. Perceived as insensitive? Find out why people think you are insensitive.** Insensitivity is a catch-all term. The authors have found 29 reasons why people might say this about you. Try to find out exactly why you are seen as insensitive. Talk to a mentor or someone you really trust will tell you the truth. It's unlikely that people will tell you directly, and even if they do, it's likely to be too general or too much based on one situation to do you much good. Of all needs, this one is probably the most complex to specify. Get a complete textured view of yourself. *See #55 Self-Knowledge.* The good news is that most people get this negative rating due only to a few aspects of insensitivity. It's also common to have some people view you as insensitive and lacking in humility and others not. That makes it easier to address. Few are truly insensitive in 29 ways!

☐ **8. Losing your cool? Maintain your composure.** It may be that you blow up and are especially bullying or pressuring under stress. Avoid instant and sharp reactions. You may jump to conclusions, categorically dismiss what others say, use inflammatory words or something of the sort under pressure.

People then see you as closed or combative and lacking in humility, when you probably want them to see you as reasonable. More negatively, they may believe you think they're stupid or ill-informed and cause them to lose face in front of others. If you're seen as intolerant or closed, people will often stumble over words in their haste to talk with you or shortcut their argument since they assume you're not listening anyway. Ask a question, invite them to disagree with you, present their argument back to them, let them save face no matter what. *More help? – See #11 Composure.*

☐ **9. Stubborn or rigid? Open up to different points of view.** You may signal being stubborn, rigid, and closed to new or different points of view. You must learn to turn off your instant evaluator/rejector filter and listen. Your first task is to understand, your second is to let the other person know you understand by repeating or rephrasing, and your third task can be to reject, with a fuller explanation of why than you now do. Ask more questions—"How did you get there?" "Do you prefer this to that or to what we're now doing?" If you disagree, give your reasons first. Then invite criticism. Turn the disagreement back to the nature of the problem or strategy: "What are we trying to solve? What causes it? What questions should be answered? What objective standards could we use to measure success?" *More help? – See #12 Conflict Management and #33 Listening.*

☐ **10. No time? Patiently build rapport.** Many signals of lack of humility are due to not taking the time to let others get more comfortable with you. Many insensitive people are very action oriented, results oriented, and very agenda driven. There's not much rapport building. One-third of the people who work around you prefer people like you. "Just the facts, ma'am. Let's get down to it." Two-thirds need a little up-front time to adjust to the situation before getting down to work. Usually three minutes is sufficient. You have to start by opening the discussion on a non-business topic. What did you do this weekend? How are the kids? Which college did your daughter pick? Did you see the Olympics? How do you like the new car? And then let them talk for a while to give them time to get comfortable. *More help? – See #3 Approachability.*

☐ **11. Interpersonally challenged? Open up to other people.** Being effective internationally requires a broader range of interpersonal skills and styles. Until you signal that you are open to others (listening with eye contact; interested in what they have to say—let them finish; share things you don't have to share—get personal; invite people to talk with you, ask questions—and then listen), little will come of this effort to be seen as more humble. *More help? – See #3 Approachability and #31 Interpersonal Savvy.*

☐ **12. Too directive? Be a teacher, not a director.** You may be highly intelligent and quite skilled in your area. You may work around people who aren't as informed or skilled as you are. You may be in a position of essentially dictating what should be done because they don't know or you think they don't know. In this case, you need to switch to a teacher role—tell them how you think about an issue, don't just fire out solutions. Tell them what you think the problem is, what questions need to be asked, and how you would go about finding out what you think some likely solutions might be. Most important, invite their thinking. If you're the expert and they aren't, help them think better by showing them how you think. Be open to the fact that uninformed people in studies of creative problem solving usually come up with the most inventive solutions. Once immersed in the problem, they bring a new perspective to it. Use that power. *More help? – See #18 Delegation.*

☐ **13. Don't care? Figure out why it matters.** Some hard-charging managers just don't think it matters what most people think of them. They think getting the results out on time and on budget is job one. They think good people can take it and those who are too sensitive aren't going to make it anyway and are not worth the time. Studies show that the vast majority of senior managers who fail do not fail because they can't get the work out. They fail because they damage people in the process and fail to keep their minds fresh. Think of the last 10 people who were forced to leave your organization. Why were they fired or asked to leave? What were the real reasons? Most likely, the problem was in relationships with others and coming up with the same old solutions to new problems. Arrogant, insensitive people don't get the benefits of the thinking of others and become stale, relying far too much on themselves and on the past. If this is you, you really need to rethink your priorities.

☐ **14. Defensive? Let down your guard.** Defensiveness is a major blockage to accurate and comprehensive self-knowledge and humility. *See #55 Self-Knowledge*. Defensive people overrate themselves in the eyes of others. If you are seen as denying your faults, you may get jumped on when people finally get the chance to give you feedback. Their evaluations of you have to be lower than justified because they think the message has to be louder to get through your defense shields. Your best chance of getting real feedback as a defensive person is to get facilitated 360° feedback where the respondents remain anonymous, or get a Human Resources professional to collect information for you and interpret it with you. If you ask for feedback directly, you are unlikely to find truth because of your history of being defensive in the face of negative criticism. Nobody enjoys giving even truthful and helpful criticism and feedback to a defensive person. It's just too painful.

- Stay calm. You will need to work on keeping yourself in a calm state when getting negative feedback. You need to change your thinking. When getting the feedback, your only task is to accurately understand what people are trying to tell you. It is not your task at that point to accept or reject. That comes later. Mentally rehearse how you will calmly react to tough feedback situations before they happen. Develop automatic tactics to shut down or delay your usual emotional response. Some useful tactics are to slow down, take notes, ask clarifying questions, ask them for concrete examples, and thank them for telling you since you know it's not easy for them.
- Listen to feedback from others. Remember, people suspect you really can't take feedback, that you believe yourself to be perfect, that you are defending against any suggestion to the contrary, and probably blaming the messenger of the feedback for the bad data. They expect the transaction to be painful for them and you. To break this cycle, you need to follow the rules of good listening. *See #33 Listening*. While this may sound unfair, you should initially accept all feedback as accurate, even when you know it isn't. You have to help others give you feedback in the beginning to overcome their fear of your defensiveness. On those matters that really count, you can go back and fix it later.

☐ **15. Low on social skills? Increase your social intelligence.** In summary form, a lack of humility is a broad form of an inability to understand and work effectively with others. For leaders, this is the most common reason for failure regardless of country or geographic assignment. Additionally, failure will happen much faster in countries where aggressive (low humility) characteristics are not valued. Ram Charan and Geoffrey Colvin studied the failure of CEOs and in a June 21, 1999, *Fortune* article concluded the number one reason for senior failure was a lack of people smarts. A lack of humility and low self-awareness are the first steps toward eventual failure.

Some Develop-in-Place Assignments

☐ Manage a project team of people who are older and more experienced than you.

☐ Manage a group that includes former peers to accomplish a task.

☐ Create employee involvement teams.

☐ Serve for a year or more with a community agency.

☐ Manage the visit of an international VIP higher in status than you.

True merit, like a river, the deeper it is, the less noise it makes.
Edward Frederick Halifax – British politician

Suggested Readings

Byron, W. J. (2006). *The power of principles: Ethics for the new corporate culture.* New York: Orbis Books.

Donoghue, P. J., & Siegel, M. E. (2005). *Are you really listening? Keys to successful communication.* Notre Dame, IN: Sorin Books.

Dotlich, D. L., & Cairo, P. C. (2002). *Why CEOs fail: The 11 behaviors that can derail your climb to the top and how to manage them.* San Francisco: Jossey-Bass.

Fernandez, J. A. (2006). *China CEO: Voices of experience from 20 international business leaders.* Singapore: John Wiley & Sons.

Gallos, J. (2008). *Business leadership: A Jossey-Bass reader* (2nd ed.). San Francisco: Jossey-Bass.

Hofstede, G., & Hofstede, G. J. (2005). *Cultures and organizations: Software of the mind: Intercultural cooperation and its importance for survival* (2nd ed.). New York: McGraw-Hill.

Hyun, J. (2005). *Breaking the bamboo ceiling: Career strategies for Asians.* New York: HarperCollins.

Kouzes, J. M., & Posner, B. Z. (2007). *The leadership challenge* (4th ed.). San Francisco: Jossey-Bass.

Moran, R. T., Harris, P. R., & Moran, S. V. (2007). *Managing cultural differences: Global leadership strategies for the 21st century* (7th ed.). Burlington, MA: Butterworth-Heinemann.

Morrison, T., & Conaway, W. A. (2006). *Kiss, bow, or shake hands: The bestselling guide to doing business in more than 60 countries* (2nd ed.). Avon, MA: Adams Media.

Stanford-Blair, N., & Dickmann, M. H. (2005). *Leading coherently: Reflections from leaders around the world.* Thousand Oaks, CA: Sage.

Trompenaars, F., & Hampden-Turner, C. (2002). *21 Leaders for the 21st century: How innovative leaders manage in the digital age.* New York: McGraw-Hill.

Zenger, J. H., & Folkman, J. (2002). *The extraordinary leader: Turning good managers into great leaders.* New York: McGraw-Hill.

Appendices

Appendix A: Competency Connections

Appendix B: Developmental Difficulty Matrix

Appendix C: Creating a Development Plan

Appendix A

Competency Connections

Competency Connections highlight how a development need or a career goal may be comprised of a few competencies. For example, if you don't make tough calls on people, you need to continue to be skilled at *Drive for* Results (53) and complement that by developing skill in Conflict Management (12) and Confronting Direct Reports (13). Or, if you aspire to be someone who can convince people to take developmental assignments, you need to be skilled at Motivating Others (36) and complement that by also being skilled at Developing Direct Reports and Others (19) and Sizing Up People (56).

Development Opportunities

Research shows that most people have similar development needs. Some skills are less prevalent in the population (see the list below). If you see a need that is critical to develop for success in your role, make sure you are skilled in the first competency and then work on the other competencies to complement it.

IF YOU THINK YOU NEED DEVELOPMENT BECAUSE YOU...	...CONTINUE TO BE SKILLED AT THIS COMPETENCY:	...AND WORK ON DEVELOPING THESE COMPETENCIES:
Understand the business as it is today but have less insight about how to make it different, unique, and aligned with the future	Business Acumen (5)	Creativity (14) Innovation Management (28) Perspective (46) Strategic Agility (58)
Care about others and it gets in the way of clearly seeing the strengths and weaknesses of others	Compassion (10)	Hiring and Staffing (25) Sizing Up People (56)
Have good decision-making skills which do not extend to making accurate people judgments	Decision Quality (17)	Hiring and Staffing (25) Sizing Up People (56) Understanding Others (64)
Believe in but have a tough time handling diversity	*Managing* Diversity (21)	*Dealing with* Ambiguity (2) *Dealing with* Paradox (40)

IF YOU THINK YOU NEED DEVELOPMENT BECAUSE YOU...	...CONTINUE TO BE SKILLED AT THIS COMPETENCY:	...AND WORK ON DEVELOPING THESE COMPETENCIES:
May not assess people well or know how to develop them	Fairness to Direct Reports (23)	Developing Direct Reports and Others (19) Sizing Up People (56)
Use technical arguments as an attack against the new and different – "It can't be done."	Functional Technical Skills (24)	Creativity (14) Innovation Management (28)
Understand how organizations work when limited to straightforward and clean solutions; have a little more trouble with uncertainty and chaos	Organizational Agility (38)	*Dealing with* Ambiguity (2) *Dealing with* Paradox (40)
Problem solve in a narrow niche	Problem Solving (51)	*Dealing with* Ambiguity (2) Creativity (14) *Dealing with* Paradox (40) Perspective (46)
Don't make the tough calls on people	*Drive for* Results (53)	Conflict Management (12) Confronting Direct Reports (13)
Write soft/easy goal statements	Written Communications (67)	Conflict Management (12) Directing Others (20) Managing and Measuring Work (35) *Drive for* Results (53)

Career Goals

Most people do not have these skills but aspire to develop them. If you see one that is critical to develop for success in your role, focus on developing the first competency and then work on the other competencies to complement it.

IF YOU ASPIRE TO BE SOMEONE WHO...	...YOU WILL NEED TO BE SKILLED AT THIS COMPETENCY:	...THEN WORK ON DEVELOPING THESE COMPETENCIES:
Can resolve differences in creating visions and establishing strategies	Conflict Management (12)	Innovation Management (28) Strategic Agility (58) *Managing* Vision and Purpose (65)
Is an accurate and candid assessor who scopes jobs and people accurately	Confronting Direct Reports (13)	Hiring and Staffing (25) Managing and Measuring Work (35) Sizing Up People (56) Understanding Others (64)
Rewards development appropriately	Developing Direct Reports and Others (19)	Managing and Measuring Work (35)
Gives direct, tough feedback	Managing and Measuring Work (35)	Confronting Direct Reports (13)
Can convince people to take developmental assignments	Motivating Others (36)	Developing Direct Reports and Others (19) Sizing Up People (56)
Can see clear strategies amidst chaos and uncertainty	Strategic Agility (58)	*Dealing with* Ambiguity (2) *Dealing with* Paradox (40)
Drives continuous improvement of systems	*Managing Through* Systems (59)	Creativity (14) Innovation Management (28) Total Work Systems (63)
Pays attention to both the team and to individuals	*Building Effective* Teams (60)	Delegation (18) Developing Direct Reports and Others (19) Directing Others (20) Motivating Others (36)

IF YOU ASPIRE TO BE SOMEONE WHO...	...YOU WILL NEED TO BE SKILLED AT THIS COMPETENCY:	...THEN WORK ON DEVELOPING THESE COMPETENCIES:
Assembles the right people to get the job done	Understanding Others (64)	Hiring and Staffing (25) *Drive for* Results (53) Sizing Up People (56) *Building Effective* Teams (60)
Can inspire and motivate units to rally around the vision	*Managing* Vision and Purpose (65)	Motivating Others (36) *Building Effective* Teams (60)

Appendix B

Developmental Difficulty Matrix

Three charts (for individual contributor, manager, and executive levels) show on a 5-point scale how difficult it would be for a typical professional person to develop any of the 67 Competencies. The charts also show the average skill rating of the average population for each competency. This information lets you know what you're up against so you can adjust your development plan, remedies, and time line accordingly.

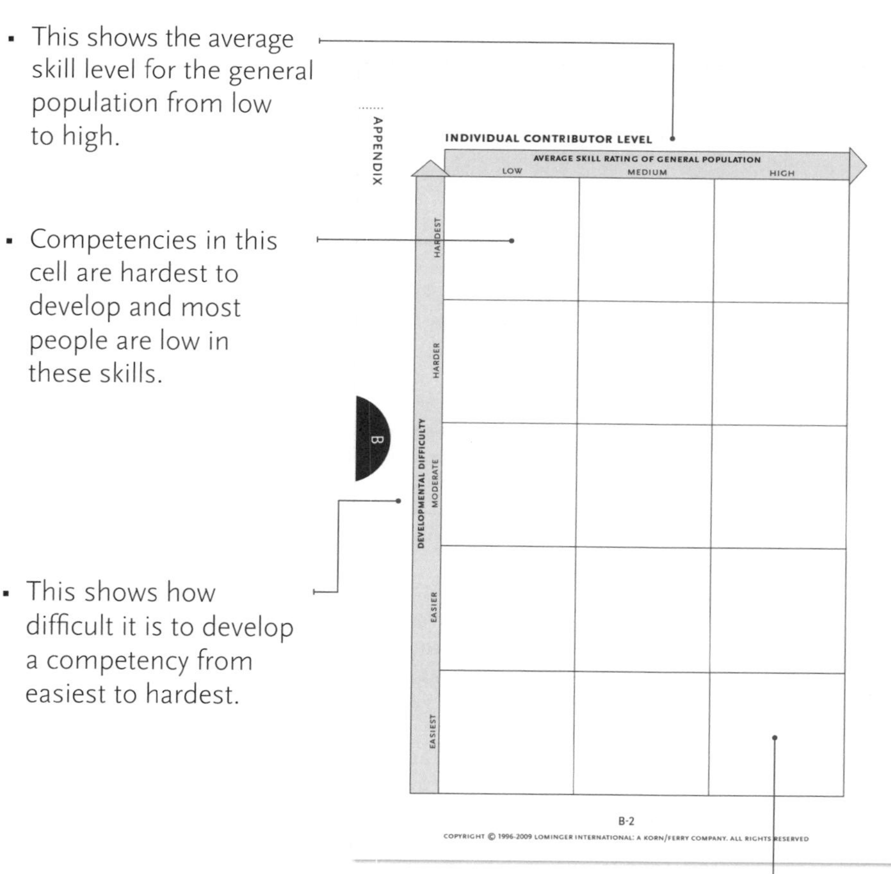

- Competencies in this cell are easiest to develop and most people are high in these skills.

INDIVIDUAL CONTRIBUTOR LEVEL

DEVELOPMENTAL DIFFICULTY / AVERAGE SKILL RATING OF GENERAL POPULATION	LOW	MEDIUM	HIGH
HARDEST	2 *Dealing with* Ambiguity 13 Confronting Direct Reports 19 Developing Direct Reports and Others 40 *Dealing with* Paradox 44 Personal Disclosure 58 Strategic Agility 59 *Managing Through* Systems 60 *Building Effective* Teams	28 Innovation Management	
HARDER	2 *Dealing with* Ambiguity 13 Confronting Direct Reports 19 Developing Direct Reports and Others 40 *Dealing with* Paradox 44 Personal Disclosure 58 Strategic Agility 59 *Managing Through* Systems 60 *Building Effective* Teams	11 Composure 31 Interpersonal Savvy 37 Negotiating 38 Organizational Agility 56 Sizing Up People	10 Compassion 21 *Managing* Diversity 66 Work/Life Balance
MODERATE	9 Command Skills 25 Hiring and Staffing 36 Motivating Others 46 Perspective 55 Self-Knowledge 65 *Managing* Vision and Purpose	5 Business Acumen 6 Career Ambition 7 Caring About Direct Reports 14 Creativity 41 Patience 49 Presentation Skills 52 Process Management 54 Self-Development	3 Approachability 4 Boss Relationships 8 Comfort Around Higher Management 22 Ethics and Values 26 Humor 32 Learning on the Fly 51 Problem Solving 57 Standing Alone
EASIER	18 Delegation 35 Managing and Measuring Work	20 Directing Others 33 Listening 39 Organizing 42 Peer Relationships 50 Priority Setting 62 Time Management	17 Decision Quality 23 Fairness to Direct Reports 29 Integrity and Trust 30 Intellectual Horsepower 53 *Drive for* Results 61 Technical Learning 63 Total Work Systems 67 Written Communications
EASIEST		16 *Timely* Decision Making 27 Informing 47 Planning	1 Action Oriented 15 Customer Focus 24 Functional/Technical Skills 43 Perseverance

MANAGER LEVEL

AVERAGE SKILL RATING OF GENERAL POPULATION →
↑ DEVELOPMENTAL DIFFICULTY

	LOW	MEDIUM	HIGH
HARDEST	12 Conflict Management 28 Innovation Management 45 Personal Learning 48 Political Savvy 64 Understanding Others	34 Managerial Courage	
HARDER	2 *Dealing with* Ambiguity 13 Confronting Direct Reports 19 Developing Direct Reports and Others 37 Negotiating 40 *Dealing with* Paradox 44 Personal Disclosure 59 *Managing Through* Systems 60 *Building Effective* Teams	11 Composure 31 Interpersonal Savvy 56 Sizing Up People 58 Strategic Agility 66 Work/Life Balance	10 Compassion 21 *Managing* Diversity 38 Organizational Agility
MODERATE	14 Creativity 25 Hiring and Staffing 36 Motivating Others 41 Patience 46 Perspective 55 Self-Knowledge 65 *Managing* Vision and Purpose	6 Career Ambition 7 Caring About Direct Reports 9 Command Skills 32 Learning on the Fly 49 Presentation Skills 52 Process Management 54 Self-Development	3 Approachability 4 Boss Relationships 5 Business Acumen 8 Comfort Around Higher Management 22 Ethics and Values 26 Humor 51 Problem Solving 57 Standing Alone
EASIER	35 Managing and Measuring Work 20 Directing Others	18 Delegation 33 Listening 39 Organizing 42 Peer Relationships 50 Priority Setting 62 Time Management 67 Written Communications	17 Decision Quality 23 Fairness to Direct Reports 29 Integrity and Trust 30 Intellectual Horsepower 53 *Drive for* Results 61 Technical Learning 63 Total Work Systems
EASIEST	27 Informing	16 *Timely* Decision Making 47 Planning	1 Action Oriented 15 Customer Focus 24 Functional/Technical Skills 43 Perseverance

EXECUTIVE LEVEL

DEVELOPMENTAL DIFFICULTY	AVERAGE SKILL RATING OF GENERAL POPULATION: LOW	MEDIUM	HIGH
HARDEST	12 Conflict Management 28 Innovation Management 45 Personal Learning 64 Understanding Others	34 Managerial Courage 48 Political Savvy	
HARDER	2 *Dealing with* Ambiguity 13 Confronting Direct Reports 19 Developing Direct Reports and Others 40 *Dealing with* Paradox 44 Personal Disclosure 59 *Managing Through* Systems 60 *Building Effective* Teams 66 Work/Life Balance	10 Compassion 11 Composure 31 Interpersonal Savvy 37 Negotiating 56 Sizing Up People 58 Strategic Agility	21 *Managing* Diversity 38 Organizational Agility
MODERATE	7 Caring About Direct Reports 14 Creativity 36 Motivating Others 41 Patience 55 Self-Knowledge 65 *Managing* Vision and Purpose	25 Hiring and Staffing 26 Humor 46 Perspective 52 Process Management 54 Self-Development	3 Approachability 4 Boss Relationships 5 Business Acumen 6 Career Ambition 8 Comfort Around Higher Management 9 Command Skills 22 Ethics and Values 32 Learning on the Fly 49 Presentation Skills 51 Problem Solving 57 Standing Alone
EASIER	35 Managing and Measuring Work 20 Directing Others 33 Listening	18 Delegation 23 Fairness to Direct Reports 39 Organizing 42 Peer Relationships 50 Priority Setting 62 Time Management 63 Total Work Systems 67 Written Communications	17 Decision Quality 29 Integrity and Trust 30 Intellectual Horsepower 53 *Drive for* Results 61 Technical Learning
EASIEST	27 Informing 47 Planning	16 *Timely* Decision Making	1 Action Oriented 15 Customer Focus 24 Functional/Technical Skills 43 Perseverance

Appendix C
Creating a Development Plan

Universal Ideas for Developing Any Competency

☐ **1. Choose wisely.** Figure out what is critically important to performance in your job or success in your career. This is a huge investment of your time and energy, so make sure that you're focused on something that matters to you and something that other people think is important, too. Be realistic about what you can accomplish. Refer to the Developmental Matrix to see how difficult it is to develop the competencies you've selected. Make sure they don't all fall in the "hardest to develop" category. If you want to develop Conflict Management (12), you will notice that it is not only rated hardest to develop but that most people are low in this skill. That's a clue that developing that competency will be very challenging. Keep that in mind when you create your action plan and set your time frame. You will feel more motivated and be more committed to your development when you feel successful and see improvement.

☐ **2. Get specific.** Get more detailed and behavioral feedback on the need. Most of the time, people are weak in some aspect of a competency. It's almost never all interpersonal skills. It's usually something specific—for example, interpersonal skills with upper management under the pressure of tough questions from two of the seven on the management committee on topics you care deeply about. To find out more about what your need is specifically, go to a few people who know and who will tell you if you ask. Accept that you have a need. Don't be defensive or try to rationalize away the need. Say you are concerned about the need and request more detailed information so you can focus on an efficient plan for growth and development. Ask them for specific examples. When? Where? With whom? In what settings? Under what conditions? How many times? Might anyone they know be of help? Get as specific as you can. Listen, don't rebut. Take notes. Thank them for the input.

☐ **3. Create the plan.** If you have accepted the need as true and you are ready to do something about it, you need three kinds of action plans. You need to know what to stop doing, start doing, and keep doing. Since you have a need in this area (you don't do this well), you need to stop some things you are doing that aren't working. In their place, you need to start doing some things you either don't like doing, haven't ever done, or don't even know about. Even if you are bad at something, there are things you do in this area that you are probably good at. Send a form or e-mail to a number of people who would be willing to help you work on this skill. Tell them you have discovered and taken ownership of this need, want to do something about it, list the specific need you discovered in step one, and ask them for the things you should stop doing, start doing, and keep doing.

☐ **4. Learn from others.** Research shows that we learn best from others when we (a) Pick multiple models, each of whom excels at one thing rather than looking for the whole package in one person. Think more broadly than your current job for models; add some off-work models. (b) Take both the student and the teacher role. As a student, study other people—don't just admire or dislike what they do. Reduce what they do or don't do to a set of principles or rules of thumb to integrate into your behavior. As a teacher, it's one of the best ways to learn something as it forces you to think it through and be concise in your explanation. (c) Rely on multiple methods of learning—interview people, observe them without speaking with them, study remote models by reading books or watching films, get someone to tutor you, or use a contrast strategy. Sometimes it's hard to see the effects of your behavior because you are too close to the problem. Pick two people, one who is much better than you are at your need and one who is much worse. Copy what the good model does that leads to good outcomes. Get rid of the behaviors that match what the bad model does. Or, get a partner. If you can find someone working on the same need, you can share learnings and support each other. Take turns teaching each other some to do's, one of the best ways to cement your learning. Share books you've found. Courses you've attended. Models you've observed. You can give each other progress feedback.

☐ **5. Read the "bible" on this need.** Every skill or competency has had one or more books written about it: How to negotiate to win. How to get along with bad bosses. How to win friends. How to be more creative. Go to a large business bookstore and buy at least two books covering your need. Take one hour and scan each book. Just read the first sentence of every paragraph. Don't read to learn. Just read to see the structure of the book. Pick the one that seems to be right for you and read it thoroughly. That book may reference or lead you to other books or articles on the skill. Use your reading to answer the following questions: What's the research on the skill? What are the 10 how-to's all the experts would agree to? How is this skill best learned?

☐ **6. Learn from autobiographies and biographies.** Try to find books by or on two famous people who have the skill you are trying to build. Mother Teresa on compassion. Harry Truman on standing alone. Norman Schwarzkopf on leadership. Helen Keller on persistence. Try to see how they wove the skill you are working on into their fabric of skills. Was there a point in their lives when they weren't good at this skill? What was the turning point?

☐ **7. Learn from a course.** Find the best course you have access to. It might be offered in your organization or, more likely, it will be a public program. Find one that is taught by the author of a book or a series of articles on this need. Be sure to give it enough time. It usually takes three to five days to learn about any skill or competency. One- to two-day courses are usually not long enough. Find one where you learn the theory and have a lot of practice with the skill. Find one that videotapes if the skill lends itself to the lens. Take your detailed plan with you and take notes against your need. Don't just take notes following the course outline. For example, if you're attending a listening course and one of your need statements is how to listen when people ramble, take notes against that specific statement; or if your need involves a task or project, write down action steps you can take immediately. Throw yourself into the course. No phone calls. Don't take any work with you. No sightseeing. Just do the course. Be the best student in the course and learn the most. Seldom will a course alone be sufficient to address a need. A course always has to be combined with the other remedies in this Universal Development Plan, especially stretching tasks, so you can perform against your need under pressure.

- ☐ **8. Try some stretching tasks, but start small.** Seventy percent of skills development happens on the job. As you talk with others while building this skill, get them to brainstorm tasks and activities you can try. Write down five tasks you will commit to doing, tasks like: initiate three conversations, make peace with someone you've had problems with, write a business plan for your unit, negotiate a purchase, make a speech, find something to fix. You can try tasks off the job as well: teach someone to read, be a volunteer, join a study group, take up a new hobby—whatever will help you practice your need in a fairly low-risk way. After each task, write down the positive and negative aspects of your performance and note things you will try to do better or differently next time.
- ☐ **9. Track your own progress.** You are going to need some extra motivation to get through this. You need to be able to reward yourself for progress you've made. Others may not notice the subtle changes for a while. Set progress goals and benchmarks for yourself. If you were working on approachability, for instance, have a goal of initiating conversations with five new people a week. Keep a log. Make a chart. Celebrate incremental progress. Noting times you didn't interrupt others or made two strategy suggestions that people grabbed and discussed will reinforce your continued efforts.
- ☐ **10. Get periodic feedback.** Get a group of people who haven't known you for long. They don't have a history of seeing you not do well in this skill over a long period of time. Get feedback from them a third of the way into your skill-building plan. Also, go back to the original group who helped you see and accept this need. Their ratings will lag behind the first group because they know your history in this skill. Use both groups to monitor your progress.

The following pages provide you with a development plan template where you can record your development need and action plan. There are three examples (unskilled, overused, and staller/stopper) to help you get started. For more details, refer to the Introduction in this book.

PERMISSION TO COPY DEVELOPMENT PLAN: *This confirms that Lominger International: A Korn/Ferry Company is granting you the right to make copies of My Development Plan on pages C-10 through C-13 of* FYI For Your Improvement™ *appendix. Such copies are for the internal use of your organization only. All copies must retain the copyright notice located on the bottom of each page.*

Sample (Unskilled) My Development Need:

Competency: 49 Presentation Skills
Factor V: Organizational Positioning Skills
Cluster L: Communicating Effectively

LEARNER NAME:
TO BE COMPLETED BY:

MY "BEFORE" DESCRIPTION *(Unskilled, Overused, or A Problem)*	SOME CAUSES FOR ME
May always present the same way, not adjusting to audiences. *(Unskilled)*	*Get nervous and emotional.* *Flat presenter.*

MY LEARNINGS FROM "THE MAP"
I realize the importance of audience sensitivity in giving a good presentation and achieving my objectives.

C

QUOTES THAT INSPIRE ME

"It usually takes me more than three weeks to prepare a good impromptu speech." – Mark Twain

MY ACTION PLAN
(Development Remedies, Substitutes, Compensators, or Workarounds)

49.3 – Read the audience:
Adjust the tone, pace, style, and even the message and how I couch it for different audiences.

Substitute:
Presentation Skills (49) is not my strength so I will leverage an area I am skilled at and substitute Approachability (3) by building rapport well.

People workaround:
Find a skilled colleague to co-present with me.

Develop-in-Place Assignment:
Present the strategy of my unit to others not familiar with my business.

MY "AFTER" DESCRIPTION
(Skilled or Not a Problem)

Is effective in a variety of formal presentation settings: one-on-one, small and large groups, with peers, direct reports, and bosses.

(Skilled)

MY SUGGESTED READINGS

The Exceptional Presenter: A Proven Formula to Open Up and Own the Room (2007) by T. J. Koegel.

Sample (Overused) My Development Need:

Competency: 18 Delegation
Factor II: Operating Skills
Cluster F: Getting Work Done Through Others

LEARNER NAME:
TO BE COMPLETED BY:

MY "BEFORE" DESCRIPTION (Unskilled, Overused, or A Problem)	SOME CAUSES FOR ME
May overdelegate without providing enough direction or help. *May have unrealistic expectations for direct reports.* *(Overused)*	*Delegate but don't follow up.* *Delegate by throwing tasks at people.* *Too busy.*

MY LEARNINGS FROM "THE MAP"
I can't do the work of the unit all by myself, so both performance and morale will suffer until I learn to delegate.

QUOTES THAT INSPIRE ME

"No man will make a great leader who wants to do it all himself or get all the credit for doing it." – Andrew Carnegie

MY ACTION PLAN

(Development Remedies, Substitutes, Compensators, or Workarounds)

18.2 – Set expectations:
People need to know what it is I expect and what the outcome looks like.

18.6 – Give a realistic time frame:
Allow more time than it would take me. Remember when I started to learn how to do this task and how long it took me.

Compensator:
I tend to overuse Delegation (18) so I will lessen the negative effect by compensating with Directing Others (20) and lay out the work in a well-planned and organized manner.

Self workaround:
Pre-declare my weakness.

MY "AFTER" DESCRIPTION

(Skilled or Not a Problem)

Clearly and comfortably delegates both routine and important tasks and decisions.

(Skilled)

MY SUGGESTED READINGS

Delegating Work (2008) Harvard Business School Press.

Sample (Staller and Stopper) My Development Need:

Staller and Stopper: 117 Overmanaging
Factor VII: Trouble with People
Cluster X: Doesn't Inspire or Build Talent

LEARNER NAME:
TO BE COMPLETED BY:

MY "BEFORE" DESCRIPTION (Unskilled, Overused, or A Problem)	SOME CAUSES FOR ME
Doesn't empower others. *Does too much of the work himself/herself.* *Is a poor delegator.* *(A Problem)*	*Excessively action oriented.* *Know too much about the work.* *Unskilled at Developing Direct Reports and Others (19).* *Overusing Functional/Technical Skills (24).*

MY LEARNINGS FROM "THE MAP"

I prefer to depend on myself to get important things done. But this is taking me away from other priorities and depriving my people of the chance to develop new skills. I realize that it's my job as a manager to make sure that my people are qualified and motivated to do the work.

C

QUOTES THAT INSPIRE ME

"A good manager is best when people barely know that he exists. Not so good when people obey and acclaim him. Worse when they despise him." – Lao Tzu

MY ACTION PLAN (Development Remedies, Substitutes, Compensators, or Workarounds)	MY "AFTER" DESCRIPTION (Skilled or Not a Problem)
117.1 – Upgrade my team's skill level. Improve on Developing Direct Reports 19.6 – Delegate for development: Take the tasks that are no longer developmental for me and delegate them to people who are ready for a new challenge. Compensator: Compensate for overusing Functional/Technical Skills (24) by using my strength in Innovation Management (28). Develop-in-Place Assignment: Manage something "remote," away from my location.	Delegates and empowers. Works to do less personally and trust others more. (Not a Problem)

MY SUGGESTED READINGS

What to Do When You Become the Boss: How New Managers Become Successful Managers (2008) by B. Selden.

My Development Need:

....

....

....

LEARNER NAME: ....

TO BE COMPLETED BY: ....

MY "BEFORE" DESCRIPTION *(Unskilled, Overused, or A Problem)*	SOME CAUSES FOR ME

MY LEARNINGS FROM "THE MAP"

QUOTES THAT INSPIRE ME

MY ACTION PLAN
(Development Remedies, Substitutes, Compensators, or Workarounds)

MY "AFTER" DESCRIPTION
(Skilled or Not a Problem)

MY SUGGESTED READINGS

My Development Need:

....

....

....

LEARNER NAME: ....

TO BE COMPLETED BY: ....

MY "BEFORE" DESCRIPTION *(Unskilled, Overused, or A Problem)*	SOME CAUSES FOR ME

MY LEARNINGS FROM "THE MAP"

....

QUOTES THAT INSPIRE ME

MY ACTION PLAN

(Development Remedies, Substitutes, Compensators, or Workarounds)

MY "AFTER" DESCRIPTION

(Skilled or Not a Problem)

MY SUGGESTED READINGS

Index

The index is designed to include key development themes that a manager or learner might want to explore in greater detail. Each entry directs learners and coaches to a chapter and remedy number that is pertinent to the theme. For example, if a learner looks up "Action Oriented," he/she will see entries that pertain to "getting organized, 1.8; perfectionist, 1.2; and procrastinate, 1.1". If getting organized is the issue at hand, the learner can go to chapter one and read remedy number eight. Please note: Index entries in italics are not alphabetized.

i